EFFECTIVENESS and EFFICIENCY

Route for entrepreneurs and business managers

Lic. Gerardo Azañedo Castillo

TABLE OF CONTENTS

LIST OF CHARTS

ACKNOWLEDGMENTS

I wish to express my deep gratitude to my family for the immense support and encouragement I have always received from all of them in my professional endeavors. To my wife, Dina, faithful companion, support, and witness to my intellectual concerns and occupational concerns. To my daughter Yesenia and my son-in-law Víctor for their committed encouragement and with whom he frequently exchanged opinions and advances on the casuistry of situations that occurred in the American and Peruvian reality. To my dear grandchildren Estefanía and Nicholas, who have always been my inspiration and entertainment in the progress and pauses that work allowed me. A special mention to my son Joel, who took the time to do a technical review of this study and suggest improvements in substance and form. The contrast of his coincidence and conflicting opinions has allowed us to improve the quality of the research. To my daughter-in-law Ana María, who, with tireless effort and patience, collaborated with me in the laborious task of editing this writing.

To all of them, I reiterate my gratitude and my apologies for taking away the time it took me to dedicate myself to this work. All of them have ratified in my experience the veracity of that popular saying: "The best company is the family; the best team is made up of your wife, and the best compensation is what your children and grandchildren give you."

I must also express special gratitude to that distinguished group of authors and professionals that would take a long time to list, but that appear in the bibliographical sources, sources consulted on the Internet, magazines, and newspapers included in this work. I do not have the pleasure of knowing most of them personally (many of them even passed away), but I feel I identify with them for sharing their ideas, and I am in intellectual debt to them. No research work starts from zero but is born from the author's concerns but is nourished and enriched by the inspiration and contribution of the lucid minds of the authors consulted. My deep gratitude goes to them because, although it may not have been their intention, they became, in fact, guides and mentors of this research. In any case, the merit of the good that is detected in this work has to do with their work, and the defects or limitations are entirely my responsibility.

NOTES ABOUT THE AUTHOR

Mr. Gerardo Azañedo was born in Lima, Perú (1952). He completed his studies in Economics at the Universidad del Pacifico (Lima, Peru) in 1974. After obtaining his Bachelor of Science degree (1979), he continued Post Graduate studies and specialization in Finance at the 1984 School of Business Administration (ESAN, Lima, Peru) and later participated in training programs in Small and Medium Business management at Florida Atlantic University (USA, 2003). He also complemented his academic experience with several years of university teaching at the University of Lima (1980-1983) where he also participated in research and presentations on Investment Funds in Peru and was a speaker on topics of Economic Integration and Stock Market.

He has had a varied professional experience both in technical assistance projects in international organizations UNDP (United Nations), Cartagena Agreement Board, and GTZ Proagua (German Technical Cooperation), as well as having held executive and management positions in his country, Peru, in private sector entities such as OSASA (Consulting in projects in the Tourism sector), Tagal (Investments and Consulting in Stock Market), Profuturo AFP (Pension Fund Administration), and also in technical cooperation projects between the Inter-American Development Bank (IDB) and the Peruvian Government (PRONAP) in the sanitation and drinking water sector. The last years of professional practice were developed in the field of business consulting.

From various perspectives, he has always addressed the issue of business management and has witnessed and participated in successful and unfortunate solutions regarding what and how things are done or should be done in the administration of private companies and local or central government entities. In this work: "Effectiveness and Efficiency," the author wishes to show elements that, in his opinion, are substantial in any management. It has been written in the reflective years close to his professional retirement. It represents a proposal from the perspective of an economist on the complicated issue of how to achieve satisfactory management.

AUTHOR'S PROLOGUE

This work shows the complexity of organizational management processes in private and public entities that, although they respond to objectives of a different nature, ratify interrelationships and reciprocal dependencies to a much greater degree than external appearances show. Caution is suggested with categorically a priori judgments or those manipulated by ideological patterns that must always be contrasted with reality. It is common to see that such judgments tend to be intentionally or surreptitiously flawed by clouding or by what we have later called training conditioning.

In the pro-liberal scenario of Western countries and capitalist systems, the prevailing approach is to consider that the excellence of private management is promoted, strengthened, and facilitated not only on the merit of private management itself without or also by excluding any vestige of government regulation, control, or participation in the economy. In the same sense, we usually hear the claim that all economic intervention from the public sector is considered harmful because it only hinders the normal functioning of the free market and private initiative.

In contrast to these principled criteria, reality shows us that the purity of the market is broken, in several cases, by the defection of the participants or private agents themselves, and therefore, intervention, correction, and even government regulation is required, especially in important sectors where supervision is necessary to defend the interests of the consumer, fragile business units or society. This is clearly confirmed in industries with notable private participation, such as the following sectors: food, pharmaceutical, financial services, commercial services, basic services (water, energy, communications, etc.), and medical assistance. The intervention of the "government arbitrator" is also imperative in areas of technical and quality standardization, such as regulations on property and patent activities, foreign trade, health, and other services.

Complementarily and for the good of the market itself, government supervision is justified when its operation is distorted by the presence of monopolies or, oligopolies, or cartels of producers that intervene or agree to alterations and distortions in the market for their particular benefit and when such distortions affect the participation of small business units vulnerable to such alterations. Due to the need to correct or solve defects that have occurred in our realities, the presence of a neutral arbitrator will always be required, and that task is the responsibility of the government to fulfill. A separate problem is when said government chooses to evade its responsibility, to delay it or finally to intervene biasedly in collusion and in favor of interests.

In addition to what has been described, it is usually observed that after cycles of crisis, the defenders of the free market "forget"; they tend to ignore and finally end up recognizing that to face such crisis situations (both in national experiences and abroad) it has been required essential "support from the government" to whom they extend their hand to request the granting of rescue packages obtained through financing at preferential interest rates, tax reduction or refund programs, differentiated exchange rates, import tariff reductions, etc.

In these cases of crisis, the sacred principles of free markets and non-intervention of the government in the economy are relaxed or "looked to the side." The unrestricted functioning of the free market usually, in extreme cases, wipes out the most vulnerable productive units but rarely of more predominant productive units. The case of the American financial crisis of 2008, the origin of which was caused by private sector agents (commercial and investment banks), was a clear example of this. Unconditional and supportive defenders of the unrestricted functioning of the free market argue that government interventions in periods of crisis are permissible because they are "exceptional and temporary interventions."

Reality contradicts them because, in recent times, we are getting used to the periodic conversion of exceptional crises into chronic crises, from cyclical crises to structural ones, that is, the seasonality of critical events becomes recurrent. In this context, necessary government intervention is allowed (and even required) to confront crises of all kinds. Accordingly, greater government aggressiveness with all its economic policy instruments (fiscal, monetary, tax, infrastructure, sanitation, health, etc.) is accepted without prejudice to correct instabilities in the economy and even counteract undesirable effects of random phenomena (pandemics, wars, migratory crises, social upheavals, etc.)

On the other hand, in contradiction to the lying transience of the crises and the evident economic interventionism that they demand, there continue to be limited possibilities and opportunities in large population sectors of the developing world to access basic levels of food, housing, education, or health. This imposes criteria of social inclusion through the implementation of subsidized management policies with the application of subsidized rates or "political prices" for certain activities and services aimed at certain dispossessed social sectors where, by necessity, free market principles must be broken and prioritize social profitability criteria.

The above reactivates the debate between the convenience of establishing direct assistance in kind (food stamps, soup kitchens, school breakfast, provision of products to pregnant mothers, etc.) or providing a monetary stipend (emergency bonuses, assistance to people with disabilities, bonus retirement, monetary allocation to pregnant mothers, etc.). This debate finds supporters and detractors for or against one scheme or another but in no way rules out government intervention. Faced with this variety of policies and beyond justified reasons consistent or inconsistent with the free market or state interventionism, the important thing is not only to consider what we do but also how things we do. Therefore, it is essential to counteract known inefficiencies or corruption of the state apparatus to ensure efficiency and effectiveness in the managed transfers.

It is also worth considering cases where, due to the difficult access to provide products or services to a certain dispersed population (Indigenous communities that are poorly accessible and far from urban areas), the private sector considers it pertinent not to venture into offering its products or services because it is considered unprofitable. In this scheme, the State is usually assigned a subsidiary role in the economy so that it assumes everything that the private sector discards for whatever reason.

Despite the defects, deviations, and limitations described, we must recognize that when the market mechanism is provided with reasonable regulation, supervision, and control schemes conducted by governmental or autonomous entities, many of the defects described are avoided or contained. For now, liberal economic doctrine does not offer an alternative mechanism to replace it. However, it is still striking that in current times and in Western and liberal spaces, greater government intervention in the economy of such countries is becoming noticeable. Are these symptoms of new functionalities? It is still premature to know.

In the scenario of socialist countries, state intervention in the economy is prioritized and defended, and they are reluctant to operate in the free-market mechanism and prefer central planning as a resource allocation mechanism. From this perspective, a government planning entity is assigned the function of determining what, how, how much, and for whom to produce, invest, and distribute resources and surpluses. In this scenario, the roles have been reversed because the incipient private sector is usually assigned a subsidiary role to assume everything that the state sector discards for whatever reason, and only with the restrictions and supervisions of the case is it allowed to operate.

In this scenario, the surprising case of China is paradoxical: it has been precisely its opening to the external market and the world of free market economies that has driven its success., which gave it the opportunity to obtain that qualitative leap of strengthening its dynamism and has allowed it to consolidate as a current economic power. This potential has been recycled internally with the important participation of the State in the economy, with state aid and promotion in financial leverage to state companies, also for meritorious and recognized renewal of scientific and technological processes, and for questioned commercial dumping schemes. (penetration and commercial aggressiveness through prices subsidized by the government) and by maintaining low wages that have placed a substantial part of the cost of its commercial rebound on the shoulders of its workforce.

Therefore, China necessarily requires maintaining an outstanding competitive position, to continue and strengthen its incursion and negotiation with free market economies. Due to this pragmatism of consented and accommodated policies between opening towards global liberalism and moderating its central planning schemes, some analysts have agreed to describe China as a peculiar model of state capitalism or also as lying socialism.

Even so, and beyond labels, the signals that China presents in other spheres, such as politics and its peculiar democratic or rather autocratic experience, leave, according to our perspective, much to be desired. As an example of events that threaten the freedom of rights and political and economic preferences of its citizens, we have on the one hand, a president of the only ruling party that has configured the renewal of his position for life. On the other hand, in clear contradiction to the ruling party against freedom of information, we have, for example, the persistence of strict limitations and prohibitions on Internet communications for purposes of internal control that contrasts with its not-very-holy aggressiveness of penetration in computer communication systems towards foreign countries and companies. Not to mention the risky situation of dissidents from your system or establishment. Until now, many continue to wonder what happened to that "student who was not there" who protested facing the tanks of the Chinese army in the so-called Tian An Meng Square massacre (June 05, 1989).

In the case of Russia, also a representative country of the socialist orbit, the civil rights situation has become, as we will explain later, much more distressing. It is striking that both China and Russia have no intention or purpose of adopting a Western democratic model or one that includes part of their important principles. Nor do we propose that this Western model should be completely imitated, which, as we have highlighted in some parts of this work, is not free from imperfections.

In Peru, as a singular example of this group of developing countries, those responsible for designing business guidelines and policies tend to overlook two important facts (economic and political): a) almost 80% of the employed workforce is in informality and b) social sectors C (poor) and D (extreme poverty) represent close to 70% of the electorate. This social curtain of contrasting inequality has been repeatedly ignored by policymakers who, through ineptitude, collusion, or corruption, have distorted and neglected this problem. Such policies have been directed towards formal spaces where only those privileged socio-economic sectors are covered and end up segregating the majority sectors whose aspirations and benefits are continually postponed.

It has been argued erroneously and boldly that the economy and political-social events unfold on separate lines. This significant and complicated informality and inequality will not be able to be successfully combated if its close relative, poverty, is not combated in parallel with which it is intertwined in that fence of precariousness. Many economic policies are ineffective because they are left aside or do not reach this underworld of an underground economy full of inequalities and contrasts. So, the doctrinal orthodoxy of both systems has been frustrating: Neither the predominant free market of today nor the emphasis on central planning tried in the times of the strengthened Peruvian National Planning Institute of the past have offered viable solutions.

For all this, we note that when we look only at the tree (that is, the particular management of any private company or government administration) without considering the particularities of the forest (other economic and social agents and other institutions of the environment), the strict considerations of a logical and scientific framework of "prototype models and solutions" limited to the framework of efficiency and in accordance with "liberal or socialist catechisms," end up being insufficient because they propose solutions with exclusive profiles and because drowned in short-term immediatism they don't know or ignore that its complexity usually evolves and mutates in a surprising and unexpected way and makes the scope and recipes of its partial solutions sterile.

Improvement proposals cannot be rigid or absolute but must aim to provide versatile, comprehensive, and multidisciplinary solutions. In these, greater detail predominates in the observation of those elements that compose it, their interrelationships and the pattern that emerges from such relationships, the behaviors and motivations of the elements that comprise it, the purpose, the direction, and results that finally achieved within the framework of the effectiveness of what is proposed.

We propose that when dealing with problems related to complex realities and systems (companies, government administrations, economies, markets, poverty, etc.), both approaches should be reinforced: the reductionist and logical approach complemented by the nuanced systemic, holistic, and patterns approach emerging. This research attempts to provide that framework of reference to address the problem of organizational management, but we warn in several of its passages that it does not aim at all to become a conventional academic text on administration because, according to what is developed in this study, we are left it is clear that the breadth, diversity, and complexity of the management problem goes beyond the strict field of administrative science.

In the final stage of this research, I did some exploring the possibilities for its publication and had an interview with an editor who asked me what my intention was for publishing it. I told him that in consideration of the low reading rate in the national scenery (Peruvian), and because of my novitiate to venture into these tasks of writer, I did not aim to obtain significant income from copyrights nor to become known in these avatars. However, I told him that by residing in the USA with a population more prone to reading and where competitive marketing with its tagged phrase "the best seller" drives expectations of novices and experienced writers, I was maturing the idea to enter this market. In this way - I told him - I could become a prospective "influencer" in the topic discussed and with projection towards broader areas. After bursting out laughing at this last witty joke, I clarified to the editor that my intention in developing the topic was to dust off old professional concerns that arose from my time as a university student and to participate in the open debate on the topic discussed.

INTRODUCTION

This work raises the debate on aspects related to the success or failure of organizational management processes in private business entities but does not exclude scenarios referring to public sector organizations and non-profit entities. The conventional perspective of business management usually pays special attention to efficiency procedures in allocating and controlling resources. However, without failing to recognize its importance, we raised important issues in the debate that complement its traditional approach; one of them maintains that in this matter, there is no room for improvisation, so it makes no sense to mobilize resources without having sufficient clarity about where we are going and how to achieve it. In this sense, the importance of planning in business management has been recognized, but in much of the business universe, especially in business units belonging to small companies, this strategy is absent or insufficiently applied.

Furthermore, the presence of a rapidly changing environment has exceeded the reaction capacity of the management bodies of companies, organizations, and governments, making conventional schemes for addressing them obsolete and inappropriate. It is necessary to complement them with strong doses of creativity and innovation, promoting timely changes, courage, and the decision to undertake new or less well-known things and get rid of obsolete schemes and patterns of thinking. During this confusion, the situation has revealed, today more than ever, that in addition to insufficient strategies, there is a notable absence of honest leaders and a leadership crisis in business and organizational management.

Additionally, the permanence of companies, organizations, and governments can be gradually or abruptly undermined when these institutions end up degraded, distorted, and vitiated by an organizational culture sustained by anti-values where dishonesty, concealment, or falsification of the truth, non-compliance with norms, the waste of resources, open or covert boycott or sabotage, widespread corruption, and others prevail in his management.

It has been preferred to intervene in the organizational management debate by presenting a somewhat more comprehensive vision that proposes, in addition to the strictly managerial nuance that emphasizes the optimal and efficient management of resources in the company, a balanced approach that complements factors such as strategy (orientation: what things to do?), leadership (driving style: how to do them?) and organizational culture (guiding management values and behaviors). The proposed approach may appear as an independent theme; however, digging beyond its apparent particularities, we find a confluent and complementary perspective. We are interested in highlighting the importance of an organizational management that reveals these unintelligible connections, which clarifies this complementarity of approaches and highlights the notorious theoretical-practical imbalance that the factors described here show as promoters of Effectiveness and Efficiency and, therefore, of satisfactory management.

Chapter one presents the conceptual categories discussed throughout the study: business or organizational management, effectiveness, efficiency, and appreciation of basic scenarios of successful and defective management. Also included is a historical review of what we have conceptualized as management styles that serve to place ourselves in the historical context of what we are interested in discussing.

Chapter two develops one of the key and controversial themes of this essay: Effectiveness. Undoubtedly, this topic can be approached from different approaches and the one chosen by us is neither original nor exclusive. Its content is distributed in what we call an effectiveness platform composed of three elements: strategy, leadership, and organizational culture, which, in our opinion, have a major impact on our inquiry regarding what must be done to "achieve those results and things correct" or also explain how the incomplete or insufficient development of the elements described explains a good part of the undesired results.

Chapter three analyzes efficiency, where ideas are outlined on how to do things or the best way to do them. This is a more conventional and less controversial concept than the previous one because there is a greater degree of consensus on it. With the help of a three-dimensional diagram, the basic variants present in scenarios of inefficiencies, intermediate efficiencies, and efficiency itself are clarified. As we maintain within this chapter, instead of describing a loose list of recommendations about "the right way to do things," we prefer a schematic presentation in line with the conventional approach to efficient management that includes three of its basic tools: Organization, Direction, and Control and Evaluation.

In chapter four, we present from a "systemic" perspective the prospection of what we understand as business or organizational complexity. A company or organization cannot be conceived, built, or progressed disconnected from its environment given that it is immersed in its specific context with which it is interrelated in permanent reciprocal effects. Notorious variants of that envelope that we call External Conditioning are exposed. Among them, the one represented by the risky populist currents of the contemporary political scene stands out. We also included in this concept the random externality with enormous economic impact, such as the Coronavirus pandemic, and we could not ignore the ever-present warmongering. For this reason, a brief overview of the economic and political connotations of recent external conditions is developed.

As we maintain below, every one of these external conditions has a significant impact on our business management problems. As a central part of this chapter, we present the main elements described for both effectiveness and efficiency, interrelated in a diagram that we call the Effectiveness and Efficiency Matrix recommended as a management tool. We conclude the topic by making special reference to the concept of Added Value, which we consider due to its connection with effectiveness and efficiency as a determining element of them and, therefore, of business management.

In chapter five, we close the study with important reflections to be considered on the topic discussed. In a world of convulsive changes like the one we live in and in the conviction that the permanence of the paradigms and the sacred cows that advocate them are ephemeral, we are interested in drawing attention and provoking the continuation of the debate on business management given that the convulsion scenario and our own mental conditioning disrupt our perception of evidence, making us see what has a substantial character as if it were complementary in nature or also what is complementary as substantial. Perspective errors are inevitable. The reflections in this chapter arose throughout the development of the topic, but in order not to divert the reader's attention, they have been grouped in a separate chapter because they correspond to the gravitational field of business management.

At the end of the book, the Conclusions are presented, where the main driving ideas of the hypotheses and approaches that make up this research are presented. With the intention that the ideas and concepts presented do not remain in the theoretical field, we have "landed" in various parts of the essay with explicit references that correspond to the Peruvian reality (native experience) and the North American reality (foreign experience). For this reason, the inevitable use of anglicisms is made more out of necessity than by fashion, and in order not to bother certain readers, these terms have been explained or translated.

The contrasts and contents between both realities have been developed within a framework of critical analysis and are quite illustrative and enriching regarding the topic presented. Perspectives broaden when different realities are contrasted. The forms, modalities, labels, and packaging vary, but in terms of substance and despite the abysmal differences, we verify the validity of the popular saying: "beans are cooked everywhere" (irregularities and sudden surprises happen anywhere).

Also, for practical purposes, we have excluded "ex professo" (intentionally), the term Efficacy as not to increase certain confusion given that in some writings and media, we have seen that it is identified as a synonym for effectiveness and in others we place it in a triangulation of combined criteria of both effectiveness and efficiency, which can complicate its understanding among those who use the word differently from those used in this work. Therefore, we leave the semantic interpretations for another opportunity and prefer that the reader focuses on the use of the terms Effectiveness and Efficiency from the perspective of decision-making and, as explained in this work.

In response to the presence of more visible business realities, this book makes continuous references to the scope of the simplest organization, the small or medium-sized business. The connotation of small businesses differs depending on the medium in question and the indicators to be used (number of workers, amount of income, value of assets, etc.). In developed countries, a small business could be classified as a medium-sized business in a developing country. Even in developing countries, we find notable differences between small businesses located in a more legal environment and microenterprises, which mostly belong to the informal sector.

For the purposes of our analysis, we maintain the realistic assumption of business behavior that establishes management aimed at maximizing profits or, as mentioned in certain texts, towards the search—as a more sustainable objective—of maximizing the value of the company in the market (which itself incorporates the lucrative purpose and integrates it with other purposes). It is worth clarifying that the market value of the company is more complex than the simple stock market price. Although the stock price must reflect the value and fundamentals of the company, regardless of whether the "share," as a representative title of part of the business property, can be listed on the stock exchange or not, experience frequently shows us that stock markets tend to be perfect and competitive, but they simply are not.

With the respective restrictions and reservations of the case, the effectiveness and efficiency instruments presented in this work can be considered valid for public management scenarios (governmental, regional, or local) and for cases of non-governmental organizations and entities

(NGOs) or non-purpose profit. Out of analytical necessity, we have focused on the treatment of management in the field of private companies, but in no way are the proposed scopes exclusive, nor are they assigned or limited to said sector.

We consider that the management problem goes beyond the limited private business scenario, which is not new and is even recognized by business leaders themselves. Therefore, throughout this research, we continuously reference the governmental and even global spheres and their respective conditions. This perspective is also another difference of our analysis with respect to conventional administration texts on the topic of satisfactory management.

This work was born with the purpose of writing a document of no more than three pages in length oriented towards journalistic collaboration. The impetus and curiosity in the topic were expanding perspectives and content, so when we reached 80 pages, we considered redirecting it toward a magazine specialized in economic or business topics. The gale of ideas continued to flow, and the events fueled more depth in the debate, so, after moving slowly and with pauses towards the 210 pages, we understood that we were heading towards an unprovoked destination such as the publication of a book. Even so, the effervescence of situations that occurred stimulated its continuity, so we had to self-impose a stop to the unquiet writing, and thus, we managed to complete a work that is around 410 pages (in Word format, one side per page). For a conventional edition of a book, this length will be reduced to just over half.

Finally, given that the importance of a piece of writing does not lie in its length or number of pages but in the quality of its content, we hope that readers are satisfied with finding it. For my part, I am pleased to have enjoyed the comfort of writing this "light baggage" work, that is, with unrestricted independence and without time pressures, work, and institutional pressures and without commitments or ideological indoctrinations. Of course, this "embarrassing backpack" can hardly be completely unloaded because we are always stalked by that "subconscious of habituality or origin" that, together with the "adherence to training conditions," ends up revealing us away at any moment. This warning is valid for the writer as well as for the reader.

1. BUSINESS MANAGEMENT: Concepts and Styles

1.1 GENERAL NOTION OF BUSINESS MANAGEMENT

According to research studies carried out in the US market, which many say represents the "non-plus ultra" (the maximum) of individual initiative and entrepreneurial freedom, it is reported that after the first five years of small business operation businesses, 80% are left out of the market and during the subsequent five years, 80% of those who continued were also left out of the market. This means that after the first decade of management, only 4% of the companies that started survived. (See: Michael E. Gerber, "The E-Myth Revisited. Why Small Businesses Don't Work and What to Do About it," Harper Business, New York, 1995, pp. 1-2).

Although the study is relatively past, we consider that, in an acceptable approximation, the substance and essence of the problem are maintained. What is happening, and why do business entrepreneurs experience a high attrition rate in small business management? Why do only a few survive and project themselves into medium or large companies? Curiously, the statistics also reflect another characteristic that is impossible to overlook, despite the high rates of dropouts and frustrations in this future of the real world, the "photographs" taken at the end of a certain period (generally annual) reflect that it is still higher the number of new companies that start the business adventure compared to the number of companies that withdraw from the market. Why does such a trend happen?

We must recognize that the spirit of the entrepreneur becomes fearless and tenacious in developing new experiences, in taking on new challenges and risks, and even being willing to accept the possibility of failing. Just as for example, in humans, couples will continue to arrange marriages (formal and informal) without taking into account the high divorce rates; likewise, the manager or entrepreneur, despite the high rates of business defection, wants to give himself the pleasure of walking "his path," on his own even at the risk of, as in marriage, being a repeat offender and defecting.

The reality described in these statistics shows us unequivocally that many entrepreneurs are faithful to punishment and willing to re-offend or undertake business adventures with an uncertain direction. Whether due to excessive daring, improvisation, disorganization, detachment, or following certain guidelines, norms, values, or for any reason, the exposed problem ignited the flame of our intellectual curiosity, and we decided to address it.

We have investigated how crucial it is to clarify what needs to be done to achieve those results and do the right things? Why are few "enlightened ones" able to foresee them and make the right choice? And what remains is how to do such things correctly or in the best possible way? Why are there many who make mistakes and few who succeed in their purpose of carrying them out? The traditional theoretical architecture with its principles, precepts, guidelines, and sophisticated normative or positivist models (what administration should be) continues to provide us with varied answers to an empirical reality plagued by complexities and overwhelmed by a majority membership of discouraged companies and managers.

When conventional theory is insufficient in the face of the reality it seeks to improve, the task of explaining and satisfactorily solving the problems of the real world envelops us in a kind of dead end, and overcoming this entrapment means, in several cases, detaching ourselves from orthodoxy learned, from the guidelines that they taught us in the classrooms and try to reexamine the problem with new approaches, perspectives, methods, and procedures, trying new routes that could give us light in the tunnel. That is our intention and our purpose.

The perspective discussed here investigates decision-making applied to the world of organizations and business; that is, it calls us and motivates us with what is related to the results of a satisfactorily administered business or organizational management. From a time horizon, these themes can be better understood to the extent that the lessons of right or wrong decisions are examined and learned in the past. However, given that realities and circumstances are changing, solutions based on historical and other experiences have their restrictions and constitute only referential aids to address management problems. Therefore, the decisions to be made in present realities must be considered, in addition to the well-known lessons of the past, new contributions and research, new analysis frameworks, and the flow of new technical instruments to face the challenges that management poses.

The development of said instruments has been broadly varied and has for decades raised the development of two major currents or approaches to addressing management problems with their respective contributions of recognized validity and influence. On the one hand, there are those who promote solutions based on sophisticated mathematical models. One of the pioneering works was that of the Hungarian mathematician John Von Neumann and the American economist Oskar Morgenstern: "Theory of Games and Economic Behavior." The works of such researchers propose mathematical instruments for what we conceive as "conflict of interest" that led to the name game theory. In this, the aim is not to provide the magic recipe to solve this or that problem but based on the principle of rationality in human action, it proposes general models of its behavior inherent to every decision process.

The prominent Peruvian historian Jorge Basadre mentions them in his work: "The random events in history and its limits," 1971, Penguin Random House Grupo Editorial, pp. 14-17, to introduce into its framework of analysis the important role of chance as a surprising and inherent factor in historical processes. We return to this random concept as a contextual element of organizational management processes that we develop in the next chapters.

In this same current, the works of A. Kaufmann, R. Fauré, and A. Le Graff have mentioned: "Business games." Buenos Aires, Editorial Universitaria, 1st Edition 1966, which highlights the contribution of computers to facilitate perspectives of rationalization in fields such as business management previously reserved for intuition and/or managerial experience. Basadre rescues from this work a very interesting thought of Machiavelli that we are going to verify in many parts of this work: "Princes who rely too much on Fortune (conceived as a favorable chance) perish when she abandons them, princes who regulate their conduct according to the political situation are rarely unhappy, and Fortune changes only for those who do not know how to adapt to current events."[1]

Basadre notes that the name "game theory" is unfortunate because, at first, it could be distorted by relating them to parlor games, but when exposed in the economic and business sphere, they are part of a board with problems and uncertainties that are difficult to foresee and confront by the manager and his team. In fact, the said team is usually immersed in different contextual circumstances, with information that is not necessarily complete and sometimes negligible, with cooperating and non-cooperative participants (internal and external) and is forced to make decisions, facing conflicts and disagreements with other individuals and being aware of the danger or risk due to the result of those decisions.

---

[1] Jorge Basadre, Op cit, page 16

One of the last and prominent exponents of this mathematical school was the renowned John Nash (1928-2015), winner of the 1994 Nobel Prize in Economics in recognition of his contribution to Game Theory. Nash suffered from paranoid schizophrenia, and part of his biography was exposed in the film "Beautiful Mind," winner of the Oscar award for Best Picture (2002). He developed a new concept of strategic equilibrium (Nash equilibrium) where agents interacting with each other choose the optimal action considering what their counterparts will do. These currents of econometric schools, in their growing tendency, come close to forming a theory of rational human behavior with the help of mathematical and computer support.

The other current is based on non-mathematical or probabilistic models but on hypotheses and qualitative arguments of the decision-making process and business or organizational management. In this current, approaches are presented that suggest different schemes for doing the same thing, such as M. Porter's competitiveness diamond, the multivariable framework of the seven "s," and the eight criteria to achieve excellence described by T. Peters and R. Waterman Jr. in his work "In Search of Excellence," the business architecture scheme of James Brickley, Smith, Zimmerman in their work Managerial Economics & Organizational Architecture, the Balanced Scorecard (BSC) of Kaplan and Norton.

We also have various approaches to the field of theory of systems for the study of complex organizations. In this current, the diagrams, archetypes, and patterns of organizational behavior that Peter Senge describes in his work "The Fifth Discipline" stand out, and we also rescue the six-step MACORE model that Peter Baltes presents in his work "The Good Life. Critical theory of living" (philosophical foundation to address problems). As can be seen, we have these and many other contributions that reinforce this growing trend of researchers in the problem discussed. Both currents have their defenders and detractors, and in this attempt to get closer to the truth and provide their contributions, some extreme positions have exaggerated their initial positions, ignoring important contributions from different currents.

Critics of the first current allude that the excess of mathematical logic ignores behavioral and psychological aspects in the teams responsible for management that, in certain cases, suffer deviations derived from partial or defective applications of the selected model. According to these critics, the mathematical current errs in taking for granted, in addition to rational behavior, which set of values and behavior patterns such as honesty, loyalty, solidarity commitment, equity, etc., on the part of the management team that does not always conform to the reality. These critics maintain that the company is not an automatically driven machine but a living organism with people who receive and emit ideas, values, and behaviors. There is also another more unpleasant and harsher self-criticism made by certain economists who point out that this current of support in mathematical and computer models is a response, as a catharsis, to a certain inferiority complex that a representative membership of the economic discipline presents in the face of the advance and distance from the exact sciences to which it aims to resemble.

For their part, critics of the second current maintain that biasing key decisions based on the personal gifts of the management team, their intuition, and sense of smell constitute factors more related to feelings or emotions and somewhat detached from guiding logical frameworks and patterns management. For this reason, in the face of the occurrence of unexpected market circumstances, potential or weaknesses of the competition and other aspects not carefully considered, fruitless results may be generated. For critics of these currents of argumentative hypotheses, organizational management should not be approached as if we had to bet on what we think are the qualities of a person or group in charge of management. This is equivalent to undertaking business management as if it were a bet, even more so when nothing guarantees that these qualities, no matter how good they may seem, will have permanence.

For these reasons, biases from one current or another have appeared that have developed a kind of symbiosis of both and have enriched their respective proposals. In this way, the mathematical current maintains the strict rationality of its econometric models but has been considering greater weighting to evaluate how and to what degree the torrent of personal, group, and circumstantial "subjectivities" affect the random probability of the model and the plausibility of its results. The current of hypotheses and arguments is reinforcing their approaches, with platforms of strict logical frameworks providing them with an architecture of greater objectivity to provide reasonable trends in their approach and greater accuracy in their diagnoses and prognoses.

Having said the above, we warn that the professional curiosity mentioned at the beginning of this work is neither original nor new since there are a legion of observers, researchers, notable academics, and professionals who for decades have been interested in the debate on decision-making in business and organizational management. Our business management approach is only an additional proposal located in the stream of arguments and hypotheses, which we have reinforced with the logical framework of an effectiveness and efficiency matrix, which is widely developed in the following chapters.

This work raises the hypothesis of validating satisfactory business management when it meets the conditions of Effectiveness and Efficiency. To the extent that performance fails to comply with such conditions, business management deteriorates toward defective results. Business management itself contains the germ of movement, change, and internal and external interaction. In this process, advances, setbacks, and strategic pauses of rethinking, and changes of direction are experienced. The key is not to lose the perspective of a continuous approach towards that proposed and desired future.

The proposed approach may seem like a truism because, for many researchers, academics, analysts, and businesspeople, these conditions of efficiency and effectiveness are acceptable, necessary, and unquestionable. However, we appreciate that its theoretical-practical treatment is usually relegated to lower levels in the hierarchy of managerial and academic importance. In fact, the usual references to such criteria are mostly isolated, unconnected, and only specific results (Example: collection efficiency, operational efficiency of machinery and equipment, logistics efficiency, advertising effectiveness, investment effectiveness, effectiveness of controls and supervisions, etc.).

Despite this, we have confirmed that in recent years, the topics proposed in this work have gained greater attention and we hope that this trend is not a simple idiom. Well, the faculties of administration and their master's programs at several foreign and local universities include specializations, among others, in topics of Business Strategy, Leadership, and Business Culture.

In this study, we dare to propose a somewhat heterodox perspective so that we invert the conventional order of treatment of this management problem and postulate that these criteria (effectiveness and efficiency) constitute pillars and axes of satisfactory management, Policies, programs, and projects, and other conventional topics (organization, direction, control, etc.) constitute complementary and reinforcing elements of the proposed criteria. But we must warn that raising priority compliance with conditions of effectiveness and efficiency in management should not lead to misunderstandings or distortions.

In this sense, we emphasize that effectiveness and efficiency do not represent ends in themselves but rather constitute means whose progress and interdependence will facilitate the subsequent achievement of satisfactory or successful management. Each of them is based on a platform that we develop in detail later. Before prejudging "a priori" whether the proposed approach is pertinent, we invite you to review the conceptual categories contained in this work that seek to clarify its scope, get rid of certain preconceptions, and, at the same time, avoid confusion.

What do we understand by Effectiveness?

Business effectiveness is about achieving the right results. Effectiveness leads us to answer the question: where to aim to achieve those correct things and results? Effectiveness corresponds to "having chosen and developed those things, objectives, and goals that must be achieved to achieve what is proposed or desired (<u>without considering for the moment how they are done in terms of resource allocation</u>).

There is a triple condition: 1) being right in choosing the product or service provision according to the characteristics required by the market, 2) being right in choosing the appropriate route and orientation to lead us towards the desired objectives, and 3) the most important, succeeding in achieving and demonstrating proposed results. This translates into feasible satisfactory achievements at the expected time and opportunity, in the right place, in the modality that the market or population requires, and that allows the company to gain positioning in the market and favorable economic impacts on its achievements. Effectiveness achievements translate into substantial increases in income, sales, profits, customers, and the market in general.

With the help of a simple analogy, we will say that to be effective, we must choose "the right bull or target," direct and correctly use the corresponding weapon toward said bull, provide ourselves with the appropriate equipment that facilitates "hitting the bull" and finally develop the optimal effort and commitment to achieve the proposed result.

It is important to emphasize the conditionalities described because it could, misleadingly or mistakenly, have been "chosen and directed toward targets" that were not the most appropriate, believing or assuming that they were. In the end, the results achieved could be insufficient or different from those expected, which is why effectiveness gains to the desired degree or magnitude will not have been met. Likewise, viable objectives and goals could be established, but inexperienced shooters were available, with frequent failures in the correct direction to reach the bull, without adequate equipment and without committed effort in their task. All of this will not allow for effectiveness gains either.

The definition is quite simple but carrying it out has its complications. After the right things have been identified and executed, the time perspective of an "ex-post" evaluation will confirm whether we have been effective based on the results achieved. But it will also be important to conduct an "ongoing evaluation" of management because it will tell us if we are on the right path and direction.

For now, we are not going to delve into whether hitting the target has been the subject of an in-depth market study or a slight market prospection. You may also have technical skills in the development of a specific, novel product or in the provision of a service that takes advantage of an unmet need. A business opportunity may also arise due to massive migration from the countryside to the city, whether due to economic expectations or social upheavals of subversion or armed conflicts, epidemics, etc., the presence of a mostly young, adult population structure may also be indicative, gender biased, etc.

In short, many reasons may have weighed in an election, but beyond the considerations indicated above, the results achieved will be those that definitively confirm whether we were effective.

Effectiveness leads in a respectable number of cases to processes of satisfying a portion of unsatisfied, neglected, or poorly attended demand, taking advantage of changes in economic and environmental environments, having adequately foreseen changes in consumer tastes or preferences, discovery, and exploitation of "betas market," etc. Economists perceive that when we refer to effectiveness, factors related to demand are involved. It is said that management has been effective because it has achieved favorable results in market goals and achievements, but more specifically, in having offered what consumers want or need and derived from the above, allowing the company to obtain favorable economic results.

The direction towards objectives and achieving adequately established goals is especially important since there have been cases where partial results were achieved without achieving satisfactory objectives and goals because such goals were erroneously overestimated. It could also happen that objectives and goals initially set were achieved, but they were artificially underestimated and culminated in modest results of effectiveness that satisfy no one. That is, deviations from over or underestimating objectives and goals must be avoided.

The panorama of a situation characterized by changes on different fronts and by conditions derived from restrictions and availability of resources means that the achievements of effectiveness and results described do not have the character of indefinite permanence and that many achievements are ephemeral. Even the effectiveness achieved and its way of impacting the market is not always well accompanied. These remarks are a strong wake-up call for traditional business management approaches to provide greater attention, do not lose sight and remain prepared to reinforce activities oriented towards continuous achievements of effectiveness.

Without failing to recognize that there are reciprocal effects between effectiveness and efficiency, fruitless debates are observed between those who consider that one of them has priority or greater relevance over the other. As we noted at the beginning, the theoretical-practical treatment of business management has strong defenders who emphasize and prioritize efficiency because they maintain the condition that any effectiveness will be obtained as a result and logical consequence of efficiency processes. As we will see later, this has certain reasonable considerations, but it also constitutes a generalization with opposing nuances. In the same way, we also disagree with those who argue on the contrary that efficiency achievements are necessarily subordinated and conditioned to previous effectiveness achievements.

What do we understand by Efficiency?

Efficiency focuses attention on the way things are done; that is, efficiency requires making the best use of the always limited resources available which will be applied in the development of the options and achievement of chosen goals. Experience indicates that taking advantage of an opportunity or market boom, although it generates initial gains in effectiveness, could be relative, insufficient, and even fade quickly if not accompanied by strict criteria of efficiency in the use of resources.

In this way, the lack of control or inadequate management of administrative expenses (logistics, suppliers, temporary contracting of services, etc.), commercial expenses (points of sale, advertising, inadequate means of distribution, etc.), and operational costs (supplies, defective materials, and machinery and equipment, etc.), can spoil any "boom" in sales and lead to a disaster of equal or even greater proportions than those generated by insufficient income.

Defenders of efficiency trends (supported by a respectable number of academics, businessmen and professionals) propose that the results of successful management require as a "sine qua non"

14

condition the prior establishment of demanding criteria of technical rationality in the management of available resources. According to this orientation, it will be the way of doing things that is decisive in achieving the corresponding efficiency and subsequently and consequently leading us to achievements of effectiveness and consolidating management support.

Accordingly, the path of effectiveness cannot be achieved without the precondition of efficiency. We leave the controversy of which condition is a priority for later and continue in the development of our theme. The forced example of spending more on washing a used shirt than a new one would cost suggests that it is not enough to orient yourself in an unrestricted and correct manner toward the proposed purposes. It is important to know how things are achieved, and there is no point in doing it at unreasonable costs. Therefore, in addition to focusing on "achieving correct results (meaning effectiveness), they must also do or carry out things correctly (efficiency) or, in other words, "do those things that need to be done in the best way."

Efficiency is found in response to the question: How can we correctly do those things that will lead us to what was previously chosen or desired? Efficiency focuses attention on the best way to accomplish such things. While effectiveness focuses on how to successfully impact demand, efficiency focuses on supply and operation through cost reduction and rationalization, use of technological improvements and information and management systems, application of new discoveries and innovations, processes of economies of scale (production increases with lower average and marginal costs) and improvements in quality and productivity.

For this reason, a conventional way of approaching efficiency is to refer to the relationship that exists between the flow of inputs and means that are combined in structured business systems. The figurative reference to what is called a "black box" represents how to do things or, also known as "Know How". The harmonious result of the set of inputs, means, processes, and systems result in obtaining the product or provision of services in accordance with the previously established objectives. Later, we will see how this relationship between production and inputs, called productivity, is constituted as a determining symptom of efficiency.

The importance of execution in resource management cannot allow itself to wait for "ex-post" evaluations (at the end of the process) but rather partial follow-ups and "in situ" monitoring must necessarily be conducted (through the extensive instruments of analysis, indicators, and ratios) that allow adjustments and corrections during operation. To avoid confusion, it must be understood that <u>when satisfactory management is developed in the use of resources in the conduct of business systems and their processes, we do not classify them as effective but rather as efficient.</u>

However, this "orientation towards the right things and doing them correctly" (effectiveness and efficiency) cannot be separated from those basic administration functions indicated at the beginning. As will be seen later, effectiveness is more fine-tuned with activities within the planning and leadership functions, and efficiency is related to management and control functions. Effectiveness and Efficiency are constituted as management qualities that will help these functions to be configured toward satisfactory achievements. As we noted before, the characteristics of conventional management functions are included in a cycle of continuity, simultaneity, and interrelation. The interconnection of efficiency and effectiveness with such functions constitutes them as independent and interacting forces and forms a support system for satisfactory management.

Effectiveness and Efficiency are two sides of the same coin in organizational management. Both (effectiveness and efficiency) are interdependent in nature. In circumstances of affinity (internal or external) or direct correlation between forces that compose it, the effectiveness obtained will affect and condition possibilities of efficiency; and in other cases, it will be the efficiency achieved that will influence and allow effectiveness to be reinforced. This interdependence can develop in a favorable or unfavorable direction, that is, it can be progressive with favorable increases in both or also regressive with unfavorable decreases between both. See Chart N° 1.

There may also be cases of independence or zero interconnection between each one. In effect, the interdependence between efficiency and effectiveness can be blocked when, for example, conditions of affinity and direct correlation of forces do not exist, but on the contrary, contradictory forces or atypical functionalities predominate among the elements and factors that comprise them, so that the occurrence of effects or impacts are blocked or reduced. Cases of effectiveness without efficiency or efficiency without effectiveness may then arise. In terms of performance of the management functions, it would relate to cases where, for example, acceptable and satisfactory management or leadership is not accompanied by good organization or also where good planning is inconsistent with poor control and supervision schemes.

Chart Nº 1: Management supports

An illustrative clarification of the functional or dysfunctional relationship between efficiency and effectiveness is found when making an analogy in sports and, more precisely, in football (also called soccer in USA). For example, a team can do things correctly by developing a coordinated game, with full control and dominance of the opponent, with good individual and group performance, with good offensive and defensive plays, with excellent tactical discipline, but unfortunately, if all this relative superiority is not manifested in the score, we conclude that said team develops its game efficiently but lacks effectiveness due to its lack of ability to score goals and goals determine results. There are even cases of teams that play efficiently well and end up with adverse results. Many times, we witnessed journalistic comments such as the home team playing a good game but unfortunately lost the match by two to zero!

The technical management of a team (like that of a company) must consider in its strategic and tactical schemes appropriate variants in the course or development of the game. Ineffectiveness means the lack of a change of direction, of a touch of inspiration, of originality, of knowing how to manage oneself with excellent psychological and emotional virtues. It is true that if a team develops efficiency, it opens greater possibilities of achieving effectiveness, but by remaining under rigid schemes, it may be difficult to achieve it and failure to achieve it is also a possibility that increases the risk of undesirable results. In the recent World Cup in Qatar 2022, the team that won, Argentina, had a frustrating start against the modest Saudi Arabia team, which it dominated throughout the match. However, their superiority did not translate into effectiveness due to insistence on the same game tactics (abuse of long crosses and aerial plays). In the end, the Saudi Arabia team, which did not have the favoritism of commentators, surprisingly ended up being more effective; he scored goals and won the match.

At the sporting level, it is proven that efficient development does not necessarily lead to effectiveness. At the managerial level, we persist in the rigid conviction that efficiency must necessarily lead us towards effectiveness and that this will not take place or be achieved without having previously achieved efficiency. In the end, comes the frustration of adverse results despite the efficiency achieved.

On the other hand, a team can achieve effectiveness and achieve a good result by scoring goals, but not due to taking advantage of its potential, but rather due to the weaknesses and deficiencies of the opponent. Accidental factors can also come into play (opponent's own goal, taking advantage of a rebound or casual deflection, involuntary infraction, etc.). Having scored goals (achieving a result) and temporarily winning the game is not a logical consequence of having been more efficient either. This is called misleading results because reality is distorted, showing a superior score that contrasts with the team's performance.

If the results are not due to their own merits but rather to external or fortuitous factors, notable inefficiencies may remain in the temporarily winning team (disintegrated play, poor marking, wrong passes, uncovered areas, lack of esprit de corps, and courage to face adverse situations, limitations techniques, physics, and tactics, etc.). If this is the case, the effectiveness achieved by having scored goals does not necessarily imply having been efficient, and not being efficient also increases the risk of undesirable results. In this case, we have also heard the journalistic comment: the narrow victory or meager draw of the local team was undeserved, and the team was saved from being thrashed! In this case, we also have evidence that, on a sporting level, one can show effectiveness without having been efficient. This condition also occurs at the managerial level.

Additionally, we must mention that the ineffectiveness and inefficiencies of the example described can also be attributed to external conditions that are beyond the control or management of management or members of each team. Among them, we can highlight climatic factors where excess heat (dehydration) or cold (numbness) affect individual and group performance, as well as the location of places of excessive height (for example, playing in areas with more than 4,000 meters above sea level) lead to breathing and oxygenation problems. Also, the conditions of the wet field due to excessive rain or snow make the normal movement of the ball difficult, and the size of the grass and the maintenance of the playing field can also be mentioned. Nor can we rule out wind conditions in favor or against refereeing errors, rigged fixture configuration, outbursts of home conditions (public hostility), etc.

Returning to our organizational management problem, we must indicate that the issue of external conditions is of vital importance and will be treated more exhaustively in the fourth chapter. Having finished clarifying the interrelation or independence between effectiveness and efficiency, we now move on to visualize the basic results of said combination.

1.2 MANAGEMENT OVERVIEWS

Once the concepts, scope, and relationship of the terms of effectiveness and efficiency have been clarified, we are going to carry out a first imagination exercise and present a graphic description that guides the relationship between the concepts presented. The attached Cartesian diagram represents, on the horizontal "x" axis, the concept of Efficiency, which has been qualitatively disaggregated into three levels: low, medium, and high efficiency. The vertical "y" axis represents the concept of Effectiveness, also disaggregated into three levels: low, medium, and high effectiveness. Any point on the xy plane represents a specific even combination of certain levels of efficiency and effectiveness. As can be seen, we have represented the concepts of effectiveness and efficiency of mixed connotation (qualitative and quantitative) on an instrument (Cartesian diagram) with the intention of providing an approximation to what we understand as a panorama or basic management scenarios (See graph No. 2).

Chart N° 2: Effectiveness and Efficiency

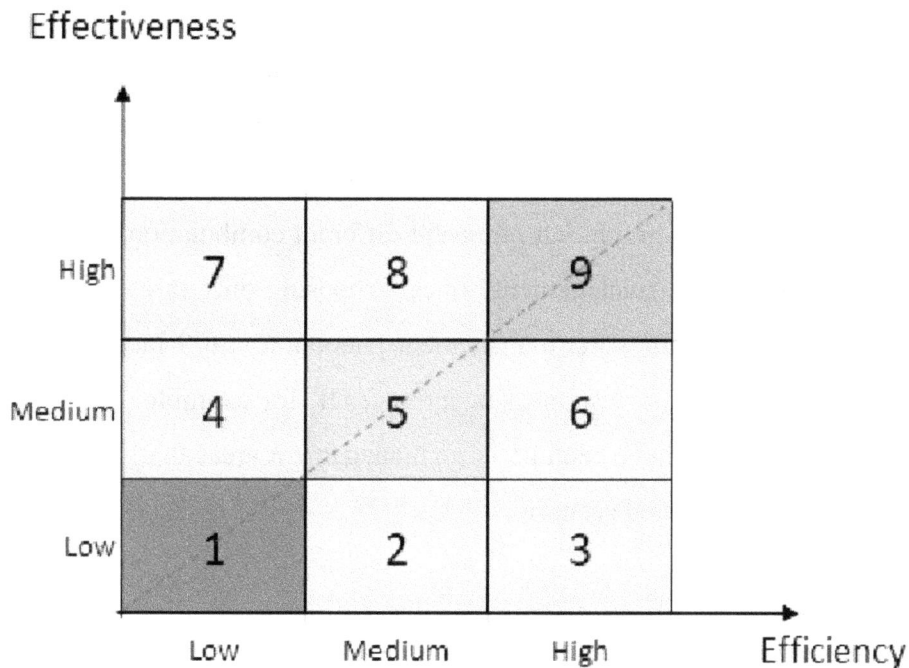

Effectiveness

	Low	Medium	High	
High	7	8	9	
Medium	4	5	6	
Low	1	2	3	
	Low	Medium	High	Efficiency

An optional way that helps to locate ourselves in the different scenarios or management zones will be that we can attribute a rating for both criteria: effectiveness and efficiency (like those given to financial instruments by rating entities). According to the observed performance, there will be good or satisfactory categories (AAA, AA, and A), average categories (BBB, BB, and B), and low or poor categories (CCC, CC, and C). The predominance of the qualification according to the categories described will determine the area or scenario in which the company is located. This qualification can be conducted by an external advisor or by the manager himself, who must proceed with the greatest possible objectivity to avoid self-deception.

An imaginary line (dotted line) can be constructed that starts from the vertex of both axes at an angle of 45° degrees, representing successive and continuous identical combinations of effectiveness and efficiency starting from lower levels to higher levels of the same. We say that it is an imaginary line because it represents a particular path of evolution, not necessarily the ideal, nor the best, nor the most plausible. This imaginary line is built only to analyze and understand the cases that are exposed and the imbalances between the two (efficiency or effectiveness). For example, it will be difficult for the same magnitude of efficiency to correspond to the same magnitude of effectiveness or vice versa.

The actual route taken by any organization will be combined with difficulties and biases in effectiveness and efficiency that will culminate in its definitive location or its displacement in different areas of the graphical management panorama. As a qualitative approach, nine basic areas have been built on the previous graph that represent different combinations of effectiveness and efficiency grouped into specific management zones. Proposing only three categories of quality (low, medium, and high) simplifies the management panorama into 9 large areas and provides clarity and simplicity in the main results of occurrence. If, for example, we had established 5 quality categories, there would have been 25 large management areas that would present us with a more demanding and complicated scenario.

1.2.1 Successes and failures

At the end of a management period or during its development, the evaluation and monitoring of efficiency and effectiveness criteria will indicate what and how the things included in business management are done. If the management has been or is being successfully or satisfactorily well administered, it will be graphically identified in the area comprised by satisfactory and elevated levels of efficiency and effectiveness (scenario No. 9 of graph No. 2). Locating yourself in this desirable area means having got it right, having achieved and being directed toward correct objectives and strategic goals and having achieved them in the best way or manner possible.

The companies included in this zone No. 9 have fulfilled or are managing management in accordance with the requirement of double-effectiveness and efficiency- in a satisfactory manner. This constitutes a similar task (using the previous analogy again), not only choosing and hitting the target but also using the ideal shooter, the appropriate weapon, with the minimum use of ammunition, in the shortest possible time and saving the other available resources. **Success or satisfactory business management** has to do with the conception of a clever idea, the correlation of its correct implementation, and a satisfactory reception by the market, that is, the achievement of effective and efficient management.

It must be emphasized that zone nine would represent, as the source indicates at the beginning of the work, that specific case of small companies with satisfactory management that initially represented 20% of surviving companies after the first five years of operation. So, of every 100 companies that started business ventures, only twenty of them assumed management in a serious, responsible, and professional manner. In the next five years, staying on this path is full of challenges and difficulties and not all the companies that remain will be able to overcome them. Only four of those samples of twenty that crossed the first fence, maintained an unfailing vocation and conviction and are the ones that were enabled to advance towards medium or large companies.

We must point out that time considerations are relative; they can be minor or major and depend on the harmonization of its components in each case. Likewise, an expansion of more demanding quality criteria (in efficiency and effectiveness), such as those of the 5 categories where there are 25 management areas, will cause the probability of a favorable occurrence to be diluted. In these scenarios, after the first five-year period, there will only be 4 companies included in the maximum level of effectiveness and efficiency (instead of 20 in the case described above). After the second five-year period, there would only be one company achieving this level of excellence (instead of the 4 in the previous case). However, despite agreeing that reality is in that order of complexity, we prefer to follow the recommendation attributed to Keynes: ... "it is better to be right in the approximation than to be wrong in the accuracy." In any case, the assessments and scope remain valid.

The conception of a clever idea can be original and new, or it can also include updated ideas and even renewed copies of existing ideas or schemes. For example, the Starbucks chain, whose idea is well known, a simple coffee shop business, had as the key to its success this new concept of offering the same thing that others offered, but in an unusual way. In this same line of action, we have the resounding success of the Cirque du Soleil, which redefined the concept and practice of the Circus business.

In the opposite case and by contrast and for exposition purposes, there is a management riddled with errors that will be in the scenario that corresponds to the undesirable and risky area of low levels of efficiency and effectiveness (see scenario No. 1 of graph No. 2). This peculiar but unfortunately common case is related to the pronounced **failure or mistake in business management**.

This situation corresponds, according to our approach, to situations where wrong or inappropriate goals were chosen (believing that the right thing was chosen) and business systems and processes were also developed in an incorrect or misguided manner (also with the "conviction" that one proceeded correctly or also due to carelessness or irresponsibility). With this, unfavorable results are obtained due to having chosen products or services that the market does not want and alternating with poor use of resources that result in excessive costs.

Continuing with the previous simile, we will say that it was far from choosing and hitting the target, and in addition, poorly qualified shooters, inadequate weapons, waste of ammunition, time, and other resources were used. The case described above corresponds to those companies that fail to achieve this duality of effectiveness and efficiency. The above translates into inappropriate goals accompanied by poor use of resources and, consequently, poor results. Therefore, companies located in this zone of mistakes are the companies most likely to exit the market promptly.

1.2.2 Defective business management

Between the two previously described cases of excellent success or overwhelming failure, there is an intermediate zone where seven zones are represented, corresponding to a hybrid situation, neither of total success nor of total failure. The companies in this area present irregular functioning, which we will call **defective business management,** where there has been partial or deficient compliance, whether in terms of effectiveness, efficiency, or both.

Again, if we bring together companies from this sector with defective management and partial performance together with companies from the previous management zone totally misguided, we will have approximately 80% of small businesses that defected and left the market during the first five years of operation which we indicated in the initial statistics of this work. The lesson is hard, but more things are required than simple good wishes to venture into the entrepreneurship of any company, no matter how small it may be. As can be seen, small businesses that fall into zones 1 to 8 engage in this morass of survival typical of defective management.

So, during the first five years of every 100 companies that started a business venture, approximately 80 of them defected due to partial or improper compliance with the stated criteria, or for whatever reason, they will tend to withdraw from the market. In the next five years of the twenty that passed the hurdles, not all will be able to overcome their detours and difficulties, and again, 16 of that sample of twenty that crossed the first hurdle will increase the group of defective companies and could also, in the long run, must withdraw from the market.

Likewise, an expansion of more demanding quality criteria, such as those of the 5 categories (before quoted), which result in 25 management areas, will give rise to probabilities of unfavorable occurrence grouped together in the majority. We then have a set of 24 among the 25 scenarios that, after the first five-year period, will direct 96 out of every 100 companies to that survival morass described above (instead of the 80 companies corresponding to the previous scenario of lower quality variability).

After the second five-year period of the 4 companies that passed the initial hurdle, not all of them will be able to overcome their deviations and difficulties, and additionally 3 of that sample of 4 that crossed the first hurdle will increase the group of defective companies and will also tend to withdraw in the long run. of the market (instead of the 16 companies corresponding to the scenario of lower quality variability).

Typical management of mediocrity: medium efficiency and medium effectiveness

Focusing on the seven zones of partial management of effectiveness and/or efficiency, we present the typical hybrid or intermediate situation where we proceeded with medium efficiency and medium effectiveness. That is, the requirements demanded by both parameters have not been satisfactorily met. The results present these companies involved in a management characterized by vicious circles of mediocrity. Graphically, these companies are specifically located in the central zone (see scenario No. 5 of graph No. 2), corresponding to average levels of both effectiveness and efficiency. The product or service provided, its quality and other characteristics offered do not fully cover market expectations for multiple reasons. This fragility makes their survival unstable and full of difficulties.

This group of companies located in scenario No. 5 are companies with notable signs of informal management; these are business experiments where improvisation prevails, things are done as they arise, and they are reactive companies where, for example, probable periods were never foreseen of crisis or boom, but they found themselves faced with them suddenly, reactively or by chance. Such companies have the characteristic of remaining attached to surviving the circumstances of their present time (as far as possible). They are companies immersed in day-to-day business, with medium- and long-term myopia, and additionally, they have the characteristic of being extremely sensitive and volatile to the socio-economic environment.

The mediocrity itself of defective management of this area is better appreciated when we focus on filters of conjunctural contexts of boom or crisis in which they operate. Here, we distinguish these sub-variants:

1. First, we describe companies that, despite the irregularities of mediocrity described, in their improvised journey take advantage of economic boom cycles that they came across by chance. This boom will have an impact regardless of whether it is effective or efficient. Graphically, they will move from scenario No. 5 to No. 8 (high effectiveness and medium efficiency) or to No. 6 (high efficiency and medium effectiveness). Due to interdependent effects between both, if they are well used, they could provide them with possibilities of heading towards the route of the area of successful companies (scenario No. 9). That depends on whether management abandons mediocrity and informality and strengthens its professionalism.

2. Secondly, there are those companies that also "manage mediocrity" and waste the boom cycle that they stumbled upon by chance. They become clouded, careless, and delayed and do not prioritize the necessary adjustments to their weak points. Their irregularities will cause many of these companies to experience frequent difficulties that prevent them from achieving the necessary sustainability that the process demands. Their strategic blindness makes them believe that the boom cycle "has just begun or that it will last longer or that, deludedly, it will be permanent." The pendulum of history has left us its great lesson, often forgotten, that "no stage or situation of boom or crisis is permanent." For those who prefer religion, we will say that the biblical episode of "the thin cows and the fat cows" has the same message.

   The result is inevitable; such companies are not prepared to live with the boom cycle, and the spring does not last long. By losing the step of effectiveness (or efficiency), the interconnection between both will make them degrade towards the areas that we graphically observe in scenario No. 4 (medium effectiveness and low efficiency) or in scenario No. 2 (medium efficiency and low effectiveness). If the problems continue, they will be exposed to descending into dangerous zone No. 1. Sailing in troubled seas will last if their endurance capacity allows, and that is why some will have greater survival than others, and few will overcome the swamp of mediocrity.

3. If <u>we find ourselves in crisis situations</u>, the phenomenon described is repeated with the addition that crises in themselves have a perverse effect. During crises, these companies with irregular performance, despite partial developments in efficiency (or effectiveness), do not obtain expected results because their effects (counteracted by the crisis) are tenuous, fruitless and are insufficient and minimized by sailing against the current or against the tide and having to deal with serious shortages and resource limitations. This constitutes a serious restriction even for companies that are in a better position, which many times, during crisis cycles, choose to park in a safe harbor and take shelter until "the stormy weather passes." There is no point in wearing yourself out in the middle of a storm.

It is evident that also during crisis cycles, the clumsiness, setbacks, and unfavorable things derived from poor management will cause these irregular companies to accelerate their own decline. As we pointed out before, these companies with "mediocre management" do not foresee or anticipate crises, which surprise them in their daily work. Their latent vulnerability to current factors will make them more susceptible to deterioration and be located in the area of companies that may exit the market because the effect of crises will generate a regressive or adverse interdependence between efficiency and effectiveness and will cause moderate and successive decreases in their performances that it would drag them more quickly towards the area of companies with clear mistakes in management (that is, towards zone No. 1). There will always be a few companies that survive, but in the long run, crises devour companies with mediocre behavior with poor management more quickly and induce them to irremediable falls and exits from the market.

Another way to typify the mediocrity of faulty management is to appreciate it from the perspective of nature, orientation, and achievement of **objectives**. For this reason, the following subvariants are distinguished:

- Firstly, there may be the case of companies that make an inappropriate choice of objectives and goals. This defect was pointed out as non-compliance with the requirement of effectiveness. The company could expressly determine itself, which sets modest goals and objectives and thereby develops an undemanding management effort. Therefore, they deceive themselves by arguing that they "met their goals," but the result achieved in terms of the market and the use of resources does not satisfy either their own or strangers. The partial results of effectiveness and efficiency of this case correspond graphically with those that are in zone No. 5 or also in zone No. 2.

- Secondly, we highlight those cases that correspond to companies that also do not make a good choice of goals and objectives, but unlike the previous case, here the companies fall into the defect of setting goal levels that are too demanding and "are self-convinced." which are appropriate goals. Such extreme situations normally culminate in partial or deficient fulfillment of the wrongly proposed goals. Your frustration is greater or less depending on the gap between what was planned and what was done. These cases correspond graphically to zone No. 2 (low effectiveness and medium efficiency).

- Thirdly, there are companies that, having made a satisfactory and balanced choice of goals and objectives, observe unfocused and inappropriate management in the management and use of resources (in a minimally efficient way). Due to this deviation, they achieve partially fulfilled goals and objectives. This case corresponds graphically to zone No. 4 (medium effectiveness and low efficiency).

Contrasting faulty management: satisfactory effectiveness with discrete efficiency

We present a category of companies involved in defective management or irregular performance that would correspond, according to our example, to a situation in which a satisfactory point of effectiveness was reached, that is, the target was hit or at a point close to it, but consuming inadequate costs, resources, and times (low efficiency). It can be satisfactorily effective with low levels of efficiency (see scenario No. 7). That is, the achievement of effectiveness does not in itself incorporate nor is it guaranteed to be accompanied by satisfactory levels of efficiency. The management team is very enthusiastic about the favorable effectiveness results and often ignores and overlooks important adjustments to its efficiency defects.

Having achieved levels of effectiveness could have been due to a correct appreciation of their environment that allowed them to anticipate, foresee, and develop timely changes, adjustments, and direction of their efforts. This allowed it to achieve the proposed goal but with defective executive or managerial progress. This possibility is quite misleading because the relative success in effectiveness (satisfactory results) shadows inefficiencies and generates "height dizziness or managerial cloudiness." The enjoyment of effectiveness successes makes us forget, delay, or cause delayed reactions to undertake the required adjustments in efficiency.

It is convenient to make a slight digression and help us review this case with the contexts of boom and crisis situations made previously. Companies located in zone No. 7 (high effectiveness with low efficiency) that encounter favorable boom environments must deploy a significant efficiency effort to move towards the area of successful companies. However, the magnitude of the change required is demanding and could be more cumbersome despite requiring changes in only one direction.

Graphically, this implies undertaking serious efficiency efforts to first move from zone No. 7 to area No. 8 (high effectiveness and medium efficiency) and continue the said effort in a sustained manner until reaching the optimal area No. 9. It must be considered that the drastic changes that must be undertaken will require a significant period. No improvement as required is obtained immediately.

It could happen that the boom fades, the product or service completes its life cycle, the productive apparatus becomes obsolete, the tastes and preferences of the market change, there is a lack of innovation, absence of strategy, etc., and then as the saying goes: "one swallow does not make a summer," the possibilities of enhancing opportunities and strengths were wasted and when the deficiencies were discovered, harsh crises ensued that not everyone understands and unfortunately the permanence of inefficiencies leads to undesirable results.

For their part, companies located in this space No. 7 (high effectiveness and low efficiency) and must face crisis situations will find it more difficult or will have less management capacity to overcome their inefficiencies. Why? Because what crises fundamentally do is make efficiency efforts sterile and they will seek to cling to their achievements in terms of effectiveness. In this case, even the improvements will not be immediate because the benefits of high effectiveness achieved are maintained. Even the probable loss or decrease in effectiveness will also have to be of a relevant magnitude and will require a good amount of time to move and descend toward the area of companies with errors in their management. But the foreseeable route of such companies in these crisis situations, except for the always imponderable ones, will be inexorably gradually descending towards area No. 4 (medium effectiveness and low efficiency), and if the attrition continues, they will head towards the undesirable area No. 1.

These are typical cases of companies that "reach the market," but their permanence is fragile; it is neither durable nor sustainable, and they fail to gain a foothold in it. On the one hand, they lacked the necessary efficiency adjustment, and on the other hand, the permanence in inefficiency generates costs that, in the long run, are paid for with expensive and incompetent products or services that imply a decrease in effectiveness. This may explain why these companies with partial results (in this case, with satisfactory effectiveness and low efficiency) find it difficult to take advantage of boom situations and tend to have greater resilience to withstand crisis situations. In general, their stay may be longer, but it will still be, in a good number of cases, agonizing.

Another contrasting management: satisfactory efficiency with discreet effectiveness

This category of companies corresponds to a peculiar situation where, in fact, it is not possible to hit the bull or the target with favorable results, achieving goals inappropriately despite developing and complying with processes that are satisfactorily efficient in the use of resources and time. We are in the zone of high efficiency and low effectiveness (see scenario No. 3). That is, insufficient (read ineffective) achievements and results are obtained that do not correspond to the efficiency effort deployed.

Here, we must be cautious when arguing that one can be satisfactorily efficient and, at the same time, exhibit ineffectiveness. The casuistry is loaded with events such as the domino effect of tiny imperfections, undetected intra- or inter-systemic errors, absence or insufficiency of greater controls and consistency of tests, absence of contingency plans, etc., that is, failures and errors could occur of strategic impact on key efficiency processes that, eventually, will compromise effectiveness. Therefore, we agree that ineffectiveness may not be due to the choice of inappropriate goals (corresponding to the scope of effectiveness itself) but rather to certain levels of inefficiency that are often hidden, tiny, or difficult to detect. Explainable ineffectiveness may correspond to certain "satisfactorily credible levels of efficiency" that simply are not so.

In the USA, some cases have occurred in the automobile industry, where companies such as Toyota or General Motors or their respective distributors have had to assume significant repair costs after several years of sales to face technical efficiency failures in part of their mechanical systems that were not detected in time.

On the other hand, efficiency problems may also be due to factors no longer linked to inefficiency but to the lack of what we could call "levers of effectiveness," which we develop in more detail in the following section. This last situation is quite typical in companies that became clouded, "rested on their laurels," believing that the successes of the past are a guarantee of the maintenance of the style and modus operandi in the present, were misplaced in their environment or reacted late to changes in. For example, there are cases of not adequately considering technological changes in their sector, changes in tastes and consumption patterns, changes in the socio-economic stratification of the target market, climatological and environmental changes, changes in the structure of productive and financial costs, absence of a culture of business sustainability, changes in macroeconomic policy, etc.

We are in the typical case of companies that "develop a relatively reasonable and satisfactory use of resources" and that, in this context of correct ways of doing things, assume that the goals, the product or service, and the chosen market are also correct, but they do not realize, do not perceive or delay in recognizing that this is not the case. These cases are more difficult to assimilate because after having done things correctly, the logical and expected consequence of effectiveness does not occur for reasons that have nothing to do with what they were doing. Management wonders, 'What happened?' A palpable example of this was the launch in 1983 of the personal computer "Lisa" by the Apple firm, which, despite its technical benefits, was not appreciated by the market.

However, we learn from mistakes since, in recent years, the same company has had notable successes with the launch of its impressive laptops, tablets, and smart cell phones. While we had called the risk exposed in the previous case as altitude sickness or managerial obtundation (where efficiency adjustments are ignored), in the current case, and although it may seem contradictory, managers get bogged down, on the one hand, in a kind of " cognitive blindness" that does not see beyond efficiency parameters and, on the other hand, a lack of reaction capacity, speed and versatility in the face of internal and external changes (where effectiveness adjustments are ignored).

It is also illuminating to review this case with the contexts of boom and crisis situations made previously. Companies that, being in zone No. 3 (high efficiency and low effectiveness), face favorable boom environments, despite the winds in their favor, must deploy a significant effectiveness effort to position themselves as successful companies. But the magnitude of the change required will also be demanding and could be more cumbersome despite requiring changes in only one direction. Graphically, this implies undertaking serious effectiveness efforts to first move from zone No. 3 to area No. 6 (high efficiency and medium effectiveness) and continue said effort in a sustained manner until reaching the optimal area No. 9. It must be considered that the drastic changes to be undertaken will take a significant period and as we argued before, no improvement as required is obtained immediately.

Companies located in this area No. 3 (high efficiency and low effectiveness) that face crisis situations will find it more difficult to achieve higher levels of effectiveness. Why? Because it is highly probable that we are facing a management team with a certain clouding of cognitive blindness that privileges the "sine qua non" condition that effectiveness must be eventually a consequence of the efficiency previously achieved. Also, because said blindness ignores that an important part of the crisis experienced may respond to factors fundamentally linked to demand and market factors that suggest a change in direction and strategy that they do not foresee.

In this sense, persistence in maintaining efficiency processes and doing little or nothing in terms of effectiveness makes efficiency efforts sterile. Marketing dislocation has its costs, and in this case, the efficiency losses will not be immediate either because the advantages of the previously achieved efficiency will still be maintained. The probable decrease in efficiency will also have to be of a relevant magnitude and will require a good amount of time to move towards the area of companies with errors in their management.

All of this concludes, as we warned before, that, despite using means and resources in a satisfactorily efficient manner, the company can be directed toward inappropriate targets. In the end, the stubbornness of the management body not undertake the required adjustments to effectiveness will cause the company to remain with a lack of effectiveness that will be devastating. The foreseeable route of such companies in such crisis situations will be to gradually descend towards area No. 2 (medium efficiency and low effectiveness) and finally toward undesirable area No. 1.

The company does not gain a foothold in the market because despite producing a product or providing a service with satisfactory levels of efficiency, it was not assimilated by the market because consumers simply do not want it, nor are they motivated by any need. The limitations and lack of factors linked to effectiveness determine the recurrence of a defective business cycle, and the "low rating" in its results makes it difficult to sustain the efficiency levels previously achieved. All of this will gradually degrade its performance and even risk leaving the market.

This may also explain why these companies with partial achievement (in this case, with satisfactory efficiency and low effectiveness) find it difficult to take advantage of boom situations and tend to present greater resistance to withstand crisis situations. In general, its permanence can also be longer, but it will still be problematic in many cases.

1.3 IMPORTANCE OF PUBLIC MANAGEMENT

Our intention is ambitious, and we want to draw attention to management problems, not only referring to the private sector. We use the term organizational management to include both public sector entities (for public service purposes) and non-governmental organizations (NGOs) (for social and community service purposes). Such organizations are not exempt from defective developments in their management. The performance evaluation parameters in terms of efficiency and effectiveness in these types of entities other than the private sector will be equally demanding, except that to the extent that they distance themselves from lucrative purposes toward community or public interests, they will have a perspective, filter, and sieve different.

An interesting approach to the topic of public and social management is given to us by Karin Marie Mokate in: "Effectiveness, efficiency, equity, and sustainability: What do we mean?" INDES Working Document. Inter-American Development Bank, July 2001. Working Paper Series I-24. Washington, D.C., in which she clarifies the conceptualizations and different interpretations of those four criteria that title her article and that, according to her, constitute the backbone of policies, programs, and projects underway. In effect, the author maintains that the scope of efficiency in social terms involves externalities that affect sectors not directly involved in the development of the project or program (roads, railways, hospitals, schools, etc.). Economists call these external economies or diseconomies that programs must consider and evaluate.

For this reason, the author maintains: "When considering these extra-market costs and benefits and making other adjustments to the analyses of private efficiency, the analysis of social efficiency is pertinent…it contemplates net social efficiency: it values with corrected prices both the contributions positive to well-being as well as the negative effects that they entail." We agree that the considerations of efficiency and effectiveness of programs or projects other than the private sphere are more precise when social benefits and costs are considered, which involve an evaluation of their social profitability.

Beyond the Manicheanism of considering that all public management of companies, by the mere fact of being under the direction of the state, constitutes a sin that will lead us to disaster, and despite the fact that the private sector will not venture into activities, sectors or spaces that it does not represent any profit; It seems a bit exaggerated to us to disqualify any organizational management in advance just because it remains in the government sphere.

For example, in the USA, the satisfactory postal service offered by the public entity has no substantive differences in terms of quality of service to that offered by its representative private peers, such as FedEx and UPS, which is why they are widely in demand. However, we cannot cover our eyes in the face of undeniable experiences of deficiencies and corruption that, although they mostly fall into the public sector, as we will see later, are not in any way the exclusive property of public activity. The cancer of corruption has no borders and operates in crossfire from different fronts and sectors.

The truth is that, regardless of whether we like or dislike the presence of public entities, the impact of what they do or do not have quantitative and qualitative relevance at both the national, regional, and local levels. This lively and noticeable presence of public entities and the management resulting from them is derived and constitutes factors of acceleration and stimulation or also of deceleration and distrust of other economic agents.

Mistakes in private business management have, as we have seen, excessive costs, waste in the use of resources and usually culminate in failure and withdrawal from the market of the company in question. Therefore, its directors will be responsible for the mistakes made and its owners and investors will be the ones who assume the losses of said management. There will also be costs shared by a) workers who were left unemployed and even unpaid, b) suppliers of goods and services who will face the breakdown of a payment chain, and c) the government itself for not collecting taxes.

In the specific case of mistakes in the management of public entities (companies, institutes, public services, decentralized, autonomous organizations, etc.), there will be no withdrawal from the market because the service offered must continue. But who pays the costs of poor management that, in addition to being inefficient, often slides into corruption? The entire nation pays for it because the deficiencies in health, education, infrastructure, and services, in general, mean higher costs, waste of scarce resources, and postponement of satisfied needs. When this management is full of mistakes becomes recurrent, it becomes trapped in a circle of incompetence where, in addition to lost resources, there is a valuable loss of time and opportunities.

In developing countries, it is observed that the best teams of technicians and professionals and the best incentives, remunerations, and working conditions are offered by the private sector, then the notorious and recurring shortcomings that are referred to in the public sector are a logical imbalance that our own system encourages. Additionally, the few qualified personnel, after training with resources from the State itself or with their own resources, end up transferring to the private sector.

Why complain that we have a basket of waste at home that contains, in large part, waste that we ourselves promote? Why complain if we do little to keep the house clean and do not provide it with adequate maintenance, renovation, and order? In matters of corruption, the double causality is forgotten, that of the corrupt person who executes it and that of the corrupter who promotes it, which sometimes falls on the same side, but other times they come from different fronts.

Certain cases of corruption are known to have been promoted by the private sector itself. With this, we have only referred to one of the aspects of the thorny problem of public management, and although there are public institutions and non-governmental organizations that are notable exceptions, they represent a minority. We are not going to delve into the problem of public management, which deserves more attention and extension than the one granted in this essay.

In developing countries, the imbalance of capacity between the private and public sectors does not allow "speaking the same language," especially when the competence and suitability of the manager are far from the efficiency and effectiveness requirements that should govern everyone who boasts of managing a company, entity, or an organization in the private or public sector. In Peru, the low execution of budget allocations in infrastructure and social development projects carried out by a good part of regional and local governments and their widespread derivation into corruption issues are a palpable example of the disability of their management.

The first step is to recognize that both public and private management are sailing in the same boat as the nation and that the uneven pace, restrictions, and shortcomings of the public sector eventually led to results that disadvantage everyone. Satisfactory management of the private sector by itself is weak and incomplete if it is not accompanied by a strengthening of effective and efficient public management that complements it. The conditions of this external envelope of public management will be discussed later in greater detail.

1.4 HUNTING FOR OPPORTUNITIES AND OPPORTUNITIES WHERE ONE IS HUNTED.

In the midst of the labyrinth that surrounds us, a panorama of changing markets, with investors interested in buying or selling goods, companies, projects, securities, etc., of uncertain external scenarios, consulting reports on diagnoses and forecasts (markets, companies and products) dissimilar and even contradictory, of intermediaries whose objectivity and honesty usually, in several cases, leave much to be desired; In the midst of this foggy and numbing context, the average man appears confused and dizzy. He sets out to hunt for investment opportunities and ends up hunted.

The "hunt for an opportunity" should not be pigeonholed into conventional parameters and, therefore, should not be limited only to the development of new investments or new business initiatives. In many cases, opportunities are at hand through the acquisition of existing companies that were mishandled or poorly managed. In this sense, the foray into a business destination different from the one to which one is accustomed should not be ruled out. There are investors in the market specializing in detecting these bargains; they are those who, after a prior evaluation and detecting potential, apply the rule of "entering the market buying as cheaply as possible even during periods of crisis and after a patient wait, clean up and strengthen the organization, proceed to sell it at the best price in boom times.

In a context where merger trends continue to be in fashion, it is worth commenting that conceptually an interesting merger alternative would be the one that corresponds (within the scenario of basic management scenarios described above) to a company in the second case (high effectiveness and low efficiency, that is, scenario No. 7) with another company from the third case (high efficiency and low effectiveness, that is, scenario No. 3). Complementation is "theoretical optimal mind" because one of them has what the other needs.

However, the success of the merger is more complex and will require evaluating other aspects such as the capacity to support consolidated cash flow, required debt margin, feasibility and complementation of new operational and commercial dimensions, the impact of reductions, or such increases in certain expenses and operating costs, appreciation of the life cycle of the product or service offered or of the life cycle or stage of each company in question, evaluation of specific competitive environment factors of each company (competing companies, suppliers, distributors ., clients) and evaluation of the global environment (economic, demographic, social, political forces), restructuring of work teams, etc.) and other factors that will affect the merger itself.

According to the above, the general recommendation on transactions to enter (buy) or exit (sell) the market, for the cases described above and for investments, is the following: Buy in periods of crisis (but a distinction must be made between bargains, extraordinary occasions and what which means buying disposable assets) and selling in boom cycles because it helps capitalize on profit margins. Given that crisis cycles can be long, and we do not know their durability, the possibility of buying and selling in the same crisis cycle is risky and can lead to losses (by selling at levels lower than the purchase made). Boom cycles are also not immune to risks. Buying and selling in a long-lasting boom cycle that is in its final phase makes it likely that the margins will be minimal (due to selling with modest margins at those who were bought or even reverting to losses).

The order of this basic recommendation can be reversed in the sense of starting by selling in boom cycles to make cash and later repurchasing second-hand options or bargains in crisis cycles. In volatile markets with frequent difficulties, such as the stock market or the real estate market, this practice is one of the golden rules. But we must complement this criterion by maintaining that this recommendation is general since specific circumstances or details attributable to the buyer, seller, or the specific market may arise that could contradict or enhance the results (manifestations of urgency of negotiation by one of the parties, imminent changes in legal frameworks, probable external economies, or diseconomies, etc.).

A key factor is to be clear in recognizing which cycle we are in and the duration we estimate its durability to remain in it, also having the best forecast of the coming cycle, observing the behavior of economic agents (buyers, sellers, regulators, intermediaries, etc.) and analyze the continuity of the legal and regulatory framework of the market in which we wish to enter. We must always be attentive because such signals and details appear unforeseen or unexpected during negotiations and are often unknown.

Despite the simplicity of the recommendation described, which does not reveal anything new, ordinary mortals do precisely the opposite. That is, people are charged with acquiring a variety of assets – companies, houses, land, boats, jewelry, stocks, commodities, shares in investment funds, machinery, equipment, resources of all kinds, etc. - which are mostly bought at high prices in boom times, and they do so with overwhelming enthusiasm because they believe or have been convinced that prices will continue to rise. Soon, the disappointments of adverse times come, and with it, the fear of continuing in investments that gradually depreciate. This makes them fall prey to desperation and panic, finding themselves in the need to withdraw, sell, and transfer their investment at bargain prices in times of crisis, and they end up drinking the bitter pill of taking their losses.

The most advisable thing (before risking money or having already risked it) is to permanently monitor the evolution of the market that interests us and thus avoid being surprised by imponderable or unforeseen factors. Conduct a prior evaluation of what you want to buy or sell and then, accordingly, take the time to improve and grow the investment made before selling or after buying it.

The various media of our consumer society, through the written press, television, specialized magazines, seminars, circles, and social, professional, business, and other networks, contribute their "quota of enchantment," play a separate role and then they spread the word and recommend: that we are in the best time to buy this or that product (gold, silver, jewelry, cement, basic foods such as flour, meat, dairy products), etc.; that real estate investment is excellent in this or that place, that there is no better investment in companies or shares in this or that sector, that the best investment funds belong to this or that activity, that the best investment advisor is this or that, etc.

In relation to this last statement of investments suggested and referred to by advisors and specialized professionals, we make a parenthesis to refer to a scandal of capital proportions in the American environment carried out by Mr. Bernard Madof, who managed, through his investment company, the largest scam and financial scandal of recent decades for an amount that amounted to 65 billion dollars (2006) through the Ponzi scheme where the investments were not applied to conventional market scenarios as supposed, but rather the funds raised from the latest investors they sustained attractive profits from the previous ones. Mr. Madof, on his continuous visits to West Palm Beach (in whose select sector resides part of the millionaire elite of America and other parts of the world), used to meet in the exclusive golf clubs with millionaire investors who were initially given the luxury of denying them access to his investment fund on the grounds that he only worked with institutional investors.

This was undoubtedly true (he raised hundreds of millions from institutions), but it was part of a ploy so that millionaire investors would insist and obtain, through references and recommendations, that they would be accepted into the select club. Word spread among them that it was safe to invest with "Berny" (Mr. Madof) because he simply "was one of us." Even though the stock market faltered in stumbles and falls, Mr. Madof's investment fund continued to report artificial double-digit annual returns to its investors. Everyone was happy and content until, as expected, this pyramidal structure, like a "house of cards" without basis or sustainability, collapsed, and with it, the hopes and dreams of thousands of investors and institutions that trusted this scammer.

In Peru, it is worth remembering the experience with the CLAE organization directed by Mr. Carlos Manrique, which attracted million-dollar investments under a similar scheme where, in a structured pyramid scheme, it was also since the funds raised from the last investors covered the profits offered to the previous ones, with the addition that Mr. Manrique had no obligation to make his deposits or their applications transparent and he was not under the supervision of any regulatory

37

or controlling entity. This scheme reached its peak during 1989-1992, where it is estimated that it mobilized up to 640 million dollars without being accountable to anyone. This system, called shadow banking, gained popularity because it offered attractive returns that far exceeded the returns offered by commercial banks. Later, word spread that it was a system set up to "launder money of dubious origin."

Despite this, at that time, in Lima, there was no talk of anything other than "the succulent profits obtained with CLAE." People were happy with the returns obtained, which were paid punctually and voluntarily reinvested month after month. This scheme, very similar to the one described above, also, as expected, collapsed and was the largest pyramid scam in Peru; that was around 500 million dollars and reached thousands of investors, many of whom, for various or obscure reasons, did not even report nor register for recovery of their funds. Although keeping the proportions, Mr. Manrique's scandal was minuscule in relation to that of Mr. Madof, the amounts and importance of it were for the Peruvian reality.

In short, many mortals like to get on the "train of quick profits with minimal effort." The second recommendation of taking the time and work necessary for a considered evaluation of the investment option is rarely observed, nor for the improvement and growth of what we have bought or what we are going to sell. People continue to act by reaction and only insist on looking at and following the well-known script of the three Bs: bueno (good), bonito (pretty), and barato (cheap). Worse still, many people "invest just to show off" and, in other cases, become impulsive buyers. Usually, they are enthralled by someone who convinces them of the magical benefits of their purchases and investments. They usually update and divulge to their friends' details of their latest investments made, but since they neglect to follow up on such investments made, they hide or cover up their disastrous results because no braggart likes to air their failures.

Returning to our topic at hand, we recommend being cautious so as not to fall into the clutches of certain intermediaries, brokers, and unscrupulous advisors in the areas of sale of companies, homes, securities, land, art objects, cars, racehorses, boats, and assets of any kind. Such intermediaries manage to present themselves and be referred to as professionals of recognized reputation and credibility, and some of them are nothing more than professionals without any modesty; they have their own rationality and adhere religiously to their credo: "obtain the maximum and best intermediation commissions or advice in the shortest possible time. So, they do what is necessary to make it happen. In a respectable number of cases, and the casuistry is irrefutable, the foundations and interests of their buying clients, sellers, or advised clients are cleverly relegated to the background.

The above should alert us to discern more objectively the goodness of the recommended product or service, the institutional prestige of the entity that offers it, the honesty and background of the intermediary, and the neutrality, impartiality, and professionalism of the other participants. The problem is that the opportunity to make the recommended investment, despite meeting the acceptable characteristics described above, is in many cases late, untimely, or in inconvenient circumstances and, normally, only facilitates obtaining profits from those who previously invested and get rid of them. The latter are the first to take advantage of the bargains provided by those who bought out of misinformation and who later sell out of desperation.

Today's relevant characteristic in the stock market, namely, "market volatility" (frequent difficulties), has been generating a certain disenchantment and disorientation. The strong shock that capital markets received because of the pandemic made most investors stumble. Only a first select group of participants with the ability to foresee, recognize, or influence the forces of the zigzagging market are those who, by being at the forefront, take advantage of it (such as billionaire investors such as Warren Buffet or the prominent businessman Bill Gates or E. Musk and other superstars), These leaders have highly qualified and specialized advisory teams and are unequivocally established, in most cases, as the market winners.

Secondly, there are the researchers and investment consultants who constantly know the trends and pulse of the market, and through contact and intelligence tactics they also know the operation of the select group above that is at the forefront. Investment advisors and analysts from large banks, brokerage houses, mutual funds, specialized magazines, etc., belong to this second group who first execute the options they have researched and then disclose their recommendations to the broad spectrum of the investing public (e.g., they report that Mr. Buffet, Mr. Bill Gates, or the fashionable Investment Fund are buying this or that stock). This second group, depending on their ability to detect and react, can be mostly winners and rarely losers.

There remains a third group made up of enthusiastic followers and customary investors of the market. This large contingent of investors maintains a respectable portfolio of securities over a medium or long-term time horizon. They normally have advice from prestigious professionals or reputable investment firms that, within a framework of trust, stability, and exchange of information, actively participate in the development of their activities. Such investors are directed to the flow of investments either individually or grouped in institutional funds to hunt what they can.

The results of this third group are disparate and combined and go on a continuum from obtaining satisfactory profits, varied results of modest profits, experiencing moderate losses, and a part of such investors do not escape experiencing unfavorable results. Always being careful to avoid generalizations, it should be noted that there are respectable brokers (intermediaries) and professional investment advisors who keep their clientele satisfied, even in adverse market situations.

Finally, there is the group of profane, improvised upstarts and curious people whose misinformation and lack of knowledge of the market makes them pay the price for their novitiate. This is the group that, as we previously warned, normally invests in showing off and lose out of obligation for not having good and timely advice. Most investors in this fourth group lack the ability to intelligently digest or assimilate a recommendation offered. Their mistakes make them easy prey for the second group described above, that is, they buy securities at high prices when they are selling, and subsequently, their desperation in the face of the fall in prices of acquired securities drives them to get rid of them and sell them at low prices, making them attractive and bought by them.

Caution with "companies in recall"

It should be noted that the withdrawal from the market of companies with irregular performance does not necessarily have to be calamitous. Just as one must have the capacity for reaction and foresight to take advantage of the boom, the same capacity is required to avoid (or mitigate) crises and opt for an optimal and timely withdrawal from the market. When this is not understood, it is inadvisable to wait until bankruptcy and painful liquidation are chosen (unfortunately, this error is repeated in many numbers of cases). This option leaves "dead, injured, and bruised" (partners, workers, financial creditors, suppliers of goods and services, etc.). Companies in liquidation become devoured by internal company vultures and are then at the mercy of external vultures. These corporate cannibals buy what is left of the company to sell it in bits and pieces.

Companies with irregular performance with the best possibilities of market withdrawal are those that, in boom times, took advantage of achieving moderate doses of effectiveness and efficiency, allowing them to show off a certain attractiveness and potential that makes it more attractive and feasible to negotiate. The experience of small and medium-sized entrepreneurs on this issue is unique because there is a certain "affection" between the owner and his company or between him and certain assets (his house, his shares, his company, his jewelry, etc.) that in many cases, it generates resistance to getting rid of it.

In the business world, as in other aspects of life, it is common for the heart (meaning emotion) to present motives that disagree with the approaches of reason. In the above case, entrepreneurs who, against all odds, emotionally cling to their company (their property, their portfolio, etc.) could lose their last opportunity to get on the train that would save them from future or greater losses.

There are skillful owners of small, medium, and large companies who withdraw from the market by selling their company at the optimal moment, that is, at the end of the expansive cycle of effectiveness or boom. They may foresee that they do not want to face the efficiency adjustment process that the company proposes, foresee unfavorable environmental situations, or consider that they are at the threshold of a mature state or a certain saturation in the product or business cycle in question; or, for any other reason, they prefer to sell, look for another opportunity and leave voluntarily. They are the ones who apply the rule of "growing the organization in boom times and exiting the market selling as expensive as possible before the crisis begins" and its harmful effects. These groups of companies are easier to sell.

The problem usually arises for those who are on the buying side who, excited by the favorable results that the sellers show them, are "convinced" of the goodness of the "product" that they offer (it is not unusual for the company to cosmetically show a certain overvaluation if there is the importance of delving into evaluative aspects before purchasing). During this seductive enchantment, he ends up paying a high price for the "sick company" that he must carry, and his investment may turn out to be riskier and not as profitable as he expected. He will have to make a serious engineering effort to improve the efficiency of the company, the property, the securities, the project, or any acquired asset. When we buy a company, and we want to avoid the "opportunity of being hunted," it is recommended that, in addition to assessing its past performance, verifying and testing its true and objective current situation, we should also estimate its future income generation capacity.

On the other hand, in the case of companies that exhibit reasonable efficiency patterns but do not present attractive economic results (scenario No. 3 high efficiency with low effectiveness), they could be undervalued given that the market values results. If the owner is not willing to continue risking any longer and estimates that the surrounding conditions will continue to be unfavorable, he will make his sales offer attractive. This may attract investors who may consider that the company and the market in which it operates still present (or will present) exploitation potential, who will be able to acquire it at a relatively cheap price, and the success of their investment will be conditional on their ability to "treat and heal the sick" with the required dose of effectiveness so that it looks reasonable in the shortest possible time.

In summary, for those of us who are spectators in the future of business management, we will see three large channels; in the first channel, there is a proportion of companies that make severe mistakes in both criteria of efficiency and effectiveness (scenario No. 1), and are the ones that, as we noted before, will be forced to quickly withdraw from the given market that it makes no sense to continue wasting resources.

The second channel is formed by this significant group of companies, the intermediate range of defective management companies (which make up the seven scenarios from No. 2 to No. 8 with partial non-compliance with some of the efficiency and effectiveness requirements). These companies will continue to fight, trying to survive and overcome the morass of difficulties and adversities along the way. Its withdrawal from the market is gradual and is a matter of time and resistance. In their final stretch, these companies with irregular performance also disappear due to starvation, liquidation, merger, or absorption by another company with better possibilities of competition.

The third and final channel corresponds to a few companies that manage to achieve what we have called successful business management (scenario No. 9) with satisfactory compliance with both criteria for effectiveness and efficiency. Unfortunately, the conditions of excellence are limited to a business minority that has tried to achieve them and maintain them. In the dynamic evolution of the real world, the business flow increases again with the participation of new initiatives that form a torrent of new companies (large, medium, and small) that, depending on their management, will take the course in any of the three causes previously described. The channel of rapid deaths, that of lethargic agonies, and that of stimulating successes. What channel are you working on?

1.5 MANAGEMENT STYLES

Before classifying those factors that can be called levers of effectiveness, it is worth making a brief reference to the contemporary historical framework that has characterized business management. The result will conform to that profile or management style that is the referential way of thinking and approaching things, although the particularities of any management are nourished by different sources: empirical or academic training of the manager, propensity to assimilate technological advances, capacity to adapt or react to emergencies, marketing, and operational priorities, etc.

This style is the response of the team responsible for management to its organizational complexity. It is the answer to the big question of what and how to do to achieve the right results and things. It is the challenge that the manager faces from his specific space and time circumstance and that forms the desired effectiveness efficiency guidelines. Historically, certain biases, trends and oscillations have been recorded in Management Styles that have evolved over time and circumstances, which we expose below.

Only for reasons of abbreviation and to avoid old references that would require more time, <u>we will take the beginning of the 20th century as a starting point</u>. In those years, a style that prioritized the product and the production process prevailed. Market demand had a receptive and complementary nature and had to adjust to the dictates of supply. The predominant management style was oriented toward achieving efficiency. The first scientific efforts of administrative science, with its theorists Frederic Taylor and Henri Fayol, established administrative principles aimed at increasing work **efficiency**.

In this sense, the approaches to division or specialization of work, studies of time and movements to improve labor productivity, establishment of acceptable levels of task performance, determination of levels of authority and responsibility, specification of rules of order, discipline, and command unity had predominance in shaping the successful management style model. As a typical result of this style, we have as a business icon Mr. Henry Ford and his prototype car "Model T" whose massive acceptance by the market confirmed a successful management style that was complemented by a peculiar superstructure of highly hierarchical organization controlling and centralized.

<u>Toward the middle of the 20th century</u> and due to the post-war dynamism, the predominant management style will successively incorporate and weigh new elements or variables. Due to business expansion into new markets, the need arises for expansion and renewal of the productive apparatus, and the concept of economy of scale (increase in significant production volumes with

reduction of average costs) gains preeminence. To achieve this, the following are of greater relevance:

- The orientation toward this productive expansion makes **the financial function** acquire greater weight in the management style. The classic Treasury function, with its limited horizon of annual cash budget management must be transformed into a vital financial management that must weave its double function: not only of efficient application of liquid resources but also of searching for financing for broader time horizons. The Capital market has become more sophisticated due to the massive attendance of institutional investors (Mutual Investment Funds, Pension Funds), the trend of companies issuing obligations in searching for and raising capital, and various financial instruments (corporate bonds, reference stocks, commodities, futures, etc.).

- The greater production and financing commitments and their necessary projection towards the medium and long term generate **the business planning function** to acquire strategic importance. The classic annual operating budget was narrowed to give way to a strategic planning scheme integrated with other business areas. The desired higher production will be conditional on its financing possibilities and the framework of previously approved planning. It is the time of mass production, consolidation of transnational companies, programming of the product life cycle, and the beginning of the race for technological innovations. As in every era, one of the theoretical references is represented by the economist J. Schumpeter, who contributed to and conceived of the importance of innovation. Another heterodox and critical contribution is provided by J. K. Galbraith and his classic works "The New Industrial State" (1967) and "The Opulent Society" (1957), his conceptions of technostructure, planned obsolescence, and defense of price and wage control. They were controversial topics of the time.

- The apex of business management, the General Manager, is overwhelmed by the growing complexity of business responsibilities and must give in to the new trend of a new organizational architecture with higher levels of decentralization and deconcentrating. **Technocracy (or business bureaucracy) is imposed**, and the admired company and example prototype has the profile of a "dinosaur" organization. The collegiate management body acquires greater relevance in management, and from the predominance of management by instructions, it moves to management by objectives, where the optimization of results becomes the new paradigm.

The last quarter of the last century continues to mark a distance from previous styles. The center of attention and paradigm ceased to be the product and the production process and had to give that privileged place to the client and the market, and therefore, **Marketing management** comes to the fore. The pattern and style of organizational management are reversed; now, the offer is receptive and complementary and adjusts to the guidelines dictated by demand. Among the theoretical references, this trend is highlighted by the renowned Peter Drucker and Michael Porter, with interesting contributions and concepts about business competitiveness. In this period, the following stand out:

- The conquest of markets becomes decisive. How to create, develop, penetrate, maintain, and defend markets? Market research in each phase of the marketing function (place, product, price, and promotion) is essential. There is no room for spontaneity, improvisation, or "shots in the air" in terms of commercial planning where inventiveness and creativity have had the right environment to develop in the context of continuous campaign launches. Marketing management has become more sophisticated and has acquired greater professionalism.

- Technological innovation processes are accentuated, and greater sophistication in products combined with the marketing support described above gives rise to great commercial impacts. The continuity of this process accelerates product obsolescence and shortens their life cycle. This also generates and accelerates overproduction or overstocks in certain products that cause a greater frequency of entries and withdrawals from the market and from the companies that support them.

- Because of the above, the Merger & Acquisitions processes are more frequent; the purchases, sales, and absorptions of companies become a financial-legal specialty that has its fundamental marketing roots. Such processes are not framed exclusively in desires of absorption due to incompetence on the part but rather respond to new competitiveness strategies where the Senior Management of companies is more open to strategic alliance schemes since not necessarily any of the companies to be merged denotes economic difficulties.

- The fierce competition focused on providing better consumer satisfaction and the accentuation of technological innovations determine that the market and technology become pillars of a process that includes not only the product or service offered but also extends to the input and the black box that symbolizes the interrelation between business processes and systems. Thus, the concept of Total Quality as an objective criterion in management arises. New concepts are becoming "fashionable," ranging from Total Quality Management, Learning Organization, Continuous Improvement, Just in Time, Business Process Reengineering, Excellence, and more that have become hackneyed and even fallen into disrepair, a topic that has not ceased to be interesting.

- In these times, the scaffolding and support of the organizational structure continues to transform. Now, everyone criticizes the "dinosaur" organization, and the current of strong reduction of hierarchical levels predominates. <u>Companies tend to present more "flattened" organizational profiles,</u> and for now, the high technocracy is entering a peculiar process of accelerated rotation of positions. The "fiefdoms" (specialized areas such as operations, finance, marketing, and planning) have made their contribution to the generation of value and wealth of the company felt, and the technical and professional staff have earned greater respect and consideration.

<u>In the initial decades of this century,</u> the management style continues to break patterns and paradigms. Business complexity continues to increase and now the conventional table of reciprocal impact between business supply and demand is altered in good proportion by factors that exceed the internal and direct sphere, and it is the external gale that acquires greater gravity. This process has been called **Globalization**. The relevant question now is how to structure and develop management in the context of an increasingly globalized environment. For the purposes of this essay, we understand Globalization as the process characterized by the greater mobilization and international circulation of production factors (capital, labor, technology, information), greater exchange of products and services that derive from it, and whose highlight is the framework of greatest interdependence and reciprocal impact between markets and participating companies.

Globalization is a kind of hurricane force with favorable and unfavorable effects for economic agents. This globalization is accompanied by accelerated rates of entry and exit from the market of companies of all sizes, permanent business mergers, accelerated labor-saving technological innovations, and a clear trend of increasing outsourcing. This reflects a disturbing symptom: There is an increase in the floating workforce (specialized or not). Companies that continue to operate are less willing to absorb and hire permanent personnel. The effect of globalization on management style stands out for the following:

- Business management now must dedicate more time to what may previously have been a light activity, that is, <u>to monitor and weigh more acutely the national and international socioeconomic environment</u>. The incidence of, for example, a drought in American grain crops, a worsening of political conflicts in the Arab world, a retraction in the dynamics of potentially emerging economies such as India, Russia, Brazil, etc., a sudden fall or rise in international market prices for minerals or fuels, resurgence of strikes or union conflicts in countries with strategic resources, war conflicts, epidemics, new variations in macroeconomic policies and many other external events <u>will impact more than expected</u>

<u>and at the least expected time</u>, the levels and structure of costs and operating income of the company.

- The domino effect clearly observable in the stock markets of developed countries is now replicated with greater notoriety and frequency in other products and markets. Changing and sudden events become permanent and hound business management with a strong dose of uncertainty and unpredictability. The management of today's business complexity is framed in the management of "critical or chaotic" systems that are difficult to predict, which require greater sensitivity and intuition to detect opportunities and threats, greater speed in the ability to react or respond to them, and greater creativity in problem-solving. The importance of the use and <u>sophistication of prediction models in the different areas of the company</u> (financial, commercial, operational) has become more relevant. Today's manager must "know how to navigate rough seas and maintain fine reflexes" to steer his boat to the right destination.

- To further complicate the complexity described above, considerations of <u>forecasting environmental impact and social responsibility arise</u> as unavoidable issues in both private and public management. A few decades ago, these topics had a sporadic place on the business agenda. In the current situation, corporate social responsibility is conceived as the business obligation (beyond its inherent legal responsibilities) to generate or maximize positive effects in its economic-social and community environment. The responsibility of minimizing the negative effects of its actions in the same environment is considered, which is relevant in forecasting the environmental impact. There is no project of relevant dimension that has not previously sifted through the social and environmental impact evaluation filters for its respective approval and implementation.

- The concepts and achievements of Total Quality are reinforced, and it becomes a distinctive element and ensures competitiveness and even more sustainability in the market. ISO quality certifications, Six Sigma, Quality Circles, and other reengineering schemes for the improvement and maintenance of Quality become more difficult and expensive, especially for medium and small companies, which, faced with the threat of being excluded from the market, must face the challenge with their limited availability.

- The organization maintains a "flattened" profile structure with few hierarchical levels, but there is greater horizontality with the appearance of new dependencies such as Quality Assurance, Management or Social Responsibility Unit, Department of Environmental Protection. But the most notable thing is <u>the increase in "outsourcing" (national and international)</u> that began in traditional service areas such as maintenance and cleaning, security, transportation, and logistics services to extend to telemarketing, market research, human resources, parts and pieces of the product, economic and financial, legal, tax, accounting consulting, etc. That is, the main or central organization, normally of relevant size, maintains dependencies that it considers necessary or strategic under direct control and supervision and subcontracts part-time or outsourced by agreeing with satellite companies (linked or not to them) in areas fundamentally of specialized services.

- In the developing world, severe political problems (terrorism, war conflicts, corrupt authorities, and severe economic crises) <u>fuel and accentuate migratory flows toward the developed world</u>, which has been showing combined advances and setbacks in its economic evolution and immigration policy. In this situation, the manager who "hooked" his medium or small company into the "satellite" circuit described above or into the radius of action of larger companies will have better chances of staying active, and those who could not do so will have a gloomier outlook and will have to trust and wait for the growth possibilities of their own internal market and subsist in the morass of underground economies.

- In accordance with what was suggested by Alvin Tofler in his work "The Third Wave," where he points out that eras are distinguished not so much in what they do but rather in how they do it, it can be stated that <u>the new international division of labor has been patterned according to the greater or lesser degree of technological advancement and innovation</u> that companies, organizations, and governments imprint on their management. The use of new energy sources, automated systems, greater use of robotics in mass production processes, global data and information management, use of microprocessors, etc., are clear examples of products with high technological sophistication (cars, telephones, cell phones, household appliances, industrial equipment, etc.).

- In this context of what and how to do things, a key tool appears: **Artificial Intelligence (AI)**, understood as that computer specialization that, through intelligent equipment and systems, enhances the use of information to support the process of decision-making, reasoning, and learning by itself. AI bases its operation on a set of integrated technological architectures that include the implementation of software, hardware, and sophisticated criteria that encompass automation, management of large volumes of information and high-performance computer networks.

In accordance with the predominant trend, its use was initially oriented towards marketing purposes: demand projections, consumer preferences, negotiation with clients, etc.; but it continues its development in applications to improve productivity and efficiencies: monitoring and control of processes and tests, supply chains, risk assessment (operational, administrative, logistical), hiring and control of personnel, counteracting corporate espionage and fraud prevention, etc.). Such advances are still at the base of the AI development pyramid and enormous potential remains to be developed.

The McKinsey company (a leader in global consulting) estimates that in the next 20 years, the application of Artificial Intelligence in marketing, sales, and other links could create added value, including profits and efficiencies, for an amount of up to 2.7 trillion dollars. (see "The Economist" magazine, March 31-Apr 06, 2018).

After having made this brief and generic account of management profiles or styles and their variants, it will not be our purpose to recommend the "best management style" (it does not exist! because changes and circumstances shape the predominant styles). Each manager will evaluate, select, and deepen the tools that best suit him/her to solve his/her specific problem and, accordingly, will adopt his/her respective dose of efficiency and effectiveness in his/her management. The Management Style constituted by that referential way of thinking, orienting, and approaching things, with its respective policies and strategic and specific guidelines, will shape the resulting nuance that the manager decides. One of the lessons that the experience described leaves us is that, given the variety of events and circumstances, there is no absolute and unique answer in terms of management styles.

Returning to our proposed approach to business management with effectiveness and efficiency, we estimate that in unbalanced schemes with high efficiency and low effectiveness (with insufficient strategies, lack of leadership and culture, and supporting values), we will be clouded in blind, sometimes insensitive growth due to inattention to variants and requirements of the market, its social environment and with risks of lack of reflection to the accelerated changes in the global context. For their part, schemes biased in effectiveness with low efficiency have the disadvantage of fruitless isolation, unsustainability, and improvisation due to the defective functioning and management of their business processes and systems. Both profiles are not exempt from the risks of management incapacity and deviations due to corruption.

The dichotomy between economic growth and income distribution options is still unresolved and is a pending subject in the economic debate and in the other social sciences. For this reason and in accordance with the criteria of reason and justice, we draw attention when the imbalance between both categories is accentuated. Likewise, in the field of business management, there is often a false dichotomy between Efficiency and Effectiveness options that distorts the weighting of one over the other and counteracts an adequate balance between the two. Each business reality presents its particularities and problems, and its treatment will be a specific task and challenge of creation and inspiration for those who assume the responsibility of managing companies and organizations.

2. BUSINESS EFFECTIVENESS

What do you do to achieve those correct results? What things lead us to be effective, and the absence of what things can lead us to ineffectiveness?

Below, we present factors that are contributors to achieving effectiveness and directing towards the desired management style. See Chart N° 3. Each of these factors to be developed in this topic has been and will continue to be the subject of abundant bibliographic publication. Our interest is not in offering the most complete or updated version of each of them, we are only motivated by the purpose of rescuing what has a unique impact on the management and perspective that we are interested in highlighting here.

Chart N° 3: Effectiveness Components

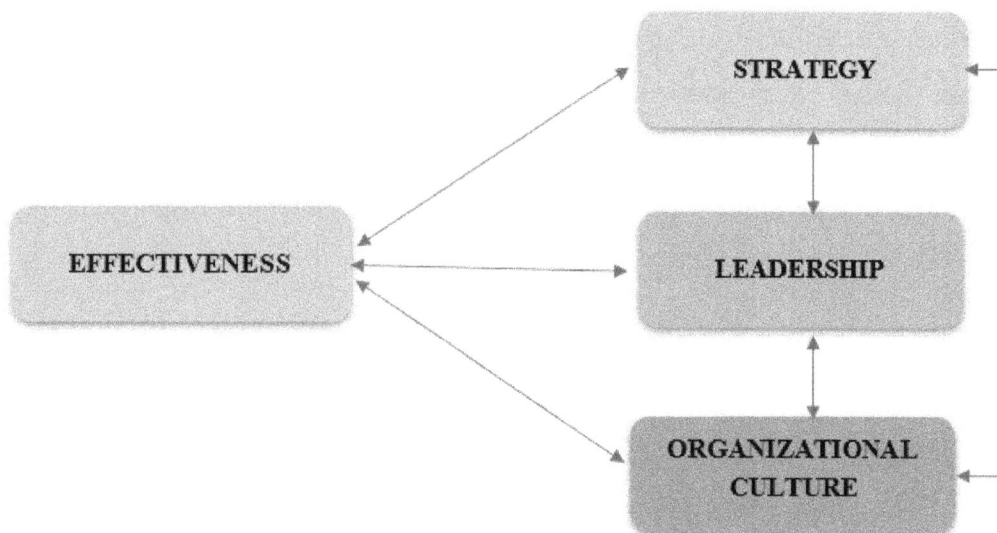

2.1 STRATEGY

Regardless of whether the strategy is formal or factual, it must always be present in any management.

2.1.1 Conceptualization

What do we understand by Strategy? We prefer to use the concept of Strategy described by Kenneth Andrews and cited by Henry Mintzberg, James B. Quinn, and John Voyer in their work: "The Strategic Process. Concepts, Contexts, and Cases", First Edition 1997, p. 72

> ".. strategy is a pattern or model of decisions that determines its objectives, purposes, or goals; It also produces the policies and plans to achieve such goals, defines the business sphere, establishes the type of economic and human organization that it intends to be, and specifies the nature of the economic and non-economic contributions that it intends to make to its shareholders, employees, clients, and customers. community..."

In this context, it is argued that objectives and goals include <u>what is going to be achieved and when the results will be achieved</u>. Policies or policy guidelines are the set of guidelines that determine the limits within which an action or decision must occur. The plans and programs constitute the design of the sequence of necessary actions that specify <u>how to achieve the objectives</u> (now, they do not describe the execution of these). Such plans define the allocation of resources, the specific activities of the different organizational subunits responsible for executing them, and a scheme to measure the proposed achievements.

Each aspect described (objectives, policies, and plans) presents a hierarchy, so those of greatest importance and coverage are classified as objectives, policies, or strategic plans. From this perspective, as these authors point out[2]:

> "...strategic decisions are those that establish the general orientation of a company and its viability considering both predictable and unpredictable changes...the **effectiveness** of the company is equally determined by strategic decisions – that is, whether its Efforts are or are not well directed and in accordance with their potential resources - regardless of whether individual tasks are performed efficiently. **Efficiency**, as well as the countless decisions that are required to maintain the daily life and services of the company, fall in the administrative area." (the emphasis and highlight of terms are ours).

---

[2] Henry Mintzberg..."El Proceso Estratégico... Op cit pages 7 y 8

This definition of strategy opens a first point of debate. On the one hand, there are theoretical prescription approaches that suggest the optimal way to formulate a strategy, or a prototype of a better organizational form derived from a rational and analytical exercise where opportunities and capabilities are combined. On the other hand, there are descriptive, case-by-case approaches with slight theoretical references, in which, instead of resorting to design and analysis, there is a tendency to form patterns of behavior based on norms and values that the members of the organization share.

The complexity of organizational reality suggests clarifying the concepts that typify it and further exploring its variability. In this context of complexity, compared to the formally elaborate, intentional, or deliberate strategy, a factual or emergent strategy appears, the latter, often built without prior purpose or intention but also in response to unforeseen or random factors so that both converge toward a final or resulting strategy. That is why we said in the title of this section: Strategy, whether formal or factual, must be present in any management.

Only for analytical purposes can we separate formulation and implementation because they are intertwined in interactive processes where aspects that we describe as leadership, organizational culture, and environments determine or imply restrictions on strategic decisions. Therefore, there is also a false dichotomy in choosing between formulation and implementation. For this reason, in the penultimate chapter of this essay (section 4.3), this interaction is exposed in the effectiveness and efficiency matrix diagram.

Although it can't be denied that strategies were formulated incorrectly, there may also have been implementation failures, or problems may also have arisen due to this strict distinction between formulation and implementation by assuming as a "valid inference" that the ideas and thinking that typify the formulation are independent of the actions that typify the implementation.

According to Mintzberg, in the creation of strategies as a learning process[3],

> " ...actions and ideas are intertwined. The organization tries something. It doesn't fully work, so it tries something else...the organization applies more changes, and the process continues in its cycle between actions and ideas...the strategy walks on two feet: one deliberate and one emergent." Management requires a light touch of skill to direct itself according to its proposed intentions (deliberate) and, at the same time, respond with openness in its patterns of

---

[3] Henry Mintzberg..."El Proceso Estratégico... Op cit page 115

actions (emergent). Both contribute to shaping and adopting the organization's final strategy (realized strategy)."

Therefore, it is relative to propose an optimal method for the development of a strategy and there is no prescriptive recipe that is valid for any organization without first having a clear knowledge of the beginnings and development of its.

From the perspective of this essay, we conceptualize the strategy as an ambivalent or dual tool because it presents useful characteristics from both the consideration of effectiveness and efficiency. Only for analysis and presentation purposes do we say that Strategic Formulation is linked to Effectiveness and Implementation is linked to Efficiency. An illuminating exposition of the integral process of Strategic Formulation and Implementation that feeds this part of our work is found in the work of Arthur Thompson Jr. and A. J. Strickland III, "Strategy Formulation and Implementation. Tasks of the General Manager", Business Publications, INC. Plano, Texas. Third Edition.

2.1.2 Content

In this part of the essay, we are interested in highlighting the impact of strategy on effectiveness. Therefore, we focus on Strategic Formulation and highlight its importance from the scope and comprehensive perspective of the company, that is, at the corporate level. The basic content of said Formulation will be made up of the following three processes:

- The first is a **diagnosis** of the starting position. What is the current situation? Where are we, and where is the prevailing trend leading us? This analysis, which includes the evaluation of interacting forces and their cause-and-effect relationships, is complemented by a SWOT exercise or determination of Strengths, Opportunities, Weaknesses, and Threats facing the organization. This part includes the analysis of the conditions of the business problem and its predominant forces. All of this will also provide us with a first analysis and approach to our competitiveness and its environment.

  The defective functioning of cases of organizational management is attributed in part to a first source of errors and deficiencies committed precisely in this diagnostic phase. The problem is detecting the real problem. Let us now see the most representative diagnostic errors:

- Fevers <u>are detected, but infection is not</u>. In this case, the diagnosis has been developed with analytical treatment of superficial and generic bias where only effects are identified and quantified. The lack of depth and clarity of analysis prevents a sequential relationship of cause and effect and adequate weighting of main and secondary problems. Logically, the deficiencies described above result in confusing, incomplete, and erroneous analyses that do not provide an adequate starting point for proposing alternative solutions. The recommendations become simple palliatives because they only mitigate superficial effects and do not attack the root of the true problem, which is still pending identification.

- Errors <u>in measurement and use of appropriate instruments</u>. Sometimes, the researcher manages to detect the true causes of the problems analyzed, but the magnitude of this and its effects are deformed or distorted by measurement errors. This has a lot to do with the fact that a deficient company suffers from having reliable and timely information, so taking data and information "as they are" can lead to errors or omissions in the appreciation and weighing of facts. that does not reflect the true levels of business problems. In this case, the analyst must appeal to his knowledge, experience, and the use of necessary technical tools to identify flimsy information, corroborate reliable information, and correct deficiencies by obtaining an accurate approximation of the diagnosed problems.

- Errors <u>in approach and conception</u>. This phrase alerts us to the possibility that the analyst develops a diagnosis where, in fact, he makes a correct identification of the cause-effect relationship and an adequate appreciation of the problem to be treated, but he can bias his attention towards urgent, that diverts his focus made details that "lead it by the bush" and neglect the treatment of the problem in strategic terms. The strategy appears as a loose list of tasks focused on the present without projection toward possible structural problems. Likewise, having identified a relevant problem and strategy, it can fall into the fragmentalism of having been analyzed in isolation as a watertight compartment, unilaterally and without an integrative and systemic conception with the rest of the elements and variables that compose it.

The above makes the company disoriented and confused between what it needs to do (what is urgent) and what it must formally postpone (what is necessary). In other words, the lack of priority criteria is evident. There are these and other types of errors or defects that accuse the diagnoses and that appear throughout the evaluative work.

- After a thorough understanding of the problem in question, we focus on the second process, which is the **determination of strategic goals and objectives**. One of the basic questions that any business manager asks is: What should we do to achieve what we want to be? What will be the desired result of the business project be undertaken or to be undertaken? This leads to outlining what planners call strategic objectives as one of the initial points in the development of a plan or strategy. Therefore, although such objectives are not part of a formally supported document, they must be conceptualized in the mind of the entrepreneur.

  Where do we want to go? What do we want to be or do in that desirable and feasible future? When and how long is it estimated to be achieved? The choice of vision, mission, and core objectives are established for medium or long-term periods. It is necessary to avoid the established goal being too ambitious since it must contemplate a feasible probability scenario because the more pretentious the goals, the greater the difficulties will be and the greater the possibilities of risks, failures, and "disenchantments" with the implementation of an unlikely strategy.

  It is usual and recommended that the elements described above be discussed, analyzed, and readjusted not only at the management level but in a consensual framework with the participation of personnel from different instances. Otherwise, the plan will only be a document of good intentions from senior management, which will never be applied, will never arouse interest, and will only adorn (as we noted at the beginning) the general manager's shelf.

- The third process aims to specify, at a conceptual level, the desired solution and includes the **Design or Formulation** phase of the Global Plan of the company or organization. What should be done or changed to achieve the proposed goals? That is, it includes a description of steps and actions to be developed in all areas and dependencies of the company. This work must specify specific actions for each department (Marketing Plan, Operational Plan, Financial Plan, Administrative Plan, etc.) that cover annual periods. Again, it is about defining what things to do and what things to define, programming for the next stages, and the how or the best way to do them remains pending. Although we have encouraged the participation of staff in these Formulation tasks, in practice, not all staff will be able to participate in all the activities; participation will be selective according to the different areas and levels.

Given that the achievement of goals also depends on external circumstances that are difficult to predict and manage, it is advisable to design from the beginning a Contingency Plan where it is outlined to face unforeseen situations that could mean a deviation or departure from the original route and goals. Likewise, this design phase is important because it helps to support and improve the prioritization of projects and facilitates outlining a gradual implementation scheme on diverse fronts consistent with the technical demands and resource availability of the entire organization.

2.1.3 Restrictions

In general, errors are carried over from one phase to another, so the deficiencies described in the diagnosis stage become evident and are carried over when the plans are formulated and designed, and in turn, the design and formulation errors are present in the Implementation phase. However, although a poor diagnosis corresponds to a poor formulation and design, the development of an accurate diagnosis is necessary but not sufficient for its correct formulation, design, and implementation. It is worth asking, then, why, in certain cases, business management was not satisfactory despite having had correct diagnoses. Let us review the answers to such a question that has to do with design problems:

- "Straitjacket" type models. Behind any formulation or design of an institutional project, there is a theoretical concept that is reflected in a model. In this model, the "know-how" is structured and reflected, where how to do things is defined; there, the content and articulation of different elements that make up the proposed systems, processes, standards, procedures, and flows of information are described. Unfortunately, the error of designers, carried away by the enthusiasm of successful models in other media and at other times, is "imported and imposed in its entirety" by trying in vain to fit the model to their reality.

- Errors and deficiencies of "serial designs." In this regard, we believe that each company should be considered as an independent reality and therefore propose a "tailor-made" solution, that is a solution that is also independent and unique. We consider that in terms of design, "serial" solutions that aim to adapt or adjust as a standard model to a varied universe of companies do not fit or are worth it. On the contrary, specific aspects of each organization must be considered (sizing, degree of relative development, cost structure, age and use of facilities and equipment, operation of existing systems, etc.) so that, based on knowledge of its particularities, your most advisable solution is designed.

- The errors of approach and conception noted above for the diagnosis stage are entirely valid and concurrent in this Design phase. We emphasize them in this part to consider that both errors (Diagnosis and Design) carry the risk of implementing (putting into practice) systems, programs, and projects whose form and substance will be incongruent with what is required.

The phase after the stages described would be the one that corresponds to the realization or execution of the Plan, which in strategic terms is called **Implementation**. How do we conduct and implement what we have formulated? This includes how to use resources to achieve the proposed goals. This purpose is more specific and will be part of the next chapter corresponding to Efficiency.

One way to express achievements in business management will be to refer to the process through which the company will evolve favorably from its inception or starting point towards the achievement of its basic objectives in accordance with its respective strategy. The evaluation of compliance with objectives and goals will provide guidelines for the success achieved. The problems begin when the company lacks a strategy or does not know its starting point or its environment and does not even try to outline an image-objective towards which it should go. Even if the company had clarity of both (start and goal) and a defined strategic design, the problems in the strategic implementation process that we will see later are not easy to overcome.

Once the idea or business project has been defined, one of the first mistakes that we have just mentioned is the absence of a strategy, business plan, business model, project profile, or whatever we want to call it, but it refers to the absence of a guiding document that tells us the basic guidelines and important considerations regarding resource allocation factors, costs, and benefits involved in the business in question. Although having a strategy does not guarantee success, its development constitutes one of those basic and correct tools that must be done.

If, as an entrepreneur or business manager, you have doubts or do not know where to go and how to do it, it is better not to undertake the journey and avoid wasting resources and time, but keep in mind that having a strategy will help you in your task. The content of the strategy will vary depending on the nature and dimension of the project or company in question. For a small company, it will be enough to have a Business Plan, and for a large company, it will be a sin not to have a Strategic Planning scheme in place. What is clear is that each business reality has its specific strategy, and tracings or copies do not work.

What is the reason for the absence of strategy, especially in small businesses? In our concept, the first aspect refers to the typical profile of the entrepreneur, with technical or professional skills and experience corresponding to the line of business that he will undertake. Although this qualifies him for the key function of the product or service to be provided, it does not guarantee that the remaining functions involved in business management are executed with the same skill as the skill that he masters. There is a tendency to underestimate, undervalue, and even ignore or postpone these functions because they are considered less urgent, one of which is precisely developing a Business Plan. This limitation is a common sin in small companies, but it is non-existent in projects and management of large companies.

For any questions on this topic or any other related to small businesses, you can refer to the work of Timothy S. Hatten: "Small Business Management. Entrepreneurship and beyond", Houghton Mifflin Company Third Edition, 2006. This and other works of copious bibliography abound in academic circles and develop the topic in a more detailed manner than that done in this work. Our purpose in this work is to highlight its importance and the general guidelines that comprise it.

The absence of strategy in small businesses also has to do with the budgetary and financial constraints of the owner or manager of the business unit, which makes it difficult to hire professionals in specialties other than their own and forces them to make risky decisions in areas of which they are not familiar. The usual result is the good cook who fails to establish a restaurant business, the good mechanic who fails to set up his workshop or factory, the prominent doctor who fails to establish a small clinic, or the lawyer or accountant who fails to set up his business professional study because blunders were made in areas (administrative, financial, commercial, legal, etc.) that the entrepreneur was not capable of detecting, understanding, or correcting and that could be pointed out and warned in the respective strategy or business plan.

On the other hand, although we consider the Strategy to be an important instrument, we do not exaggerate in conceptualizing it as a "sine qua non" (indispensable) condition to guide any management. The real world will continue to show us notable examples of entrepreneurs who achieved success without having a formal strategy but did establish a factual strategy based on their exceptional "nose" and intuition to avoid risks and identify opportunities. Not everyone has such skills, and the number of entrepreneurs who failed because they did not have a strategy is greater than those who achieved success without having it formally conceived.

Like any work tool, the strategy is not an unrestricted instrument that must be followed. On the contrary, it must be instrumentalized, perfected, and adapted to the contingencies in the development of one's own path. The strategy, after a certain period of regular operation and evaluation, will be made up of successive approximations and the demand for unforeseen changes towards a more elaborate profile, being subject to feedback, renewal, and respective adjustment (Reformulation of the Global Plan).

Despite the advantages of having a strategy, even in its simplest version, we believe that, unfortunately, it will continue to have little roots, and small businesses will continue to be ignored by drivers. It is likely that the entrepreneur who has achieved initial success will not recognize the usefulness of a strategy and will continue to trust in what he considers his "infallible" sense of smell. The successful small businessperson runs the risk of becoming a creature bristling with an enormous ego and self-sufficiency so that he will consider that nothing and no one could tell him where to go or how to do it. His initial successes will convince him that he does not need any strategy, and until the probable changes in the business environment cause such a shake-up, he will not consider the need for a strategy.

The less successful and more informal entrepreneur also downplays the importance of strategy because he usually sets out on his entrepreneurial journey without a compass, or a map, or a road map, and with a mediocre crew. He suddenly navigates stormy seas without knowing how or why and ends his journey in unexpected destinations. He will continue to survive as long as circumstances and his ability to endure allow it. Every trip and fall experienced could rethink the need for a strategy that either could be too costly due to the use of resources and time that compromises its solution, or it would be inopportune to undertake any rescue because the ship is about to capsize. Better said in the process of imminent bankruptcy.

The strategy becomes, in cases and without intending it a remedy to cure bumps and falls for those who still survive. However, we hope that the increasingly widespread use of strategies is breaking this structural and generational resistance in the education and praxis of small business owners. In this, we consider that in terms of business management, there is no room for improvisation, and chance (always present) works, in most cases, against it.

2.2 LEADERSHIP: How to understand it?

2.2.1 Leadership and Management

The Direction management function is one of the central activities of all management and involves processes committed to obtaining better results in the execution of the company's resources. For the purposes of this essay, we are going to separate the management function into two large groups of activities. One of them is of administrative or executive orientation that responds to how to conduct or modify actions, tasks, and processes, has a short-term horizon, and executes the allocation of resources that necessarily come together in daily problems. In planning jargon, these activities correspond to what is called the Implementation of that which has previously been formulated and designed. These are activities that set the tone for what we will discuss in the next efficiency chapter.

The other group of activities related to the management function that we develop in this part is more related to effectiveness and refers to that part of Management in its role of **strategic orientation**. It is about the conception of that set of guiding activities that influence the activities in their direction (or redirection) and focuses its attention on activities that have a strong impact on the future of the organization. It outlines its approach for a medium and long-term horizon and perspective. This does not mean at all ignoring the present, but rather, not neglecting, within the tumult of functions and activities of the present, those that have greater preponderance in that perspective and desired horizon. That is, these are management activities included in the field of strategic leadership.

A summary of the difference between leadership and management is that **the leader** represents an image of the architect who foresees and knows how to navigate through chaos or critical situations. To do this, he uses his instruments of creativity, intuition, and innovation, while **the manager** represents the image of the solver of everyday management problems. To achieve this, he uses rational procedures in his usual management, control, and supervision tasks. We make this distinction of the directive function between leadership activity and executive activity only for analytical purposes and to facilitate the understanding of differentiated roles. In practice, the manager must combine both roles; as an executive, he must have leadership skills, and as a leader, he must possess executive qualities.

Both activities are intermixed to the agenda. Management without leadership encourages a style lacking inspiration and innovation, with routine development of stationary activities and without development. Leadership without management forms a style disconnected from reality or neglects the necessary activities and challenges of the present. Both perspectives considered in isolation are not favorable because they could generate destabilizing drag, promoting disorder and chaos in any organization. (See Gosling and Mintzberg: "The five minds of a manager," 2003, Harvard Business Review 81(11) 54-63).

A distinction must be made between management development and leadership development. Management development involves training management teams with sufficient knowledge, techniques, and skills to improve business performance through tested and learned solutions. Leadership development is oriented towards establishing a collective leadership capacity that allows us to anticipate changes or even seek and implement those changes, which means taking advantage of opportunities and facing unforeseen challenges and contingencies. Leadership is conceptualized as an effect instead of a cause, with an emerging peculiarity that is to strengthen (with contributions of innovation, creativity, conviction, intuition, and honesty) the effectiveness of previously designed business systems where each person is considered a leader.

In this context, executive development is related to managerial development roles, while the leader has to do with the development of people in leadership roles. Management development involves investment in human capital that strengthens the interpersonal competence of selected individuals, and leadership development involves a collective process involving investment in social capital by strengthening interpersonal networks, communication, and collaboration between people and the organization. The distinctions described here between executive development and leadership development are important because we saw that academic efforts have traditionally focused on individuals (executives), leaving behind the focus that we are interested in highlighting in this essay, which is leadership from a collective and organizational perspective.

The generalized concept of a leader is one that involves a person who brings together a set of skills and virtues that allow him to stand out in his respective context and, at the same time, establish links of influence between him as a leader and the group of followers where he operates. This bond is born, grows, and develops in a framework of respect, admiration, and roots and determines a commitment to collaboration and follow-up. This individualistic conception predominates in popular thought and perceives the leader as "the hero of the movie" and his group as the mass of devoted followers. This conception has determined that leadership is usually associated as an ascribed and inseparable property of the leader. Being a leader empowers one to act with the seal of leadership, and leadership must correspond with being a leader.

However, reality shows us contrasting examples of people who have not necessarily possessed or exhibited excellence in leadership skills and virtues and have developed successfully within the leadership framework (e.g., the introverted and conscientious Bill Gates, founder of Microsoft). At the same time, the fact that the person possesses most of these qualities of excellence does not guarantee that they are necessarily inclined or interested in developing leadership (e.g., Mahatma Gandhi and Mother Teresa of Calcutta never set out to be leaders of anything, but leadership was the consequence of a lifetime dedicated to helping others).

There are also notorious examples of people who, in their excessive political ambition, reach positions of power using more tricks than merit, but no matter how much they remain or are re-elected in such positions of power, they are usually accompanied by notorious ineptitude (few skills and virtues required) that disqualifies them from becoming authentic leaders. Whether due to obstinacy, egocentrism, dark interests, or whatever, the truth is that reality confronts us with that endless species of "toxic" leaders and leaderships that correspond in scenarios with varied shades of pro-leftist, centrist, and pro-rightist tendencies such as Nicolás Maduro (Venezuela), Vladimir Putin (Russia), Xi Jinping (China), Donald Trump (USA), Boris Johnson (Great Britain), Jair Bolsonaro (Brazil), Alan García (Peru) and others. Later, there will be an opportunity to refer to the predominance of this risky trend of various populisms that reappear and/or are accentuated in the current political scenario.

The opportunity is conducive to remembering what was pointed out by Miguel Ángel Cornejo (See journalistic note in the newspaper "El Comercio," Lima, Peru. Nov 13, 1994) regarding the difference between being a boss and being a leader:

> "...for the boss, authority is a privilege of command, for the leader a privilege of service. The boss pushes the group, the leader goes to the front, committing his actions. The leader does not need to display credentials of legitimate authority, his Generous commitment, his magical dynamism, and his attitude of dedication are the best cards with which followers find out about their authority....The boss inspires fear, the leader inspires confidence, injects enthusiasm, strengthens the group...The boss says go, the leader says let's go...The leader is the one who gets real commitment from all the members,...permanently motivates his people to want to do their things, supervises everyone's work, and spreads a mystique, a profound ideal. The boss arrives on time, the leader arrives early. He who sees further than others are a

leader... a leader is he who is not content with the possible but with the impossible."

In addition to what a person can possess or do to strengthen specific skills that make him or her a leader, the leadership process is the result of a complex interaction of factors. That is, who can be appreciated as leaders; the way they behave and the results they achieve will be determined not only by their intrinsic individual characteristics but by the weight of social and cultural factors in which they operate.

The environment in which leadership operates is by no means homogeneous or uniform but rather varied in form and content. For example, an environment that demands urgent decisions, such as a battlefield, disaster, or emergency response, requires a leader or a team of leaders who have a certain relatively autocratic style that executes decisions from the high hierarchy "in situ." This is a person with "field marshal" qualities. For its part, an environment of advertising, consulting, or journalistic industries will require a greater degree of participation, so, in said environment, consultative style leadership would be the most suitable. Due to the multifaceted nature of the environments that leadership faces, it cannot be said that there is a single best way to develop leadership or behave as a leader. For this reason, we share the concept of:

> "...leadership as a process of social influence of complex personal interrelationships to guide, structure and facilitate behaviors, activities, and relationships oriented toward the achievement of shared goals whose results matter not because of the specific individual qualities of a small group." number of admirable people (read leaders), but because said process allows achieving organizational effectiveness."

(See "Exploring Leadership," published by Richard Bolden, Beverly Hawkins, Jonathan Gosling, and Scott Taylor. Oxford, University Press, 2011. Pages 167-170). The highlighting and comments in parentheses of the quote are ours.

Given that one of the characteristics of our current society is the occurrence of events where uncertainty, complexity, and constantly changing landscapes predominate and coexist. One of the keys to facing this environment will be through the development of leadership that involves and commits all those who have interests in the organization (leaders, shareholders, workers, creditors, suppliers, authorities, etc.; English terminology has coined the word "stakeholder" to refer to such groups). It is then myopic to perceive and conceptualize the development of leaders or leadership individually or in isolation without considering the broad context in which they develop.

2.2.2 Visualization of Opportunities and Risks

Due to its implication in the concept of effectiveness and going a little deeper into visualizing the complex relationship between leadership and management, it is important to make a prior digression regarding the topic of opportunities and risks. The business and organizational leader must, as we economists say, see not only the tree of his organization but also the forest that constitutes a complex amalgam of environments. He must feed on a panoramic perspective of space and time that will enable him to have greater clarity of analysis in the perception of opportunities and risks that affect his organization. For this reason, it is stated that management will become more effective to the extent that whoever directs it "sees and goes further than others."

The perception of an opportunity constitutes the identification, at a given moment, of development potential. The business, project, or organization manager with strategic and entrepreneurial ability develops that sense of smell, perception, intuition, and glimpses within that complex and diffuse reality, the possible opportunity, and the appropriate moment or "timing" to take advantage of that opportunity and implement it what you have already identified goes. Failure to do so is simply a missed opportunity, and since, just like the availability of resources, opportunities are also scarce, a good manager cannot afford to waste them and must be alert and on the hunt for them.

It must be recognized that not all managers have this important ability to identify and take advantage of opportunities, especially when they are immersed in complicated and confusing processes that are volatile, random, and with time restrictions on daily emergencies. There is no rule or formula to identify an opportunity; it often presents itself casually, suddenly, and without any announcement. Therefore, we must keep our eyes wide open, "be aware of seeing what we are looking at, and have the courage to undertake the opportunities detected."

In this regard, it is worth reflecting on the statement of "being aware of seeing what you are looking at." In this sense, we refer to a broader concept that consists of developing a "capacity for sensory awareness," which includes becoming reflectively aware of something that cannot be so easily perceived or that is apparently confused or hidden. This sensory capacity allows us to identify or sense an opportunity, a problem, an unforeseen event, etc. and empowers us to act in accordance with said knowledge. Sometimes, we observe or perceive phenomena or events in a superficial, generic, or routine way without paying greater attention to details that make them imperceptible, but which are indications of deeper content. This sensory capacity through vision suggests that "being aware of seeing what you see," that is, developing that thoroughness that allows you to appreciate things without leaving aside details and apparently unconnected behaviors that the majority does not appreciate, relate, or ponder.

If we refer to other senses other than vision, such as smell, taste, hearing, or touch, this olfactory, gustatory, auditory, or tactile capacity must be developed so that through their respective organs, they can perceive those respective sensations and have knowledge of them without even requiring visual ability. How do we apply this in management? In the case of vision, certain guidelines have already been suggested, but the capture of externalities and events through the other senses has its share of intuition, interpretation, accurate inference, and categorization of events that have occurred or are about to occur. Having well-tuned senses will make it easier to raise awareness of such events so that the "translation or interpretation" of a piece of news, a discovery, a strike, a military conflict, a defection from competition, a shortage of supplies, a market upturn or fall and in general any possible external economy or diseconomy and others, have a reading of appropriate concepts.

By simply tasting a spoonful of liquid container (coffee or tea), we perceive whether it is adequate or slightly sweet or sour and we do not need to have seen the amounts of sugar previously poured or taste the entire container. In the same way, our sensory or gustatory capacity is perfected with the perception of a simple sample (that is precisely the technical foundation of surveys), which will allow us to infer the possible impact on that market or population segment under observation and estimate the possible sympathy or aversion of said segment toward some event.

Likewise, the olfactory capacity can give indications of how things have been presenting a receptive or hostile environment (they smell good or bad) long before they are presented or exposed to the market (they are served at the table). In the same way, your hearing ability will warn you if you are close to stormy winds with lightning, thunder and lightning or if calm has already prevailed in the convulsed scenario. Finally, the touch capacity will inform you if the weather continues to winter if spring has already appeared, or if you should prepare for a warm summer and clear skies. That same tactile ability will make you aware of painful profiles (economic and political) of social impact that must be considered before developing any management.

This capacity, which many describe as smell and intuition, has nothing subjective, intuition, hunch, or chance. This capacity is the result of a keen perception and comprehensive evaluation of ponderable and concurrent factors in management that are not learned in university classrooms but in the experience of business life through bumps and stumbles. The business manager complements, filters, and weighs his decisions with the unavoidable use of his judgment, criteria, and intuition and with the help of important technological advances and information management and processing instruments (surveys, opinion polls, and projection with model statistics).

Sometimes, opportunities derived from trade agreements, completion of investigation processes, competitive errors, pre-announcements in fiscal, exchange, monetary, tariff regulations, new infrastructure works, etc., can also be foreseen or detected. That would allow an advanced period of preparation to capitalize on it.

Opportunities are not necessarily linked to the prevention or visualization of favorable situations. In a respectable number of cases they are a prelude to, are accompanied by, or are a consequence of one's own or others' critical experiences. In Asian culture and China in particular, the word crisis has a double meaning: the first and most conventional refers to the dramatic situation that arises in terms of threats, severe problems, conflicts, restrictions, absences, and shortages in availability. of resources. The second great teaching for these cultures refers to the fact that consequently and because of the crisis itself, "opportunities" may arise that appear as new options or alternatives, which remained hidden or not visualized in situations prior to the critical contingency.

For people of this Asian culture, the occurrence of a critical situation can lead to the development of a flourishing opportunity. Not everyone can discover it and take advantage of it. The word crisis is so widespread in our environment and in all sectors, and the only thing it generates is complaints and lamentations. It is necessary to develop that skill that allows, amid that ocean of crisis and chaos, to identify those scarce opportunities and capitalize on them. History is full of cases where opportunity was a consequence of critical situations. Ingenious popular sayings send the message: "There is no evil that does not come with good."

An illustrative example was captured by the renowned film producer Steven Spielberg, based on a real case, in one of his masterpieces, "Schindler's List." In it, Mr. Schindler visualizes and develops a business opportunity because of a critical situation derived from a war conflict (World

War II). He decides to set up a factory to supply the German army with household utensils. However, the importance of doing business accompanied by criteria of ethical values, as a preview of what we will explain in the next section, also meant an opportunity for a group of prisoners of war of Jewish origin to be saved from the Holocaust.

A variety of contextual factors may intervene in the identification of an opportunity (as we pointed out in the conceptualization of leadership): climatic variations, seasonality, life cycle of a product or service, potential of a place, discovery of a market niche, renewal technological change of equipment or plant, changes in demand preferences, replacement or obsolescence of products, fashions and variants of products and their use, economic situation, armed conflicts, temporary policy measures in the event of emergencies, etc. There must be an evaluation of weighted criteria to perceive both the opportunity and the circumstances of the immediate environment that make it feasible.

The presence of external economies and diseconomies also play a vital role. (Example: construction of new infrastructure - roads, railways, ports, airports, leisure centers, etc. - establishment or closure of shopping centers, transfers, or establishment of public service entities such as ministries, hospitals, universities, etc.) that cause the flourishing of new businesses and clients or the loss of these. If prudence advises it, the project (launch of the new product or provision of service) can be launched, but it could also be recommended to be postponed or the need to make certain adjustments, suspended, or canceled to avoid further losses.

Hand in hand with the identification of opportunities, **the perception of risks** must be considered. We must be attentive to red flags that are a warning of limits and adverse circumstances. Risk, defined as a possibility of losing something (income, clients, market, profitability, productivity, etc.) that has grave consequences, is not only exclusively linked to those who coexist with risky activities. Indeed, the risk can end with the most intrepid, who end up jumping into the "empty pool," but it also tends to affect even the timidness that "decide" not to make or postpone decisions for fear of making a mistake. The latter, due to their aversion to risk, "paradoxically fell into the risk of not taking risks" because by trying exaggeratedly to avoid it, they came closer to it.

The risk must be considered not only in attention to the object or destination that contains it but also the peculiarities of the subject who faces it, the origin, circumstances, and contexts that compromise its realization. In terms of business management, decisions (especially strategic) set the course and determine, depending on their nature, major or moderate risks. The economic and social situation and the external panorama add to management a specific correlation of imponderable risks.

But it will be the degree of knowledge and tolerance towards risk on the part of the management body; it will be its availability of contingency plans to counteract them, it will be its capacity to react and willingness to "adjust and provide its management" with precise and timely changes in the face to the foreseeable trends, which, together with good judgment, will allow the business boat to be carried out, overcoming the difficulties of risky contexts. As we pointed out in the topic of "opportunities," in this topic of "risks," we also reiterate the recommendation to develop sufficient capacity for the development of sensory awareness: "Keep your eyes wide open and be aware of seeing what is happening and look" at the signs that we intuit with the help of the other senses.

The problem of risk arises both for the most experienced, who constantly risk their business boat by sailing on rough and stormy seas in search of new horizons and for the extremely conservative, who only resort to what is known when they face unforeseen events or unfamiliar problems. The latter tend to end up lagging in obsolescence and lack of innovation. Both groups, by risking too much or by preferring never to risk, can be left out of the competitive business race. In fact, risks can be taken in conditions that do not become suicidal recklessness. A prerequisite to becoming an organizational leader is facing and assuming manageable and responsible levels of risk.

2.2.3 Development of the Leadership Process

Leadership development and management development are integrally related and strongly influenced by the culture of the society in which they operate. From the perspective of the Eastern world, cultural norms and conventions (different from those that prevail in the Western world) are determining factors in the conception of leader, leadership, and favor and prioritize relational aspects, participation, service, and guidance.

According to what was noted by the Leadership Development Center [4], for the development of a business system to be **effective**, it must be integrated with different processes of the organization, such as, for example, management planning, selectivity of the employment process, establishment of rewards, recognition, control, and detection of erroneous or deviated processes. It is necessary to provide a feedback and support scheme between management and leadership responsibilities. Every organization should find ways to assess its management development and leadership development capabilities and be understood as part of an integrated strategic framework.

Successful companies have leaders behind them who lead them on the path of achievement and sustained growth. As we mentioned, the number of successfully managed companies is a minority, and this is due to the absence or shortage of leaders in today's modern world. This deficit of authentic leaders with the required excellence of intrinsic qualities represents a strong call for attention and self-criticism of modern society and its educational systems. Why does corruption run rampant, lord it over, become endemic and become a distinctive characteristic of business and political systems of our time?

Are leaders born or made? There will be people who, as in other areas or disciplines such as science, arts, or sports, will present aptitudes that reflect innate qualities that place them in a better disposition to perform what a certain function requires. This does not imply that because of this fact, they overlook the necessary enhancement of their learning. There will also be other people who will have to forge their managerial or organizational leader profile in the permanent effort of training, constant training, and in the practice and learning of trial and error. Although we face a situation of lack of authentic leaders and the numerous list of qualities required to be one is demanding and difficult to concentrate on a single person, in practice and in a good part of management and academic circles, the conception predominates (debatable and controversial) that "leaders are born" and that the seal of their personality is decisive in determining who will become one and who will not.

It cannot be ignored that one of the preponderant factors in management has to do with the requirements and personal qualities that the driver or manager of an organization must have. In fact, if there is no solid support of qualities, skills, and virtues that fit with the functions of

---

[4] R. Bolden, B. Hawkins. Exploring Leadership" op cit pages. 71-72

organizational management, it will be difficult to achieve leadership that promotes sustained changes, of forming an organizational culture inspired by values, of maintaining a spirit attentive to the hunt for opportunities and detection of risks, exploring innovation and value creation processes and finally outlining a vision and vocation as a strategist.

But we must also warn that it would be biasedly implausible and even forced to make leadership depend solely on the personal attributes of the leader, even if he possesses them (even embryonic). Here, we touch on a controversial topic. In most management selection processes, candidates are subject to psychometric tests to evaluate their psychological profile. Such tests assume that personality characteristics can be identified, categorized, and measured with an appreciable degree of precision and acceptance, and in addition, it is assumed that this personality profile remains stable and even independent of any situation or context in the environment that takes place. For this reason and according to this presumption, the person who meets an acceptable degree of such qualities will be disposed of and capable of assuming managerial functions. According to this conception, the leader and his identified profile form a predictable pattern of similar and optimal reactions in any context, circumstance, and time.

From another perspective, researchers Cooper and Baker: "Fair play or foul. A survey of Occupational test practices in the United Kingdom" 1995, cited in "Exploring Leadership…" [5], draws attention to the failures in many organizations in the monitoring of psychometric tests due to the lack of confirmatory signals offered by the relationship between personality and performance and question how true it may be the fact that our identities are sufficiently constant and stable over time. According to these authors, our identities and psychological profiles, instead of existing independently, are supposed to emerge as we progress in our relationships and interactions and in the context that characterizes our lives. If the latter were true, it is not strictly conclusive that personality measurement corresponds to fixed and stable identities because these identities probably vary in a state of constant flux (and ebb). If so, the scope of the measurement described is relative and only referential.

This approach raises the digression that even the same person could have a different response to different or similar contextual situations. There will not be two identical responses with the same strength or weakness in situations of crisis, risk, boom or bonanza, emergency, etc. Even

---

[5] R. Bolden, B. Hawkins, Exploring Leadership" …op cit pages. 43-45

when considering the temporal variable, it could even be stated that an honest (or corrupt) person from twenty years ago can surprise us today with a response contrary to what was expected.

In this regard, history shows us a peculiar case, the French general Philippe Pétain (see https://es.wikipedia.org/wiki/Philippe_P%C3%A9tain), considered a national hero for stopping the German advance in his important victory in the Battle of Verdun (Feb. 1916) during the First World War. His reputation led to an impressive career as he was promoted to Marshal of France (Nov. 1918), Minister of War (Feb. 1934) and Head of State (July 1940). From then on, he began his debacle by giving his management a pseudo-dictatorial turn, establishing or deviating towards a collaborationist policy with Hitler's Nazi Germany and sharing with him a certain complicity in the Holocaust.

In effect, power was reprehensibly transformed: he suspended public freedoms and party activity, encouraged union manipulation, deported 149,000 Jews from France, and promulgated laws to exclude French people of the Jewish race from participating in public activities and administration. He was so committed to the German regime that he fought the French Resistance itself by keeping close to 70,000 people in prison, of which 10,000 were sentenced to death. In abundance, he ordered his generals based in Algeria and Morocco to combat the Allied troops that landed in North Africa (Nov 1942).

After the war, his disgrace precipitated; he was accused, tried, and sentenced for high treason. In August 1945, he was sentenced to death, although the death sentence was later commuted to life imprisonment. His health was declining, he was losing lucidity, and he died in July 1951.

In light of the experience described, we could reflect on to what extent if we persist in believing, like the common mortals, that personalities and their complex behavioral envelope have little probability of change, then maintaining intact the presumption that "leaders are "born" will imply that it will only be enough to make an effort to find them (even if it is with a magnifying glass) and the help through specific training, training, and leadership development programs will be limited or marginal.

In addition to the intrinsic characteristics that a leader must possess, the things he does and how he does them are equally important. What do management functions require of a leader? In addition to the executive functions described in your conventional roles as an efficient manager of organizational resources (human, financial, technological, etc.) in which you must conduct yourself with honesty, discipline, and perseverance, as a leader, you are expected to address specific issues, for example: Maintaining an entrepreneurial spirit, open to new experiences, new opportunities and willing to take considered risks.

Additionally, a manager must know how to negotiate with other agents with organizational interests, such as shareholders, workers, suppliers, distributors, clients, authorities, and the community in general. This presupposes a certain predisposition of an extroverted, sociable, expressive character and of knowing how to manage relationships with different people and even have a good relationship with them in a framework of mutual respect.

Another skill is managing critical or emergency situations (a good example was the meritorious performance of the former mayor of New York, Mr. Giuliani, in charge of the attack on the Twin Towers on the fateful September 11, 2001. Regrettably and in reinforcement that psychological patterns and responses do not remain constant, this same character would throw his prestige overboard by assuming, as a lawyer, an unconditional defense of the insidious Donald Trump and accompanying him in the support of lies that cost him his suspension in 2021 of professional practice at the New York Lawyer bar.

In abundance of what leaders and leading companies should or should not do, we cite as a bad example the regrettable reaction of the senior management of a well-known (Peruvian) brewery, Cia. Nacional de Cerveza CNC, which in the eighties of the century past they ignored the taste and preference of the consumer and their strict daily quality control and tasting tests. Unfortunately, by continuing to place a defective product on the market, the company caused, in addition to large returns, serious economic problems that took years to correct.

This issue of critical and emergency situations is one of the most difficult to manage given that managers or directors are, in the context of these emergency situations, burdened with responsibilities of such quantity, variety, and simultaneity and do not have time to structure schemes conscientiously and rationally pre-prepared. The panorama of permanent changes harasses you in such a way that the capacity for immediate reaction is crucial, demands an urgent response, and rules out, due to temporal restriction, the advisable action with greater reflective weighting.

Given this, management must base its decision-making process under a panorama of conditions of uncertainty, with partial and incomplete information, with time pressure, and only with the help of a rapid analytical perception of the complexity to be treated and with its good judgment, common sense, and intuition, you will be empowered to perceive a conceptual synthesis of your problem and the approach and solution to the complexity of its management. This will make it easier for you to focus on the substance of the problem to be treated and avoid "beating around the bush." Even so, the manager will not be able to have clear certainty that the results to be achieved are those expected by the always imponderables out of control.

The absence or limitations of the qualities described are something like the goalkeeper of a soccer team whose lack of reflexes in urgent or critical situations can generate disastrous results for his team. The failures or errors of a goalkeeper are, compared to those of any other player, gravitational in the results. This calisthenics or mental agility that drives effective responses is hardly learned in university master's training but in the mastery of lived experiences and is complemented by the personal gifts of the leader.

It is not our intention to discard the importance and contribution of case studies based on the presentation, analysis, discussion, and solution of cases or business management problems widely used in university master's programs. They constitute a framework of reference, but their "solutions" in no way can be conceived as unrestricted recipes or magic formulas applicable to any other situation. **The phenomena and events that occur in the field of social sciences are unique and unrepeatable**. Similar events may be experienced, but the contexts will also be different and the variability of scenarios (business, community, local, regional, or national) are also different. So, it will be the experience and learning of the successes and errors of each case that will have to play a determining role in its knowledge and solution.

The trend of business events and the challenges of the environmental and global panorama suggest that these phenomena, with their concomitant situations of crisis and emergencies, will be the ones that will have a frequent impact on business problems in the medium term. Therefore, we call attention to greater theoretical-practical learning in the leadership topics discussed here in the business management debate.

Additionally, the Leadership condition is because the manager and his respective team of managers who accompany him must display important qualities such as demonstrating consistency and showing good examples to follow, being a good communicator, motivator, and good strategist, and persevering in guiding the management route toward the organization's goals. Nor can it be denied that he must present a certain charisma, which beyond physical qualities means personality with such a degree of roots, enthusiasm, fortitude, and human warmth that it inspires adhesion, following, and influence on the behavior of those who accompany him. Historical examples abound, from biblical and religious figures such as Moses, Jesus, John Paul II, and Mother Teresa; from the political sphere such as Abraham Lincoln, Winston Churchill, Martin Luther King Jr., John F. Kennedy, Mahatma Gandhi, Nelson Mandela and from the business sphere such as Henry Ford, Konosuke Matsushita, Warren Buffet, Bill Gates, Steve Jobs, and others.

Just to be indicative and exemplify the relationship of certain skills with the management roles indicated, we will mention skills, in addition to those described in this section, which will always require management attention and commitment. In this sense, the manager must have an analytical skill that enables him to correctly evaluate and diagnose any specific problem, distinguishing the effects from the causes that originate them and without neglecting to locate and understand the context of the total complexity of the organization with a perspective that surpasses short-term immediacy.

This faculty will also facilitate your role as an entrepreneur by being able to identify and have the resources that allow you to take advantage of opportunities and avoid risks. This analytical capacity will also enable you to better handle emergency situations and to be a perceptive forecaster and anticipator of changes.

The organizational manager must promote tasks, schemes, and projects that generate synergy, that is, processes where the result of interacting elements and factors is greater than the sum of its parts. This means possessing fluid, accessible communication and coordination skills without formal or bureaucratic obstacles, complemented by the ability to motivate people and cohesive work teams committed to organizational goals with enthusiasm and passion.

According to several researchers, **emotional intelligence plays an important role in this area**, that is, the ability to perceive and regulate one's own, others, and empathetic emotions to understand their impact on the members of the organization. All of this is crucial for establishing network groups, resolving conflicts, and strengthening relationships between leaders and followers. In this specific topic, we must highlight and confirm the notable rise in female leadership that due to their greater capacity in developing and practicing emotional intelligence (empathy, intuition, reestablishing and maintaining relationships with all participants, team management, negotiations, etc.), has taken advantage of male leadership and its presence in CEO positions (highest executive level) in renowned corporations is no coincidence.

In accordance with the old but current and recognized principle that "authority, at any level, must be accompanied by knowledge," its defender, Mary Parker Follett (1868 – 1933), argued that knowledge and experience are pillars of administration (see Gareth Jones and Jennifer George: "Contemporary Management," McGraw-Hill Irwin, Third Edition, 2003, p. 55). We must mention that the set of skills that correspond to the field of technical or professional knowledge compromises not only the head of the organization but the entire management or executive team, including middle management. It is not strange that, when this principle is violated, whoever has authority but lacks respective knowledge his position is questioned, and his authority is not recognized.

We make a parenthesis to indicate that part of the problem of the Peruvian political situation lies partially in the non-compliance or lack of that principle described. In recent government experience, citizens, the opposition, and former President Pedro Castillo himself recognized (both on his part and his main collaborators and advisors) limitations and deviations to govern the country's destinies. Of course, in addition to the ineptitude, the opposition to the regime, from different fronts, had its collaborative share in his defenestration. It is striking that this same opposition has a complacent behavior towards the current regime of President Dina Boluarte, whose profile of ineptitude is close to that of her predecessor. Shared interests, conveniences, and collusion between representative leaders of the powers explain this opposition complacency.

Here, we outline an approach that well-known traditional politicians (from the right and left) and well-known personalities and leaders of the other powers (formal and factual) refuse to recognize. Our reading of the situation outlines **three complementary approaches**. The first approach is of a symptomatologic nature that alludes to effects on the complicated social field. For decades, our electorate, especially the most dispossessed social sector, has been tired of the frustrating contrast between what the ruling elites say vs. what they do. Therefore, the confirmation of the lack of integrity and coherence of political operators generates little confidence and no credibility. As we propose in the following section, we live in the context of a permanent leadership crisis.

In this electorate, notorious symptoms of fatigue, discontent, and disappointment in the functioning of all the powers of the state are identified (through successive surveys and opinion polls). Citizens do not feel represented or supported by anyone. The few and respectable exceptions do not come to eclipse the critical perception of the endemic situation. The new political options try to capitalize on this leadership crisis and seek to capture the preference of said electorate that, with anxious expectation, wants to believe what fresh faces and successive outsiders are offering them (Fujimori, Toledo, Humala, Kucynsky, Castillo) but, unfortunately, the disenchantment has continued.

The second approach has a causal foundation. Why do such elites not want to understand, see, and hear this deep feeling of popular satiety that even goes beyond the scope of dispossessed sectors and incorporates the educated middle and upper classes? We find an initial reason in that the leadership of formal and factual powers only pay attention to the short-term immediacy of their decisions and policies, which, of course, do not see beyond the maintenance of their interests and benefits. This fact alone disqualifies them as authentic leaders and disqualifies the direction of their decisions, which we must admit do not constitute solutions to the problem described, nor are they intended to be.

The third approach is prescriptive in nature, not so much to outline plausible solutions but to explore, for now, probable ways to find them. The appropriate forms will allow us to arrive at better possibilities to explore the root of the problem and its feasible solution. In this third approach we highlight three steps: First, accepting the previous "mea culpa" described in the second approach. This implies overcoming fierce resistance that the clouded leadership class is not willing to admit. Even blindness and insensitivity are of such magnitude that it prevents them from visualizing that the worsening of this same state of things even goes against their own interests. The effects derived from political and economic instability, a climate of uncertainty, citizen insecurity, and generalized discontent among economic and social agents, ungovernability, interference between powers and institutions, improvisation in decision-making and public management, lack of strategy or guidelines of an inclusive national plan, etc., only generate an undesirable autarky for everyone.

Secondly, given the denied assumption that the elites admit the mea culpa, they will have to, out of responsibility and civic conscience, assume commitments of true leadership and not generate power vacuums or conflicts and imbalances between them. Assuming this responsibility implies that they must impose a change of course, a redirection, which is consensual, which means getting rid of their biased short-term interests to compensate them with medium and long-term perspectives that consider the needs and interests of displaced sectors and populations that are part of our reality.

Thirdly, the details, content and profile of this redirection of strategic leadership necessarily have to take into account three bases: a) a critical examination of the historical past, although it is not required to be very distant, it is enough that it be contemporary because history repeats old ties; b) a most objective and comprehensive evaluation of the present problem based on its causal elements, its interrelationships and its emerging patterns; c) the design of the agreed vision, with its respective objectives and goals of what we want or expect as a nation in the future.

Subsequently, the implementation phase of what has been described is much more complicated because it will typify how we are going to manage and advance this change of course. It will be important to define participatory and inclusive schemes so that the regulatory, decision-making platforms, and execution mechanisms and instruments reach all strata. Only by imbuing this provision will it be possible to strengthen sustainable solutions that go beyond simple calls for new general elections where changes in membership in executive or legislative powers do not mean any improvement but rather a continuity of deterioration.

In line with recent global and regional trends, options from a strengthened conservative right are emerging with renewed vigor. There we have the new face: Mr. Rafael López Aliaga, recently elected mayor of Lima, who has defined his new National Reconstruction party as "popular center-right," which we can rather recognize as "populist right." Continues Mr. Fernando de Soto, with a discreet profile who, in the recent presidential elections with the Avanza País group, had the merit of dispersing the right-wing vote. Accompanying this trend is the well-known Mrs. Keiko Fujimori, a repeat offender in second-round races, who has not finished accepting that a large part of the population repudiates her. This group is completed by the Alianza Para el Progreso party, led by Mr. César Acuña.

These main right-wing options have appeared revamped with populist messages to gain popular favor in the next elections. Currently, they live enthralled and "twinned" in common efforts, even with support from leftist sectors, to prepare the terrain (with legal provisions in its favor to control organizations of the Electoral and Judicial Power) for the next call for general elections. The low blows between them will come later.

The left-wing options in our midst will find it uncomfortable and not so easy, after having initially supported former President Castillo, to tread very finely to get rid of the undesirable burden of his temporary coexistence. As happened previously with the traditional parties (APRA, PPC, and Acción Popular), the well-known parties of this local left remain divided and could go to the hothouse for not having renovated or modernized their ideology or political and doctrinal praxis. They have continued to reduce their party-political capital, and their main effort has been to distance themselves from the current government in power (of Dina Boluarte). The opposition forces (from the right) and the gale of concentrated press media will oversee covering a veil of confusion and discredit to this diverse leftist current so that the electorate does not distinguish between them and discredit them all as coming from the same bag of failures communists.

Closing this parenthesis of ineptitude and corruption entrenched in the Peruvian powers of state, we return to our theme of effectiveness and efficiency. It is then confirmed that any manager or director requires a satisfactory range of knowledge and skills related to his or her function. However, given that he can hardly gather knowledge and skills understood in all areas, it is acceptable for him and his main collaborators to seek advice from specialists on specific topics. We are referring to the set of technical knowledge that each manager must possess and apply in their specific field or area in compliance with their organizational role (marketing, finance, production, research and development, human resources, etc.).

From the above, the task of successfully fulfilling the multiple functions of business management, and on the other hand, being endowed with a select set of personal qualities make it difficult for this challenge to concentrate on a single person. Therefore, in small companies, the driver becomes a kind of "one-man orchestra," developing multiple functions and roles that demand more than his capacity allows. This, in turn, is the cause of certain errors and management failures that explain, in part, the high rate of desertions and withdrawals from the market initially discussed in this essay. This also explains the better possibility that larger companies have in forming management teams that allow them to counteract the exposed rigidities.

Assuming that some of those people who read this essay have a managerial vocation but do not possess all of that select group of qualities for management (a realistic assumption that we economists usually use), then they will have to be aware that, like many things in life, in this purpose, you cannot burn stages and successful management is not achieved overnight, and it will take time to perfect it. These personal qualities will be learned and acquired gradually as a result of processes and stages of formation, experimentation, and training.

There is an alarming paradox in which, on the one hand, the advances and discoveries of scientific and technological knowledge in all disciplines and areas of knowledge only evacuate skilled and capable technicians, scientists, and professionals in the specialized quadrature of their field and discipline. On the other hand, these advances have not been accompanied by a sufficient provision of suitable human capital in terms of management and organizational and political leadership, or having produced it, said human capital is wasted or hindered by imperfections of ineffective or corrupt systems that make it difficult to access the sphere of strategic decisions.

2.2.4 Leadership Crisis

The concrete thing is that we have had to live in a global leadership landscape with few successes and many setbacks. For example, on the political front, deceitful and imperfect democracies are known both in national political situations and in foreign governments, impasses between powers of the State are also common, and, finally, social representation systems function inefficiently. In distinct parts of the world, there are always continuous outbreaks of confrontations and war conflicts. In developing countries, institutional vulnerability and a chronic panorama of widespread corruption become common.

On the economic front we have deterioration and/or slow economic recovery, global and local markets that operate more unstable. Inflationary processes and imbalances in foreign trade, risky growth of public debt, increase in informality, and underemployment are more difficult to contain. Never like before, are we hearing a broken record of the words of mistrust and uncertainty among economic agents and a shortage of qualified managerial and technical personnel.

On the social front, the intensification of immigration processes for labor and war reasons is visible. The social crisis acquires notable manifestations in the permanence and increases in levels of unemployment and levels of poverty, a greater degree of social violence and breakdown of the principle of authority, greater outbreaks of citizen insecurity, segregation, and racism, violations of civil rights, etc.

In this turbulent reality, the absence and need for leadership that reorients, reconstitutes, and strengthens the pillars of desirable socioeconomic structures becomes more noticeable. Since we have the use of civic reasons, we have experienced a leadership crisis, and the characteristic note of current times are the continuous corruption scandals of leaders in public and private entities, in developing countries, in developed countries, and in countries with political systems and different faiths.

Corruption has become endemic and has become a kind of institutional cancer that overwhelms and does not respect conditions, size, borders, spaces, systems, creeds, and cultures. It advances stealthily, gains followers, becomes widespread, and when it is detected, it is often too late or too costly to counteract it. Our present shows us more than ever <u>the lack and, at the same time, the urgency and need to have authentic leadership</u>.

Again, in the <u>Peruvian case</u> and in a situation where corruption scandals compromise former presidents and high officials and where tentacles of penetration of drug trafficking, terrorism, and crime in domestic politics are beginning to be discovered, an outstanding Peruvian journalist and political analyst, the Mr. Gustavo Gorriti who, from his own experience, suffered the misfortune of being a victim of corrupt civil dictatorships, (Fujimori-Montesinos), said in the Magazine "Caretas," Lima, Peru, Edition 2299, Sept 05, 2013, the following:

> "If there is something clear in the history of this country, it is the prevalence of corruption in its governments. There have, of course, been some regimes that have been more corrupt than others and some serious attempts to clean up the State. Sooner rather than later, however, these efforts end up bogged down, tangled, and weakened before withering or corrupting themselves. It is depressing, but it's always been that way."

We fully agree with what Mr. Gorriti pointed out, but with the precision that corruption is not the exclusive property of government administration but that certain sectors of civil society and its representative institutions (judicial power, legislative power, certain sectors of the armed forces, certain private business sector, etc.), also suffer from the same problem.

Towards mid-July 2018, a scandal of major proportions occurred in Peru in the direct sphere of the Judiciary that has compromised the behavior of high judicial authorities. Beyond the ruffians' attitudes of certain judges, the audios revealing the scandal reveal shameful compromises that unmask a crisis that is not cyclical but structural of the Judicial System. The axis of this atrophied system was the predominance of a platform of corruption made up of networks in different institutions such as the Supreme Court, Superior Courts, National Council of the Judiciary - entity in charge of appointing and removing Judges and Prosecutors - the Public Ministry (Prosecutor's Office), etc. All of them have links and tentacles in other institutions and powers of the State, such as the Legislative Branch (Congress and Legislative Commissions) and the Executive Branch (Ministries) and other authorities.

This platform is woven like a dark plot that places operators and moves participants in a kind of transient puppet controlled by this kind of hidden power. The main objective of this scheme is to access, maintain, manage, and perpetuate its power and interests. In situations where said hidden power is diminished or with deterioration in its position or control, it has the option of negotiating and exchanging favors with its adversaries.

In situations where their open advantage in management and control of power is evident, they attack to the maximum, painting their management with an authoritarian tone. In this context, those eligible for key positions in the different powers of the state normally upstarts with ambitions for a political career, with a hunger for notoriety and representation, and are chosen not so much for personal qualities but for their commitment to strictly enforcing the instructions of omnipotent power.

The current situation has placed Peru in this latest and depressing scenario, that of political authoritarianism of the forces that control the power regardless of what political sign they belong to (right, left, or center), but the intention of using power to satisfy petty political and economic interests prevails. In contrast to this, the social scenario that accompanies the process is that of social polarization with unpredictable results.

It was the same as Mr. Gorriti mentioned above, who, as an investigative journalist for a well-known NGO (Non-Governmental Organization), unintentionally became the protagonist of a major scandal for having disclosed to the press videos and telephone recordings that exposed the crisis regarding culpable dialogues held by high judicial authorities is brought to the fore. In them is latent the rot of an atrophied judicial system in force in Peru where shameful verdicts, influence peddling, and other anomalies are directed that make up this scourge entrenched in the structures and institutions of the judicial power with ramifications in the other powers of the State.

We could ask ourselves: What does this scheme of corruption formed in a different space - the judiciary - have to do with our issue of effectiveness and efficiency, limited to the economic and business space? It has a lot to do with it; therefore, although the crisis that occurred arises in another scenario with different contents and problems, there is a "domino" effect of concatenations and consequences that, like expansive waves, reverberate and affect surrounding spheres. Therefore, there do not exist, such as those who hold "separate ropes between economics and politics," but, on the contrary, such ropes are very close together, braided, and related.

Let us start with the conception that a State is based on the formation of three pillars and basic and independent powers: the Executive, Legislative, and Judicial. Each one has its own areas but with interrelated actions and content. The "normal" development of this tripartite superstructure of powers facilitates, promotes, and stimulates the development of society. On this tripartite scaffolding, societies increased their degree of civilization and coexistence by learning to evolve from primitive societies to modern societies today with perfected and even perfectible systems of government, legislation, and justice.

In modern societies, the tripartite system has established a scheme of "weights and measures" that allow a balance of powers so that when any of them exceeds the limits in the development of their functions (without prejudice to the fact that within these their respective mechanisms and means of control have been established), the validity of this balanced system allows its adjustment and correction. In this context, nations have experienced the advances and disappointments of having good and terrible administrators of government, good and terrible legislators, and good and terrible administrators of justice.

The lack of suitability or inefficiency of any person in the exercise of their responsibilities can be corrected with simple replacement, replacement, or training, having to assume the respective direct and opportunity costs that this entails. However, when societies and citizens do not learn from their mistakes, the risk remains of continuing to be immersed in disorientation, indifference, ignorance, and manipulation; then deception prevails, and the cycle of terrible rulers, shameful legislators, and deplorable judges is repeated.

In this context, electoral processes and systems of political representation become lost opportunities. When the sovereign people do not find adequate channels for political participation and ways of expressing themselves, when they lack a fine perception of analysis, when their thinking is arbitrarily confused or distracted, when they can hardly shake off flaws, conditioning, indifference, and manipulation, When it has limited capacity to make its own and improved decisions, then the stability and survival of the nation is at risk, which is trapped and exposed to the tyranny of minorities or civil or military dictatorships.

The variability of crises of cyclical immediacy that we experience in our environment are manifestations of a profile of chronic and structural permanence that can be typified as a social phenomenon of **endemic hypertrophy**. The Peruvian reality seen through the medium- and long-term lens is a tragic example of this phenomenon. Since the economy is that structure that, like a locomotive and wagons, rests and slides on the rails of the tripartite scaffolding. Any defect, anomaly, distortion, disruption, or destruction in said scaffolding will cause undesirable effects whose result will mean delay, involution, chaos and, according to the analogy used, the derailment of the economic train.

When one experiences the insanity of an executive branch deviated by incompetence and/or corruption, there is the expectation that the remaining powers (legislative and judicial) will direct it toward the path in accordance with the law. Likewise, when the legislative branch is also trapped in the same ineptitude or even finds itself involved in collusion with the executive branch, there remains the hope that the judicial branch will prevail with its verdict in accordance with the regulations. But when the imbalance and defection of powers also includes judiciary, the integrity of the judiciary and the stability of the system will have been fractured and degraded. When the scourges of corruption penetrate the judicial sphere, they will be curtailed, debased, and coerced their ability to function as a guarantor of the rule of law, distorting its suitability as an impartial arbiter of rights and duties between natural and legal persons.

The interrelation of powers suggests that even; despite having satisfactory executive and legislative power, the defection of the judicial power will be decisive in the results to be achieved. Although we should not fall into generalizations out of respect for the existence of the still few honest judges and prosecutors who continue to serve, the challenge of removing this cancer of corruption will require a difficult and long process because, from the shadows, the hidden powers of corruption will not remain with their arms crossed and will opt for all means at their disposal, to oppose stiff resistance.

Addressing the issue of corruption and, specifically corruption in Peru goes beyond the scope of this work. Every time the subject is delved deeper, the results in past and contemporary history are painfully frustrating. Serious researchers have treated the issue of corruption with greater prolixity and scientific rigor than that offered in this work, and for further reference, we cite the work: "The Infamous Pact. Study on corruption in Peru", Felipe Portocarrero S, (editor). First Edition, March 2005. The work contains 430 pages, important advances by sixteen researchers from different disciplines, and the Pontifical Catholic University, the University of the Pacific, the Institute of Peruvian Studies, and the support of the Ford Foundation participated. As the editor points out on p. 7:

> "The fight against corruption...has revealed that its persistence is associated with deep historical roots and patterns of social behavior that are very difficult to eradicate. The media report on the judicial processes initiated against those who made the public service a source of illicit enrichment.
>
> The multiplication of news is of such magnitude and so accelerated... that it exceeds the individual possibilities of any researcher. Furthermore, its manifestations are so diverse and its ramifications so extensive, complex, and profound that its study requires a very broad collective reconstruction effort that can only come from professionals from various disciplines.

In the same study cited, we have as an example the article by Mr. Alfonso W. Quiroz [6]:

> "The cost of corruption can be counted in two ways: first, as value that did not reach its assigned destination, as it was diverted by corrupt interests (it may be monetary or in-kind values). To these deviations, we can add the opportunity costs in terms of private investment (national and foreign that ultimately does not come to fruition due to the same degree of existing corruption) and in terms of administrative efficiency; and second, as the institutional damage that corruption causes by distorting or weakening key institutions for stability and investment. The first calculation is quantitative; the second is essentially a qualitative calculation. In the long run, these costs will mean that the more corruption there is, the less investment and growth." (the highlighting is ours because they emphasize the efficiency and effectiveness criteria that we propose in our work).

According to the author, the infamous decade (1990-2000) belonging to the Fujimori-Montesinos government became the period of the greatest corruption in republican history. An

---

[6] See "Costos históricos de la corrupción..." pages 76-82

authoritarian government is established by a small group made up of ties and tentacles in various sectors that manage to capture the power of the State for the purposes of illicit enrichment and specific political ends. All this corruption develops aided by informality and lack of transparency and becomes generalized and becomes something accepted and natural to the system. According to the figures shown, the average annual cost of corruption in said period was approximately 1,400 million dollars, reaching an amount of fourteen billion dollars for the entire decade, which represented almost a third of the average annual budget amount and close to 4% of the average annual GDP during the same period.

But the problem does not culminate in the quantification of figures, which are estimates, since the same author [7] concludes:

"The institutional costs incurred during the infamous decade were enormous in terms of both the inefficient and distorted functioning of key institutions and the damage caused to the civic community fabric...the institutions that suffered the greatest damage were the armed forces, police, and intelligence system. The Presidency and Congress have fallen to the lowest levels of public respect (imagine this statement was held 7 years ago! Not to mention the critical situation of December 2022 or June 2023, where levels of acceptability of both institutions have been lower than those)...in addition to the crises in the judicial and educational systems, the fact that a reform of the 1993 Constitution, necessary to avoid the institutional traps of the Fujimori past, has no signs of being carried out by the political opposition that prevails today...Corruption has bequeathed to Peru perhaps the highest value and institutional costs than any other contributing factor to underdevelopment." (The comments in parentheses and underlined are ours).

A close idea that quantifies the effort to develop is provided by the information disseminated in the editorial of the newspaper "El Comercio" of July 28, 2018, in which, according to the 2018 World Economic Forum report, in the Competitiveness ranking In the Category of "**Efficiency** of the legal framework to resolve disputes," out of a total of 137 countries, Peru occupies position 129 and in the category of "Institutional Pillar" it occupies position 116. As we pointed out before, this specific problem of remaining lagging behind in institutional development constitutes an

---

[7] See Alfonso W. Quiroz, "Costos históricos de la corrupción..." pages 82 y 92

anchor for economic takeoff. Again, although the information dates to 2018, the indication is valid because even the current situation denotes greater institutional deterioration.

From this perspective, a company or organization that operates in the context of satisfactory management of effectiveness and efficiency may encounter a judicial or governmental structure and framework that defects, which is corroded by corruption, which is incompetent to manage matters of its competition and to resolve disputes and claims. In their normal management, companies must resort to said legal or governmental framework to conduct multiple tasks, from simple procedures, temporary permits, obtaining and renewing licenses to more complex processes such as dealing with complaints, participating in bidding contests, auctions, awards of services, tax audits, etc.

In this process, you will have to overcome obstacles, time and money costs that come from abuses, excess bribes and cumbersome bureaucratic obstacles. Additional costs for protection or physical security (plant, equipment, people) and impacts on intellectual property and patents, all this coming from operating in the underworld of chaos and corruption.

In reinforcement of the aforementioned where corruption breaks borders and infests realities, certain information (August 2018) coming from another reality such as Argentina, reported another scandalous case of corruption when secret notebooks were revealed where detailed and scrupulously noted bribes collected from certain businessmen (mostly linked to infrastructure contracts and service concessions) by the government authorities of the administration of Néstor Kirchner and that of his wife, Cristina Kirchner. As an example of the seriousness of the scheme set up by the government administration, the investigative journalist of the newspaper La Nación, Diego Cabot, revealed such facts that were confided to him by the driver who recorded the respective collections and deliveries (including places, people and amounts of money).

The journalist was careful to refer such information directly to the judicial spheres before disseminating it to the press. According to preliminary estimates in this isolated case derived from the notes in the notebooks by a driver and endorsed by investigations initiated by the prosecutor's office, the number of bribes is approximately 220 million dollars and only represents the tip of the iceberg given that the entire flow of corruption was not exclusively through that channel. The research process is in development.

On the other hand, and in honor of the truth, it should be noted that unethical behavior can also originate not only from the government side but from the business side used to it. At the Latin American level, the uncovering of scandalous corruption orchestrated by the private construction company ODEBRETCH of Brazil (2015-2017), which tilted international tenders in its favor by granting million-dollar bribes in the underhanded form of contributions, donations, and collaborations to high officials and governments on duty from several Latin American countries, disguised consultants, etc. has revealed a major scourge entrenched in that plot of political and business power. The example described above of the Brazilian company, which has become the central axis of a corruption scheme at the regional level, shows this scourge of corruption as a two-way street.

In summary, the absence of an adequate legal and institutional framework and the persistence of a scourge of corruption that distorts it leads to increases in operating costs and expenses and stagnation or decline in productivity for any private and public management. The same source cited by newspaper El Comercio of the same date refers to a study by the Inter-American Development Bank, which highlights that in Peru during the period from 1970 to 2015, productivity remained stable, decreasing by 0.3%. With such restrictions and the absence of improvements in productivity and competitiveness, it will be difficult to achieve or maintain optimal levels of efficiency. (We will go into more detail about this topic later in section 3.3.2).

As part of the complementary measures to combat corruption and compromises in the Legislative Branch, the last government administration of Peru (Martin Vizcarra) proposed a Referendum project to avoid the immediate re-election of legislators and other corrective consultations on the functioning of the legislative branch and electoral. This may seem like an illusory initiative for other realities, but for ours it has a justification based on the poor experience for decades of a legislative power (with honorable and rare exceptions) that has successively been made up of a majority with little qualification, full of blunders, prone to compromises and other tricks, operating in the style of successively re-elected cliques that, in the purest style of the "cosa nostra," execute partisan slogans that obstruct governability by questioning, disavowing or "shielding" authorities from other powers. For this reason, they represent the most discredited power for many citizens.

Additionally, peculiarities and imperfections derived from our electoral system (preferential vote, distribution figure) determined that, for example, the option of the Fuerza Popular political party led by candidate Keiko Fujimori despite having obtained 32.6% of the votes in the 2016 general elections votes in the first round, taken as a basis for the party distribution of seats in parliament, finally obtained an improper oversizing of the congressional majority, monopolizing 73 of a total of 130 elected seats, that is, it boosted its participation to reach 56.2% of the existing seats. Given that the Referendum proposed constitutional reforms, it should be previously discussed in Congress and approved by a majority that reaches three-quarters of it.

This being so, we remain immersed in a trap of "legal impasse against democratic institutions." That is to say, the contradictory situation arises in which the predominant legality threatens and coerces democracy because it prevents and breaks the rights of a large part of the citizens. Democracy will continue to be conditioned by the tyranny of a minority that, due to legal accommodation, became an oversized legislative majority. The other way to achieve said majority is through pacts and collusions where the differences and contrasts of doctrine and principles between parties, regardless of who the pact is made with (it may be an opposition party), are subject to the shared and immediate convenience of the interests of the party agreement.

An anomalous situation then occurs where a flawed reality and a legal structure that reinforces it correspond. This distorts the spirit of the Law, which is called to correct flawed realities and not perpetuate them. Just as internal citizen security does not exclusively concern police spheres, the problem of democratic risk described here poses a complicated pending issue for jurists and non-jurists, parliamentarians, and non-parliamentarians.

All of this, like an echo of a paraphernalia that only seeks to distract the attention of unsuspecting citizens from whom it is hidden, distorts and confuses the substance of the matter through the imprisonment of scapegoats who intend to put "cold cloths" and alleviate the fever of protests, counteract the discontent of public opinion and manage to protect or free the true perpetrators to end a repetitive cycle of impunity, leaving the mafia and corruption networks almost intact.

It must be understood that the crisis described today does not represent a temporary manifestation but rather a structural one that for decades has been wrapped in a platform of "hidden power" that encompasses other powers of the State, other institutions with operators at different levels and even incorporates possible applicants to the Executive Branch and well-known figures on the political scene. This corruption has as its champions conspicuous representatives of Parliament compromised in the telephone recordings released, others whose cynicism and audacity in defending the indefensible provokes nausea, and others whose complicit silence betrays them. Only a respectable parliamentary minority has protested and saved the honor of this State power, which only confirms the discredit and popular discontent regarding said institution.

Back to our topic at hand: How can we address the issue of Leadership in the company or organization? We have outlined the characteristics and demands of entrepreneurial leadership, the basic qualities and skills required of the driver or leader, and the dangerous situation of prevailing leadership crises and corruption. Faced with the complexity of this panorama, we consider that leadership development should **not be left to improvisations; it should be a matter of management,** and for this, we propose the same tools previously explained to configure the business strategy.

As stated in the Strategy topic, here we also recommend the three processes: From this perspective, we also propose a first step of recognition of the predominant problem, that is, a diagnosis of the specific situation of the current Leadership scheme. What is the current situation or existing management and leadership profile? As it currently works, where is the prevailing trend leading us? Is it leadership compatible and congruent with the formulated strategy? This analysis includes the evaluation of forces that interact, that is, of the leaders (formal and factual) and the teams or people led, and identifying problems, causes, effects, strengths, and weaknesses of both forces.

Understanding the current problem will lead us to the second process, which is to refine the goals, objectives, and general guidelines of the desired Leadership scheme compatible with the strategic goals previously defined in the strategy. Towards the formation of a centralized Leadership scheme in the upper management spheres or towards the formation of a backbone of leaders (managers, middle managers, team leaders, and key officials)? Do towards a leadership that legitimizes values that reinforce a change in the existing organizational culture? Do towards a leadership scheme that consolidates the qualities, skills and expectations of the leader and followers? Do toward a motivational and participatory leadership?

The third process refers to the conceptualization of the solution and includes the formulation or design of the desired Leadership Plan. What should we do or change to achieve the desired leadership direction? How to guide and specify entrepreneurial tasks, how to identify and direct projects in the portfolio, or how will management face changes or adaptations of technology? How to improve leadership for efficient execution and allocation of resources? That is, the proposed processes include the formulation, even at a conceptual level, of the steps and actions to develop the entrepreneurial leadership function, with how to execute them still pending.

The three processes described above also turn out to be weak and incomplete if they do not converge in their proper execution and implementation. The leadership described here (as well as what was raised in the Strategy topic) requires a complicated and correct Implementation. This last question will be addressed in the chapter corresponding to said topic.

Additionally, we draw attention to the fact that to promote a comprehensive process of business leadership, leadership schemes must also be reformulated and perfected in other spheres of social reality. For example, at the political level, conventional mechanisms, channels, and procedures of democratic functioning have been questioned, which has led to inefficient and false democracies. We have the well-known cases of Venezuela, Cuba, Russia, North Korea, China, Peru, the USA, and other places where questionable democratic processes predominate and the representativeness and development of institutions of the legislative, judicial, and electoral power are not sufficiently convincing.

Both in these and other cases, the answer is usually that this is because it is established by the constitution and the laws of the country in question. It seems good to us that the established laws and rules be respected, but in the face of the appearance of new and changing circumstances (different from those that gave rise to or based on the original rules), it is worth examining and contrasting these laws and rules of the game in light of new conditions, especially in transcendental matters that do not necessarily have to remain unchanged but could be perfected.

There must be a correspondence univocal relationship between normativity and reality. When this correspondence is broken, the dilemma arises between the obligation to respect and abide by the current regulations and the right to question, to protest (civilized), to express disagreement, and even to rebel in abiding by a rule or law that, no matter how much it is invalidity, it is unfair, fruitless, inoperative or a "dead letter." Centuries ago, the libertarian and independence movements of our American countries offered a sample of response to this challenge.

The topic is quite thorny and sensitive, and there are, of course, interests at stake. Leadership, whether in the private or public area, has the intricate attraction of its dose of power and its responsibility and ability to influence the socioeconomic events of the area in which it is responsible. The prominent philosopher Comte commented about the work "The Prince" by Niccolò Machiavelli that the author had the great merit of "showing us not what men should do, but what men do." The experience of past and present cases often shows us that when the power of the gun, of money, and of civil or military dictatorships impose their forces. Anything can happen; the price of life loses value, action based on ethical principles and respect for civil rights and the principles of equal opportunities are replaced by dark and unspeakable purposes where the end justifies the means. This is so even though both the end and its respective meaning are highly questionable.

It has been overlooked that, in terms of organizational leadership and political leadership, an authentic leader (business or political) can win or lose, for example, a tender, a market, an election, a claim or complaint, etc., but doing so in good lid applauds and praises the participants. We witness cases of triumphs or victories that embarrass or taste like defeat and other cases of defeats that exalt, fortify, and leave a victorious taste.

Regarding the latter, once again, sport offers us an exemplary case that went viral and went around the world. On December 2, 2012, a unique race (Hiru-Herri cross) was held in the town of Burlada in Navarra (Spain), where the African (Kenyan) athlete Abel Mutai, who had recently won the gold medal in the 3,000 m steeplechase In London, he was very close to the finish line and on the verge of winning the event. He suddenly became confused; he thought he had reached the goal, so he slowed down and began to greet the public. Behind him was the Spanish runner Iván Fernández who, upon realizing Mutai's mistake, did not try to take advantage of the opportunity but, displaying a deep sense of honesty, urged his opponent to cross the finish line first and prevent him from winning the race having could do it.

(see:https://santodomingocorre.com/index.php/categoria-noticias/937-la-honestidad-del-atleta-ivan-fernandez-al-dejar-ganar-a-un-atleta-despistado published on 10 January 2013.

When asked why he did not win the test, he said: "that the test already had a winner, that there was no merit or glory in winning the test by taking advantage of a confusion, and that having done what I did has given more fame than if I would have won. And that is very important because today, the way things are in all environments, in football, in society, in politics, where it seems that anything goes, a gesture of honesty comes in very handy,"

(see https://elpais.com/deportes/2012/12/14/actualidad/1355506756_770952.html)

Representative companies of the private sector are not immune to this leadership problem, and as we pointed out before, the notorious cases of corruption do not only concern public officials, nor are they exclusive to developing countries, and currently, but the presence of spontaneous leaders also appears widespread and lacking suitability. The well-known Peter principle ("people advance until they reach their maximum level of incompetence") seems to reign without limits or borders in rich, poor, capitalist, socialist, Jewish, Arab, Christian, Asian, White, Black, Hispanic, etc.

How to avoid newcomers to such important positions? Does access to such positions in several cases appear to be tainted by flawed processes? Have systems been created that defend and promote "freedoms and rights" but, in fact, distort them? In many realities, manipulation, chaos, and cheating seem to have been institutionalized. Here we present another pearl: in the current congress, Keiko Fujimori's political group has made its political weight prevail so that Mrs. Martha Moyano, an unconditional supporter, presides over the important Constitution Commission. Unfortunately, the lady lacks technical and professional qualifications; she is not versed in law issues, nor does she hold any academic degree in said discipline. She is only a political operator who has been conducting legal and political reforms that interest her party and the opposition. The business leadership proposed in this essay needs to be complemented and reinforced with leadership at the political level with the same demands and requirements for efficiency and effectiveness that are described here for the business level.

In the Peruvian case, the thorny issue of projects in the mining and energy sector, such as Camisea (natural gas exploitation), the Conga project (gold exploitation), and several projects for the exploitation of copper and other minerals (Las Bambas, Tía María) that are representative examples of political entrapment. Many mining and infrastructure projects were and continue to be suspended, and with it, the paralysis of significant investments worth billions of dollars. A platform of minimal consensus has not been achieved because disagreement and distrust between participants still predominate. Whether due to myopia, pettiness, or excessive political calculation, the fact is that, in such projects, the problems, far from being solved as everyone would like, seem bogged down, credibility is lost, and the "status quo" of aggravating or perpetuating problems is maintained.

If a defective, manipulative, and dependent leadership scheme persists, the solution to problems becomes more conflicting. From this perspective, there is a co-responsibility in the leadership - labor, community, business, and government - where the conflicts and protagonists seem trapped in a complexity where it does not predominate that everyone has access and the right to obtain benefits (that is, that 'everyone wins') but that when any participant considers that his relative position of obtaining benefits is disadvantaged or unbalanced by the benefits obtained by other participants, then he will oppose the other participants winning and will do everything possible so that everyone loses.

Even knowing that it is impossible to impose criteria where everyone earns the same or that everyone can never be satisfied with 100% of their requirements, the margins of tolerance are broken, and no consensus is produced. In decision theory, this is called "zero-sum games." There is no progress, and everything stagnates. One of the most perverse effects of the problem has been the loss of opportunity for a significant contingent of available technical and professional workforce to be prevented from developing its full potential. Untapped talent persists, and the country sees, once again, postponed its possibilities of future growth and development.

Hopefully, we will have future opportunities to have researchers who develop an evaluation of the economic and social opportunity cost of not undertaking or indefinitely postponing large-scale projects such as those mentioned above, which, of course, must consider different evaluation perspectives. From our perspective, we rebel by becoming a country of lost opportunities and we rebel when there is no government arbitrator trained and determined to ensure the interests of all participants are respected.

In some cases, viable solutions have been found that harmonize the rights to business freedom with the rights of communities and workers to enforce the social, environmental, and labor responsibilities of the projects in question. It requires leaders capable and committed to finding effective, timely, and stable solutions. We need leaders who have the commitment, vocation, ability, and convening capacity like the one shown in his modest scope and actions by that Peruvian saint, San Martin de Porras, who managed to "gather dog, mouse, and cat, to eat from the same dish."

By way of reflection and bringing to light recent and past problems of the Peruvian reality, we agree with what renowned social researchers (Rosemary Thorp, Jorge Basadre, Julio Cotler, Aníbal Quijano, Augusto Salazar Bondi, and others) have concluded that **during its republican life, Peru has been a recurring example of frustrated leadership**. They maintain that, in the context of economic and social dynamics, the leadership of the dominant classes (political, business, military, religious, merchant, and other institutional leaders), given their limited autonomy and incompetence historically endorsed throughout contemporary life, have not been capable enough to promote and become a transforming force for social changes.

To calm outbursts of interpretation, we will say that the defense of supporting changes or promoting social development in a structurally neglected society does not necessarily imply being supporters of communist or socialist positions. Even the most recalcitrant right-wing or liberal positions are not openly opposed to these changes. To begin with, the need for such social changes responds to historical emergency services that date back to colonial times when communist, socialist, Marxist, etc. experiences or models or doctrines did not even exist or were known.

In those times (as well as in current times), the links between politics, economy, and society cannot be separated. The comprehensive vision of this reality reflected the predominance of dominant classes (mostly Spaniards and certain sons of their born in America) who formed a scheme of colonial domination in favor of their own interests that overexploited natural resources (mineral and agrarian) and native human resources. In this scheme, the majority Indigenous population, their family, and communal environment were subjugated and exposed (for almost three centuries) to a system of servile exploitation, in poor living conditions and relegated to a pitiful position of a marginalized social class with minimal or no possibilities of improvement.

The references described do not correspond to biased ideological positions (the lucidity of the broad-spectrum postulates: liberal, socialist, and libertarian ideas of the French Revolution and its authors were not yet flourishing in those times), but there are recorded written testimonies made by that scarce, but there is an existing character of some educated characters, among whom Felipe Huamán Poma de Ayala (1534-1615) stands out, a Peruvian chronicler (from Ayacucho, Peru), in whose works "Nueva Crónica" and "Buen Gobierno" and from a different perspective from the chronicles existing, recounts the experiences lived in his time where he exposes the abuses of the "encomiendas" (an institution made up of indigenous people subjected to servile or forced labor) used by the officials and relatives of the Spanish crown. In such works, he makes explicit his denunciation of the bad government represented by the viceroyalty and the contrasts of the colonial society of those years. (see https://www.biografiasyvidas.com/biografia/p/poma.ht)

In abundance of the above, we quote the article by colleague Carlos Lecaros Zavala (economist and philosopher): "Injustices, Claims and Repression" of January 12, 2023, which includes a historical episode starring José Baquíjano y Carrillo, precursor of our independence, following his welcome speech that he read when Viceroy Agustín de Jáuregui took charge of the viceroyalty of Peru (1780-1784). (see http://korazondeperro.com/elmundo/injusticias-reclamos-y-represion-la-espiral-de-la-violencia/).

The author of the note clarifies that, according to historians, even though the precursor was not in favor of an absolute break with the crown, he sued the viceroy with fine subtlety, demanding for him to have a better government compared to those who preceded him. Here is the reproduction of the quote from the precursor who, referring to the subjugated peoples, said:

> "For them, your excellence will not spread tears, displeasure, and disconsolation under his peaceful and gentle rule. His great soul contemplates that good itself ceases to be good if it is established and founded against the vote and opinion of the public, that each century has its chimeras and its illusions, disdained by posterity, dissipated by time, and that this brilliant light has convinced that improving man against his will has always been the deceitful pretext of tyranny; that the people are like springs; when they are forced more than its elasticity suffers, bursts, destroying the reckless hand that oppresses and holds it."

The author of the note points out in his article:

> "…the message is an invitation to the viceroy to act by listening to the population…what it expresses is a will for change along the path of the right of the governed…The message also invokes not to go against the will of the people with measures that only apparently favor them because they have always been deceptions of tyrannies. Finally, the culminating message is to alert you that any exercise of authoritarian power can cause the breakage of that popular spring that will destroy the reckless hand that oppresses it".

At the end of said colonial period, it was no coincidence that libertarian attempts arose in Peru from native leaders such as Tupac Amaru II (1780) and Mateo Pumacahua (1814). They and their partisan hosts sacrificed their lives and fought to achieve these social changes and indigenous demands, but they were drastically silenced. However, the sacrifice of their lives, their messages, and their examples were not in vain and served as an inspiration that lit the fuse of subsequent emancipatory movements in other Latin American countries.

When it was thought that with the consummation of Peruvian political independence (1821-1824), the conditions would be generated that would allow the qualitative leap of desired social changes to be consolidated, the great disappointment arises: Now we can no longer hold responsible to third parties and to colonial domination, the impossibility of transforming the established order, but rather blaming the ineptitude of the political class that took over the management of government. In the first five decades after independence, the nation was governed in a framework of blatant instability with the predominance of an alternating scheme of military and civil leadership. The only thing that remained stable was the scheme of social domination where only the foreign ruling class was replaced by the new and nascent local aristocracy composed of Spanish born in Peru sympathetic to emancipation, mestizos, military, merchants, landowners, supervisors, and others close to the circles of power. Since that time, the pejorative term "la indiada" (native and indigenous class) was coined to refer to that large, marginalized population sector.

As confirmation of this constant historical burden, the subjugation and marginalization of the large Indigenous majorities continued throughout the rest of republican life. Such majorities were once orphaned and without support from forces, media, and channels that vindicate their demands and claims. The priority interest of the dominant classes at that time was not to address the postponed demands of these dispossessed classes but rather to focus on how to find the ways, means, and mechanisms to access, enjoy, and maintain power. Applying the golden rule of "the end justifies the means," we better understand the succession of leaders, open and covert coups, political cannibalism, pacts, and other betrayals and vandalisms that partly explain the history of our kleptocratic political class. Once they came to power, with very few exceptions, the said political class continued to be faithful to its purposes of enrichment and other corruption derived from staying in power.

Two hundred years of political independence have continued in Peru, and the history described (with its understandable variants) seems to be repeating itself. It is depressing to admit it, but only the protagonists who interpret the same script change. In the international concert, Peru became linked with the new centers of world hegemony (England and the USA), where it plays the role of supplying raw materials to said economies. The ties of domination become more subtle when moving from the sphere of political dependence to the sphere of economic dependence. It cannot be denied that there have been periods of progress, boom, modernity, and an incipient development of economic and social scenarios, but the presence of economically concentrated elites with enormous political influence has also prevailed.

Currently, the challenge of counteracting large gaps of inequalities and social exclusion that confirm the hypothesis of social scientists remains latent. In the last quarter of 2022, the intention of opposition politicians was accentuated in achieving the presidential vacancy of Mr. Pedro Castillo, which finally came to fruition, more due to errors and clumsiness of the former president himself than due to the merits of the opposition. The citizen asks: what after that? Uncertainty and instability are rampant; the delayed claim continues to be ignored: Peru is not Lima!

The political crisis has, as we have seen, an endemic source and connotation. In the current situation, signs of an open polarization between positions and political parties with extreme positions have become more noticeable, revealing a clear situation of decadence, deterioration, and unbearable decomposition. To this panorama must be added a biased social fragmentation with gaps in political representation and authentic leadership and a presence of power elites more inclined to their own immediacy. With all this, we have the breeding ground that has been leading us towards a scenario of growing anarchy and chaos that is good for no one and harms everyone.

In that sense, we quote the isolated opinion of a Peruvian jurist, Mr. Fernando de Trazegnies (See newspaper El Comercio de Lima, May 21, 2018), whom no one who knows his career (university professor, professional consultant, and former chancellor) could call him leftist and would seem rather a refined representative of reactionary sectors. The column states that from his own first-hand experience, his disenchantment with Peruvian politics and politicians, pointing out the following:

> "There is no doubt that every politician is – or should be – an unforgettable character because of what he contributes to the development and well-being of

his country. Unfortunately, this is not always the case. I would even say that, in most cases, shortly after concluding their public activity, the image of politicians is lost because they have not provided an important contribution to national development. What is worse, their activity is often reduced to the production of unacceptable chaos. **The history of Peru shows us this political crisis**" (text highlight is ours).

The quote was written years ago (2018), and from what we currently experience, it seems like it was written yesterday. The current opportunity puts us in conditions (which are difficult to repeat) to assume and lead, with conviction and action, to the challenge of attempting a transformative change within consensual frameworks. Are we going to repeat the mistakes of history or learn the lessons that they have left us? To do so, you must have the courage and lucidity of that rare lineage of Peruvian leaders and intellectuals such as Jorge Basadre, Augusto Salazar Bondi, José Carlos Mariátegui, Víctor Andrés Belaunde, José Luis Bustamante y Ribero, Víctor Raúl Haya de la Torre, and others who, from their respective and even contradictory ideological spectrum, bequeathed their contributions of intellect (not necessarily coincident), from their own perspectives and of course with values of national transformation.

Beyond nuances and colors, the legacy of such leaders challenges us to be generators and promoters of our own changes and to shake ourselves off from conformism or the inaction of the indifferent. Will we be able, in these celebrations of this bicentennial of (Peruvian) Independence, to achieve a national agreement that allows us to treat and solve the problems of our multicultural society under a stable scheme and for a horizon of at least three government administrations? Will we have the courage, conviction, and capacity to undertake and lead changes under a consensual style and oriented towards what the various protagonists of our socioeconomic events need?

Until when will we continue in Peru from failure to failure and from postponements to postponements. We have been labeling failures for five centuries. From the well-known failure of the past colonial model continued by the controversial failure of the republican model, followed by the failed neoliberal model and the recent decades with failures of trials of conservative and pseudo-leftist options, both disguised as populist. Are we only left to continue complaining, lamenting what certain interested groups did or continue to do arbitrarily, colluded, and with impunity?

In these notes on political leadership, it is worth bringing to light the reflections made by Mr. César Pérez Vivas in his article "Political Fragmentation," published in the newspaper La Nación on July 20, 2021, which seems written to describe our current political situation. (mid-2023). The author points out:

> "Solid democracies have parties, unions, academies, clubs, churches, corporations. All of them constitute the social base that supports and guides the life of man in society. We are faced with entities or fictions called <u>parties that are nothing more than an entelechy, managed by a person who owns it, who attends the electoral fair with the aim of placing his franchise</u>".

> …We are living, without a doubt, in a diminished time for the institution called a political party. Multiple causes have contributed to this, and it is fair to say the first is within itself, when it changes from institutions with solid programs, with regulatory bodies respected and obeyed by all, to groups managed by an aspiring leader for life who demands democracy for the country, but denies it within his own political family…In the heart of a sick society with values disrupted by a set of cultural, economic, and spiritual elements, the climate for the development of reliable parties, authentic channels, and mediators between citizens and the state becomes more complex." (emphasis is ours)

Due to indifference, irresolution, ignorance, plotting conspiracy, alliances, or secret pacts or whatever, <u>we have not understood enough awareness that what happened at other times on the national political scene ends up affecting and compromising everyone and all the socio-economic scenario of the present and of course conditioning our future</u>. It seems that as protagonists of our reality (leaders and followers), we suffer from blindness or presbyopia for not grasping the bottom of the problem and deafness for not listening to postponed demands. If we have finally grasped and listened to it, it is even more regrettable for not having developed the need and commitment to change said fund.

We have not yet been able to put on the table valid options for authentic change where a serious debate, analysis, and discussion of reasoned intelligence is imposed instead of confrontations, where political sectarianism or rigidity of arguments, the denial of weighing positions different, or finally the imposition of violence (raised either by insurrectionary forces of the left, by reactionary forces of the right or by the unbreakable "manu militari" or Coup d' état). Are we only left to leave "freedom" to those courageous people who want to impose their changes under insurrectionary styles or by force of arms? What must happen to move us towards the true and desired changes?

It should also be noted that for some time now, part of our Armed Forces has not felt totally inclined to play the traditional role of gendarme nor to be protagonists of open or covert military coups that politicians and powers of yesteryear foisted on them. Given the disapproval earned by the current executive and legislative power and the latent political-party crisis, certain lucid sectors of such armed forces will not be willing to fall into undesirable excesses such as serving and favoring that questioned partisan democracy as guardians or executioners' policy that, as we have seen, does not have all its merits. The facts will show us whether their willingness to repress dispossessed majorities for longer at the cost of blood, fire, and regrettable loss of human life will predominate and assume the consequent costs of political trials that accrue from this.

It cannot be ruled out that part of this sector of the armed forces, with clear civic responsibility, may coincide with the popular cry: let them all go! and that they can agree that an orderly and agreed call for general elections (presidential and legislative) be conducted as a transitional measure.

We understand the demand: let them all go! It conditions us and subjects us to an immediacy (new elections, change of protagonists in the executive, legislative, and judicial powers) that, although it suggests changes demanded by the plebs, combats short-term effects but not causalities and can lead us to successive repetitions (such as the of changing presidents annually). Therefore, such prescriptions are insufficient to undertake broader processes. It is then worth asking that, given a visible and widespread panorama of crisis, <u>what and how do we do to direct ourselves toward a necessary and authentic process of leadership</u> and changes in the country?

There are some preconditions that should be considered and that we have already outlined previously: <u>Firstly</u>, whoever conducts the important role of national leadership must **assume an inclusive policy** that recognizes the spirit and intentionality of the historically postponed demands of the majority displaced by minorities who held and used power in their favor. It is worth clarifying that the defense of inclusiveness does not obey a charitable, alms-giving, or pious nuance but rather responds to a reading of a crisis that compromises the recognition of those postponed demands and puts aside segregationist criteria and policies.

When, instead of learning from our mistakes, they are repeated in cycles of continuity (as in our battered history), then what is required are fundamental changes of social transformation within the democratic framework and not simple adaptation or cosmetics. If we cannot learn from our own mistakes, at least we learn from the successes of others.

Secondly, and as a reinforcement of the above, those who lead the country must be convinced and aware that one of the distinctive features of these neglected majorities is their **multicultural mix due to differences in ethnic, geographical, religious, customs, and other** origins, which confirm or explain congenital population differences in our society. This demands government policies that, in addition to being inclusive, recognize such differences. The burden of backward educational levels of these sectors located outside the metropolis or center of Lima made them the object of marginalization, ignored (politically and socially disqualified) because they are pejoratively considered second-class citizens, manipulable and lacking criteria for what they need, and it suits them.

This conditioned political consciousness, both by Lima residents and even by provincial residents in Lima, would seem to be presenting certain curiosities. The messages from centralized news media and their political allies have always had a greater impact on these Lima strata (upper and middle), but they, in turn, have been showing a certain boredom with the same tired repertoire of poor arguments and very contradictory with the feeling of the majority whose result in the face of the suffocating ineptitude of members of state powers spreads in disbelief and distrust. For their part, the provincial mestizos and their ancestors have always felt, from a social perspective, authentic representatives and owners of Peru. The result of neglecting the needs of this multicultural society is a warning sign of that noisy social polarization that sociologists, anthropologists, and others have been warning us about, with greater notoriety than before.

Thirdly, whoever leads the process will have to rely on ideals and values that are sufficiently defined and agreed upon with respect to the diversity that is going to lead and whose behavior patterns (of leaders and those led) are desired to change. Here comes the great difficulty: because we start from the beginning with a polarized society like ours, with edges of endemic corruption, with habitual styles of government closer to the maintenance of privileged interests. So, the dose of this prescription of cultural renewal will take time and hard work to implement and will face resistance to change that could condition and make any change sterile.

A pragmatic objective could be proposed to aim toward sustainable governance management in successive government administrations through a leadership process made up of a collegiate and renewed body of leaders who make it feasible to accommodate this simultaneous requirement between **unity and diversity**. The challenge will be to enable a minimum of cohesion between Lima and the other provinces to achieve a national project of integrative unity that recognizes, respects, strengthens and commits an equitable participation of rights and opportunities of sectors of which we are part.

Fourthly, we have proposed the fulfillment of the previous difficult conditions under the uncertain or denied assumption of: "whoever leads the process," when in truth, we are discouraged to see that in our midst, there is no authentic leadership or visible leaders and probes. The crisis of leadership and leaders to which we referred to before is a typical characteristic of our shortcomings. Looking at the political scene we confirm (with honorable exceptions) that its main actors and parties are mere upstarts and agreed opportunists on the lookout for the benefits of power or with a criminal vocation. The right-wing parties (now call themselves liberal or libertarian) accumulated successive failures, and the left-wing parties (now calling themselves progressive) ended in notorious frustrations that ruined hopes for change.

It would seem like a dream that the conditions and changes described above would be undertaken in our environment. **We find ourselves on the verge of a dark panorama of a power vacuum** in which extreme positions on the right or left could become unnecessary, or perhaps, as has been the case in recent electoral experiences, we will be imprisoned with the advent of new outsiders reiterating messages of hope that people need to believe. Will citizens grant new opportunities to the same old parties, or will they give their trust to new parties and characters with renewed clothing but with the same attitude as always?

A renewed political class is required that at the same time promotes an economic dynamism that generates trust and is not contaminated by subordinate interests, a new political class that, with a defined propensity for justice, combats inequalities and postponed social frustrations. This requires new generations willing to commit to changes that, unfortunately, we do not have now, and they do not emerge now.

In this regard, it is important to note that Dr. Francisco Durand, in the same work cited above, "The Twelve Apostles..." op cit. p. 338-341, expresses his disappointment by stating that:

"The main GPE (economic power groups), their bosses, and the large business unions, as the main national elite, do not seem to give strategic direction to the country, which requires ideological development, national plans, and public presence... Although the Lima groups have greater cohesion, they have not shown greater capacity for collective leadership, nor have they expressed an interest in public service...

...power in society and the State is a space that cannot be empty. Someone must occupy it to direct it. If the strongest economic elite does not point out a path for everyone and does not even relate to each other, others will do so, and the country will be adrift... This is the problem of the management of Peruvian society that emanates from the type of elites that we have and their internal differences."

The emphasis in the quotes is ours, and the concepts expressed by someone who has studied in depth and objectivity the complicated issue of elite leadership and its links with power structures in Peru confronts us with the pitiful controversy that one thing is to develop as a dominant class in the economic sphere and quite another thing is to develop management capacity and leadership in the political-social sphere. This last challenge extends to those who claim to represent the country's working and middle classes.

Who assumes leadership in the country?

Given that currently, the representativeness of the partisanship in the sectors of the right, the left, and the center are, to say the least, unpresentable, detestable, unreliable, and in collusion with their low interests, the strict political-partisan scenario remains for now, it is tainted and toxic, and its prophylaxis will take a long time. For the demanding conditions and changes described in previous paragraphs to be met, one can think about resorting to the same social frame so that, without political intermediaries and through its own representative bodies, authentic leaders of the business class, the professional middle class, and of the working class.

Unfortunately, as Dr. Francisco Durand suggests, the elites called to take on the challenges of directing the country's destinies show a lack of long-term vision by focusing on short-term immediacy and a regrettable lack of collective direction, of conviction, willingness, and commitment to take on such challenges of transformative changes. Sarcastically, some of their representatives could argue, from their perspective, that it is not necessary to change what is going well. This blindness prevents them from seeing the snowball that will eventually attack themselves.

If they do not act on the matter, others will take it for them. When that happens, they will have already physically left the country because their capitals left a long time ago.

If we review our search for options in the majority classes, we find serious restrictions on channels of representation. Who claims its authentic representation? The current left-wing parties continue to be dispersed and discredited; they have also disappointed popular trust, and their possibilities of increasing their representation are very doubtful. On the other hand, it will be very difficult for the factual powers that be to allow the emergence in the working class of an authentic Peruvian leader (not because he cannot be found, but rather because they would end up silencing him), given that he would be proscribed as a terrorist.

In this process, the absence of an emerging, independent, and authentic middle-class sector that exhibits the same shortcomings has also been noted for decades: little conviction and transformative capacity. It is not surprising that when this middle class disappears or is diminished for various reasons (pauperization, indifference, sectarianism, lack of commitment and social awareness, corruption, collusion, or complicity), true independent options or political center and differentiated options of extreme right or left, also disappear. Its weakening leaves a void felt that makes its poor social representation latent due to the same process of polarization.

Additionally, we point out that this limitation of an absent political center has been strongly reinforced by obtuse positions from the extreme left or right that attack its weak presence because they consider that they diminish their political capital. In this way, by stifling the possibilities of a professional and intellectual middle class that could provide an expected stabilizing support and prone to governability, the way is left open for the exacerbation of more contradictions.

Aware of their potential technical contribution, the conventional political parties of the right or left compete to attract part of the membership of said middle class that has ended up relocating to such parties. However, the true political strategy of conventional parties is not at all to annihilate the political center but to use it as a figurehead in election periods to shadow or overshadow its true authenticity and dress in populist and centrist clothing to attract its preference. This is how, in recent years, Peruvian politics has presented most outsiders (fresh faces and parties) in a formal and lying political center lane.

The above does not mean to disqualify the existence of an authentic, conscious, and responsible middle class that can occupy a respectable position at the political center. As this option is dangerous for the interests of the traditional classes and parties, it is no coincidence that these traditional sectors tend to falsely regroup under the mask of self-proclaimed center-left and center-right options.

In summary, at the business, organizational, and governmental levels, it is useless to have the best strategic planning system if those responsible for management and leadership become overwhelmed by their context and circumstances and end up vitiating their management and performance due to recurring inabilities and ineptitude of improvised experiences (or improvisers) or end in scourges such as corruption (the most risk of our times) or finally due to indifference, deviations or complicity, they will allow the same interests and the same postponements of the past to take over.

2.2.5 Complementary aspects

To round out the required leadership profile, it is worth specifying some scopes. First, like many of the things discussed above, **leadership is also changing**. Previously, the figure of the individual, messianic, egocentric, virtuous, and even idolized leader, was decisive, injecting enthusiasm and adhesions to the front of his organization. The relationship between leader and followers became highly dependent, close, direct, and continuous. Both were needed, and to this day, we would say that features of this trend persist. The old medieval phrase of "to dead king, substitute king" has a certain basis in keeping alive and intact that customary bond between subjects and monarch that, of course, favored and accepted the continuity of the monarchical system.

Currently, the organizational complexity and its environment have proposed reinforcing concepts toward a **collective leadership** scheme (shared and distributed) where the presence of teams that accompany the leader is enhanced. Organizations tend to form a collegiate body of leaders at diverse levels that allow the sustainability of the innovations undertaken, that avoid vacuums or gaps in power, and that promote adequate renewal. The relationship between the leader and the followers is less close and direct due to the presence of the intermediate body of leaders.

This scheme is reinforced with the presence of an Organizational Culture composed of current, shared values (by leaders and those managed) that are sufficiently motivating for changes and improvements. **There is no leadership without a culture that supports it**. Even a crisis tends to provoke the emergence of a leader because the population will always look for a leader who, with honesty, courage, hope, and innovation (and other supporting values), drives and motivates them to face the challenging future in a shared way.

Secondly, **leadership currently faces** the challenge of functioning in a panorama where the **imbalance or contradiction between internal factors under control versus external factors with little or no control** is manifested or becomes more latent. The presence of factors, spheres, means, circumstances, and resources that are more autonomous suggests the development of capacities that are often absent. On the one hand, it requires analysis skills, intuition, recognition of substantial problems, and management of emergency situations, and on the other, tools such as the power of persuasion, influence, and negotiation skills at various levels and positions are crucial to resolving crises and conflicts.

In this scheme described, the leader may have a formal designation of authority (manager, president, director, etc.), but lacking the skills described (analysis, intuition, persuasion, negotiation, influence), it will be difficult for him to be recognized as an authentic leader. While on the contrary, he who, without having a formal designation of authority, effectively exercises these skills will, in practice, be an authentic leader. Given that, in the midst of such events and problems, these needs are continuous and repeated at different levels and circumstances, the true leader will not be enough to follow the proverb: "create fame and go to bed," but for the on the contrary since changes are permanent, leadership will be the result of permanent work and the leader will have to know how to earn his own leadership day by day.

Thirdly, **the key to successful leadership** would be, for example, getting it right or **influencing enough so that people who are not under control do what is expected**. What has been described leads us to consider, within the context of leadership, the issue of power. A broad definition of power refers to the ability to ensure that third parties are willing, act and motivated in accordance with guidelines and results desired by us and to prevent those results not desired by us. Although there are people capable of exercising power without becoming leaders, leaders are immersed in power relations.

Lukes[8] explores the combination of leadership, politics, and power and argues that power works in three modalities or dimensions: The first is the <u>ability to influence decisions</u>, that is, the

---

[8] Lukes (Quote by: R. Bolden, B. Hawkins: "Exploring Leadership" …op. cit. page 75

ability of "A" to ensure the obedience of "B." This dimension is widely used in diplomatic spaces but can, depending on the tactic used, lead to some form of visible conflict. The second dimension involves a leader's ability to establish established topics for discussion. This dimension, called "agenda determination," is important because it can prevent the occurrence of conflicts and because it reveals how, through agenda control, you can manage (introduce, eliminate, or direct) desired aspects in decision-making.

The third dimension is called social, institutional, or cultural dimension based on the proven fact that cultural values are assimilated, shaped, and remain internalized in the individuals and groups of our society to the point of being consensually accepted and reproduced without the slightest question. Accordingly, a respectable proportion of people tend to accept the "status quo" even though it does not fully represent their own interests. Therefore, the author suggests that groups with access, management, and control of power (minorities with economic or political power) can, through this cultural amalgam ("predominant or dominant culture"), influence and control groups that lack said power (also understood as dispossessed and little influential majorities and masses).

This social and cultural dimension does not have perpetual durability but can reach the limit where "the elasticity of the social contract" breaks. In this situation, a crisis of such magnitude is generated that it causes a rupture or vacuum of power and entails a restructuring of the current scheme and/or replacement of the power scheme with a new one. For this reason, we reaffirm what was previously stated that leadership is changing because the conditions or forces determining power are also changing.

That is why empires rise, but they do not last forever, and eventually, they fall. In this inexorable process, historical evolution usually brings us closer to situations like the one we are living in, where the predominant hegemonic power (for example, in the global context) does everything possible to maintain itself and where the aspirants to said power also do everything possible to replace the current power and consolidate their own. Unfortunately, in this dialectical panorama of confrontations, there are repeated cases where power, on the one hand, debases, corrupts, leads astray those who possess it, and, on the other hand, obsesses, overwhelms, and disturbs those who aspire to it. The warmongering that we currently experience is a clear manifestation of the confrontations described.

A careful analyst and researcher, Mr. Pedro Baños, in his book: "World Dominion - Elements of Power and Geopolitical Keys," Editorial Planeta S.A. First Edition 2018, pp. 13-15, refers to the fact that at the level of nations and their desire for power, certain key elements are appreciated that facilitate or explain the maintenance of a power scheme, namely:

"Military force (material means and number of combatants in activity or mobilizable, Economic Power (available financial resources and reserves), Diplomacy, Intelligence Services (Information), Availability of Natural Resources, Territory (extension, geographical location and orography), Population and Intangible Potentials (number, education, culture, history, willingness to work, effort, trust, loyalty, etc.), Knowledge and Technology, Strategic Communication (psychological wars, media manipulation, propaganda and population perception of transmitted images)."

The author of the cited work develops each exposed element in greater detail, and, with due restrictions, certain analogies could be transferred to identify in the context of business management certain ways to access and maintain power and leadership. However, the intention of this essay does not point in that direction at all. Furthermore, given that our preferential attention falls on the effective and efficient management of small and medium-sized businesses, their possibilities of accessing power schemes are scarce, and any exercise of diligence would only be preventive in nature and would serve to enable the entrepreneur of small and medium-sized businesses to identify, perceive, anticipate, and counteract the tentacles of predominant power coming from levels of government or larger companies. We will deal with this problem in more depth in section 4.2, External Conditioning.

The sequence of the above leads us to delve into and examine in some detail another thorny issue that constitutes the third pillar of enormous importance in this Effectiveness platform. As we stated before, there will be no leadership without a culture that supports it, therefore, we develop below the topic of Organizational Culture, whose content and characteristics we will examine immediately.

2.3 ORGANIZATIONAL CULTURE: Revaluation of Ethics in Management

2.3.1 Concept

The success or deterioration of any management also includes, in addition to the well-known quantitative aspects (income, sales, profits, costs, productivity, etc.), qualitative aspects such as prestige or discredit of the company or its managers, satisfaction or loss of consumer confidence, identification, commitment and mystique of the worker with the business objectives or, on the contrary, distrust and even covert sabotage of the worker with such objectives. Among external factors, we can mention the social projection of the company towards the community or disregard of said reality and indifference to the needs of its community environment, the impact and favorable feeling of the public and consumers towards the image, presence, business brand or apathy and reluctance to them, etc. These other aspects are, in many cases, more sensitive and crucial than the quantitative aspects in the operational and usual development of the company and are even more difficult to correct.

The achievement of effectiveness and its maintenance has to do with those intangible factors mentioned above and they mark the route towards what we call "management quality." Success or failure in these qualitative aspects is felt and perceived, but they are not always easily quantifiable and weightable by themselves but by their indirect effects in other fields.

Within this context of intangible aspects, we have to refer to the Organizational Culture, constituted as the predominant philosophy in the company, **structured based on a set of values and beliefs** that determine the "modus vivendi," the mystique, the behavior, the way of approaching problem-solving and the degree of effort and resulting commitment (at the individual and/or group level) of the members of any organization both within the organization and its external relationships. This "is perceived and felt" from the initial contact, from the first time we set foot in any company or organization.

As indicated in the Strategy section, regardless of whether the Culture and values are formally established, designed, and reflected in a document, in every company, organization, or institution exists, de facto or by default, a predominant organizational culture with its respective current values. On the other hand, the values acquired and assimilated in our individual training can contrast or be reinforced with those that predominate in the organization or in those that it promotes.

What is the scope contained in the word "value"? In this regard, what is highlighted by Salvador García and Shimon Dolan in their book: "Management by Values," McGraw-Hill/IESE. Espana, 1997, pp. 61-65, who distinguish three dimensions of the word "value," namely:

- The ethical-strategic dimension includes criteria or guiding concepts established for strategic learning processes (for the medium and long term); they are stable over time and are made up of deliberate choices regarding criteria for action in response to specific situations. (example: honesty, competent service, customer satisfaction, mystique, commitment, and loyalty, etc.). In contrast, there are anti-values or reprehensible concepts that typify opposite responses to the values described, and that complete the behavioral problems of people and their relationships (e.g., dishonesty, incompetent service, customer dissatisfaction, disloyalty, etc.)

- The psychological dimension includes qualities that describe the predisposition in people who are sufficiently motivated to resolutely undertake challenges and large undertakings and face without fear the dangers involved in their decisions. Among such qualities, we have courage, bravery, and open confrontation with critical or problematic situations. Also, for better understanding and by contrast, we have opposite concepts: the fears and prejudices that typify unresolved, ambiguous, and pusillanimous personalities whose effects on any attitude, management, or decision process are crucial.

- The economic dimension is related to the utilitarian nature of the significance or importance of something or someone (objects, products, ideas, projects, processes, technology, knowledge, people, etc.). Value in its economic dimension is related to its intrinsic character, its scarcity, the interest it arouses, the price it commands, its appreciated quality, its relative circumstantial or strategic merit, whose final impact is to "add greater value" to the product or to the usufruct by the owner who owns it.

In this section, we will refer to the concept or category of the term "value," referring to the first two dimensions stated. Regarding the economic dimension, it will be discussed more fully in the fourth chapter of this essay.

The management of a company will not simply be conducted within a framework of effectiveness and technical efficiency but must also contemplate forms, channels, or means that allow and facilitate the people who make up be it realized yourself professionally and personally. In the disciplines that study human behavior (psychology), the person develops and enhances his capacity when he truly believes and trusts in what he does and in what those who accompany him

110

in his work do, that is, when there is **reciprocal reliability**. This reinforces both business objectives and the personal fulfillment of those who work.

Human behavior, individual and group, is complex in nature and difficult to predict and manage. People are normally prey to their own preconceptions, prejudices, feelings (sympathies, antipathies), interests, phobias, and particular fears. The psychological environment that results from personal interrelationships is initiated, developed, and nourished with reciprocal effects between, on the one hand, positive values such as trust, creativity, honesty, esprit de corps, etc., and on the other hand, anti-values, defects or personality deviations such as greed, selfishness, fraudulent behavior, fears, rootlessness, etc. also present in the members of an organization.

In certain circumstances, the effect of these interrelationships has been as important or more important than the achievement of quantitative goals and objectives in the company (e.g., increases in productivity, reduction of average costs, satisfactory rate of profitability, etc.) because the correlation of forces of the relationships described between people has determined a succession of concatenated effects either towards strengthening their growth and development or there are also cases towards the deterioration of the company or organization.

We must clarify that the values of a person, institution, company, community, and entire nation will not be sufficiently assimilated with the simple invocation, exposition, or motivational talk of ideas and concepts. This is convenient but never sufficient. Leaders of companies, organizations, groups, communities, and authorities in general must keep in mind that it is more relevant when **values are preached by example and coherence between what is said and what is done**.

In this sense, if instead of instilling values through good example, the opposite happens, that is, if the leaders of private or public organizations are open or disguised examples of dishonesty, abuse, corruption, manipulations, compromises, and subterfuges of purposes covert or criminal, etc., then one of the pillars that support any interrelation is broken, **the loss of trust**, and it takes a lot of time and hard work to reestablish it. For a Nobel Prize in Economics (1972) like Joseph Arrow, "mutual trust is a critical lubricant for the functioning of social systems.

2.3.2 Deterioration in the existing Organizational Culture

In the same way that we reviewed what we call a crisis of leaders and leadership, this time, we are going to refer to the problem of deterioration in organizational culture. We had said in the initial part of this essay that we were going to refer to other realities such as the American one

111

where "beans are also cooked" (that is, any place is not exempt from experiencing irregularities). In the last three decades, there has been a notable increase in events related to business ethics in the United States that led to notorious scandals and loss of confidence in the American business landscape.

As noted by O. C. Ferrell, John Fraedrich, and Linda Ferrell in: "Business Ethics: Ethical Decisions Making and Cases," Houghton Mifflin Co, New York, Sixth Edition, 2005 page. 4:

> "...the debate surrounding the behavior of a number of well-known companies that border on legal issues and ethical gaps, among which Enron, World Com, Arthur Andersen LLP, and Tyco, among others, have highlighted the need to integrate ethics and corporate responsibility in all business decisions..."

According to studies reported by the authors, 57% of the public believe that the values and standards of business leaders and executives have declined, and in another study, two-thirds of respondents believe that recent scandals have created a crisis of trust and reliability in the form how business is done in America.

Business ethics begs the question: To what extent are specific business practices acceptable or not? As an example, the last crisis in the American stock market and financial system had to do, in addition to certain recessionary winds in the global economy, with the deserved distrust that was generated among economic agents inside and outside the USA. Previously solid companies collapsed (Leman Brothers), others had to be absorbed in mergers, other companies were involved in forced bailout programs (Aetna, Fannie Mae, Merry Linch, etc.), others suffered shameful financial scandals where the falsification of information such as the cases of Enron, Arthur Andersen and in others, multimillion-dollar scams (65 billion dollars) were uncovered, such as those of Mr. Bernard Madof, a conspicuous representative and member of the high sphere and former leader of the New York stock market.

In abundance, there were complaints about manipulation in the use and abuse of risky mortgages (subprime or Underwater mortgages) and of representative securities on them ("toxic" papers) that major investment banks such as Goldman Sachs, Morgan Stanley, Citigroup, and other banks have had to respond in separate investigations before the American Senate. How was the mortgage bubble created, which had the American economy in recess for almost 7 years?

When the flagrant irresponsibility of the private-financial sector itself became latent, a government intervention with regulatory policies was provoked. The supervisory entity of the securities market in the USA (Security Exchange Commission, SEC) established procedures to correct deficiencies in the capital market and to investigate suspicions of fraud by Investment Banks that participate within it. However, just as in times of pro-liberalism, trends that seek to correct excesses and advocate for a greater degree of regulation and control emerge through reactions; in times of government interventionism, zealous defenders of the free market make their appearance, "lobbyists" appear to shield those responsible and build a scaffolding that seeks to dispel attempts at regulation and control.

The financial industry alludes to rising costs and reducing returns, forcing pressure for the freezing or disappearance of regulatory reforms that have given rise to what has been called banking shadowing (a kind of very well-calibrated lobbying shield) that in one of the recent issues of Time magazine (September 23, 2013) were cited by academic Rob Johnson, Director of the Institute of New Economic Thinking, as responsible for spreading greater risk and volatility in the financial system.

In this situation of banking expansion and globalization, academics such as James Galbraith, a professor at the University of Texas and expert in financial crises (cited in the same source), have put their finger on the sore point, pointing out that the conventional banking business model by which was created, that is, providing loans to the real sector of the economy, has become relatively the least attractive model. Speculative and profitable deviations in other fields that we have mentioned before have had to do with this. It is no coincidence that, in the current situation, the pendulum of history returns us with strong winds and impulses (which found an echo in the administration of Donald Trump) towards deregulation.

We must note that, at least in the American community, the uncovering of the scandals described are known and were initially tried and punished. We say initially because according to what was published in The Economist magazine (Volume 412 No. 8902, Aug 30-Set 05, 2014. Pages 9 and 21-24), the central article makes a critical analysis of the issue of the increase in criminalization in American business. For example, and just to refer to the financial sector, the consequences of the mortgage bubble began to develop.

To show this button, according to said magazine, in 2014 alone, a select group of financial companies: Bank of America, JP Morgan Chase, Citigroup, Goldman Sachs, and other banks, have disbursed to the authorities no less than the incredible sum close to 50,000 million dollars (an amount like the total of Peruvian exports in 2012). This amount **was made to arrange agreements to avoid going to trial** and/or paying large fines for alleged deceptions in mortgage-backed bond investments (that is, to fix part of the problems derived from the negotiation of the famous toxic bonds, bonds based on risky mortgages).

As stated in the cited article, why do these large companies make such payments if they know they are innocent? Although it may seem strange, they prefer to follow the well-known rule that lawyers foist on us: "a bad agreement is better than a good trial." Indeed, pursuing a long and cumbersome trial with criminal charges is something like being left at the expense of losing your operating license and receiving a subsequent death certificate for the business. However, it appears that under such agreements, "everyone wins," the way in which such agreements are developed and concluded is very deceptive. They are normally covered by a veil of jealous discretion between regulators, prosecutors, and lawyers of disputing parties (or, to put it openly, negotiating parties). The entire process takes place in secret, and transparency is avoided until the final agreement is only made known to the media in very brief terms so that many questions about it remain in doubt.

We say that everyone wins because, <u>first</u>, only large companies that can make such payments have access to such agreements. The scheme is exclusive, and the postulate that "justice is equal for everyone" should be added, "for all those who can pay." <u>Secondly</u>, this peculiar way of administering justice confers absolute powers on prosecutors and regulators since this prevents (despite signs of fraud) the scandal from being aired in an open and public trial because such officials have the power to "non prosecution" (do not go to trial).

By leaving the judges on the sidelines, a matter that far exceeds the boundaries of business and is a matter of public interest is managed with subterfuge. <u>Thirdly</u>, both defenders and opponents of the capitalist system have as a common point and agree that this "modus operandi" of the American judicial apparatus does a disservice to the credibility of the system because it institutionalizes and allows "shielding" and shameful deviations regarding clear facts regarding corruption.

The problem of selling bonds with risky mortgage backing also dragged down important European banks. According to a journalistic article in "The Wall Street Journal" (March 30, 2018), Barclays PLC (a British bank) agreed to pay the US Department of Justice the sum of 2,000 million dollars to settle a pending lawsuit. In 2016, Deutsche Bank disbursed just under $7 billion, and Credit Suisse paid the sum of $5 billion. These banks made such disbursements by declining to continue litigation over similar charges.

Regarding the American financial crisis, someone has pointed out:

"It has not been a random event. It hasn't been due to business cycles. The crisis had a real cause, and that cause was fundamental and structural. Our government, our financial market, our largest financial institutions, and our largest corporations entered corrupt businesses to scam consumers and taxpayers. The entire mortgage financing business, and much of Wall Street itself, was corrupt, and through donation campaigns and lobbying, they were able to corrupt our government."

We note that the person who holds the ideas in the previous paragraph is not a rabid communist, nor a socially resentful person, nor an anti-system (capitalist), but rather someone we would classify as an "insider," a former investment banker at the famous Goldman Sachs, is Mr. John Talbott, who, among his published books on economics and politics, knows first-hand "the ins and outs" of the operation of the American financial system. The quote corresponds to his book: "The 86 Biggest Lies on Wall Street." Seven Stories Press, First Edition, New York, 2009, p. 1.

His appreciation beyond sympathies or antipathies has a basis for objectivity because, as we explained before, the opinions of Times magazine and The Economist regarding the same topic have points of agreement, and as our grandparents said: "when the river sounds, it is because they bring stones." Although there will be no shortage of those who discredit his points of view, arguing that the only thing that such assessments achieve is to play into the hands of left-wing positions (anti-system) or also to obstruct practical solutions for financial rescue where "the goal (in this case, preventing the weakening of the financial system) justifies the means." Finally, it is also argued that such critical appraisals only hinder alternatives that allow defects and irregularities to be covered with the veil of the "lesser evil."

On the other hand, we can ask ourselves what the undesirable consequences would have been if we had allowed ourselves to be influenced by those sectarians or ultra-conservatives who, in close defense of the classic liberal script of "let it be done or let it go," would have allowed a foreseeable financial and economic crack (breakdown) and after that, wait for the "invisible hand" of classical liberal theory to rebuild or restart the recovery of the system with one's own private effort. Faced with this, it was considered that there was no need to be too attached to the liberal catechism; it was enough to admit with a certain blush and embarrassment the anomalies and flagrances of the private-financial sector and appeal in this case to "the visible hand of the government" to request emergent aid through the so-called rescue packages (billions of dollars of financial leverage) that were finally granted to the big banks to overcome the crisis.

In this case, the banks and the defenders of the liberal catechism only accept "intervention and certain government regulation" as an exception. The principle prevailed that "the goal of avoiding at all costs the economic collapse of the financial system justifies the means" of temporarily allowing certain state interventionism. History will tell us if Presidents George Bush (Jr.) and Barack Obama chose with "good intentions" to safeguard the system or if they simply gave in to extorting and taking advantage of critical circumstances by large financial groups. It is striking that after having received government aid, these financial groups kept more distance from regulatory intervention and began to sing the praises of deregulatory liberalism.

In most developing countries, the outlook is darker; many of the scandals are covered with "smoke screens," the crimes are unknown, and when they are known, the majority go unpunished due to the latent corruption in the political systems themselves and judicial. In Peru, towards the end of 2017, a payment made by the Brazilian firm ODEBRETCH to a consulting company linked to the former president of Peru, Mr. Pedro Pablo Kuczynski, was revealed when he was a minister in the government of former president Toledo (also required by justice for having received million-dollar bribes from the same company).

Given that the president had previously repeatedly denied having had any relationship with the ODEBRETCH company, given the evidence presented, the former president was forced to go to parliament to face an accusation of declaring a vacancy due to permanent immorality, from which he escaped by a tight sentence voting margin. Versions circulated that there were negotiations "under the table" where it was exchanged in a "quid pro quo" style, saving Kuczynski from the presidential vacancy in exchange for a pardon in favor of former president Alberto Fujimori, which was finally granted in record time. However, months later, the pardon was annulled by court order.

Such events engulfed the country in a climate of instability and mistrust from, which it has been difficult to get out of in the short term. In this context, the disclosure on March 21, 2018, of some videos where efforts by some parliamentarians to save President Kuczynski from a second request for a vacancy in Congress were revealed led to him presenting his resignation from the position of president who, without pain or glory, remained only 18 months, being the first president forced to resign due to the scandals derived from the ODEBRETCH company. The network of economic and political links of said company (and others of a similar nature) with local companies and authorities confirms the conviction of the population surveyed that considers a good part of local companies more accomplices than victims of corruption.

116

However, it must be noted that in the case of smaller companies (medium and small), corruption, although less burdensome than in the case of large businesses, is also part of an overwhelming system in which, for example, to culminate any regular procedure, established bribes must be disbursed. All this only confirms that corruption is a two-way street between the public and private sectors.

But even before that, the list of scandals is long and suggestive: "Telephone Sucking (the clandestine telephone tapping scheme for purposes of political and economic advantage has turned the daring to border on what is prohibited into a national sport, and we continue to have scandals at the same "Watergate" style but with the particularity that impunity prevails). Another scandalous issue was that of the "Narco pardons" (condescending presidential grace of former president Alan García, who released from prison a group of people convicted of drug trafficking, several of whom, once released, returned to repeat their crime). The recent revelations of authorizations, regularizations, and fraudulent negotiations of real estate and land by private mafias and government officials colluding with them have also been scandalous.

This only reflects the scourge of our society and once again ratifies the perception that there is no point in achieving economic progress if institutional delays and corruption persist (both in the State Powers and in private institutions). We should not be surprised that growth is paralyzed, and investments are discouraged because this scourge plays the role of an anchor that hinders the continuity of any economic achievement. The detachment from values and the proclivity to break the rules feed the predisposition to commit crimes and exceed the limits established by laws, and the crimes of robberies, kidnappings, assaults, femicides, and other corruption have become the "bread of the day" and take over even 90% of the news scoops from the Peruvian television press.

In this context, the growing problem of citizen security has become a generalized crisis and a forced electoral platform for candidates at all levels of government. It must be kept in mind that this citizen security problem manifests itself as the growing risk that ordinary citizens face of suffering aggression, assault, robbery, kidnapping, and even the possibility of being a victim of murder by juvenile or professional hitmen (whether by adjustment accounts, by extortion or even by simple mistake). All of this, in unforeseeable circumstances, whether walking or driving on public roads, conducting daily activities in a commercial, work or banking establishment, or while relaxing at your own home.

This security problem has equal and greater implications than those of terrorism in the eighties and is one of the current critical manifestations of major causes. Attacking problems by focusing on the effects is necessary, but insufficient actions. Addressing the problem only with greater police and judicial rigidity addresses emergencies, but they are palliative and temporary relief. Unfortunately, such actions remain superficial to the problem. To put it in terms of our approach, the late reaction and inefficiency of police activity or the central government is criticizable due to the insufficiency of a criminal intelligence strategy and the absence of a Plan to counteract it. Here arise the immediate economic and judicial restrictions that the police spheres demand, which are a wake-up call for the problem to be addressed from broader perspectives.

Even when criminals are arrested, some of them, using tricks, penetrate the corrupt spheres of the judicial system to emerge free of all guilt. <u>The problem described has a structural nature; it is deeper and corresponds to the degree of criminalization present in our society and in our culture, which vitiates and debases the behavior of people, institutions, and powers</u>. By "structural," we want to highlight that this crisis has an internal basis, is persistent, is not occasional, and worsens over time. As we argued before, it is a type of endemic hypertrophy present in our social system whose solution is more complex and requires more work and time. The analysis, research, and contribution of solutions provided by professionals from various disciplines, such as sociology, psychology, education, law, economics, and others, will be important in this issue.

What is referred to in Peru in relation to problems of power structures invites us to develop an important parenthesis to analyze in some detail a panorama with special peculiarities that occur in the American reality. Indeed, democratic praxis (government of the people, by the people, and for the people) acquires different manifestations in also different realities (presidential, federative, monarchical democracies, etc.). **In the United States**, during this century, two "sui generis" (very particular) results are observed in its electoral processes. In 2000, candidate Al Gore defeated the opposition candidate George W. Bush in the popular vote by a narrow margin of 0.5%, but the latter became President, and later in 2016, Hillary Clinton also won (48.18% of the total), with a margin close to three million votes (2.1% additional), to his opponent Donald Trump (46.09% of the total) who finally ended up being sworn in as president.

Those of us profane to this democratic scheme asked ourselves: How is this kind of electoral magic that makes it possible to "win by losing" woven, and why has it manifested itself in recent times more frequently than before? How and on what basis is a break in the majority permitted? The answer responds in part to a scheme designed by the founders of the American country who were concerned about the vices of a dangerous concentration of political power, and to avoid it, they considered representativeness distributed not only on a population basis but also

118

geographically (especially in consideration of small towns far from cities). For this purpose, the so-called **Electoral College was established as an indirect election system.**

The last determination and distribution of the College was made on December 15, 2018 (Ver https://es.wikipedia.org/wiki/Colegio_Electoral_de_los_Estados_Unidos). Currently, this College forms a total of 538 members, which corresponds to the total number of members of Congress (100 Senators, 435 Representatives and 3 from the District of Columbia). Based on this, the candidate who manages to obtain the key figure of 270 (minimum majority over the 538 delegates or voting members) is assured of the presidential election.

Each State has a certain number of electors equivalent to the number of Senators (always set at two for each State) to which are added their respective members of the House of Representatives, which is determined based on population and political criteria. (for example, Texas has a total of 38 Electors, Pennsylvania 20, Virginia 13, etc.). The number and variability of such members in different States is agreed upon and consented to by both parties before the elections.

The Constitution determines that each State is responsible for the way in which it chooses its respective Elector Members. In general elections, citizens, despite marking the presidential candidate of their choice on the ballot, may have the sensation of voting to elect their presidential candidate, but in practice, they are voting to elect the members of the College. The candidate who obtains the most votes from a particular State ends up winning all the votes committed to the Elector members of the respective State (also called electoral delegates).

With this, a "sweep of the voting members of the losing party is institutionalized as if the victory on the part of the winners had been 100% of the votes. Although electoral delegates are free to choose any presidential candidate, in practice, they end up doing so in favor of the candidate of their political party. The race then consists of adding as many voting members as possible until reaching the key figure of 270 members of the College to guarantee electoral victory.

In the 2016 elections, Hillary Clinton won the elections in 20 states (plus the District of Columbia), which earned her a total of 227 votes from voting members. For his part, Donald Trump won the elections in 30 states that, brought him a tally of 304 votes from electoral delegates, thus exceeding the minimum threshold of 270 votes required for victory. Although these results explain and clarify this democratic scheme of indirect voting through the Electoral College system, they leave us with certain doubts and deserve (as foreign observers) following reflections and

- First of all, it must be recognized that the rules of the game are known by all participants in the electoral contest and are also predetermined before the elections so that "there is nothing dark under the sun" nor any irregularity that must be reproached by any participating party or candidate.

The founders of independence established the rules of indirect voting through the Electoral College since 1787 and present a respectable tradition of 236 years. During the twentieth century, the validity of this system meant an acceptable alternation in power by both parties, and it never drew attention that the winning candidate in the presidential elections, computed according to the accumulated total of popular votes, ended up being the normal winner to become head of government. However, in the recently noted cases of candidates Al Gore and Hillary Clinton, there was no such correspondence. How did this tuition system determine the balance toward who won?

- In the category of Senators, the figure is quite clear, given that it is established that each State (regardless of its population density, its territorial extension, or its geographical location) will be represented by two senators, then the race to obtain a majority in the Senate chamber (for a total of one hundred seats) consists of winning the vote in the greatest number of States. This strategy has been skillfully managed by the Republican Party in the 2012 and 2014 elections (midterm elections) and by candidate Trump in the 2016 elections, where they carried out important political proselytizing work in States with a significant presence of rural areas of lower population, while the Democratic Party did so with a notable bias in the urban areas with the largest population but which in the end included a smaller number of States. In this way, while the Republican Party accumulated a total of 46% of senatorial votes in 2016, it achieved 51 of the 100 available seats because they were distributed in a greater number of states.

He ensured key control of the upper house of Congress, which is difficult because senators are elected for six years divided into three-thirds, so only enter the electoral competition a third of these (33 senatorial seats are put to the vote) every two years (one-third in presidential elections and another third in midterm elections). By partially renewing the Senate, the aim is to prevent the entire legislative body from ever entering the electoral race. This partial renewal strategy could be adapted in the Peruvian environment where, for years, we have been experiencing vices of execrable parliamentarism and ungovernability.

- The House of Representatives is made up of 435 members elected in proportional representation to the voters of each state and previously agreed upon political considerations. Representatives are elected for a fixed period of two years and can be **re-elected. Representatives compete** every two years for the complete renewal of the lower house. That is, in the American midterm elections (two years after the presidential elections), the entire number of the House of Representatives is renewed with the option of re-election.

In the last election in 2016, the same strategy described above of the Republican Party of trying to win in the greatest number of States (although with tight margins) meant that in this House of Representatives, it accumulated 241 seats, which represented 55.4% of the total. In the end, the Republican party achieved 304 voting members (adding both chambers), surpassing the 277 voting members gained by the Democratic party, and were the ones who, due to the powers delegated by the constitution, tilted the presidential election in favor of its candidate Donald Trump. Unobjectionable triumph is finally recognized by his opponents. According to the Constitution, the approval of any law must pass the approval of both chambers. Hence the importance of having achieved a congressional majority.

As mentioned before, Trump won the elections in 30 States (50% additional to the number of his opponents), marking a difference that is difficult to overcome. The Democratic Party maintained its victory in its main strongholds (California, New York, Illinois, and New Jersey) and lost in States with a significant presence of undecided voters, also called "**swing states**" because they usually elect one candidate in different elections or another party (such as Florida, Ohio, Arizona, and North Carolina).

Finally, the Democratic Party's priority attention to densely populated states and swing states caused inattention and unfavorable results in smaller states. While the Republican Party also maintained its strongholds in States with significant populations (Texas, Pennsylvania, Oklahoma, and Kentucky), it won in certain swing States and ensured its victory in the numerous States of "minor" population importance but of great collective importance (Kansas, Louisiana, Indiana, Missouri, Tennessee, etc.).

- Secondly, we must draw attention to an irreversible fact derived from different environments and circumstances that typified the social reality that the founders of independence had to live with respect to that experienced by citizens in the current reality. Between both milestones, an important evolution has been experienced in the socioeconomic and political configuration.

121

In the beginning, the analysis, evaluation, and projection of that social reality made by the founders of the country led them to design a democratic system that established the electoral college as the most plausible entity to distribute power and avoid its concentration. More than two centuries ago, America went from having formed an agricultural society of little relevance in the international arena to a current industrial power of significant relevance and global impact. On the social level, this meant a gradual displacement and concentration from the disintegrated rural areas towards the big cities. For example, in the article "Representing Americas. The minority-majority" from The Economist Magazine, Jul 14th-20th, 2023, p. 23, the information is recorded that in 1950, 36% of the population lived in rural areas, in 1990, 25% did so and in 2016 this participation decreased to 19%.

But this trend not only reflects quantitative change but also a different qualitative panorama. The citizens of the rural area and the citizens of the urban area have roots, desires, beliefs, expectations, and a different worldview. In rural areas, we find the typical "red neck" peasant with strong and traditional political and religious convictions. In these areas there are also respectable families and entrepreneurial groups with a higher degree of technical qualifications who develop their agricultural activity with modern technology, supplying large cities and even with export projection.

Urban areas have grown at faster rates because their industrial advances have provided them with greater and better employment opportunities (migrations from the countryside to the city) and because they have brought together a population mix with a tendency and reinforcement of immigrant majorities. Industrial growth and that of cities fed each other and, in turn, led to parallel growth in the provision of diverse services (commerce, finance, hotels, etc.) with greater relevance and presence than that existing in rural areas.

The diversity of the working class of urban conglomerates (of different immigrant origins such as white Europeans, African Americans, Hispanics, Asians, etc.), with varied aspirations for rights (gender, freedom of religion, sexual choice, protection of children and the elderly, anti-war, anti-racism and anti-segregation, and others), has found in the cities the most favorable medium to demonstrate and have their points of view respected.

- In the political sphere there is a conformation of State representation that went from the thirteen original States to the fifty States of today. At first glance and without considering the applicability of electoral registration, this is a growth that materializes a greater distribution and dispersion of power. It is not strange that, throughout history, several such

States justified their existence by obtaining legitimate democratic representation and by biased partisan intentions.

In America, political jargon enshrined Macchiavello's principle "divide and rule" by coining the term **"Gerrymandering"** <u>as a partisan tactic that seeks to redesign limits and borders in electoral districts with the purpose of maximizing partisan advantage or influence in electoral results</u>. Through "Gerrymandering" manipulation, a relative representation is converted into a victory of absolute representation by diluting the relative weight of the opposition votes and converting the relative weight of one's own votes into a one hundred percent majority.

Over time, the term became generalized to refer to situations with a negative connotation. Under this tactic, the power of opposition votes can be concentrated or encapsulated in districts with less relative weight compared to other districts or to the national conglomerate (between States). The manipulation described can also be directed to highlight or minimize the presence of some ethnic, religious, or racial group in national representation. Finally, the accumulation of the tactics described has led to the Gerrymandering result, where a minority with popular votes can become a majority in Electoral College votes. The small states that typify rural areas became minor bastions of the Republican Party whose strategy has been to obtain sufficient political clientele in the greatest number of them. All this, without detriment to maintaining its traditional bastions in large states and in important cities.

The Republican Party, to put it in our terms, was more **effective** for its correct directionality within the framework of the established rules. However, it should also be noted that the effectiveness that led him to an electoral victory ended up relatively blurred by <u>doubts of unethical behavior</u> in indications of having made use in his favor of certain cyber interference by Russia in the past electoral process and certain legal irregularities that we explain in detail later.

For its part, the Democratic Party, motivated by population bias, has become the party of the big cities, where it has had to work very carefully to attract a diverse clientele so that various groups with varied interests do not rub or clash among themselves (immigrants vs. residents, whites vs. Hispanics, permanent vs. temporary workers, Catholics vs. evangelicals, etc.) raising "flags" that are not necessarily related or coincident (gender claims, sexual harassment, discrimination based on criteria of age, sex, race, dissimilar positions regarding controversial issues such as abortion, permissiveness regarding homosexuality, etc.).

All of which meant a harvest of sympathizers but also adversaries. In this context, the Democratic strategy (referring to the terminology of our essay) was not effective enough to gain enough support in that polychrome stream of urban conglomerates, nor was it convincing enough to tip the balance in its favor in the swing states and came up against an insurmountable barrier in small states.

In all honesty, we must point out that the Gerrymandering tactics described above cannot be entirely attributed to the responsibility of the Republican Party because they are part of the inheritance of the democratic game of the current system that both parties have ultimately developed, consented to and with whom they have lived alternately electoral processes. With this, we do not even want to justify its continuity but simply to point out (as we pointed out before as foreign observers) the bipartisan co-responsibility regarding it. Curiously, the origin of the term Gerrymandering is in honor of Elbridge Gerry (1744-1818), Governor of Massachusetts who in 1812 promoted a redistribution of electoral districts to favor his "Democratic-Republican" party (together at that time!) against the Federalist party of the same era.

The midterm elections (in November 2018) have meant a certain modification of the political map. The pre-electoral environment had as unfavorable factors President Trump and his continuous blunders: embarking on a trade war against China and its European allies, contradictory position in front of his Security Cabinet regarding the Russian intervention in the last elections, separation of parents and children minors with illegal immigrant status (after the wave of internal and external protests he was forced to retract), suppression of temporary residence status, rejection of environmental protection agreements, discrepancies within NATO, sudden removal of senior officials government officials, decreased spending on social services, etc.

As favorable aspects, President Trump was able to show a revitalization of the economy with satisfactory levels of growth, a decrease in unemployment rates, an absence of inflationary pressures, and monetary stability. The fact of having obtained victories in the last presidential elections in 10 more states (50% additional) than his opponent gave him a significant advantage that was difficult to overcome in the short term.

However, it was to be expected that the avalanche of internal and external criticism of his management and his person, together with the rethinking of the Democratic Party's strategy, would mean a decrease in his supporters, especially in the swing states and in the female vote. Indeed, in the House of Representatives of the total of 435 seats, the Democrats obtained a majority in such midterm elections with 235 seats, and the Republicans reached 200 seats.

In the Senate, since it is only renewed by thirds of the 33 seats in electoral consultation, the Democrats obtained 24 seats, while the Republicans managed to obtain 14 seats. However, the

Republican majority weight in the remaining two-thirds (outside the electoral dispute) allowed them to retain their tight majority by monopolizing 52 seats of the total of 100 existing.

The prevalence of an indirect voting system that biases and privileges electoral victory based on victories in the number of States, together with the dispute to maintain preferences in large States, have been counterbalancing factors so that the new electoral map reflects a more balanced correlation of existing political forces. Indeed, it was more difficult for President Trump to overcome the difficulties of a closed opposition, and in the last general elections of November 2020, candidate Joe Biden obtained favorable results in the general elections and greater margin in the House of Representatives by a narrow margin, but the results of the Senate vote were not strong enough to achieve a majority in said chamber.

- Thirdly, what is happening in relation to the **Supreme Court of Justice** deserves special attention. In the USA, this court is made up of nine members (a president and eight associate judges). Belongs to the president of the nation to appoint the supreme judges, who are normally chosen by the affinity of political-judicial ideals and must be confirmed by the Senate. Such judges serve for life and can only be removed by Congress or can also resign from their position of their own free will.

Currently, Republican presidents have appointed 5 judges, and Democratic presidents have appointed 4 of them. Each judge is supposed to make their decisions within the framework of impartiality and autonomy. In a strict sense, they act with independent criteria without this implying being linked or committed to the expectations of the president who appointed them or that of his political party. The decisions of the Supreme Court constitute precedent that obliges other courts to respect them, its rulings have the capacity to repeal laws that oppose them and are also unappealable. Finally, the Court has the power to declare unconstitutional any law established by the Legislative Branch, as well as any act coming from the Executive Branch.

One of the critical analysts of the current political situation, the former Nobel Prize winner in economics, Mr. Joseph Stiglitz (see article "American Democracy on the Brink" dated Jun 29, 2018, https://www.project-syndicate.org/onpoint/american-democracy-on-the-brink-by-joseph-e--stiglitz-2018-06), a well-known tendency of anti-conservative thought sharpens his aim against the Supreme Court, which he recently accuses of having established a series of rulings that favor companies against workers as well as extreme right-wing positions against most Americans. According to this critic, the Supreme Court has followed Donald Trump in his trend of disregard for the rights of women and the family, of racist phobia and prejudice, biased protectionism, and deepening inequalities. This maintains the critic and presents us with a gloomy panorama where another pillar of democracy (the judicial power) seems to start to weaken.

Given the seriousness of the accusations, it is advisable to present certain details about the Court rulings. One of the decisions to which Mr. J. Stiglitz refers is the one where the Court rules in favor of American Express so that merchants are required to make certain payments by accepting the credit card of said company in their respective businesses, which according to the author is forcing anti-competitive practices. Although the divergent opinions of the supreme authorities and that of the economist are debatable, it is striking that in the current circumstances, the controversy has been resolved in favor of large corporations and against smaller businesses.

He also refers to another ruling in which the Court prohibits public sector labor contracts where government workers can make contributions to unions that are negotiating on their behalf. The Court's opinion was that unions cannot force workers to pay payments that support approaches with which they do not agree, which represents a violation of the 1st constitutional amendment (right of free expression). However, the author reveals this forced interpretation when comparing it with that ruling established by the Court in 2010, where it authorized corporations to make unlimited contributions to political (electoral) campaigns, which also make disbursements of money in favor of options electoral decisions that could be contrary to the opinion of a respectable majority of shareholders and workers.

Another criticizable ruling, according to the author, is when the Court established that a State cannot force an authorized reproductive health center not to inform patients about the availability of abortion options. Stiglitz states that in another perverse interpretation of the 1st Amendment, the Court held that freedom of expression includes the **freedom not to say certain things** (even in this case, in legal health centers). Faced with this, the author points out that, for example, cigarette manufacturing companies would also have the freedom to omit from their packages and advertising the warning that smoking is or can be harmful to health. That is, the Court must balance the right of free expression with others of equal importance, such as, in this case, the right of a woman to be informed about aspects concerning her health.

Finally, the author refers to the Court's ruling ratifying President Trump's executive order prohibiting the entry into the country of travelers from Islamic countries. According to the author, the Court based its ruling on the interest of national security. It is always postulated that we are all equal before the law, but it seems that some are (to put it in Orwellian terms) more equal than others because the strange thing about the case is that according to what the author points out, being the citizens of Saudi Arabia responsible for the terrorist attack of September 11, 2001, said country is not on the list of prohibited countries.

Although for Mr. Stiglitz, like a good economist, he tends to look beyond political events to find economic causality, and therefore, he maintains that this omission is due to the dark, lucrative interests of the presidential family in that country. We give the benefit of the doubt to the president (without this meaning agreeing on the underlying issue) and we consider that the main reason responds primarily to the character of said country as a strategic ally in the Middle East.

It should be noted that the Republican Party's handling of this Supreme Court issue is daringly risky because it lights the fuse of a political confrontation with unpredictable consequences. In addition to the evidence revealed by the recent controversial rulings of the Court, let us review facts that leave traces of irresponsible manipulation by the Republican majority:

- Having regained control of the Upper House in 2014, the Senate was responsible for approving the nominee for supreme judge proposed by former President Obama, Judge Merrick Garland. However, the Senate, with a Republican majority, did everything possible to delay its decision until it was canceled. This is part of what is called "Filibusterism" in American political jargon.

The reprehensible slowness suddenly became accelerated, and three months after Mr. Trump took office (April 2018), the Senate provided a hasty approval of the candidate nominated by Trump, Mr. Neil Gorsuch, to replace the deceased Supreme Antonin Scalia 14 months before said confirmation. Without questioning Judge Gorsuch's suitability, the speed with which the president summoned him, and the Republican-majority Senate ratified him.

Nor does it escape the detail of having summoned a relatively "young" 50-year-old to such a high judiciary in comparison to his supreme colleagues, who have a mature average age of 71 years. The reason for this situation is that, as mentioned before, the supreme serves in office for life, and with this, President Trump intends to ensure a Republican nomination for at least two generations.

- Additionally, President Trump, given the resignation of Supreme Justice Mr. Anthony Kennedy, also had the opportunity to present or appoint his replacement, and to do so, he proposed Mr. Brett Havanaugh, who was also confirmed as Supreme Justice by a Republican majority during a heated debate where he was accused of sexual harassment. The candidate is a renowned judge who has the approval of the conservative legal organization Federalist Society. Once the stormy senatorial interrogation was over, Trump ensured the maintenance of the supreme nominated by the Republican Party and with ideological affinity with it. Finally, in reinforcement of the previously mentioned trend, this candidate also corresponds to another "young" 53-year-old, with which Trump not only secured a majority of seats on the Supreme Court but also (acting within the legal framework and the tricks of the case), consolidates a long Republican permanence in the highest court of justice.

- If the described trend continues, there may be a risk of moving the Court toward a "relatively young profile of members with little experience" in the highest court. Given that the life expectancy of today's citizens has lengthened significantly compared to what existed two centuries ago (when the fathers of independence established the "lifetime tenure of supreme judges"), it is not out of place. The re-establishment of a limited permanence (for example, 12 years) and, at the same time, setting a minimum age for entry to the Court that ensures having an honest and experienced judge (for example, from 60 years of age). This simple initiative becomes complicated because it will require a constitutional amendment that is currently impossible.

- One of the first signs of having imposed a conservative tone on many of the supreme judges was evident last June of the year (2022), where the current Supreme Court annulled the rule that declared abortion as a constitutional right. Although the issue is extremely controversial and full of divided opinions, the truth is that the decision of the supreme authorities is taking a civil rights issue into the realm of political manipulation. Conservative states and opponents of the Biden administration are incorporating regulations that have the same direction. This issue has led to political controversy that set a certain tone in the midterm elections in the USA (Nov 2022). There are still other critical issues on which the Supreme Court will have to rule. For example, we will be attentive to how it would react to the likelihood of lawsuits and accusations related to former President Trump.

- <u>Fourthly</u>, where is this overwhelming eruption that has taken over the executive branch and controls the Senate in the legislative branch heading and which seeks to perpetuate a certain condition in the judicial branch, leading to? This situation contradicts the purpose of the founders of independence, who sought to avoid a government administration prone to risky boundaries of **political concentration of power**. Trump, as expected, induced a management style where he transferred his usual business aggressiveness to aggressiveness in the political field. Nobody warned him that it is one thing to win an election and quite another to fall into the risk and temptation of gaining influence and conditioning the normal functioning of the other powers. Nobody warned him that the "gluttony of power" finally becomes indigestible and causes a self-deterioration of, which we have already witnessed.

In his peculiarly overwhelming mood, Trump, ignoring pertinent advice from advisors, imposed a style that ignored elementary principles of government coexistence. One of them, enshrined in the constitution itself, is the aforementioned "Checks and Balances." It conceptualizes that each sphere of power establishes its own type of "checks, measures and balances" with which it exercises influence on the other powers to avoid abuses, errors, accumulation of power, and incompetence of the other powers. For example, a bill must be debated and approved in both chambers and, after this must be promulgated by the president, who in turn has the power to veto it and return it for modification in Congress. Congress can make the necessary modifications (or not make them) and approve them with a two-thirds majority and overcome the presidential veto. Finally, if the law were the result of compromises between the legislative and executive powers and had fundamental defects, it would be up to the judicial power to express itself regarding the incompatibility or unconstitutionality of the norm.

Another way to maintain this principle is through the "advice and consent" procedure that corresponds to the Senate to approve nominations of senior officials proposed by the president. As stated before, these "checks and balances" have become flawed. The Republican Party exceeded its actions in several cases. Although it is argued that he acted within the legal framework, his prominence led him to penetrate tentacles of influence in the three branches of government and thereby break the cornerstone of balance and reciprocal control of powers.

In summary, this system of indirect voting through the Electoral College is completely legal, but it has been generating a certain disproportionality that reveals a hidden paradox where the feat is achieved in which "a minority prevails over the majority" with the aggravating circumstance that not only power is monopolized in the area of the Executive Branch but, as happened recently, the current electoral system facilitates its extension so that it is also monopolized by the same minority in the Legislative Branch and finally exerts dangerous influence in the Judicial branch.

A palpable example of the disproportionality referred to is when, for example, in a State assigned with 10 voting members, a result is recorded where the Republican party obtained 60%, and the Democrat 40%, and the ten electoral members are assigned to the winning party (as if there were obtained 100% of the vote). Although the same occurs in the States where the Democratic party is victorious, the most reasonable thing would be for each party to be assigned, in any case, the voting members according to their corresponding participation in each State. A separate issue is the determination of the number of voting members for each State in which history and Gerrymandering practices (agreed upon by both parties) would partly explain the distributive magic.

For a renowned professor at Harvard University, Lawrence Lessig, and another renowned litigation lawyer, David Boies, cited in The Economist magazine from Jul 14th-20th, 2018, p. 23, the assignment of all the votes of members of the college to the winning party is unconstitutional because they consider that the votes not assigned to the losing party have been in effect "disenfranchised," that is, they have been deprived of their legitimate right to vote obtained at the polls. Therefore, such lawyers have attempted a legal route, equally difficult and different from the constitutional amendment route. In this direction, such professionals have filed a lawsuit in four States with the expectation that their claim will travel the long path of confirmation to the Supreme Court.

As a culmination or complementary effect of this indirect voting system, it reinforces and **consolidates a two-party political model** and, in practice, excludes the participation of third or minority options. Small political parties that try to compete have little chance of obtaining a victory in any State, and in the current circumstances, it is difficult for them to achieve 51% in any State. At most, this minority vote is achieved, which, in the context of the current system of indirect electoral registration, keeps "swept away" and are unable to obtain votes from electoral members.

The votes that these small parties obtain are lost; they disappear in the void of a **minority without representation, without voice, and without vote**. The only way to achieve political representation in this country is to be Republican or Democrat; any other option is "anchored" and restricted in the starting signal of electoral competition. It should be noted that the derivation of a two-party electoral system was not an effect desired by the founders of independence nor is it one for our modest assessment as foreign observers.

Additionally, in reinforcement of the fact that the present two-party political model is not the most conducive to co-governance, its disturbing effect is observed by having exacerbated a growing panorama of partisan polarization (between adversary parties and within each party). This is seen, for example, in the lengthy debates for budget approval that in the last years of the Obama administration caused a certain paralysis of the State apparatus and the risk of declaring in "default" (non-payment) the financial commitments of the American public debt. Under Trump's presidency, it was in his own administration that it self-generated, due to said polarization, a few weeks of paralysis of the State apparatus.

The co-governance panorama was also affected by the accentuation of the so-called **"filibusterism,"** <u>understood as a tactic of indefinitely lengthening or delaying the debate on a law that is not desired to be approved</u> (e.g. comprehensive immigration policy, temporary residences, renewal of immigration facilities for young "dreamer" students, etc.), <u>or also as a tactic to block a presidential nomination for a high position</u> that the Senate is responsible for approving with its "council and consent."

In the context of said polarization, <u>party positions have become more extreme</u> because the differences in ideological realignment regarding crucial issues of governability and social coexistence have become more felt. As a result of this, currently, extreme positions have been empowered among, on the one hand, the conservative wing of the Republican Party, which has been noticeably strengthened within it. This faction has unique support received from religious sectors (specifically evangelicals with increasing incursion into party activity) and from representative populations of the rural area.

This conservative wing shows greater prominence compared to the moderate faction of the Republican Party itself and has been exploiting with singular success the underlying phobia of a large part of the American citizenry regarding the intentionality of the Democratic Party, which it accuses of wanting to implement obsolete socialism schemes and, regarding anti-immigrant sentiment (mainly anti-Hispanic). Both factors formed the backbone of the Republican programmatic base in the recent and subsequent presidential elections.

On the other hand, in the Democratic Party, the liberal wing faction, despite its minority representation within the party, has seen its position strengthened thanks to President Trump's own mistakes. This liberal wing leads heartfelt criticism and open opposition to the Republican administration on controversial issues such as racial discrimination, access to health benefits, recognition of the rights of women, children, and families, tolerance of sexual options, legal status of immigrants, abolition of abortion, equal opportunities, etc.

This faction has been pigeonholed by its opponents under the label of "socialists" (tremendous absurdity for American reality). But beyond considering itself discredited for this, this liberal Democratic wing reaffirms itself in criticizing the insensitivity shown by its Republican opponents to solving the priority needs of a significant and growing neglected population sector. In practice, the crossfire between conspicuous representatives of these extreme sides has only hindered the possibilities of better governance and prevented the achievement of consensus and agreements between both parties.

- Fifthly, we consider that, under current regulations, the electoral results discussed distort reality and distort the principles that founded American democracy. If the founders of independence were to witness the results presented, they would be absorbed and disillusioned because the Electoral College established by them as the purpose and strategy of avoiding political concentration of power has led to precisely that. That is, power "is dispersed in the appearance of formality, but ends up concentrating in the party that manages that dispersion."

Just as a child's clothing is too short when he or she becomes an adolescent and, in turn, his or her clothing is inappropriate when he or she becomes an adult, as we pointed out before, despite the significant evolution and growth of this "corporeal reality." social American," the democratic clothing that accompanied her from birth to adulthood is essentially the same and no matter how much stretching is undertaken, said clothing does not fit her, so that it looks like a kind of "straitjacket" causing contortions and deformations to the body that binds it.

There is a group of respectable citizens who consider that perfecting the clothing of this democratic system, whether through the difficult constitutional amendment or through the long and complicated legal route, represents something like betraying the will of the "sacred" fathers of independence and, therefore they are reluctant to undertake any reform. This "loyalty" has translated into permanent conservatism due to its presbyopia in detecting or underestimating contradictions, fissures, and clashes between evolution and transformation of reality and the obsolete legal and institutional framework that comprises it.

History is full of examples where the resolution of such contradictions has given rise to abrupt, conflictive, traumatic, bloody, etc., solutions, such as the independence of this country and other countries in America and the fight for human rights. Civil rights (8-hour workday, women's suffrage, segregation of minorities, and others) that meant years of struggles and sacrifices.

This conservatism and determination to maintain the "status quo" is responsible for endangering the survival of a democracy that has begun to deform, taking a course different from the desired one. The protagonists of the complicated reality that we are witnessing, or more specifically, the spokesmen of the present bipartisan configuration, are faced with polarized positions, mutual recriminations, and endless debates where the possibility of achieving consensus becomes increasingly difficult. What one of the parties proposes or defends is a matter of opposition from the other party.

Consensus becomes difficult because each party has its own truth and is conditioned by its own perspective and interests. When narrow visions prevail for the simple reason that "each one pretends to be judge and party" or "each one provides water for his own mill without caring about the rest," then the entrapment arises that prevents progress, improvements, reforms, agreements, and so on changes that the situation demands.

In such a situation, the conventional arbitrator responsible for the resolution of conflicts and critical controversies at the highest level is the Judicial Branch and, more specifically, the Supreme Court. Hence, the importance of the judges that comprise it meet requirements of suitability and, technical and professional experience and of impartiality, and autonomy. Let us remember that the Supreme Court of the USA has the power to declare unconstitutional federal or state laws issued by their corresponding legislative powers, as well as declare unconstitutional any act of the federal and state executive powers, and its decisions are final.

What happens then when the respectable magistrates that make up the highest court of justice show signs of questionable decisions that derail the impartial and autonomous trajectory of said institution? When this supreme arbiter begins to defect, reliability is broken, and the governability of the nation and its democratic institutions is endangered.

The way the parties and powers have been functioning, the management balance presents a panorama of risks where partiality, mistrust, polarization, and obstructionism predominate instead of leading us to a healthy institutional order, neutrality, trust, and a climate of shared purposes and agreements. In this perspective, the last administration of President Trump placed us at risk of a deceptive tyranny of minorities characterized by a partisan protagonism that influenced and attacked various branches of government. For this reason, his attempt to re-elect himself by appealing to his well-known tricks, the fragile memory of the citizens who will continue to ignore his lies, and the discreet performance of his opponent, Biden, return us to the risk of his probable second term.

During the administration of current President Biden, the recompositing of the political map made it possible to partially contain the anti-democratic avalanche, but it has not been immune to the current political erosion and deterioration. There is no perception of a consolidation of changes, and the feeling persists that political polarization has extended to the sphere of the socioeconomic macrosystem because continue the lack of trust and credibility, which is the key lubricant to achieve consensus, progress, and social coexistence.

- Sixthly, as the panorama is presented, it is crucial to ask who to turn to get out of this democratic trap. Something that can help us resolve this crossroads is to make the imaginative artifice of transporting the fathers of independence in the time tunnel, from the past to the present, and sitting them on a platform in a kind of open popular town hall so that in light of the experience of the democratic scheme established by them and in consideration of the severe changes in the socio-economic and political context of the past 236 years, let us ask them if they would recommend us to continue and face the future following "faithful to the form of the same scheme" (that is, that the indirect election system through the Electoral College remains in force and that the system of weights and measures that support the "checks and balances" of reciprocal influence between powers also remains in force without any variation). Or if, on the contrary, they would recommend that we change said democratic framework and adapt it to the present circumstances, what would they respond to us?

- We venture to outline that beyond considering that we maintain or change the scheme they suggested, the first appreciation of the illustrious thinkers would be that their message has been misinterpreted, that the "fidelity" to what they proposed must have been mainly to **the substance and not to the form**. The substance line is related to avoiding the vices of the concentration of political power, maintaining vigilance that guarantees the deconcentrating of this power, and promotes the functioning of the balance of powers. Said fund is the one that has a profile of permanence and an incorruptible essence. The form refers to all that architecture or mechanism that makes governance viable and, by its very nature, has a changing character.

- The founders of the country would reproach us with a frown that we have done things the other way around, that is, we have kept the form and its stagnant democratic scaffolding constant without the capacity or the intention to adapt it to the changes experienced, and rather we have changed to wrong, that unbribable fund promoting precisely what they set out to avoid, that is, deviations towards the concentration of power.

- The second assertion of the founders would be the suggestion that we must ask ourselves, as honestly as possible, for an examination of conscience so that, when deciding on the true matter of change, the subsequent question is: What will we achieve or where will the decision be taken lead us?

- Interesting options arise here. A first group of such options falls into what we could call the persistent **"conservative" current of maintaining the form** (which in turn bifurcates into two subcategories of options). The first subcategory is the one that proposes maintaining "the form" because they argue that this will maintain "fidelity to the substance" proposed by the founders. This option is curiously tricky because it raises an argument that, in practice and as we have seen, ends up distorting it.

- The second subcategory of the conservative current is the hidden or covert option and proposes maintaining the form without explicitly mentioning it, given that its stratagem consists of maintaining the form in fact without revealing it in words (doing it, but not saying it). Why would this option be feasible? Because those who propose and execute it have the tacit recognition of the impossibility of maintaining fidelity to the fund proposed by the founders.

- What is the similarity between both subcategories? Both maintain the obsolete formalities of the democratic framework and the maintenance of distorted and conservative forms of institutional and legal frameworks of social coexistence. For this reason, they are incongruous because they disrupt the essence of that background proposed by the founders.

- The second group of options falls into the **"liberal" trend of changing the way,** which is also subdivided into two subcategories of options. The first subcategory of this current will propose changing the way to avoid deviations from the substance proposed by the founders. In this case, it is crucial to define what to change, how much to change, and how to change, which requires undertaking a series of important reforms that transform this governance architecture, a design engineering that can involve constitutional amendments, changing the indirect voting scheme, ensuring the representativeness of minorities, suppress or prevent the redistribution of electoral districts through the well-known "gerrymandering" practices, prevent "filibustering" and obstructionism in the nomination process of senior officials, adjust the system of "Checks and Balances" that promotes an effective and reciprocal influence and balance between powers of the state, changing the system of election, composition and validity of judges of the Supreme Court, etc. As can be seen, this is a necessary but difficult and complicated challenge that could take several decades to implement.

- The other subcategory of this liberal current is the option that proposes changing the form and, at the same time, perfecting the substance proposed by the founders. With good reason there may be citizens who suggest that after 236 years is enough time for the nation to redefine its vision for an equally long future. In order not to fall into utopian territory, a feasible approach would be that, without separating from the strategic objective of deconcentrating of political power, some others of equal importance are complemented or added, such as equal opportunities without discrimination of any kind, recognition of minority rights, ensuring social services in health, education and housing, environmental protection, alleviating and reducing poverty, avoiding deformations in income distribution patterns, etc.

- These and other strategic objectives must be debated by society and its representatives' entities, and so that they do not continue in the limbo of good intentions, they must be instrumentalized with specific complementary and additional measures to change the form described above. If the previous subcategory was, as we maintained, difficult and complicated, the present one will be, to say the least, titanic. However, let us keep in mind what someone suggested: "We will never put an end to unfavorable things in the past if we allow this past to continue destroying us."

- Finally, given the citizens' insistence in the imaginary open town hall to define themselves between the general's options of the "liberal" current of changing the form or the "conservative" current of maintaining the form, surely the wise founders of independence, as a third assertion and in order to avoid annoying impositions or manipulations, they would suggest that it is up to us and not to them (who have already done their thing), the responsibility of proposing, debating, developing, perfecting the desired changes or also the responsibility of maintaining and letting go the existing scheme intact.

We have been careful not to present the options described under the categories of Republican or Democrat because we understand that in the American partisan heterogeneity, there are conservatives and liberals within both parties. Although the doctrinal biases of each political reality will not be lacking, we trust that the contribution of lucid minds on either side will be evident. Therefore, regardless of where lucidity comes from, America needs imaginative and innovative approaches that resolve the crossroads and the democratic trap in which it has been developing. The first step is the recognition that a process is being experienced that corrodes the institutions, the functioning, and relationships within and between Powers of the State.

Considering that the deformity of the democratic system has been partly the result of bipartisan co-responsibility accepted and consented to for more than two centuries. The solution to this problem will also have to be, above electoral triumphs or defeats, a political challenge for this same American bipartisanship of this century. The challenge requires that the political class know how to get rid of the myopias inherent to knowing that it is in permanent dispute over electoral contests and place itself in a perspective that integrates, with greater tolerance or understanding, its own and others' points of view and, above all, with a long-term vision.

This requires getting rid of that numbing lethargy that comes from self-serving subterfuges, from distorted perceptions that make it difficult to get rid of rooted points of view. It is necessary to overcome short-term conceptions and false remorse of "fidelity or mea culpa" when sacrosanct traditional schemes are questioned. All of this constitutes barriers that prevent the proposal and development of renewed political coexistence schemes.

We have made this long parenthesis of conjunctural and structural problems in the American and Peruvian reality to highlight how the complicated aspect of Culture, Values, and Leadership affects subordinates, makes viable, restricts, and conditions what we understand as the effectiveness of business or organizational management. We need intelligent, mental "daring's" like those Albert Einstein had when challenging the sacred venerated cult of Newtonian Physics that was in force for more than 200 years.

We need to break with old paradigms and perceive reality differently with the help of special lenses other than those we usually use to detect the confusion and harmful gravitational and magnetic fields of any management more clearly and to glimpse, design, and develop alternatives and future solutions. In this determination, Mark Twain's impulse of wisdom will be important: "Twenty years from now, you will feel more disappointed by the things you did not get to do than by what you did. So, take risks, sail away from safe harbors, explore, discover…"

2.3.3 Initial step: Toward agreement and consensus

Returning to our management problem, we highlight that the continuity and aggravation of conflicts within any company, organization and community, or nation will not be surmountable if the two basic elements described above persist: **imposition of interests** on the some interested parties and the **loss of trust** between the main protagonists. This will make the company, organization, community, or institutions enter a swamp or vicious circle that restricts and conditions the possibilities of overcoming its difficulties.

How to moderate or reconcile positions and how to restore trust? It cannot be denied that people act in consideration of motivations, interests, and particular benefits (remuneration increases and bonuses, greater responsibilities and professional experience, obtaining promotions, technical

137

training, achievement goals, increased profit rates, expectations discrepancies in risks and benefits, decrease in costs and increases in productivity, etc.).

This is how human beings function; we act under the expectation of compensation (not only economic but also professional, political, or a combination of them). On the other hand, any company, organization, or government has its own policies and goals that it will try to enforce and comply with, but it must also consider the expectations and points of view of the other economic agents that accompany it in its task (workers, technicians, employees, suppliers, bankers, local authorities and even competitors). There will be situations in which the different perspectives (own and external of each agent) present affinity and complementarity of interests, and there will also be circumstances in which conflicts of interest predominate. How to make these conflicting interests compatible?

The first step consists of finding the framework of institutional, political, legal, economic, and social consensus in which a scheme with sufficient degrees of tolerance, openness, and recognition regarding the distinct positions predominates. In an open and serious negotiation process between two or more parties, it is not easy to bring to light different objectives, different points of view, and different desired results. In this, the foundations must be laid to facilitate the development and consensus on balanced proposals that make incentives, benefits, prizes, incentives, and other interests compatible and make a situation of reciprocal and shared benefit viable.

We insist on the search for new and original solutions; they must be established under a climate of concertation and consensus and supported by reasonable convictions, which meet the fair expectations of the participants or affected (direct and indirect) – businessmen, entrepreneurs, workers, governors, suppliers, consumers, communities, etc. - and achievements in general well-being. Once again, we find the same warning: a recommendation that is easy to state but difficult to undertake and implement.

We recognize that unraveling the tangle of problems incubated in long processes will also require complex and gradual advances not subject to immediate pressures. Likewise, it must also be admitted that it will be impossible to fully meet the expectations of all participants. Any negotiation scheme implies admitting on the part of each participant a certain margin of tolerance with respect to positions different from their own. A less belligerent position must predominate and, after separating the total problem into parts, begin to deal with it by the less critical and conflictive parts that allow progress in partial consensus.

We have heard the argument that poverty cannot be distributed and that we must first grow and then distribute. Once again, the labyrinth of false dilemmas arises; both things must be done because neither growth nor poverty can wait. Starting from a level of poverty such as that existing in our reality and the Peruvian experience of sustained growth in recent decades, the necessary simultaneity of both is confirmed. According to the "EL Comercio" newspaper of Lima (April 29, 2018), the level of extreme poverty, as reported by the National Institute of Statistics and Censuses, was reduced by 20.7%, falling from 42.4% in 2006 to 20.7% in 2016.

However, despite the important improvements in the reduction of extreme poverty income levels (remunerations, wages and salaries of teachers, health sector professionals, police, public employees, etc.) compared at the regional level (Latin American), they have gaps to be improved. The debate on poverty is much more complex than what can be discussed in this study; it is enough to reaffirm what was maintained by a renowned statistical researcher from the aforementioned newspaper (April 06, 2018), Mr. Alfredo Torres, who affirms that poverty statistics Poverty (measured only in monetary terms) draws a misleading line and that any multidimensional calculation of poverty (that is, including greater variables and indicators of the standard of living such as quality of health, sanitation, education, housing, etc.) will have to reflect higher rates or levels of poverty.

The concerns of multilateral organizations such as the World Bank or the Inter-American Development Bank (IDB) are not in vain, as they see with concern that the fragility of social results in the Peruvian economic experience could easily be reversed and that population mass that has barely exceeded the limit of extreme poverty could relapse at the slightest symptom of economic deterioration, which we have nearby. Unfortunately, this negative forecast has been confirmed, and in the current situation, in mid-2023, extreme poverty levels increased again to 30%.

In any employment relationship, an implicit agreement is established, beyond regulations, regarding mutual expectations between employer and employee that are not formally established in a legal contract but that constitute daily conduct. Just as what happens with the "Social Contract" that the French philosopher Jean Jacques Rousseau (1712-1778) taught us when, in extreme situations, said agreement deteriorates and breaks, then the social bond is eroded, giving rise to extreme situations such as violence, social disorders, repressions, and tyrannies. For this reason, although the tripartite working groups between employers, workers, and the government do not show gratifying results, the search for consensus must continue to be supported.

During any social tension, the employment relationship becomes merely utilitarian. On the one hand, the worker is only a physical presence in the workplace; his dreams, ambitions, and illusions are elsewhere, in other things, and the law of minimum effort and, with it, minimum (or zero) performance prevails in them. On the other hand, when the company neglects the worker's requirements, this becomes a simple numerical code on a payroll and the law of maximum profits at minimum cost prevails. I am reminded of reading a comic illustration from a misleading social dictionary where the word Hypocrisy was defined as a scenario where the worker acts as if he were doing a decent job and the boss acts as if he were paying a good salary.

When interests become irreconcilable, some group tries to impose privilege, violently or with subterfuge, its interests over other groups. The lack of capacity for cohesion and integration of values will make it impossible to achieve progress and put the continuity and even survival of the organization at risk. When instead of cooperative, constructive, and tolerant dialogue, typical of a supportive organizational culture, prevails confrontation, aggression, and indifference regarding the role to be played, then the **organizational culture of destruction** will have prevailed in which the rigid dogmatic and sectarian positions supersede the interests of the entire company, organization, or community.

Messrs. James Brickley, Clifford Smith, and Jerold Zimmerman, authors of the book "Managerial Economics and Organizational Architecture" Third Edition, McGraw Hill Irwin, 2004, suggest important criteria that are directed towards other topics but that deserve to be considered in any concertation process. They propose, as a conceptual framework for their management model, a management architecture platform that, as a kind of support bank, is based on three pillars: Correct decision-making (assignment and execution), Performance Evaluation System (as part of a permanent control) and Reward System (benefits for achievements).

The authors assume that each company will have defined, as part of its management architecture, its own strategy, which must be compatible and coordinate the operation of these three pillars to obtain increases in the value of the company. They add that any variation, change, or defective or correct movement in any of these pillars without careful consideration of the remaining two will cause a functional imbalance that will cause a decrease in the value of the company. They also present important cases that support their approaches.

The above is so true in the Peruvian case that, for example, around January 10, 2022, according to the report of the Ombudsman's Office, (https://www.comexperu.org.pe/articulo/659-de-los-conflictos-socioambientales-registrados-en-enero-de-2022-corresponden-a-actividades-

<u>relacionadas-con-la-mineria</u>) there were a total of 203 conflicts: 154 active and 49 latent. Socio-environmental conflicts amounted to 132 cases, of which 87 of them are related to mining activity.

There is an alarming inability to resolve conflicts in population communities near mining centers, which means stoppages of production not only in the mining center but also paralysis of labor activity (commercial, tourism, transportation, services, etc.) in sectors surrounding the center miner. As a result of these conflicts and political instability, international financial instrument rating companies raised their country risk criteria and downgraded the rating of national public debt bonds. With this, in the immediate future, the cost of financing to obtain will increase for higher interests.

In recent decades, business leaders have found it difficult to face an environment that is constantly changing and is being redefined by the presence of forces that act more rapidly with respect to the assimilation and response capacity of the drivers of companies, organizations, and governments. This is reaffirmed by consultant Mr. Dov Seidman in Fortune magazine (Sept 15, 20017, page 90), where he argues that the redesigning of our management capabilities, our institutions, and our leadership models lost pace and lagged behind the redesign of the world.

This author maintains that the forces that support this change are: a) greater global interdependence, where what a company or government does can affect many other entities in a more accelerated and direct way than has ever happened before; b) greater intercommunication, where internet technology, the multiplication of social networks and all the paraphernalia of artificial intelligence have broken or shortened the distance between economic agents (governments, consumers, employees and companies); c) greater transparency, where it is increasingly easier for competing companies and governments to penetrate or obtain (by licit and illicit means) what was previously jealously guarded (client list, production technologies or strategic weapons, strategies market, telephone spying, disclosure of documents and private conversations, etc.).

Based on what was stated in the previous paragraph (interdependence, communication, and transparency), we can maintain that we perceive more clearly the message of the so-called "butterfly effect," which describes, metaphorically, that the flapping of a butterfly's wings in Asia will cause successive concatenations, a hurricane in the Caribbean. To this effect, we can also add another one, also known as the "Boomerang Effect," where things leave and return to us (sometimes in dimensions, characteristics, and consequences that are not so desirable). With this, we want to emphasize that these forces described have been the cause of advances and setbacks in companies and governments and of abrupt economic, political, financial, and social scandals, claims, and accusations between parties in conflict.

Regardless of the good or bad things that have taken place, what is evident is that many leaders and followers have not yet fully assimilated the changes. In the socioeconomic and business environment, there is a certain disorientation, confusion, uncertainties, delayed reactions, discouragement, low morale, lack of support, and even mixed feelings that reveal a clear **loss of trust** between economic agents, companies, organizations, governments, and citizens in general.

This loss of trust is seen, for example, between voters vs. political parties vs. party candidates (the advent of outsiders to the political sphere is not a coincidence), between powers of government (executive vs. legislative vs. judicial), between government and taxpayers, between companies vs. suppliers and between companies vs. customers (return of defective products) and between employees and employers (strikes, confrontations, boycotts), between borrowers and lenders, etc.

Events leave no respite and far from presenting themselves gradually and smoothly, they often happen abruptly, like a "snowball" breaking out and in a "mare magnum" of confusion. This implies the collapse of candidates, political parties, companies, organizations, and leaders who will hardly be able to recover from the situation. Even so, those who manage to reposition themselves through tricks may exhibit authority but not leadership because trust does not exist.

2.3.4 Values: Engine and Fuel in Organizational Culture

Here, then, comes the crucial question: Is it important to form an organizational culture that constitutes one of the pillars or supports of management? What is the best reference pattern to support this organizational culture? On the one hand, there are those who argue that the formation of a corporate culture is difficult to shape because it is impossible to satisfy all participants due to their conflicting interests. They also maintain that discrepancies will continue to exist, and we can only try, within a narrow margin, to make them coexist. It would make no sense, they say, to waste all the effort in creating a new culture that will solve little or nothing.

Likewise, there are also those who allude that companies already have a de facto business culture. Although it is not the best, it is the predominant one, and it would only be enough to revamp it and put it to work towards the company's objectives. There is also no shortage of those who "add more fuel to the fire" and discard the establishment of organizational culture because it

142

can deviate toward a sinister totalitarian [9] attempt that seeks to control not only the actions but also the emotions of employees. It has been suggested that this corporate culture represents, especially in authoritarian settings, a simple pretext to implement brainwashing aimed at adopting beliefs and behaviors in line with certain values and discarding others.

We leave in suspense the concern of having or not having an Organizational Culture to continue delving into three interesting approaches. **The first is**: Are the values that should make up any Organizational Culture fixed and untouched, or do they vary according to time, space, and circumstances? In this regard, we must highlight the current of relativism in ethics. This begins with the observation that diverse cultures also have different moral systems and opinions regarding diverse topics such as abortion, premarital relations, tolerance of homosexuality, social roles and autonomy of women, protection of minorities, genetic surgery, etc.

Accordingly, different realities show disparities in the way of conceiving, admitting, and, therefore, implementing different values. For example, we have important values such as Freedom (in its broadest sense, freedom of thought, expression, assembly, worship, mobilization, etc.), Equal Opportunities (to work, to be educated, to live in conditions of health, safety and environmental conditions that protect life and nature, etc.) and a desired Justice that develops on a plane without discrimination of any kind (race, gender, social, economic or political condition, age, etc.) and that promotes distribution patterns of wealth in accordance with the effort developed and human dignity.

The unique way in which a dictator interprets and implements freedom of expression, environmental protection, imprisonment, and trials of dissidents or opponents then acquires peculiarities and disparities that we all know. For these reasons, the approach described considers that morality and ethics are relative.

In opposition to said relativism, we have, as a second approach, the current that demands the validity of universal and untouched values. Values are clothed in objectivity, equanimity, and impartiality, and what are subjective are the assessments made by people who tend to be clothed in partiality and tendentious passions. Although values are interpreted or valued in diverse ways depending on the prevailing social norms, this should not prevent us from evaluating whether one

---

[9] Willmott, quoted by: R. Bolden, B. Hawkins en Exploring Leadership...op. cit. page 94

system is better than another. The apparent relativistic neutrality makes it impossible, for example, to condemn the Nazi genocide, intolerance of political dissent, condemnation of discrimination based on gender, sexual option, race, religion, etc., because they only recognize, justify, or explain such facts due to the existence of differentiated moral and ethical systems, but not worse or better than others. This neutrality usually avoids degrading considerations against the essential freedoms inherent to human nature and the validity of universal values.

The third approach outlines the old dilemma: do the ends justify the means? In this regard, we can maintain that the forced interpretation of some proposed value enables the implementation of means, tools, programs, and procedures to achieve purposes with a marked tint or particular interest (even those that are not correct from a humanitarian perspective). This can vary in a very broad spectrum that, in the purest style of authoritarian dictators or terrorists, ranges from "collateral damage related to people's lives" such as systematic torture, kidnappings, imprisonments, expatriations, and overlapping crimes against dissidents, etc. to equally condemnable matters related to the usufruct of power such as the granting of concessions or special licenses, facilities or favoritism in electoral, financial, tax matters, boycotts, harassment, etc. The affirmative answer to this third approach - that is, accepting that the end justifies the means - takes us back to the problem of relativism.

From another perspective, the interesting position of José Ortega y Gasset in his work "El Espectador" deserves to be rescued, Salvat Editores S.A, Spain, 1970, page. 49, where he "lands" the values (from the plane of ideas) towards reality (on the plane of facts). For him, these are two conceptions (values and reality) that are never isolated but linked to each other. By relating values and reality, the author maintains that there are no absolute values nor absolute realities, especially when these are shown or conceived independently. We add that this approach departs from previous relativistic or universal conceptions because it does not conceive them independently but always linked or contrasted to their reality environment.

The reality, according to the author, is presented on two levels: an external, apparent, manifested level and another internal level of conviction and substantive connotation. External reality has the unavoidable mission of being a corresponding (or coherent) expression of internal reality; otherwise, it becomes false. According to this, the word (what is said) and the action (what is done) must be a concordant manifestation of the spirit. On the other hand, the internal reality has the mission of manifesting and externalizing itself in its external reality counterpart, so that if it does not do so or does so in a manner that is discordant with it, it is also converted into falsehood.

For Ortega y Gasset, the authenticity of a man, society, or culture is realized when there is a bi-univocal correspondence between, on the one hand, the manifest word (or action) and, on the other, the spirit, essence, and values that make up that substantive connotation. If this condition is not met or becomes inconsistent, then the man, the society, and the culture that surrounds him turn out to be false, hypocritical, or fake. For this reason, he gives as an example that the man who usually exuberantly defends opinions, ideas, principles, and values that deep down he does not care about is a fake. In the same way, the man who really has those opinions and values but never defends and demonstrates them is also another fraud. The author rounds off his idea by stating that "the truth of man is based in the correspondence between gesture and spirit, in the perfect adequacy between the external and the intimate."

The position described is interesting, but it could also be counter-argued that, for example, a "convicted and avowed" Nazi is acting in congruence with his conception of racial supremacy by supporting, agreeing with, or "turning a blind eye and overlooking" war crimes of that unfortunate war episode. It can then be argued that, in this case, there is no farcical attitude but rather a coherent one between "gesture and spirit," even if it is in that murky side of human existence.

In safeguarding Ortega y Gasset's approach, we can argue that respect for life (both as a principle and as a real fact) is out of the question and said value has a universal and priority connotation. This being so, we maintain our disagreement with the supposed neutrality of ethical relativism, and we find it advisable that, first, we can be guided by the universality of values but never keep them idealized in the cloud of our imagination, but rather compare and revalidate them permanently, as suggested by Ortega y Gasset, with the circumstance of our reality.

Given the above, the big question arises: why are values, organizational culture, and ethics important in the business world, in organizations, and in government administrations? Its importance lies as pointed out [10] by O.C. Ferrel, Fraedrich, and L. Ferrel in "Business Ethics, op cit. P. 6 and 7, in which:

> "…in business, politics, and science, specific actions are taken that are judged right or wrong, ethical, or unethical by the community made up of

---

[10] O.C. Ferrel, Fraedrich y L. Ferrel in "Business Ethics op. cit. Pages 6 y 7

consumers, investors, employees, interested groups, and public opinion in general. If society judges such actions as unethical or wrong, even though the manager or ruler believes in the goodness or righteousness of that action, the social verdict will be relentless and will directly affect the organization's ability to achieve its goals. Said verdicts will have a determining influence on society's acceptance or rejection of the organization and its activities."

Palpable proof of this was the disastrous impact that the falsification of information and unethical behavior of the company Arthur Andersen had on the business and social community after its connection to the Enron scandal became known. This disaster prevented the auditing company from continuing to operate normally and culminated in its withdrawal from the market.

But what happens when history shows us that said implacable social verdict was wrong or was manipulated by interested groups, by opponents, or even by the media? What happens to people, managers, rulers, companies, or organizations unjustly condemned and punished with disgrace? To avoid risky detours, the task of shaping an organizational culture will be necessary and will require overcoming the narrow perspectives of interests, whimsical political convictions, or extreme ideological positions.

Building an organizational culture of cooperation and integration that translates into commitment to action and mystique among the members of the organization is as important as having a good operational structure with a modern industrial plant or commercial support with an updated marketing strategy. Today more than ever, **the revaluation of ethics in the business world** and in organizational management becomes essential. When this is not understood, when the organization is led without the support of principles and values, when improvisation and spontaneity prevail, the organization and the company are exposed to the risk of corruption or to the stalking and voracity of business and organizational cannibals who wander in and out of them.

To avoid confusion, it is necessary to clarify the differences or similarities involved in concepts such as ethics and morality. In this regard, in the work of Robert Salomon and Clancy Martin, "Morality and Good Life," Fourth Edition, McGraw-Hill Companies, 2004. Pages. 2-12 offer an interesting perspective. Such authors point out that, for example, morality is specified through rules of conduct, which discriminate against what is right or wrong about an action. For its part, ethics aims, through the study of values, norms, and justifications, to delve deeper into why certain actions are considered correct and others wrong. Ethics raises the demand for explanatory justifications or discrepancies for those actions finally chosen.

According to these authors, ethics and morality are closely related and mutually influential. It cannot be determined whether an action is right or wrong in a vacuum, but rather the other aspects or agents involved in making the choice must be considered and filtered with values that involve them. They refer to the classic example of euthanasia, where it comes into play whether medical assistance in suicide is morally permissible versus the right of a terminally ill person to be assisted in his or her intention to eliminate himself. The right or wrong of the action goes beyond circumstances and leads us to deepen the theme of human values. In this sense, they point out:

"The problem with justifying an action or principle is that a good reason for it must be shown. But there may be other better reasons for the chosen alternative. What makes ethics difficult is that not all conflicts are easily solvable, and some are not. Some crucial questions of our time have nothing to do with justifying one value system over another because several value systems coexist. This context of plural society has different arrangements of values and opinions regarding what is correct. Therefore, a primary function of ethics will be to provide a way to evaluate conflicting ethical views that present different pictures of morality and the good life".

The construction of an organizational culture is achieved through the establishment of action programs that exemplify those strategic and operational values that will make up the new desired organizational culture. In the training course, those new and unknown values and concepts will have to be assimilated, and, on the other hand, those already known and considered unscathed or unquestionable but no longer fit into the new scheme will have to be unlearned. The task becomes complex because, in both senses (learning and unlearning), Resistance to Change must be faced. If we want to modify the relationships between the protagonists and reinforce certain values such as commitment, sense of belonging, mutual trust, responsibility, etc., with the objectives of the organization, it will be necessary to change the organizational culture because the values that contain it and the attitudes to be generated are the engine and fuel to optimize a Management oriented towards achieving better results.

Curiously, the "administrative rationality" of certain managers becomes blind and tends to ignore and even undervalue the importance of the set of desirable values and existing redeemable values in their organization. Culture is not classified as a true "asset" that requires management.

Far from shaping and developing the permanence and fulfillment of shared values, they are not taken seriously when it is desired to promote behaviors toward organizational success.

As pointed out by Salvador García and Shimon Dolan [11]:

> "In a sequential cycle of experiences and learned behaviors, its basis is made up of that set of beliefs that, as though structures, conceptualize our existence (its conservation and improvement) and will be configured and fed back into values and principles and ethics (own and others) ... In practice, the subject actor or group will exchange information and, after positively or negatively evaluating the facts, people, or things, will predict the tendency to act in a certain way or mode of conduct, which in turn maybe it will reflect results. Therefore, when you want to change behaviors, instead of directly changing attitudes, you have to work on modifying, changing, and learning the values and beliefs that precede them."

One of the most important reasons for the failure and interruptions of many change projects (strategy changes, system changes, structure changes, process changes, policy changes, etc.) or the failure to continue is because many attempts at change lack the intention of addressing something as important as cultural change based on values that promote the attitudes that demand such changes.

It is naively and mistakenly considered that cultural change will be a secondary effect that will occur due to the force of circumstances or due to the weight of the changes initially proposed. The harsh reality will demonstrate that they are not effects but a prior (or simultaneous) condition, and unless values and beliefs change, the new proposed changes, no matter how well designed, will never work. They will remain at a superficial level where they only generate an initial expectation and then later frustration. After a certain time, excuses will be found that justify its ineffectiveness where the deficiency described above is usually omitted.

Many of the difficulties of mergers and acquisitions processes are that they frequently focus on the quantitative valuation of assets, resources, and economic results of the operation, leaving aside what concerns the results of the overlap between the organizational cultures of the purchasing entity and the one purchased, absorbed, or merged. This not only implies the physical dismantling of complete areas and dependencies with personnel included but also the disappearance of the

---

[11] Salvador García and Shimon Dolan: "La Dirección por Valores...", op. cit, Pages. 72-73

organizational culture of the absorbed entity or area in which there could be values, ideas, beliefs, and attitudes that are salvageable and feasible to maintain in force in the organization merged entity with the capacity to positively enhance the merger. Overlooking this issue (culture and values contained in it) could imply risks of deterioration in the resulting merger. As a summary of what was described above, the signs that typify effectiveness are presented in the following graph.

Chart Nº 4: Signs of Effectiveness

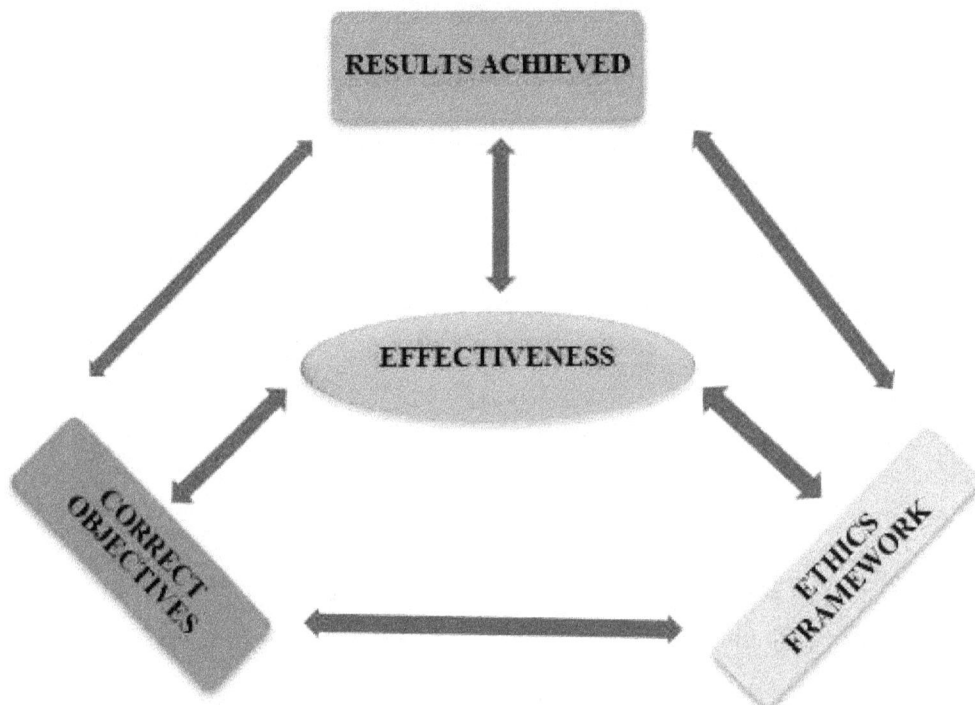

The other important reason for ethics in business and organizations is the recognition, or greater awareness, that exists today in business circles about the beneficial relationship between the improvement of ethical conduct and the economic performance of the organization. In the work of O. C. Ferrell, John Fraedrich, and Linda Ferrell [12], the authors describe that the formation of an ethical climate in the organization simultaneously impacts the **reliability** of three important strata, which are reinforcement of employee commitment, investor loyalty, and satisfaction of consumers. The final consequence of the is a notable contribution to the company's profits. From the

---

[12] O. C. Ferrell, John Fraedrich and Linda Ferrell: "Business Ethics…", op. cit. pages 14-18

perspective of this study, it is these recognized impacts on business results and performance that allow us to ratify the consideration of organizational culture as one of the key factors in achieving business effectiveness.

Given that in organizational management, there are a number and variety of matters that lead to ethical problems, the authors, O. C. Ferrell, John Fraedrich, and Linda Ferrell [13], draw attention to aspects of singular relevance, namely:

- "Honesty and Justice" - Honesty involves truthfulness, integrity, and trustworthiness; Justice includes the quality of being fair, impartial, and equitable." When such standards are broken and, for example, the consumer is subject to deception or fraud in the acquisition of a good or service, or it does not meet the expectations offered, when a company verifies the poor quality of its product and service supplier, when the lender confuses the borrower with charges and subterfuges that increase the effective costs of credit, when the "ordinary" citizen perceives corruption or incompetence in the officials in charge of public management, etc.; then trust is destroyed, and it becomes difficult and sometimes even impossible to continue carrying out private or public management. When it is unknown or not accepted and persists in continuing in such conditions of discredit and mistrust, the results will be calamitous.

- "Conflict of interests" - It is a typical situation where the dilemma arises of choosing between an option that results in the interest or benefit of some party involved. The problem requires attention and supervision so that employees, even managers, should avoid personal interest or benefit regarding that interest that has to do with the organization in which they operate. There are even cases where acting against the interests of the organization tends to tip the balance in favor of third parties. In all these cases, the principle of "avoiding being judge and party" is broken. The correct thing to do will be to step aside and exempt yourself from assuming responsibilities that compromise or cast doubt on behavior that conforms to the rules. When the person does not do so or is not clear about it, it must be the organization itself that establishes the parameters that avoid situations of potential conflict of interest.

---

[13] O. C. Ferrell, John Fraedrich and Linda Ferrell: "Business Ethics...", op. cit. pages 31-40

- How are conflicts of interest caused? On this topic, receiving, giving, or granting benefits in the form of bribes, personal payments, gifts, attention, special favors, etc., is quite deep-rooted and involves employees, executives, and government officials committed to influencing the outcome of some decision (purchases, contracts, bidding, obtaining or renewing licenses, etc.).

- In our Latin American region, we have already cited the notorious case of the Brazilian firm ODEBRETCH, winner of tenders for infrastructure megaprojects, engaged in millionaire bribes granted to high government officials and in facilitating the financing of presidential electoral campaigns in exchange for being favored in such tenders. In Peru, said firm acknowledged having paid bribes for an amount of $29 million dollars between 2005 and 2014 that compromised the governments of Alejandro Toledo, Alan García, and Ollanta Humala, and the recent contributions to the presidential campaign are being revealed, such as the candidacy of Keiko Fujimori, (daughter of former president Alberto Fujimori) and who was a finalist twice in second round elections.

- "Fraud" - It occurs when systems or forms of deceptive practices are established to benefit the self-interest of the person, the organization, or third parties. Fraud is done with the explicit intention to deceive, manipulate, or conceal facts and create a false or misleading situation. Among the most common forms of fraud, we have:

- "Accounting Fraud" - They refer to the usual accounting audit reports that provide valuable information to investors, shareholders, authorities, and other interested entities, which base their decisions on the accuracy and veracity of the information disclosed. To define criminal responsibilities derived from fraud or conflict of interest, the legislation of many countries, in addition to penalizing those directly responsible for fraudulent information, has contemplated the express prohibition of both auditing and consulting services being offered simultaneously by the same company because There were notorious cases where the granting of juicy consulting contracts conditioned the veracity of audit opinions.

- "Marketing Fraud" - When the communication derived from the integral marketing process, from creation and distribution to the promotion and price determination, is misleading, deceptive, and combined with tricks and half-truths, the only thing that is obtained is the destruction of the trustworthiness of the consumer public, supervisory authorities and other interested groups. There are cases of false advertising where something that is not said, offered and advertised, which unfortunately occurs after having completed the purchase of the product or service received. Another very sneaky way of lying in this marketing process is through messages attached or sometimes overly understood in the product labeling.

- In this regard, in Peru, the prestigious company Gloria S.A. recently had a serious problem with this last issue. In addition to selling its classic evaporated milk product packaged in 454 ml cans, it launched another product with the same can packaging pattern, but whose label showed an overflowing dairy cow that the consumer public interpreted as a variant of its well-known evaporated milk. However, it was only through the claim of authorities from another country (Panama) that it was discovered that the milk in the new product was not evaporated milk itself but rather milk made with inputs from dairy products. Even though the company argued that the label of the product did not make any reference to the fact that it was evaporated milk, the discredit, the distrust in the product, and the pressure from local authorities, the company was ordered to withdraw from the market said product and was subsequently fined financially.

- In other cases, fraud is usually committed by corrupt employees. In a respectable number of bars and restaurants, cases of fraud involving the sale of liquor and other products have been discovered without proper documentary support. The physical stock of products in stock does not match or is lower than the report of what was formally sold. This flawed scheme is repeated in other areas of many conventional businesses (clothing, footwear, cosmetics, etc.).

- Consumer fraud. These are problems committed not by personnel (workers, administrators, bosses) of the company itself but by agents external to it. In this case, clients usually deceive and commit fraud for their own benefit and to the detriment of the company or organization. The best known is theft inside commercial establishments. The ways are varied and range from hiding items in your own clothing, item exchanges and changing price tags to taking advantage of generous return policies on merchandise after you have even used it.

- "Discrimination" - Racial, sexual, gender, age, physical, social, or legal discrimination constitutes a topic of current debate, especially in the workplace, social, and political spheres. In the American environment and with the current trend of discrimination and harassment, minority groups must face traditional hostile social displays and patterns of behavior.

- An event that occurred on May 25, 2020, reported by American and international media, caused public opinion to be shaken by the execrable scandal unleashed by some white police officers in the city of Minneapolis, USA, who, upon arresting an African-American citizen, George Floyd (47) for an alleged crime (possession of counterfeit bills), in flagrant excess of their powers, they abusively attacked him until he suffocated and caused his death. The event was widely disseminated in viral images and sparked a wave of widespread protests throughout the country that degenerated into acts of looting and social violence, which in six days reached close to 4,400 people arrested in the main cities of the country, five deaths, and millions of dollars in property damage.

- Technological information - It must be clarified that the problem is not the technological information itself but the abuse that is made of it when it affects the normal development of other people, other organizations, or third parties. As notable advances occurred on the Internet and other forms of communication, the number of people and companies that used it with tricks and traps for their own benefit also grew. One of the first problems that began to arise was evidence of people using the company's technology for personal matters during business hours. The response of most companies has been the implementation of monitoring and supervision systems for e-mail and web visits not related to work.

- The current situation has revealed a serious threat faced by people, companies, and other private and public organizations. These are **cyber-attacks** where, due to economic or political interests, the privacy, property, and secrets of any strategy, project, instrument, or tool of any entity are violated. Here we already surpass ethical aspects to fall into areas of flagrant crimes.

- According to what was reported by Time magazine (July 21, 2014), IBM's security division reported in 2013 that the number of attacks on American companies with computer viruses was around 17 thousand and with a tendency to increase. An illegal market has been formed where the weapons that are sold are computer viruses. In this dirty game that responds to created interests, economic and political motivations have a lot to do with it.

- Who participates in this market? a) virus brokers, specializing in intermediating the sale of all kinds of vulnerabilities. b) attacked companies that pay cash for viruses that affect or threaten their products or computer systems. c) computer criminals who use such viruses to market stolen secrets and information of all kinds. d) the governments and intelligence agencies of the country's most active in developing and defending viruses as a tool of intergovernmental espionage (USA, China, Russia, Israel, and others).

- According to sources from the magazine, the Microsoft firm had an offer limit of one hundred thousand dollars to hackers who find threats to their Windows system; the Google firm has paid hackers nearly 3.3 million dollars since 2010 for rewards against vulnerabilities to its systems, the Facebook firm paid 1.5 million dollars in (2014) to defend itself against 687 viruses that affected its system. This source also maintains that a hacking group based in China uses vulnerabilities in Internet Explorer to launch attacks against important American companies, spy on human rights activists, and conduct intellectual property theft.

Whether for commercial or internal security reasons, the real fact is that both companies and government agencies have taken the threats described as sufficient justification for the violation of privacy of people. The scandal of the famous WikiLeaks (about 20 thousand e-mails containing classified information from the American government) that in May 2013, Mr. Edward Snowden – former contractor of the US national security agency – began to make known to the world through the press, put former President Obama's administration in serious trouble and spy systems were exposed, including personalities and allied governments.

Mr. Snowden, sued by the American government, subsequently obtained asylum in Russia, where he remains to this day. Controversially considered a traitor and dissident and a hero and patriot by others, the truth is that his disclosure put the issue of security vs. privacy on the table for debate. See (https://en.wikipedia.org/wiki/Edward_Snowden) to what extent is the violation of the privacy to which we all have the right permissible? What is the limit, circumstances or exceptions that allow it to be exceeded? Once exceeded, what disclosure will be allowed and what will not? How do we restore the dignity, image, and honor of those who were unjustly compromised in matters where they had nothing to do with it?

Another delicate problem on the topic of technological information has arisen when the scandal involving, on the one hand, the well-known company Facebook, as a provider of social networking services to one of its special clients, the British consulting firm Cambridge Analytica, and on the other hand, the latter's relationship with it special client, the then-candidate Donald Trump, to whom it provided support in the 2016 Republican election campaign.

To what extent can customer privacy be openly violated by using data for commercial purposes or to enhance or provide a third party with a certain electoral advantage? Everything seems to indicate that there are no limits because according to what is stated in https://en.wikipedia.org/wiki/Facebook#Privacy, the following is cited:

> "Facebook has faced a constant stream of controversies over how it handles user privacy, repeatedly adjusting its privacy settings and policies… On April 4, 2019, half a billion Facebook user records were found exposed on servers in Amazon cloud, which contained information about users' friends, likes, groups, and registered locations, as well as names, passwords, and email addresses."

Lawyers illustrate a key principle of social coexistence: **"the rights of any natural or legal person end when the rights of another begin."** With the prism that this principle offers us, let us analyze the problem in question that involves a very sui generis organizational triangulation.

Firstly, Facebook, in the pre-election period, had among its main achievements a volume that exceeded 2.3 billion active users. It represented approximately 45% of the world's population aged 15 to 64. We took this population base because to access Facebook, you must be 13 years old (a rule that is hardly met in practice).

Indeed, Facebook has had admirable success in its attempt to develop a community of people based on the Web, where it allows them free access and information about world events with news of all kinds, exchange of experiences, communications, notes of sympathies, photographs, opinions, etc. The success of its marketing effectiveness has been skillfully reinforced through strategic alliances with other developers such as YouTube, WhatsApp, Instagram, iTunes Store, Messenger, Microsoft, and others.

For this reason, in the last decade, the growth of users has multiplied almost tenfold. This impressive growth has made it easier for the company to accumulate an invaluable treasure, which is the creation of a valuable directory with the data of its clients in the USA and in the world where, in addition to general data such as name, date of birth and age, sex, place of residence, marital status, etc., important features of preferences and psychological profile of its users are revealed. According to a recent Netflix documentary ("Nothing is private" title of the Spanish version and

155

The Great Hack of the English version), Facebook has up to five thousand items referring to the personality of each user.

According to the cited source from Wikipedia, Facebook established in March 2012 the obligation to activate (update) the user biography. If it had not been done by the users themselves, the Facebook bodies oversaw doing it. Why is this activation important and what to do with said data? For example, one button is enough. Mark Zuckerberg (president of Facebook) commented, "there are 200 million people on Facebook identified as single, so clearly there is something to do here." In May 2018, the company announced plans to launch a dating service. As well as Mr. Jeff Bezos, president of the giant Amazon (the e-commerce company) and Mr. Jack Ma, president of Alibaba (a leading Chinese company in online e-commerce); Mr. Zuckerberg also foresaw, several years in advance, that there would be no hesitation in doing business over the Internet.

Facebook offers social networking and online social media services, but the commercial ownership of the large database managed through a complex high-tech platform gives it the basis of enormous market potential (zoned, stratified according to varied and specific marketing criteria) capable of targeting a wide spectrum of advertising coverage, so the bulk of its income comes from advertisements that appear on its users' screens. By 2019, it had growing revenues close to $146 billion.

Secondly, the consulting company Cambridge Analytica specializes in data collection and analysis to support advertising and political campaigns. What and how does that company do specialized work?

According to what is reported in https://en.wikipedia.org/wiki/Cambridge_Analytica , the company collects data on voters (demographics, consumer habits, internet activity and, other public and private sources on preferences and opinions).

This data is processed by applying the instruments of models, research, and statistical segmentation and with the support of Artificial Intelligence software to manage high volumes of information, determining a complete profile of the behavior, motivations, and tendencies of the consumer or of the electorate. Therefore, the company offers its commercial and political clients the desired behavioral change in the target population or market.

The company was accused in March 2018 by media outlets (The New York Times, The Guardian, and The Observer) of having misused information from 50 million users of the Facebook platform. This information was revealed by a former Cambridge Analytica employee, Mr. Christopher Wylie, a computer expert, who stated that the company had created a machinery to manipulate voters' decisions and that when he retired from the firm (2014), he warned Facebook regarding the actions of Cambridge Analytica.

For this reason, The Guardian denounced that Facebook had been aware of this for two years and that it did nothing to protect its users. In a delayed reaction and after the facts became known, Facebook tried to shake off the mud of the scandal and banned Cambridge Analytica from advertising on its platform.

The strategy consisted of acquiring the database for academic research purposes and finally ended up managed by the consulting firm for use in the presidential campaigns of Ted Cruz (2015) and Donald Trump (2016). As also important background, his notable participation in the faction that supported the withdrawal of the United Kingdom from the European Union (Brexit, 2016) and important support for the electoral campaign of Mauricio Macri in Argentina (2015), who was finally elected, is described.

In videos made on hidden cameras that were revealed by a British television network, the executive director of the consultancy, Mr. Alexander Nix, boasted in front of an alleged client (undercover journalist), explaining the various "dirty tricks" used by the consultancy in their electoral campaign work for their clients (discrediting opposition candidates by implicating them in cases of corruption, sexual scandals, spreading lies, etc.). After these videos were revealed, the senior management of the consulting firm, also seeking to shake off the scandal, decided to suspend Mr. Nix, implying that it was a regrettable boast on the part of said executive and arguing that Mr. Nix's statements "do not represent the values of the firm."

Subsequently, in May 2018, the consulting firm Cambridge Analytica announced the closure of its activities, and months later, it declared bankruptcy in both England and the USA. Aside from the certain foundation of said bankruptcy, the intention to shield itself from probable and future demands from large clients whose data was used without their knowledge and authorization was obvious. The cited source reported that Facebook, in addition to appearing before a British parliamentary committee to determine responsibilities, received in October 2018 a significant fine from the United Kingdom judiciary of £500,000 for violating laws on the protection of personal data.

For its part, the Federal Trade Commission (FTC) of the USA faces accusations against Facebook of having inappropriately shared the data of 87 million users with the consulting firm Cambridge Analytica, and after more than a year of investigations confirmed (July 2019), responsibilities and imposed a multimillion-dollar fine on Facebook of the order of five billion dollars as a sanction for bad practices in the management of data security of its users for violation of their privacy.

Thirdly, from this triangulation, we have Mr. Donald Trump and his election campaign (June 2015). The successful background of the consulting firm Cambridge Analytics in the Brexit campaign tipped the balance in its favor so that Trump and his campaign committee decided to hire his services. This was confirmed by the directors of Cambridge Analytica themselves, who (in the same videos released) admitted to overseeing the investigation, data analysis, selection, and execution of Trump's digital and television campaign.

The chosen slogan was: "Let's make America great again." The formal body of the campaign's workhorse was its opposition to illegal immigration border security (the construction of a wall on the US-Mexico border and the temporary ban on citizens from certain Muslim countries entering the country). In the economic field, he promised to raise employment levels, favor private investment, protect the national business community by raising tariffs on imports, and mark distance by opposing the predominant free trade. In terms of fiscal policy, he proposed a significant reduction in taxes for companies. Additionally, his inclination towards military interventionism had its correlation with an increase in the defense budget and military expenditures, offset by decreases in social expenditures.

Criticism was immediate, and his opponents described his administration as racist, segregationist, inciting violence, a macho inclination that violates women's rights, neglect of children and the helpless or unprotected population, xenophobia, religious intolerance, disassociating themselves from environmental protection policies, disagreeing on international politics with Western allies, incubate a potential fiscal deficit, aggravation of public debt, authoritarian management bias and disregard for minorities.

The slogan, with its hopeful message and the briefly described campaign body, aimed to capture the desire, aspirations, and fears of that undecided electorate with a typical middle-class psychological profile supported by those pendulum states to which we referred in previous chapters and in which the consulting firm Cambridge Analytica worked hard to tip the balance in favor of the Republican option represented by Donald Trump.

For those of us who witnessed the experience of the 2016 presidential election campaign, we have no doubt that behind the formalities of a campaign, secret strategies, a set of tricks, tricks, and "dirty tricks" were being cooked up behind the scenes of which were known, and others remained in jealous reserve. Much of this electoral paraphernalia was more clarified after the electoral event and not throughout the process itself. Below, we present some of them:

When throwing darts at the opposing candidate, it was necessary to simultaneously consider arming the shield or armor in self-defense against probable opposing darts. Knowing the elevated risk that the disclosure of a sexual slip of the candidate Trump with two "top models" from the defunct Playboy magazine could mean and given their threat of disclosing it, it was considered necessary and strategic to buy their silence. So that there is no doubt that the slip described by the Republican side as an absurd and defamatory journalistic accusation was Trump's own personal lawyer, Mr. Michael Cohen, who, after the campaign and elections were over, admitted to the judge, having made the respective payments to said models by Trump's express order.

There was no shortage of those supporters who referred to the fact as a simple precedent for a minor offense. However, the issue was controversial because it was alleged that the disbursements were made with funds from the electoral campaign, which did constitute a serious crime, and the trial has not yet been finalized in a New York court. To make matters worse, Mr. Cohen, accused by the prosecution of co-responsibility in the events, availed himself of the benefit of a reduced sentence, collaborated with the authorities of the case to clarify the fact, and declared himself guilty.

On another issue, the Republican campaign cleverly and endlessly exploited the disclosure (March 2015) that candidate Hilary Clinton used her own email and private server when she was Secretary of State instead of using the servers of the Department of State. Since some of such emails could be under the category of highly classified, the Federal Bureau of Investigation (FBI) began an investigation to investigate how the issue was managed.

Candidate Clinton was called to testify (October 2015) before a parliamentary commission (Benghazi Commission) for more than 8 hours in a public hearing that did not provide any more information than what was already known. It did not fail to draw attention that after the email controversy subsided, just one week before the elections (October 28, 2016), the FBI decided to reopen the investigations into the email scandal. This left a bitter taste for the Democrats right near the end of the campaign and was the stab of strategic influence on the results.

In confirmation that crime never pays and always gets paid, in August 2022, the FBI surprisingly raided the luxurious residence of former President Trump in the town of Mar-a-Lago, Florida, on suspicion of having secret and classified information that he had access to in the White House. The process is under investigation, and the former accuser of privately managing secret information has now been accused of the same thing. One more pearl in the accumulation of serious legal demands that he will have to face in the short term. We could ask ourselves suspiciously if when he faces his future litigation, they could take us to the Supreme Court, and it would not be surprising if the latter, with the bias imposed by him, shows its best predisposition and speed to smooth the way for his candidacy for the next re-election.

Given certain indications about Russian interference in the 2016 electoral process and the clarification of this fact being of public interest, in March 2017, the prosecution appointed Mr. Robert Mueller (former director of the FBI) as special prosecutor of the Department of Justice for investigate any links and coordination between the Russian government and people close to the Trump campaign.

American intelligence agencies had indications that the Russian government interfered in the American elections by hacking the servers of the Democratic National Committee and the Google email account of Hillary Clinton's campaign chairman, Mr. John Podesta, to support the dissemination of fake news through social networks and for trying to penetrate the electoral systems and databases of the different States of the American Union.

(https://es.wikipedia.org/wiki/Investigación_del_fiscal_especial_de_los_Estados_Unidos_de_20 17).

See:https://es.wikipedia.org/wiki/Investigaci%C3%B3n_del_fiscal_especial_de_los_Estados_Un idos_de_2017#:~:text=La%20investigaci%C3%B3n%20del%20fiscal%20especial%20de%20los %20Estados,que%20surjan%20in%20the%20course%20of%20this%20research%C3%B3n .)

Among the clues are telephone audios that reflect contacts maintained between Russian intelligence officials with Michael Flynn (Trump's former National Security Advisor, who is awaiting sentencing), Paul Manafort (Campaign Manager until August 2016, convicted of a prison sentence and pleaded guilty to financial fraud) and other members of the campaign.

In July 2019, special prosecutor Mueller, after two years of investigation, was summoned before Congress to present the results of his report in which he concluded that President Trump could not be accused of any crime, but neither could he be exonerated. He also concluded that his team found evidence that the Russian government worked to interfere in the outcome of the election but could not establish criminal collusion.

The Democrats were left with the disappointment of not hearing a devastating report that supported a presidential impeachment trial, and the Republicans were also left with long faces for not hearing a claim that was formally discarded.

The above described sets a very suggestive precedent so that, faced with the dance of millions represented by future electoral campaigns and faced with the struggle for power and interests that come into play, influential groups of economic and political power rethink their scheme of entering into the dangerous paths described and look for innovative strategies so that they can continue competing (with third-party support) with new letterheads or a different company name, the same social networking services from firms like Facebook and the same political consulting services from firms like Cambridge Analytica to the same or new clients (understand parties, movements, coalitions) and the same or new candidates with ambition for power. We will be attentive to analyzing whether new formalities are successful in their attempts to maintain the same gloomy and rugged backgrounds.

From an isolated and formal perspective, each participant in this tripartite scandal played their specific role adjusted to the functionality that corresponded to them, that is, offering services on social networks (Facebook), consulting in data collection and analysis (Cambridge Analytica), development and execution of a competitive electoral campaign (Trump and his campaign team). But from a comprehensive perspective and considering real facts, the concatenated conjunction is disturbed by a tangled chain of vices with questionable profiles and contents. In what circumstances or moments are legality and the boundaries of ethics violated to achieve, at any price, a business and/or electoral attack in which the end justifies the means?

A professor at my university study center (Mr. Fernando del Carpio) enlightened us in class about a wise lesson (also taught to him during his student days) about the nature and risks of professional activity. He told us that because of our academic training, we faced our professional future with a weapon in our hands (such as a pistol). You, the professor stressed to us, will have the ability, but also the responsibility and awareness to determine for what, when, and how to use said weapon. Indeed, over the years of our own and other people's experiences, we can affirm that each person follows their own path and their own "jungle" (context and circumstances), and said journey is full of temptations and challenges.

In the scandal described in this part and the performance of the participants involved, there will be those who are for or against this or that position (that of Facebook, that of Cambridge Analytica, or that of Trump and his electoral campaign in 2016) or none of them, but beyond sympathies or antipathies, this situation confronts us with an old dilemma of knowing how to orient ourselves in that complicated continuum where on the one hand the law of the jungle and the "Darwinian" principle of survival prevail and on the other side, reason and respect for a healthy coexistence. Later, we will touch on this topic in more detail.

2.3.5 Social Responsibility: from and to where?

Currently, the actors of business and organizational management are incorporating in their management a greater emphasis on Social Responsibility criteria where, while promoting healthy competitiveness, mechanisms of collaboration and integration of the company with its social environment are also sought. In a broad sense, the concept of social responsibility is made up of several aspects. Author Archie Carroll [14] presents the idea in the form of a pyramid diagram. See Chart N° 5. We prefer to expose it as enveloping layers due to the dynamics and variability that constitute them.

Accordingly, the base of the pyramid, or rather the first surrounding layer, is of economic responsibility. This economic responsibility is self-imposed and is limited to obtaining economic results that satisfy the expectations of owners and investors, which provide attractive and stable employment to people in the community, and that produce goods and provide services that contribute to general well-being. Any failure or defect at this level generates a direct and

---

[14] Archie Carroll, quoted by O. C. Ferrell, Fraedrich and L. Ferrell: "Business Ethics... op. cit. page 48

circumscribed impact on the business scenario, towards shareholders, workers, creditors, suppliers, and consumers who are the main affected.

The second surrounding layer is <u>legal responsibility</u>, which is made up of a set of rules, laws, regulations, and other provisions that the company must abide by and comply with. This regulation includes economic or administrative aspects (tax, exchange, tariff, labor regulations, and competition and supervision regulations) and in relation to consumer protection, promotion of equity (non-discriminatory treatment), and security (to life, environmental protection). Said regulations are normally established by government administrations as a guarantee of compliance with the company's own obligations to the community and with the State. Any failure at this level results in the application of sanctions that the same regulations stipulate. For example, financial fraud scandals forced the establishment of more severe laws in the USA with civil and criminal liabilities against managers who approve false accounting audit reports.

The third envelope is <u>ethical responsibility</u>, which refers to the orientation, implementation, and monitoring of standards of behavior that are acceptable to all groups with interests in the company (in addition to shareholders and workers, it also includes consumers, creditors, authorities, community, etc.). We have developed in this section and with a description of real-world references, the importance of values and ethics in the world of business and organizations. This responsibility is also voluntary and self-imposed. We will only add that the defection on this issue can certainly, in some cases, it may lead to criminal acts (e.g., corruption, tax fraud, discrimination, money laundering, etc.), as well as the withdrawal or disappearance of the company from the market because social rejection for unethical behavior has greater consequences than penalties for failing to comply with administrative regulations.

The fourth envelope of <u>social responsibility</u> is the best known and refers to philanthropic aspects related to the contributions of the company or organization to its local, communal, and social environment. Philanthropic responsibility is strictly voluntary; there is no obligation to carry it out, but its implementation, in addition to being consistent with ethical aspects (e.g., social solidarity), promotes patterns of harmony, goodwill, and support for communal well-being. This is the most popular envelope because it is directly assimilated with the favorable or unfavorable impacts on the social environment.

However, the interrelated effect between the envelope layers described above should not be ignored. In effect, the development and evolution of these responsibilities (economic, legal, and ethical) will have a favorable impact on making the philanthropic commitment effective, and this, in turn, on those. It should also be noted cases where a company can continue its commitment to social responsibility despite having pending lawsuits, tax debts and other types of claims with local or government authorities.

Chart N° 5: Levels of Business Responsibility

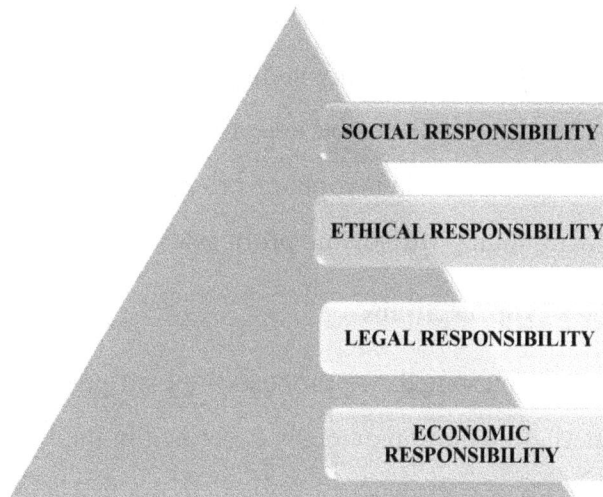

This concept has been assimilated by corporations and brands known worldwide, such as Coca-Cola, Microsoft, Toyota, McDonald, etc., which have recognized examples of social responsibility and has also been assimilated by companies in the local environment of Peru such as Inca Kola, Cristal, Telefónica, Banco de Crédito, etc. who, regardless of positions or disputes with authorities, carry hand in hand both their economic and legal responsibility as well as their ethical and philanthropic responsibility. Such companies have shown their social responsibility and continue to contribute to reducing the social problems in their environment. They collaborate in the development of social infrastructure works (roads, hospitals, schools, nursing homes, etc.) and sponsor the development of art, culture, science, and sport in the environment in which they are located or the environment that needs it. They even contribute with material and economic aid in cases of emergencies and natural disasters and achieve a healthy coexistence with unions, employees, and the community in general.

When this concept of social responsibility is neglected or defects occur where the philanthropic dimension is lost in the void; then we have the case of companies that, despite successfully undertaking their economic and legal responsibility, will be classified as greedy and unethical entities (since they ignored the principle of solidarity with their social environment). They will be seen as companies that only enjoy profits and surpluses obtained without the intention of sharing a voluntary portion of these with the community where they operate.

Some managers of these companies where the philanthropic dimension is fractured argue in the face of the criticism received that their social responsibility culminated with their legal obligations and specifically with their tax contributions. In effect, they save their economic and legal responsibility, but they will not be able to save themselves from the social affront that accompanies them. In this case, the myopia of prioritizing short-term profits prevails versus the important criterion of obtaining sustainable profit rates in the long term.

2.3.6 Complementary Appreciations

For all the situations presented, we propose the configuration of an Organizational Culture structured under criteria like those previously described in the topics of Strategy and Leadership, that is, it will be made up of three basic processes. In the first process, an audit and evaluation of the predominant values in the organization will be conducted, contrasting what is said with what is done. What strengths and weaknesses exist in the organization at the level of values? How do these values currently function, what is the risk of them being maintained, and where is the prevailing trend leading us? Are these values compatible and congruent with the formulated strategy? This analysis includes the evaluation of interacting forces, that is, the people, technical, and professional teams of the various areas in terms of their adherence or not to the prevailing values. Its operation will allow the evaluation of problems, resistance to change, and its causes and effects.

The diagnosis made of values will facilitate the perception of the second process, referring to determining which values will support the vision, mission, and other strategic objectives, that is, which essential or final values are compatible and reinforcers of those strategic goals. Towards a new Organizational Culture that promotes values that simplify business complexity, promote conflict resolution and direct it as guides or guiding elements towards the desired goals? Towards an Organizational Culture supported by ethical principles that inspire attitudes that consolidate those desired qualities, skills, and virtues among people in the organization?

The third process will have to support the conceptualization of the solution and includes the Formulation of the proposed Organizational Culture phase. What will we need to learn or change to achieve the desired culture? In addition to the essential or final values of the previous step, what instrumental values can be counted on to serve as support to achieve the first ones? What operational values are directly involved in the implementation and resource allocation process? How to instrumentalize that organizational culture through meetings, events, recognition, symbols, uniforms, colors, logos, slogans, motivational phrases and concepts, stories, etc.?

If you ask us, what are the best values that should be included in a business culture? What will be the best organizational culture? When and how do we start cultural change? Is it necessary to undertake light changes of gradual adaptation or changes of radical transformation? We do not know the answer because that will be part of the challenge that the manager or executive will have to face and resolve in his or her environment.

Throughout this section, we have referred to certain values such as mutual trust, respect for positions and interests different from our own, honesty, credibility, collaboration, participation, shared commitment, dialogue and cooperative communication, exemplarity, etc. There are, of course, other notable values, such as teamwork, creativity, initiative, diligence, quality of life, customer satisfaction, environmental protection, improvement, etc. All these values and others not mentioned for now make up a totality that must be a matter of evaluation, selection, and filtration in each business reality.

Mr. Seidman, [15] previously mentioned, proposes four guides that, as pillars, will constitute a leadership moral capable of correcting this gap or delay of business managers with respect to their environment, and we will also say consistent with the maxim that there is no leadership without a culture to support it. It is curious that such recommendations are careful not to refer explicitly to specific values but rather to conceptual categories that will facilitate the adoption of subsequent values. So, we have:

---

[15] Revista Fortune, set 15, 2017 page. 91

- Manage and lead the organization toward a noble purpose or objective. This generates dedication, devotion, and hope.

- Maintain a management style that inspires followers. For example, loyalty must be inspired. In the USA and most countries, the oath of loyalty to the Constitution is even formalized. Leaders must seek to inspire loyalty in people, not to themselves but to the purpose and mission of the organization. Here, we consider that giving a good example and coherence between what is said and done is crucial in inspiring, following, and adhering to followers.

- The leader must be encouraged and willing to act with both courage and tempered patience. They must conduct themselves with courage in the face of uncomfortable situations, vulnerable places, or territories, that is, they must show resolve to face and not avoid difficult situations, but they must also know how to conduct themselves with patience and tolerance to give confidence to their citizens and allow them time and opportunity to be more careful, rigorous, and creative.

- Maintain and continue the construction of a "moral muscle." The author recommends a kind of moral calisthenics, exercise, and continuous practice of values so that successes and actions do not have sporadic nuances or "they are the flower of a day." This will educate in developing persistence and consolidation of values. Initially, good habits are formative for the development of consciousness and character; once acquired, they are affirmed and strengthen the personality.

We also must resolve how these values are articulated, mixed, or done within the company itself. From the above, we confirm that there is no cliché or prototype of any organizational culture that is the subject of a model to copy. In the end, the shared values that make up the desired culture form a kind of neuralgic network spread by the management body and intermediate leaders throughout the organizational body that are not seen but are perceived and facilitate management to be directed at the boundary's effectiveness towards strategic goals and objectives.

As well as what is described for the business strategy, we were talking about a previously formulated formal strategy and another factual one (conducted according to praxis) and finally about a resulting strategy in response to the symbiosis of both. The same thing also happens in this topic of Organizational Culture. That is, we can have an intentional, directed, expressly conceived

Organizational Culture and a de facto Organizational Culture based on the commitment and shared practice of its members (a widespread option in Asian environments where existing and new personnel are aligned and disciplined towards the modus vivendi of a pre-existing culture).

Finally, we have the Organizational Culture resulting from that mix between the theoretical and the practical, between the formal and the real. Whatever the case may be, our recommendation will be that this culture does not remain in the window of good intentions, but rather that we persist in putting it into motion and that it in no way be left to chance, to mere improvisation, to the taste and orientation of only some of the "enlightened" in management.

We have referred to three basic factors – strategy, leadership, and organizational culture – necessary to obtain what we call Effectiveness. These factors are perceived not as objectives per se but as contributing means through which "choosing, orienting and achieving the right things" will be facilitated, that is, making effective business management of choosing and hitting the target of the objectives, the most important business (strategic) objectives. It is true that we will gain effectiveness and optimal results by doing what is suggested, but we do not think that they are exclusive and exclusive factors.

In fact, there are other factors that remain in the pipeline that were not specifically addressed—improvements in productivity, research into market strata and niches, training, media, etc.—and that could be confused with those factors that will be discussed further forward because they have directly to do with what we categorize as efficiency.

Therefore, we must be cautious; the importance of the factors described is relative, first because it will depend on the specific situation of each company, which will require specific refinement of greater need in one or another factor. Second, we cannot escape the important elements that contextual reality suggests to us. The business world will continue to give us notable examples of effective entrepreneurs forged more in practice than in the laboratory of university classrooms. From there comes our hope and optimism in the entrepreneurial strength of small business owners.

These entrepreneurs do not know how to make a formally conceived strategy, but they have a real strategy, simple and clear in objectives and procedures, crafted and put into practice through pure effort and dedication. These businesspeople possess that sense of smell and intuition in their businesses that makes them congenital leaders because they see and go further than others. In terms of organizational culture, they are addicted to work, an important value that does not require divulging it in words because they lead by example, and finally, due to their uncompromising honesty, they inspire adhesion and enthusiasm.

Based on the above, we reiterate that we have come to this point to show business candidates who are trained in "school and laboratory" what some of their "practical" colleagues execute with singular mastery in the field of facts. In all countries these rarities emerge of successful entrepreneurs who started from modest levels and gradually grew. In Peru, the recent case of the Añaño family empire (beverage industry) became a representative group of national economic relevance and constitutes a typical example of the above. There are other exemplary cases that are omitted for the moment. (See Francisco Durand: "The twelve apostles of the Peruvian economy," Pontificia Universidad Católica del Perú. Editorial Fund, 2017.)

Today's most successful people were forged through trials and errors committed yesterday; they dreamed big but started small. It is no coincidence that certain common characteristics are held by, for example, the five wealthiest men in the world, announced annually by Fortune magazine (USA), among whom the names of Warren Buffet (investments), Bill Gates (software), Carlos Slim (telephony) and some other tycoon from the energy world, the technology sector (Elon Musk) or some prominent entrepreneurial business leader (like the current Jeff Bezos of the Amazon firm).

First, they did not start with substantial amounts of capital but with modest resources and premises (workshops implemented in moderate environments) that were gradually and successively strengthened. Second, none of them have high academic degrees beyond the qualification standard training to conduct their management. It is necessary to point out that, in Peru, the custom prevails of requiring high qualifications of master's degrees and doctorates to apply for or access certain positions. This is initially appropriate, but unfortunately it is only a formality because regardless of whether such credentials later turn out to be of dubious quality and origin. No one has thought to propose that the results achieved validate the degrees obtained or presented.

These people began their activities without having been empowered with either money or knowledge, and, lastly, they have in common an unfailing and selfless dedication, or rather an addiction, to work and a "nose" and comprehensive intuition that normally leads them through the path of success.

The message is clear, and perhaps these factors, and not those we have described before, are the most important to consider in achieving effectiveness and, therefore, business success. This is what the prominent businesspeople described above have done. The only thing we provide in this work is a route that paints one of the probable routes (among the existing ones) through which to undertake this journey that, considering the advantages described, we hope will be kept in mind.

Experience, the teacher of life, suggests that we must "learn by doing." This idea has several examples, but Paulo Coelho explains it very well in a passage from his famous work "The Alchemist" (Harper Collins Publisher, New York, 1st Illustrated Edition, May 2007, page 134.) where he relates: "...only There is a way to learn, and it is through action. Everything you needed to know; the trip taught you." (it was the alchemist's response to the boy who was making a pilgrimage in search of treasure).

It is also appropriate to quote the reflection of the notable scientist Albert Einstein: "Do not try to be men of success instead, try to be men of value." Only him to bear witness that the first part of his sentence (man of success) will be a simple consequence of the second (man of value). Presumably, the connotation of the term "value" refers, from your own experience, to having the courage or worth to do new, unknown things that lead to creative or entrepreneurial results.

The desired emphasis on achieving successful results will be difficult to achieve if you do not have that enterprising spirit, that courage to take weighted risks, that search and development of new and unknown routes. Such successful results will not be achieved if you do not have the courage to operate inspired by a culture of shared values. This may be the route to overcome old paradigms and create new ones in the form of new products or services, new ways of impacting the market, and of fixing the management of resources, systems, processes, and technologies to serve it.

3. BUSINESS EFFICIENCY

3.1 PRELIMINARY ISSUES

From the perspective of effectiveness, we saw that business actions point to longer-range considerations such as strategic orientation, change of course, ethics, values, culture, and business leadership. That is, the functions described demand from the manager a strategist-entrepreneur role. We have proposed visualize the effectiveness from the perspectives of Business Strategy, Leadership, and Organizational Culture, and we reiterate their nature as long-term tasks due to how difficult they are not only to formulate them but fundamentally to implement them. These are complex and delicate tasks that normally involve several years of management.

However, this should not lead us to mistakenly think that the manager, in his role as an entrepreneur, is a contemplative seeker of opportunities who, through his creative and innovative ingenuity, spends his time concentrated in a workshop as a "thinking bubble" or looking at what that his "crystal ball" informs him about a distant future and in the end, he spends his time concretizing little or nothing. This category of entrepreneur is even disparagingly called a mere and even naive dreamer. Quite the contrary, in his entrepreneurial function, the manager is an active promoter who includes in his own short-term tasks those that have long-term perspectives and scope. As an entrepreneur, the manager acquires the nuance of promoter of ideas, strategist of programs and new projects, but since the search for opportunities does not necessarily guarantee success, the orientation of these ventures makes him a risk taker.

From the perspective of Efficiency and the techniques that comprise it, business management involves activities that compromise the management and allocation of resources. In this case, a managerial role predominates in the manager and the development of executive functions of organization, direction, control, and evaluation of systems, processes, and procedures that involve daily activities with greater impact in the short term.

Likewise, this concern of the manager in his managerial and executive function should not lead to thinking that he remains assigned or trapped in the daily grind without considering or evaluating how his daily decisions will impact the future of his organization. What happens is that, in the exercise of this managerial function, time constitutes a pressing constraint, and he must face a scheme of multiple decisions with varied coverage, greater time pressure, and content with greater variation than what he faces in his entrepreneurial function. In this sense and precisely by not stopping thinking about the future of his company, it is up to the manager, for example, to execute actions in the present that reduce the risk that he took in his entrepreneurial role.

This managerial-executive approach to management has been criticized for its accentuated inclination in that daily grind that sometimes leads it to neglect its attention to the changing requirements of its clients and external agents (consumers, suppliers of inputs and materials, service providers). , also of its internal clients (workers, shareholders), and to downplay or not adequately weight technological changes and other exogenous factors that, in the long run, end up impacting the company in unsuspected magnitudes and opportunities. When this happens, and customers perceive that their needs are not satisfactorily satisfied, they will search for find alternatives in the market.

For example, what happened due to the impact of the internet on the crisis in the recording industry and currently in the publishing sector, newspapers and magazines are a clear example of this. But it should also be noted that the same crisis described has meant the emergence of some opportunities that business managers in these sectors themselves are beginning to glimpse.

In summary, both roles of Efficiency and Effectiveness (with their respective executive and entrepreneurial approaches) and their respective activities are interconnected and simultaneously and gradually interweave the bases of sustainability or collapse of the future of the company or organization. The manager cannot afford to structure his work agenda if the current day, week, or month will assign only exclusive efficiency or effectiveness tasks. The programming will only be referential since the specific problems you face, and your day-to-day life will set your real agenda, and you will have to manage the balance or imbalance that best suits your own circumstances and the needs of the company.

As we pointed out before, Effectiveness and Efficiency are two sides of the same coin; they are part of the same organizational management process. If a direct and fine correlation of forces occurs, the interdependence between them will mean that, in certain favorable circumstances, the resulting Effectiveness can favorably affect executive management and will enable positive achievements of Efficiency. In the same way, the Efficiency achieved will also be a factor that will reinforce the Effectiveness to be obtained. Conversely, in unfavorable circumstances, ineffectiveness can also cause inefficiencies eventually. Inefficiency will condition or cause ineffectiveness.

Efficient management responds to the scheme initiated with the selection, availability, and allocation of human, material, technological, financial, and physical capital resources (equipment, plant, buildings), which are articulated under guidelines, standards, procedures, processes, and systems to obtain the product or service provision that responds to market expectations. The normal thing should be that high standards of Efficiency correspond to satisfactory levels of Effectiveness and vice versa. But, as mentioned above, it must be kept in mind that the coexistence of satisfactory levels of Effectiveness with modest levels of Efficiency or also presumably satisfactory levels of Efficiency that are not compatible with modest levels of Effectiveness achieved may also occur.

In the previous chapter we referred to the dual nature of the Planning component both from the perspective of Effectiveness and Efficiency. We said that what concerns the Formulation of the Strategic Plan corresponded to a task framed in the field of Effectiveness. In this part, we maintain that success in Efficiency refers to the optimal application or execution of business resources, which is specified in the related activities in three large areas: Organization, Direction, and Control and Evaluation of systems, processes, and resources in general. All of this is included in the cycle that goes from the allocation of resources to obtaining and placing the product or service on the market. From a planning perspective, this is called "Plan Implementation," or if there is no plan, this process simply corresponds to the implementation and development of the Management itself.

It is worth clarifying that the Formulation of the plan has a guiding nuance and is conducted as a laboratory or workshop task, but it is not divorced from the reality to which it must resort to analyzing and corroborating its approaches. For its part, Implementation has an executive nuance and is conducted as a field task, in the field of facts, face to face with reality, and for this reason, it does not remain divorced from the thinking, logical, and restructuring discernment of necessary changes during the management process.

A second clarification is that the order shown is only referential. In practice, the use of the planning tool is more informal. The separation between formulation and implementation is mostly of analytical importance because they go hand in hand, feeding each other and perfecting each other mutually and simultaneously.

The conceptualization of solutions to the business problems that are configured in any Strategic Formulation is necessary because it guides in practice the achievement of effective results. Without it (without formulation), executive management is reduced to mere improvisation. On the contrary, if we remain in the strictly conceptual sphere of Formulation, without landing in praxis (without implementation), management will remain mere mental exercises of theoretical speculation.

It should also be highlighted that on the one hand, moving in the field of Implementation implies moving in dark terrain that is difficult to predict, and on the other hand, the conceptualization that underpins all Formulation has its own limitations and will not be clear enough to foresee or detail unforeseen events, nor the course of reciprocal effects between the leading forces of business activities, nor the way and opportunity to overcome obstacles or emergency situations.

Therefore, both (Formulation and Implementation) considered independently offer an incomplete contribution with important gaps or absences. Given that successful management is not suitable for improvisations nor for theoretical or speculative fantasies, it must then be nourished by both the guiding and theoretical contribution of Formulation, as well as the contribution of practice provided by Implementation. In this way, theory guides practice, and practice, in turn, updates and reformulates theory. The independent contribution of each of them (Formulation and Implementation) is limited and weak, while their actions in an interrelated way complement each other, enhance each other and multiply.

Regarding this interdependence, it is worth remembering the phrase attributed to Mr. Keynes: "Practical men, who believe themselves free from all intellectual influence, are generally slaves of some deceased theoretical (economist)." (Note taken from Keynes' classic work: "General Theory of Employment, Interest and Money," cited by Samuelson in his work "Economics," Eleventh Edition, page 13). Since we consider ourselves practical men and not coming from learned academic spheres and aware of the slavery alluded to in the before quote, we comply with the bibliographical notes of all the authors – deceased and surviving – with whom we have an intellectual debt.

Just as we observe duality in the functional character of planning, we also observe ambivalent duality in the managerial function. From the perspective of Effectiveness, we highlight the orientation of the Management in its nuance of entrepreneurial leadership, especially in that which commits to the business future and evaluator of opportunities and risks, while from the perspective of Efficiency, we will highlight the profile of the management activity in its nuance of executive function of resource allocation in current and specific tasks, that is, in the day-to-day operations of the Implementation itself.

Additionally, we noticed that, in terms of Organizational Culture, there was also a characteristic of duality that manifests itself, on the one hand, when structuring that set of **essential and strategic values** that will be congruent with the way of thinking about things (Formulation supported by effectiveness) and on the other hand, structure that group of **instrumental values** compatible with the way of doing things (implementation supported by Efficiency). That is, there are aspects or approaches included in planning activities, management activities, and Organizational Culture activities that are not only assigned to Effectiveness but are also included in the scope of Efficiency.

Until this part of this essay, we have exposed enough categories of analysis that allow us to specify the concept of what we understand corresponds to a successful and satisfactorily administered business or organizational management. In this sense, we propose a more structured concept that includes:

- A management that promotes substantial transformations aimed at achieving its vision and strategic goals in which, starting from a knowledge of its initial situation, it projects consolidating its strengths and overcoming its internal weaknesses towards the construction of new and improved systems, structures, patterns, and processes.

- Said transformation process will be achieved through successive and gradual approaches within the framework of conditions of Efficiency in management, employment, assignation, and control of resources (labor, financial, technological, time, etc.) and conditions of Effectiveness in which, guided by its strategic route, it does not neglect the visualization and exploitation of opportunities and the forecasting of risks of the changing environment.

- In this transition process described, management will necessarily have to be supported by leadership that is sufficiently entrepreneurial, legitimizes changes, facilitates achievements, and motivates attitudes and stimuli. All of this, complemented and supported by an organizational culture made up of values that, as sources of inspiration, will drive the Efficiency and Effectiveness schemes through the appropriate channels.

The tasks to achieve correct implementation and satisfactory efficiency are of such quantity and variety that they are framed in policies, systems, procedures, and guidelines with different degrees of specificity depending on the area or system (operational, commercial, administrative, informatics systems, logistical support, etc.), according to indicators to be measured, time periods, etc. All these aspects are categorized into what we call Management Techniques, which, due to their nature and content, have to do with Efficiency processes.

As stated in the previous chapter, **it is not** our intention to expose "in extenso" every one of the Management Techniques in all areas of a company. Its particularities will have to differ depending on the line of business, size, business cycle, technology, and specialization of each business unit. We understand that this is the subject of abundant bibliographic publication that would exceed the purpose of this essay, which in no way intends to become a conventional Administration manual or executive recipe book.

One way to understand business efficiency is to describe the main successes and errors that are committed in the application of the various Management processes. Instead of presenting, as has always been done, a loose list of them, we prefer to present the concepts related to Efficiency from the analysis framework of the three aspects described above: organization, direction, control, and evaluation. Its advantage will be a more comprehensive appreciation of internal, external, technological, marketing, etc. factors committed to Efficiency and, in addition, clarify its complementation with the Effectiveness factors described in the previous chapter.

3.2 BUSINESS EFFICIENCY. How do things do correctly? How to avoid falling into inefficiencies?

3.2.1 Efficiency Profiles

We have pointed out that efficiency is included in the development of activities that begin with the selection, availability, and allocation of human, material, technological resources, financial capital, and physical capital (equipment, plant, buildings), and that will be interrelated under guidelines, standards, procedures and processes in business systems in order to obtain, as a result of this complex articulation, the final product or service provision aimed at satisfying needs in accordance with market expectations.

The "corporeal or physical" elements included in any organization are composed of that variability of "inputs" (humans, materials, physical facilities, etc.) that must pass the initial filter of adequate selection, qualification, and evaluation. These tasks were already designed in what we call Strategic Formulation, where the required input profiles were defined. At the beginning, such inputs make up "loose pieces," but later, they will have to be interrelated in a complex gear, or **"black box"** made up of the set of business systems, processes, and procedures also previously defined according to the nature of the company.

In the next phase, which we call Implementation, we activate the efficiency guidelines and processes and proceed to specify the availability of inputs, and the equipment required by the respective systems (operational, commercial, administrative support, technological, etc.) and thus launch the business apparatus. In this process, inputs and systems described above will be coupled and interconnected, and the corresponding tests will be developed, fine-tuning the business complex in all its areas and will allow the obtaining of products (outputs) or provision of services that will be indicative of quality management.

The name "black box" must be used in part because the business manager will start from the predetermined laboratory and workshop tasks to articulate them and make them viable in the face of the complicated and always-changing reality. The manager is preparing to enter darker terrains where the emergence of new and unforeseen events will present obstacles and problems to be resolved. Considering that not everything can be foreseen, the physical instruments and equipment are inert capital without the presence of that powerful human capital whose capacity, experience, and creativity will be influential in obtaining results for efficient management.

Reality, with its multiplicity of elements that make up both the inputs and the black box systems and their way of articulation, makes their interweaving and distinction much more complex. The consequence of this interrelation of inputs and systems, depending on the quality of their components depending on the ability to know how to integrate them, harmonize them in their respective gears, and make them work and control them, will show us a range of results (outputs) with particularities and distinguishable cases. Therefore, only for simplification purposes, we will assume a **basic variability scenario** corresponding to a predetermined arrangement of inputs and business systems and their respective resulting efficiency management prototypes which we explain below.

To avoid complications or deviations derived from its relationship and impact with Effectiveness, we will also assume that the platform that constitutes it (strategy, leadership, and organizational culture) operates at standard levels within a neutral functionality that does not restrict or condition effects efficiency. That is, only for the purpose of clarifying a more independent analysis of efficiency factors, we leave their interrelationship with effectiveness in suspense.

With the help of the following three-dimensional diagram, we are going to describe an illustrative architecture of prototype modalities of what we understand in **business efficiency management**. On the "y" axis, we represent **the inputs (y)** that could be classified as low (y1), medium (y2), and high quality (y3) categories. On the "x" axis, we represent **the business systems (x)** corresponding to systems (operational, commercial, administrative, IT, etc.) coupled, structured, and implemented in their specific Know How that we could also classify in a gradual quality as low (x1), medium (x2) and high (x3). In this three-dimensional plane, we represent on the vertical axis, "z" axis, the **results in terms of Efficiency** of those products or services provided by the company. Here comes the hand of the manager, who must achieve an optimal interaction of inputs and systems that we symbolically propose are made up of their respective black box.

Accordingly, the results will also be grouped according to their quality into inefficient management (z1), moderately efficient management (z2), and efficient management itself (z3). The result of the combination of the relationship between "x" (systems) and "y" (inputs) will determine "z" (the resulting management efficiency).

The management panorama diagram described in chapter one (see section 1.2) showed an introductory two-dimensional management scheme of various basic scenarios between effectiveness and efficiency. In this part, we show combinations of what we understand constitute basic profiles referred exclusively to efficiency management. The difference between the present profiles and those previously described is that in this case, we propose a design with categories referring exclusively to the field of efficiency (without any reference to effectiveness considerations) and add it in a three-dimensional diagram and not two-dimensional diagram context such as the opening chapter diagram.

As a result of the above, we will appreciate three significant spaces. In accordance with the assumed assumptions, the first will correspond to scenarios of inefficient results, according to the assumed assumptions, based on the three-dimensional surface, whose main variants will be explained below. Then, there will be intermediate characteristic scenarios on a second level of the three-dimensional surface located above the previously mentioned scenarios, and finally, scenarios located on a third level of the three-dimensional surface that correspond to efficient profiles will be shown.

Chart N° 6: Total Inefficiency

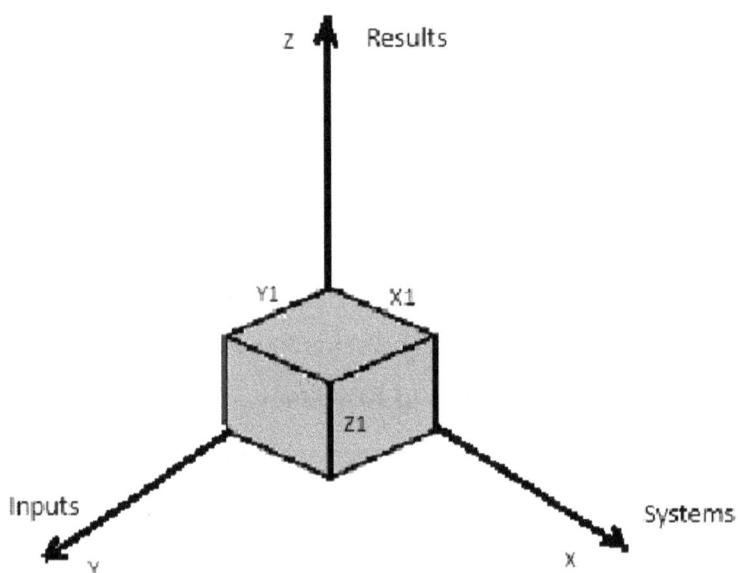

The major features are the following:

1. Inefficient combinations of results

A simple but sometimes forgotten observation must be considered: business management cannot work magic, so if it is fed with inputs of low-quality standards and/or with also defective business systems, one can conclude "a priori" that it is highly probable that the resulting management will evacuate disposable products or services. This situation (See Chart N° 6) which corresponds to the Total Inefficiency scenario, which relates the combination between low inputs (y1) and low quality of systems (x1) and, therefore, inefficient results (z1).

Companies immersed or trapped in this cube, where "inefficiency oozes out of the pores," <u>tell us what should not be done or the terrible way of doing things</u>. Missteps are the order of the day, and therefore, they are obvious candidates for companies and organizations to quickly exit the market or disappear for reasons of inefficiency. These companies are, to put it in medical terms, "terminal patients."

We can also analyze a combination (y1) and (x2) that represents the combination of poor-quality inputs and medium-quality business systems and, additionally, the combination (y1) and (x3) that corresponds to inferior quality inputs and high-quality business systems. These two mixed combinations keep constant the unfavorable permanence of inputs of inferior quality. What will happen?

From a realistic perspective, the presence of harmful elements (in this case, inputs of inferior quality) will predominate a correlation of contradictory forces (positive vs. negative). The relationship becomes difficult or blocked. This will have major importance in the resulting products to the point of conditioning, making it difficult and complicating the formation or ascent towards a higher stage. In this way, defective inputs play an anchor role, preventing the undertaking of any improvement or even ending up vitiating or corrupting the normal functioning of the favorable elements. Therefore, regardless of how said black box was configured in terms of medium or satisfactory quality, the permanence of low-quality inputs will play a drag role that will restrict and condition efficiency management, tilting results towards inefficient scenarios (z1).

An example of this on a business level would be the production of a well-designed and made line of dresses but with fabrics, yarns, dyes, etc., of inferior quality that do not respond to and are far from market requirements. Another example at the economic level will be the one mentioned in previous sections, where the economic growth achieved is insufficient to achieve better levels of economic development due to the anchoring role that corruption plays in the political and institutional spheres.

According to the above, two new cubes resulting from the mixed combinations just described will be added to the total inefficiency cube. Such cubes (y1, x2, z1) and (y1, x3, z1), also of inefficiency, would be represented on the "x" axis towards the right side of the initial cube and constitute what we could call the **"inefficiency fence."** For practical and simplification reasons we have omitted its graphic sample.

In an analogous way, let us now consider the combinations (x1) and (y2) that correspond to an inferior quality of systems with medium quality inputs and, additionally, the combination of (x1) and (y3) that relates a combination of poor quality of systems with high quality of inputs.

For the two mixed combinations described where the quality of the inputs is improved, but the poor quality of the systems remains constant, we maintain the working hypothesis previously indicated, that is, the relationship of forces or elements of contradictory content (favorable and/or positive with unfavorable and/or negative) will determine a correlation of forces prone to deterioration that prevents promotion to a higher stage. Therefore, regardless of the quality (medium or satisfactory) of the inputs, the permanence of business systems of poor or terrible quality will also have the same drag effect on results framed within the framework of inefficiency (z1).

These two mixed combinations would add two new inefficiency cubes (x1, y2, z1) and (x1, y3, z1) to the left side of the initial total inefficiency cube on the "y" axis. This determines an **extension** of the fence of inefficiency, but now, due to the permanence of poor-quality business systems.

Unlike the companies included in the total inefficiency cube whose presence was ephemeral and disappeared quickly, the companies that remain within the **inefficiency fence** (due to the presence of either inputs or systems with improved qualities) will have greater flexibilities and ability to survive, but its permanence is a matter of time, and its possibility of being able to overcome and escape the circle of inefficiencies are also limited because its restrictions lead it inexorably towards inefficient scenarios.

An example of this would be the production of a line of footwear with decent quality leather, soles, glues, linings, etc., but with outdated designs or defective construction and workmanship. The market does not accept them, problems of increases in expensive stocks, auctions of inventories or returns are generated.

Although such companies are, as is often said in medical terminology: "patients with severe damage," respecting the principle that every event, no matter how rare or strange, also has its probabilities of occurrence, it cannot be ruled out that under the direction of an efficient manager, (with knowledge and experience in knowing how to manage scarce, limited or poorly trained resources), one could achieve the feat of asserting oneself in one's limited scenario, "getting out of the swamp" and ascending to a second level of medium results. Efficiency results also depend on the capacity or ability of the executive or director to know how to manage (organize, integrate, handle, control) such components of inputs and systems.

We are referring to cases where management causes results that do not have a passive or dependent role on inputs and systems but rather play a role as an independent variable and generate favorable or unfavorable impacts on that combination of inputs and systems.

For example, in addition to the five combinations explained, there would be four others that end up even in the foreground despite comprising combinations of intermediate qualities with high input or system qualities (even between high input and system qualities) that were not included in the assumptions described above but which deserve comment.

It is not difficult to imagine, for example, what will happen when an inept car driver with little experience and ability is put to compete. No matter how much we equip it with a car with sophisticated technology and an adequate and well-designed roadmap, it is highly likely that the results will be adverse. This hypothetical case refers to the combination of $(x3, y3, z1)$, where even with high or satisfactory qualities of inputs and systems, disappointing results $(z1)$ are achieved.

The above is worth highlighting the fact that combinations of medium and high-quality inputs or systems will not be sufficient if they are accompanied by inept or corrupt management. Due to the above, the results obtained in these five last-mentioned combinations will be assigned to the first plane of inefficient platforms.

2. Next, we examine combinations where we adopt the assumptions of **medium quality**.

We start with the representative combination $(y2)$ and $(x2)$. It is an easily distinguishable option, that is, one of medium-quality inputs with medium-quality business systems. The qualitative improvement of both elements, even if they are not satisfactory, will allow an improved product or service result compatible with the medium efficiency category $(z2)$. In this case, we start from an improved combination of inputs and systems (compared to those described in the previous cases), and therefore, we reach a higher stage of results consistent with the case described.

The cube that configures this combination $(y2, x2, z2)$ appears in Chart No. 7 (yellow) as if it were suspended in a second level of three-dimensional space. The companies immersed in this suspended cube remain, pardon the redundancy, "in suspense" because despite having overcome the danger of pitiful inefficiencies, they maintain restrictions that condition them to continue their ascent towards areas of greater efficiency. They do not do things wrong, but they do not do them completely right either. Such companies are those that have the particularity, from the perspective of efficiency, of "doing things halfway."

Many of them (especially small companies) sometimes do so due to serious budget restrictions, but a large part of them, from the management body to employees in general, fall into the bad habit of following "the law of minimum effort," developing management in a blasé manner, as if to get by and save appearances. The lack of conviction, commitment, and greater discipline are obvious.

Another characteristic linked to the latent mediocrity in such companies is their instability in terms of income, markets, clients, operational irregularities, discontinuity of supplies, bottlenecks, etc. All of this entails tightness, financial gaps, and cost overruns that make her live "up to date" on her accounts. For this reason, endemic mediocrities disable them from facing the challenges of changing environments in the face of which they tend to accentuate their defects.

Chart N° 7: Average Efficiency

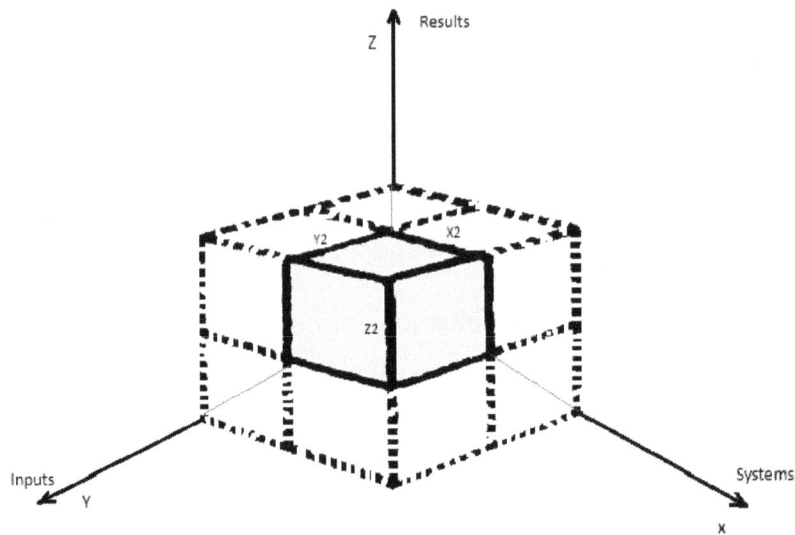

The remaining combinations included in this second level present several cases that deserve comment.

Firstly, we can mention combinations of medium-sized elements with poor qualities (of inputs or systems) that we have previously treated and classified, due to their unfavorable contradictions, as risky. We also make the exception here to mention an atypical case that combines inputs and systems of inferior quality but that exhibits a medium result ($x1$, $y1$, $z2$). Said cube can be seen stuck at the origin of both axes but at the second level. This contradicts the previously assumed negative drag characteristic. The only explainable reason for this is that, in this case, exceptional management of such quality has predominated that optimizes and makes of their limited resources and systems that allow them to achieve a result that exceeds expectations. Many times, we have verified this phenomenon that happens in the real world, but it happens infrequently. For this reason, we consider that its permanence in the second level could be temporary.

In Chart N° 7, two dotted cubes are additionally shown corresponding to such cases of mediocrity and theoretically formed at the second level that appears on the lateral and posterior sides of the cube (yellow) of average efficiency. In these cases, inputs and systems of inferior quality are combined with their peers of medium quality. It is highly probable that, if exceptional or saving management is not presented, the cubes representative of said combinations will hardly remain at this second level and will gradually drift towards lower scenarios of the first plane of inefficiencies.

There are two other cubes that comprise **low and high qualities** (of inputs or systems) that respond to the combinations ($y1$, $x3$, $z2$) or also to that of ($y3$, $x1$, $z2$). In practice, the carryover effect mentioned above derived from combinations of high and low qualities, although thanks to favorable management, they could generate initial intermediate results ($z2$), in the long run, it will be difficult for them to remain at second level, and it will be very likely that the cubes of such combinations descend to the foreground of inefficiencies.

Here, it is also worth highlighting the same comment noted above regarding the restrictions of unequal combinations of inputs and systems. However, its inertial tendency towards descent to the foreground does not rule out that, due to factors related to efficient executive management, the possibility could arise in one of the five cubes described, either to remain firm at this second level and to lay the foundations for his later promotion.

Secondly, we have a combination that is also unequal but with the presence of medium-quality inputs ($y2$) with high-quality business systems ($x3$). Here a correlation of contradictory forces will predominate and will end up complicating the ascent to a higher stage. Therefore, regardless of whether the business systems that make up the black box were configured in terms of high or satisfactory quality, the permanence of medium-quality inputs will play an unfavorable drag role in the combination process that will lead to results of medium efficiency (z2) and prevent any ascent.

This new cube resulting from the mixed combination (y2, x3, z2) will be added to the medium efficiency cube initially described (y2, x2, z2). Such a cube, also of medium efficiency, will be represented on the "x" axis but at the second level and towards the right side of the yellow cube. For simplicity we have omitted to represent said cube in the average efficiency graph to expose only the most representative cube.

We have another variant of this combination of medium with high qualities, but this time, it includes high-quality inputs (y3) with medium-quality business systems (x2). In this combination, we maintain the before-working hypothesis. That is, the presence of medium-quality business systems constitutes unfavorable elements that promote a correlation of forces with a tendency towards deterioration or defection and prevent promotion to a higher stage. Therefore, regardless of the satisfactory quality of the inputs, the permanence of medium-quality business systems will have a role in driving results that fall within the framework of mediocrity (z2).

This mixed combination (y3, x2, z2) also adds another new cube of medium efficiency represented on the "y" axis at the second level and towards the left side of the yellow cube previously indicated. The two lateral cubes (of medium and high qualities) that we have just described, together with the yellow cube initially presented, determine what we could call a **"platform of medium efficiencies."** It must be recognized that the companies that make up this intermediate results platform are better equipped and have better attributes than those described in the combinations described in the first-level inefficiency cubes.

This allows them to have a greater degree of freedom to take advantage of situations that may favor them, and therefore, they have greater permanence in the market and have a greater capacity to withstand the difficulties of their business coexistence. Despite this, as they normally "live from day to day," their greatest risk comes from the shocks of changing environments, sudden crises, or facing emergency situations for which they are not sufficiently prepared. For this reason, the unequivocal and endemic mediocrity that characterizes them, together with the accumulation of their own instabilities, can make them prone to the risk of falling toward the level of inefficiencies.

We are left with a final combination of this second plane that comprises combinations of high-quality of inputs and high or excellent quality of systems but with medium management results (y3, x3, z2). This unique case would correspond to management defections or ineptitude or management that wastes the valuable resources available due to management inability, corruption deviations, or ineptitude in handling emergency situations. For all these reasons, the company that presents this combination remains at that second level due to management problems and will be added to the platform of companies with medium efficiency.

3. Finally, we enter the terrain of **high and satisfactory qualities**.

The representative combination of this is (y3) and (x3), where both the inputs and the business systems that make up the black box are of optimal and satisfactory quality.

On this occasion, the combination is complemented by efficient management developed in satisfactory parameters, which will generate a relationship between favorable elements or forces and will feed back with reciprocal strengthening effects. The interacting elements (inputs and systems) are related, harmonized, and function correctly. Therefore, they constitute a correlation of synergistic forces that, accompanied by satisfactory management, generate a result that can be greater than the sum of the parts.

Chart N° 8: Total Efficiency

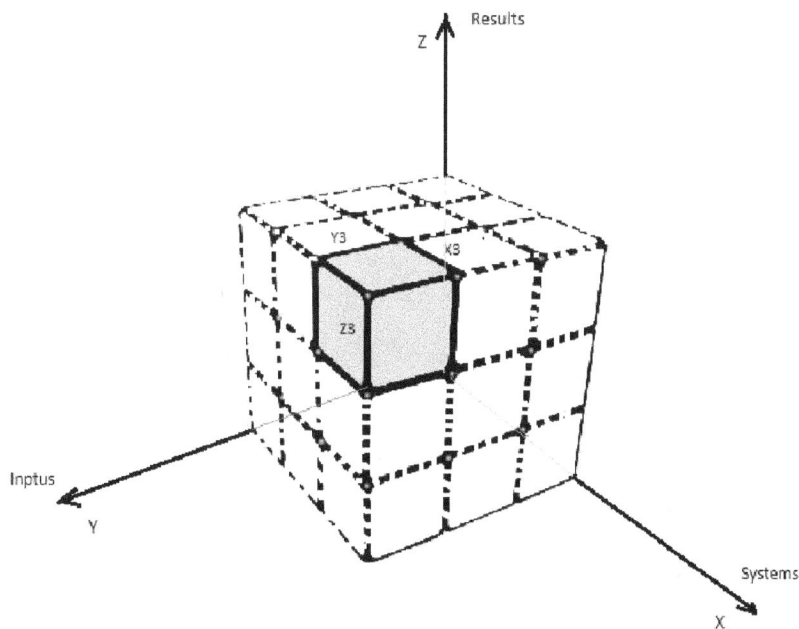

186

The three-dimensional Chart Nº. 8 shows the **"total efficiency cube."** It is represented by the sides (y3,) (x3) (z3) and is in a diagonal direction opposite to the vertex of the total inefficiency cube (y1) (x1) (z1) initially described. Furthermore, it is located on the third level and at the highest level of efficiency. One and only one combination, corresponding to the use of inputs and business systems of optimal and satisfactory quality (y3 and x3) with efficient management results (z3). Indeed, doing things in the best way or correctly (meaning satisfactory quality) does not offer anything new, but despite this, even though everyone knows and accepts it, not everyone has the predisposition and conviction to do it, and not all those who decide to do it could achieve it.

The interrelation of high-quality levels of inputs and systems will fuel high quality and probability of satisfactory results. We must emphasize that we are referring to results in terms of efficiency, that is, doing things correctly or doing them correctly. The results in terms of effectiveness have to do with other factors described in the previous chapters.

It should be noted that the total efficiency graph is represented by a figure like that of the well-known magic cube, made up of a type of 27 dice, of which only one of them corresponds to the total efficiency graph. But it must be admitted that configurations different from the one presented may occur depending on how we relax some implicit assumptions. For example, the qualities between inputs and systems can correspond indistinctly in different dimensions of magnitude and time. If so, the represented cube and its respective dice could present amorphous figures, more elongated in height, length, and width, which, in the present analysis we have discarded for simplicity.

Companies immersed in this efficiency cube "make excellence their modus operandi" not only in the implementation and conduct of important and priority tasks such as, for example, operational systems that define production lines, marketing strategies, and policy execution, financing, and credits, etc. but also those minimal and detailed tasks that complement any simple or even routine procedure, such as for example, courtesy and diligence in baggage reception (hotels or airlines), personalized attention to customer preferences and complaints, ex-post monitoring of the customer's opinion on the quality of the service or product received, etc. The companies included in this cube pay special attention to the quality of input in use, to the maintenance and improvement of their business systems and to the ongoing training of the personnel involved in them.

The notable benefits of operating efficiently are, among others:

- Contribution to the stability and/or rationalization of costs and expenses.

- Stability and financial planning: Skillful management of deficit and/or surplus flows, short and long-term financing strategies, etc.

- Consolidation of business strengthening and sustainability of the company through obtaining added values, management of product or service life cycles, technological innovation, daily monitoring of clients, the market and environments, etc.

- Sustained growth in operational results: operational volume, operational income, profits, etc.

- Stability and/or growth in market share: number of clients, market niches, new and external markets, satisfied consumers, etc.

By these last two benefits exposed, it is understood why and how the fruits of efficiency, with its instruments, result in and impact effectiveness scenarios. But with the differentiation, they respond to varied factors mentioned above that are related to the Strategy, Leadership, and Organizational Culture platform.

In confirmation that "nothing is free," that there is no free lunch, and that every benefit has its price, the route to reaching the peak of business efficiency is difficult and requires a lot of effort and sacrifice, but once achieved, it is more difficult to stay there. For now, it is important to mention that the mere fact of living in this cube demands constant efficiency and calisthenics, not only on the part of the management body but also on the entire company's staff.

The eight cubes that accompany the total efficiency cube on the third-level platform also deserve a separate comment. What happens in these cases? Each of these eight cubes has the advantage of having a high-quality component (inputs or systems) combined with remaining elements of medium or low quality. However, these are cubes that are located at the closest level and on the way to becoming total efficiency cubes. The only possibility that the effects of unfavorable carryovers will be blocked is that an efficient management process has been developed together with skillful management that will have a leverage function to remain at that third level of high efficiencies, otherwise, they will also decline.

188

The comment made above deserves to be reinforced about what we consider this "manager's ability." When faced with differentiated conditions between low, medium, and high qualities of inputs or systems, he manages to surprise by generating unexpected but satisfactory results. They are those managers who, with scarce, modest, and deteriorated resources, produce an optimal articulation that gives rise to synergistic effects where more is achieved than the sum of its parts or more is also achieved with fewer (or reduced) components.

These "efficient management architects" know how to relate the pieces of their puzzle and ensure that companies at that first level of inefficiencies advance towards the second level of intermediate efficiencies, and when they manage companies at the second intermediate level, they combine their management with discipline to lead them towards the desired third level. Once there, not everything is said, and they must make the appropriate adjustments and finishing touches to direct them toward the cube of total efficiency.

So, the first lesson that those who reach levels of excellence learn **is not to let their guard down**. Any neglect of performance, relaxation of standards and prerequisites of efficiency, overconfidence, etc., will mean that the risk of any unequal combination of qualities arises. This imbalance, for the reasons explained above, can cause them to descend towards the area we call the "platform of intermediate efficiency," or even if it persists and the appropriate corrections are not made, it could descend to the inner level of the "fence of inefficiencies."

3.2.2 Determinants of Efficiency

The elements that typify an efficiency process are of a varied nature and we wanted to present them under categories that are related to the efficiency topic presented here and which we will review immediately.

Chart N° 9: Efficiency Components

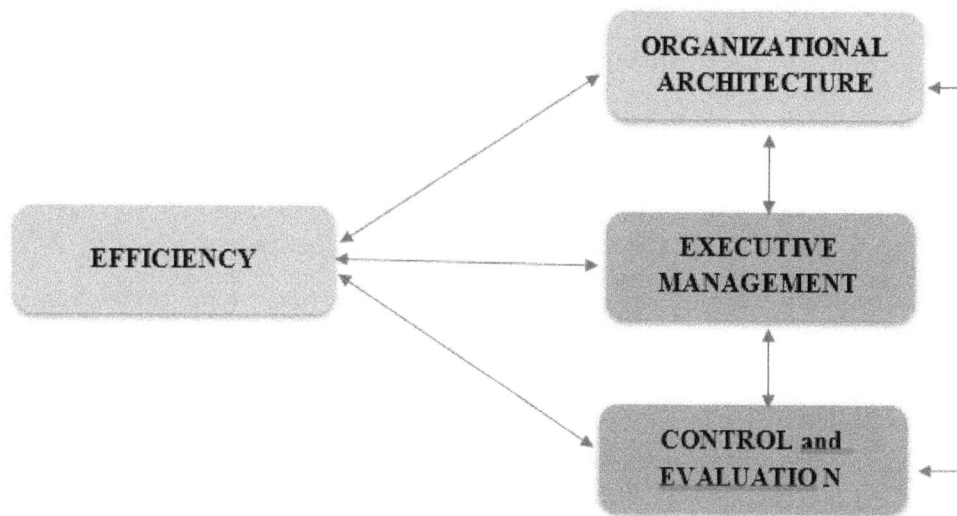

3.2.2.1 Organization

The first thing we must point out regarding this organizational component is that it should not be misinterpreted as the simple arrangement of a business organization chart (which we will discuss later). The component presented here is much more than that. This item includes the development and implementation of those favorable conditions for the beginning of the Implementation. Here, the support structure for the desired change must be formed, that is, the **organizational architecture** of the company. It is the organizational macrosystem composed of the set of business systems and subsystems that compromise the entire company.

When it comes to a company that is going to start its activities, we are referring to the trial and testing phases until "fine-tuning" the operation of the different inputs and the functionality of the different business systems, namely: Operational System (How will what is planned be produced in the plant?), Commercial System (How will what is produced be sold in the market? Administrative and Financial System, Planning System, Information and Network System, etc. In the case of a company in progress, it will have to be organized and coordinated how to conduct the changes and reforms in the respective areas and activities previously identified.

We define a **System** as the arrangement of elements, resources of any kind, actions, ideas, and information that have the particularity of interacting with each other to generate what will be a product for the same system or an input for another system. The quality of what the system generates, the adequate opportunity, and forms of interconnection, communication, and coordination will affect (favorably or unfavorably) the functioning of both the system itself and the system(s) with which it is interconnected or related. The efficient functioning of a system is not an end but a means or management tool.

The systems will be formed by answering the question: How to do things correctly in this area of the organization? The structuring of business systems and subsystems is a kind of "tailor-made suit-making" according to each user (companies) and will vary depending on the line of business, the size of the organization, technological availability, and the business cycle, the economic situation, budget limitations, etc.

For the purposes of this document, we will understand **Processes** to be the combined set of actions that, corresponding to different systems, interrelate and interact to enable the achievement of the company's goal activities, which are the production and sale of a good or provision of a service. The Processes answer the question of what things to do in this system and in its interrelation with the rest of the systems with which it is contacted. For example, the computer system, in addition to the elements that make it up, has the peculiarity of receiving and providing information connected in networks and processes with the rest of the systems (commercial, financial, logistics, etc.) with which it is related.

Procedures, in our category of analysis, correspond to the ordered group of specific actions that enable the achievement of a specific objective. Such procedures are included in both the Systems and the Processes, but while in the Systems, the procedures and their components are developed entirely within it, in the Processes, such procedures and their components are developed by reinforcing linkages and interactions between production activities and different systems.

For example, there will be procedures included within the Operational System, and they are made up of a set of technical-operational activities limited to the scope of said System and that makes its operation possible. There will also be procedures included in Operational connection processes with activities of different systems and yield a specific result within the general linkage of the organization.

Parallel to the above, the organizational architecture must include the choice of an organizational structure that will be the framework where the systems will function. Said structure, in addition to contemplating and obeying the characteristics and restrictions included in each system, must be sufficiently compatible with the desired change and flexible to adapt to future adjustments. The chosen structure will be made up of its respective management, line, and support bodies and will have the profile and levels that senior management decides. In this, it must be considered that there is no "ideal organizational structure" that is the object of tracing. It will accompany the chosen structure - as well as the different business systems - their respective Organization and Function Manuals, Regulations, as well as the Standards, Procedures, and Policies as the case may be (payment, collection, inventory policies, and others).

Another of the basic aspects that will be defined in this organizational phase will be the legal makeup of the organization. There are variants that range from the simple individual limited liability company to the large corporation such as a public limited company. Each one has particular and specific rights, responsibilities, and functionalities regarding tax, accounting, operational issues, responsibility of directors, etc., that are established before the organization is launched. Like the organizational structure, the defined legal structure does not have to be a "straitjacket" since, according to the experience and evolution of the company, it can vary and adapt to the most convenient changes. When it comes to specific matters (tax, labor, planning, etc.), the small or large organization must have adequate professional advice, whether permanent or temporary.

The organizational landscape should also allow us to have a structured "Company Policy," which responds to monitoring and treatment of that part of "external clients": suppliers of inputs, parts, and pieces, and other services, and commercial, financial, and tax creditors. A good part of what is called efficient working capital management (credit from suppliers, promotional lines of bank financing, taking advantage of tax advantages, etc.) comes from the optimal management of the items described above. We reiterate that in this part, the policies and processes are defined and organized, but their management and implementation correspond to the heading of Management explained below.

Since the time factor is one of the scarcest for the management, a recommended way to organize the work of the general manager and area managers is to conduct a schedule of their various activities. A simple and practical way to do this is with the help of the well-known Gantt charts. When things are good and effective, they last. Henry Gantt, a little over a century ago

(1913), proposed this tool that has become more sophisticated with the use of the modern computer but maintains its principles.

Using this diagram, a detail of the activities and resources that will be developed to achieve a specific result is made on the vertical axis on the far left. On the horizontal axis, the time (weeks, months, quarters) of the beginning, development, and end of the activities described above are programmed. This diagram is usually accompanied by the specifications of those responsible and the classification of the activity (for example, it could be an activity that is a prerequisite for the start of another or requires simultaneous or parallel coordination with another activity). With the current technological support of the well-known application software called Microsoft Project, the task described is strengthened.

Additionally, independently, professionals or technicians involved in initial tasks of implementing processes and procedures proceed to organize their tasks in what is called a "pending list," or they also tend to use the useful "aide-memoire" to facilitate the coordination and assignment of assigned tasks.

Finally, the organizational actions described should extend to preparing the organization of those other components that make up the Effectiveness theme. Given that, as indicated before, the respective Leadership Plans and the Organizational Culture Plan will already be formulated, we will begin by appointing those responsible - within the company - and respective work teams that will conduct and adjust the activities previously designed in the areas of Leadership and Organizational Culture.

The tasks involved in these leadership and culture activities will be new or unprecedented for many companies, and the shortage of specialists in the subject means additional tasks to those normally conducted unless specialists in the subject are hired. This could imply that at the beginning the personnel involved notice what we have called "resistance to change." In staff participation, it will be relevant to find ways to guide, motivate, and incentivize them.

Throughout this organizational phase, as noted before, tight budgets and time restrictions will force gradual advances. It must be kept in mind that the undesirable, but necessary "organizational bureaucracy" must start from the simplest and gradually and, according to needs, advance towards the most complex. In the case of small businesses, this last recommendation is a necessity.

3.2.2.2 Direction

The previous Organization phase will have made it possible to conceptually design and formulate the tasks to be undertaken, the individual managers, teams and organizational areas in charge of executing said tasks, as well as defining the functionalities of the business systems and processes. After that, the development of this other macrosystem continues, which is the execution or management of activities aimed at starting, modifying, improving, or strengthening business activity. That is, we are referring to the direction phase, management itself, that involves purely executive tasks of launching the continuous operation of the company or organization.

Among the first issues that management will face will be to resolve the gap between what it needs and the resources it has for it. This will mean defining the initial dimensioning of the organization, determining priorities, and scheduling gradual steps in the process. According to this and knowing its budgetary restrictions, it will define which and how resources – human, material, financial, technological – it will require for the beginning of the management. The optimal quantity and quality of such resources are related to the volume of activity desired, to the particularities of the product (or products) to be developed or service to be provided, and, of course, will determine the limits of quantity, quality of inputs, equipment, and systems to be implemented.

It must be kept in mind that the implementation or management of business systems such as operational, commercial, IT support, financial, administrative, logistical, and other systems will be adjusted to the particularities of each company's line of business, its size, access to available equipment and technologies, the training and experience of the selected personnel, the availability of financial resources, market rigidities, and other details specific to each reality. It would, therefore, be extensive to refer to describing the particularities of every one of the aspects related to this directive phase for different business realities, but it is also worth reviewing specific aspects that must be included in any Directorate.

What is the basic condition to achieve efficient Management?

It is often stated that the most important capital in any company or organization is its human capital. The suitability of said human capital will provide management with adequate direction and clarity regarding both "What things to do" to achieve effectiveness and to define "How to do such things" to achieve efficiency. That is why we emphasize that one of the important issues for achieving efficient management is the careful and strict selection of personnel. **The capacity and**

experience of the management team and the accompanying technical staff will be crucial in any start-up or management development stage. For this reason, we reiterate not so much the individualized importance of the manager or leader but the presence of a body of executive leaders who will be key in the results to be achieved and because they are directly responsible for the implementation and launching of processes and activities of the entire system of business systems and activities.

The lack of suitability, the influence of traditional recommendation, and favoritism will make the selection of human resources defective at all levels (executives, middle managers, and workers in general), which puts at risk the quality of competent and efficient management. This deficiency is much more latent in cases of small and medium-sized companies and is quite critical in cases of companies dedicated to providing services, where the performance of human resources is key, and errors in this matter translate into poor results in the short term.

Organizations and companies that ensure suitable personnel, in terms of capacity and experience, will be more likely to offer and guarantee competitiveness in their production process or service provided. If there is a shortage of qualified personnel or there are budget constraints, a basic training program must be considered to prepare those personnel who are still unprepared. It goes without saying that if, in addition to hiring personnel lacking honesty, training is not provided, the costs of inefficiencies will be appreciable (repetition of processes, greater uses, and costs of inputs, wasted man-hours, delays in procedures, high percentages of products, defective processes, and services, bottlenecks throughout processes and procedures, high level of complaints and returns, etc.).

Despite the warning that generalized savings in human resources are not a good advisor and that the quality of personnel exposes companies and organizations to undesirable and frequent risks of inefficiencies; the common mistake begins with wanting to save on salary expenses and thereby sacrifice quality in the services contracted, especially in key positions. In the end and as always, cheap is expensive.

This misleading and false short-term savings in human resources will have repercussions on the company itself when, in the short term, it remains involved in a context of suffocating mediocrity and inefficiency due to the inability to solve daily problems and when in the medium and long term it faces limited possibilities of survival due to not having a team capable of facing changes, undertaking innovations and managing contingencies. This problem has been clearly defined by the companies that market their franchises, and to counteract it, they have scheduled and demanded from the franchise acquirer the obligation of prior and strict theoretical-practical training of the personnel they hire before starting their daily work.

The qualification of human resources takes us back to a delicate topic of structural limitation in developing countries, which is the shortage of technically qualified labor. This brings to the fore the political responsibilities of technical and professional educational systems of public and private entities of questionable quality and out of date with what their reality demands.

In summary, human resources will underpin efficient management to the extent that their suitability and competitiveness are acquired and maintained. Which will depend on your qualifications and training that is in no way sporadic or occasional but rather as renewed and permanent as possible. This competitive and valued human resource is what we recognize as part of the guarantees of efficiency achievements. The other important part will be given by the contribution to the productivity of this human resource, where labor ingenuity is enhanced with the appropriate material and technological resources that will multiply their capacity to contribute to the production cycle.

Which business systems and activities can be considered essential "central axes," and which constitute "gears" of peripheral character and support?

It is necessary to take this differentiation into account, but the recognition of differentiated functionalities of systems or processes should not determine a certain preferential bias or disadvantage of attention between them because the operation of the business machinery requires harmonization, coordination, and complementarity between both types of systems. (axle systems and gear systems). Both will require an appropriate type of attention, care, and monitoring, and the specific circumstances will determine their priority. This factor is a source of frequent disputes and disagreements between managers of areas that require the greatest and prompt allocation of resources for their land. General management, as part of knowing how to manage internal diversity, will have to be decisive and define, based on the interests of the company, the corresponding order of priorities.

The Operational System has the important responsibility of developing the content, composition, quality, and other characteristics of the product or service that the company offers to customers. Quality processes began in this system, and it is the one where technological advances are usually at the forefront. Whether it is an industrial, mining, agricultural, commerce, financial services, or other company, the layout of the plant and infrastructure, machinery, and technical equipment will be decisive and will mark the difference and typification of its operational performance. Additionally, the human resources required in any operational system is quite particular and demanding in terms of technical qualification due to the strategic importance that this area has within the organization. For example, in companies like Microsoft, the need to have highly competitive professionals in the IT area has even forced the demand for foreign professionals to incorporate them into their organization in this field.

The Commercial System is another important pillar of the company whose function is the placement of the product or service to the consumer public and thereby facilitates not only the important recycling of financial resources towards the company, but also establishes a presence in the market. Therefore, its function is projected beyond the important task of selling to understand broader criteria within the conception and activities of marketing (place, product, price, promotion).

This commercial area, in its desire to form its own army or sales force for its product or service, usually undertakes training processes on a regular basis that demand time and permanent costs. The remuneration of this sales force is based on a policy of commissions on sales made (remuneration according to results). Since performance standards are demanding, a good contingent does not meet them and must be replaced, which is why there is usually a high degree of turnover in this type of personnel. Companies in the financial sector (commercial banks, mutual funds, insurance companies) are a clear example of this.

In every company, there are areas such as administration, finance, IT, logistics, human resources, quality control, and others whose function is to provide support to the areas described above. We have previously highlighted the importance of its functionality not only because of how essential its complementarity with the rest of the systems is to achieve satisfactory management but also because the notorious cases of defections, irregularities, and other setbacks and corruption described in previous chapters frequently originate and development (although not exclusivity) in the inefficient development of these support areas.

In this complexity of business management, how to efficiently manage transversal factors included in various internal systems and processes? One of the controversial aspects in terms of task execution are those that demand beyond individual or group commitment within the same functional area, coordination, and intertwined sequences of activities between different areas. This gives rise to frequent friction, conflicts, and bottlenecks in business operations. All of this translates into inefficiencies and increased costs when such dysfunctions are not corrected adequately and in a timely manner.

The better the activities, processes, and systems described in the previous phase (Organization) have been defined and programmed, the less will be the misunderstandings, the gaps or voids of unforeseen sequences, and the discretionary margins that give rise to different and even contrary interpretations (in the current Execution phase). The proper order, standardization, fluid sequence, compatibility, and integration of the different areas and systems will make the entire company function as an orchestrated concert. The establishment of intra- and inter-area meetings and the management and leadership of multidisciplinary work teams are an advisable alternative to partially solve the problems. The leadership referred to in this part includes not only Senior Management but also middle management.

To reinforce its efficiency standards, senior management usually uses two management mechanisms. **Decentralization and deconcentrating**. Through decentralization, authority (and the power that this entails) is distributed to different areas and levels of the hierarchy (Divisions, Management, Deputy Management, Departments, etc.). Depending on the complexity of the organization, there will be diverse levels of decentralization. In small or medium-sized companies, decentralization completed by the management team will be sufficient. In larger companies, it will be necessary to extend decentralization to lower hierarchical levels or different regions and, if necessary, establish specific representatives. The delegation of authority is assigned to decision-making matters in the specific field that corresponds with the consequent commitment to inform and account for it. When the latter is ignored, it gives rise to deviations, excesses, abuses, and even illicit derivations. The casuistry of corruption cases for this reason is frequent.

Through the second mechanism, deconcentrating, the apex of the organization (general manager) proceeds to delegate functions, responsibilities, and tasks (but not authority or power) to the different areas, levels, or people of the organization. This mechanism responds to the need to alleviate the burden of tasks and responsibilities that usually clutter the general manager's desk. Again, in small and even medium-sized companies, there is a defective tendency to concentrate an enormous number of tasks at the top of the organization because the manager-owner of the business wants "everything to pass through his hands." The absence of delegation of tasks tends to blur your focus and neglect what is most important because you become distracted by tasks that you could well delegate and only ask for accountability.

In small businesses, it is common for the owner to be the central axis of the operational function because he normally has the qualifications, experience, and mastery of the most relevant technical qualities of the business line (mechanic, cook, merchant, independent professional). The bias and attachment to this function that you know the most and dominate determines your tendency to centralize tasks and your unwillingness to delegate responsibilities. In other cases, this overload leads him to neglect or ignore other responsibilities that are as much and even (in certain situations) more decisive than the operational activity that he dominates.

What aspects complement an efficient Management?

Given that the different tasks and activities, even those carried out with the help of equipment and automated machinery, are executed, controlled, and coordinated by and between people, aspects related to <u>communications</u>, interrelationships, their forms, and styles require considerations that they go beyond the regulations, a "very sui generis fine-tuning touch" that under any cover, <u>be it motivational stimulation, be it mutual respect, good treatment between supervisor and supervisee</u>, be it by delegation of responsibilities, or by consideration of executing risky activities, whether due to the perception of mutual trust, or any other factor; all of this gives the employee the willingness to carry out his task efficiently and at the same time the satisfaction of knowing he is recognized.

The activities in this execution phase correspond to short-term periods, and in daily actions, it must be kept in mind that in parallel, those activities that correspond to <u>longer-range processes must be prepared and executed</u>, such as those related to research activities and development, business intelligence, plant expansion projects, etc.

Finally, the actions of the Execution phase should not be limited to the conventional plan of the Business Strategy previously designed but must also conduct the execution and implementation of processes and activities in the other components of the Effectiveness topic. That is the execution of the already formulated Leadership Plans and the Organizational Culture Plan.

How to conduct efficient Direction?

Again, we say there is no magic formula nor the best recipe. Detailing a single and specific path would be fruitless, and each manager will have to find his way out according to his situation. There may be similar situations, but each reality has its own starting point, its own goal, and route. Even for that specific situation, there will be different solutions because imagination and creativity have no limits and as the saying goes: "different roads lead to Rome" (there are diverse ways and means to reach the objectives and goals).

In this "executive" stage, it is crucial that first, the problems of "resistance to change" that we described before are satisfactorily overcome. In this regard, management must probe and know the idiosyncrasies, culture, and values predominant in its organization. You must also identify conflicts of interest and circles or groups of formal and informal powers to perceive the open or covert boycott of the proposed changes. Finally, in your direct contact with the staff you must explore and draw your conclusions regarding the integration, mystique, and commitment of the workers with respect to the organization's objectives.

Additionally, we must face those difficulties that we previously called "transition problems". These problems, as we pointed out, are a direct function of the level of relative development of the organization and function of the magnitude of the desired change. If it is considered that in the case of quite ambitious projects and programs, it is recommended to address it through a gradual strategy and in stages of annual or biannual periods.

We must consider that in the management of a company, you cannot "burn through stages" and the achievements and difficulties of the various stages of Implementation must be assimilated. In this, it must be recognized that among the main limitations of this phase are, on the one hand, the limited availability of human, material, and financial resources and, therefore, there is always the restriction of being able to count on them in the required quantity and opportunity (especially in small companies).

The Implementation phase will evaluate management capacity in its crucial executive phase. This difficult and delicate task will involve managerial talent so that, in response to internal and external constraints, senior management knows how to resolve and articulate their knowledge, experience, and management style to "produce" efficient and effective management. This talent and managerial skill are what allow us to succeed in the face of unpredictable events that always occur and affect the company and allow the organization the security and confidence to take on the challenge of change.

Just as the good rider knows the virtues and defects of his horses, he knows the routes and their dangers, he will know how to direct them, he will know how to "temper the reins", how to lead them on flat roads and on winding and steep paths, he will know how to rein in and how to by correcting your deviations at the right times, you will know how to recognize and what to do when your horses feel like running or trotting, when they are hungry and thirsty, and when they are exhausted and need rest. Likewise, a good organizational manager must know, understand, and perceive the situation of his company, the expectations and limitations of his staff. He must know how to choose where to go and how to arrive at his destination, how to make the necessary adjustments, to arrive healthy and safe, satisfied with the task accomplished, and ready to embark on a new journey.

3.2.2.3 Control and Evaluation

This component describes activities that aim to obtain an adequate measurement of business performance. This measurement may correspond during the execution of the management phase or when a pre-established chronological cycle (quarter, semester, year) has ended. It must be evaluated whether the path taken allows us to get closer or further away from the established goal. The manager forms a judgment about the quality of the partial or total results. If he recognizes what has been achieved as satisfactory, he will set new goals or, depending on the time horizon, he will continue to reinforce and make appropriate adjustments so as not to lose sight of achieving the desired goals.

In the event of an insufficient or unfavorable result, the activities undertaken must be reviewed and evaluated from the perspective of how efficiently they have been conducted. It should also be examined whether other means or methods could have offered better results. Finally, instead of questioning or abandoning the established goals, it is necessary to evaluate whether, during unforeseen circumstances or unpredictable emergency situations, the organization was not able or was unable to undertake the timely and necessary changes in course.

This Control and Evaluation macro system also has a dual or ambivalent character in the sense that, if we consider an evaluation of what is being achieved "on the progress" and during the execution process itself, adjustments will be determined along the way that do not require waiting for the end of the process. We are interested in highlighting this type of Control and Evaluation as a key task that makes up the Implementation stage because it is a control and monitoring conducted "in situ" (that is, in the same place) that allows adjustments to be made during the same implementation process, avoid detours and correct defects and failures "on the road." When this on-site monitoring is ignored, the severity of failures known after the completion stage are more difficult and costly to correct.

On the other hand, we call the evaluation conducted at the end of the Execution phase "ex-post" evaluation (that is, after the fact), carried out at the end of the realization stage no longer as a field task but as a workshop task. Therefore, it is appropriate to exclude it as a phase belonging to the implementation itself and consider it as part of a subsequent Formulation or, to be more precise, Reformulation. In this case, changes and refinements of processes, systems, people, and methodologies are required for subsequent periods.

In summary, this stage of Control and Evaluation, both the one conducted "in situ" and the one we call "ex-post," are important because it will facilitate the integral feedback of the process, that is, both in its conceptual part (reformulation) and in its executive part (implementation).

A recommended way to conduct these controls and evaluations is to monitor what we previously called the activity schedule. For this monitoring, so-called "Road Maps" are usually used, which contain more detailed information on the set of activities included in each process or procedure, those responsible, and resources committed throughout their execution. The complex nature of simultaneous jobs coming from different departments of the company requires careful management of activities that require parallel or consecutive sequence conditions and prerequisites for others. This involves supervising the order, coordination, and sequence of the tasks undertaken.

It is also worth noting that the manager and bosses must keep in mind the old popular adage: "the eye of the master fattens the cattle" and make effective their own role of control, supervision, and monitoring in specific areas and functions that involve corrective actions against to internal and external changes. As previously stated in the Execution phase, the current Control and

202

Evaluation function will be executed not only at the top management level but also at intermediate and work team levels.

It is always recommended that this control and supervision function be conducted by a person other than the one executing the activity. We must avoid falling into schemes of "being judge and party" that lead to situations of conflict of interest, falsification, or concealment of reality.

Finally, in these Control and Evaluation tasks, the actions should not remain only at the conventional level of the Business Strategy but should also include attention to the fields described above in the topic of Effectiveness, that is, establishing Control and Evaluation. of results in the components of Leadership and Organizational Culture.

Why do we insist on the need for control in an organization?

Because behind any organization are the men who manage and develop it, and in a respectable number of cases, <u>many men, for various reasons and in the absence of control schemes, are prone and vulnerable to defect</u>. The circumstances vary, the protagonists vary, and the environment and times vary, but the motivations and deviations in behavioral patterns are the same. This is human nature, confused and disturbed with old ties (of insatiable search for money, pleasure, power, etc.) that few can unravel and shake off. Unfortunately, there are frequent cases where people become disturbed, debased, clouded, and succumb to or become more entangled in such deviations.

When this disturbed membership penetrates the life of companies, government administrations, political, welfare, cultural, sports institutions, etc., the absence or insufficiency of control, audit, and supervision systems will lead to everything from negligence, irresponsibility to deviations of criminal or corrupt nuances that fit into the cases of organizational defection described in the first chapter.

In effect, what is stated in this section brings us to the frequent conflict of elucidating between personal interest and its compatibility with organizational interest. In terms of business management, one of the common conflicts in a transition process toward successful management is the coupling between the person and the organization. We can refer to such a situation in a similar way to the footwear between foot and shoe. For some people, the defects that the foot already had have ruined the shoe. For others, defects in the model and design of the shoe are what have deformed the foot. For others, walking defects that explain the deformation of the foot and shoe. For others, it has been the mistreatment and poor maintenance given to their shoes or their own feet.

Anyway, we could outline more reasons "why things don't fit well." To prevent this from happening, one of the basic tasks is the establishment of efficient Control and Evaluation systems, but with the aim of finding the right balance for the specific situation of each business reality so that it is not insufficient to generate destabilization and even criminal chaos, nor excessive controls because they are demotivating, cumbersome and end up being breached.

In summary, as has been seen, each of the elements described that constitute the Efficiency platform: Organization, Direction (or executive management), and Control and Evaluation have specific content and their respective importance in each stage of the Implementation process, and they complement each other to achieve what we call "doing things correctly." These factors are the most representative and direct factors of efficiency, and the actions included within each one will affect the result of efficiency achieved, but there are also other specific factors that lead to inefficiencies and, which we describe below.

Chart N° 10 presents a particular idea of how the efficiency components can be related. Through a system of axes and gears, it can be seen, for example, on the left side of the graph that the relationship between the components or support axes (Organizational Architecture and Evaluation) are operated independently to make the central axis (Executive Management) operate in the direction clockwise which in turn complements and reinforces the functioning of the system.

On the right side of the same graph, another form of relationship is shown where there is a direct and simultaneous actuation of the support axis on the central axis (Executive Management) that also causes the actuation of said central axis in a clockwise direction, which also reinforces the functioning of the efficiency system. It should be noted, as explained before, that a dysfunctional or regressive operation could occur in the components of both the support axes and the central axis so that when the direction of the arrows is altered or reversed (due to abnormal reasons of deviation, ineptitude or corruption, the direction of the gears will be altered, causing inefficiencies.

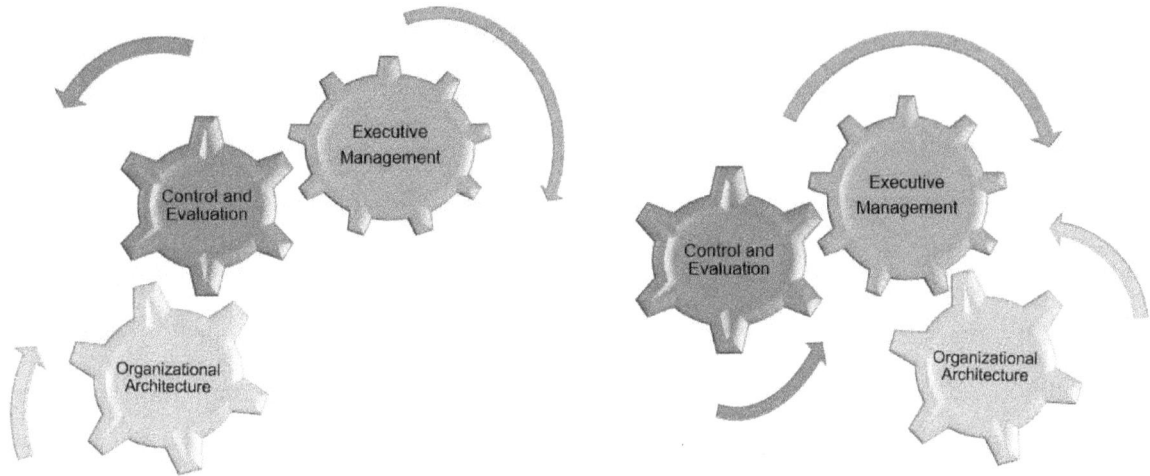

3.2.3 Constraints on Efficiency

In addition to the elements described above in the Implementation process, it is important to consider transversal factors that affect all its components differently. Let us look at some of them.

3.2.3.1 Cognitive Blindness

The term "cognitive blindness" usually refers to certain aspects, problems, or criteria that, in certain circumstances, the managerial body unknown or unaware of, when they recognize them, simply deny or minimize them. Cases of cognitive blindness may occur in the distinct phases included in the implementation: organization, direction or control, and evaluation. Among the various existing cases we are going to refer to two perspectives related to our topic.

1) Cognitive blindness due to efficiency factors

The most widespread cases have to do with inefficiencies that remain hidden by undetected or unknown failures. One can be inefficient, but the management body "does not see" and remains "convinced" that it has proceeded in accordance with scrupulous standards of efficiency when this has not truly been the case. Undetected faults are misleading because they even pass preliminary rehearsal tests. However, it must be kept in mind that, for example, above a certain temperature level (heating or cooling), some parts, its coupling or its operation becomes defective. Machines, equipment, and people do not have the same performance when working at sea level or at 4,000 meters above sea level. The same occurs when, after a certain distance, mileage, or time of use, the manufactured product fails and does not present or maintain the expected resistance or quality standards.

An unfortunate example of this was the detachment of certain high-temperature-resistant ceramic plates that covered part of the exterior of the Challenger shuttle rockets (January 28, 1986) and triggered a fatal accident during its launch into space, a fateful explosive accident where the seven members of the crew lost their lives. The NASA technical staff were convinced that they had taken all necessary precautions and that they proceeded correctly and efficiently during all stages from organization to control and evaluation. Up to this point we consider this case as typical of inefficiency due to cognitive blindness of unknown failures.

However, when we investigated more details about this case, we verified that the example cited goes beyond the framework presented as it is a fact that is flagrantly serious. According to the journalistic article by Francisco Basterra (El País newspaper, Jun 04, 1986), the report - leaked to the press - of the Roger Commission (former Secretary of State) appointed by former President Reagan that investigated said disaster for more than four months (considered the most serious accident in the conquest of space), the accident had to do with negligence and bureaucracy on the part of NASA that allowed the launches to continue without correcting previously known failures. Even three years before the first shuttle launch in 1978 (there is written evidence of such defects known as failed rocket booster joints). This is a clear case of negligence that triggered a reorganization of NASA and confirms what the journalist said, "the story of an accident that did not have to happen."

The specific reference in the article published on the Internet dated June 20, 2022, see: "Challenger space shuttle accident" continues to draw our attention.

(https://es.wikipedia.org/wiki/Accident_del_transbordador_espacial_Challenger).

The Commission determined that it was NASA's organizational culture and decision-making system that contributed to the accident. This accident confirms, according to what is discussed in this study, two causes, one of them due to internal efficiency factors, that is, to the existence of a quality business system related to Management (the one referring to decision making) deficient (technical recommendations from launch engineers were ignored) and the other, to the validity of an organizational culture where the concealment of defects was placed above the will to correct them.

The latter (culture and values that constitute it) is one of the factors that we have already highlighted as keys to effectiveness in the preceding chapter. As we argued before, efficiency and effectiveness are not isolated, so, in this case, they occur in reciprocal and simultaneous affectation. The lack of effectiveness due to the predominance of a deformed organizational culture led to and was reinforced by inefficiencies in the decision-making system.

2) Cognitive blindness due to factors external to the direct context of efficiency

A good number of managers consider that only the efficiency achieved or to be achieved will be sufficient to succeed in this bull of effectiveness (this group makes up the "efficiency current"). For them, the achievement of effectiveness will come of its own weight and as a logical consequence of the implementation of previous efficiency processes. According to this approach, there will be no effectiveness if efficiency is not achieved. If effectiveness is a subsequent achievement of efficiency, there cannot be effectiveness if there was inefficiency before, or cases of combined presence of inefficiency and effectiveness could not arise. When managers of this current are asked about their lack of key aspects of effectiveness (planning, leadership, values), they usually argue: "Neither my company nor my management team requires or needs it." This is a denialist approach to effectiveness as an independent factor since it is always considered dependent on efficiency.

In fact, their positions regarding the three factors described above as key elements of effectiveness are the following:

They accept planning reluctantly and for the simple formula that "the company must have a plan more for display purposes than for execution." For them, the plans are merely theoretical and futuristic speculation of the organization that "are never fulfilled and are of no use." Without doing enough research into why they are not being fulfilled or of no use, your organization's plans are frozen in their formulation phase and accumulate in updated versions that adorn the shelf in the manager's office.

Regarding leadership, they consider that having reached the high positions of their organization and due to the authority and power linked to them, they are fully enabled and automatically converted (he and his team) into leaders.

In the leadership section developed above, we have discussed in greater detail the relationships between leadership, authority, and power. In it became clear that a manager, although usually involved in relationships of authority and power, does not necessarily require such conditions to exercise and make his leadership prevail. Therefore, not all those who possess authority and power are guaranteed leadership, and there are also personalities who are finally recognized as leaders, even if they do not hold managerial positions vested with authority and power.

There is not necessarily a direct correlation between management and leadership. This must be confirmed in practice. The idea is that both complement and reinforce each other, but reality shows us representative cases where this is not necessarily true. Furthermore, the cases in which the arrival to managerial and leadership positions came about using forbidden tricks are illustrative. The serious thing about the above is that the described false perception of leadership is not exclusive to those who consider themselves leaders without being one but also to the biased mass of followers who consider them as such.

Representative examples of "toxic leaders" include Hitler, Stalin, Franco, or those closer to us, such as Pinochet, Videla, Trujillo, Chávez, Maduro, Banzer, Velasco, Noriega, Somoza, Stroessner, and others. Most of them are of military origin and authoritarian profile, with demands and accusations that violate human rights (kidnappings, murders, torture) and with pseudo-tragic later years involved in scandals, illnesses, exiles, and even murders. The end (established unilaterally by them and for the benefit of themselves and their favored circle of relations) justified the means imposed by them (a clean slate to their opponents). It is not difficult to deduce the type of organizational culture and values that predominated in such government administrations.

Regarding organizational culture, they usually have different reactions. In the case of some government administrations and companies, their disdain for issues that they consider accessory or not a priority is reaffirmed. In some cases, it is preferred that the values that make up the culture run through another body of authority and power, which has mostly been the church (in its wide spectrum of creeds and sects). Some authoritarian administrations began allied with the Church, but over time and, as the abuses and corruption increased, these Churches began to express discrepancies to be uncomfortable, and then friction and disagreements occurred.

At a business level, for managers of this current it is in some cases more comfortable to let each person, from their spiritual, religious, or personal perspective, contribute (or support) what they can regarding the issue of values and culture. In other cases, and in recognition of the importance of organizational culture, they consider that it cannot be left to the free will of people, but far from promoting a participatory and voluntarily convincing style, some administrations opt for the extreme of imposing the purest Nazi-style a framework of indoctrination, proselytizing, and propagandism to shore up the support of the masses.

3.2.3.2 Resistance to change.

The situation of resistance to change is one of the main difficulties manifested in the implementation phase. Every process of restructuring, reorganization, and redefinition of procedures and positions involves changes that, to a greater or lesser extent, generate a climate of uncertainty, especially when such changes are imposed from the outside in (or also from the top down). Many people see this as affecting their interests or personal positions, so they react by hindering the proposed projects and doing everything possible to make them fail.

This "overt or covert boycott" is reinforced by the group of people who react negatively due to considerations of insecurity or fear of change. Such people mistakenly believe that they will not be able to respond satisfactorily to the challenge of the greater effort in training and dedication that change demands in their future work, and despite being poorly paid and lacking in preparation, they anecdotally turn out to be the main architects of maintaining the "status quo." of your organization. They apply the motto: "The old known is better than the new unknown."

By putting their personal interests before business interests, such people consciously or unconsciously ignore the advantages of the proposed projects. Therefore, they do not feel identified or committed to the success of such projects or the changes they involve. In such circumstances, there is no teamwork, no mystique, nor work integration because "each one attracts water for his own mill," and the continuous friction and conflict of interests prevail and hinder any improvement that is desired to be implemented.

Thomas J. Peters and Robert H. Waterman Jr., coauthors of the best seller "In Search of Excellence," Harper & Row Publishers, New York, 1982, described that organizations are a kind of creatures of habit that, like people, tend to be strongly influenced by last. Before any change, the company, in fact, has a pre-existing organizational culture, and the set of predominant values and beliefs can be facilitators or detractors of the participation capabilities, the development of the innovative spirit, inventiveness, and creativity of the staff.

Finally, the group of people who could be more receptive to taking on the challenge of change and understanding the benefits of the proposed project are not encouraged to commit to it because those who design and implement it have not contemplated sufficient dissemination or participation schemes or encouragement towards staff. As a tactical approach to the leadership and culture implementation phase, it will be up to management to apply a scheme to enhance those values that facilitate the desired support culture and the defense or shield to counteract anti-values that detract from said culture.

3.2.3.3 Transition problems.

Even in the case that critical cases of cognitive blindness or resistance to change are overcome, every implementation process takes time and resources that are in direct proportion to two factors: From what level do we start, and what is the magnitude of the desired change? How short or long is the route to take?). Once again, specific and unique considerations for each company come into play here, given that the complexity or particularity of the business model, its respective business systems, and its processes to be implemented depend on it.

In addition to what has been described, the main problems of transition towards the proposed models face the following practical difficulties:

- Financial constraints to acquire all the material, equipment, and human resources required by the proposed systems. Financial restrictions are always limiting for any company, even more so when changes are implemented. The availability of financial resources will be decisive in achieving the intensity and speed of such changes.
- Lack of human resources in the quality and quantity necessary to assume the responsibilities derived from the implementation. In developing countries this shortage is very evident and is further deteriorated by the presence of cronyism, corruption, and political favoritism.

- Limitations of available physical infrastructure given that the facilities and equipment are insufficient and obsolete to provide adequate support for the execution of new scheduled activities.

- Organizational difficulties due to lack of adequate regulations and lack of definition of procedures, responsibilities, and communication between areas. The coexistence of old systems but still in force and new systems that are tested and still incomplete generates delays and confusion.

- Different degrees of advancement or development in the different business systems (operational, commercial, administrative support, etc.) to be implemented make their interrelation difficult because they have been conceived and applied in isolation, unilaterally, and on different occasions. There is a lack of a balanced and harmonious balance in its execution.

- Transition problems derived from differentiated executive capabilities and managerial leadership in different areas of the company also deserve to be noted. Managers may have varied knowledge and experience in modified subjects and will have their own conception of diagnosis and solution to the problems raised. Management capacity gives managers a certain margin of discretion to direct what, according to their own criteria, they deem a priority and what is not. Many times, this perception does not necessarily coincide with what is proposed by more neutral entities such as external consultancies. Such discrepancies should be discussed sufficiently until consensus positions emerge and general management finally settles.

- In addition, the style that management imprints on its management plays a separate role, that is, the consensual or authoritarian form, the decentralizing or concentrating form of functions, the reserved and professional profile or that of leadership with overflowing enthusiasm, the preference for imprinting to its management gradual adjustments or rapid changes, the friendly, condescending and warm character or the circumspect, hard and cold behavior with internal clients (staff, shareholders, board of directors) and external clients (consumers, suppliers, distributors, etc.) All this shapes the way of doing things and is decisive in the results achieved.

- It is also worth mentioning problems of discordance between short and long activities term. That is, not all activities that aim at short-term results are necessarily compatible with

211

activities with a long-term time horizon and vice versa. For example, the strategic reformulation of a company may propose a diversification of the production line that implies plant expansion, which represents a committed investment for several years.

If, for his part, the general manager is more focused on achieving economic results (profits) in the short term because he understands that this will bring valid points to his management and to his pocket (to the extent that, as usual, have established benefit packages or bonuses for results achieved), then their orientation to postpone future reinvestments will be obvious. To overcome this conflict in which "the manager cannot be judge and party," it will be up to the Board of Directors to clarify this issue. Otherwise, who controls the controller? Limits must also be set for the manager to avoid involuntary, reckless, arbitrary deviations or where conflicts of interest arise.

The conductor of a symphony orchestra selects the repertoire, prepares scores, structures variants, and arrangements, coordinates the intervention of the different instruments in the various parts of the musical pieces, and after that, develops sufficient rehearsals and adjustments and is finally ready for its performance stellar (there is no room for improvisation!). Only then, with clear mental recognition of its opening, course, and completion, does he prepare to direct the execution of his musical piece, with the help and collaboration of his specialized instrumentalists, for the delight and satisfaction of his audience.

In the same way as the symphony director, general management must execute his management by giving the organizational touches that are required. "Getting the company going" implies that the systems that make up its business engine, such as the commercial system (sales) and, the operational system (production), and the main support systems, have the priority of being fine-tuned and ready to get going. Subsequently, the manager also prepares to carry out sufficient trials, adjustments, and tests and, after that, direct and execute his management with the help and participation of executives from various areas.

From a temporal perspective, three typical moments can be formally distinguished in this implementation phase that compromises efficiency processes: before completion (Organization), during completion (Direction and execution of actions and tasks), and after completion (Control and Assessment). However, we must again point out that we avoid rigid interpretations. That is to say, the exposed sequence helps with its conceptual clarity and logical order, but in the labyrinth of reality and after having started the process according to the established scheme, a different direction could be determined. Accordingly, after initial management periods, on-site evaluations may suggest that, in response to imponderable internal or external problems, management must be readjusted or redirected with different and complementary activities that even imply a certain reorganization and reallocation of resources initially formulated.

This hustle and bustle in the real world and its overwhelming problems constitute the great challenge of this platform of efficiency that the person responsible for any management must navigate. Along this path, he will strengthen his experience with advances and setbacks, with successes and failures that will be indicative of the fulfillment of your purposes.

3.3 KEY SIGNS OF EFFICIENCY. How can we be sure that we are leading and immersed in the path of efficiency?

If we assume that the entire Implementation phase, with its respective stages of organization, execution, control and evaluation, were carried out within satisfactory parameters of efficiency, that is, after doing things correctly and in addition to adequately managing the restrictions described above, several types of effects or symptoms will be distinguished that will allow us to confirm if we are immersed in the correct path of efficiency or if we are deviating from it. Some of these symptoms present quantitative effects that are feasible to measure, and other symptoms are characterized by presenting qualitative effects of notable perception but difficult to measure. Here, we go on to describe them.

Chart Nº 11: Signs of Efficiency

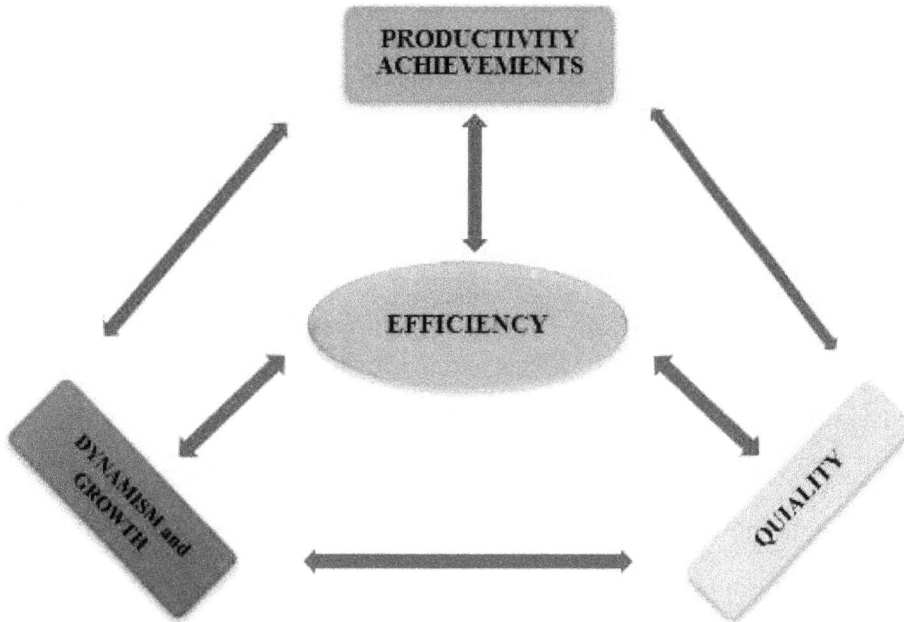

3.3.1 Stable and sustained dynamics: a referential symptom of efficiency.

When things are done correctly, the business engine is tuned, oiled, and prepared to show (and usually does) a performance of continuous, stable, and sustained growth. Production volumes, sales revenue, customers served, market positions worked, workers hired, facilities and material resources used, financial capital used and required, investments and new and complementary projects, etc. Everything is going in harmony and within a notable framework of growth and impressive dynamics. The conventional ratios and indicators to measure this dynamic are easily measurable and quantifiable and are found in all finance texts in the existing literature.

Although business dynamics show positive and advantageous symptoms, caution must be taken regarding growth. Just as driving a car in accelerated gear allows us to quickly arrive at our destination, such accelerated driving also presents unavoidable risks such as unexpected loss of control, the inexperience of the driver, appearance of unforeseen events on the road, overheating of the machine, lack of knowledge of complicated characteristics route (curves, detours, winding roads, speed bumps and potholes), lack or poor signage and lights, etc. Business management must be sufficiently cautious to consider its accelerated growth and know how and when to slow down according to the internal or external circumstances or restrictions that arise in its path.

Growth, just because it is such, is not necessarily beneficial and a priority; in certain cases, it is inappropriate. For the same reason, any slowdown, pause, or even decrease is not harmful and can be timely and convenient. For example, if the company and its main activity are in a life cycle where they have already surpassed their introduction and growth phase and are in a maturity and/or decline phase, accelerating the pace of growth can lead to an undesirable overturn stock due to placement difficulties with the consequent extra costs that this entails. It would rather be advisable to slow down (liquidate inventories, attend to order sales, reduce shifts, etc.) until reorienting or defining a new marketing strategy.

In fact, it can be recognized that business management is preferable when its dynamics present stable and sustained growth instead of unstable growth or even decline. But how to achieve this sustained and controlled driving without losing that satisfactory growth rate? Here, several factors come into play, among which we can highlight innovation, creativity, adaptation to modern technologies, market monitoring and others. Indeed, in the introduction and growth cycles, it was necessary to take advantage of this boom phase and have the greatest possible growth and generate attractive levels of profits and profitability. But in the subsequent phases of maturity and decline, the way to reverse product depletion in the market is through product innovation that meets the variability of consumer preferences.

For example, the predominant trend in these times regarding body care and health has forced the competitive soft drink industry that Coca-Cola and other competing firms, in addition to offering their leading product, classic Coca-Cola (which surely must have shown drops in consumption compared to the body care fashion), was forced to offer the variants: Coca Cola Diet, Coca Cola Zero (calories), Coca Cola Lime, Lemon and Vanilla, Berry, Coca Cola without caffeine. In addition, to also offer drinks linked to its brands, such as Sprite, Seagram's, Lemonade, Minute Maid (fruit), Powerade (sports), Dasani (table water) and others. Its main competitor, Pepsi-Cola, has done the same.

The McDonald's chain criticized for providing "junk food" had to sharpen its market focus and meet the demand for light or vegetarian food and complement itself with a salad menu and previously non-existent soft drink variants: coffees in varied styles, frozen drinks, and continue with the success of food packages for children (happy meal) and entertainment (playground) for them. In these cases, and in others (Toyota, General Electric, Apple, Samsung, Bayer, Hilton, etc.),

215

there has been a creative and even ingenious response from management to quickly adjust to the new winds of the market without losing the representativeness and essence of the business.

The above corresponds to strategies to counteract or foresee the imminent advent of an unfavorable life cycle. Failure to undertake such innovations in a timely manner would have meant a decrease in its market share, a decrease in its dynamism and in its income.

In many cases, prudence recommends keeping business operations "at a minimum," that is, a level of operation that covers fixed costs. Even if this is not possible, companies are swept away by the crisis. If, on the other hand, it manages to "shelter itself from the storm," remain at minimum speed and cover the costs fixed and up to a part of its variable costs; You will have done what is advisable to stay afloat and face a less harmful environment in the future. If we had to judge this company only based on the growth achieved due to its minimal operation, we would have disqualified it. For this reason, we title this section: Stable and sustained dynamics: a **referential symptom of efficiency**.

Another unfortunate case is what we conceptualize as "overheating of the business machinery." When we refer to the term "machinery," we are not only referring to fixed assets (plant, machinery, equipment, and other material resources) but also to other resources (technological, financial and, of course, human resources). In effect, business efficiency will be lost if, to maintain high growth, we drive the business machinery at a forced pace. Maintaining high growth rates over extended periods (more than seven years) is very difficult and often risky. Machinery and equipment, material and human resources wear out, and the law of diminishing returns will be felt, reducing the ability to generate favorable results. If we add to this the lack of an adequate maintenance culture for said "machinery," its main axes, parts, gears, and interrelationships are going to break down, then by wanting to grow more, we lose efficiency and end up growing less.

Here, what is convenient is even a reduction or paralyzation of business operations or those required parts. However, we must recognize that there are companies that cannot afford to stop and have replacement equipment planned. It is highly recommended because it guarantees scheduled maintenance to areas or equipment that are overused. Carrying out a kind of comprehensive "Overhaul" of machinery, systems, and business processes, like the comprehensive maintenance that airlines carry out with their aircraft after having traveled a certain number of miles, has undeniable advantages.

The term "stoppage" should not be interpreted "totally" because the company could schedule, during this period of stoppage, an event for celebration and awards for goals and achievements, redefinition of business strategy (global and for each department) or consolidation and adjustment of the business culture. That is, "paralyzation" must be conceived, as noted at the beginning of this essay (Page 1), as strategic pauses for rethinking and does not necessarily involve "non-productive" or lost time.

An illustrative case regarding the issue of how to manage business dynamics with technological adaptation and market sensitivity was what happened in the entertainment industry and within it to the video movie rental service of the Blockbuster chain. At the beginning of this century, it was the undisputed leader of its market, with thousands of retail establishments in the USA and the rest of the world, millions of customers, enviable operational efficiency and large marketing budgets and expenses. His competition at that time, the small firm Netflix, avoided the excessive costs of retail distribution establishments, ventured through its online platform and under the concept of subscriptions (not rental), offering an interesting variety of movies that began to distribute at significantly lower costs and free of the annoying late delivery charges.

Netflix deepens its computer operations by strengthening its online subscription at a low monthly cost of nine dollars by offering movie packages with a wide variety (almost 100 options) renewed periodically. Their online movie deliveries overcame the difficulty of delays experienced by mail deliveries and the time savings from visits to rental centers. When Blockbuster wanted to react, the competition had a good advantage. What happened? Why couldn't the firm react with a timely technological adaptation? Some data record certain hidden and misleading weaknesses: the late fees for video returns, in addition to being annoying for their clients, were quite relevant to the firm's total income.

Entering this fierce online network competition would have meant that Blockbuster, to be on equal terms with the competition, had to give up significant income from penalties and invest a respectable sum of money in establishing its online platform. This could not have been done without reducing its usual high and outdated rental rates. With operational costs being high, the options described (giving up penalty income and reducing rates) were impossible. In 2010, Blockbuster declared bankruptcy.

Netflix's path continued to consolidate continuous successes in effectiveness and efficiency, and today it has become one of the technological giants imbued with arduous competition in the production of great television series, setting guidelines for what will be the future of global television. Here we show the results of its management that, according to the Fortune Magazine report, among the 500 largest companies in America, based on turnover, Netflix was ranked 261 and rose to 115 in 2021, registering revenue annual payments that were around $11.7 billion in 2018 and rose to nearly $25 billion in 2021.

In 2018, it obtained a level of profits of around $600 million, which rose to $2.7 billion in 2021. In the said three-year period, it multiplied its profits by 4.5 times. In accordance with the concept that things are worth what the market considers them to be worth, the same magazine reports a market value (market value towards the end of March 2018) of the order of 128,000 million dollars, which rose to close to 239,000 million in 2021.

3.3.2 Productivity Achievements: Key symptoms of efficiency

One of the recognized ways to measure the efficiency and progress of a company, organization or country is through the economic indicator of productivity. What is productivity, and how is it measured? Productivity is a technical coefficient that measures the resulting relationship between the product and the inputs used in its production process. That is, there is a recognition of knowing that one is more efficient when one obtains more production while keeping the quantity of inputs constant or also obtains the same production with a smaller quantity of inputs. In both cases, productivity will have increased. We can also complement the topic by adding the concept of marginal productivity to refer to greater increases obtained in production with respect to the increases in input.

Productivity can be measured both at the general level of the company and in reference to a specific part of it. In the first case, the productivity ratio or indicator is obtained by dividing the total production by the total inputs (labor, material resources, energy, capital and others). To overcome the inconvenience of the different measurement criteria for the various inputs (hours worked, tons required, kilowatt-hours), all components are usually worked on in monetary terms. In certain cases, management may be interested in obtaining productivity ratios related to a specific input, for example, labor productivity (production/labor), materials productivity (production/materials), energy productivity (production/energy used), etc.

218

The topic of labor productivity in service provision activities deserves special mention. Unlike what happens in manufacturing activities, service activities are more labor intensive. Therefore, what was mentioned before regarding training, coaching, direction, and control are of vital importance in the results of productivity of said service sector. What the staff does or does not do and how they do it will be determinant in the productivity achieved.

The productivity ratio is a representative indicator of economic efficiency, that is, how efficiently or in what way and how the arrangement and allocation of resources has been made to achieve said production. Here, we must keep in mind that the quantity and quality of the inputs used are related according to an arrangement of processes in systems (symbolized by certain analysts as "black boxes") whose heterogeneity responds to the varied structure and diversification of each business unit or also of each economic reality.

A widely used productivity indicator is the labor productivity ratio, but not only in a specific manner but also by observing its dynamics. In it, we will see that not only is the growth of production or the growth of employment seen as unilaterally important, but when observing the evolution of labor productivity, we distinguish three typical scenarios:

a) **Decreasing productivity**: If we have an economy or a company that, starting from its respective beginning, achieves increases in its production in the final period, but the economy or company does so use a greater number of workers, then its labor productivity will have decreased. The case could also arise that both (economy or company) do not register productive growth, but the economy or company in question ends up using a greater number of workers. In this case, it is also argued that they will have obtained a result of decreasing productivity.

b) **Constant productivity:** The case may arise that the economy or company experiences the same proportion of productive and occupational increase, then the resulting productivity will be the same. One can also consider the case of zero growth in both production and employment, which will also indicate constant or stable productivity, regardless of whether the previous level of productivity is satisfactory or not.

c) **Increasing productivity:** This is the opposite case to that initially described. That is if the economy or company starts from its respective starting point and achieves increases in its production in the final period, but the economy or company does so use a smaller number of workers, then its labor productivity will have increased. The case could also arise that both (economy and business) do not register productive growth, but do so with a smaller number of workers, then their productivity result will also increase.

The interpretation of labor productivity results must be cautious and the causal factors of the probable increases or decreases in it should be delved into. For example, results of decreasing productivity may be because the worker, no matter how hard he tries, is tied to the use of obsolete or outdated systems or equipment (manual planting, irrigation or harvesting systems vs. mechanized systems). A vital factor in increasing productivity is the use of advanced equipment and technology in operational, logistical, distribution, commercial and administrative information processing, etc.

In an abundance of factors that affect productivity, a brief survey on the internet (see https://concepto.de/productividad/) shows us that among factors directly attributable to workers, the following are cited, among others: their educational training, motivation, work behavior (punctuality), physical condition during working hours. Among those factors linked to the organization of work (coinciding with what we previously called the black box) are poor design of products and services, work methods, layout and use of physical workspaces and systems of business planning and management.

Among factors related to inputs other than labor inputs are the quality of raw materials, quality of equipment and machinery and their maintenance, and types of energy used. Finally, factors attributable to external conditions include marketing techniques, potentially underemployed or unemployed labor, needs and variations in demand, local or international economic environment (globalization), technological advances, changes in legal or administrative provisions, etc.

Why is productivity so important?

Because first, apart from being an indicator of efficiency, that is, apart from confirming the correct way of how things are being done, the achievement of increasing productivity means a leap that enhances growth in terms of lower costs. The fact that obtaining greater production while maintaining constant inputs (or with a relatively smaller increase in them) or also maintaining the same production with the use of fewer inputs will have a favorable impact favorably in the cost structure (total, average or marginal) allowing a rationalization of these to the point of facilitating higher profit margins and operating surpluses.

Secondly, the productivity indicator poses a more demanding condition in achieving Efficiency with respect to the previously described condition of stable and sustained dynamics. In fact, the achievement of productive growth, growth in income and surplus will always be welcome and constitute referential symptoms of Efficiency, but when such increases in production and income occur in the middle of a cycle of severely decreasing productivity (or even slightly decreasing as happened in the Peruvian economy during the boom of the last two decades), then the growth experienced constitutes, strictly speaking, only an illusion of efficiency.

This illusion of efficiency presents a characteristic like what in economics we call a "monetary illusion" that results when, in a certain period, the welcome increase in salary has been in lower proportion to the inflation experienced in the same period. In this case, we believe we are earning more, but the price increases in the economy end up liquefying the increases received, and with a long face, we verify that after a certain period, the purchasing capacity of the highest salary received is less than what we had before the "deceptive increase." That is why it is argued that we remained in the monetary illusion of having received a higher nominal salary when, due to inflationary effects, "the real salary" has been negative and has decreased.

In the same way, for efficiency to be assured, the necessary and sufficient condition is that positive and increasing productivity is experienced. Otherwise, the decreasing or negative productivity transmits to us an illusion of efficiency generated by "deceptive productive growth" because, in the bottom line, we continue to remain in areas of diminishing returns (where increases in production present higher incremental costs). Normally, companies that have improved their efficiency have been because, among other things, they have been able to complement it with significant growth in their productivity levels.

For example, at a macroeconomic level, the ratio of total production to the number of employed population (GDP/EAP) is usually used as a signal of labor productivity and thus obtains the indicator of product per unit of employed labor. The importance of what GDP means as the main economic indicator, its composition, its growth, and its implication as a generator of income, jobs and well-being is recognized.

At a macroeconomic level, obtaining increasing productivity, that is, increases in production proportionally greater than the increase in inputs used, confirms higher levels of efficiency and increasing trend of improved production and resource use systems. Production grows, employment grows, and economic and social returns grow due to the efficient use and allocation of resources.

Since before the coronavirus pandemic emerged, technological advance was empowered as a strategic factor in the achievement and increase of business productivity in operational, marketing, administrative, logistical, financial, etc. supports, which marked the difference between leading companies and follower companies of those. But, although the pandemic brought us unfavorable impacts in terms of aggravation of costs and capacity to generate surpluses, we must thank the pandemic and specifically the confinement, for having put us before the challenge of resolving the crossroads of how to continue operating during said scenario.

From then on, it became clear that a portion of the staff could continue carrying out their work at home and that their physical presence in the workplace was not essential because they could connect to the Internet, access the data and information network, and prepare their respective reports. Finally, the executive staff also had the opportunity of monitoring and supervising the work of previous staff outside the workplace. Like any beginning, there was no shortage of setbacks and initial difficulties that were overcome, and currently many of them have the support of specialized systems companies called "Software as a Service" (SaaS).

This system configures application models included in a platform where both the software and the data it manages are centralized and hosted on a single server external to the contracting company that uses the service. The company in charge of providing the service is responsible for providing the software in what is called "the cloud," which is already configured, as well as maintenance and technical support. The contracting company accesses the software from any computer and from anywhere. These response and improvement processes have been feasible in formal economic sector scenarios, but in less formal or informal contexts, the situation, as we will see later, is different.

One of the few serious studies on productivity carried out in Peru was sponsored by the National Institute of Statistics and Informatics and was commissioned by Dr. Joel Jurado Najera in April 2000. See details at the following link:

https://proyectos.inei.gob.pe/web/biblioineipub/bancopub/Est/Lib0173/RESUMEN.HTM

Despite the years that have passed, the findings and conclusions of the research continue to be important, accurate and confirmatory of what happened in subsequent decades.

The study shows a worrying reduction of around 40% in productivity during the last two decades of the last century, going from 6,831 dollars (in 1999 prices) in 1981 to 3,967 dollars in 1998. According to the study, the increase in the employed population (EAP) played a key role in the reduction of productivity (the absorption of the employed population grew in greater proportion to production). To this, we must add that in the same period, the productive apparatus did not show any substantive dynamism due to obsolescence, lack of technology or other factors. In the first two decades of this century, there are informative references that, despite the cycle of economic boom and dynamism, productivity did not experience improvements and remained at almost stable levels.

It is curious that, on the one hand, in times of crisis accompanied by unfavorable productivity behavior, with irregular productive growth, with lower levels of efficiency and exploitation surpluses, they have not been able to be counteracted during boom times because the growth in production and occupation they did not have adequate relationship patterns to improve productivity and generate higher levels of efficiency.

The study offers us a clue to clarify this apparent contradiction. The reason is found in this dichotomy of the local economic structure. At the EAP level, towards the end of the last century, a large occupational partition can be seen that is accompanied by an asymmetry of productivity where only a third of said EAP belongs to the sector that the study classified as work in the "market context." that is, salaried and state work (in a traditional environment of a dependent worker-employer relationship, in the urban sector or modern sector) that, on average, has the highest levels of productivity. On the other hand, **the remaining two-thirds of the EAP are in a "non-market" context**, that is, in that multi-sector area of urban and rural-peasant informal market. Even according to recent information (see https://gestion.pe/economia/inei-informal-pais-sigue-crezando-formal-266936-noticia/ de mayo 15,2019), said informal employment would be reaching levels close to ¾ of the PEA.

In this sector, an explosion of microenterprises survives, where low-skilled labor is hired with meager remuneration and income and, therefore, also exhibits the lowest levels of productivity and profitability. The above leads us to reveal the directly proportional relationship between levels of poverty and informality, where the increase or decrease of one of them impacts the other and vice versa. But in the middle of them, and as a backdrop, productivity comes into play. It is no coincidence that elevated levels of informality, such as those seen in the Peruvian reality, are involved in low levels of productivity (and that areas or sectors with lower informality exhibit higher levels of productivity).

As we explained before, lower productivity records generate inefficiencies, increases in cost patterns, and reductions in profitability and complete the vicious circle of greater poverty, greater informality, and lower productivity, consolidating a permanent spiral of deterioration and precariousness.

An essential element in productivity achievements is related to technological advances. Alvin Tofler, in his work "The Third Wave," highlights that what differentiates one era from another is not so much what is produced but how it is produced. Indeed, the technological revolution of recent decades has had a tremendous impact on productivity. In the operational aspect, for example, mass production arrangements were experimented with, the use of conveyor belts and electromechanical equipment rapidly evolved towards automated production with robotic equipment, the use of computers of increasing potential and sophisticated electronic and computerization processes (hardware and software), the establishment of greater precision in quality controls and processes, greater volumes, and diversification of production levels, etc.

The purpose has been to improve productive performance using new and improved machinery and equipment that were initially applied to the productive area. However, this process of technological innovation supported by research activities, development of inventiveness and creativity, has been extended to the remaining spheres of business management. This is how the areas of marketing, finance, administration, accounting, human resources, logistics, planning, etc. They begin to benefit from the use of computerized equipment connected to the network, Internet access, and the use of software that expands their ability to obtain, organize, store, process, and transmit voluminous information internally, externally, and automatically.

It should be noted that regardless of the area in question (operational, commercial, administrative and others), greater productivity due to technological innovation will always require the presence of qualified personnel - operator, technician or professional - to make it viable and enhance it. It is true that technological innovation has a favorable impact on productivity, but not all improvements in productivity result from technological improvements. If this were the case, all new productivity would be an exclusive achievement of researchers and scientists linked to technological innovation. However, there can be improvements in productivity based on the ingenious contribution of professionals and technicians with less scientific backgrounds but innovative. For example, there are frequent cases of the design of new products, new processes, new systems, new resources or a new mix of these; all of them within the same scheme of existing technologies.

The potential for new opportunities that technological innovation offers us in the field of computing and communications has been notable, but as we explained before, the identification of risks derived from its widespread use has also emerged. There is an open war and crossfire in cyberspace, and hackers, using sophisticated "computer viruses" or spyware, have circumvented conventional antivirus programs and penetrated the most "secure" networks and information systems of companies.

Beyond the difficulties noted above, it cannot be denied that the efficiency achieved by technological and non-technological innovations reinforces productivity improvements and, in turn, contributes to reducing costs and, as we noted before, increases the company's profits. The expectation of companies that undertake technological innovations is, of course, to increase their profit levels, which in many cases is achieved by establishing lower unit prices but placing greater production volumes on the market so that they increase and consolidate their competitiveness.

What has happened with the price of televisions, personal computers and their laptop variants, tablets and microprocessors, electronic audio and video equipment, and others are a clear example of this. It should also be noted that in the case of smartphones, with the reinforcement of impressive launches and marketing support, it is possible to place improved products and even with a higher price.

The above confirms what we pointed out at the beginning regarding the fact that productivity improvements reinforce efficiency processes, which in turn have a favorable impact on effectiveness because it allows the company to obtain and maintain satisfactory economic results.

3.3.3 QUALITY: Distinctive touch in efficient management

Previously, we referred to quantitative results (income and production growth, increases in productivity, rationalization, and cost reduction, etc.). However, to dispel the illusion of numerical mirages that may be seasonal, cyclical or misleading, it is important to refer to a qualitative element that points out efficiency processes from broader perspectives. In this regard, we consider that one of the symptoms and distinctive characteristics of efficiency is Quality, which we understand as a process of continuous improvement of the product or service offered.

The efficiency of any management is reinforced by developing "Quality," and this, in turn, after being recognized and preferred by the consumer, will provide the basis of consistency, sustainability, and recognition of the company in the market so that it is projected towards processes of longer range that surpass short-term optics. That is, efficiency will be reinforced through quality processes and, in turn, <u>maintaining quality schemes will underpin efficiency processes and, consequently, effectiveness</u> due to their positive impact and recognition in the market.

Initially, quality acquired a restrictive scope, limiting itself to the operational context, where emphasis was placed on the degree to which the product or service conformed to the established standards of quality, desired operational performance (improvement of the production process, redesign of plant size and operational functioning, cost optimization, acceptable tolerance range, number of defective products per production volume, production increase ratios). Subsequently, quality is updated, acquiring a broader meaning and points, in addition to the above, to the degree to which the product or service responds or even exceeds customer expectations. This last approach goes beyond the operational reference and incorporates the marketing variable, that is, an "optimal" product or service (from the operational perspective) is not enough but must also satisfy consumer expectations.

To the extent that such expectations, preferences, and tastes are changing and substitutable, marketing support was formed to listen to, take the pulse of the market, and direct the most convenient market strategies so as not to lose (or rather gain) market share. In other words, structuring a quality commercial system will be feasible to the extent that its efficiency is that which keeps us aware of "what people like." The result of this work led to reversing or restoring processes in the operational area to make the respective changes, adjustments, and modifications in accordance with market guidelines and signals. Failure to do so would run the risk of maintaining an outdated, obsolete, productive apparatus and losing competitiveness.

However, as we noted in the previous chapter, recent management styles more frequently incorporate external variables. The greatest impact of this global panorama (with its economic, social, political, international forces, etc.) on internal variables (costs, expenses, income, prices, rates, taxes) and on the immediate future of business activities. It shakes up not only the predominant patterns in operational and commercial systems but also the business support systems (planning, research and development, financial, administrative, IT, logistics, etc.).

For this reason and, in a sense, more open to the outside, we understand the term total quality today as the reengineering process that is inserted into the entire company. That is, without undermining the quality efforts in the respective operational and commercial systems ("axis" systems in any quality process), said purpose will have to be expanded to strengthen such efforts towards the other systems (financial, research and development, computer, etc. ("gear" or support systems), by redefining improved and automated processes within each of them. The quality in the "support systems" complements and reinforces the quality in the "axis systems."

In the understanding that an organization comprises an integrated system of various areas or subsystems, which are not conceived as isolated watertight compartments but as systems that interact with open borders between themselves and with the outside world, if improvements are not experienced in the support systems, their inefficiency may affect and perhaps spoil the good functioning of the operational and/or commercial systems. The casuistry shows us cases where, for example, poor financial management or lack of control has caused serious problems and even business falls and vice versa, efficient financial management supported and made possible a rebound in business management.

Why is quality in management so important?

First, because it makes efforts not only in relation to the result of the product or service offered but, as we described before, it involves the entire company and is not limited to the functionality of a particular area. Although many organizations have currently created a Quality Assurance area, the responsibility for the resulting quality does not fall exclusively in said area. Its function will be to supervise, control, and inspect the integrity of the quality process that is desired and proposed throughout the organization, which includes various areas and those responsible for the distinct phases and stages of business operation, from the inputs and resources used, their respective processing and transformation systems into final products or services, including even their distribution to the consumer. That is, establishing quality schemes energizes the company. The reconsidered quality in business systems and processes will result in the quality of the final product or service.

Secondly, quality is important because when a company delivers to the consumer public a high dose of quality in the form of a product or service offered, this means not only increases in the company's profits as fair compensation for the effort to achieve it, but they also involve an increase in the quality of life as that specific need is largely satisfied. As we argued before, the economy of a country or a company should not only be measured in quantitative terms but also qualitatively. The quality coming from an organization to society, as we noted before, can be accompanied not only by lower prices but also by higher levels of quality of life for society.

Thirdly, we share the conception that quality is in no way a result of chance, improvisation, or luck, but rather as John Ruskin (English, writer, and art critic 1819- 1900), whose artistic works were cataloged for achievements of excellence in their style: "Quality is never an accident, it is always the result of an intelligent effort." That is, quality corresponds to the effect of an intentional effort of imagination, creativity, and inspiration that leads to an improved level of the product or service offered.

It is worth referring again to the case of the Netflix company. In July 6, 2018, edition of The Economist magazine (pages 11 and 18) confirmation of the achievement of said company in having transformed the content and orientation of television into its traditional version and having become one of the important technology giants (on the heels of Facebook, Google, Amazon). Indeed, the main American television networks (national and local) are being affected by the impressive competition from Netflix and other similar companies that have been achieving a significant reduction in viewership on traditional television. Netflix has (towards mid-2018) close to 125 million subscribers, which represents double the number it had in 2014 and who are "stuck" to its vast programming that registers an average viewing time of two and a half hours per day.

What are the keys or lessons that this overwhelming success leaves us with for entrepreneurs, for existing companies and even for their large technological competitors?

First, the orientation, search, and achievement of irrefutable quality in the services offered deserves to be highlighted. To counteract how difficult it is to satisfy the immense volume of subscribers, this quality is accompanied by a first characteristic of variety in which the company spares no effort to achieve. In its recent entertainment production, it contains more than 80 samples of films, original and contracted series, documentaries, etc. which far surpass any other television network with respectable production such as HBO, BBC, or studio such as Hollywood can make (Warner Brothers reaches 23 film samples or Disney with only 10).

In its attempt to make its productive variety compatible with the variety of users that make up its clientele and considering that it has more subscribers outside the USA than within the country (57 million in the USA alone), films are offered that reach 21 countries and with streaming options, subtitles and audios in different languages. Furthermore, considering that the final subscriber corresponds mostly not so much to individuals but to families, large-scale data management has allowed it to classify, offer and recommend different specific menus according to the preference of each family member. For this reason, the company prioritizes keeping its clientele satisfied and supporting a television production whose expenses, despite the risk of over-indebtedness, exceeded (in July 2018) 12 billion dollars annually.

Secondly, the quality and variety mentioned above are added to the important factor of offering your subscription at comfortable and accessible prices. The monthly subscription cost that includes the transmission of the signal from up to two receivers simultaneously amounted (initially) to eleven dollars (towards mid-2023, said subscription was around $18). Additionally, in consideration of what we previously pointed out regarding "dynamism" as a symptom of efficiency, the following button is enough. In the first quarter of 2018, the company registered an increase in new subscribers amounting to 7.4 million, which represents a significant amount of cash sales. A simple extrapolation of its subscriber volume (125 million) and monthly subscription cost ($11 on that date) reflects annual gross revenues of around $16.5 billion.

A short parenthesis is necessary to clarify that from a financial perspective, "apparent" contradictions between cash flow performances (Cash Flow) and operating results performances (Losses and Profits) may be of concern. The surplus cash flow position does not imply a direct obtaining of profits and, in turn, a deficit situation in the Cash flow does not mean an inevitable loss. This last case is the one that corresponds to Netflix, where the aggressiveness of its operating expenses (production, marketing and technology) cannot be financed or fully covered with its current income. That is, it incurs permanent cash flow deficits and tight liquidity but continues to generate extraordinary profits.

The combination of the first and second factors described above means that, in this growth cycle, it has the imperative need to operate continuously, financing its working capital and given its potentially suitable position to attract long-term financing, investment banking is very willing to facilitate said financing. Not many companies can afford the handicap of meeting their short-term liquidity requirements with long-term financing. This makes it easier to leverage its operations by generating sufficient current income to meet the current portion and interest expenses of said debt in addition to covering the remaining operational expenses.

Additionally, if the forecasts of some analysts regarding its possibility of achieving 300 million subscribers by 2026 are fulfilled, the company could achieve the feat of, on the one hand, overcoming the growing trend in its debt levels (rising towards mid-2018 to 8.5 billion dollars) and on the other hand continue managing as before in the context of a difficult deficit cash flow position combined with favorable operating results. Management has ratified its willingness to continue - for several more years - borrowing, to continue operating on the tightrope of cash deficits and, despite this, to continue showing profits in its financial results.

Thirdly, it is worth highlighting a management style that has kept it (unlike other technological giants) away from scandals, disclosure of facts, misleading or fraudulent news or linked to electoral manipulation or political cannibalism. It is worth mentioning that, despite maintaining a respectable number of subscribers, the company does not sell or contact advertising with third company, which frees its clientele from overwhelming and annoying commercial breaks such as those presented by companies that transmit conventional open television signals. This, in turn, constitutes one of the important advantages of Netflix's innovative style and one of the reasons for its marked success.

It is even worth highlighting the deep investigation and objectivity shown in his historical or political series on controversial topics regarding the American reality itself (crisis of the war in Viet Nam, trends in the Trump administration, civil rights conflict, the murder of John and Bob Kennedy, etc.). For this reason, the zeal of administrations of authoritarian governments such as China, where the predominance of regulators or controllers has prohibited its operation in said territory. We estimate that the conjunction of the three key factors described above explains the resounding success exhibited by Netflix, whose management has maintained until now a manageable balance between this amalgamation of internal (shareholders and investors) and external (consumers, suppliers, lenders, and regulators) envelopes.

On the other hand, we cannot rule out that Netflix's competition (Amazon, Disney, and others) will not remain mere spectators, and their response will not be long in coming. Business management, with its evolution of advances and setbacks, will have to mark the corresponding pauses, rethinking and rearrangements. In confirmation that large companies like Netflix do not have it all easy and cannot avoid the impact of the current crisis (decrease in production due to the coronavirus, suspension of service in Russia) and the strong reaction of the competition.

According to the report from https://www.eluniverso.com/entretenimiento/television/netflix-pierde-20000-suscriptores-en-lo-que-va-del-2022-nota/, the company, after almost a decade of continuous growth in its number of clients, it lost close to 200 thousand subscribers during the first quarter of 2022. This announcement is a prelude to the impact on its income stream, so its net benefits during said quarter amounted to 1,597 million dollars, which represented a decrease of 6.4% compared to the same period of the previous year, and its shares fell in the market by 28%.

Back to our scheme, when things are done efficiently, that is, when management organizes, executes, controls, and evaluates activities in a satisfactory and coordinated manner, the results and adjustments implemented will allow us to overcome obstacles and advance toward the proposed goals. The Efficiency platform described above (Organization, Executive Management, and Control and Evaluation) will have to be carefully achieved, and in the transition process from inefficiency profiles to efficiency, implementation problems will be glimpsed and faced, but important successes and favorable symptoms that we have described before will also occur such as sustained growth (with the indicated restrictions), productivity achievements and quality processes. These symptoms are external manifestations that accompany and reinforce Efficiency processes, which prioritize diligent action, thoughtful evaluation of management and its feedback and strengthening.

4. VALUATION OF ORGANIZATIONAL MANAGEMENT

4.1. THE COMPLEXITY OF THE ORGANIZATION

4.1.1. Sui generis nature: complexity prone to destabilization

So far in this essay, we have made descriptions of the conventional functions that are useful in any business or organizational management. To appreciate the complexity embedded in every company, it is convenient to briefly digress into other structural characteristics that surround it. We have argued that companies do not correspond to static realities but dynamic ones with forces and components whose properties have the particularity of evolving and changing over time. These changes affect the way its components interrelate and, in turn, their mode of external interconnection. This characteristic gives it a structure with components of reciprocal and variable affectation and relationship.

Unlike the events that occur in the physical or exact sciences, where the phenomena are verifiable experimentation in each repetition, in the case of organizations and companies, the events (although they seem similar) are different, irreversible, and unrepeatable. The results of management may also be similar, show a certain recurrence of successes and failures, and may even be experienced in cycles of continuity or alternation, but their content, intrinsic characteristics, and their contexts and circumstances will be different. Such results, beyond our desires to repeat previous successes or avoid previously experienced failures, will have their own particularity.

The peculiarities described (versatility of content and relationship and differentiated and unrepeatable uniqueness) determine that the business entity must be conceived as a complex system because it is highly influenced by internal changes, innovative processes and technological improvements, and random events typical of the business environment. (pandemics, wars, natural disasters) and due to their high sensitivity to exogenous factors (economic, political, and social), which in general transfers a tendency to destabilize, become unbalanced and even orient itself towards a propensity for chaos. Given that such events occur at unpredictable times, frequencies, and magnitudes, They normally escape or remain outside the control of the management body and are not always the result of intentions and decisions of those responsible for management.

Therefore, business predictions with a high degree of certainty are difficult. The problem goes beyond the use of modern statistical instruments in the projection of models that attempt to forecast by including many more variables and much more time. Without detracting from these efforts, which will continue to be used and provide usefulness, the point is to advance the challenge of finding alternative schemes that facilitate the understanding and successful development of management.

Professor P. Samuelson reminds us in his classic university text "Economics" [16] that economic laws are laws of probability and do not have the accuracy of laws as in the exact sciences. They are laws referred to and limited to the "average." If the observed event fits what is understood as a normal probability pattern (corresponding to a probabilistic system of normal distribution with little dispersion), then the regularity of behavior and correlation are highly predictable. But as is often the case with a good part of economic and business reality, it does not always fit into probabilistic systems of normal distribution and shows considerable dispersion, so it is difficult to guarantee "average" behavior with precision. Therefore, predictions with conventional instruments show certain limitations and are not completely accurate in all cases.

In this perspective and to better understand the dynamics of these complex realities, we mentioned before that their components present a reciprocal and variable impact. This, together with changes in the environment, gives any organization a sui generis content and behavior that is difficult to predict. Within these complex (living) organizational systems, the categorical statement that "numbers don't lie" should be taken with caution. The recognized accuracy of conventional mathematics acquires a certain relativity and surprise in complex systems.

Indeed, it is often suggested that when it comes to living organizational systems (such as that of a company), sufficient caution must be taken when appreciating the content and evolution of its components included in any process. For example, the equality 2+2=4 could be altered and give us a result equal to 5. In such cases, a synergy effect has predominated, where cooperation, commitment, and the mystique of the participating parts make the whole greater than the sum of its parts. In other cases, equality can also be transformed and result in 2+2=3; in this case, a situation of negative synergy occurs, where the antagonism, disagreement and lack of motivation of the participants make the whole less than the sum of its parts. For this reason, for example, a

---

[16] P. Samuelson: "Economia" op. Cit. pages. 10,11 y 12

merger of two companies may yield unexpected results (major or minor) that differ from the simple aggregate consolidation of their financial statements.

In the same way, if an organization intends, for reasons of cost restructuring, to reduce to a smaller size (plant reduction, reduction of commercial spaces and premises, divisions, etc.) and decides to eliminate a certain number of areas or personnel. You will have to anticipate or consider possible negative synergy effects to avoid "backfiring" on you. By simple extension of the negative synergy criterion applied in a subtraction or subtraction, the case 4-2=1 may occur (in this case, the company has gotten rid of the most valuable participants, areas or components that contributed and added the most to the results, so after its removal, the result is more affected). But the case may also arise where 4-2=3 (in this case the company has gotten rid of disruptive or less valuable participants who contributed less to management, so after their reduction, the result is less affected).

Likewise, it can be said that the division of $4 \div 2 = 2$ can, in certain cases, become an inequality $4 \div 2 \neq 2$. For example, if the Management of a company decides on a new zoning in its commercial area so that its 12 main cities where it operates are grouped into 4 divisions or regional zones and, with the purpose of being equitable, assigns an equal number of 3 cities to each region. In each division, there will be some of them that, due to their content, size and number of clients, quality, or social stratification of the same, advantageous or disadvantageous location to distribution or outlet centers, etc., will have greater or lesser potential than others. So, when a complex system disaggregates or separates a whole into supposedly "equal" parts, the resulting parts may be different. The above allows us to conclude the important lesson that complex systems such as those of <u>an organization suggest the need to go deeper and pay greater attention to the quality and content</u> of the individual factors or elements that enter the measurement of any operation, interrelation, and analysis.

4.1.2. Management of complex systems

Systems Theory responds to a theoretical framework that has been applied in various disciplines of natural and social sciences. This framework proposes concepts such as organization, totality, dynamic interaction, and the replacement of linear functionality concepts with circular functionality. The concept of a System responds to a set of elements with relationships of interaction and interdependence that give the entity that makes it up its own entity within a unified totality. (https://idoc.pub/documents/ley-de-la-variedad-requerida-d49oj3j38649)

The management of complex systems proposes one of its principles known as the Law of Required Variety or Ashby's Law, named in honor of the person who formally proposed it and who is considered one of the promoters of cybernetics. This principle distinguishes, within the formation of a system, the identification of a regulated entity (or subject to regulation) whose function will be to transmit information to another entity that has a regulatory nature, which, based on the information received, determines an action to follow. The set of actions and reactions of both elements (regulated and regulators) determines what we observe, also called the variability in the behavior of a system. We arrive at "Variety" as a concept referring to the various changes and states included within a system.

A summarized way of stating the Law of Required Variety is: "only variety absorbs variety." For a better understanding of this principle, it is usually referred to by stating that for a system to tend to achieve stability, the variability of the regulatory entity (R1) must be equal to or greater than that observed by the regulated entity (R2). That is (R1) ≥ (R2). In other words, a system is prone to destabilization when the regulated entity (or subject to regulation) contains greater variability than the regulatory entity, that is, when (R2) > (R1).

This principle is best appreciated in the example of the system made up of the air conditioning subsystem (regulating entity) of a room and the temperature subsystem of the same room (entity to be regulated or regulated). The regulatory entity captures or perceives the information of the entity by regulating it through a thermometer or thermostat, which has a variability of temperatures so that, from a certain pre-established or programmed level, the cooling of the room provided by the subsystem is activated. of air conditioning for a certain period, after which it also turns off automatically with a clock that activates it. After a period with the air turned off, the room will heat up again, and the adjustment cycle will be repeated.

Another interesting example of appreciating the law of Required Variety is when comparing the functioning of the immune system of the human body (regulatory entity) and the appearance in the external environment (entity to be regulated or subject tom regulation) of a virus or bacteria that causes a disease or plague (malaria, AIDS, Ebola, tuberculosis, flu, Covid 19, dengue, cholera etc.). The existence in the environment of the virus or bacteria penetrates the healthy human organism in many ways, and the action of the virus or bacteria causes a variability that cannot be blocked or counteracted by the immune system, which destabilizes the organism with consequences that can be fatal. In this case, the application of the vaccine will strengthen the immune system and/or counteract the actions of the virus.

What does the Required Variety Law have to do with the complexity of business systems? Very much. Firstly, the business structure presents components at different levels, processes and systems that have a regulatory function (understood as supervisory, controlling that determines a decision and/or action to be taken when an anomaly or deviation is detected) and components subject to being regulated (supervised and controlled that transmit information, data and indicators to the previous ones). Unlike the example of the air conditioning system (where, for clarification of the concept, a single regulatory entity and a single entity to be regulated were assumed), in the business and organizational world there is variability of regulatory and regulated entities. This is one of the reasons that also explains the systemic complexity of a company or organization.

Secondly, according to its functionality and hierarchy, an element of any system or subsystem can have multiple functionalities, that is, it can perform its regulatory function and can also be regulated by another regulatory element or subsystem. In the same way, it can inversely perform the function of a regulated entity and can also exert regulation on other regulated elements or subsystems. Multiple functionalities also refer to the fact that a regulated element or subsystem can receive regulation from several or different regulatory elements or subsystems and exert a certain regulatory character towards one or more regulated elements or subsystems from other areas or levels.

Thirdly, an entire system of reciprocal interrelationships is interwoven where a predominance of the variability of regulated entities can be presented jointly and comprehensively, which, being greater than that of regulatory entities, determines a persistence towards imbalance, destabilization, and chaos. The key to successful management is to find means, also called "variation filters," that allow balancing the inequality between (R1) and (R2) so that the variabilities in either of the two parts of the equation decrease. We prefer to use the term "balance" and not "equalize" because strict equalize, in the context of a changing nature such as the company, will be impossible or quite transitory.

Fourthly, one way to appreciate Ashby's Law in complex organizations such as a company is when, for example, within it, the Evaluation and Control system (entity regulatory) could not timely detect the occurrence of systematic theft in the operational or commercial area (entity subject to regulation). Another example in the external business environment (entity to be regulated or subject to regulation), an unforeseen event may arise that is even outside the decisional scope: natural disaster, increase in oil prices, new technological discovery, changes in consumer tastes, sudden variation in tax, fiscal, monetary, exchange policy, appearance of a sudden epidemic, etc.; that have not been foreseen by the company's senior management (regulatory body) and that could not even contemplate pre-established strategies for such variants. Therefore, the absence of contingency plans and emergency response could generate chaos with unpredictable consequences (R2 > R1).

Fifthly, identical components (personal from the same section) do not necessarily have, despite the determination of the same regulatory procedures, identical forms of reaction or equal ways of relating to external effects. In the real world, people give a certain particularity to their performance (satisfactory, complacent, lackadaisical, apathetic, distant, lazy, opposite, etc.) so that they also make their way of relating differently and give rise to different results. The company is not a mere set or sum of resources, machinery, equipment, technology, and other inert assets. Being made up of human people means that their performance, capabilities, and circumstances in which they operate grant management a range of alternative options, decisions and versatility whose final choice will allow obtaining different and unique results.

It is important to analyze, from the perspective of this law, the way business problems present and evolve. In the example of air conditioning, a failure in the operation of the levels or limit times can lead to overheating the room to unbearable levels. In the example of the immune system, the absence or impossibility of applying a timely vaccine or special treatment would also generate fatal outcomes and in the business organization, the inefficiency of its control system will also cause disorder, destabilization, and even criminal propensity.

It is important to mention in this part the approaches of Donella H. Meadows in her work "Thinking in Systems." 1st Ed, Rio de Janeiro, Sextante, 2022. Translated into Portuguese by Paulo Alfonso. P. 25-29, where she points out the following:

"A system is composed of three types of things: elements, interconnections and their function or purpose... A system is more than the sum of its parts and can have adaptive, dynamic behavior and a defensive purpose (resilient) and sometimes evolutionary (mutant). When a living being (also conceptualized as a system) dies, it loses its systemic qualities, which are the multiple interrelationships that keep it functioning as a whole...The elements of a system are easy to notice since many of them are visible and tangible. But the elements do not need to be physical things. Intangible things are also part of a system.

Many interconnections in a system operate through a flow of information (sent or received). This information holds systems together and plays an important role in the way they operate...These types of interconnections are often difficult to perceive...For this reason, information about the existence of a problem may not be enough to trigger action. ...The best way to identify a purpose (or problem) of a system is to observe it for some time to see how it behaves...Purposes are demonstrated by behavior, not by rhetoric or stated objectives."

The acuity in observing how any of the three components of the systems vary, substitute, or alter is essential. It is common for the elements of a system to be renewed or replaced. If so, if the interconnections are not altered and remain intact, then the system will also remain unchanged or will vary very slowly (for better or worse, depending on the quality of the system) replace, for example, members of a technical team). We make the reservation that if any strategic element is removed or added (that has the quality of altering certain interrelationships, purposes or functionalities), important variations could then occur, but if they develop their usual behavior, the same functionality will be maintained, and no alterations should occur.

On the other hand, if what changes are the interconnections, whether the elements are replaced, the system may be substantially altered. In the same way, a variation in the purpose or functionality of any system will also substantially alter it, even if the elements and their respective interconnections do not change. In summary, the author asserts that the behavior and evolution of the three systemic components are equally important.

However, we must add that the incidence or preponderance of said components is different. As the author herself tells us, the variation in functionality or purpose is decisive and is not subject to variations of the other components (elements or interrelationships). Secondly, the invariability of the interrelationships between elements will remain unaltered regardless of the regularity of variations or renewals in the elements that make up the system.

Thirdly, there is the variability of the elements that can initially accompany the interrelationships and systemic functionality in the same direction of change. But in the reinforcement of what we previously called "quality of the content of the elements that are considered in any relationship," the strategic quality that certain elements possess in their capacity to alter interrelationships and functionalities could cause adverse effects to variability or invariability of these interconnections.

The majority of "solutions discussed," adds the author, correspond to partial methods and specific reductionist approaches that, although they are based on correctly rational procedures, <u>are not effective in their solution</u>. Despite the excellence of its analysis and techniques of such approaches, in several cases, the problem remains current because it is derived or transformed into other problems.

So, the recommendation of her proposal raises the complementarity of approaches. The reductionist approach must be completed with a comprehensive approach to intrinsically systemic problems that help us expand and reinforce the perspective of understanding the problem. The evaluation of this complex systemic reality (business or social) derived from internal and external interactions of its components will facilitate a better understanding of its operation and results.

The author recommends investigating why there are times when a system accelerates or decelerates, why the system happens to behave in an unexpected way and why it mutates. It must be observed in some detail how they behave and how their elements are related, replaced, or renewed. It is necessary to understand how the multidirectional and simultaneity of its components affect its operation. In this way, the problems will be clarified, making their solution more feasible.

4.1.3. The pendulum from order to chaos and vice versa.

The now "fashionable currents" about the occurrence and conception of change are in no way an invention of the modern schools of administrative science; the Greek philosopher Heraclitus proposed their pillars more than 2,500 years ago when he proposed his principles of perpetual flow and eternal becoming. According to him, everything is in motion, and nothing lasts forever. Everything flows, change is the only thing permanent. For this reason, he maintained: "one cannot bathe twice in the same river; when I do it a second time, neither I nor the river are the same."

Continuing in this line of thought, it is valid to assume that neither chaos nor boom are permanent situations; just as after the storm comes calm, so also forces and elements will emerge within the chaos, which will counteract it and gradually promote self-organization of the system. That is, the system develops within a continuum whose extremes are stability and instability, like a kind of pendulum between order and chaos and vice versa.

Here, we must warn that in addition to there being no permanence of absolute or extreme situations of booms and chaos, the stability and instability in which they are involved are relative because management develops a capacity for "business homeostasis" where relationships, variability and alterations the internal and external elements that comprise them will be channeled, filtered and mobilized through the conglomerate of their business systems that attenuate and compensate for said variability to make the business organization operate within a viable margin or range of functionality and competence. In this process the skill of the management team is decisive.

But this does not happen with simple spontaneity. It is the conditions prevailing in each situation that, throughout its own evolution, determine the appearance of new forces or elements, and it will be those evolutions, changes and their interactions that gradually impose a certain order within the disorder or also a certain disorder within the order. **Order and chaos develop and incorporate their own components of change and self-regulation.**

In contexts of chaos, business management must find ways to manage it and know how to behave within it, that is, find attractors to chaos that facilitate the self-organization of the system. However, it is also valid to ask: In a situation of an orderly and balanced system, can we think that it would be better to refrain from doing something that could alter it or rather deploy only those efforts to stay within it?

Regarding this, we must consider several aspects: first, as we argued before, nothing is permanent. In business life, events of a variable nature and additionally of a random nature often occur that may exceed the control capacity of the team responsible for management. Such events beyond our will or desire (action or inaction) will condition management until it is directed toward unexpected changes.

Many times, during the chaos caused by unforeseeable factors, the most technologically sophisticated tools, such as software and automated systems, observe insufficient designs and processes or have not been programmed to deal with such unforeseen situations and normally collapse. Only ingenuity and human capacity can confront and resolve them. A clear example of this was the collapse of computer systems in the implementation of the discussed American health insurance program "Obamacare." The applications to access said program were of such volume that the original design of the software did not contemplate the simultaneity of its operational volume. The government administration faced serious criticism and had to turn to the most qualified professionals in its field to solve an urgent problem and they achieved it after a few months.

Another example was the occurrence of an earthquake measuring 7.9 on the Richter scale in the city of Pisco, south of Lima, Peru (August 2007). The event caused a loss of 597 human lives. After the earthquake, telephone communications were saturated and collapsed for many hours, which further aggravated the emergency that arose. Telephone exchanges of authorities, hospitals, residential telephones, and sophisticated cell phones were left with a deadline. To further complicate the situation, the earthquake generated road blockages, river overflows and other problems that made it difficult to supply food, logistics and humanitarian assistance to several towns that were temporarily isolated. The city was cut off and lacked supplies for several days and the problem was finally resolved. In previous earthquakes of similar severity, this severe problem of telephone and communications blocking had not occurred.

Secondly, as the defenders of Systems Theory maintain, if nothing is permanent, then it will be pertinent to have careful diligence to detect the pendulum dynamic from stability to chaos or from chaos to stability and if the tendency of business performance overcomes or counteracts this pendulum movement. Given that maintaining an organization in strict and permanent equilibrium is almost impossible, in the event that it is denied, this would not be entirely advisable either because a situation of stability or permanent equilibrium (questionable theoretically and practically) would present among its peculiarities an undesirable risk of condition the advance of creativity (why change what has been working well?) and thereby reduce the need to introduce innovations to the system.

In the hypothetical context of permanent equilibrium and its concomitant effect of reluctance to make changes, a kind of permanent business arteriosclerosis could be fostered that will discourage the ability to respond to the challenges of the ups and downs of the environment and, therefore, could cause a certain stagnation where the company, considering that since everything is under control and in order, decides to "not decide" or rather remain in limbo of do nothing or do the minimum.

Although it may seem paradoxical, an extremely stable situation, in apparent order and strict control of rules and procedures, where the business machinery works like a clock, is convenient from the perspective of its operation, but not so much for the development of inventive mechanisms and creativity that may remain dormant. Indeed, when chaos occurs or when problems worsen amid it, that focus of inventiveness, creativity and innovation is activated and stimulated, showing all its potential to find viable solutions to the problems experienced.

Furthermore, self-organization from chaos to stability will require complementary conditions, such as freedom of action and mobility to facilitate the development of initiatives, the creation of new methods and technologies and the innovation of business systems that converge toward solutions to the problems at face. In our concept, this situation explains in part the fact that China, after the death of Mao Tse Tung (1976) and under the subsequent leadership of Deng Xiao Ping, found a certain escape valve when directing its country towards a pragmatism of reforms, opening to foreign investments and privatization of state companies, creation of economic zones, modernization of economic policies that were urgently required. By breaking the rigidity of its system and taking the difficult anti-system solution of promoting a certain degree of freedom and initiative it meant achieving sustained economic and commercial dynamism for several decades.

Complementarily and in the reinforcement of the conditions of freedom for this outbreak of creativity, a lucid mind like Einstein's maintained (See Walter Isaacson: "Einstein His life and his universe. Debate, 1st Ed, Sep 2008, page 594):

> "...freedom constitutes the wisdom of creativity... the development of science and the creative activity of the spirit requires a freedom consisting of the independence of thought with respect to the restrictions of authoritarian and social (even religious) prejudice. Nurturing that independence had to be the role of government and the mission of education. "This creativity required, in addition to nonconformity, a spirit of tolerance and criticism whose basis is the belief that **no one has the right to impose their ideas and beliefs on others.**" (emphasis is ours)

In addition to freedom in its broadest sense to move forward in problematic situations of chaos, another condition to consider is the issue of **incentives**. To which should be added, as a close relative, the issue of sanctions. While incentives seek to encourage correct things to be carried out; Through sanctions, we will seek to discourage incorrect things from being done. The human person strengthens his conviction to commit to something when a personal or group incentive stimulus that motivates him is offered or presented.

Likewise, to stop excesses in which such personal motivations conflict with or affect the rights of other people or the organization itself, sanctions are established to avoid deviations in organizational behavior. Popular wisdom coined in a few words the summary of what was stated in the phrase: "the carrot and the stick." Despite this, and as we have previously stated, in the review of national and foreign situations, there are a good number of company directors and organizational, governmental, and political managers who, due to their excessive enjoyment of carrots, risk experiencing blows.

It is pertinent to point out that, in situations that affect individual freedoms and rights and in undesirable situations of extreme control and excessively regimented, characteristics that are regularly related to authoritarian regimes; the lack of incentives and other government intolerances harass and oppress individual initiatives to the point of sometimes making them subject to persecution, prohibition, sanctions and punishments. Even many times, such sanctions occur not so much for having committed legal infractions but for the simple fact of disagreeing with the minority tyrannies that hold power. In this scenario described, there is no motivation, meritocracy is disrupted, and desertions become escape valves.

When we talk about incentives and sanctions, we are not only referring to those of an economic nature. It cannot be denied that the economy has stimulating energy, for example, the perception of a bonus at the end of the year for results achieved is not a bad thing for anyone, in that same sense we have the cost of training or specialization programs or courses, bonuses for special festivities, promotion based on merit, obtaining discount coupons to clients and others.

But there is another type of incentive that is not economic but is also important and has to do with the encouragement and recognition of values that the organization is interested in highlighting. There are companies that usually, for example, distinguish the efficient performance of the staff and establish a special distinction: the employee of the month, the star salesperson, honor for the merit of inventiveness and creativity, honorable mention for punctuality and attendance and others.

These conditions of freedom of action and mobility and of incentives and sanctions, of promoting correct, pertinent things and avoiding incorrect, unethical and improper things, lead us again to the thorny issue of values. This framework must be widely agreed upon at the business level. How to define and prioritize strategic values and instrumental values that promote increases in the Added Value (a concept that we will expand later) of the products or services offered by the company? What key values are underpinning for Efficiency? Finally, do we raise the crucial question if such values implemented at the business level are consistent or contradictory with the policy of the government administrations in power? The response to such concerns serves as a prelude to what we will develop in section 4.3 External Conditions.

4.2. INFORMALITY IN SMALL BUSINESS MANAGEMENT

The effectiveness and efficiency framework exposed so far fits into mostly "formal" scenarios, and includes business units that remain under the scope, supervision and regulation of central government regulations, tax administration, and other provisions of local governments and other entities. But we must admit, as part of the complexity of the business scenario, the dispersed presence of atomized business units corresponding to small businesses that mostly make up this informal sector or underground economy as it is called lately.

In this context, there is a small portion of small companies that are part of this formal sphere and another small group of small, truly informal companies that may be motivated to responsibly incorporate the set of technical instruments suggested in this study (strategy, culture, architecture organizational, monitoring, evaluation and feedback of systems and processes). However, reality presents us with external conditions (as we will see later) that are of such magnitude that they work against said purpose.

The critical reality shows us in the Peruvian case two unavoidable contrasts: first, around seven and up to eight out of every ten employed people do so in informal business settings and second, the work of these people in small businesses whose production or services are estimated to represent around a fifth of the economy's GDP. From this, it follows that in general terms, three-quarters of the workforce employed in this informal sector contributes only one-fifth of total production. The low productivity, which affects or determines the overall national productivity, has significant implications. This harsh, objective reality, verifiable in this sector of small businesses, demands concrete solutions.

If we start from a more precarious and vulnerable situation such as that which corresponds to small companies, we have the obligatory obligation to delve into the characteristics of this business unit in its respective context of informality. A good reference source is the publication of the National Institute of Statistics and Informatics of Peru, dated Nov. of the year 2019:

"Informal Production and Employment in Peru."

(https://www.inei.gob.pe/media/MenuRecursivo/publicaciones_digitales/Est/Lib1764/libro.pdf)

Without detracting from the advances of other existing research, the criteria and recommendations collected from various sources and international organizations and the results shown in said research are adjusted to the purposes of this work.

It is then necessary to classify informality as that socioeconomic phenomenon that brings together activities carried out by economic agents who prefer to remain outside the rules and provisions established by the authorities (central government, local government, tax administration, etc.). The national business reality also exhibits many cases of companies that, in parallel to their activities within the framework of formal regulation, partially venture into the informal sphere when, for example, they carry out sales or purchase transactions "out of accounting records" with informal companies themselves or even when they maintain informal practices with the consuming public.

The labor market of this informal sector presents its own patterns and differentiated features compared to the formal sector, which also maintains labor relations with the informal sector (sporadic temporary employment or hourly or seasonal employment or promotional seasons). For this reason, some analysts prefer to use the category of "underground economy" to encompass the informal sector itself, plus that part of formality that crosses the border and is connected to said informality.

Informal goods and services production activities seek to generate income and employment for those who participate in them. These activities are made up of small-scale productive units (micro-enterprises) with an organizational scheme characteristic of family or sole proprietorships. In most cases, they do not constitute legal entities formally registered in public registries. The assets that the company has belong to the owner or boss of the business. Transactions and agreements are entered into in a personal capacity with the owner, who raises his own funds and assumes in his personal capacity all loans and other commitments made. The informal management of activities without taxation or accounting book records makes it difficult to distinguish between expenses assignable to regular business activities with regular household expenses.

In this informal scenario, activities with a reduced profile but permitted by authorities are formed, such as retail trade in food, clothing and footwear, outpatient food establishments, personal services (domestic repairs, car cleaning, domestic services, personal care such as hairdressers, massages, etc.) manicure, therapy and medical care, distribution services and delivery of documentation or products, etc.) and there are also clandestine activities that border on illegal or prohibited by authorities such as smuggling, drug trafficking, prostitution, crime, etc.

This labor market operates in that representative scenario of microenterprises where 82% work in units of less than 5 people, where three out of every four people hired do not have the usual social security benefits, health care, unemployment, and others. In this context of informality, ¾ of its workers have a degree of elementary education (primary and secondary) people are hired with low salaries where the average monthly remuneration represents a third of what a worker in the area receives formally.

The study confirms the asymmetrical and social inequality in income. In the four lowest income deciles, 2/3 of households with income belonging to the informal sector are concentrated, and in the four highest income deciles, ¾ of households with income exclusively from the formal sector are grouped.

Due to this, this sector of small informal businesses exhibits the lowest levels of productivity and profitability. The difficult and complicated thing will be how to create the conditions to generate a gradual transition that channels informal activities towards formal ones and ensures that said informality has less preponderance in the total economy. In other words, we are asking how to break part of that vicious circle of poverty where a trap of precariousness persists in which a large part of people, families and small businesses in our economy are involved.

Even in developed economies, informality is still absent and reaches between 10% and 15% of total production. In Peru, around 2018, the informal economy reached, as we previously stated, almost a fifth of the GDP, but various private investigations on the underground economy (with informality included) estimate an average from 30% to more than 50% stake.

Based on this, our doubts are partially cleared up as to why, in recent times, we have noticed a suspicious contrast between the macroeconomic indicators recorded by the formal economy against the buoyant purchasing and spending capacity in urban sectors that contradicts it. Foreign and occasional visitors and observers notice that retail distributors of formal and informal establishments for the sale of products, restaurant services, accommodation, travel, recreation places, etc., are full of consumers and crowded with people with a notable spending capacity. and belonging even to middle and even low social strata.

This means that there is an entire parallel chain of production, marketing, financing, distribution of inputs, parts, and pieces, and collateral services (transport, storage, etc.) that involves a significant participation of economic agents and the population that supports it. These are indications that in today's Peru, the word crisis has a relative connotation; what exists is an overwhelming informality that is felt in all sectors and levels, and that moves the wheels of the economy more than it seems.

Therefore, if we persist in the goodness of the spirit and validity of the proposed model of effective and efficient management, what proceeds will be to explore the best way to simplify its content, to adapt it to that sector of reality, prioritize the adjustments of the case and revalidate it in trial-and-error testing.

There is a first condition that is met with acceptable empirical evidence in the Peruvian economy and other similar ones. The point is that the cycles of greater dynamism and economic growth of the formal economy drag the flow of its current, growing productive units of the informal economy with those who are connected in the supply chain. Informal entrepreneurs or independents, due to their interest in remaining attached to this dynamic, also tend to grow and move towards formalization.

The inversely proportional relationship is fulfilled: the greater the growth, the less informality and vice versa. In the chain of positive (or negative) effects, the increases (or decreases) experienced in productivity of the formal sector also come into play, which, by incorporating a greater unit of previously informal production and commercial companies, increases the national average of productivity.

What would most motivate the informal entrepreneur to formalize?

We must start with the hypothesis that the informal entrepreneur in no way begins his activity with the exclusive intention of evading taxes but to self-generate income and employment in the simplest, fastest, and least expensive way possible. However, it cannot be overlooked that as things stand, the informal entrepreneur enjoys his precarious spell of tax evasion and non-compliance with other regulations (labor, municipal, environmental) and his "relative" unfair competition in the face of formality.

This benefit of obtaining lower costs in the short term by remaining unregistered and in the shadow of the authorities' provisions is, in turn, one of the factors of the heavy anchor that makes it difficult for it to expand its radius of action and grow. It is a dilemma between being born and dying in the confinement of its small scale or growing with the possibility of generating, in the medium term, greater and growing income compared to what it started with.

However, we should not generalize because there is a respectable, well-directed minority. Unfortunately, a large part of informal entrepreneurs and their social environment tend to be poorly accustomed, poorly trained, or carry with them behaviors inappropriate to that tangled social fabric that we call "chicha culture," whose main characteristic, beyond externalities and appearances, is your predisposition or stubborn inclination to break and contravene norms, procedures and values of social coexistence.

Also, for the sake of greater objectivity, said Chicha culture is not exclusive to informal spaces but has expanded throughout a large part of the social scene, becoming embedded in other sectors and strata. From simple attitudes such as not respecting traffic laws, exceeding norms of civility, decoration and neighborhood respect, criticizable behavior in public places in front of children or the elderly, disrespecting authority, to violating regulations of fiscal authorities (taxes), municipal (license and permits) and governmental (fees and fines). This complete set of things characterizes that "domestic liveliness" that, in many cases, leads to breaking commercial commitments that discredit and disqualify them in the business world, no matter how small they may be, and even leads them to exceed the border of what is legal.

The possibilities of starting a formalization (having legal status, tax and municipal records, keeping accounting books, bank accounts, etc.) would enable the informal entrepreneur to opt for formal financing (less expensive than the informal financing channels to which they usually access) and have sufficient working capital to maintain and grow its operations by multiplying its contacts with both suppliers and customers.

Decades and successive governments of different shades have passed (right-wing, centrist, left-wing) that, in fact, forgot about offers in their electoral campaign and postponed addressing those always postponed demands towards small businesses. It seems unfortunate that, in contemporary Peru, there has not been a government capable of confronting a problem head-on and developing a political front to deal with the problem of informality and, through it, counteract poverty.

There are two aspects mentioned above that deserve reflection in this part. We highlighted the first in the introduction of this work by indicating that we had to be careful to try different approaches to deal with old and permanent problems (poor business management, poverty, informalities, corruption, etc.) that hold us back and prevent us from breaking and shaking off circles vicious that condition our social realities. The second aspect is to self-recognize or convince yourself that it is possible to achieve challenges. We must shake off low self-esteem, get rid of vestiges of defects and generational complexes and trust in our own abilities.

So that this does not remain a chimera or fiction, it will help us to verify that within these same critical realities, they have been presented, although in a restricted manner and with all the limitations of the case, real experiences of economic agents who did get it right and developed a satisfactory activity. Each of us, whether as entrepreneurs, professionals, technicians, or workers, has those dreams and desires that we must dare to achieve.

As a typical example of what has been described, we have the case of the Flores family, mentioned by the researcher Francisco Durand in the work "The Twelve Apostles..." Op cit. Page 296, as one of the representative elites of the economic power of the emerging provincial groups. The origin and evolution of the group and its leader, Aquilino Flores, is known by an aura of legend. He came to the capital, Lima, from a rural town of extreme poverty located in Cusicancha, province of Huaytará, department of Huancavelica. He began making a living washing cars and selling candy. Subsequently, developing his sense of smell to detect the tastes and preferences of the sector that focused his attention on that segment of the poor and middle class, he dedicated himself to selling custom clothing from third-party producers.

After a few years he innovates his activity by adding a stamping process to his merchandise. This added value allows him to increase his clientele, obtain greater profits and end up venturing into his own manufacturing. The entrepreneur continues to grow and integrate vertically backward with his own supplier companies until forming his own business emporium around his leading company, Topitop. The origin and destination of his production were initially informal and without any registration. However, its own growth inevitably pushed it towards greater visibility before the tax authorities, so much so that it had to be formalized.

The higher cost of this had the advantage of allowing it to operate on a larger scale, even venturing into exports. At that same address, in 2009, he inaugurated a cotton yarn plant in an area of sixty thousand square meters. In accordance with the FTA (Free Trade Agreement) agreement with the USA, the yarn used by the company had to be made in Peru. According to the study cited, around 2015, one of the indicators of the group's economic success was that 70% of its production was destined for the United States and, to a lesser extent, for Europe.

This casuistry is a kind of light at the bottom of the tunnel and suggests that there are achievements that counteract the endemic problems we face. But they also suggest us rethink, undertake and try different styles, new attitudes, and less orthodox postures. Authors Abhijit V. Banerjee and Esther Duflo, in "Poor Economics. A radical rethinking of the way to fight Global Poverty", Reprint Public Affairs, USA, 2012, criticized the vein effort of some governments and non-governmental organizations to guide their work on not-so-valid assumptions such as that microfinance is the cure-all balm, that schooling is equivalent to learning and that a dollar a day spent on food is an extreme limit when income is low.

According to these researchers, after the worn-out debate in the Western world discussing the main causes of poverty, the conventional model proposed to counteract the productive inability of poor economies, and their limited self-generation of investments came to propose significant external financing aid of selective investments and in the context of formality of market mechanisms. Through this, it was sustained, this qualitative leap will be possible to get out of the so-called "poverty trap." The authors' approach disagrees with the thesis presented because they consider that continuing to debate the right or wrong of any external aid is hiding what really matters.

For these authors, more important than discussing where, from, and how such funds should be channeled is addressing the problem of where and how they should be applied. Instead of investigating the cause of poverty and the design of a refined generic strategy, it was necessary to choose to advance step by step, in a set of tasks from the particular (visible, tested and verified effects) towards the general.

In the context of the approaches presented in this work, the approach of these authors suggests that based on the knowledge of specific complexities in different areas, solutions should be undertaken on the fly and along the way, which, due to the urgency of this stage, prioritize more effectiveness than efficiency. In the beginning, the options chosen will not be the best (technically speaking); they will have the limitation of being palliatives that will initially cure the fever and not the disease, but the emergency are of such magnitude that patients cannot wait and if immediate action is not taken, they will continue to die from the effects of such fevers or from starvation.

The procedure to follow will be the same therapy in the face of a starving, malnourished patient with severe signs of physical and mental fragility (infants, older adults, or pregnant women). In that case, it is inappropriate to recover it with solid foods and in an accelerated manner. The pertinent thing will be to treat him initially with a balanced diet and gradually, as his vital signs strengthen, reinforce his diet with other components.

That is the harsh reality of poor countries, where some present more dramatic pictures than others. So before financing the construction and equipment of a modern hospital (of unquestionable necessity, but which bureaucracy and corruption will complete tomorrow, afternoon and never), let us think, as a first step of putting into operation medium-sized outpatient clinics, medical posts and basic complementary services (laboratories, tests, vaccinations, etc.) in less accessible places. In the same way, instead of installing a modern drinking water and wastewater treatment plant (also of unquestionable necessity), epidemic outbreaks of cholera can be prevented or reduced by installing wells to obtain natural water with basic chlorination treatment and septic wells. Both small and, for the moment, for community use.

In the area of housing, one way to counteract the marked overcrowding in large cities would be to consider the development of basic social housing modules with accessible financing for low-income families. Finally, on the educational level, the most practical thing will be the installation of primary and secondary schools in rural areas where educational needs are most pressing. For such rural families, the urban areas where this service is offered are inaccessible.

Each area described has its specific problems that are difficult to address and solve in depth. The first step is to overcome extreme poverty and the alarming conditions of precariousness.

Therefore, in the short term, measures and policies that accentuate effectiveness (results) must be conceptualized and applied. Subsequently, through gradual procedures and during the ongoing process, methods and efficiency improvements will be perfected.

Faced with the dilemma of waiting for the long-awaited financial aid (external or internal), we must address the urgency of "putting out the fire we have at home" that is in danger of expanding or not wait for the flood to spoil the situation. the harvest or the fragile home. We must, therefore, make use of the available resources without abandoning the perspective of more complex processes and more ambitious goals. That is, act immediately and urgently in the short term without removing the prospects of generating viability conditions in the medium term.

Specific circumstances - such as extreme poverty - usually raise the dilemma of whether, on the one hand, it is a better strategy to combat it with that unquestionable instrument of sophisticated logical frameworks with valid but complex and far-reaching diagnoses and solutions, or if, on the other hand, rather, than another perspective is more appropriate, less attached to complicated models and more focused on addressing urgent problems of each reality, according to simple guidelines and procedures, but supported by the common sense that experience, knowledge of the environment and budgetary restrictions pose.

When pure rational conventions are sometimes inopportune or untimely, the best option will not be to exclude them but to combine and complement, balance, and harmonize both perspectives in a mix between reasonable processes with criteria of suggestive map of intuitive clues, instincts, and others. "Olfactory or auditory" signals that are captured by those who are immersed in the specific problem. This will lay the foundations for subsequent, more complete solutions.

Curiously, in the process of developing oriented projects described above, small companies (both formal and informal with a propensity to formalize) may have potential opportunities to develop. Informality cannot be successfully combated without also combating in parallel and frontally its close relative, poverty, with which it is intertwined in a labyrinth of greater entanglement and complication. In this process, the reorientation of public spending on supporting and promoting small businesses is essential. We believe that only to the extent that this fence of precariousness is gradually broken will there be possibilities for informality to move towards more formal spaces.

The details and particularities of the titanic effort to attempt a prophylaxis of business informality or the underground economy goes beyond the intentions of this work, but we pose it as a challenge for future research efforts.

4.3. EXTERNAL CONDITIONING

In abundance to the problem of business complexity and its peculiar conformation with dispersed and atomized business units of special qualitative significance, systemic thinking warns us about the variability of the environment that, by causing a succession of causes and effects, generate changes and amplify imbalances within the organization. In this way, the erratic dynamism of the set of external conditions threatens the effectiveness and efficiency of any management.

A prominent exponent of this current of thought is Professor Peter Senge, who, with other authors like Charlotte Roberts, Richard Ross, Bryan Smith, and Art Kleiner, published the book: "The Fifth Discipline in Practice," Ediciones Granica S.A. Barcelona, 1995. (This work is after his original work, the Fifth Discipline). As the author mentions, the publication includes experiments and research that diagram the behavior of dynamic systems where it details recurring patterns, which, beyond the superficiality of the effects, allow clarifying causal elements such as typical "snowballs" of cyclical problems generated in an organization. The systemic approach points out that small events separated in time and distance can be the cause of significant changes in complex systems in another scenario. This is known as the "butterfly effect," which figuratively states that the flapping of a butterfly's wings, for example, in Asia, causes a hurricane in the Caribbean.

The evolution of social, economic and political systems and their corresponding models or mechanisms has unleashed permanent controversies among participants in economic reality (businessmen, workers, suppliers, shareholders, financiers, rulers, etc.) and continues to be the great headache of politicians, academics, researchers, social scientists and other brilliant minds who, as more than two hundred years, persist in the sociopolitical debate that clarifies the conceptions, divergences and imbalances in force in that complex systemic trilogy of economic, social and political factors that tries to elucidate or resolve: a) what, how and for whom to produce and grow b) how to refine criteria of equity for a better way of distributing income and benefits derived from that production and growth c) what criteria of reason and justice should be established to respect the rights and civil liberties of all members of society.

The "snowballs" of cyclical problems, the tangled skeins of systemic relationships, and the "butterfly effects" pointed out by Peter Senge have configured different socioeconomic macrosystems in different spaces and times and continue to be the subject of mixed controversies, the choice of system most convenient. The nuance of the debate is outlined and takes on particular forms in the economic-business space between, on the one hand, those who staunchly defend economic liberalism with its components of free enterprise and markets and, on the opposite side, those who only view it positively eye strong participation, regulation and control of the state apparatus in all areas and sectors of the country (economic, social and political) where centralized planning is the key to said order.

Between the two profiles, there is no shortage of nuanced mixtures. On the one hand, those who, from a liberal position, are tolerant of a certain degree of state intervention and regulatory entities different than the private sector and, on the other hand, those who, from a more statist and centralized position, consent to and endure a moderate and directed private participation in the economic sphere.

Behind each option described, there is a different way of conceiving, prioritizing, and specifying production and growth; a different way of conceiving and distributing the income resulting from such growth and a different way of considering individual rights and freedoms. Defenders and detractors of both currents have had a place in government administrations of different times, in different countries and with dissimilar results in each current.

The researcher, Peter Baltes in his work "The good life. Critical theory of living", Lima, Universidad del Pacífico, 1999, pp. 138-139, reminds us that the Germans coined the theoretical concept of "social market economy" during the post-war period as an attempt to overcome criticism of lack of respect for individual freedoms and rights in centrally planned economies and also as an attempt to present alternatives to the extreme effects of market economies, where the cult and bias towards individual interest became the predominant and sectarian criterion of the economic and social order, causing disturbing distortions and inequalities.

According to the author, with the understanding that man is an individual composed of nature and reason; an economic model that rejects, distorts or is openly contrary to self-interest (which is intrinsic to human nature) cannot and should not be imposed. Nor can it be imposed a model that ignores or excludes equality of rights based on the reason. The "social market economy," according to the author, offered an alternative that was conceived as an attempt to overcome these restrictions because, as a market economy, it accepted self-interest, and as a social system, it was oriented towards respect for equal rights between people. Beyond agreeing or not with this position, time and experiences will confirm, as in the cases of other recognized models, whether the socioeconomic model of the German proposal was a success, an incipient experiment, or a simple delusion.

In Peru, our current constitution (since 1993) curiously welcomed the concept of a social market economy and inserted it in its article 58°, but it has a more formal than factual connotation. We have in Peru an entity (Constitutional Court) that prevents acts committed by citizens, authorities, institutions and norms in general from being contrary to what the Constitution establishes, but we do not have an entity that makes the authorities see what the Constitution established, but it has yet to be implemented, or there have not been sufficient channels and mechanisms for its full functioning.

Practice, customs and experience have repeatedly brought us closer to repeated realities that make up what are called mixed economies. Although a wide mixture can be brought together under the label of a mixed economy, it is appropriate to consider some reasons that explain why this mixture exists. As Professor Juan Ignacio Jiménez Nieto points out in his work: "Politics and Administration," Tecnos Editorial, Madrid, 1970, pp. 36-37, there are sectors that are entirely public, such as Defense, Internal Government and International Relations, because their "final products" are indivisible and there is no individualized demand for them offered and satisfied by the market. Such services, the author points out, are grouped in the category of General State Services and must be provided in any case by the public sector under any regime or political system and under any party platform (the emphasis and underlining are ours).

In this category of General State Services, the direction of public spending can be done through direct discretion or bidding schemes. This does not rule out the provision of goods and services by allocating monetary resources totally or partially towards public sector entities or involving private sector entities (through tenders for the provision of products or provision of services), which leaves the possibility open of a mix of state and private.

The mixture becomes more latent from sectors where the management acquires its bias towards the pro-liberal or the pro-interventionist. Thus, for example, we must distinguish between two subsectors. Firstly, the subsectors classified as Social Services - Education, Health, Housing, Work, Social Security, etc. - and secondly, the Economic subsectors (Agriculture, Mining, Energy, Industry, Commerce, Transport and Communications, Financial, etc.). In the framework of a liberal state, both subsectors acquire a majority absorption and monopolization by private activity, leaving only general services in charge of public responsibility.

However, in the recognition that the market mechanism has its limitations, it is common for even the most liberal states to maintain a certain shared participation (individually or as a co-participant) of private entities with public entities, especially in social services. (basic and higher education, sanitation, social housing, pension or retirement funds for retirees, food assistance, health, etc.).

The economic sectors in a liberal state are developed exclusively and mostly by private action and initiative. However, there, too, liberalism recognizes the need for a certain state participation and an important part of the development of, for example, physical infrastructure (construction of irrigation canals, ports, airports, roads, bridges, highways, hospitals, schools, etc.) are usually delegated to public activity. It is well known that the implementation of such works is carried out through bidding and competition systems with private participation.

Additionally, in a liberal state, the public sector usually assumes in certain areas the "promotion" or support of private activity (for example, financial support through development banking, regional banking, municipal banking, sector banking). Also support to small businesses, scientific and technological research, promotion of productivity and competition, etc.

There are also many business activities carried out by the private sector that, by their very nature and to avoid excesses or oligopolistic deviations to the detriment of small companies and in defense of consumer interests, require (even in more liberal societies) a certain control, supervision and regulation exercised by state entities.

According to this, and beyond biases and nuances of greater or lesser regulation, supervision and control, we are accustomed to the fact that in certain sectors or scenarios, such as certain regional or local banks, insurers, and entities participating in the securities market, setting rates for public service companies (water, electricity, telephone), price control on certain provisions of the basic basket (bread, milk, flour, noodles), certain crops (grains), granting health authorizations for food and drugs, and others, should be carried out mainly by public sector entities or independent organizations.

Finally, there are economic activities (especially in developing countries) in places or areas that are quite remote and dispersed from the urban environment where private activity is simply not established because it is not profitable or lucrative for them. In such a situation, activities must be carried out by government entities (banks, air transport, hospitals, schools, provision of health or food services, sanitation, etc.). That is, the private sector ends up granting the public sector activities of a subsidiary or relegated nature that are not of its interest.

From this perspective and given the nuances shown (volunteers and forced) of participation in private activity with public activity, we can conclude that "pure liberalism" is fiction. Despite the sympathy of supporters of said pure liberalism, it is fiction because it does not exist as a verifiable reality. This is how we classify it despite earning the antipathy of supporters of this model. It is not surprising that the renewed term "neoliberal" has come into vogue, which seeks to shake off extreme positions but without abandoning the liberal essence.

On the other hand, in states with a statist or interventionist bias, government administrations monopolize the General State Services without any discussion. In addition to this, public activity acquires notable preponderance in taking charge of the Social Services subsectors, reaching the majority coverage of these. However, budgetary restrictions make it difficult to fully cover such services for growing and needy populations, which is why in many countries, private activity is allowed to participate, covering a moderate part of the offering of such Social Services (education, sanitation, health, pension funds, etc.).

Regarding economic sectors and in the context of interventionism, the government moves between a spectrum given on the one hand in a strong direct participation in the production of goods and services in different sectors of activity through various forms of public entities (ministries, decentralized organizations, autonomous institutions, state companies, regional and local governments, etc.). The above is complemented by the guidelines of a central planning body that determine what, how, when and for whom to produce and invest.

On the other hand, also in countries with statist predominance, a moderately permissible intervention is observed towards private activity that will seek to condition it towards areas and objectives previously defined by those in power. For the latter, they will make use of persuasive tools of control, supervision, regulation, and induced promotion.

The emphasis of one trend or another will mark higher or lower levels of state interventionism. However, as mentioned before, the direction of state spending does not exclude the participation of private companies in calls for tenders for the construction or acquisition of goods, services and infrastructure works required by interventionist government administrations and in temporary concessions of public services.

Before prejudging the results of countries with an interventionist tendency and generalizing that everything that remains under state administration is bad and harmful, it must be noted that a good part of public activity, especially in social services, many of the services are offered to prices lower than the costs of producing them because they are partially or totally subsidized. Beyond classifying the provision of such services as deficient because they are focused from the traditional perspective of income vs. costs, it must be considered that certain public administrations set priorities, guidelines and policies aimed at providing the greatest possible coverage of social services to dispossessed populations.

Additionally, many state companies that participate in economic sectors usually establish "political prices" that do not cover their operating costs either – such as the price of gasoline, rates for health services, education, food assistance, water, etc. - and therefore in these cases, as in the cases of social services mentioned above, the usual surpluses are not recorded (in the conventional style of private companies), but they do manage to provide benefits in terms of social profitability.

The debate on how to correct social gaps – via subsidized political prices, direct assistance through public spending, higher tax rates and contributions, through improvement of tax administration, through bias and sectorization of social assistance to highly vulnerable sectors, etc. - they remain in force, as do the gaps.

Currently, even in the most representative interventionist states – such as China or Russia – there is a margin for private, domestic or foreign activity and initiative, which the state reality itself is assimilating. Nor can it be ignored that, in the current situation of globalization, the interventionist architecture of such countries is being restructured by the majority contact with an external world of private predominance. Chinese, Russians, Cubans, Venezuelans, and other supporters of state paradigms have had to accept, although reluctantly, that the development of their models requires a necessary openness to count on the private counterpart from abroad.

By the above, it is also valid to conclude that, in these realities with a state and centralized profile, chemically pure state interventionism is also another fiction. As described with the sympathizers of liberalism, in this case, we will also earn the displeasure of supporters of this statist scheme, but again, we remain, beyond sympathies and antipathies, faithful to observed realities.

And what do such external conditions have to do with our topic of business management?

In this continuum between liberalism and interventionism (and the nuances of mixture that derive from them), <u>organizational management is affected and conditioned, for better or worse, by that socioeconomic and political envelope.</u> In this interaction, organizational management has come and gone, experiencing successes and failures, keeping pace with the gale of such currents and "dancing to the tune that they play" in the parade of specific socioeconomic and political envelopes.

This means that variability external to business management has a nuance like that of a mother and child linked by the umbilical cord so that before birth, the dependency is strong, and what affects the mother will also affect the child. After giving birth, cutting the umbilical cord and first years of upbringing, the creature adopts the habits and customs of its immediate environment. Then he acquires the use of reason, becomes more conscious, learns to fend for himself, evolves towards greater independence and undertakes a long learning process until he reaches maturity. <u>Business management will have independence and degrees of freedom, depending on its affiliation with the environment that conceived of it, welcomed it and where it was developed.</u>

Additionally, business management will also face throughout its evolution another variability other than those described above that correspond to unforeseen and fortuitous events such as war conflicts, natural disasters, plagues, epidemics, new technological discoveries, fires, social disorders, work stoppages, terrorism, etc., and come to form a **random envelope** of that universe of statistically unpredictable or difficult to predict events that do not fit into what are known (from a statistical perspective) as random events with a normal distribution.

These external conditions (including the two types of envelopes described) are restrictions that have in common being outside management control. The ability to influence them is little or none. According to this, it is usually considered that there is an elevated risk in external conditions, and therefore, the generation of imbalances that destabilize management processes is enhanced. For this reason, things that are not under control tend to be considered riskier than those that are. However, without discarding the above, as we will see later, generalizations must be avoided.

Within the field of management, we must be cautious when, for example, when referring to the Control and Evaluation System (integrant of the Efficiency process), we are prone to think that because the said system is part of a scheme under internal control of the things that are supervised (material, human, financial resources, processes, relationships, communications, partial results, etc.), would be less risky than the external conditions described above over which there is no control. This should not lead us to conclusive generalizations either.

To clarify what has been described, let us admit that, in principle, every event, fact or activity has a probability of occurrence (even random events). This is clear to insurance companies when they calculate the insurance premium against them to estimate the probability of losses, but it is not very clear to ordinary mortals when they evaluate risk options. The authors S Levitt and S. Dubner of the best seller: "Freakonomics," Haper Collins Publishers, New York, 2006, (pages 135 and 137), illustrate this point by reminding us that, for example, the mortality rate from vehicle accidents is much greater than that of plane accidents, people consider it more risky or experience more fear traveling as a passenger in an airplane (where they do not even have any control) than as a pilot of their own car (under their own control). The empirical evidence cited confirms with indicated statistics the contradiction between considerations of fear of risk and the generic appreciation regarding control or not of the situation.

The same authors present the case of parents who agreed and were satisfied with their decision to authorize their minor daughter to play preferably with her friend who has a pool at home instead of playing with another friend whose parents have a gun in his house (of course with the care of the case). What these parents did not know is that the rate of minors drowning in swimming pools was one in eleven thousand, while the rate of deaths of minors in gunshot accidents was one in a million. In the case described, it was not the lack or lack of control of a hypothetical situation but rather fear, a strong emotional factor and contrary to rational argumentation, which determined opting for a riskier decision believing that it was not.

Next, we have another illustrative case. On March 24, 2015, an unfortunate plane accident occurred where the ship of the German company Germanwings, belonging to the group of the well-known firm Lufthansa, crashed in the French Alps, and all 149 people on board lost their lives. After rescuing one of the black boxes, it was concluded that it was the co-pilot, Andreas Lubitz, who caused the fatal accident. What happened? Apparently, said co-pilot suffered from unknown mental disorders and suicidal inclination. Weeks later, it was known that until the day before the tragedy, he was researching suicide methods on the Internet. He took advantage of a moment when he was alone inside the cabin to close it and prevent anyone else from entering. He did not answer the pilot's heartfelt calls and steered the plane toward its destination of a fatal disaster.

After the attack on the twin towers in New York on September 11, 2001, airlines established rules, procedures, and security protocols to prevent terrorists or hijackers from entering and taking control of the cabin crew of an airplane, one of which was to secure and block the access of strangers to said cabin. This provision was put into effect, but the remote probability that a member of the crew itself was the one who caused the possible accident or attack was not considered. The problem did not come from outside but from within the organization itself. Currently, new control provisions are being put into practice that will take more into account the rule that every event has its probability of occurrence.

Returning to our topic, we could affirm that failures in the control systems managed under the direction of the company could have a specified probability of occurrence and may be riskier and cause defective management with respect to what we have called external conditions outside the internal control. However, this does not detract from being prepared and establishing contingency or emergency plans in the face of such external conditions. These issues of probabilities, emotions and their weighting in risk matters cannot be excluded in the management evaluation and control.

4.3.1. The threat of populist currents in private and public management

As we said, the dynamics of business management lead her to experience successes and disappointments and to dance to the tune that is played in that troupe composed of the gale of said envelope, whose effect is to set the pace and direct it. Given that the business entity cannot be conceived as an isolated entity, this envelope is constituted, according to the "systemic" approach, as an 'external variability' outside the control or desire of those responsible for management who will have greater or lesser independence and degrees of freedom according to the envelope where they develop.

This envelope has to do with the framework of a superstructure archetype of component guidelines and economic, social, and political conditions. The following are determinants: the economic framework, which is where the predominance of property systems, resource allocation systems, operating systems and/or market regulation and basic prices are determined; fixation, release or control of interest rates, exchange rates, gasoline, energy, determination of rates, taxes, tariffs, processes to encourage production, consumption in impoverished or border locations, etc. In the social framework, the public and private educational system, health system, pension and retirement systems, social assistance, labor regulations, etc., are configured. The political framework determines the system of citizen participation and representation, existing political organizations and institutions, etc. Sociologists call this entire sociopolitical superstructure a system.

And in these scenarios described, what role does the Constitution of a country play, and why is the debate on updating it or including modifications so important? The Constitution of a country represents the supreme norm and is located at the apex of the legal structure, the "law of laws." The Constitution of a country is part of the necessary instruments to support, build, and model the superstructure archetype. Any law, regulation or legal provision emanated by any power of the state must conform to the guidelines established by the constitution; otherwise, it is void due to its unconstitutional nature.

The choice of options raised in the frameworks (economic, social, and political) described determines the desired society and the establishment of regulations in the relationships between citizens. In the context of a rule of law and social coexistence, these frameworks are provided with their legal covering that ensures and consolidates their development according to the chosen pattern. So that the absurdity of maintaining obsolete norms or regulating non-existent realities does not occur, the changing reality will correspond to changes in regulations previously analyzed, debated, and finally chosen and aimed at correcting gaps or deviations that reality presents.

The sociopolitical model chosen and configured will form this systemic envelope that acquires a specific profile, locating itself in that continuum that goes from an extreme of ultra-conservative liberalism, a right-wing neoliberalism (USA, France, United Kingdom) to the opposite pole of regimes of leftist bias, authoritarian and quasi-dictatorial (Russia, China, Cuba, Venezuela). Within this continuum, there has also been a predominance of centrist options (right and left) that are quite typical in the socio-political realities of the West (Germany, Spain, Sweden, Chile, and Mexico). We are not interested, nor is it our purpose to apologize and praise advantages or criticize and condemn the disadvantages of any sociopolitical system inserted in the broad panorama of environments described.

Our interest is to reveal how our unit of analysis, which is business or organizational management, is affected by these environments or, more specifically, how this external variability (composed of the social, economic, and political envelope) acquires nuances, trends and currents of influence such magnitude capable of generating both processes of boom, growth, and progress as well as imbalances, instabilities and chaos in business and organizational management.

History has shown us how, in this complex framework of every society (from tribes, communities, cities, towns, empires, kingdoms, nations and even the current sophisticated democracies and dictatorships), elites of economic and/or political power are usually formed, the which, to arrive and remain as such, configure these envelopes according to their interests. These same elites have learned the historical lesson of not grossly neglecting the population nor acting divorced from the masses under the penalty of leading to the breaking of this tacit social contract and provoking abrupt revolutionary or coup exits whose drastic changes in the predominant envelope would prevent them from preserving it.

Therefore, one of the first political lessons for a political power to be structured and consistent on a stable platform is that it must **consolidate the elite and people binomial**. The crux of the matter is how to find the appropriate strategy "ad captandum vulgus," that is, to capture and conquer the vulgar (the plebs, the masses, and some even refer to it as the rabble as a qualifier for popular class people with little culture and with superficial or scarce knowledge on any subject).

What do elites usually do to gain popular preference? Here, we find everything from the well-known and historical tactic of "bread and circuses for the plebs" developed by Roman emperors to populist touches of palliative gifts for their basic needs. The definitive thing is that the elites must grant something "quid pro quo" as an exchange to encourage the functioning and coexistence of the elite-people binomial.

In this type of compensation hypothesis, history shows that both what the elites offer and what the people receive are not necessarily material goods but also promises and hopes to improve the lacking material life status of the masses, regardless of whether, in the end, such promises are just "white lies." To be stricter, in the last electoral campaigns of many countries in the region, only hopes and unfulfilled promises were given away.

In regimes with a democratic profile (or their crude simulations), the key tool that the economic power elites must arrive and remain in power is to have brought about the emergence (and in certain cases re-emergence) with valiant force and renewed brilliance, populist currents within the democratic partyocracy. This populism surreptitiously and subtly shades its democratic garb by trying to direct and manipulate the conscience of the masses and voters to finally guide them to the benefit of interests, economic and/or politics.

In this context, contemporary populism is not attached to exclusive doctrinal paternity and is observed in chameleonic shades from right-wing conservative populisms through centrist populist options to left-wing interventionist populisms. Many tear their clothes to identify, qualify and criticize what or what type of "populism" happens here or there, but when the clothing and makeup are stripped, the forms are diluted, and the indistinct populist reality emerges with the same background and essence assigned to different and even opposing party currents.

Populism in dictatorial or authoritarian regimes has a more political than economic basis and is openly shameless. Governments of this nature subtract, dodge, and evade the true democratic and participatory garb and have no qualms about doing so using force.

In short, **populism corresponds to a particular democratic guise of the broad partisan political spectrum (right, center and left, or autocratic) implemented by the economic or political elites of any social conformation to consolidate and control the support of the masses and guide the system to benefit their interests.**

What is it that identifies populism within the broad contemporary political scene? It would be ostentatious to grant populism a label of political doctrine in the work: "The reason for populisms. An analysis of the populist rise of the right and left on both sides of the Atlantic", Ediciones Deusto 2017, Spain, several authors outline clarifying concepts regarding the populist phenomenon. Mr. Fran Carrillo [17], coordinator of the collaborations that constitute said work, includes in his writing a classification that should be highlighted:

> "The term populist refers to a way of doing politics characterized, regardless of the ideology that supports it, by the attempt to emotionally and vehemently attract popular favor by offering simple and poorly founded solutions to real and complex problems."

Firstly, the authors point out that the symptomatic of the case is that by appealing to and taking advantage of popular sentiment, the populism proposed alternatives and solutions are not as plausible as if they really were. However, one must be cautious with the pejorative charge used by those who disqualify populism or the populist because, in the first place, it is not simply a mere attempt to cajole large sectors of the population that may be gullible or manipulable and that, in the end, after all, any politician from the broad ideological spectrum does well to gain popular favor. The principal issue is that we must <u>pay attention to the form, manner, procedures, and tools that populism uses to obtain what they seek</u> (and that, in many cases, they achieve).

Secondly, by ignoring and minimizing its procedures, the populist phenomenon is granted advantages in its stealthy advance. Therefore, one of the reasons for its relative success compared to the options offered by the traditional partocracy is that the populist currents have known how to better read and interpret the social problems of their environment more correctly, while the traditional partyocracy continues clouded in its internal struggles to access or remain in power. In this way, populism implements a more daring, more heterodox, and different strategy to achieve its goal and takes advantage of the traditional partyocracy. These are adversaries who have a good social sense of smell and unerring sagacity and cunning.

Additionally, populism, on the one hand, focuses its attention on the short term to make its interests profitable and continue gaining followers, and on the other hand, it irresponsibly incubates collateral effects that, in the medium and long term, can threaten the survival of the

---

[17] Fran Carrillo in: "El porqué de los populismos. ...", page. 136

system itself. From this perspective, signs have appeared in recent years that indicate that the pendulum of contemporary history is leading us, whether we like it or not, toward political-economic options of populist predominance.

The concern of those of us who distrust and disagree with this option is that it contradicts the principles, values, and central ideas with which we were educated because it is clear to us that in this scenario, the risk of democracy being broken, diminishing the balance of powers, increases more distant and even utopian the feasibility of directing society towards more harmonious levels of well-being, freedom and justice becomes. The predominance of populist options makes evident a trend of greater confrontation, contradiction, and polarization.

As the opponents of populism maintain, one of the dilemmas to be resolved will be that this populist current only embodies proposals with weak foundations, clothed in a mere demagoguery that seeks the favor of the people by appealing to sentimentalities such as the return to longed-for and bygone eras with their respective visions, principles, and customs. This populism usually re-establishes, as a form of nostalgia, the phrase "every time in the past was better," and therefore, its true intention is to oppose or resist the advances and changes that are supposed to distort the type of democracy that they understand and defend.

On the other hand, those who defend these populist currents maintain that populism represents political and institutional renewal, the rebirth of collective identities missed by the predominant political establishments (power groups), and, therefore, it will mean the expansion of the democratic bases and true popular representation. This sounds good, but we will have to be very attentive in observing how each step built by this populism in the short term ratifies what they propose or ratifies our distrust.

Why does populism emerge or renew itself today as a protagonist of the contemporary political scene?

First, we must start by admitting that, as in any confrontation or contest, the triumph or empowerment of one party means failure or loss of the other. In this case, the first reason that explains the reappearance of recent populisms (which covers varied options of the party-political scenario) obeys both the innovative strategy of the populist currents described above and the latent failure of the traditional partyocracy whose political proposal and praxis has become outdated and misplaced with respect to the demands of the masses and modernity and has only caused disappointment and distrust.

Secondly, the inefficient actions of a good part of the traditional political class due to their ineptitude, their incompetence and their share of corruption have created favorable conditions for a breakdown in the loyalty of the masses, a leadership vacuum, an uncertainty that is being taken advantage of by outsiders (upstart characters from outside the political environment) who embrace and incorporate populist currents and burst onto the contemporary political scene as a spokesperson for that massive feeling of protest against the hegemonic establishment.

Thirdly, as a rule, and by professional default, economists tend to verify that mostly behind every socio-political event, there is some causality or economic reference, and the current populist wave is no stranger to this. <u>The processes of globalization, economic and market opening, and technological modernization are generating winners and losers</u>. In recent decades, the main variables of global economic events in developed and third-world countries (production, investment, trade, consumption, savings, salaries, employment, interest rates, etc.) continue to experience uneven evolution not only between countries but also within them.

In the same country or economic region, there is a duality of industrial sectors, companies, professionals, technicians, and other workers that have become more prosperous and other activities or sectors are observed where the opposite is true. In the latter, irregularities, difficulties, and instabilities have become noticeable, whereas words like crisis, chaos, and deterioration are recurrent. This critical situation then became a breeding ground for this group of losing countries and economic and social sectors to express, openly or covertly, a certain disenchantment and distrust towards the traditional political class, towards the parties, factions within it and before the systems of representation, which began to be questioned for not meeting their expectations and thus reinforcing the first cause indicated above.

Fourthly, this populism has skillfully structured a rhetorical argument that is demagogic enough to take advantage of the critical economic and political environment described above and manage to satisfy the interests of the few winners and, at the same time, try, with relative success, to satisfy the expectations of the losing majority without it it doesn't matter if you must lie to do so. In this regard, the reflection of the writer and journalist Mariano José de Larra (Madrid 1809-

1837) comes to mind: "The heart of man needs to believe in something and believes in lies when he does not find truths to believe in."

To this, we should add that when rulers and governed cling to or become clouded in these lies, a pernicious course is opened where an excessive cost of lost opportunities, deterioration of state powers, prolongation of suffering and even regrettable losses take place of human lives. Our region has been observing failed populist experiments. For samples, we have as representative examples of left-wing populism the recent Venezuelan and Nicaraguan experience (with Maduro and Ortega at the helm) and, as an execrable experience of right-wing populism, the past Brazilian experience (with Bolsonaro). The Peruvian experience, which we will delve into later, has been representative of a mixture of populisms of disguised centrist options (right-wing and left-wing). Due to the importance and singularities of the case, we will deal with American populism in the following section.

4.3.2. Populism in the United States of America

When referring to Donald Trump's electoral victory in the USA in 2016 (section 2.3.2 Deterioration of Organizational Culture), we find an explanation for this by referring to the peculiar electoral registration scheme in force in American democracy. Hillary Clinton's electoral setback was clarified from a normative and quantitative perspective. In this regard, we raise our doubts and reflections on the risks that, in our understanding, the predominance of said electoral system meant, which even for a sector of its own citizens also has. In this part, we will clarify from a qualitative perspective the causes of the electoral victory of Donald Trump in 2016 and clarify how said candidate broke the mold by becoming a conspicuous representative of American conservative populism. Let us see there are some facts that confirm what was maintained.

Before doing so, it is also worth pointing out that our intention is to reveal the pernicious populist nuance wherever it comes from. In this case, in these times and in this country (USA), said nuance is attached to the Republican current in the figure of Trump, But the Democratic representation was also not exempt from having had in its rank's populist models such as the former governor of Alabama, Mr. George Wallace, also a furious and undisguised defender of racial segregation and opponent of the countercultural movements of his time.

In the world of politics, there are no coincidences, and therefore, it is no coincidence that Trump and the Republican Party "found a marriage fit like a glove" and agreed to work on the populist route that suited the interests of both. Trump emerged until that moment (2016) as the outsider candidate "without a questionable political past" in need of obtaining the support of a popular base. In this case, the one with the greatest affinity with his experience and creed was that of the Republican Party. An important part of his program was his drastic opposition and criticism "of the power represented in Washington." This opposition virulence was not so much anti-systemic, but rather it was political anti-establishment of the hegemonic system that at that time was represented by the Democratic administration, to which the Republican Party had been losing in two successive presidential elections and urgently needed to overthrow it with renewed strategies.

Trump skillfully managed to capitalize on this discontent over the social decline in certain segments of the American middle class and articulated a populist message where, as a harangue, he defended, before the masses, their right to recover what (according to his perspective) the elites of power represented in Washington had usurped them. Once Trump's front was consolidated with the Republican Party, an aggressive government program was created, which broke with formal schemes and was consistent with the harsh anti-establishment message mentioned above. On the domestic front, his first pillar was to present himself as the standard-bearer of an anti-immigration policy (biasedly Hispanic and Islamic) justified by national security criteria.

After almost thirty-four years of that historic milestone of November 1989 that marked the fall of the Berlin Wall, where much of Europe and the rest of the world watched in amazement its singular effect of dissolution of the system and block made up of the former -Soviet Union. Donald Trump, against the current and against the trend of history, in accordance with his anti-immigration program, promises in his electoral campaign, in the purest authoritarian style, the construction of an ominous wall on the border with Mexico to counteract Hispanic immigration.

While the Berlin Wall was a symbol of the Cold War and the artificial separation of Germany, the Trump Wall will be the symbol of racism and xenophobia. According to official figures, the volume of terrorist criminals and other crimes that violate the Mexico-USA border is negligible. The majority of Hispanic immigrants who cross this border with difficulty do so for reasons of building a better future for their families and are engaged in tasks that the average American citizen shies away from; they simply do not like them, and they will never do them because the considered unremunerative, degrading and some of them even risky (manual agricultural tasks, minor trades such as gardening, garbage collection, cleaning of public roads, commercial and domestic cleaning, plumbing, masonry, installation of roofs and floors, cleaning of glass and windows of buildings, restaurant dishwashers, courier service, delivery and collection of products, food and others, etc.).

For any social researcher in the American environment, it is a latent fact that in certain sectors of the American middle and upper classes, there is an anti-Hispanic racial phobia, and there are also concepts of shared or accepted white racial supremacy (tacitly and even in some cases even violently). These feelings were repressed and concealed by the high cost that the demands of the African- American population had five decades ago in their fight for their civil rights and against racial segregation. Today, not even Trump himself would dare to declare himself openly racist; otherwise, he would commit political suicide. However, he has found the populist device to be so without manifesting it.

On this occasion, xenophobia (hatred, antipathy, disdain) resurfaces and targets against the Hispanic community. This hidden and concealed feeling, but "on the surface" in certain social strata, was excavated and made profitable by Trump and his populist current through the design of an anti-immigrant policy as one of the elements keys to gaining adherents, strengthening their election, and seeking their re-election. With this strategy, this populist candidate managed to make a proficient reading of his social reality and align with the middle and upper social class that was comforted to find someone who openly expressed thoughts and feelings that coincided and related to theirs. They found someone who "sings the music and songs they like."

Then, the reasons given to justify anti-immigration for reasons of internal security only constituted simple pretexts, and the real reason responded to a latent racial phobia. It cannot be denied that a sector of white, middle-class American citizens from rural areas and large cities have that predisposition or desire for white supremacy and see with some concern how Hispanics have become the first national minority.

Hispanic immigrants, especially of the second and third generation, are no longer illegal. Many of them are bilingual, have acquired technical and professional specialization and have made their presence felt in the competitive workplace. Nor can we deny the continuity of a mass of immigrants with low job qualifications, little culture and prone to crime that unfortunately gives reason to the animosity of said white American minority. Above this immigrant mix where "just pay for sinners," the main concern of this reactionary white minority is the existence of a growing Hispanic population that has become more cultured and intelligent, which has become electorally more relevant, to the point of being able to become a faithful balance in tight electoral disputes.

Therefore, as confirmation of said anti-immigrant policy, former President Trump's conservative strategy meant that after coming to power, he made use of all government machinery to counteract the immigration flow. Among the measures implemented are children of undocumented immigrants born in the USA will no longer have the right to American citizenship, and repeal of the permanence benefits (DACA) available to young immigrants who are pursuing secondary and higher education (called "dreamers") increased costs and greater obstacles to immigration administrative processes and procedures, use of special budget items to allocate them to the construction of the questioned border wall.

Along the same lines, there is the modernization and equipment of border patrols, diplomatic and commercial pressure on Mexico to reinforce the containment of Central American immigrants to the USA, the relaunch of raids against undocumented immigrants in workplaces and factories, the threat from the federal government of cuts budget to those States considered "sanctuaries" due to their tolerant policy towards undocumented immigrants, family separation of parents and children of undocumented Hispanic immigrants detained at border crossings, etc. It is evident that the entire battery of fire described was directed against the Hispanic immigrant class.

The border wall with Mexico began to be built in isolated sections, and during the Trump administration (until September 2019), only 102 kilometers were built. It should be noted that the total extension of the border with Mexico reaches almost 3,200 kilometers. Given that walling the entire border would be, except for Trump, absurd, Congress, at the request of the Republican Party itself, had agreed in December 2005 to the construction of a wall of only 1,123 km. In fact, the construction of a work of such magnitude could not fail to be considered the most dilapidated monument in American history.

Therefore, to avoid a major mistake, the American Senate during the last government of Republican George W. Bush approved (May 2016) the amendment that reduced the construction of the wall to 595 km in length (952 miles) plus an additional 800 km of barriers to prevent the passage of vehicles. Despite the reduction described, the work will still be onerous when compared with other social requirements and emergencies. So that Peruvians have a comparative idea of what it means, we will do an imagination exercise. If we move the extension of the wall to Peruvian territory, we would be walling off more than the coastal distance between Lima and the northern city of Trujillo, which reaches 558 km, and to appreciate it in its entirety would take us a car ride of almost 9 hours.

Trump's election campaign promise that the wall would be paid for by Mexico was exposed as another of his big lies. This promise only sought to catch unwary people who were pleased to hear and believe such a lie. In his desperation to fulfill this promise and in consideration of the fact that the Congress, now with a Democratic majority, approved 1.375 million dollars (a quarter of what was requested) that will only allow him to build 132 km of new and replacement fences, Trump has gone so far as to declare a state of national emergency (Feb 2019) in order to direct part of the funds from the Departments of Defense and the Treasury in order to be able to allocate them to complete the construction of the wall.

(see: https://es.wikipedia.org/wiki/Muro_fronterizo_Estados_Unidos-M%C3%A9xico).

However, with the issues of international affairs, the economy and domestic politics being hot, it was clear that Congress, the press, and public opinion were very attentive to the way Trump determined his priorities.

The Berlin Wall extended over a perimeter of 155 km, a height of 3.6 m, built of reinforced concrete and lasted for almost three decades (1961-1989) before finally being demolished. If Trump's wall is completed, it will have an extension of 595 km (almost four times the Berlin Wall), with a variable height between 5.4 m and 9.1 m and built on imposing walls whether made of concrete or steel slats. However, the tight time remaining for the Trump government and the delicate internal political situation made it unlikely that his great promise to build the wall will be completed during his mandate and will remain, for now, as the great unfinished work.

Trump strongly returned to the issue of the wall in his re-election campaign, alluding that "the opposition (Democrats, press and other media) obstructed him and prevented his mission, which would be achieved in his second term." To the admiration of locals and strangers, once again, his supporters, sympathizers and undecided people believed him. Otherwise, he would not have had such a tight electoral defeat against Joe Biden in November 2020, having registered the support of more than 70 million voters' favor.

In the contemporary international sphere, the external envelope that we have referred to presents a particular scenario. Mr. Diego Macera, opinion columnist of the newspaper "El Comercio" of Lima (05/23/2019), presented an interesting parallel of how the USA and China appear as the current protagonists in the modern version of those ancient hegemonic disputes that occurred in the history and known as the "Thucydides Trap" in honor of the Athenian historian who gives an account of the Peloponnesian War between Athens (emerging power) and Sparta (dominant power). From this historical perspective, the USA and China, beyond the skirmishes of a trade and tariff war that the entire press focuses on and distracts from, are engaged in an arduous dispute for current hegemonic dominance.

In macroeconomic magnitudes at the beginning of this century, the Chinese economy had a Gross Domestic Product (GDP) that represented almost a quarter of the US economy, but according to estimates by the International Monetary Fund itself towards the end of 2019, the Chinese economy represents about two-thirds of the US GDP. This dispute for hegemonic predominance has been fought on different fronts (economic, scientific, military, technological, political and social influence, etc.) and will take more years or decades to elucidate.

The current scientific and technological advances are determining that this field will be one of the fronts where the most important battles will be fought, and the three decades to which we previously referred to in the fall of the Berlin Wall are not out of place to estimate what will be a spectacular competition and current hegemonic definition. That is, towards the middle of this century, the struggle could have been resolved.

The author of the journalistic article, the newspaper El Comercio, refers to the count made by Harvard University where in the last five preceding centuries, 12 of the 16 historical scenarios involved in the Thucydides Trap, that is, 3 out of every 4 episodes were resolved, through war. The rest was resolved through difficult negotiations and political and economic compromises. Although history shows us the predominance of force in the majority of solutions to such conflicts, the warlike alternative in the current circumstances is less likely and does not suit any of the parties involved or the rest of the world, which is why Mr. Diego Macera raises the question of whether the protagonists in the current controversy, the USA and China, manage to behave at the height of the circumstances and that, beyond being wounded, bruised and reluctant, they prioritize reasonable criteria and are forced and pressured to negotiate.

We have referred to the issue of hegemonic conflicts because, in this context, international reactions and convulsions are generated in which another crucial element appears that has been acting with notable singularity as a spring for populism. It is about the resurgence of an immaculate and renewed **nationalism** (see "The reason for populisms…" [18] Op. cit. pages 24,25 and 46). For example, in the American case, Trump and his policy on the external front meant that the USA, considered for decades as a champion country of free trade, has given up on said purpose and alleging an imbalance of perceived benefits with respect to its main competitors, embarking on a trade and tariff war, generating actions, reactions and expectations unfavorable to the continuity and dynamics of global trade flows. Trump ended up becoming the standard-bearer of protectionist nationalism.

In this same direction were their complaints and renegotiations of agreements previously signed within the framework of the World Trade Organization, the North American Free Trade Agreement (with Canada and Mexico), and raising tariffs on imports of steel and aluminum from Europe. According to reports from "Trade negotiations between the European Union and the USA (see: https://www.europarl.europa.eu/news/en/headlines/world/20190214STO26415/eu-us-trade-talks-the-issues-at-stake), the President of the International Trade Commission of the European Union (EU), Mr. Bernd Lange (German Member of the European Parliament) acknowledged that: "the negotiations on the TTIP (acronym in English of the Agreement on free trade and investments between the European Union and the USA) will be difficult because the American government intends, on the one hand, to reinforce investment in its country through protectionist measures and, on the other, to keep China below it and try to reduce its influence."

In this unabated populist nationalism, the Trump administration interpreted that the participation of the USA in many international and multilateral organizations has become to the detriment of its sovereignty and interests, which is why it was inclined towards distancing itself and even withdrawing from some organizations. The information disclosed in the New York Times on May 26, 2017 (https://www.nytimes.com/2017/05/26/world/europe/nato-trump-spending.html) where criticism and disagreements with Trump are reported with allied countries and NATO members, whom he rebuked that they should spend more money on their defense.

---

[18] "El porqué de los populismos…" Op. Cit. pages. 24,25 y 46

This led German Chancellor Angela Merkel to express her disappointment that Europe can no longer fully trust other countries (in reference to the USA and the United Kingdom) and that it will have to fight for its own destiny. In the same sense, in an interview given by the President of France, Mr. Emmanuel Macron, to The Economist magazine (Nov 9, 2019, pages 9 and 18), he expressed his disappointment and concern about the future of Europe, which will no longer be able to depend of America because its priorities have changed. Macron refers to several facts: the non-penalization of former President Obama for the use of chemical weapons in Syria, Trump's abandonment of his Kurdish allies due to the withdrawal of American troops from the conflict zone in Syria, leaving them exposed to the immediate war attack of the government of Turkey. With the aggravating factor that both the USA and Turkey, members of NATO, did not bother to inform and coordinate their respective actions with said organization, undermining its functioning and representativeness.

Additionally, the fact that the USA and China allocate large sums of money to the issue of artificial intelligence to consolidate technological hegemony and that, on the other hand, authoritarian governments such as Russia and Turkey develop military actions on the edge of the European border, suggests according to Macron, a strategic and political rethinking of Europe whose attention was more focused on enhancing its market economic condition to the detriment of the formation of a political bloc that strengthens its current vulnerability.

Likewise, in relation to Trump's open disagreement with international agreements and environmental protection practices, the aforementioned source (BBC News Mundo), in its report of June 1, 2017, confirmed Trump's decision to withdraw the USA from the Paris Agreement on climate change, ignoring the warning voice raised by the scientific community to stop global warming, which has been registering dangerous levels due to the emission of greenhouse gases emitted by human activity, among which carbon dioxide (CO_2) stands out.

China and the USA are responsible for 40% of the world's CO_2 emissions, and their progressive reduction implies gradual changes in their energy sources. Among the presidents of both countries, China's Mr. Xi Jinping at least observes cautious composure and remains committed to the Paris Agreement, but Mr. Trump, displaying his illiterate knowledge and understanding of environmental protection, chose for retirement.

In both cases, that of NATO and the Paris Agreement and in many others, it was revealed that for Mr. Trump his clear opposition to cooperation between countries is because he privileges what he interprets as sacred national interests. In this sense, to the extent that maintaining leadership in cooperation organizations has the counterpart of assuming certain financial commitments, he prefers to detach and shake off such commitments, arguing, as he did on the issue of climate change in the Paris Agreement, that it only means (according to the last source cited) "a massive redistribution of American wealth to other countries."

With this and by focusing on a perspective that does not see beyond the short term and to the detriment of American leadership, Trump himself became trapped in a policy of self-isolation with respect to his traditional European allies, playing into the hands of his rising hegemonic rival whom, in the end, gives him space to continue gaining influence. The new administration of Joe Biden has been redirecting the route of its predecessor and reestablished, through an executive order (January 2021), the return of the USA to the Paris Agreement that seeks commitments to avoid or reduce climate warming and signed another executive order to prevent the departure of the USA from the World Health Organization.

However, in the previous wake of disappointments and criticizability interventions (Iraq, Syria, Libya) made by previous American administrations, the regrettable errors in the way the withdrawal of troops from Afghanistan was carried out left the Biden government an image of humiliating defeat to the point of causing a reduction in approval ratings of less than 50%. It also remains to be clarified how the current Biden administration will adjust and strengthen its trade policy toward China.

An important lesson from history remains unchanged, and the elites keep it in mind: in a large part of the electoral processes observed, the citizen exercises his right to vote guided not so much by programmatic or doctrinal considerations but fundamentally by emotional subjectivities. That is, the judgment and criterion that prevails in voters has to do with emotional issues, intuitions, sentimentalism, affinities, prejudices, preconceptions, etc., to the point that using reasons, facts and palpable and important evidence goes to the background or they are simply overlooked.

According to this background, the strategy of populist options will consist of giving priority to emotion over reason. In a multicultural society made up of a diversity of values and cultures, populism will persist in its strategy of creating a synthesis of messages that provide the people with an illusion, a desire, or a hope for what they had currently lack and which provided them in that past certain security and/or satisfaction. Much better if this message of hope were announced by some new character without a critical political or electoral past (outsider).

Political advisors, the Republican Party found in the 2016 election the ideal candidate in Trump for their strategy and coined the key campaign phrase: "Make America Great Again," which became the motto of his electoral victory. The phrase impacted large, unstable, indecisive, and uninformed social sectors who were captivated by that longing for a return to a past that was better for them and hope for a promising future. Time would confront us with that laconic romanticism of idealizing a past that no longer exists as another false promise.

In this context of false and unfulfilled promises, populism, in its permanent intention to deceive the masses, does not cease to use open and covert lies without worrying about them being exposed because what matters most to it is the media effect they produce in accordance with their interests. At the end of 2019, some American media, including the Washington Post, reported that, in the 1,055 days in office, President Trump had made 15,413 false or misleading statements, which means an average of almost 15 lies per day.

(see: https://es.wikipedia.org/wiki/Veracidad_de_las_declaraciones_de_Donald_Trump)

According to Mr. Frank Bruni, columnist for The New York Times (Aug. 07, 2019), he said: "There is no greater farce than when a president denounces what he himself represents. That is the case of the president of the United States." For said columnist, this phrase summarizes Trump's biggest and most dangerous lie. According to the cited source, among the most common lies are: "We are building the wall" (160 times), "We made the biggest tax cut in history" (143), "We have the best economy in the history of the USA" (134), "Democrats want to allow uncontrolled immigration" (123), "We are paying almost 100% of European defense" (102 times).

The list is long and would be redundant to expand on the same, but as a reflection, we can ask ourselves: Did the American people care little or nothing that their president lies repeatedly, or did they already get used to it? Why has Trump made a habit of his rude, inconsiderate, and even disrespectful way of lying to citizens? Why did the relationship between this sleepy mass and the lying populist politician become perverse? And not the slightest hint of change is observed in any of the intervening parties, and on the contrary, this unhealthy relationship is strengthened and consolidated. Where does the fact that citizens experience a contradictory duality lead us in which, on the one hand, they become complicit and co-responsible for a smelly scheme of domination and, on the other hand, they become the suffering and sacrificial recipient of it?

It is worth putting on the table the observations of a study carried out by the Royal Society: "Processing political disinformation: understanding the Trump phenomenon," cited in: "The reason for populism…" [19] where it is reported that the political class, unlike than what happened before, it is less affected by lies. Among the curiosities of the study, it is shown that when it came to Trump's statements, even if they were false, the attribution of truthfulness increased regardless of the substance of the point of view expressed, but the value judgment and previous feelings of affinity. The study cited concluded that:

"Voters do not value truthfulness as a sine qua non-condition for supporting a candidate but will campaign for the one who best connects with their previous prejudices about what is correct and what is not."

According to other references, such as the Gallup survey cited in, the approval rating for Trump's administration started at 48%. During the first quarter of 2020, it reached its highest level with 49%. The average acceptance percentage was 41% (2017-2021), and finally, the lowest point of approval was 34% in January 2021. What is notable about the trend described is its relative stability without presenting sudden variations.

(https://news.gallup.com/poll/203198/presidential-approval-ratings-donald-trump.aspx)

When it comes to a candidate in an electoral campaign, the issue of lies is a matter of controversy. On the one hand, his supporters, sympathizers, and those who are undecided about him can tolerate, ignore and even take as true the lies that are presented to him because their obtundation, feelings and subjectivities allow it. On the other hand, opponents also seek to confront, criticize and demonstrate these lies. The repercussions of party competition are limited to the revenues, profits, tricks, or tricks typical of any electoral dispute.

But when one observes, as in the case of Trump, that in his presidential role, he continued to lie and behave as if he were still in the electoral campaign, attracting all the media noise that only sought to privilege the rating more than the content of the information said, then the repercussions of this irresponsibility take on a risky profile. It is as if the president were walking "on the edge of

---

[19] op cit pags 143-144

a knife," giving his decisions a high degree of incredibility, inconsistency, and instability. This is how it was perceived on the internal front by citizens, part of the business sectors, opponents, and the press, and it was also perceived by external observers.

Additionally, the drag of an aggressive, imposing personality, little predisposed to accepting recommendations that do not fit with his preconceived schemes and Trump's style of managing public affairs as if it were his private company gave rise to notorious cases of separations, forced resignations or volunteers of a good number of collaborators who, due to the daring to disagree or wanting to amend the plan, were replaced to give greater space and presence to an entourage of unconditional people always willing to say "Yes, Sir" than to in the long run, they would not prevent him from outbursts such as the one related to the Ukraine scandal that led to the impeachment trial he had to face at the end of 2019.

In the first presidential election bid, the scheme worked satisfactorily for Trump. But in his first re-election attempt, he was no longer an outsider and was saddled with a questionable political past that did not allow him to achieve his goal. However, he was left with the feeling that he could have been re-elected, and currently (July 2023), he persists and attacks in an aggressive re-election campaign in which he must carry a heavy backpack of major and serious judicial charges against which he has appeared as a victim of the present establishment, what will happen? There is still a lot of ground to cover and appreciate in these unique forms of populism.

Back to the theme of our work, what does the mess of populism describe have to do with business management? It has a lot to do with: first, when turning the page from the electoral environment to that of the economic and social reality, the quality that any public administration develops is no longer determined by promises, intentions and words but by actions, progress and achievements. The latter are the specific and objective signals that are provided to economic agents (businesspeople, producers, investors, merchants, consumers, workers, professionals, technicians, etc.) who, based on them, will make their respective decisions in the economic environment in they are faced with concerns.

So, if in the field of facts (and not cheap, misguided and lying talk), such signals are not clear, do not exist, or simply show a wrong direction that ignores the recommendations of responsible advisors, specialists, and scientists, it fosters a climate of uncertain and unfavorable expectations.

Secondly, the challenge of effective and efficient public management will influence the behavior and trends of economic sectors, industries, and the market in general. Depending on the orientation, dynamics and priorities that are imposed on management (and its attention not only to short-term problems but also to alleviating longer-term problems), the expectations of the described sectors and their partners may or may not be satisfied and clarify their uncertainties. In the end, it will be clear what and who is privileged and what and who is deferred.

Thirdly, the human dimension cannot be separated from any public management and will determine whether the relationship between rulers and the governed is harmonious or conflictive if it is developed within the framework of ethics and adherence to values or if, on the contrary, lies prevail, the bad example, the permanence of lies and falsehoods, the disregard and intolerance of cultural diversity and basic civil rights. The authoritarian audacity to overwhelm other powers and institutions, the tricks of political demagogy and other absurdities of those responsible for public management have their limits.

When such practices persist, living with them and accepting them as if they were normal will lead, whether due to ineptitude or blindness, to exceeding these limits and promoting recurrent overexposures and unsuspected aggravations of social crises. For any public administration or business manager, the Latin sentence "res non verba" (realities, not words) is clear. With this, we want to emphasize that beyond populist masks, the importance of the issue of reciprocal trust between rulers and citizens, between a company, its workers, and its community prevails.

4.3.3. Populism in Peru

Regarding tricks to gain the support of the masses combined with lies and posturing, my father told me that during the time of the Peruvian electoral campaigns in which he lived (1950s), Mr. Manuel Prado, while still a candidate, presidential in Peru, gathered masses in his electoral campaign in the sugar establishments of northern Peru and promised that, if he reached the presidential position, he would return to the area to "mingle with peasants and workers in the agricultural work of the people." In response to my admiration for such demagoguery, he confirmed to me that the people believed him and applauded him.

Since that time, the Peruvian citizens and the traditional political representations showed and confirmed that, in terms of elections, popular sentiment prevailed. This candidate, an illustrious representative of the rancid Lima aristocracy and its interests, was finally elected president of Peru for up to two periods (1939-1945 and 1956-1962) and, as far as is known, in his subsequent visits to northern Peru, he never was confused with peasants doing agricultural work.

In this "quid pro quo" game of exchange, the people stretch out their hands and receive everything: in Peru, according to relatives, it was known that the candidate General Manuel A. Odría, to gain popular sympathies, ordered a sandwich of ham to those attending rallies during electoral campaigns. Also, during the time of Fernando Belaunde, modest monetary compensation was distributed for attendance at rallies. During the military government of General Velasco, attendees at rallies were also compensated and facilities were granted for titling plots of land for housing. In addition to the trivial lies and the handouts received, in that military era (1968-1975), when I had my first political experiences, the official propaganda machinery proclaimed the populist message: "the solid binomial formed by the People-Armed Forces." Message spread in all media and ad nauseam so that the opposition and the masses keep it in mind.

The recent Peruvian (and Latin American) political scene in the last decades was not exempt from the populist phenomenon. Over there, we have the elected political outsiders such as Alberto Fujimori, Alejandro Toledo, Ollanta Humala, Pedro Pablo Kuczynski, Martin Vizcarra (by uneven succession) and recently Pedro Castillo and Dina Boluarte (also in uneven succession). All of them, in the heat of the electoral processes, in an "express" manner, with the urgency and improvisations of the case, created their own political party or were invited to join presidential boards of weak existing parties (without substance, form, or doctrine).

To keep up appearances, they developed their brief program or government plan (a conglomerate of generic, loose and unconnected ideas from which effective phrases with massive impact are rescued) and formed an improvised call to a good part of collaborators, several of whom were already in the enjoyment of high positions of power (ministers, parliamentarians, magistrates and high-level technocrats) removed the masks of loyalty, separating themselves and marking the distance from the group that brought them to power.

In the Peruvian parliament, this style of desertions and rearrangements became commonplace, and the term "turncoats" (deserters) was coined to refer to those congressmen who, with the greatest self-confidence, abandoned the initial political group to end up joining another group forming a group "new" or integrate the independent label of "non-grouped congressman." In practice, all of them ended up allying with one another with greater predominance and even with an opposite tendency to the one they initially formed.

This execrable parliamentary class with little or no political party and doctrinal affiliation was not aware of or was not interested (even until today) in the contempt and resentment it accumulated in popular sentiment. The masses were and continue to witness the sad spectacle of such divorces and "happening" marriages. Mr. Winston Churchill, in his two-term administration as English Prime Minister (1940-45 and 1951-55), must have witnessed similar problems since he is credited with the phrase, "Some men change parties for the good of their principles, and others change their principles for the good of their parties."

As an example of "populist" measures, Peru is rewarded by a fatality since the Congress elected in 2019 was expected to be more weighted than the previous one. However, the rule that each new congress is worse has been confirmed than the preceding. In that sense, said congress approved a series of measures with a heavy populist bias: formalization (in the midst of a pandemic) of passenger transportation in "collectives" (private cars that transport people in overcrowded conditions), early and partial releases of supposedly intangible funds for retirement purposes under the management of the Pension Fund Administrators (AFP), suspension of toll collections on land transportation routes, projects to reformulate the existing pension system, project to establish a wealth tax, etc. These initiatives were populist in nature and had in common undressing a saint too, with the same clothing clothes another.

In the opinion of an analyst, Mr. Roberto Abusada (see Diario "El Comercio," Lima, Peru, May 14, 2020), in these measures, in addition to being approved without prior passage through the relevant commissions, "the economic rationality and the Legal and constitutional locks are left aside... A diligent Congress would debate each initiative in committees, gathering opinions from experts to report on the impact of each project. Sectors potentially affected positively or negatively would be called to express their opinions."

The analyst maintained that the legislative branch is undermining trust, "which will be even worse when this Congress finishes ruining it with its short-termism, clientelism and its unbridled populism" (underlining are ours). Indeed, the cycle of parliamentary ineptitude has been repeated with the current congress (with a right-wing majority) corresponding to the presidential term of Mr. Castillo (with a leftist tendency) and his successor Dina Boluarte.

In Peru, for a long time now, the absence of values and tainted practices of anti-values are leading us towards a growing number of politicians without principles or principles hidden by them. The "liveliness and unscrupulous" of a certain class of Peruvian politicians has no limits. This is a clear sign that the problems of crisis of leadership and values described in previous chapters go beyond the business sphere explained above and are also highly visible in the political sphere. There is no point in having adequate cultural support in the business sphere if we do not also have the same support in the political sphere and institutionality.

Peruvian citizens have been spectators of how, in their crazy race towards the presidential seat, the politicians described found it easy to catch unwary people and reach power, but once in power, it was extremely difficult for them to stay there and conduct satisfactory management. The lack of a sufficient political "background" emerged, either due to inexperience, ineptitude, inexperience in public management, and due to getting mixed up in the cocktail shaker of dependence on de facto powers and corrupt temptations (many of them fueled by the Odebrecht gale and other more recent ones, but always with the same background). The truth is that in the end, such characters have ended up in serious problems with the law and with the risk of conviction and imprisonment (already materialized in several cases).

A case that deserves to be highlighted was that of Alberto Fujimori who had an arduous electoral competition with another famous outsider in politics, the writer Mario Vargas Llosa. In the novel "The Fish in the Water" (Editorial Seix Barral, S.A 1993), the writer recounts this electoral experience in which he reveals, as a "mea culpa," his electoral setback due in part to his reluctance to ignore that the electoral competition should have been between outsiders because the electorate was fed up with the country's traditional political class.

Although the writer initially formed an independent movement ("Libertad") in which he could have had better fortune, he ended up agreeing to a new political front (FREDEMO), allying himself with that political class that the people detested and distrusted. As he himself relates in said novel (p. 97) regarding his electoral marketing advisors:

> "I ignored a lot of advice...because it crashed against considerations of principle......One of those pieces of advice, from the first in-depth survey, carried out at the beginning of 1988 to the last one carried out on the eve of the second round, was: break with the allies and run as an independent candidate...the polls showed from beginning to end of the campaign that in the social sectors "C" and

"D," (corresponding to the poor and very poor Peruvians) that represented two-thirds of the electorate, there was deep disappointment and great resentment towards the parties, especially those that had already enjoyed power."

The precision in parentheses is ours. This same discredited political class generated a thousand problems in the management of his electoral campaign, and that same political class allowed him, in his own words:

"...make a depressing discovery. Real politics, not that which is read and written...but that which is lived and practiced every day, has little to do with ideas, values, and imagination...and, to put it crudely, with generosity, solidarity, and idealism. It is made almost exclusively of maneuvers, intrigues, conspiracies, pacts, paranoia, betrayals, a lot of calculation, not a little cynicism and all kinds of juggling. Because **the professional politician, whether from the center, from the left or from the right, what really mobilizes, excites, and keeps him in activity is power, reaching it, staying in it or occupying it again as soon as possible"** (see "The fish in the water," the emphasis added is ours).

The people, like theater spectators, watched in amazement as groups and people happily and contentedly boarded the victory train of the probable winner, according to the pre-election polls. But the popular verdict, whether due to distrust of that political class or the fear spread in the counter-campaign over the probable package of measures that FREDEMO would take, determined that the balance tilted in favor of Fujimori.

In the end, and against the forecasts of pollsters and despite the million-dollar propaganda campaign of FREDEMO in all the media, it was demonstrated that in politics, negative synergy can also be experienced where "the whole can be less than the sum of the parts," especially in cases where the characteristics, qualities and contents of the elements that make up the summative operation play against it. This fact could be classified not so much as Fujimori's victory but as Vargas Llosa's great defeat because "the vote against" prevailed (antipathy to the candidate, his partners, and the image they projected). Curiously, this "vote against" factor is repeated with other protagonists in subsequent elections, where candidate Keiko Fujimori was repeatedly the loser.

For greater clarity of what happened, we must separate Mr. Mario Vargas Llosa (MVLL) in his version as a writer and novelist of unquestionable quality and prestige from the person who attacks the Peruvian political scene in his version as a superstar candidate. No one questioned that being an outstanding writer does not necessarily entitle one to be a good ruler or statesperson.

Precisely, the party platform that supported him was supposed to provide him with the support required for his future government administration. What was it about taking advantage of his reputed literary prestige as a lever to access power. For his part, the writer, a novice and aware of his political orphanhood, believed he saw in that political support the sufficient party base that every politician requires.

As usually happens in Peru, an agreed marriage was consummated and based on the interest of both parties. A marriage that would only last the period of electoral euphoria. The lack of background and sense of smell of the political candidate makes him doubt and ignore the advice of his electoral advisors (leave the front; your associates are repudiated by the electoral majority!). But the enthusiasm from his auspicious converted position (initially an enthusiastic defender of socialism and currently a fervent defender of liberalism) gave him the opportunity to embrace and champion a liberal front with political parties of doctrines that he ardently defended and promoted.

This, combined with his clear favoritism in the pre-election polls, together with the gale of sycophants, second-guesses and careerists who always surround every favorite candidate, ended up elevating him in a cloud of cotton wool and consummating his obnubilation. Years after an examination of conscience and according to the last quotes presented, the writer would have to recognize his own unease about "that depressing discovery" of the political class of the center, the left and the right, that notoriously supported him.

Throughout this process of electoral competition, as highlighted by Mr. Atilio Boron, one of his harsh critics and opponents of his political position, his shortcomings and blunders were evident that, as a political protagonist, led him down a lost path to his electoral defeat. (See: The dream of the marquis. Mario Vargas Llosa, a pen at the service of the empire." Monte Avila Editores Latinoamericana, 1st Edition, 2021.

The writer, despite the recognition of his "mea culpa" of ignoring his campaign advisors, despite the recognition of that deplorable discovery of the country's politics and politicians and despite evident recurring phenomena in various realities in the rest of Latin America, continues to reaffirm himself in his converted position, his fervent ideological position and the dissemination of his liberal political creed have not changed one millimeter. As we noted before, his work propagandizing liberal (or neoliberal) positions is independent of his qualified work as a renowned writer. Another issue is that, according to Mr. Boron, the writer uses prestige and literary fame, in addition to the support of all that paraphernalia of the big press and related international institutions, to continue influencing public opinion and in the framework of political decisions of the region.

We have a pending ideological, political, and doctrinal debate on the table in which we can be in total or partial agreement or disagreement with the positions of MVLL or Mr. Boron. Of course, an interesting debate that we keep in mind, but that goes beyond the scope of this work.

Writing this part of history after the battles have been fought gives us a certain advantage in observing the mark of an important milestone for everything that came after. The people, always forgetful, find it difficult to learn, ponder, assimilate, and reconsider the cost of their election and become, in each electoral dispute, an influential and even manipulable sector. Popular emotionality and sentimentality prefer and reward the candidate who presents himself as a victim of having suffered something (again, compassionate sentimentality).

This was very well used in the presidential re-election campaigns of Fernando Belaunde (triumphant return as a victim of deportation) and Alan García (triumphant return as a victim of persecution and political asylum). The oratory demagoguery of both candidates deceived the masses and validated their re-election regardless of whether their previous government management was average or terrible or if what they offered had any basis.

We dare to maintain that in the case of Alberto Fujimori, if he had not been legally prevented from holding any public office again, he would surely have run again, and the masses, to compensate for it, would have re-elected the "poor man" (triumphant return of voluntary self-exile). We have highlighted this last word (poor man) in quotation marks because, although the statement may seem perverse, perhaps a large part of the population is unaware that, according to a respectable organization such as Transparency International, Alberto Fujimori appears on the "top list" of the ten greatest international kleptocrat leaders with a record of having raised the trifle of 600 million dollars between 1990 and 2000.

The reference only includes Alberto Fujimori and not his close collaborators such as Vladimiro Montesinos (intelligence advisor, who for representing power in the shadows was considered the Peruvian Rasputin) currently imprisoned and from whom nearly 200 million dollars from illegal activities (influence peddling, arms and drug trafficking) were recovered from his secret accounts

286

in foreign banks. Nor does it include a certain corrupt circle in the armed forces that supported him and to which he ended up demoting.

In a kleptocracy, the ruling elite of the system uses power to amass personal fortunes. They often use money laundering mechanisms or divert funds into secret bank accounts in tax havens as a tactic to cover embezzlement or theft. The distinctive note of the scheme described in most Peruvian cases is impunity, where a system of endemic corruption prevails at all levels of power.

This theoretical description is familiar to Peruvians. Our very condescending, paternal, and forgetful people, not being able to do the favor of re-electing Alberto Fujimori, have been on the verge of doing so with his daughter Keiko, who by endorsement, took the baton and ran in the three recent presidential election processes and went on to contest in the second round a final election that he lost by tight margins. How long will the Peruvian people continue to be clouded and dependent on what the Fujimori dynasty does?

The current Fujimori leadership, monopolized by the figure of Keiko (who was in temporary prison accused of money laundering, obstruction of justice, and influence management), will be expected. Firstly, it will be difficult to counteract the significant political wear and tear due to the irresponsible obstructionist work of his party when it had a congressional majority due to its shameless shielding (parliamentary protection to prevent judicial processes) of notorious figures of corruption (prosecutors and judges) and members of his own group, ignoring obvious fragrances.

Secondly, given the events that occurred at the end of September 2019 that led to the dissolution of the congress by the former president in office, Mr. Martin Vizcarra, the Fujimori group lost its main bastion of struggle and was tasting (temporarily) relative wear and tear of power and the only thing evident is the weakening of its platform in various instances of power. However, it cannot be ruled out that even in retreat, any wounded beast can counterattack and surprise its rivals. We will see later how the events continued to happen.

The Peruvian economy presented a decade (2006-2015) of respectable dynamism, but the erratic international crisis (slowdown in external demand for exported products, recessionary trends in the main world economies, worsening of conflicts in trade agreements) and unfavorable factors in the internal sphere (slowdown of foreign direct investment and national private investment, political instability, worsening of social and citizen security conflicts, continuation of high rates of informality), have caused the last five years to experience the resumption of a worrying slowdown that became accentuated, as we highlight later, due to the emergence of the Covid 19 pandemic.

If what we previously called a severe institutional crisis is added to the economic panorama described above (critical individual and interconnected functioning between powers and institutions, questioning of the schemes and results of citizen representation), a panorama is formed that is not conducive to a desirable architecture. Legal-institutional that supports the economic and social development of the country. In an environment where the irresponsible corruption of certain authorities is colluding with certain civil and criminal strata, the lack of respect for the authorities, the propensity to fail to comply and evade legal and regulatory provisions, domestic violence, crime, citizen insecurity, improvisation, informality, etc., it becomes more difficult to initiate and carry out reforms. Peru is a kind of patient with a generalized infection.

The pollution is to such a degree that the few honest and upright authorities and citizens who happily exist appear as heroes and saviors when all they do is fulfill their normal functions. The task of **social prophylaxis** is titanic because the authorities elected and appointed to exercise this function (that is, both the representatives of the old and stale political class and the latest generations of outsiders) have fallen into the same cycle of incompetence, corruption, and lack of reliability.

In this sequence of Peruvian political instability, the following stood out: the load of the political opposition (with repeated failed attempts by parliament to request a presidential vacancy against Pedro Castillo), the tenacious offensive and speed of the Attorney General's Office, which came to the forefront to accuse and investigate President Castillo's family circle for signs of corruption that have been uncovered and that ended up seriously compromising him. Finally, we must also add the permanent harassment of the mainstream media against the president since months before he assumed power and that he also sought to direct public opinion against the newly released executive branch at that juncture.

Of course, no one can deny President Castillo's ineptitude and incompetence in managing a public administration as complicated as ours. Added to the above is the orphanhood and lack of political operators who contribute to its management and provide communicating vessels with the other political forces and its mistake in surrounding itself with close people who only sought access to the spheres of power to take advantage of this. The ongoing investigations will determine, according to the evidence, whether the president was finally colluding and was part of the corruption mechanism that is beginning to be revealed.

The country would have been grateful if the president, aware of his limitations, his inexperience and inability to summon capable and honest people, had stepped aside and resigned from office to avoid greater evils. Unfortunately, this possibility was overshadowed by the myopia of the conception that if I - the executive branch - lose or give in, you - the legislative branch opposition - win (or vice versa). What prevails in negotiations is called a **"zero-sum game,"** where the benefits or successes obtained by one of the parties are equal to the losses or failures by the other party. Neither party wants to give in because they understand that giving in means losing, and this means making the opposing party win.

Reaffirming what we stated before, in these circumstances, distrust, hostility and lack of cooperation prevail between the parties. In this, the absence of an agreed strategy between powers to overcome the increasingly aggravated trap in which the country found itself becomes latent. Meanwhile, during the term of the Castillo government, we witnessed critical confrontations and exchanges of mistakes between the executive and legislative branches.

The opposition only wanted, "in a tantrum and in the midst of a desperate wait," the immediate presidential vacancy without having made an outline, nor being clear about the best way to carry it out, nor the reasonable options for the subsequent transition period. Options in which, despite the popular clamor for everyone to leave, the parliamentary opposition turns a deaf ear and excludes the option of withdrawing from the current political scene.

On the other hand, in this situation, President Castillo, faithful to his political reading since his time as a candidate, loaded his work agenda, deciding to reinforce his attention, priority and contacts with the provinces with which he felt more connected and found it less hostile than Lima. The presidential strategy described exasperated the fierceness of the parliamentary opposition, the Prosecutor's Office and the systematic media hunt of the written and television media that could not understand how "despite the evidence they showed," President Castillo was beginning to rebound in approval polls.

It is curious that a large part of the citizenry seems tired of the fact that newspapers and news programs have had the same script for a year and a half and that, because of this, they have lost their audience and are dangerously incubating a kind of **social apathy**. A representative part of the population shows a certain reluctance, lack of interest and little will to develop critical consciousness. Citizens were not sufficiently motivated to support the discredited parliamentary class in their persistent attempts to vacate the presidency, nor to support an inefficient government with signs of corruption. The popular cry, as we pointed out before, was and continues to be everyone leave and the people do not feel represented by any of the competing powers (executive vs. legislative).

Additionally, in the context of experienced social conflicts, the media have ignored a phenomenon that should also be a matter of verification. The popular sentimentality of the common citizen has a kind of effervescent effect that tends to favor those who are considered the victim (we showed this before in the favoritism of the candidacies of former presidents and unknown outsiders) or also favor those with whom they consider themselves subliminally identified. What we notice subliminally corresponds to cases with little or no conscious perception of the senses of reason but with a defined emotional impact on population behavior.

We mentioned before in the American populism, the lies, fallacies and all that set of distortions of truth and reason propagated by former President Donald Trump during his campaign and his government gave him approval advantages because studies showed that it mattered little or nothing if the person lied or said things inappropriate to reason, what mattered was having gained his sympathy and identification and the dissemination framework media for it.

The truth is that despite the load of the offensive described (opposition, prosecutor's office, and media), it has been of such magnitude and ferocity that, paradoxically, it is promoting the opposite effect to the desired one. Whether due to apathy or popular sentimentality, for both reasons and for whatever reason, the truth is that these factors play a peculiar counterweight in the load described. Before the former President Castillo was vacated, he exhibited a 30% of approval rate. While his successor, Dina Boluarte, currently (second quarterly 2024) exhibits a very low 5% of approval that, jointly with its colluding parliament, also shows similar and embarrassing approval rates.

However, it must be recognized that the recent congressional attack for the presidential vacancy (the third attempt raised towards the beginning of December 2022), unlike the previous motions, presented a forceful arsenal that was the most serious attempt at a vacancy that had to be faced. Having predefined their respective strategies, the opposition and government were on the verge of debating the motion for this third vacancy (December 07, 2022) when suddenly the unusual and unexpected decision of political suicide by President Castillo to declare a self-coup without counting occurred with the support, nor basis, nor any legal justification for it.

We do not know if the clumsiness of what happened was the result of an unusual reaction to an erroneous reading of the situation or a poor perception of the actions of the forces and agents of the political scene (for or against). We suspect that he may have been misinformed or poorly advised by intimate circles of his trust, or he may also have been the victim of betrayal, as some suspect. His notorious nervousness during his speech and the disconcerted look on his face after it also denotes having been gripped by panic, fear, confusion or suffering from a chronic and severe depression that could have incapacitated or unbalanced him to make lucid decisions at important moments crucially.

Whatever the reason or for a combination of the possibilities described above, it became latent that a president must be an intelligent consumer of the recommendations of his advisors. But if we admit that advisors also suffer from technical incapacity, the circles of incompetence exceed the criteria of reasonableness and good sense. In this case, once again, the ineptitude and precarious management of Castillo and his team became known. The consequent and forced defenestration will cost him and the country dearly. The truth is that the illegality of his act, through a statement that ordered the dissolution of Congress and the reorganization of the judicial system, focused attention on what the Armed and Police Forces do or do not do, which already had certain signs of such clumsiness and ended tipping the balance in favor of the rule of law. A few hours after his failed statement, he was arrested and must face constitutional charges.

The majority opposition of the congress found itself with the table set to vacate him. Now, with justified reasons for constitutional violation, they set aside the previous vacancy motion based fundamentally on indications of corruption. However, making evident the exchange of clumsiness that we mentioned before, the also inept congress, in a summary process, without debate or defense, proceeded with the greatest pleasure to execute it politically through to the "immediate voting procedure" to decide a singular "vacancy express."

Immediately after that, "the Majesty of Parliament" burst into "delirium tremens" in jubilant celebration in the center of the parliamentary chamber, the congressional opposition confused in

291

hugs and celebrations, even crying, with exalted praise, compliments and photos to remember. The opposition "celebrated their great triumph". This spontaneous celebration was broadcast live on national television stations. What was the congressional opposition celebrating with so much hubbub? The congress did not obtain any triumph because it was Castillo himself and his stupid clumsiness who was also annihilated. The only thing that such celebrations achieved was to inflame resentments and animosities among a large part of the non-Limeño population (both those who reside in the interior of the country and those of non-Limeño origin who reside in Lima).

The enthrallment of the parliamentary opposition meant that they were not aware of the sad spectacle they were providing to the country. Their mediocrity made it impossible for them to consider in fair measure and with sufficient prudence that, no matter how justified the reasons for the well-deserved vacancy were, the bleeding of one power into the hands of another, carried out as the lawyers maintain, "with premeditation, cruelty, treachery and advantage," a depressing spectacle was offered that provoked greater rejection of the executioner and, contradictorily, a certain adhesion (of non-Lima majorities) to the culprit who clumsily tried to get rid of a repudiated Congress whose true achievement was to turn him into a victim. As confirmed by the surveys that we discussed later, these congresspeople, in their permanent disconnection from reality, did not keep in mind that they had such high disapproval, discredited and even worse than the also high disapproval of the government they had just liquidated.

So that it is not said that the previous criticisms of the opposition majority come from extreme leftist positions, we quote the opinion of Mario Vargas Llosa, whom no one could call leftist, published in the newspaper "El Comercio" of Lima on January 08, 2023, where regarding what happened at the juncture, he said: "Perhaps it is ridiculous to celebrate what happened, since the international image of Peru has been seriously affected in recent weeks." We agree on the ridiculousness of the celebration, but we disagree that said celebration and the events surrounding it are criticizable only because they damage the international image of the country. The international image of the country has been damaged and deteriorated for a long time and due to more serious factors than the congressional celebration.

We found the opinion of Mr. Max Hernández, psychiatrist and executive secretary of the National Agreement, to be very considered, an institution that seeks to promote dialogue and understanding between guardianship organizations and powers of the State, who in an interview with the newspaper El Comercio on the same date outlined what following:

"...I believe that many sectors have contributed here that have attributed Castillo's vacancy as if it had been an achievement of a congressional agreement when it was simply the moment in which Castillo had committed that hara-kiri...if you carry out a procedure (referring to the vacancy de Castillo), the correct thing was to maintain a correct silence. Using excessive relief, I think, encourages me to say that what we have lost is a lot of correction. I believe that that unwritten code that allowed us to relate with a degree of trust, with a degree of good faith, has been destroyed.

When the interviewer from the newspaper asks, in the face of this absolute distrust, how does this nostalgia and sympathy for Pedro Castillo arise now? The interviewee responds: Very deep, historical, cultural, and social reasons are at play, which points to a sort of valuation of certain dimensions of the identity. There is a particular way of understanding identity, that is, Andean, rather peasant, rather poor, rather suspicious of Lima."

As can be seen, the circumstances of the congressional celebration and the critical situation reveal to us the existence of deeper and more complex factors - trustworthiness, diversity, inequality, misunderstanding, exclusion, and others - that have predominated for a long time in this deteriorated international image of the country mentioned above.

The flood of votes from provincial citizens who garnered preferences for Castillo in the second round of the last electoral contest (although won by a narrow margin) has had a lot to do with that identification with the candidate of provincial origin, from rural areas, a professor of school, of modest social status, defender of labor rights, etc. Therefore, it is possible that on this occasion and in scenarios outside of Lima where the impact of the press media is lower, there may be traces of this subliminal identification (especially in social sectors D and E) mentioned above. If this is so, it is more understandable why, in the platform of the struggle of the provincial protesters coming to Lima, the demand for Dina Boluarte to resign or withdraw from the presidential mandate responds to the fact that, in fact, rather than being against her, they consider her a traitor to Pedro Castillo for whom they maintain traces of that nostalgic sympathy despite its illegality.

The parliamentary left has also had a discreet, uncoordinated, and dissimilar profile. After initial and auspicious support for the government, as the corruption scandals worsened, disenchantment was increasing, and it has been difficult for it to distance itself and rather its usual splits, dissidence and sometimes zigzagging and sometimes discreet and circumspect. This left, in its vain attempt to shake itself off the mud, has ended up more compromised than freed from it. Also, like their right-wing colleagues, they compete in performing clumsy, sad spectacles and curiously, to the admiration of locals and strangers, they have shown astonishing agreement with right-wing sectors in controversial votes negotiated under the table.

In short, the right and left members of the current congress will never accept that they are also co-responsible and are part of the problem of crisis and political instability that the country is experiencing. They only continue to reproach each other for this, but they come together when their interests coincide (prolonging their mandate until 2026, attacking the institutionality and independence of powers).

It should also be noted that the current opposition majority in Congress displays its agreed immediatism and has acted in recent times as a faithful leader of the Prosecutor's Office, which, as part of a process that has been called judicialization of politics, has been determining the agenda politics of the country. <u>This has made evident a coordinated strategy between both and with the audacity to act through the intermediary needs and interests of the Prosecutor's Office.</u> The congressional majority and its respective board had no problem, for example, in calling, on a Sunday at three in the afternoon (December 11, 2022), a meeting of the full congress (extraordinary and urgent) with the sole purpose, finally achieved late at night, to remove the presidential immunity that belonged to Castillo and that the Prosecutor's Office needed to annul it so that he can be tried like any citizen and request his preventive detention for up to a year and a half.

What was signed in the preceding paragraph has been confirmed in the last months of November and December of the year 2023, where the collusion and embarrassing exchange of favors between the Prosecutor's Office and votes granted by conspicuous members of Congress were evidenced, with evidence from chats and audios who decided on agreements that favored the interests of both parties. In this way, the election of the head of the Ombudsman's Office, a key position that presides over the Commission who elects the members of the National Board of Justice (JNJ), which in turn is in charge of the election of and removal of judges and prosecutors. In this conflictive agreement (between congress and Prosecutor Benavides), they decided the forced separation of the supreme prosecutor, Zoraida Avalos (contrary to the intertest of Prosecutor

Benavides), and it was in the last stage to decide the defenestration of all the members of the current JNJ. The problem is just beginning, and there is still a lot to untangle.

It should be noted that if, for this opposition majority, former President Castillo was the cause of the crisis and that with his vacancy and arrest, a good part of the country's problems was resolved, they would have to be reproached for their major miscalculation. The novel has not yet finished, and it takes a while. Firstly, from a technical and judicial point of view, many things (in defense and against Castillo) will continue to come to light, but the lack of restraint, prudence and some clumsiness committed by the opposition forces that in their desperate attempt to process his "express vacancy", they did not carefully respect each and every one of the procedures of a delicate process that should have had all the formalities of the case, such as, for example, an elementary political trial given that even having been detained in flagrante delicto, he was still president.

Although the opposition justified its immediate action due to the exceptional and extraordinary situation that the self-coup gave rise to and which made it possible to shorten formalities, Castillo's defense has denounced such non-compliance, and it will possibly be a matter observed in the report of the Inter-American Commission on Human Rights that has just been published visit Lima in mid-December 2022. It must be clear that we are not defending the illegality and clumsiness of Castillo, but we are only saying that in the case of a special case such as that of a sitting president, all the requirements had to be scrupulously complied with legal guarantees. All of this will finally be clarified, along with the substance of the complaints, in a still-long judicial process.

Secondly, from a political point of view, the permanent frustration of a large part of the citizens who do not feel represented or identified with the current opposition parliament nor with Castillo and his government due to obvious signs of corruption that have engaged. When the channels of representation and citizen participation break and collapse, the people demonstrate habitually as they usually do, in the streets and with mobilizations where they make their protests, complaints and demands felt, which began to spread throughout the country. The popular demand that everyone leave (executive and legislative power) is still in force and includes the current provisional government of Dina Boluarte, and of course, the demand to close congress and advance elections also remains alive.

It cannot fail to be recognized that, as always amid protests and in troubled waters, elements outside the law, illegal miners, criminals and other agents who see in popular discontent the opportunity to take advantage of their interests and further destabilize the system. In this sense, attacks against public and private property, against ambulances and police posts and attempts to take over airports, which have nothing to do with popular protests and demonstrations, are equally condemnable.

The current situation proposes to the present administration a strategy of "fine surgery social" very distant and different from the old resource of appealing to police and armed forces repression. It is evident that the current administration lacks such a strategy, is neither qualified nor has enough political operators to implement it, and, finally, is not interested. The popular clamor has been to accentuate the demand for early elections. Given this, both the government led by Dina Boluarte and the congressional majority have had to, in the face of pressure from the popular marches, retreat from their initial position of wanting to remain on the political scene until 2026 and reluctantly agree to debate a proposal to advance elections. Unfortunately, given the shamelessness of mutual recrimination and hypocrisies between both powers (executive and legislative), said proposal became part of the unimportant file of this parliament.

The newspaper El Comercio de Lima interviewed Mr. Alberto Vergara, a Political Scientist (December 11, 2022), about the events of the Peruvian political situation who highlighted the following:

> "… let's be honest, this result (in reference to the current crisis) has been cooked up by the entire Peruvian political spectrum. You would have to be either very sectarian or very naive to believe that Congress or the Peruvian right has any appreciation for democracy. That is the misfortune of Peru, there is neither democratic left nor right. And from that comes this turbulence, it is natural that instability is our most stable trait.

> As Roberto Gargarella suggests, the rule of law and democracy must be based on a conversation between equals. If conversation is non-existent and we despise each other, democracy is unviable... ultimately what we have is a tremendous crisis of trust.

> …What has rotted is political representation. We can have a new Constitution, new laws, new elections, whatever you want, but what has rotted is the raw material of politics. There are only birds of passage with a tendency to pickpocket. The medium-term and general interests have disappeared. If we only have selfishness and immediacy, progress is impossible."

So, due to the experimentation of this system of corruption and endemic degradation, a good part of the Peruvian people have been for a long time been in the limbo of a trap of indecision, they have no one to choose; they do not know who to choose nor who to trust and he has spent the last elections plucking daisies among outsiders to finally opt for the one who represents, in his opinion, "the lesser evil" (This one yes, This one no), and the one who is finally elected, is for reasons that have nothing to do with parties or programs but with popular affinities, sentimentalities and antipathies towards the adversaries. The offer of electoral options leaves much to be desired.

In the current circumstances, when in the interview, the political scientist is asked how President Dina Boluarte should govern, his response returns us to the topics discussed in the initial chapters of this study (strategy, leadership, and values):

> "…She has not yet built the legitimacy that allows her to govern… What is her purpose in the presidency? We do not know, if she does not propose something transparent to the country, something that aims to get it back on track, instability is going to eat her up… and much worse if she considers that repression is a way to stay in power.

> …I do not think we can improve if citizens do not return to the political scene. Politicians are going to continue doing their thing if there is no citizen pressure, why doesn't it appear? Citizens know that the main problem in Peru is not a party or a person, it is not Fujimorism or Castillo, as the basic left and the basic right believe... our problem is not a person but a situation, a system. And it is difficult to mobilize against something so multidimensional. It is easier to do it against someone or something. And yet, what has us stuck is a situation. I am afraid that without a citizenry that puts in line the politicians who take advantage of this troubled river, things will not calm down."

Meanwhile, the absence of honest leaders is conclusive, and the trap of indecision is highly capitalized by those who never lose or rather by those who always win, whatever the political-social situation and circumstance and whatever the forecasts and results of any electoral process. Such winners are campaign advisors, polling companies and the media. These agents oversee highlighting barbs, sarcasm, lies, insults and prohibited tricks of all calibers, orchestrated debates, biased advertising and some dubious surveys "at the request of the client." These winners are in charge of putting together the electoral feast that keeps the voter from being dazed and enthralled, and stunned. They lead to the distracted electorate, with simulated pulling of hair and ears, towards details of formalisms, ignoring and overlooking the substance of that "state of affairs" referred to earlier by Mr. Alberto Vergara.

To expand on what has been pointed out, the jealously structured and disseminated propaganda feast has its peculiarities: The presidential candidates usually attend their proselytizing visits wearing fake costumes and different clothing from the place they visit (coast, mountains and jungle) and even pretend to dance their typical pieces, in this populist masquerade they are usually accompanied by some local entertainment character who lends himself to the game to collaborate in gaining followers. In the final period, there is no shortage of low blows to weaken the opponent or the one who is leading the polls.

Finally, on voting day, it has become customary to put on the absurd televised show of the "popular breakfast" in a marginal neighborhood of any city where the only aim is to show an artificial popular sympathy of the current candidate towards the people. Regardless of whether he is elected or not, the candidate's visit and his "populist" electoral breakfast with said population and locality will be forgotten. But since memory is fragile, this last act of disguised proselytism will be repeated in the next presidential vote.

The problem of populism in third-world countries like Peru is that, in addition to promoting vulnerability and institutional decay, it cannot hide serious economic restrictions that make it difficult to address and solve alarming social problems in health, education, housing, employment, retirement pensions, care for vulnerable populations (children, women and the elderly), citizen security, etc. An example of this was the manifest social explosion in Chile (Oct 2019), which, despite its respectable political and economic stability in recent decades, has awakened amid an abrupt manifestation of popular discontent with a reserved prognosis.

Writing these lines, I stopped to listen to a Peruvian television news program regarding a problem of robberies and assaults that are common in the current Peruvian reality. He was an entrepreneur who, with valiant effort, accumulated his savings to travel to Lima and established a small business, a hairdressing business in which he invested nearly ten thousand dollars. Less than three months after starting its activities, its premises, despite having security provisions and being in a relatively central location, were the victim of robberies on up to four occasions, stripping it off its main tools and work equipment. Despite this, he remained unwavering in his intention to get up and continue in his entrepreneurial endeavors.

The above is enough to discourage anyone, and I wonder if any of these populist politicians from the right and the left, who tear their clothes apart in talk, have ever had or will have the courage and predisposition to risk what, based on their own effort (without government help, favors, bribes, etc.), makes them understand or undertake what it means to build and develop a business initiative. The anonymous entrepreneur mentioned above is a true example of persistence, of fighting against the adversity of the environment and of firmness in the purpose of continuing the path of carving out a better future.

The intricate connection of this triangle between economy, politics and society leads us to rescue interesting approaches made by Dr. Francisco Durand [20] in "The twelve apostles of the Peruvian Economy…," where he maintains the following:

> "According to Eduardo Anaya, economic groups can be defined as a set of companies of diverse nature and specialties, directed according to a common policy,.. maintaining their legal autonomy within the group. Economic power groups (EPG) constitute an established topic of study. The predominant focus among academics and the press is economics. For them, groups are a market phenomenon. They see them as organizations that generate employment, develop technologies, and obtain profits.

> There is another less frequent but equally important approach, they come from politics. The GPE are studied as de facto powers, powerful entities that have the capacity to project their enormous material resources into politics, relate favorably to parties and congresspeople and maintain a close relationship and, to the extent this is possible, productive, or collusive with the State. This approach allows us to understand how GPEs act and the mechanisms they use to translate their enormous wealth into influence over public decisions: campaign financing, lobbies and "revolving doors." In recent times, the discussion also includes the use of bribes…

> …The GPE are entities commanded by influential elites, select minorities who control today more wealth than any other business sector or social group…they have a strong dominance of the market and profit levels, they are the main employers and taxpayers in the country, they are the ones that make the greatest investment in advertising and the ones that project the most in social and philanthropic works. They are also the largest contributors to political parties, the best clients of law firms and consulting firms… in short, they are people (these elites) whose power is known, respected or also rejected in political circles."

---

[20] "Los doce apóstoles…" op. cit. pages14-24 and 62

From the above, it is inferred that it is necessary to distinguish between what the gale of external variability means for that small circle of companies that are part of those elite business groups and, on the other hand, that an enormous number of small and medium-sized companies or sectors that do not belong nor are they linked to the conglomerate of GPE companies and their elites. For that first and select business conglomerate that makes up the GPE, the elites are in charge, through their pressure and influence in the spheres of government, of tipping the balance in their favor by structuring an artificial scheme that will increase, maintain or recover their economic power (exemptions tax exemptions, exemptions from procedures, tariff reductions on imported inputs and "blind protection" with high rates on the import of foreign products, preferential exploitation concessions in public services, differentiated exchange rates, preferential credits, financial rescue packages, etc.).

For its part, for that other vast majority of small and medium-sized companies lacking influence, patronage, and protectionist umbrellas, given their own limitations of size and operation, they are normally, in practice, excluded from the generous and compensatory invisible government hand.

They lack any representation and pressure scheme. So, when that gale of external conditions occurs (global supply crisis, foreign inflation, increase in the cost of external and internal financing, strikes, wars, epidemics, etc.), which are beyond any control and are not generated by them, they are left to the expense of managing with their scarce resources through winding routes, adverse weather conditions and other types of risks. They will have to make do with their limited ability to generate marginal profits to which they have access. For all these reasons, they are called for their own survival to redouble their efforts at effectiveness and efficiency in their business management.

The triptych scenario mentioned above (economy, politics, and society) is completed in connection with the social sphere with peculiarities of our environment and that should not be ignored because of what they mean and represent. Again, let us take note of the specific reference that Dr. Francisco Durand, op. cit. pags. 14-24, tells us about the topic discussed:

> ...The GPE operate through the articulation of the economic, with the
> political and social, largely because "wealth marries wealth." Hence, marital
> alliances and social coexistence consolidate them if there are no racial fissures
> or of social and geographical origin. The incessant profit and wealth

accumulated in property and money allow corporations to have primacy as the most important economic agents, which goes hand in hand (adds the author) with access and influence on the State and social influence and recognition."

...In the same way that they have de facto influence, they have power as elites who develop habits. This fact differentiates them from ordinary mortals and begins with their social isolation...generating imperial mentalities...some scholars argue that they feel like a class apart, a special elite that does not live, think, and act like others. We are facing a new aristocracy of money.

The background is inequalities of all kinds, not only those due to the enormous concentration of resources in the hands of the GPE and property-owning families, but also because structural conditions of injustice have existed that are deeply rooted in society. Institutions have traditionally excluded the poor and have not given them opportunities because they have been subjected to racial discrimination. "(The underline is ours)

It is well said that the economy manifests itself in the political, social, and (we add) it is reflected in the cultural scenario that maintains links of connection and, at the same time, independence with those. We can present pieces of evidence of this, and we have selected two pieces of evidence that we find interesting. The first is the claim made by the prominent Peruvian bard Felipe Pinglo Alva in one of his greatest musical creations, the waltz "El Plebeyo" (published in 1934), where he reflects the echo of those facets of the conservative Lima of that time, and it describes the drama of an unrequited (or impossible) love due to social inequalities and prejudices ostensibly manifested since those times. Let's pay attention to the lyrics of the song that describes the following:

"...♫♫ The night already covers with its black crepe. Of the city, the streets that people cross with slow action. Artificial light with weak projection fosters the gloom that hides revenge and betrayal in its shadow. After working returns to his humble home, Luis Enrique, the commoner, the son of the people, the man who knew how to love and who is suffering from that infamous law of loving an aristocrat while he is a commoner,

Tremulous with emotion, he says this in his song: Love, being human, has something divine, loving is not a crime because even God loved. And if the affection is pure and the desire is sincere, why do they want to steal the faith of my heart from me? My blood, although commoner, also dyes red and the soul in which my incomparable love nests, she of noble birth and I a humble commoner, the blood is not different nor is the heart different. Lord, because beings are not of equal value!

Thus, in mortal duel, lineage, and passion, in silent struggle, they want to condemn me to such cruel pain, seeing that a love, because he is a plebeian, commits a crime if he claims the gloved hand of a fine woman. The heart that sees his ideal destroyed reacts and reflects in great rebellion that changes his humble face. Yesterday's commoner is today's rebel who everywhere proclaims equality in love..."

The underlining is ours. My preference for the musical genre emerged in this part of the work and I considered it pertinent to highlight the context of social inequalities since those times manifest in the artistic-musical scene. Despite this, no one has thought of the stupidity of calling it a revolutionary song, much less a terrorist one. However, so that you do not criticize for having chosen a topic that, inappropriately for some, may be light or trivial; I invite you to consider a more reflective theme where the same inequalities and discriminations caused a social explosion that inspired Mr. Ricardo Dolorier to compose the huayno "Flor de Retama" whose origin is more recent than the previous theme, dating back to June 21, 1969.

On that occasion, students and parents from the town of Huanta (Ayacucho) demonstrated in the streets in protest a decree given at the time by the military government of General Juan Velasco that eliminated free state education. As a result of the confrontation between the population and the police, and the Sinchis (elite police group), twenty people died. After the event, the military government backed down and repealed the controversial decree. (see https://es.wikipedia.org/wiki/Flor_de_Retama)

Those who issued this decree did not even have in mind that the Ayacucho region had been suffering from a situation of extreme poverty for decades. Indeed, it is a "protest song," and it is not surprising that each performer transmits it in their own way. For this reason, conservative sectors have vetoed it for wrongly considering it as an apology for terrorism. But as was noted, its origin had nothing to do with it (subversion occurred on the political scene in the 1980s), and neither was the song composed by terrorists, much less as a tribute to them.

Not even a dictatorship like Velasco's, supported by severe police repression, could subdue an authentic and fair popular demand. I hope that the memory of this historical lesson from more than fifty years ago awakens the conscience of today's forgetful political class. If not, the people singing the huayno "Flor of Retama" will remind them. Below, we reproduce the lyrics of the controversial song:

(see https://www.cancioneros.com/letras/cancion/739535/flor-de-retama-ntologia)

"…♫♫ Everyone see. Oh, let us see! Come, brothers and see. Oh, let us see! In the small square of Huanta, yellow broom flower, yellowish, yellowing Broom Flower. The Sinchis are entering on five corners. In the small square of Huanta, the Sinchis are surrounding. They are going to kill heartfelt Huantinos students, yellowish, yellowing Flower of Retama; They are going to kill heartfelt Huantine peasants, yellowish, yellowing Flower of Retama.

Where the life becomes colder than death itself, Taita inti (express reference to the Sun God, Inca divinity) burns indignantly. The great snows thaw, and the great lakes begin to fill. The great flood is about to arrive to bury worlds that oppress. And on the new land, the Retama will flourish and thus the applauses that sound above ta, ta, ta.

Where the blood of the people is spilled, where the blood of the people is spilled, right there the yellow broom flower blooms, the yellow broom flower blooms Retama Flower. The blood of the people has a pleasant perfume, the blood of the people has a pleasant perfume; It smells of jasmine, violets, geraniums, and daisies, of gunpowder and dynamite. It smells of jasmine, violets, geraniums, and daisies; Gunpowder and dynamite, damn it! Gunpowder and dynamite! Damn! Gunpowder and dynamite! "

Towards mid-December 2022, the serious Peruvian sociopolitical situation reached superlative levels and encouraged researchers and analysts to demonstrate, as everyone felt moved to express their opinion. We collect comments from personalities such as Mr. Raúl Asencio -Historian and principal researcher at the Institute of Peruvian Studies IEP- who has maintained aspects that we also previously discussed in various sections (see newspaper El Comercio, Lima, Dec 18, 2022)

"…As a result of the economic and social changes of globalization, Andrés Rodríguez-Posse maintains, a polarization between "winners and losers" territories would be occurring… As economic and political power concentrates, peripheral territories see opportunities diminish, spreading a sense of frustration and grievance…

In Peru, this fracture is based on other previous racial, political and cultural (fractures) and on a history of two centuries of exacerbated centralism that has led to a concentration of wealth and political power in the capital (Lima)...Polarization territorial division derives from situations of imbalance and inequity...Territorial fractures are increasing and have political consequences...Meeting the demands of relegated territories is an ethical issue but also an imperative for the preservation of democracy.

If the violence has reached the current point (23 deaths around December 19, 2022), it is not only because there are structural grievances but because of the actions of political actors: the inability of the Boluarte government (current president) to understand the magnitude of the challenge, the indolence and arrogance of Congress, the pressure of those who ask for more repression and militarization of public order and the irresponsibility of those who play to extreme the contradictions.

All these factors must be included in the equation. But <u>neither new elections nor a change of government, even if they are the only way to stop the massacres, are going to solve the problems derived from territorial polarization</u> and the frustration of millions of relegated Peruvians... who, in order to make themselves heard, they are willing to support extremist options, whether from the right or the left. And to follow them even down the path of coup." (emphasis is ours).

Similarly, another political analyst, the journalist Patricia del Río, whom we could in no way call leftist, has expressed, in the same source and date previously cited (El Comercio), a singular point of view regarding certain political protagonists national:

"Peru is burning and between bullets... and the perplexity of a country that wakes up more confused every day, the pettiness of a political class that abandoned its mandate of representation to make villainy its true standard is being drained. Congress no longer must pretend that it wants to stay, and from Almirante Montoya and Maricarmen Alva (conspicuous members of the right-wing opposition) to Waldemar Cerrón and Guido Bellido (members of the left wing of Congress) have voted to keep their seats while the country it falls apart (and we also add, it bleeds into the interior of the country).

The message of those who march (in the streets) is overwhelmingly forceful, and you must be foolish not to listen to it: they do not want this Congress, not even one more day... Although it is difficult to accept it, Pedro Castillo, with his scarce 30% acceptance, has managed to. According to the latest IEP survey, 44% of Peruvians support his coup adventure... How bad does this Congress have to be for an openly corrupt president to have been applauded for wanting to make them disappear?

As happens in situations of misgovernance, the legitimate indignation was joined by violent and criminals who have unacceptably looted and destroyed... However, instead of understanding the origin of the fury and seeking a strategy of dialogue with those who do have fair demands, the plan was to shoot them all without asking and indiscriminately brand them as terrucos" (for clarification to foreign readers, this term refers to those who are terrorists).

In the recent quotes, we must also indicate that the comments in parentheses are ours. The government, the parliamentary majority and certain press try to generalize and delegitimize all protests and all protesters by using the nickname terrorists. By "placing all protesters in the same bag" and due to the obvious presence of vandals, the aim is to stigmatize legitimate protests and, worse yet, justify indiscriminate and brutal repression.

It is also worth mentioning that the Congress question should take note that the recent survey conducted by the IEP shows that a significant 83% of the population approve of bringing forward elections. Faced with this obvious reality, the current congress is indifferent and indolent to the acute crisis that is being experienced. What seems clear is that, contradictorily, the evasion of responsibilities shown by both powers of the state (legislative and executive), despite having in their hands the ability to smooth out the crisis, their open intention to remain in power is generating a worsening of this crisis. They will pay dearly for the ineptitude and incompetence of their management.

That is why we say that the novel continues and what is coming in the coming months will have a lot of tragicomedy. From the political scene, we have learned the following phraseology: "Politics is the art of the possible." (in effect, we have just seen how the votes of opposing sides have agreed on the part of the extreme right -Renovación Popular- with the extreme left -Peru Free to oppose the early elections). In politics, there are no coincidences; what prevails are the interests that can be manifested or covert, which is why those paradoxes are understood where conveniences of formally divergent political options converge.

In that same scenario, we hear phrases like: "today for me, tomorrow for you." At the negotiating table, the "quid pro quo" predominates, that is, what do you give me in exchange for what I give? The uncomfortable observers, journalists, critics and the populorum (town) are calmed by arguing that "dialogue is not agreement." We will always remain attentive to see what, how and between whom shameful agreements are negotiated. Another well-known phrase: "walking slowly, you get there quickly," is part of the usual trick to favor proposals or people through cases of "shields and locks" to those who are interested in maintaining in his position or also of extensions or impediments to disfavor proposals or political adversaries such as for example, keeping draft laws on hold or "blocking" people proposed for high public office.

It is worth the opportunity to remember the phrase: "a fish dies through its mouth." In the American case, we said that the accusations by Trump and his campaign to discredit Hilary Clinton for having classified and confidential government information in her personal email were finally discarded. On the contrary, the attorney general's office discovered in recent months that, as a former president, Mr. Trump possessed, in his Mar a Lago residence in Florida, a large amount of classified national security information, for which he will have to face serious criminal charges. To this will be added two other serious charges: for defrauding the United States (responsibility in the assault on the Capitol for inciting, assisting, and aiding an insurrection) and for obstructing an official electoral procedure and the right to vote of third parties (alleging electoral fraud pressured authorities in some States to alter the results of the vote).

In the Peruvian case, I cannot fail to draw attention to the allegations of electoral fraud that the candidate Keiko Fujimori and the opposition forces raised before the National Election Jury with the help of a select law firm and the entire Lima press against Pedro Castillo when he won the second round of elections. After months of costly efforts for her, also for the government (parliamentary investigative commissions) and where she was made ridiculous by the nonsense of a delegation that traveled to the OAS headquarters to substantiate what only said delegation believed, no fraud could be evaluated. They had the bitter taste of seeing him sworn in as president-elect, but the de facto powers - political opposition, power groups, certain sectors of the armed forces, and concentrated press - agreed in making life impossible for that weak administration and exert all kinds of pressure amid a unison and permanent opposition charge that we witnessed and do not remember any precedents.

Curiously, a coincidence is observed in both candidates, Donald Trump, and Keiko Fujimori, in having appealed to the appeal of fraud when they were defeated at the polls. Currently, Trump is facing serious charges for fraudulent and hostile acts against the law. It is not going to be that our well-known Keiko's tricks, compromises, and provoked abuses by the current congress led by her political party against judicial institutions will also prove insufficient when she must face the final stretch of her legal claims. However, as we mentioned before, the unthinkable also has its probability of occurrence; it would not be strange to outline the possibility that both Keiko and Trump would leave us absorbed if they managed to obtain their acquittal.

Real examples in the anecdotal history of American and Peruvian politics were widely described in the previous chapters. That is why the expression that Politics is dirty is widespread and, with honorable exceptions, a good part of Peruvian politicians are mixed up in their impudent indecencies that even border on acts against the law and good customs. Taking as a backdrop the framework of reference described the debate on necessary political reforms in Peru, despite promises from the current congresspeople, continues in a long wait, and sleeps the sleep of the just and rather reforms are being implemented to taste and measure e the current parliamentary majority.

Additionally, it is also often argued that, in a typical context of political instability, extreme options begin to emerge that aggravate governability. Well, our political dashboard shows the surprising rise in options with radical nuances. In the left sector, there is the surprising appearance of the ethnocacerista party led by Mr. Antauro Humala (ex-military and brother of former president Ollanta Humala), which has been advancing in some pre-electoral polls and has become the ghost that alerts and displeases the right, to the traditional left itself and to conservative sectors of the Armed Forces. For no analyst, it is a mystery that such armed forces have become, in fact, thanks to their own historical positions and the complacent satisfaction of right-wing political parties, into a figurative "omnipresent political institution," and although they do not formally accept it, they demonstrate deciding and even veto capacity within the Peruvian political scene.

It is still premature to see how the option will be cleared in the right-wing party sector, but in recent times, there are signs of marking distance between them. In any case, it will be expectant to see how, within that "brute and angry" right (made famous for its violent nuance), they will try to close the way and block Don Antauro and his forces and make their way between them, aiming with elbows and trips to achieve this leadership and becoming "primus inter pares" (first among equals).

We have expanded on dealing with the current problems in Peru because what happened with former President Castillo, beyond the immediacy of his illegalities and blunders for which he will face justice, allows us to sift this experience in light of that background of atrophied imbalances, structural inequalities, and postponements of our economic, political and social reality. The current political upheaval and labyrinth enables us to, as a form of self-observation, look from the outside through the window, towards the interior of our house and confirm that "state of things" recently typified by that territorial polarization and frustration referred to by historians, anthropologists, political scientists, journalists, and other analysts mentioned above. From this perspective, we can agree that palliative short-term solutions such as new elections, new governments, new laws, new taxes, new congresspeople, or governors correspond to a necessary superficial ordering but by no means sufficient.

Why is this issue of territorial polarization important? Because as Mr. Raúl Asencio mentioned above pointed out, said polarization results in situations of imbalance and inequity. On this same topic, the notable Peruvian historian Jorge Basadre expresses his point of view in his work "Perú: Problem y Possibility and Other Essays," Penguin Random House Grupo Editorial, 2022, pp. 288-290. The author died in 1980, and his work was initially written in 1931 and had subsequent reissues, but the solidity of his approach takes on admirable validity that seems to have been written for the current situation. The author pointed out the following:

> "The Peruvian Constitution...ignored local life (refers to life in the provinces). It left the capital... It recognized the department and the province (political divisions of the Peruvian State) as mere subordinates. But those were nothing more than an arbitrary tattoo on the skin of the country...And the province lived only to vote for a remote and abstract Parliament. All the rest of the life of the country was, as the Constitutions mandated...life of the capital. <u>The solution is...to forge, through localism, the self-awareness of the nation, which does not exist.</u>
>
> It is urgent that the Peruvian be taken by his concerns and then, by an appropriate mechanism, be forced to get involved with other Peruvians in broader pursuits, to fight, to be enthusiastic, to undertake enterprises, to demand more, to be responsible. Think more, try more, be more impetuous... (we add that you are more committed to your reality)
>
> In what organ of local life will this therapy be based? There in the cotton valley, there in the cattle pastures, there in the mining factories is the solution. In the nuclei of the territory and the population that have a life of their own... through production, distribution, or consumption, in the economic unit... How many things can the men of each economic unit talk about? It must be departed from to reach national life. (if the economic unit itself corresponds to the company, the spirit of Basadre's proposal to constitute the Nation is necessarily inclusive and decentralizing).
>
> ...<u>Organize the State over the nation...no longer the nation humiliated and forgotten by the State</u>...The history of Peru in recent times is perhaps nothing

more than the subversion of the provinces against Lima for the first time, or Lima concedes and grants, or Evils will occur that will no longer be those that the provinces passively endured but rather those that will emanate from their rebellion" (Once again, Peruvians today are warned by what we should do or what we should not do).

It should also be noted that the comments in parentheses and underlining are ours. Obviously, the complexity of the problems mentioned will demand comprehensive, multisectoral options, with various considerations of space, size or sizing, short, medium, and long-term time horizons and other technical considerations that pertain to each specific area and that entail a debate, analysis, and agreement on where and how to direct them.

The appreciations of this topic of territorial polarization are complemented by the crucial point made by the anthropologist and historian **Luis Guillermo Lumbreras** about his position and defense of what he calls Cultural Rights (different, he points out, from human rights), among which he stands out the first place the right of peoples to maintain their native language.

(See https://www.youtube.com/watch?v=0IrEZvVklsc)

(appointment with restriction due to temporary availability) in an interview by Mr. Modesto Montoya, host of the space "Where are we taking Peru" to Mr. Luis Guillermo Lumbreras on December 21, 2022).

In addition, we can also include, in addition to their right to maintain their native language, their right to preserve and promote the integrity of other cultural expressions. That vast wealth constituted by the plastic arts: painting, sculpture, drawing, architecture, engraving, ceramics, goldsmithing, crafts, mural painting, and, of course, we also add musical, vocal, and instrumental and literary expression. Complementarily, we must highlight not only the intrinsic value of cultural expressions themselves but also what exists behind them and what is linked to it. Culture and art are, in turn, repositories and reflections of that set of idiosyncrasies, worldviews, values, customs, modus vivendi, etc., that typify a community, region or society. These contents are different in nature in the provinces and are sometimes contrasting and even contradictory with those that prevail in the capital.

"What is happening currently, maintains Mr. Lumbreras, is a confrontation between the country of ours and the country of others; we have access to a series of services that most others do not have or have precariously (education, medical and hospital care, retirement, food, etc.). The things and problems of others are different in each place and people try to solve them differently. We ignored each other. Most of the problems are on that other side, which corresponds and understands the others. What is happening is that the others are starting to get up.

…we must unify nationality criteria, recognize our differences and that the claims of others are true. The rights and obligations are not the same…The Constitution assumes that we are a unit, but we are not."

Mr. Lumbreras maintains that in the current crisis, this diversity, those "differences that exist between us and others," are unknown or not understood in their true dimension. For this reason, the policies inspired and conceived for us are, in many cases, ineffective for others.

As an example, and because of these references, I was reminded of the story that a professor told us in class during my time as a university student (Mr. Pedro de las Casas) regarding a curious experience he had at a Sunday fair in the middle of the country. Warned about the artisan beauties of the town visited, our teacher rushed to arrive at the fair early in the morning to make personal purchases, and for family and friends. After locating the desired crafts, he suggested to the woman he sold them that he buys all her merchandise displayed on her temporary table. The woman, who also came from a community near the fair, gave up on closing the deal and argued that, if she did, since she had nothing to sell the rest of the day, she would have to return home and miss enjoying an entire day fair. The professor had no choice but to buy him a portion of what he wanted and distribute his purchases among the other exhibitors.

Here, we have a clear case of how the strict economic rationality of the capital visitor collided with the ancestral custom of a provincial artisan merchant whose rationality was dual and simultaneous, that is, for her, it made no sense to sell without participating in the fair. Fair activities in the provinces are usually accompanied by various performances by musical bands, songs, folk dances, communal parades, craft exhibitions, typical food, etc., that give it a special color and attraction. Therefore, the purpose was not only to sell but also to enjoy the pleasure of participating in the fair. Although it may seem strange to us, the "rationality and economic satisfaction that is understandable and prioritized for us is in no way totally compatible and may be subordinated to the sociocultural satisfaction of fair participation in the case of others."

The purpose of what has been stated above is to highlight that the dimension of diversity exposed must be understood and assimilated so that it is included in the scaffolding of technical-legal instruments that support governmental and political management decisions. So that the designed measures do not go to waste, it will be important to demand strict management from all the protagonists and political actors in our reality (members of the three branches of government, political parties, businessmen and citizens of the center and peripheries included) a strict comprehensive quality management in their respective decisions. This harmonious set of decisions in the public sphere represents the required condition that will complement effective and efficient business management in the private sphere. The development of coordinated actions in both spheres is not a simple desire; it is a necessity and a requirement for general well-being.

Why has it become so difficult for the country's rulers and politicians to apply integrative quality management? Why is our political class so reluctant to understand the evaluations and diagnoses that recognized social scientists have made about our reality, and why do they turn a deaf ear and ignore the recommendations and suggestions they put forward? Why do even when fresh-faced political options come to power, they end in successive disappointments? Regarding the endemic flaws, ties, scourges, and other structural anomalies that our reality exhibits, "barriers of resistance or protection" seem to have been created that are difficult to overcome. These problems are not new, and the compromises "under the table," the vested interests, the truncated attempts, and the political operators in the executive or legislative branch who function as front men acting through the interposed interest of third parties in lobbies are also not new. They are open or covert corruption or collusion, whether due to misinformation, blunders, ineptitude or complicity.

Will it be possible to make this political class understand the need and urgency of long-awaited and postponed changes? Is it possible for them to understand that privileges should not correspond to the interests of people or companies but to the interests of society as a whole? Is it possible that the irresponsibility and myopia of our political class has them so numb, and they are not aware that due to their crude actions, we have the discredited record of having had six presidents in the last five years and that this corresponds to a deep cause of deterioration of the country's external image, to the point of considering ourselves an "ungovernable country"? Is it possible that we do not reach or want to understand that misunderstandings and collusion of the de facto powers gradually bring us closer to undesirable extreme situations such as the exacerbation of social contradictions and, with it, to expand more instability and democratic fragility towards the rupture of that tacit social contract between governed and rulers?

311

Just like the Doctors in extreme cases have no choice but to amputate the member with gangrene to avoid a generalized infection, so also social surgery, led by authentic representative forces of the country and by citizen participation, must separate and leave out of the scenario (through of the combat of ideas and not the brute force of physical elimination) to that group of clueless and corrupt political operators who are never willing to engage in constructive dialogue, but only to hinder, destroy and obtain the maximum possible benefit.

These bad apples must be replaced by that sector of upright citizens who still exist, who are aware and have the will to overcome these "barriers of resistance," and who are willing to agree on solutions that we know are difficult but possible. It is up to us, and it is up to us to find the appropriate mechanisms for democratic participation. Knowing how to choose, knowing how to decide, knowing how to control, knowing how to demand and ensure respect for the institutional life of the country. Other countries have achieved it.

Our purpose, in addition to exploring a framework for satisfactory management, is also to advocate for providing opportunities to that enormous number of entrepreneurs (technicians, professionals, artisans, small businesspeople, etc.) who exist in our environment and dream of establishing their own economic unit. Faced with handouts and false promises of cheap populism offered from outside the worker's individual environment, we propose to vindicate entrepreneurship as a responsible activity that arises from its own initiative.

If we reread the quotes from Basadre and Lumbreras, it is clear to us that our multicultural and multiracial (racial variation) nation constitutes a conglomerate that will take a long time to "organize as a Nation State." Both suggest guidelines of an inclusive and inductive nature, that is, from the peripheral to the central and from the particular to the general. Relying on the terminology of physical science, we agree that this centripetal force must be generated from the peripheral to the center, necessarily supported by the action of agents that promote it, in this case, from the executive and legislative decision-making bodies (different by course to those that currently predominate in the current Peruvian scenario).

The question then arises and its answer: Why do we defend the postulate of entrepreneurship? For two important reasons. The first of them has to do with what is stated in section 4.2 regarding informality as a characteristic of small businesses. In that part, we argued that the conventional and embryonic way in which entrepreneurship arises and appears is in the context of personal microenterprises: mostly commerce or individual sales activity in small mobile units (carts, tricycles), selling food, fruits, food, clothing, and other products or also offering basic services (car cleaning, shoeshine, repairs and others), offered mostly on an outpatient basis and on public roads.

This birth is characterized by taking place in eminently informal and precarious contexts. Here, the individual effort of the entrepreneur comes into play, his discipline, his honesty, and his conviction to obtain and increase family sustenance in, which sometimes he even begins subcontracted by a third party. If he stays on the right path, the volume of his activity will grow, and he will move to a higher level of operations that involve leaving the outpatient nature and entering commercial premises, although small, but with greater projection. As it evolves, its own growth levels will demand the need to formalize and achieve better commercial and financing opportunities.

His own experience will be key to strengthening that individual initiative (based on the values described) that we consider to be of incorruptible essence in human nature and any society. Entrepreneurship constitutes that cell that will begin motivated by these individual initiatives, and that is nourished by work, effort, and dedication to initially convert from small business units and later, with the same spirit, underpin its strengthening towards medium and even large ones' companies.

The second reason has to do with the aggregate effect generated by entrepreneurship. As contingents move from informality to formality, their contribution of approximately 20% of GDP will increase as they join the formal productive stream. This incorporation also implies greater technicalities and modernization with subsequent gradual increases in the average levels of productivity and resulting growth at the national level. Along with the above, almost 80% of the employment that informal activities absorb, or concentrate are going to have the opportunity to also be gradually channeled into formal activities with the consequent benefits of health care services, retirement, and unemployment compensation for workers.

On the other hand, the effects of entrepreneurship on the flow of income, in the enhancement of its distributive effect, will be, in a certain way, palliative to counteract patterns of concentration and will contribute to reducing (even modestly) social imbalances and inequities in magnitude that exceeds the cost of not doing them. Entrepreneurship suggests potential toward an economic scheme of democratization with openness to private initiatives, although on modest or moderate scales, but with doors open to larger sizes. Of course, we are not arguing that entrepreneurship is the panacea to solve the complex business problems exposed in this work. These are only policies that will mitigate and have a moderate scope in the enormous challenge that informality poses to us.

Entrepreneurship is often criticized because, see Francisco Durand [21], it is maintained "that it only promotes individualism assigned to a quite heterogeneous, dispersed, and disorganized social group that does not include the whole social... The thesis of entrepreneurship affirms the author, does not translate into State policies and, therefore, does not serve as the basis of a social pact...they do not receive protection or aid from the State and are at the same time socially discriminated against, including the most successful. In this regard, it should be noted that the defects and discredits described for entrepreneurship, far from being a limitation, are part of that scourge of sectarianism, discrimination and challenges that precisely must be overcome.

We must not forget that the promotion of entrepreneurship is not justified by mere charitable and welfare policies, but rather, as we pointed out before, in those areas where formality does not interest participation, entrepreneurship has ample room and much to contribute because despite its own limitations and deficiencies in operation and productivity, contributes to launching projects that combat poverty. It is true that entrepreneurship may have limited scope but promoting it head-on will be a valid option to mitigate inequalities, and doing so will be better than doing nothing.

4.3.4. The Coronavirus pandemic

What we previously typified as populism is part of enveloping external variability that we call the predominant sociopolitical framework or model. But we also warn that this envelope is not the only one because, in the context of this turbulent variability, business management is not exempt from being affected by a set of unforeseen, fortuitous, sudden, and random events that range from natural disasters such as droughts, floods, and earthquakes, to war conflicts, social disorders, fires, epidemic outbreaks, plagues, etc. All of them represent that chain of events that are statistically difficult to predict (random) but that always occur. Their characteristics may be dissimilar, but in any case, they represent, for business or organizational management, a risk that affects without distinction all the members of the system.

---

[21] "Los doce apóstoles...", op.cit. pags. 340-341

In this part of the essay, we take a conceptual support of what chance represents for the Peruvian historian Jorge Basadre in his work "Chance in History and its limits" [22]. The author maintains that:

> "Chance is foreign to all law, it does not emerge every day, nor is it very frequent. It implies the unexpected coincidence of two series...that may obey a more or less strict determinism, but those encounters escape, in fact, any attempt at law." Time in history - adds the author - is made up of moments **full of the possible that has not been realized**.

> The history of men is... a succession of phenomena within which the individual can, to a certain extent, think, intuit, and, above all, choose his actions. For this reason, human events are... a flow of more or less unstable balances and reserves against chance... History as a whole is a process, and chance can... only help or delay the design." (The highlighting and underlining are ours).

In effect, we agree that, in the scenario of possibilities, the option finally chosen and realized will always be less than the number of possibilities not realized and that the choice takes place amid unbalanced contexts affected by chance. In his interpretation of the phenomenon of chance in the field of history, the author reinforces his conception by quoting the French writer Elie Halevy (1870-1937) [23], who states:

> "...by applying the methods of historical research to us, we can discover the reasons for our beliefs and find that good part of them is accidental, that is, they come from circumstances not governed by us. And perhaps a **lesson in tolerance emerges from this...one can ask whether it is worth it for some to kill others, or vice versa, for convictions whose origins are so fragile**."

The highlighting and underlining in both quotes are ours. The reflection of the French author is necessary to keep in mind both for those who support the use of a brutal repression as a means of maintaining the status quo and established order, as well as for those who consider armed struggle and subversion as the only means of accessing power and impose a new order.

The characteristics of a random phenomenon can, as recorded by the facts, explain or clarify a historical event, determine a scientific discovery, or advance or inspire a work of art. The aftermath of chance may be gravitational and different in the fields of science (whether exact or social, such

---

[22] op cit pages 23, 24 and 29.
[23] Quoted by Jorge Basadre in "El Azar en la historia..." Op. Cit. pages 21 and 30

as history) or in the field of art because its protagonists, their methods and the paths taken are different. <u>Chance, as a sudden, unpredictable, and unexpected phenomenon, without any obedience to established patterns, will continue to exist and be part of reality</u>. We could summarize by stating that chance is consubstantial, congenital and an unavoidable presence in the real world.

But, as our renowned historian Basadre points out:

> "The margin of uncertainty (which typifies chance) is not always indeterminate, nor is it always determined. <u>There is no absolute chance. There is only a relative chance.</u> Man, because of the autonomy of his existence, carries within himself the ability to conceive and choose his actions, but up to a certain limit." For this reason, Basadre agrees with Alexis Tocqueville [24] (19th-century French writer), who brings us an intelligent statement: "It is true that around each man, a fatal circle has been drawn and no more than it can pass; Yet within the wide margin of that circle, he is powerful and free."

Finally, we must keep in mind that chance and its favorable or unfavorable connotation does not necessarily have to be a harbinger or aftermath of misfortunes and regrets but also a preamble and beginning of advantages and benefits. There have been cases where a physical limitation or disability, hereditary or contracted disease, epidemic, a personal disagreement, or an accident can lead to developing a stimulus for scientific or artistic creativity or an unknown opportunity (e.g., the admired metaphysician Stephen Hawking and his illness quadriplegic, deafness in the prominent musician Beethoven, the rise of teleworking as a result of epidemic confinement are some examples of them).

Now, with a more clarified concept of random phenomena, we will develop in this section the appearance and expansion of the **Coronavirus (Covid-19)** pandemic as part of that **random envelope** of the field of external variability, but of a different nature and connotation than the variability previously described as Populisms. The surprising and unforeseen expansion of said pandemic and the implementation of containment policies have generated an unfavorable impact on the economic sphere of magnitudes, content and expansion never experienced, which have underpinned the year 2020 as a new milestone in the socioeconomic events of the point of obligatory reference differentiating the before and after of it.

---

[24] Quoted by Jorge Basadre in "El Azar en la historia…" Op. Cit. page 31

According to figures published by one of the most authoritative sources, John Hopkins University (Baltimore, USA) (see: https://coronavirus.jhu.edu/map.html). Towards the end of 2022, when the pandemic had been almost controlled, the balance two and a half years after its outbreak reflected the following figures. The number of confirmed Coronavirus infections in the world exceeded 661 million people and the number of deaths from the pandemic was around 6.7 million people. In this total, the USA occupies first place with a total of 100.7 million infected people and 1.1 million deaths. Among other countries in America is Brazil with 36.3 million infections and 693.9 thousand deaths. In developing countries like Peru, 4.5 million infected people and 218.2 thousand deaths were registered.

The characteristics of its expansion in different countries where the outbreak has been significant show a particular trend similar to that of a curve in the shape of a mountain or bell that shows three defined and distinct cycles: a first cycle with increasing and rapid rise of infected; then a second cycle with arrival at a plateau-shaped peak that temporarily stabilizes; and finally a third cycle of gradual and definitely downward trend in the contagion curve. As has been experienced, such cycles are not definitive, but according to the mutations in the epidemic and the efficiency of its control, these cycles reappeared in the form of second, third, fourth and more "waves" periodically according to the particularities of each country and region.

Given that home confinement was one of the highly consensus and recommended practices to contain the epidemic expansion, and even though it leads to inevitable consequences of deterioration and economic recession, an arduous debate on priorities and preferences between options was put on the table related to health crisis (save lives) vs economic crisis (save the economy). In this regard, Professor Richard Baldwin, a seasoned researcher who has spent more than three decades studying issues of globalization and trade, settles the discussion of this kind of entrapment by maintaining that it is a false dilemma between saving lives vs. saving the economy (see https://www.bbc.com/mundo/noticias-52578840). Let us take a brief look at what each option meant:

Save Lives.

The epidemic containment policy contemplated, on the one hand, direct actions under the control of the health sector itself (expanding and improving the availability of beds, medical equipment for intensive care, infectious test sets, respirators, professional and technical personnel, masks, gloves, medicines, oxygen, uniforms, etc.) and, on the other hand, social confinement actions related to the collaboration and behavioral commitment of the population. Within the latter, the imposition of home isolation, quarantine, social distancing, curfew, restrictions on public circulation, and the closure, prohibition, and restriction of the operation of businesses and activities or events (sports, cultural, recreational, etc.) considered non-priority and potentially prone to contagion.

First, we highlight that from a health point of view, no health professional team (at the national and international level) has stopped supporting and recommending confinement measures, and the nuances of this correspond to national possibilities. Ignoring the recommendation of confinement meant, in practice, being lazy and irresponsibly tolerant of the growing expansion of the pandemic. Another discussion is the issue of how, in what way to implement it and until when to prolong the confinement and whether to reimplement it with moderation or severity.

Since its inception, there have been opponents of confinement measures and among the most frequent reasons for such opposition are those who fly the libertarian flag of free movement. These defenders of "freedom in the broadest sense" see confinement and the obligation to vaccinate as an affront to the unquestionable right to freedom of choice.

In this regard, we would have to debate that the same right that those who disagree with the need to be vaccinated have, to oppose and protest moderate or strict confinement measures, also have those who accept the recommendation of respectable health professionals and are willing to abide by confinement or distancing measures. The problem is that we participate in a reality with the characteristic of unavoidable social coexistence. So, the sacred principle of individual freedom should not violate the same rights of any other member of our family, communal and social environment. As lawyers and legislators emphasize, "your rights end when the rights of others begin."

Secondly, it must be understood and accepted that there is a direct correlation between confinement and economic recession. It can be said that the greater the confinement, the greater the recession. The confinement centered on the disposition to "stay at home" is a direct cause of the inevitable recession. The dilemma arose because, faced with the growing number of infections and deaths due to the pandemic, there was strong public pressure to reinforce health and confinement policies. At least in the initial stage, counteracting this pressure based solely on the argument of not affecting economic evolution or unwavering defense of free choice principles was technically inadmissible and short-sighted.

Additionally, strict conventional patterns of public finance management were extraordinarily suspended. In this way, it was inappropriate to display fiscal savings or surpluses, and it was advisable to make orthodox criteria more flexible and to manage with care in the field of debts and deficits in an exceptional manner because circumstances deserved it.

Thirdly, there have been political leaders who, guided by their intuition, prejudice, intuition or suggested recommendations (right or wrong), determined their priority, preference, opportunity, speed or indifference with which they implemented their specific containment policy. In several cases, initiating a containment policy more out of force than desire and pressured by an ethical obligation to do something to counteract the growing number of infections and deaths turned out to be inopportune, delayed, and ineffective. It is no coincidence that countries with leaders initially reluctant or hesitant to implement confinement modalities and more inclined to not affect the progress and economic dynamics (USA, Great Britain, Brazil, Mexico and Iran) have found themselves paying the price for accelerated expansions of the epidemic because of its delayed reactions.

We must always keep in mind that all science, whether around health, economics, politics or any field and discipline, has as its fundamental principle to be oriented in an unrestricted and unequivocal manner to safeguard human existence and to facilitate the conditions for its improvement. Whatever the alternative is chosen (save lives or save the economy), it must respect the ethical imposition that all science must abide, be at the service of man to help him solve his problems and difficulties and never complicate or deteriorate his living conditions.

However, from a perspective that clarifies the false dilemma (saving lives vs. saving the economy), we must keep in mind that the implementation of confinements without considering necessary and compensatory economic rescue programs or establishing such programs late and poorly administered will lead to worsening undesirable effects of economic recession and health.

Therefore, there is no alternative to choosing confinement to the detriment or discarding of economic reopening; the most advisable thing would be complementarity between confinement and its corresponding rescue program.

Even in the reluctant American administration under Trump, Congress, with majority approval of both parties (Republican and Democratic), gave the green light to a significant program to rescue the order never seen before of 2.3 trillion dollars (about 10% of its PBI) to compensate for the recessionary effects of its late-initiated confinement program. Bridging the differences, it is important to note that, in Peru, at least in this first phase, the decision was made to start its containment program (Mar 15, 2020) and to allocate 12% of its GDP for its rescue program. The big problem in our case has been terrible management and serious infrastructure restrictions.

Given that it was unknown with a certain degree of certainty when and how the pandemic would end, new cycles or outbreaks of the epidemic continued to be experienced depending, among other things, on the way and timing in which both home confinement and the restart of the economic opening were managed. Each country, based on its specific health care provision and infrastructure and its economic capacity, faced its respective containment policy whose design and content were adjusted to its economic availability.

Save the Economy

As stated before, confinement measures have a direct and serious impact on economic activity because they imply an abrupt break in the chain of monetary and physical flows (suppliers) in the basic cycle of sales-income-production, causing a sudden paralysis and cessation of economic activities that results in increasing shortages, business closures, underutilization of plant and equipment, unnecessary accumulation of inventories, paralysis or postponement of investment decisions and new projects, massive and generalized unemployment, partial or total retraction of salary income, collective unrest and panic, etc.

Confinement policies used to be accompanied by rescue packages designed from the economic perspective to mitigate and counteract the recessive effects that they generate. Such packages are designed to recover the spending capacity of economic agents (individuals, families, companies), to prevent the risk of business bankruptcies and to fundamentally support the desired economic recovery. In this sense, it seeks to reactivate private consumption, alleviate the lack of resources in vulnerable social sectors and provide small, medium, and large companies with sufficient

320

liquidity (via accessible credit) that allows them to be provided with working capital and enables the continuity of their business and its operations.

Even so, prolonged confinement accompanied by insufficient or late rescue packages not only directly impacts the economy but also leads to lower levels of health and, in the long run, regressive consequences on the spread of the original epidemic and others, as well as of worsening nutritional conditions and poverty, especially in the dispossessed social classes. For this reason, those opposed to any nuance of confinement and quarantine maintained that "said cure could be worse than the disease" to the extent that they have a perverse effect on the problem they wish to combat.

Additionally, it would also be risky to prolong home confinements for longer than is prudent in societies such as Peru and other Latin American countries, with a population that is mostly poor and in extreme poverty and is informal in nature. On the one hand, developing countries have the forced restriction of not being able to continue in confinement for a long time because fiscal coffers and debt capacity have (to a greater or lesser extent and, depending on each reality) their own limits. So sooner or later, no confinement could be established for prolonged periods, and they would have to give way to economic reactivation and make use of scarce resources for it as well.

In understanding that the economic problem is not only reduced to negative production figures and other important national accounts but is also intertwined with the social sphere that accompanies it, the forced recessive cycles determined a degradation in the population's standard of living, and these in turn, they are partially seen in lower levels of health and increased levels of poverty.

That is, to achieve and maintain optimal levels of health such as easy access to hospital care, good provision of health infrastructure, availability of sufficient specialized personnel, equipment and laboratories, number of beds, etc., and maintain satisfactory levels of sanitation (coverage of water and sewage services) the support of a good running of the economic locomotive is required.

However, we must note that, in cases of developing countries like Peru, the experience of this implicit correspondence between economic improvement and improvement in health has not been clear and direct. Here, we encounter a structural problem of public management efficiency since the country's limited health infrastructure is latent, and even in the best stage of the Peruvian economy (2006-2011), the opportunity for a comprehensive reform of the health sector was not taken advantage of. I hope that the current pandemic experience will once again prioritize your immediate attention.

On the other hand, the endemic social problems that typify societies in the developing world with impoverished lower classes (and also the visible poverty cushions in the large cities of developed countries) are usually affected by various problems such as social exclusion and segregation, lack of health services, malnutrition and infant mortality, citizen security problems, low educational quality, high crime levels, lack of respect for authorities and rules, generalized corruption, etc. All of this reflects the very poor condition of many households with a lack of basic services and surviving in overcrowded conditions that when their indicators are added to poverty statistics (traditionally measured in monetary terms), they are astonishingly increased (in Peru, the poverty cushion considering these last indicators it increased by almost 10%).

Such social segments, being unable to work and being deprived of an income for their daily food support, are highly prone to breaking the fragile fence of social compliance and obedience and out of desperation, they can even commit crimes. These social sectors are susceptible to swelling protest groups that easily deviate into acts of social disorder (looting, assaults, and other criminal outbreaks).

The concrete fact is that, in scenarios with gradual or severe confinement, recessionary effects have not stopped being predicted since their inception. For the year 2021, there was a readjustment or resurgence of productive progress at the global and regional level, but it must be taken with reservations because it is based on the recessionary economies of the previous year. Indeed, the world economy experienced an abrupt recession of -3.3% in 2020. After this, a certain expansive rebound was seen in 2021, and the growth rate was 5.7%. For the year of 2022, hopes for a moderate economic recovery faded due to a slowdown aggravated by the war between Russia and Ukraine. The world economy was estimated to level close to 2.9%. (see: https://www.bancomundial.org/es/news/press-release/2022/06/07/stagflation-risk-rises-amid-sharp-slowdown-in-growth-energy-markets)

The same effects were expected for most countries with advanced economies, which in 2020 experienced a decrease of -4.6% and after that, a rebound growth of 5.1% and for 2022, a moderate growth of 2.6% is expected. This is how we have the USA: from 5.7% in 2021 to 2.5% in 2022; Germany: from 2.8% in 2021 to 2.1% in 2022; France from 7.0% in 2021 to 2.9% in 2022; Italy:

from 6.6% in 2021 to 2.3% in 2022; Spain: from 5.1% in 2021 to 4.8% in 2022; Japan: 1.6% in 2021 to 2.4% in 2022 (see: https://www.imf.org/en/Publications/WEO/Issues/2022/04/19/world-economic-outlook-april-2022)

In Latin America, the 2020 recession was -6.4% and then from 6.7% in 2021 to an estimated 2.5% in 2022; Brazil from 4.6% in 2021 to 1.5% in 2022; Mexico from 4.8% in 2021 to 1.7% in 2022; Argentina from 10.3% in 2021 to 4.5 in 2022; Chile from 11.7% in 2021 to 1.7% in 2022 and in Peru from 13.3% in 2021 to 2.8% in 2022. In summary, the critical challenge of the current situation for most entrepreneurs, companies, and society has been the search for alternatives to face the crisis and adapt to new circumstances.

Unfortunately, applying a rescue program without having covered the optimal conditions for flattening the infection curve or even if a recovery program is poorly executed presented the risk of generating a resurgence of the epidemic, a second wave of infections that had to be corrected with a new confinement program. When the process became recurrent, a vicious circle was generated that formed a particular profile like the letter W ("W effect") on the contagion curve. All of this was caused by improper applications of rescue programs and, therefore, aggravations in the continuity of the epidemic outbreak.

For its part, when it was decided to prioritize economic dynamics and postpone or minimize the design and scope of any confinement program, leaving aside the well-known recommendation of health experts, in practice, it encouraged giving a free pass to the outbreak and epidemic expansion. No government administration could endure for long the discredit, repudiation, and severe criticism of public opinion for allowing the epidemic to spread with increasing numbers of infected and dead people. Therefore, the choice to prioritize the economy at the expense of the option of saving lives implied risks of outbreaks and incurring technical and ethical questions that also made it inadvisable.

If the dilemma between saving lives or saving the economy was misleading and unviable, **what was the recommended choice to get out of the false dilemma?** The most advisable thing, according to Professor Baldwin's recommendation, was to start as soon as possible with both programs: the confinement program (pro-health) and the rescue program (pro-economy). The contagion curve is usually represented graphically in the shape of a bell or mountain where the vertical axis quantifies the number of infected people and the horizontal axis temporal units (weeks, months, or quarters). See graph No. 12. An epidemic problem was being faced that, due to lack of knowledge, made it impossible to foresee its outbreak and counteract its rapid global expansion that took all authorities by surprise. This forced the undertaking of ex-post (after the epidemic outbreak), confinement and health programs that aimed to counteract the infections and deaths that the pandemic generated, or to put it in graphic health terms, an attempt was made to flatten or hammer the contagion curve.

In the understanding that confinement causes recessionary effects, the corresponding rescue program must necessarily be applied with fiscal measures to also achieve a desirable economic reactivation. We can represent the recessive curve graphically in the lower quadrant of the contagion curve, and it will form an inverse bell to the contagion curve, where the vertical axis, in this case, will quantify the depth of the recession (measurable, for example, in negative growth rates) and in the horizontal axis will represent the same time units.

According to the professor, the recommended strategy was to apply the double hammer blow that manages to flatten both the contagion curve and the recessive curve to reduce both the infections and deaths of the epidemic and, at the same time, mitigate and counteract the recessive effects. However, without failing to recognize the theoretical validity of the recommendation to "hammer" both curves, we considered that certain particularities of its implementation and the characteristics of each cycle of the process should be considered.

Chart N° 12:

Covid-19, The double medical and economic curve.

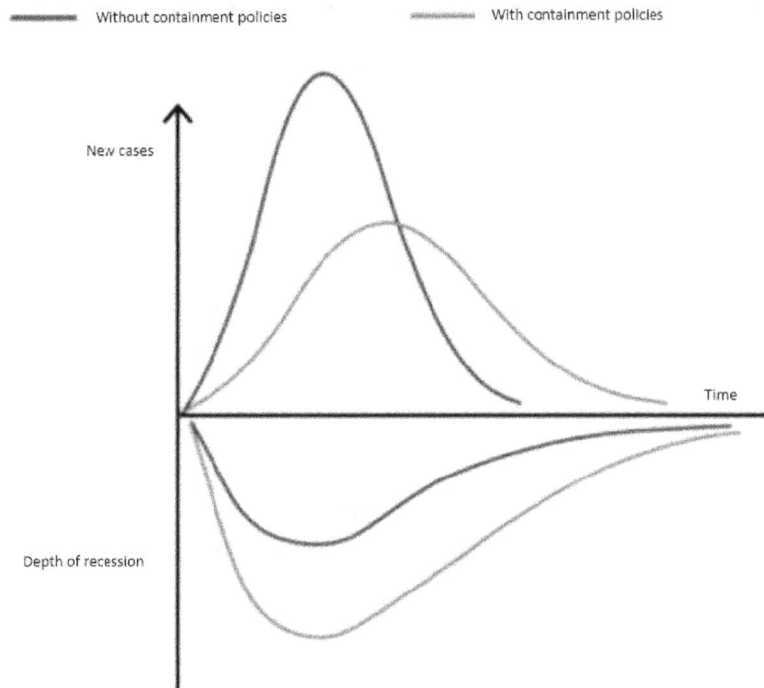

Source: Chart proposed by Researcher Richard Baldwin. http://enfermed.mx/wp-content/uploads/2020/04/Curva-Pandemia-Recesion-400x435.png

Let us review the typical characteristics of the distinct phases of the epidemic process:

First cycle of epidemic expansion: Lock yourself in and keep your distance.

In addition to strict sanitary measures, confinement was suggested as a basic approach to a praxis of physical or social isolation that was summarized in the phrase: "stay at home." For its part, any rescue program with recovery and economic opening must necessarily contemplate a population mobilization toward work centers. Although "working at home" is widespread due to the possibilities of computer connection on the Internet having some compensation, a large part of work activity still requires physical presence. The incompatibility described suggests the simultaneous and overwhelming impossibility of both options.

At the beginning and with an epidemic in full expansion, the emergency meant, in accordance with the recommendation of health experts, starting the process with the implementation of an intense containment program (both in its content of sanitary measures and confinement). In this context, the rescue program was conditioned and could only be carried out through a gradual process so that, in its first stage, it included only palliative measures facilitating money transfers to compensate as much as possible for the lack of income of vulnerable social sectors, with limited resources and maintain minimum levels of care for basic needs. Also, at this stage, there was the possibility of establishing partial or total subsidies for the payrolls of small businesses and independent entrepreneurs.

As the confinement program progressed, it was expected that its results would show certain slowdowns in the number of infections, deaths, hospitalizations, patients in intensive care and other indicators. This process could take, depending on each reality and the efficiency of public management, an approximate period (from the beginning of the epidemic to the arrival on the plateau) of six to nine months. From a health perspective, the results of this stage were partially satisfactory, given that the epidemic began to be contained but was not completely overcome.

In that same period and from the economic perspective, the recessionary effects generated by confinement – paralysis of economic activities (productive, distribution and services), closure of companies, increase in unemployment, a significant decrease in salary income, suspension of the chain of payments, etc. - continued to worsen because the palliative transfers previously made were usually insufficient to contain the recessive debacle.

On the other hand, it should not be thought that just by decreeing the end of a confinement or quarantine process, it will continue with an immediate start of reactivation. The first reason for this is that we are dealing with an emergency that took the authorities by surprise, which has been demanding quick solutions and that there are also no references from previous experience. In these circumstances, there has not been enough time to strategize well in advance.

In practice, these strategies are designed at a general level. With this, the responsible team runs the risk of executing uncoordinated, disorganized, incomplete, improvised actions, etc., which translate into poor results due to the costs of procedural failures and errors, repetitions of failed processes, lack of coordination, and voluntary and involuntary omissions and in general, a pernicious waste of resources.

The experience obtained in the initial cycle of the rise of the epidemic curve showed in Peru and many countries pitiful failures: shortages and delays in the acquisition and import of health equipment and materials, lack of technical and professional personnel, inter-institutional lack of coordination, bottlenecks and unpredictability even in the collection of corpses from the epidemic, irresponsibility and indiscipline of certain population sectors in abiding by the quarantine and curfew, outdated population registers to channel government transfers to needy sectors, excesses of bureaucratic procedures that do not correspond to a situation of emergency, changes of addresses and a number of unregistered deaths, corruption in the marketing of medicines, hoarding and shortages of supplies, medicines and equipment, etc.

For this reason, the confinement and sanitary measures did not show convincing results, and after a reasonable time, there were no signs of having reached the flattened area or plateau. The first indicator of approaching the subsequent cycle of the plateau is determined by the arrival of a first inflection point on the contagion curve that marks the beginning of decelerations in infections and deaths. The existing team and professional staff, with the support of professionals specialized in emergency management and complex situations, should, after a quick assessment of the situation and with the experience of the process, focus their attention on identifying the causes of the delay and undertaking selective actions to correct it. "Put out the fire" of main problems and complementary actions on secondary problems.

From the beginning of this essay, we have stressed the importance of being clear about what must be done and how to do it. Many politicians, seeing themselves pressured both by representative sectors of the economic and business sectors and by massive protests by social sectors on the brink of violence, allowed economic reopening under inadvisable conditions. Therefore, by not taking much care to propose an unrestricted and generalized lifting of confinement measures during the expansive phase of the pandemic, it meant, in practice, giving free rein to the runaway horse of infections.

The liberalization of confinement measures and other restrictions on business operations due to justified economic reopening measures require high management surgery that considers specific circumstances. Within each country, the dynamics of contagion, availability of resources (human, physical and monetary), hospital infrastructure, etc., are different and ignoring them had the elevated risk of causing a new outbreak of the epidemic (second or third waves).

The recovery programs, regardless of their intensity, imposed a "return to work" that collided with the health mandate to "stay at home" characteristic of confinement programs. **Given that the factor in the spread of the epidemic is people**, the impetus for returning to that long-awaited work activity accompanied by unwise forms of economic reactivation led to new population torrents being exposed to the epidemic outbreak. For this reason, executing indiscriminate reopening programs at this stage is as if we wanted to put out the fire with gasoline.

So, it was not strange to see ourselves trapped and involved in those vicious circles mentioned above and their respective "W effect" profiles (difficulties) in the contagion curve. Some researchers opposed to the widespread reactivation pressure, such as the economist Mr. Noah Smith, argued that "Reopening too soon will do more harm than good.

(see:https://www.infobae.com/america/agencias/2020/04/17/reabrir-demasiado-pronto-hara-mas-dano-que-bien-noah-smith/ from April 17, 2020).

According to the researcher, there will be certain groups of people and families who will be wary of going out freely to shop and eat in restaurants until they are convinced that the danger of the coronavirus has been substantially overcome. If it is proven that infections rebound again, people will fear going out again and will remain in a kind of voluntary self-confinement." This learning and forced self-awareness of the pandemic was what happened in the USA, a country that led the number of deaths and infections worldwide.

With the accumulation of unemployed and the outbreak underway, public pressure increased to reinstate a new confinement that would add its respective recessive cost and simultaneously destroy more lives. This repetitive cycle affected and conditioned the effectiveness (results) of inappropriate reactivations. For this reason and in reinforcement of what was stated above, the author of the cited note held an interesting point of view that is worth highlighting:

"…it is not a choice between the economy and people's lives. It is a choice between short-term economic losses (understood as arising from confinement with recession) or prolonged economic losses combined with mass deaths (understood as arising from reopening the economy in inappropriate conditions) **reopening the economy is a matter of if the conditions are met, not when.** We must wait until there is a public health regime capable of containing the virus."

The comments in parentheses and the highlights made in the quote described are ours. Few countries could boast of having reached this level of public health system capable of facing the crisis. For example, in Peru, the economic reopening was inappropriately established when the conditions of a health regime capable of containing the virus were not yet in place. This has meant falling into those repetitive cycles of epidemic outbreaks or a cycle of elongated plateaus that confirm to us that "the wash cost us more than the purchase of the new shirt" because both issues, pandemic and recession, remained pending, unresolved and with longer permanence longer than expected.

Second cycle of arrival at the plateau: He who awaits despairs!

This cycle is identified by a slowdown in infections typified by a certain constancy in its evolutionary dynamics that configures a straight line like a plateau. This meant that the epidemic continued to show a stable trend and was still far from having disappeared. This stability is due to the positive effects of the implementation of health and containment programs from the previous stage. It is a partial work that requires continuity of the effort to contain the latent epidemic outbreak.

The route of ascent on the epidemic curve must show a second inflection point on said curve, which confirms the direction towards a plateau profile. Only at this time of slowdowns in infections and deaths is it possible to empower the economic rescue program, which will be made up of frontally anti-recession and opening and economic recovery measures such as access to soft loans, lowered interest rates, grace periods, promotional payments, flexible payment horizons, affordable amounts to finance working capital deficits, leverage with external financing, making fiscal policy more flexible with taxes reprogrammed in terms of periods, terms and rates, preferential treatment for small businesses, streamlining bureaucratic procedures, intersectoral programming and coordination, etc.

This is a package of measures whose refinement requires agile inter-institutional coordination with various sectoral participants and regional and local governments with management experience and knowledge of their respective realities. Otherwise, the bureaucratic process will reduce its efficiency. The government, businesses and consumers became aware of how easy it was to shut down the economy and how difficult it is to get it going again. The only certainty is that undertaking the reactivation will take longer than planned and to the anguish of the previous stage, the impatient wait will be added to overcome the difficulties of this flattened phase and continue the fight.

Given that the objective in this cycle is not only to continue the development of economic reopening but also to prevent and contain any inertia of rising infections, this stage presents the best circumstances to act simultaneously in both programs, that is, a **double hammer blow. The first to counteract the epidemic advance, and the second to promote reactivation**. The containment program includes, in its health part, an improved strengthening of the measures undertaken that overcome the difficulties experienced in the previous cycle and in its confinement part, a lifting of its restrictions under a selective and gradual scheme and, at the same time continuing monetary transfers to sectors social aspects that were not included or postponed in the previous stage.

The continuation of the palliative transfer measures undertaken during the previous cycle also depended on the fiscal capacity of each country and the way in which the recovery program was implemented. It should be kept in mind that the appropriate strategy for what was described was to do it in a framework of greatest efficiency.

Some of the experts on the team responsible for the containment program had to reorient their attention towards reformulation tasks, such as helping to redefine and refine the actions required in this new cycle. Failure to do so ran the risk of repeating the inefficiencies of the previous cycle, with advances, setbacks, inaccuracies, and greater waste of resources. Therefore, aware that this brief reformulation effort is carried out in emergency circumstances, after being evaluated and analyzed, it would have to be put into practice on the fly to, on the one hand, consolidate permanence on the plateau, which will mean having achieved mastery in containing the advance of the epidemic and, on the other hand, facilitating economic reactivation.

Beyond our wishes, getting the wheels of an economy in recess moving again depended on the gradual nature of the complex economic structure. To begin with, it is known that, on the global demand side, consumption and investment expenditures (private and public) have their own factors and forces that influence within them and in stimulating or discouraging the dynamics of GDP. In the context of an emergency, where the recession has been a consequence of a cause that has not been strictly economic but as a result of a sudden and unpredictable health crisis (whose origin and duration were unknown), affected confidence, preferences, caution in restricting expenses and savings, the perception of risks and returns, the willingness to go into debt to strengthen existing capabilities, restraint in the use of credit cards, and the criteria for postponing or canceling new events or projects were also re-evaluated.

The payment chain was deeply affected because the cessation of business activities meant, on the one hand, the cut of regular income and sales in companies and, on the other, less private consumption spending by people due to the growing unemployment that every recession entails. In this sense, when the expectations and provision of resources for expenses and investments are affected or blocked by the forced absence of income, the decisions regarding them are re-examined, left in suspense, and take their respective time to recover their usual dynamics. These decisions are not automatically driven; politicians, businesspeople and other economic agents had to be made to understand that facing the recession was not achieved by normatively decreeing the immediate economic reopening.

Likewise, a sudden rupture of the value chain with its respective physical flows of goods and services (supply chain) and its corresponding monetary flows (payment chain) are not recomposed overnight. On the supply side of goods and services, there is a heterogeneity of sectors, industries and activities of a variable nature in their composition, in their propensity, susceptibility and dynamics, both their own and in relation to the dynamics with other sectors and with the economic totality. For example, the construction sector, in good times, usually accompanies the GDP with average growth rates equal to or higher than this. Conversely, in times of crisis, its dynamics are usually lower than that of the economy.

Additionally, mass consumption industries (food, beverages, clothing, and footwear) are more susceptible and more volatile to the difficulties of the economy in general. For their part, there are other industrial sectors that are more stable and less affected by economic cycles, such as the capital goods, machinery, and equipment industry. Similarly, in developing countries, there are activities linked to exports, such as metal mining, oil and agroindustry, and there are also other activities, such as the pharmaceutical industry, household appliances, and telecommunications, which are highly dependent on the import of inputs and industrial equipment and products of greater technological sophistication. Sectors highly linked to the external sector have their own dynamics.

On the other hand, there are certain activities that are highly linked and dependent on other sectors. For example, commercial activity, whose immediate recovery will seem more feasible, is conditioned in part by its availability of inventories and by a gradual recovery of demand that it serves (the dynamics and activity of retail stores are good indicators of this). When these inventories of variable durability (from two to four weeks, depending on the activity to which they belong) begin to run out, the commercial sector will depend on its suppliers. The latter, also coming from different industries, will respond to the reactivation stimulus by initially supplying orders from the commercial sector with their own inventories. If this is the case, industrial stocks, in accordance with the policy of each company, may present a variability that allows them to supply periods between four to six weeks.

The above suggests that we can deceive ourselves with an illusion of perceiving growth and recovery when we are only experiencing a "burning or consumption of inventories." The replacement of inventories can be considered as the first anti-recession indicator, but this has to do with the restart of the operation of plants, furnaces, machinery, boilers, and equipment, with their respective inputs and supplies that, in turn, will require tests, quality, and set-up, etc. so they cannot be activated by a simple economic reopening provision either. If we add the replacement times of the commercial and industrial sectors and their respective links (packaging, plastics, cardboard, glass, stationery and printing, painting, services, etc.), the restart of the supply chain could take a period of a quarter.

Two or three quarters could be the average permanence during the plateau cycle, after which, depending on the gradual reincorporation of the rest of the sectors, we can only speak of a slow start of reactivation and growth. However, here we must also make the point that the recommendation of gradualness (acceptable from the perspective of confinement that seeks to avoid massive overcrowding) may be counterproductive in its implementation (from the perspective of economic reopening) given that the intersectoral connection of certain industry and its respective network of suppliers may not necessarily be compatible with the generic gradualness that is programmed.

If so, there could be cases of suppliers or distributors scheduled to restart their activities three months after the start of activities of the producer or main client they serve. This gap is another critical point that will have to be resolved along the way and as we go. It is required that, in each category of companies or sectors, provision is made and "keep these inter-business mechanisms ready and tuned" because otherwise, bottlenecks will appear that will lengthen the time spent on the plateau and, therefore, delay the desired reactivation. For example, the paint manufacturer restarted its activities, but its main distributors were scheduled for later, or the plumber may be prevented from serving his clientele because the hardware stores that supply it remain without authorization to open their establishments.

Therefore, just as what is recommended in the health field, also in the economic area, due to demand and supply considerations, selectivity and efficiency criteria will have to be imposed. Each country, with full knowledge of its reality, must decide which sectors will begin the process and how to add them to the reactivation stream. From an economic perspective, the period that the permanence on the plateau could last represents only the beginning of the frontal fight against the recession (let us remember that in the previous cycle, the palliative transfers will not have had a greater impact). It is even highly probable that at the end of this period and given its duration, the economy will continue or face recession cycles and will require more time to recover its dynamics.

The team responsible for managing this plateau cycle with curves with a flattened profile (epidemic and recessive) faced greater demands than before because their work required "spin thinner" in reinforcing and refining details of both the rescue program and, at the same time continuing, with the containment program. The time restriction faced in any emergency makes it impossible to have a strategy completely formulated and reasoned in advance. The emergency will then have to be faced by simultaneously taking initial, gradual, and alternating steps of execution (implementation) and design (or reformulation) of trial and error. In this way, the strategy finally applied on the road and on the fly will be built to face an emergency.

Third cycle of reduction in infections and economic recovery: Beginning and progress of the hardest, longest, and most difficult stage.

If any reader thinks that reaching this stage means having overcome the epidemic outbreak, we regret to disappoint you and tell you that the previous cycles were a kind of preamble and preparation because the decisive fight against the pandemic was just beginning.

In this third and final cycle, a decreasing epidemic curve and a progressively improved recessive curve with an upward trend are confirmed that will continue to gradually transform towards a reactivation and growth curve. The objective in this cycle will also be double: accentuate the economic recovery and reaffirm the decrease in infections and deaths. This means continuing to work intensely and simultaneously on both programs (containment and rescue) but refining and perfecting the criteria of gradualness, selectivity, and efficiency.

Why does this stage require finer surgery than the previous ones? Because it is a cycle that supports more complex scenarios that pose the challenge of facing and overcoming several red alerts:

- Firstly, health in many countries (especially developing ones) presented, to a greater or lesser extent, a certain precariousness and limitations that, at this point in the process, will show signs that place the **health system on the brink of collapse** (and some will even have already experienced it). We have witnessed critical experiences where medical staff had to make the painful decision of choosing which patients to assign scarce resources to (read ventilators, transfer to the intensive care unit, hospitalization, medicines, oxygen, etc.) and to which patients to suspend them.

Such dramatic decisions have become latent even in developed countries (Italy, Spain). Additionally, the collapse also has an impact on another critical problem, which is the greater number of cases of contagion and unfortunate deaths of the health system's own personnel and of the personnel safeguarding the confinement (local and national police). That is to say, the pandemic starkly revealed to us the acute vulnerability of a worn-out and limited health system that affected the first front of the battle against the epidemic and its urgent need to reinforce it.

- Secondly, the fiscal coffers have limitations inherent to the size and capacity of each country, its level of tax pressure and its respective collection management, the existing fiscal balance or imbalance (income vs. expenses) and the capacity and availability of financing and reserves. Therefore, as we mentioned before, **income transfers to vulnerable social sectors also have their limits in amounts and time**. Their permanence and durability in recessionary times (with a cessation of economic activity and a significant decrease in tax collection) requires that they be temporary and extraordinary in nature.

Therefore, as the containment program (both in its health and confinement aspects) faces budget restrictions, a scheme of attenuated reductions will necessarily have to be adjusted that will require, on the one hand, greater selectivity when focusing on addressing or prioritizing the points critical issues (e.g. ensuring the availability and equipment of intensive care rooms, attention to extremely poor social groups, and other "critical issues" such as a shortage of oxygen cylinders and other supplies) and on the other hand limiting or reducing transfers to sectors unprotected social

334

- Thirdly, the confinement measures and their variants of social isolation, quarantine and curfew, established for justified reasons to counteract the spread of infections, have had the undesirable collateral effect of **aggravating the recession**, leaving in their wake the pitiful balance of growing unemployed, loss or decrease in labor income of employees, technicians and professionals, suspension of usual economic activities, business deterioration due to illiquidity and insolvency, abrupt rupture of the value chain, business bankruptcies, etc.

Although this process has exceptions, such as not paralyzing activities related to health, supply of food, medicine, and certain services. In the long run, the weight of the rest of the economic sectors will be felt in the economy. In the end, considering that the reactivation is still pending, the imbalance between a restricted supply and an unsatisfied demand will exacerbate a greater shortage of many goods and services necessary to the population and the economy. The inflationary effect will begin a series of subsequent aggravations.

- Fourthly, reality left open the possibility of a simultaneous effect of the three previous red alerts is described: a) collapse of the health system, b) collapse of public finances with its risk of not continuing or reducing transfers to unprotected sectors and c) economic collapse of increased scarcity and shortages of goods with its risk of aggravating severe recessionary effects, inflationary and hinder economic recovery programs.

All of this will make us reach the critical point and the limit where, as basic needs cannot be met, society breaks out, first in demonstrations of discontent and protest and later in **outbreaks of social violence** with a reserved prognosis.

The appreciation of the perspective of the process and its corresponding cycles allows us to maintain that the alerts described, as has been observed, have been present in different intensities and in many countries. Undertaking economic reopening programs inappropriately during the initial cycle of the epidemic's expansion was risky. Undertaking reactivation in subsequent cycles will depend on the economic capacity of each country and how efficiently it manages the red alerts mentioned above. Just as in the first cycle, the priority was focused on the fight against the epidemic expansion; without diminishing said effort, the central attention during subsequent cycles was and continues to be the fight against recession.

Likewise, as if to emphasize attention to acute problems that even solvent economies are experiencing, we highlight, as an example, the unemployment button. Towards the end of April 2020, in the first economy in the world (USA), unemployed workers registered to apply for unemployment benefits rose to an astonishing figure of close to 30 million people (14% of the unemployment rate that fortunately dropped favorably to 4% at the beginning of 2022).

However, the fears of a resurgence of inflation were confirmed when its levels reached 9.8% towards the end of 2022. Even so, the strict and aggressive management of a restrictive monetary policy (raising interest rates) generated greater stabilization and a decrease to 3% (end of the second quarter of 2023). (see https://www.global-rates.com/es/estadisticas-economicas/inflacion/indice-de-precios-al-consumo/ipc/estados-unidos.aspx)

As an example of what is happening in developing countries, in Peru, unemployment among people between 25 and 44 years old reached its peak during the pandemic expansion around June 2020 with an unemployment rate of 16.3% and has gradually decreased until reaching the level of 6.7% in December 2021 and finally stabilized at 6.0% towards mid-2022. Towards mid-June 2023, the pressing problem was the economic recession that, according to official sources and private analysts, would border towards the end of the year at a negative rate of -2%. The problem described is not foreign to the rest of the countries of the world, so to mitigate it, the financial leverage of multilateral agencies granted under advantageous conditions would be of enormous importance.

(https://estadisticas.bcrp.gob.pe/estadisticas/series/mensuales/resultados/PN38067GM/html/2020-1/2022-7/)

Finally, we cannot fail to mention the fact that the short-term financial relief received during the pandemic may entail risks in the long term. This complicated recovery process will leave companies with a heavy financial burden. If, in the foreseeable long reactivation process, they do not manage to recover, such companies will have to juggle to solve their operational expenses and the financial obligations for credits received in rescue packages. It cannot be ruled out that several of them, faced with the difficulties described, will not be able to service these debts and, given the impossibility of refinancing their debts, will be on the verge of bankruptcy due to insolvency.

On the other hand, it was not surprising that a good number of countries, due to the need for the emergency, were forced to aggressively increase their public spending and reached extraordinary levels of fiscal deficit (in the USA and Peru, such levels with respect to the size of

GDP reached up to 10% and 12% respectively). In the management of their public finances, the conventional way in which countries partially cover their short-term deficits is through long-term financing that normally comes from sources of external debt or through the placement of Bonds or obligations that also increase their public debt in the international financial system.

In these cases, the risk of countries becoming unable to pay their debt service ("default") is becoming part of the blacklist of disqualified countries to obtain future credits. In any case, regardless of the ability to face credit obligations or not, this Coronavirus pandemic has left an indelible mark in its wake that our companies and governments have a greater financial vulnerability due to the need to have committed themselves to heavy financial burdens.

For the purposes of this essay, we highlight that, in general terms, this forced incremental debt towards levels higher than those existing prior to the pandemic will determine that business management will remain more conditioned, more vulnerable, and trapped in difficulties that are more difficult to overcome for a long time and whose effects we have unfairly transferred to future generations.

In confirmation of the above, we have that the World Bank states in its recent report of January 10, 2023, the following:

The following: "Global growth is slowing sharply due to high inflation, rising interest rates, reduced investment and the disruption caused by Russia's invasion of Ukraine. The global economy is forecast to grow by 1.7% in 2023. Emerging and developing countries face a multi-year period of slow growth driven by heavy debt burdens and low investment; At the same time, global capital is absorbed by advanced economies facing extremely prominent levels of public debt and rising interest rates. The low level of growth and business investment will exacerbate the already devastating setbacks in education, health, poverty and infrastructure, as well as the growing demands derived from climate change.

(https://www.bancomundial.org/es/news/pressrelease/2023/01/10/global-economic-rospects)

The Coronavirus pandemic has affected all countries around the globe and will condition, to a greater or lesser extent, their future possibilities for development and growth. The magnitude and variability of the effects of the post-coronavirus puts the majority of countries (developed and developing) in delicate positions, struggling to overcome or survive their own crises so that, on the one hand, on the internal front, overcoming the obstacles derived from the pandemic will be a long, difficult, complicated and gradual process due to their limited possibilities, the complexity and economic and social vulnerability they face.

On the other hand, on the external front, the Coronavirus pandemic has accentuated the impact on globalization in the essence of its configuration (see The Economist, May 16-22, 2020, pages 7 and 57). The free movement of people, goods and capital is taking on greater restrictions that could last beyond the pandemic and will have to alter the forms and contents of a new and diminished globalization with an indefinite course. The intensity and urgency of this will depend on how acceptable it is to abandon the idea that companies and products are treated equally regardless of where they come from (it is understood which country they come from).

The above implies that the equal, unrestricted, and absolute treatment in force in (past) international rules and agreements will give way to treatments of relative equality or, to put it more clearly, to treatments of exclusivity, affinity and/or segregation. Powers and trading blocks that share such ideas will be more likely to establish bilateral or more restricted participation agreements between them.

As a summary, what is described in this Coronavirus Pandemic section has confirmed adverse effects on economic and business progress. As we stated at the beginning, business management faced Covid, an event of external vulnerability, random and difficult to predict, and the management body was surprised by the opportunity and novelty of its expansion, by the inability and restrictions to exercise any control over the same and to which their ability to react was conditioned to what was permissible by the health and government authorities.

This "sui generis" experience has come to be called by certain analysts a "black swan" phenomenon. According to the author and investigator of the event, Mr. Nassim Taleb, it corresponds to a metaphor used to describe an atypical case outside the scope of regular expectations, which entails a great socioeconomic impact and which, once the event has passed, is rationalized by hindsight, making it seem predictable or explainable. (see es.wikipedia.org/wiki/Black Swan Theory).

However, Taleb himself and other analysts have rejected that the coronavirus pandemic should be considered a black swan. The most questionable requirement has been its probability of occurrence, which, according to some reports, was predicted by several researchers and even by the WHO itself. What was not certain was when it might occur.

Regardless of how it can be classified by this or that name, the truth is that the other characteristics do remain valid (among which we are interested in highlighting their high economic and social impact). Taleb himself points out that banks and companies are very vulnerable to dangerous black swan events and are exposed to losses greater than those predicted by statistical and mathematical models. Typical examples of black swans are the beginning of the First World War, the Spanish flu, and the attack of September 11, 2001, in New York. To them could be added the fall of the Berlin Wall.

The disruption of the pandemic to business management comes from the subsequent effects of any economic recession caused by it, among which we have: cessation of business activities, suspension of sales income, shortages and neglect of customers, cutting of the value chain (supplies and payments), chronic liquidity deficits, inter-business disconnection, blocking of linkages and complementary services, accumulation of inputs, materials and inventory stocks, underutilization of plant capacity, equipment and transport units, non-compliance, rupture and postponement of commercial agreements and contracts with chains of suppliers, distributors, advertisers and clients, accumulation and sanctions for non-compliance with financial and tax obligations, suspension of external advice, impact and shortages of usual flows of goods and cargo in foreign trade, making complicated decisions of personnel reduction and layoffs, facing processes of plant closures and company bankruptcy, etc.

The above means facing a gale of business dismantling, a kind of destructive hurricane, which in its wake left us with a regrettable balance of injured people and companies that ceased to exist. Since business management is based on the principle of going concern, its purpose is to survive and overcome crises. Business recovery will become more difficult because the reconstruction of the business framework will be, for many companies, a kind of rebirth and starting again, removing debris, and restarting a long reactivation and restructuring of the effects.

However, since we have reached the last cycle of the epidemic process, its economic consequences will last for several more years. In Peru, many mistakenly consider that the problem has already been overcome when we can argue that the only thing that happened was the suspension of confinement measures, but the drama of economic recession, shortages and high levels of inflation are latent and tend to worsen due to the imminent occurrence of the El Niño Phenomenon in the coming months and also because the precarious conditions of health care, sanitation and environmental protection continue its deterioration.

We have intentionally expanded on the topic of the pandemic, the development of which was exposed in phases or stages and independently and sequentially for the purposes of analysis and presentation. Our purpose was <u>to highlight characteristics of what government and business management was in unforeseen and emergency conditions</u>, whose symptoms, successes, and failures will set the tone and reference for future emerging environments. Reality, as always, was plagued by multiple and simultaneous events and showed us evolutions, mutations of singular repetitive and even overlapping sequences that typified second, third and successive waves. All of this suggests to us that despite the decreasing trend registered by the pandemic, we will have to get used to living with its consequences (physical and economic) for a long time and have an obligation to prepare respective contingency plans against variants of this pandemic or another pest.

4.3.5 The Inevitable Warmongering

To the delicate post-pandemic situation described above, another random external condition is added that also deserves to be highlighted. The events of Russia's invasion of Ukraine (Feb. 24, 2022) affect the global panorama in a peculiar way because it is generating political and economic effects of greater impact and longer duration than initially expected. As if to further complicate this war scenario, since the first quarter of 2023, the aggravation of acrimony and differences related to China's claim on Taiwan has also begun to get hotter, which has provoked US support for the continuity of its independent status.

Finally, with this study in its final phase, a complicated military confrontation broke out in the conflictive Middle East between Israel and Hamas, a Palestinian political and paramilitary organization as an Islamic resistance movement which is established in the strip of Gaza (border territory between Israel and Egypt). As a sign of a conflict that tends to become more serious and far from justifying the initial surprise attack by Hamas that lit the fuse, Israel's aggressive military attacks in Gaza have caused, towards the end of December, a death toll of almost 20,000 Palestinian citizens deaths among a civilian population that even registers deaths of women and children. This disproportionate Israeli reaction has been criticized within international organizations and by some political leaders who have forced a temporary truce to exchange hostages, but which is very far from meaning a ceasefire. The issue of human rights once again becomes relevant.

The worsening of the conflict between Russia and Ukraine is manifested in the regrettable loss of human lives (mostly Ukrainians), a greater flow of refugees (elderly, women, and children) who emigrate from their country, and the bellicose Russian aggressiveness that recalls the purest Nazistic style of past experiences with ferocious attacks and bombings on civilian populations that the Ukrainian people will hardly forgive or forget.

This scenario has reactivated geopolitical axes, and now the USA is committed to rebuilding and strengthening the Western Front with Europe. In the other block, a combative Russia initially appears, but with undeniable tacit and political support from China, whose discreet position was revealed with its vote against the UN resolution that condemned Russia's invasion of Ukraine. Later, it will have to be confirmed what, how, and when the "Chinese Panda Bear" will provide, for mutual convenience, probable economic and financial support to its fellow species, the "Russian Brown Bear". In any case, we remain attentive to a stage performance that will take place for a while.

In the present conflicts that occurred in Ukraine and Taiwan, in addition to being focused on territories close to military powers, they present characteristics of the threatening possession of a military arsenal with enormous destructive capacity that means a potential risk of projecting a zonal or regional controversy in controversy with edges of character and global impact. Disagreements to unbalance or make hegemonies prevail have singular incidences on the military level.

As if to "add more fuel to the fire," the Russian Ministry of Defense reported, according to the newspaper El País (see https://elpais.com/internacional/2022-03-21/que-son-y-como-funcionan-los-misiles-hipersonicos-kinzhal-que-rusia-ha-lanzado-contra-ucrania.html of March 21, 2022), the use a few days ago of Kinzhal hypersonic missiles (confirmed by the USA) that can reach a distance of up to two thousand kilometers, transport nuclear charges, reach a speed of up to Mach 10 (that is, ten times the speed of sound) and also have a maneuverable trajectory capacity that makes interception difficult. This display of Russian military power fulfills its function of sending a deterrent message to the West.

The USA has warned that if Russia uses nuclear weapons or chemical or biological weapons, it will provoke an immediate response from the Western Front. In previous typical conflicts of the past Cold War, indirect confrontations occurred between the hegemonic powers (USA and the Soviet Union) in the territories of third countries, Viet Nam, Angola, Korea, Cuba, etc. Currently, the conflict presents the peculiarity of direct intervention by a recognized military power such as Russia, which takes place on part of its own border. This makes us enter, after a relative pause of almost three decades, a recent version of the Cold War between the fronts where the spark of a war risk of greater intensity and spread becomes more potential.

If the military balance of the conflict continues strongly in favor of Russia, it will have to weigh the input of more time than expected, the regular human costs, and other resources of staying in the line of combat (also with casualties and injuries, although minor) and the immediate and significant logistical support and military aid from the Western Front. All of this generates a deterioration that may predispose Russia to not having to wait for an outcome and to be inclined towards negotiated solutions.

Meanwhile, the economy of unavoidable presence before, during, and surely after the conflict will continue to increase its strategic role to the point of being able to induce, with a similar impact of the missile deterrents, a greater willingness to carry out peace negotiations. Why would it be feasible to agree to talk? Because the strong economic sanctions that the Western Front imposes on Russia mean a significant decrease in its income from oil exports and future gas exports to Europe. In addition to this trade blockade, the freezing of assets of main Russian banks in American and European markets and the withdrawal of the SWIFT system (international transfers) of important Russian banks in the USA and Europe will block their access to American and European financial markets and reduce their ability to maintain their commercial and financial flows.

Additionally, specific restrictions were established in certain areas: such as the prohibition on exporting equipment for the oil sector to Russia to make its maintenance and modernization difficult. According to BBC News (see, 2022), the Russian Civil Aviation infrastructure has significant external support from supplies from Europe, the USA, or Canada, which is why the sale of aviation equipment to Russian commercial airlines has been prohibited. The restrictions also include limiting Russia's access to high-tech products such as semiconductors.

On the other hand, the Russian economic scenario shows us that even with less economic power, towards 2020, it maintained an expectant eleventh place in the world economy, making us realize that what it does or fails to do in the global concert of economic interdependence will have a significant impact. Let us see why:

- As a result of the conflict, the shortage and increase in oil prices are leading to an energy supply crisis and a global inflationary impact with undesirable consequences in the West. Russia, as an important oil producer (seven million barrels a day and the third largest producer of crude oil in the world after the USA and Saudi Arabia) and as an exporter of this (7% of the world's supply), has left, due to its forced withdrawal from the market, a void difficult to fill.

- Given this, the International Energy Agency (IEA), according to information released (see: https://www.motorpasion.com/industria/nueva-liberacion-masiva-barriles-petroleo-tratara-relajar-precios-frenar-hegemonia-rusa-sector-energetico) announced that to avoid Russia's dependence on the market, its 31 member countries agreed to release 60 million barrels of oil from their emergency reserves. However, the price of crude oil continued to rise towards a new range between 100 and 120 dollars per barrel. The countries of the oil cartel (OPEC), which also makes up Russia, look with expectations at the evolution of the market and were initially reluctant to increase their supply and increase their production, and export volumes to stabilize the market.

- Knowing that the use of part of the US strategic reserves is provisional and requires replenishment, flirtation has arisen for the US to increase its purchases from Venezuela as a feasible alternative to the requirements of both countries. A US delegation traveled to Caracas to address this issue (March 8, 2022, See https://www.france24.com/es/minuto-a-minuto/20220308-acuerdo-petrolero-con-eeuu-servir%C3%ADa-a-venezuela-ante-sanciones-a-rusia-dice-experto)

The needy Venezuelan economy will not miss the attractive premium price of crude oil that the situation of higher prices offers it.

- It will be confirmed once again that when needs are pressing, the possibility of reaching a consensus and making the motto: "business are business" always remains open. On the one hand, ideas flow with their differences and contrasts and on the other hand, transactions continue that sustain a peaceful survival. We must not forget that Venezuela was partially evading the oil embargo that the United States imposed on it since 2019 through the support of the Russian bank, which, as it is currently sanctioned, would also affect Venezuela.

- On the other hand, the supply of gas from Russia to Europe, despite its sudden rise in price, has continued since the beginning of hostilities in an untouchable manner, safe and flows imperturbably "as through a tube" or to be more precise, as through a gas pipeline. We only must add that Russian natural gas production amounted to almost 680 billion cubic meters in 2019, representing 17% of world production and it also has the largest gas reserve with 38 trillion cubic meters.

- In abundance of the same, Russia's strategic position as a fertilizer producer (50 million tons annually representing 15% of world production) fueled its reaction (in the face of Western measures) to suspend since mid-March 2022, its Fertilizer exports represent about 17% of global exports.

The continuous demand for fertilizers in said market is already registering a normal increase in prices. The situation of shortages, high prices, and reduced availability generate a lower use of fertilizers and will directly affect the productivity of crops, which is why the European and Asian agricultural sectors, and the distributor chain are concerned about a probable shortage of food and fruits in their markets and their respective increase in price. In the wheat sector, the joint presence of Russia and Ukraine represents a quarter of world production, and its impact on the conflict will also aggravate the inflation.

We have put this warmongering on the discussion table as a clear example of an external condition where its implications go beyond the scenario of the litigants and acquire special geopolitical and economic connotations in the rest of the world. How far can we go in this unequal confrontation between Russia and Ukraine? Why does Russia persist in its desire to turn Ukrainian territory into a graveyard? Will the western front of the USA-Europe and its indirect participation in the conflict (limited to economic sanctions and military support) have sufficient deterrent capacity?

The hegemonies will continue to play their cards, but what and how much do the litigants of the conflict loss or gain by prolonging it? Let's look at some guesses:

Russia, beyond its well-known military supremacy over Ukraine, used the invasion of neighboring territories to, under the pretext of supporting the independence desire of these areas, end up annexing them to its area of power (just as it did several years ago in Crimea). With this, it has wanted to strengthen what it considers its zone of influence where Ukraine represents, due to its location and extension, a strategic area in its desire to recover part of the power of the former Soviet Union. The determination of their military incursion sends a clear message to the USA: "Do not advance further into my area or establish more military bases that threaten my border." Without trying to justify the exaggerated Russian war effort but only to frame it in the geopolitical context, we will say that it has been very similar to the reaction that the USA had against the former USSR in the missile crisis (Cuba) in the sixties of the century past.

Russia will continue in combat, but it will not be willing to mortgage its future and will continue with the war accelerator until it considers that the balance of the accomplished facts is irreversibly in its favor. So, after consolidating her position and with greater negotiating power, it will be willing and determined to negotiate peace in which it will seek to impose its conditions and soften its weakened warlike image. More than a year and a half after the conflict began, peace negotiations remain stalled for the moment.

The latter is a clear indication that time could be working against Russia, which is facing more difficulties than expected. First, this military incursion was not as smooth and rapid as the previous annexation of Crimea eight years ago because, on this occasion, it was met with greater Ukrainian war resistance and greater civil repudiation within Ukraine that Russia did not foresee or minimize and that will end up fueling an anti-Russian sentiment for several decades in the post-conflict.

On the other hand, there was also a faster and more intense reaction on the part of the Western Front with economic sanctions that Russia also underestimated. Affecting the vulnerable side of the Russian economy by undermining the flow of present and future foreign trade of its natural resources (oil, gas, fertilizers, grains, etc.) is a hard blow with pernicious and cumulative effects that will take their toll as time progresses and aggravate its economic fragility.

If the conflict persists and beyond probable promises under the table (what Russia can negotiate or receive from China), it will not be easy to quickly find substitute buyers of its supply capacity, nor will there be few immediate suppliers to their affected commercial demand. Additionally, it is possible that with the financial aid (loans) to be received from the large Chinese coffers, it will have the opportunity to strengthen its economy by redirecting it to make it less dependent on its natural resources and try to repower its obsolete industrial and technological capacity.

Finally, as mentioned before, the wear and tear generated by any warlike impact, together with the growing discontent of its internal civil front (whether due to disagreements over the military incursion and its manner and results), transfers it to the government elite Russian, certain margins of instability that over time could increase resentments and hidden dissidence.

The USA-Europe front will continue with military aid to a weakened Ukraine and will continue with economic sanctions against Russia that, although they prolong the Russian wear and tear, do not seem to be enough, and new or reinforced strategies will be required to contain it. Let us not forget that after the fall of the Berlin Wall and the collapse of the former USSR, the strategy of the West and the USA was to destabilize and keep at bay a Russia that was left economically bankrupt.

All of this resulted in the majority of the former independent republics of Russia and many other Eastern European countries being received with open arms by the USA-Europe front, ready to provide them with financial, commercial, and technological support through their incorporation into the European common market and also military support, making it easier for them to access NATO and obtain the installation of American military bases in several of them.

From this perspective, the hypothetical strategy of premeditated Western provocation against Russian interests made foreseeable the possibility of the outbreak of a conflict that was a matter of time. The outbreak arose in Ukraine, where the annexation of Crimea to Russian sovereignty (March 18, 2014) was a prelude and warning of a risk of war that the Western Front did not consider in its proper dimension. They also underestimated that in the last thirty years, the enormous potential of Russian natural resources became its main economic support to facilitate its continued technological leadership in the military field to say to the West: Here I am, and they do not go from here!

China will continue to stealthily move its pieces on a board that suits it quite well. In the first stage, it will continue to advocate from the audience and, for the audience, a diplomatic solution to the conflict, but behind the scenes, it will continue to encourage the combative Russian participation and its encouragement of military advance. The extension of the conflict is in China's interest because, on the one hand, the greater the economic wear and tear on its partner and the greater its vulnerability to the conditions that it imposes on Russia in exchange for its "selfless help." On the other hand, the extension of the conflict also implies the continuity of the charge from the Western Front to Ukraine, without which it would be at the expense of an imminent Russian defeat.

The war may continue until, on the economic level, some front is not willing to continue assuming greater burdens, nor is any front willing to assume greater wear and tear on the military level. It will then be the balance or imbalance on each front and between both fronts that will be decisive not in reaching a stable solution to the conflict but in reaching a conditional peace agreement or a weak ceasefire.

In the second stage and after a long and expected process where a peace agreement is formalized, China will be able to proceed, free of external pressures, to provide help to Russia to recover the economic wear and tear of its military incursion by purchasing and compensating it, even partially the volumes of oil and gas that Europe stopped buying. Unraveling the trade blockade with the West will not be easy or immediate either.

As if to ensure that everything remains the same and even better than before, China, without assuming any cost in this conflict and externalizing its diplomatic stance as a great compromiser, will be in a better position after the armistice is signed to offer Russia an attractive financial assistance package of loans in highly advantageous amounts and conditions (long terms, low interest rates and with sufficient years of grace) that Russia will hardly be able to rule out. Nothing detracts from the fact that in this exchange, gold will be the precious metal that comes into play for China to include in its present and future conditions and acquisitions. Both have what the other needs, so everything will be facilitated by establishing in such credits as "simple collateral" the fixing of sufficient availability of gold, oil and gas to support them.

China's main interest in its supposed "solidarity aid to Russia" is motivated by his convinced appreciation that such aid is simply a means to consolidate its own hegemonic path. This has to do with the time it takes for the development of the conflict and the completion of the negotiation process. If this continues, it will be unofficial and frowned upon for China to abandon its apparent discretion and openly undertake any aid. Even more so, given the contrary position of the West, there is a risk that it will also be subject to economic sanctions.

China remaining discreet and circumspect will potentially prove to be the biggest winner. The cost of its financial aid to Russia will be less than the cost already borne by the Western Front during the conflict and what it will have to bear after it. While the Western Front will have to bend its efforts to carry out a supposed Marshall Plan for Ukraine, China's support for its Russian comrade will have, in return for its purchases and financial aid, guarantees of increasing its availability of strategic products and reserves (gold, oil, and gas) that will support the dynamics of its future growth. If we add to this the enormous preponderance of China in current global trade flows, this country will continue to advance its potential hegemony and continue to influence the course of future economic relations in the world.

The next step will be to advance in the field of international finance, payment and transfer mechanisms and foreign exchange and virtual currencies (dethroning the dollar will take time and will not be easy). China has been experimenting since May 2020 with a digital version of the yuan initially conceived as a domestic payment platform. Currently (Sept 2022), according to official sources, the digital currency has involved 260 million transactions, including 12 billion dollars since its testing. The next step will be to see ways to internationalize its use so that it achieves a faster and cheaper payment system than the current ones. (see The Economist magazine, Sep 10-16, 2022, pages 74-76).

The losing protagonist will be, as in other episodes of hegemonic controversies, the country where the theater of operations took place, in this case, **Ukraine and its people**. Which will be devastated with a regrettable balance of greater loss of life, destruction of physical facilities (homes, hospitals, buildings, and other material resources), and with their inalienable right to claim what they consider their own. Its recompositing will be long and tedious and will depend on the help to be received from the Western Front.

New airs and hegemonic renovations?

A prominent scholar of empires in the history of humanity like Mr. Krishan Kumar in his book: "Empires. Five imperial regimes that shaped the world" Ediciones Pasado y Presente, SL, 2018, Barcelona, pp. 17-55, raises certain premises that can help us understand the hint of historical and present geopolitical profiles. The author maintains the following:

> "Empires, and everyone agrees on this, have a negative and pejorative connotation. Nowadays no one advocates empire... empires are generally

considered bad... it is difficult to imagine any state trying to materialize it in a formal way... This being so, the author asks why suddenly the study of empires has become so popular and fascinating?"

Antipathy for the empire is not the same as indifference towards it or the study of it, and among the reasons for the notable interest in its reappearance, the process of long-term changes in the world economic and political order known as globalization has been cited. Empire, the author notes, can be the prism through which examines many of the pressing problems of the contemporary world, perhaps even the pains of the birth of a new world order. Everywhere we look, we will find problems and situations for which there are precedents in historical empires."

During this futurology indicated in previous paragraphs, we are left with the suspicion that, if in the coming decades, the dominant influence of probable aspiring hegemonies such as the Chinese front and its junior partner Russia is accentuated, individual rights and freedoms face a dangerous risk like the one that currently persists in these countries. The leadership of two autocratic monarchs and their respective styles of government will be obvious signs of false democracies as we conceive them in the Western world.

We must start from the fact that since their origins, empires beyond the expansive territorial or overseas profile and their political dominance have had, as the quoted author states, a civilizing mission and justification. The implicit assumption in historical experiences was that barbarism prevailed beyond its borders. Therefore, their incursion was justified because it provided mechanisms of legal, institutional, and security order to their domains. From the perspective of this essay, we are interested in highlighting how the leadership responsibility of the empires in their challenge of managing said diversity of regions and geographical spaces could be carried out with the best effectiveness and efficiency to extend and export their own institutionality from the metropolis to the periphery so that the culture, values, and interests of the metropolis prevail in said connection and bridge.

As historical background, the author points out that [25]:

"When the empires had already been formally dissolved, in the decades after the Second World War, their place was quickly taken by the superpowers, which, in many cases, were empires, although they were not given that name... The

---

[25] Kumar: "Imperios. Cinco regímenes..." op. cit, pages 36 and 37

empire is the rule over a multitude of people. Imperialism and colonialism are attitudes and practices related to empire."

We then pose a first reflective question with a pending answer: What and which characteristics would that legacy of institutional order have that both the hegemonic aspirants and the current protagonists in the predominance of it will try to sell, impose, or maintain on us? The trend of the geopolitical panorama seems to show us important changes: substitution and regrouping in the sides that fight for predominance, changes in functionalities to achieve their purposes, the presence of relatively inverted hegemonic roles or relationships to which we were accustomed and that are heading towards a new strategic balance in a new version of the cold war.

In the last Cold War, the Western front with the USA at the helm exhibited potential and economic dominance. Its vulnerable flank came from social, political, and ideological crises derived from demands for social rights, racist segregation, coercion of women's rights and sexual freedom, youth dissent motivated in part by warlike interventionism, and the propensity of an important part of that force youth towards a peculiar modernism of "hippie culture", with a deviation towards drug addiction or leisure.

In this trend, a society attached to values of consumption and physical or material possession (the American dream distorted to the extreme with its paradigms of the luxury car, the luxury house, the luxury trip, etc.) and towards a violent society prevailed with extremism profiles of pseudo-religious or political sects, political polarization and in favor of a disturbing lobby culture very well structured in the powers of the state. For example, for a long time now, and in the face of continuous scandals of deaths due to shootings in public places and schools in various places in the USA, initiatives to control the sale of weapons have vanished because they encounter stiff resistance from the entities responsible for carrying them out.

We could conclude that economic progress itself was sowing the seeds of deterioration of values and weakening of ideological and partisan positions that eventually were undermining the cultural and social panorama of the system itself.

On the other hand, in this same past Cold War, the Soviet front and its followers were at a disadvantage in having less economic power, but they had a strong ideological and political structure that supported the prevailing sociopolitical system. The cult and veneration of socialist ideas, principles, values, and praxis made up the dominant culture directed by an elite and political party superstructure. However, this supposed perfection of the ideological model (Russian, Chinese, Yugoslavian, etc.) was offered, sold, exported, and propagated to the rest of the world, but it could not avoid its imperfections precisely in the field of ideas and values, which is the lack of tolerance for dissidence and rather its gross degradation with the use of force to criminalize or eliminate it.

Even so, this socialist ideology instilled a certain attraction and enchantment in dispossessed realities (peripheries and neo-colonies of Western powers), which ended up betting on such options, moved by the hope of change and supported by the respective center of hegemonic power. In this way the mission of the Soviet empire spreads reason, science, and culture (with values included) in the form of communism to indoctrinate laypeople into its system. This is how revolutions were exported to the world by supporting subversive movements in Cuba, Viet Nam, Angola, Nicaragua, etc., converted into a theater of operations of this past Cold War with indirect intervention between the hegemonies of that time (USA and the USSR).

In the recent version of the Cold War, we notice the presence of a new protagonist, China, a rising power (seconded by its junior partner Russia, a declining power), which is moving towards prioritizing the consolidation and strengthening of its economic front which could achieve in the coming decades. If said supremacy is consummated in its favor, it might not be so forceful but rather moderate. It will not be easy or quick, nor will it be unbalanced because the Western Front will maintain sufficient financial and technological support, which is the field where the toughest and most definitive battles will continue to be fought.

Let us also not forget that, in this new rearrangement, China has for decades recorded an economy that is at the forefront in terms of global growth and predominant participation in international trade. Even so, observers estimate that China has begun to record the decline of its boom period and that the times ahead will not be entirely favorable either due to the probable economic slowdown (slowdown typical of any trend) that it will have to face.

In addition to the recent loss of its high economic dynamism, the most vulnerable flank of this socialist front is the one that was previously its stronghold. Currently, his socialist ideology is anachronistic, and its political-party doctrine has been vitiated by a praxis of authoritarian and contradictory bias between what is said and what is done. In practice, such countries (China and Russia) have given up on their original and main socialist principles to become a kind of autocracies commanded by elites screwed to power in single-party schemes. China's opening to the West has turned it into a sui generis example of State Capitalism, whose party leader, Mr. Xi Jinping, established the legal arrangements to remain in the leadership of the party and government for life.

In the historical development of Chinese culture, we can ask ourselves, what has been its experience in democratic matters? It has been little or none. They have been ruled for centuries by dynasties of emperors, and in recent decades, after the brief authoritarian regime of the Kuo Ming Tang led by Chang Kai Shek, they passed into the period of the Chinese Revolution led by Mao Tse Tung. They have not had a democratic experience; they have not been able to enjoy the benefits (and dangers) of living in a democracy. Therefore, China does not find it attractive to try or share the Western democratic experience, it is only interested in a utilitarian relationship with the West in which it can obtain the greatest economic benefit from it.

Unlike past imperial patterns, China does not aspire to a predominance of its culture in the rest of the world. According to Kissinger's careful assessment (the details of which will be explained later), China's Buddhist-Confucian inspiration has more relevance than its Marxist inspiration, and its projection towards a hegemonic predominance has the main purpose of consolidating respect, gaining influence, and consideration of their interests. Although China does not seem committed to exhibiting profiles of political expansionism, it will welcome those countries that help strengthen its leadership. As we have always maintained, nothing is free, and China currently has enough capacity to, through subtle exchanges of goods and services, obtain the desired power and influence.

In the conception of a seasoned researcher of empires like K. Kumar, the recognized pattern was established in the formation of an empire based on the purpose of imposing its peculiar institutional framework from the center to the periphery. This being so, we wonder why China would be willing to break this classic pattern of imperial predominance by not being interested in transmitting its legacy of culture and institutions. It seems to us that, in this dialectic between Principles and Praxis, China would seem to choose to consolidate its position by prioritizing its pragmatism for now. Will this scheme be feasible and sustainable for the future coexistence of the new center and its periphery?

In the Russian case, the preponderance of an example of an autocratic government with clear biases of profiles of tyranny, dictatorship, and the empire of coercion of the population is observed. Its leader, Mr. Vladimir Putin, has remained in power for twenty years and is likely to remain in power for at least fifteen more years. The collapse of the former Soviet Union is too fresh for the export or imposition of its obsolete institutional system to have the possibility of foreign reimplantation. His concern lies in recovering as much as possible an area of geopolitical influence in which he can prevail its relative hegemony.

Both countries (China and Russia) have hegemonic aspirations in common, but for the moment, they prioritize achieving or recovering material potential (economic, military, technological). Given that its current priority is to consolidate and strengthen its economic flank, this will continue to be achieved at the expense of its sacrificed populations located at the base of the social pyramid that have been clamoring for some time to find forms of relief and escape valves and social relaxation. In both cases, it is the political power elites that exercise iron control over the socioeconomic system over which they spread their tentacles and networks to take advantage of power and keep the masses subjugated and captive.

Only after reaching a new strategic balance in their favor will, they attempt to consolidate and strengthen this institutional and cultural superstructure and induce it toward its externality. This last step of forced or surreptitious imposition of dominant culture will be another controversial issue given that, as stated before, there is currently no visible interest in its export on the Chinese front and, on the other hand, in Western spheres a marked antagonism and even rejection of autocratic and pseudo-dictatorial governments that detest the renewal of leadership cadres and usually, for enjoyment, usufruct and enchantment of power, screw themselves in it for decades.

An interesting recreation of this situation is made by George Orwell in his novel **"Rebellion on the Farm"**, 19th ed., Ciudad Autónoma de Buenos Aires: DeBolsillo, 2022, where he seeks to represent with animal's certain nuances of the Russian revolution and such animals as at first, they raised their voice against the master's oppression and the humans (Farmer Jones represents the Tsar) and manage to triumph. But when they exercised power, they turned out to be more tyrannical than the regime they overthrew. The revolutionaries were the farm pigs to whom Orwell gave a certain military aspect, and some are represented by Napoleon (Stalin), Snowball (Trotsky), the selfless, faithful, and sacrificed workers for the revolution, they were the Horses, and the crow Moses represents the Russian Orthodox Church.

When the situation becomes tyrannical, the pigs who hold power, dominion, and privileges in their favor, impose their new government regulations in replacement of the previously established seven commandments: **"All animals are equal, but some animals are more equal than others"** (Orwell op. cit. page 121). This sentence summarizes the author's satire on egalitarian contradictions of totalitarian regimes. When his work was ready to be published, the Soviet Union was a country allied with England in the world conflagration; his fable faced, for that reason, the pettiness of intellectual modesty and surreptitious censorship of government sectors and private publishers of his medium and his time, but he finally managed to overcome obstacles and published his writing and achieve international recognition in the post-war years.

George Orwell died relatively young, at the age of 47, in 1950, and it never ceases to amaze how, in the middle of the Cold War and in a context where "the egalitarian benefits" of the communist system were exported, a simple fable, the size of a book of pocket of 140 pages, had the enormous impact of eroding the communist system and ideology despite the fact that it was also the victim of shameful scenes of book burning. It also caught our attention that when making inquiries about his career, the name George Orwell was a pseudonym used by the Indo-British journalist and novelist Eric Arthur Blair. (See article by Ybrahim Luna: "The crisis of journalism" in the weekly "Hildebrandt en sus trece," March 22, 2024, page 15. Lima, Peru, Year 14, No. 678).

For this reason and among other reasons, we reaffirm what we previously maintained that, in such aspiring hegemonic socialist countries, there are gross caricatures of democracies that border on farce and hypocrisy. This does not mean that Western democracies are models or champions of perfect democracies, to which we also pointed out certain deviations before. Let us not forget that in the West, it is usually the elites of economic power who determine the rules of the game in their favor.

In addition to the deformed democratic profile of this socialist front, another flagrant vulnerability of said front is the oppressive and intolerant nature of the spheres of power against certain fundamental individual freedoms such as the right to freedom of opinion, disagreement, and dissent, the right not to be arrested, criminalized, and even eliminated due to ideas not necessarily compatible with those defended by the powers that be. The writer Sophie Pinkham specialized in Russian culture, history, and politics, maintains in her New York Times article: "The Exodus of anti-Putin Russians" of March 22, 2022, several embarrassing events:

(see:https://www.nytimes.com/es/2022/03/22/espanol/opinion/rusia-oposition.html)

> "…millions of Ukrainians flee the brutal Russian invasion. But Russians are also fleeing their country at a speed likely not seen since the collapse of the Soviet Union. They are not fleeing foreign bombs, but their own government...Faced with the forced closure of almost all independent media and the announcement of draconian punishments for any criticism of the war...tens of thousands of members of the political opposition are rushing to escape…"

Among the most prominent characters, the author points out those of Boris Nikolsky, a professor of classical literature who fled with his family to Yerevan (Capital of Armenia), one of the few destinations that did not require a visa and that could still be accessed given that airlines Russian authorities began to prohibit exit to most Western cities. The professor and his son were arrested in protests that broke out in Moscow in favor of another opposition leader, Alexei Navalny, whom they tried to assassinate with lethal medicines and who was finally arrested at the same airport upon his return from Germany, where they were able to prevent his death. He was held in a prison in the Arctic area, where his mysterious death was finally consummated (February 2024) at the hands of the Russian authorities. Adding to the list of the same phenomenon is the dissident and linguist Igor Melchuk, who maintained (1970) that there were only two ways to avoid the Soviet regime: go to prison or emigration. The list is continued by the poet and academic Tomas Venclova (1977), the exiled writer Sergei Dovlátovy, and the poet Joseph Brodsky (1972).

Nor can we fail to mention the renowned writer and critic of the Soviet regime Aleksandr Solzhenitsyn, who was sentenced to seven years of forced labor in icy Siberia (1945), expelled from his country in 1969 for denouncing censorship of his literary work and who was subsequently awarded in 1970 the Nobel Prize in Literature. It has also continued to draw attention to the recent unfortunate "air crash" (Sept 2023) that caused the death of Yevgeny Prigozhin, Putin's initial shadow collaborator in his attacks in Ukraine and Africa at the command of the well-known mercenary organization Wagner, who sinned by rebelling against his boss in June of the same year. According to internal and external versions, Putin does not forgive betrayal, but some doubt that beyond dissuasive displays of power, it constitutes signs of loss of power.

Additionally, with greater or lesser intensity, there is also a certain intolerance towards the establishment of equal opportunities for personal, labor, and business development in activities that only the established power allows or considers permissible, that is, subsidiarity on the part of the government towards the private sector. In the case of China, due to reciprocal benefits from trade reopening, this policy has had to be partially made more flexible.

In this new version of the Cold War, the front of the USA and Western countries does not have everything in its favor. The economic flank has in recent decades accused continuous instabilities derived from external conditions (among which the pandemic and some wars stand out) and certain internal imbalances (financial crisis, unemployment, market volatility, slowdown in domestic demand, etc.) that have affected its dynamics, have slowed its growth.

The current Biden administration has undertaken strategic reorientation to strengthen the economic and technological front. In its attempt to make the USA consolidate and lead its industrial advance of the future, it has planned large investments in the computer, biotechnology, and research fields (clean and renewable energy, semiconductor plants, electric charging stations for vehicles, emerging industries, etc.). It remains at risk of bureaucratic obstacles that could exacerbate this process due to the fact of having lost political weight in the last midterm elections in November 2022. (See The Economist set17th-23rd 2022, page 25) and due to the late reactions to the Chinese strategy in the face of such situations.

Curiously, and as a reaction to demands for social achievements and the support of countercultural movements, the struggles for civil rights and freedoms that predominated in the last Cold War continued to be raised on that Western Front (USA and Europe). Its ideas, principles, and critical values have been able to renew, consolidate, and expand both in that group of already existing freedoms such as freedom of the press, freedom of opinion and protest, free movement, and free enterprise, as well as in new conquests of rights, civil rights such as the rights of women (as mothers, wives and workers), of the LGBT community, of the population with physical limitations, the right to health services, the right to non-discrimination in the workplace based on race, sex, age, social status, religion, etc.

Thanks to all these achievements of principles, ideas, and values that can still be perfected, the Western Front shows progress in terms of respect and individual rights that contrast with their deterioration on the China-Russia front. It is no coincidence then that, in this context, the USA is now the country that, since the fall of the Berlin Wall, has been eager to export "the libertarian benefits" of its system precisely in several countries dismembered from the former USSR and in countries formerly part of the Iron Curtain (Eastern Europe). Some analysts are reluctant to recognize a new Cold War but maintain that it is a simple revamp, with the incursion of new participants and exchanged roles, of the previous Cold War after a relative pause of almost 30 years.

Regarding this, we cannot ignore in this Cold War issue the death (Aug. 30, 2022) of Mikhail Gorbachev, considered by many to be the architect of the end of the last Cold War, the fall of the Berlin Wall, the dissolution of the former Soviet Union and the change in the course of history that came with it. For his defenders, he wanted to seek a way out through reforms (Perestroika) to the broken Soviet economic and political system but could not obtain full internal support.

Like many figures in history, this last president of the former Soviet Union spent his last years of life with sorrow (due to his widowhood) and without glory in a peculiar ostracism, relegated from political life with nothing to fear, but also with nothing to shade (unlike the ostentatious assets of well-known current leaders). Having appeased the threat of a nuclear conflict earned him the Nobel Peace Prize (1990), whose monetary compensation would have given him some economic tranquility in his final years, but he decided to award it to strengthen the Russian liberal newspaper Novaya Gazeta (See The Economist, Obituary page 78, Sep 3rd-9th 2022).

The opportunity is conducive to collecting opinions from a controversial figure in international geopolitics, Mr. Henry Kissinger, former Secretary of State of Richard Nixon and consultant to companies and governments on international affairs. Admired by some and criticized by others, our interest is simply to rescue his judicious analysis of the international situation. At one hundred years old and a few months before he died, he noted his lucidity in a recent interview in The Economist magazine (May 20, 2023, pages 16-19). Precisely in consideration of the current problems in the Taiwan Strait and other issues, he expresses the following:

"We are on the path towards a confrontation between great powers. And what worries me even more is that both sides have convinced themselves that the other represents a strategic danger... When **we are in an adversarial world with mutually assured destruction**, you must morally avoid it for your society... the Taiwan problem is a special problem that it involves fundamental principles… **the margin for concessions here is limited**. On the other hand, with the way things have evolved so far, it is not a simple matter for the United States to abandon Taiwan without undermining its position elsewhere..." (The highlighted words in the quote are ours).

How did this situation come about? From the Chinese perspective, nothing is free, and everything costs effort and sacrifice, and the results are not achieved in the short term either. Here comes Kissinger's recognition regarding the evolution of China as a power, and we can listen to it as an approach to what we have called public management with efficiency and effectiveness. Mr. Kissinger maintains:

> "China has become a strategic power and has acquired technological capabilities that make it a genuine rival...My perception of the Chinese is that they are more Confucian than Marxist in their basic thinking...China's strength has historically been that the selection of staff through the education system and through appointment has brought forward nationally trained individuals. So, the Confucian system teaches two things: achieve the maximum strength of which you are capable and want to be respected for it..."

Precisely in the face of this fear of what the perception of a powerful China means, the magazine's interviewer asks Kissinger, "Where is the USA in that pendulum, (which we have also outlined before), between its idealism that is essentially part of this country, and the realism that tempers its idealism". Kissinger outlines certain guidelines to be considered:

> "The key question is whether the fear of China is justified. And if it is justified, is our policy adequate to deal with it? I do not believe that China, in its history, has aspired to world domination. They have aspired to the maximum evolution of their capabilities, inspiring so much respect that other countries would adjust their policies to Chinese preferences...So, over time, if they achieved a superiority that could be genuinely used, would they take it to the point of imposing Chinese culture? I don't know. My instinct says no, but I don't want to put it to the test. "I believe we have the ability to prevent that situation from occurring through a combination of diplomacy and force."

When asked by the interviewer about what the current situation requires, Mr. Kissinger points out some characteristics that coincide with what we described in previous chapters on **strategy and leadership**:

> "Identifying where you are... this type of analysis is useful for constructive things. Define objectives that can recruit people, find means,

describable means, to achieve these objectives. Link all of this to your internal goals, whatever they may be."

We pointed out in the first chapter of this work a distinctive sign of current and recent management styles related to the emergence of Artificial Intelligence in the field of business management. Today, we must return to it as a key element in the technological race that gives it a uniqueness in the consolidation of future hegemonies. Precisely confirming current signs to the present version of the Cold War, Mr. Kissinger warns us:

> "…incredible things are happening… I'm talking about technology here…. if you look at military history, you can say that it has never been possible to destroy all your opponents… [Now] there are no limitations. Every adversary is 100% vulnerable…destructiveness becomes virtually automatic…due to mutually assured destruction and artificial intelligence…we are at the very beginning of a capability where machines could impose global plagues or other pandemics, not just nuclear, but in any field of human destruction. Circumstances require responsible leaders who at least try to avoid conflict."

History reflects, according to the prestigious academic on these topics, Mr. Krishan Kumar [26], interesting antagonisms between empire and nation that deserve to be considered:

> "Nations and empires are rivals and opposites…The principle of nationalism is homogeneity, often considered in ethnic terms. Try to embody a common culture. Nations express a radical egalitarianism…they are extremely particularistic…the only thing they care about is their own path and they are convinced of their superiority to that of other nations…
>
> Empires are multiethnic or multinational. Instead of seeking a common culture, they emphasize the heterogeneity of cultures, especially that which exists between the elite and local cultures. Empires are hierarchical, opposed in principle to egalitarianism… they aspire to universality, not particularism.
>
> …They consider that they are at the center of the world, that they are responsible for bringing the civilizing process to all corners of the planet and they consider themselves an instrument of a broader purpose, of a religious or moral nature."

This being so, we raise a second question: to what extent will the leaders of the current nation-states aspiring to consolidate hegemonies (e.g., Xi Jinping, Trump, Putin, Johnson, Macron, and

---

[26] See in "Imperios…" op. cit. page 38

others) continue to move towards obedient nationalisms that, as we have seen, they display principles and purposes that are different and even opposed to the imperial nature and essence? In response to this, we will say that the element of power that superimposes them is so tempting that it can generate blindness and detours on the path taken.

For the same reason and despite the basic antagonisms described, the author also finds singular similarities [27]:

> "…There is another way to tell the story of the relationship between nation and empire. In this story they are not opposed but are considered alternative or complementary expressions of the same phenomenon of power. Empires can be large-scale nations; Nations are empires with other names…In both cases we are witnessing an attempt to carry out a fusion, a symbiosis between a people and a political entity."

The underlining is ours. The contradictions and similarities between empires and nation-states suggest that divergence and convergence both display both their origins and, in their evolution, but this confusing and tangled envelope with which they are presented to us in modernity will not fail to remove the mask from empires with nation-state labels that never stopped aspiring to be empires and whose objectives and scope are global and not local or regional. And the curious coincidence between empire and nation in their "populist" intentionality, as we defined it before, synthesized in the consolidation of that "elite and people" binomial.

We make a parenthesis to highlight a curious particularity throughout this triangular process between warmongering-hegemony-partisanship. Parallel to this process of hegemonic rearrangement, it is no coincidence that in recent decades, "socialist or left-wing" political parties have appeared and reappeared with singular notoriety in well-off Western realities, which have incorporated renewed political classes that compete as equals with traditional parties with different options. These parties invested with a socialist background have tried to access power or its channels, but without the shock of the use of force or revolutions but within the system of political-party representation. Some of them have achieved their goal and joined from power or from the opposition to the debate, criticism, and evaluation of alternative solutions.

But in observance of the physical principle that "every action generates its reaction of equal intensity, but in the opposite direction", this process has not led to the appearance of renewed

---

[27] See in "Imperios…" op. cit. page 41

versions of conservative and right-wing options that brilliantly seek a leading role with new and traditional political parties of their respective scene.

As expected, and because "the authors do not rule in tastes and colors," these political scenarios present a nuanced political-partisan version that ranges from ultra-conservative right-wing positions center political options to the extreme left. Due to the necessary interaction, dialogue, discussion, and debate inside or outside the parliamentary precinct or between powers (legislative and executive) and interactions with citizens and press media; the political scenario has been acquiring special characteristics such as being sufficiently moldable, flexible, with variability in its meaning, in its orientation, in its form and substance.

The result of this partisan mix with its corresponding reading (analysis, evaluation, and diagnosis) of its reality is determining a varied and alternating capacity to influence, represent, and satisfy the aspirations of citizens. In this part of history, we recently find ourselves with winds that blow the pendulum from positions from the left to the right but with a citizen expectation that remains attentive to verify what is said with what is done in both currents.

In this electoral game, it is not surprising that opposite poles abandon their original political positions and end up coinciding for the convenience of specific interests. At the same time, it is not surprising that attachment to rigid sectarian positions makes any understanding and agreement on other issues difficult. In the end, it is difficult to understand political behaviors that break patterns of logic and violate principles of good living. We still must verify the validity of the sentence that theorists taught us: "Politics is the art of the possible."

In short, we admit that business and organizational management were seriously affected by the Coronavirus pandemic, which has imposed a complicated future on us with foreseeable higher debts and financial costs. Additionally, in the development of this section, it has been seen how the random external conditioning of warlike nuances will impose on business management, for several years to come, a dose of inflation, scarcity, and increase in the cost of energy sources, inputs, food, and other goods of significant impact on cost and productivity levels and structures, making it more difficult for us to produce the same thing and making survival more difficult (see Chart N° 13).

Chart Nº 13:

External Conditioning

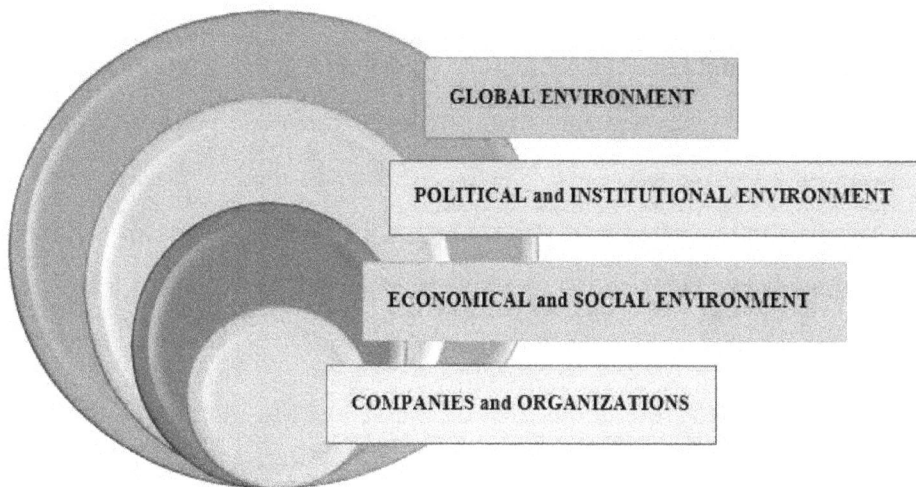

The Company's Management is warned that in addition to the well-known "populisms", the additional and random external gale of pandemics and wars will compromise management towards risky and undesirable scenarios that will affect achievements of efficiency and effectiveness for what it will have - now and how much better - than fine-tune, adjust and develop changes, innovations, and improvements in your business systems and processes. Failure to do so or to remain within the same management schemes will mean being exposed to risky deterioration.

4.4. EFFECTIVENESS AND EFFICIENCY MATRIX

It has been argued that effectiveness and efficiency are two sides of the same process, that is, business management. We have explained how the absence of both, the partial or incomplete formation of any of them, leads to a representative cause that drags companies towards defective management or full of errors and that eventually can culminate in their withdrawal from the market. In chapter one, a diagram was presented where the relationship between effectiveness and efficiency was displayed and a basic overview of management scenarios with typical cases derived from said relationship.

In our attempt to elucidate how these determining elements of management (Effectiveness and Efficiency) are constituted, we have explained what we understand as representative components of each of them. In this analytical description, the most important of its formation have been shown separately for exposition purposes only, knowing that they intermingle and interact.

Both factors (effectiveness and efficiency) are by no means independent or isolated, but rather, they are interdependent and have the capacity to affect each other. This affectation is experienced both in a favorable sense when the empowerment of one of them positively impacts the other or also in an unfavorable sense when the defection of one of them causes negative effects on the other. Cases were also mentioned where the functionality between the two can be blocked by the presence of contradictory forces so that the enhancement of, for example, effectiveness does not favorably impact efficiency or vice versa.

Chart N° 14 shows us a referential idea of the sequential manner of the effectiveness and efficiency processes, however, we reiterate that reality will present alternation and even simultaneity of both processes.

Chart N° 14: Effectiveness and Efficiency Processes

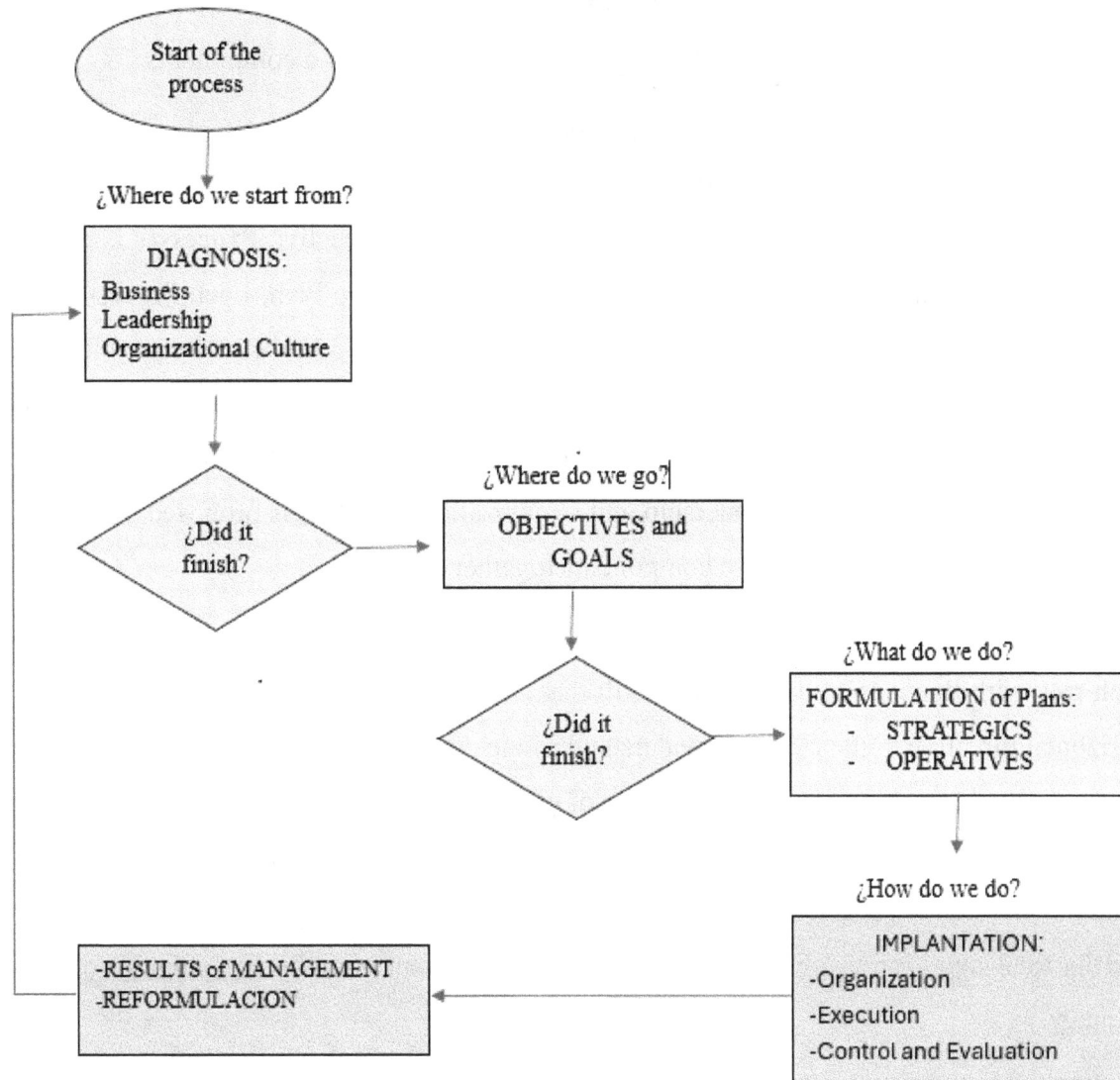

Below is the **Effectiveness and Efficiency Matrix**, which relates to both criteria, but unlike the diagram shown in the initial chapter, this time, this relationship is shown with its respective interconnected components. The interconnection of such rows and columns is represented in their respective cells and shows qualitative information (except for those contained in the evaluation and control column). This does not prevent listening and examining the character and meaning of the relationships between them.

The interacting nature of the effectiveness and efficiency matrix represented in its respective rows and columns, finds in the cells that make up the matrix, the interconnection nuclei that we are interested in analyzing to determine the functional relationship (dependence, conditional, sequential, prerequisite, etc.) between said cells and also the use of references that involve quantitative categories (maximum, abundant, much, minimum, scarce, little, medium, regular, etc.), examined throughout processes and procedures in the analyzed components.

Effectiveness is represented from the perspective of the rows of the matrix and has been referred to with its three major components: Strategy, Leadership and Organizational Culture and in turn, for each of them, the development scheme of their respective **Processes** is exposed: a) Diagnosis, b) Goals and Objectives and c) Design of the specific Plan. Each Process will detail activities described in each cell so that their execution, displayed horizontally, results in partial results for the consolidation of each component. Also, in an analogous manner, the need to prepare and develop the respective activities of each process independently for each of the other components of Effectiveness: Leadership and Organizational Culture is proposed. For simplicity, the matrix shows activities of these components together.

From a horizontal perspective, reading the matrix shows that the intersections of the cells of each row with the cells of each column will describe successive activities whose progress (in a horizontal direction to the right) we understand as the development and culmination of a specific **Process**. We then have, from the perspective of effectiveness, three basic processes to develop: a) Diagnosis, b) Goals and Objectives, and c) Specific design of the Plan. When we position ourselves from this horizontal perspective, the integration of the activities included within each subprocess, and its total aggregation gives rise to what is usually known as the Formulation of Business Strategy.

Efficiency is represented from the vertical perspective, that is, from the columns to which we have related to the Implementation scheme and shows its three basic elements: a) Organization, b) Direction, c) Control and Evaluation. The intersection of rows and columns are also determined in the formation of cells. For exposition reasons, the matrix and its respective cells have been simplified, and only basic and representative actions that complete and indicate the meaning of what is proposed are presented in each intercept cell. For example, the cell that results from crossing the Design (Effectiveness) row with the Direction (Efficiency) column will describe a set of actions to be undertaken that will be much more detailed than those that have been described due to the peculiarities and specific requirements of any organization.

In turn, from a vertical perspective, the intercepts of the cells of each column with the cells of each row describe activities corresponding to **Procedures** that we understand correspond to different components of the Efficiency scheme whose progress (in a vertical downward direction) will allow the completion of a certain **System**. We then have, from the perspective of Efficiency, the formation of three large subsystems described and the integration of the procedures that correspond within each subsystem gives rise to what we usually known as the Implementation of the Business Strategy.

Each cell makes up an arrangement of processes or procedures to achieve a specific end or represent a specific means to another end. Reality will disaggregate in greater detail the visualization of any "interception cell" between the element of Effectiveness with another element of Efficiency. From our approach, we insist that in addition to what is described in the field of conventional Business Strategy, a similar effort must be developed to constitute Formulation and Implementation for the areas of Leadership and Business Culture. Once these additions are completed, the Company's Comprehensive Strategy will have been completed with all its components.

The matrix gives us a comprehensive overview of the elements involved in business or organizational management. It is a kind of referential map in which the different pieces, loose from the puzzle of management, find forms, paths of interconnection and location in the integral context of any management. Each company or organization, according to its size, line of business, operation, experience, technology, etc., will have it specify matrix configuration, which should not be understood as rigid or inflexible, but rather, according to its own dynamics, will vary over time.

When contact and interrelation occurs between components of Effectiveness and Efficiency and their respective cells, a set of activities will be defined that are required, executed, and transmitted in a spectrum of concatenations whose characteristics we describe below (See attached table):

MATRIZ de EFECTIVIDAD y EFICIENCIA

EFECTIVIDAD (PROCESO) · ESTRATEGIA · OBJETIVOS · DIRECTRICES · DESARROLLO · INSUMOS

EFICIENCIA (IMPLANTACION)

	ORGANIZACION	DIRECCION y GESTION	CONTROL y EVALUACION	Resultados Parciales de Efectividad
DIAGNOSTICOS	Diagnóstico Eco-Fina. (antes Implantac.)	Supervisión de la performance empresarial y del proceso de implantación.	Seguimiento a indicadores económ, financ, operacio, comerc. etc.	Evaluación Eco-Financiera después de la Implantación.
	Sistemas Empresariales Existentes	Asignación de recursos y responsabilidades	Control Presup,histórico vs proyectado	Tendencias y factores de riesgos y de oportunidades potenciales o desaprovechadas
	Entorno Socio-Económico	Lineamientos de Política por áreas	Proyección Modelo Empresarial resultante vs programado	
	Análisis FODA	Pruebas de Insumos y Sistemas		
	Diagnóstico del Liderazgo existente	Liderazgo existente vs deseado	Indicad. de Liderazgo Globaly por Equip	Evaluación de Liderazgo resultante
	Diagnóstico de Valores Culturales	Valores vigentes vs propuestos.	Incorporación de valores en la nueva cult	Eval de Cultura Org. resultante
OBJETIVOS	Determinación de Visión, Misión y Objetivos de la Estrategia	Evaluac.de objetivos a nivel de áreas y de proyectos especiales		
	Objetivos de Liderazgo	Redireccionamiento en Liderazgo	Seguimiento en la aproximación o desviación de objetivos propuestos	Evaluación y Actualización de Metas y Objetivos
	Objetivos de Cultura Organizacional.	Aprensión y desapreensión de valores estratégicos y operacionales		
DIRECTRICES	Selección y Diseño de Insumos: materiales, humanos, equipamiento, etc.	Ejecución y desarrollo del Plan Global y por áreas: Programa de ajustes y contingencias		
	Diseño Sistem. Empres.: Operac., Comercial, Financ, Inform., etc.	Ajustes en Diseños de Sistemas ven la interconexión de Procesos y Procedimientos	Sistema de Información Gerencial	Evaluación de resultados de Efectividad en los sistemas y la gestión global
	Formulación del Plan Global, por dependencias y Plan de contingencias	Gestión de proyectos especiales y contingencias	Formulación vs Implementación	Evaluación del Plan Globaly Rediseño de Planes Operacionales
	Formulación Plan de Liderazgo	Gestión del Plan de Liderazgo	Auditoría de gestión liderazgo	Evaluación de Planes de Liderazgo y Cultura Organizacional
	Formulac. Plan Cultura Organiz.	Gestión del Plan Cultura Organiz.	Auditoría de gestión de valores	Cultura Organizacional
Resultados Parciales de Eficiencia	Conformación de Arquitectura Organizacional	Resultados de Eficiencia en la gestión global y en sistemas empresariales	Ajustes al Sistema de Control y Evaluación	**RESULTADO FINAL** — En procesos y procedimientos de Efectividad y Eficiencia Feedback y Redireccionamiento de la Gestión Organizacional

1. The actions described in each row-column interceptive cell present a quality of **dual functionality**. That is, they fulfill a specific purpose in themselves and, at the same time, can serve to achieve another goal of a different scope or order. For example, if we focus on observing the matrix from a horizontal perspective, we can verify that, given the nature of the "Diagnosis" item, it includes those actions that fulfill a specific purpose within the respective cell.

   In turn, continuing with the linear perspective, each cell forms a concatenated sequence of activities included in different Systems (Organization, Management and Control) but corresponding to the same Process (Diagnosis) whose aggregate will allow the definitive formation of the corresponding Diagnosis and Evaluation to the entire business (far right of the row quoted) as part of the Strategy and that make up one of the components of the Effectiveness category.

   Likewise, observing the matrix from a vertical perspective allows us to identify in each cell those actions (or part of them) that fulfill a certain purpose in themselves. In the same way, a vertical view of such cells allows us to identify these cells as means or part of Procedures related to different Processes (diagnosis, objectives, and designs) that will enable the completion of a Business System belonging to a certain component of the category of Efficiency. According to the nature and importance of each company or organization, subsystems can be detailed and formed, such as the Computer Subsystem (monitoring of procedures and their partial results), Logistics, Human Resources, etc.

2. In relation to the previous point and in accordance with what is described regarding systems theory, within certain cells, the quality of regulatory entity and regulated entity (or subject to regulation) must be distinguished. Organizational complexity contains a multiplicity of regulated and regulatory entities. According to the functionality of the activities, this unique **simultaneity** must be highlighted in the matrix. The latter refers to the fact that **the same cell can fulfill a regulatory function and, at the same time, can fulfill the function of a regulated entity** for another regulatory entity and vice versa. For example, the cells belonging to diagnostic processes allow us to appreciate signals that will be evaluated by the control and evaluation process cells, which in turn will be shifted into indicators of utmost importance for the execution process cells.

3. Regardless of whether it is means or ends or regulatory or regulated entities, the interrelation does **not imply a unidirectional, linear relationship with adjacent cells, but rather a multiple relationship** (several cells, with different interconnections), ambivalent, back and forth which indicates variability of causes for the same effect or variability of effects due to the same cause. Any cell, regardless of its position, can be related to another (or others) with distant and distinct positions. Organizational complexity is articulated in an increasingly diffuse network of intertwined relationships that will outline an organizational behavior where the original cause and its consequent effects, as well as the main forces with respect to the accessory ones, become unintelligible. Therefore, having exposed the relationships in a matrix form responds to the purposes of exposition and order, but in the facts, the dynamic functionality of business complexity goes beyond unidirectional and sequential relationships.

4. It must be kept in mind that the actions included in each cell are conducted by people (individually or in groups) or also by a combination arrangement between people and mechanical or automated equipment. These **"living organs"** committed to their execution do not always have coincident and shared interests but also different and even contradictory ones. If among the participants in conducting different actions, there is a commonality of interests and mutual trust, then it will be highly probable that the results of the <u>interconnection will be positive</u> and direct, that is, satisfactory effectiveness results favorably impact efficiency results (and vice versa).

    On the contrary, if conflicts of interest and mutual distrust predominate, the result of the <u>interconnection will be negative</u>, and it is very possible that unsatisfactory results in efficiency will also translate into unsatisfactory results in effectiveness (and vice versa, depending on the case). Since people are responsible for conducting the activities that make up systems and processes, what such people do and how they do these activities will be decisive.

5. This last case of negative interconnection can also lead to what we previously called **blocked interrelation**, that is, where effectiveness does not impact efficiency and vice versa. In such cases, contradictory forces predominate, and it is possible that the actions are incomplete, unbalanced, communication absent and deficient, and that the participants

in carrying them out are disintegrated or disunited so that the favorableness of some category of effectiveness or efficiency is insufficient to impact on the other.

6. In the case of activities that are prerequisites for subsequent activities or that require a coordinated sequence, **functional conflicts** usually arise, such as between the so-called line bodies (operational and commercial) and support bodies (finance, human resources, logistics), which are the ones that provide inputs to the previous ones. In a scheme of scarce resources, all dependencies justify their urgency and priority to obtain their requirements, and general management, in response to the company's priorities, must resolve differences. The area manager will have to do the same when conflicts appear within each unit or system of the company. For example, financial management may bias its priority toward stabilizing the company's finances with short-term financing to finance budget deficits and, on the other hand, the same management should not neglect long-term financing of operational and commercial plans. The company's general policy and corporate strategy will set the guidelines.

In addition, area management and, in extreme cases, general management itself will have to face the amalgamation of **externalities**. That is, an external envelope is presented conforming to requirements of regular and potential clients, suppliers, inspectors and local authorities or supervisors of public organizations, central government, competitors, external consultants, etc., with whom you must resolve specific issues. All this, mixed with that other external envelope (economy and national and international politics) whose influences, pressures, negotiations, and commitments constitute restrictions on management, increase the stress of the management body and the risk of making decisions that are more emotional than rational. Nor can we fail to mention what we previously called external conditions of random occurrence (pandemics, wars, etc.)

Here, we must pay attention to seeking and achieving synergy effects (the whole being greater than the sum of the parts) and enhancing the capacity of the components to "achieve more with less." There is no other option or time to waste because, in the management of interpersonal relationships, not undertaking such processes leads to the undesirable route of ineffectiveness and inefficiencies with negative synergies (the whole is less than the sum of the parts) and disabilities where achieve less with more.

7. The matrix shows specific cells whose row and column intercept summarize partial **results** corresponding to each management component. The cells on the extreme sides (corresponding to the last column on the right side and the last row on the bottom side) describe these partial results of the Effectiveness and Efficiency components, respectively. For example, from a vertical perspective, the partial achievement of the "Organization" System (one of the components of the Efficiency platform) is identified in the cell that intersects the first column on the left side with the cell in the last bottom row of the matrix. Said cell is the partial result after having satisfactorily (or poorly) developed the procedures included throughout said column, the activities that in organizational matters were formulated and served as support in Diagnosis, Objectives and Goals and Plan Design tasks. The resulting cell at the end of the column shows us how progress could be made in forming a complete (or incomplete) Organizational Architecture for the company.

Similarly, the partial achievement of the "Design and Formulation" element of the Effectiveness category (third row) is seen in the last right-side cell of the same row that contains it, and its partial result will be the effect after having developed satisfactorily. (or poorly) the respective activity processes in the fields of Organization, Management and Control and Evaluation. In this case, the resulting cell at the end of the row will show us to what extent the Formulation should or should not be the subject of Redesign and Update.

Another way to highlight the same thing is by observing the linear interrelation of the elements that make up a single row with the other elements of the columns with which it intersects horizontally or also of a single column with the other elements of the row with which it intersects vertically. For example, the Diagnosis element of the row the Effectiveness intersects horizontally with the elements of Organization, Management and Control and Evaluation. As a result, the satisfactory performance of the activities included in each intercept cell will result in (see the last cell of the diagnosis row with the results column to the right) a complete and comprehensive evaluation of the organization with the correct identification of the problems that face in your transition process.

Likewise, let's see the vertical interception of the "Direction" element of the Efficiency column with the elements of Diagnosis, Goals and Objectives, and Design and Formulation; once their respective activities have been satisfactorily completed, satisfactory management will be obtained (see the last cell of the Management column with the row of partial results towards the bottom), in its strategic, executive, and applied values dimension.

8. The analysis of the matrix can also be deepened and appreciated with more versatility by relating various components of the Efficiency column to some components of the Effectiveness rows. That is, cases of **simultaneous interrelation** can be experienced. For example, a problem detected in the cells of the "Organization" and "Direction" columns (Efficiency components) with the Plan Design row (Effectiveness component) could be due to errors in organization and formulation of executive management or also poor managerial management of a well-formulated design. Likewise, problems in cells of the columns of two components: "Direction" and "Control and Evaluation," with the Goals and Objectives component, could indicate unsatisfactory achievements in the fulfillment of well-formulated objectives and goals or also satisfactory management of goals erroneous established (at the level of areas, work groups, specific projects).

9. There may also be a problem derived from the appearance of **"external factors"** (competitive product, technological change, change in consumer tastes and preferences, etc.) or from **unforeseen emergencies** (drastic change in economic policy, climate change, war conflict, pandemics, etc.). This will require us to concentrate on the activities that make up the intersection cells of the Design and Formulation row (of Effectiveness) with the elements of the Direction and Control and Evaluation columns (of Efficiency). To do this, the impact of the specific problem will have to be evaluated and controlled, a correction or adjustment program designed or, if necessary, a corresponding Contingency Plan to face its effects, carefully and diligently executing said program and monitoring the progress and results of its implementation start-up.

10. Every comprehensive Control and Evaluation process suggests a weighting of the actions described for each cell of the matrix and must be evaluated to determine whether the results and the way of executing them were conducted satisfactorily or indifferently. Depending on the result of these, a rating calculation can be established on a continuum that ranges from excellent, satisfactory, moderately acceptable, discreet, and even dismal. It is important to highlight the character of the last cell, in the extreme right and lower vertex,

which represents the joint weighting of the partial results corresponding to both the last row and the last column described above. This cell summarizes the culmination and results of the Effectiveness and Efficiency processes, and as such, it will have to support the corporate health of the company and its corresponding "feedback" from organizational management. With this result we can conduct the necessary adjustments and corrections for the immediate future in terms of both efficiency and effectiveness factors.

11. Conversion of the **planar matrix into a volumetric sphere**. We are going to allow ourselves to use our imagination to alternatively represent the complexities of the matrix described. To do this, let's imagine that the sheet that contains the matrix of relationships between effectiveness and efficiency, its components and their respective cells are written on a transparent sheet, and we use it to cover a transparent sphere from one end to the other, so that it can be Its reading can be distinguished by rotating the respective sphere. The matrix has been converted into a volumetric sphere. Why is this change in perspective from a flat figure to one of volume?

To help us perceive, in addition to the visible relationships corresponding to contiguous and sequential cells shown in a two-dimensional matrix, those poorly intelligible, covert, or hidden relationships that correspond to relationships between discontinuous, intersecting, multiple and ambivalent cells (regulatory or regulated, causes and effects, receptive and signal transmitters) that are better appreciated within the sphere (within the company).

The normally visible or detectable relationships are those that are easily subject to registration, measurement (ratios, indicators, quotients, etc.) and projection. All of this makes up, in conventional business results reports, what we could call reports on "the flat or two-dimensional superficiality of the matrix." Most common evaluations remain at this level.

This is like the clinical examination conducted by a primary or family doctor who, with the help of his basic instruments and preliminary tests, will carry out a general check-up of the patient. If no major problems arise, your prescriptions will be sufficient to correct the recorded abnormalities. On the contrary, if the symptoms and preliminary tests present signs of risks and severe abnormalities, the patient will be referred to the respective specialist doctor.

So, faced with relationships that are difficult to detect in general or superficial tests, the company or organization will have to go through a more specialized and comprehensive evaluation that allows us to appreciate, within this concatenation of effects and causes, the unintelligible, covert, or hidden, relationships that cause these symptoms detected. The most affordable way to do this is for the evaluator, whether external consultant or professional member of the organization itself, to insert himself into the business complexity or "penetrate into the sphere" and through his technical instruments and analysis tests specific, which we can figuratively call a viewer, probe, specialized surgery or any other visual or auditory means, can detect either the infectious focus, the functional anomaly of the affected organ, abnormal growth, hormonal excess or absence or any other problem within the organism.

By "penetrating the interior of the sphere" (internal evaluation), it will be possible to inspect in greater depth and detail the functioning of the different systems and processes of business complexity, that is, it will be possible to monitor this neuralgic network of relationships and appreciate the functionality, dislocation and simultaneity between regulated and regulation centers that typify a system. Likewise, it will be detected by investigating the interior of each process or procedure, to what extent the prerequisite activities of other activities are met, to what extent accidental conditioning arises from and towards other activities and whether they respond to a programmed sequence.

In the same way, only by visualizing the interior of the sphere and focusing on the problem areas this network of intertwined and multiple interrelationships between discontinuous cells will be more clarified, which would explain whether several symptoms and effects arise, derived from and due to the same causality, or if they are more well various causes attributable to the same effect.

It will not be strange that in a less expected future, artificial intelligence applications such as the so-called black box algorithms (see The New York Times, "Artificial Intelligence." Special Edition, May 2020, page 16) can become the algorithmic instrument that helps us untangle the complex decision-making scheme existing in business systems immersed in the described sphere.

12. Finally, as we noted before, every company or organization, beyond the materiality and modernity of its physical assets and satisfactory formulations in the designs of its systems and processes, companies and organizations are made up of people and are constituted, figuratively and metaphorically speaking, in "living organs."

Again, only by penetrating the interior of the sphere and being sufficiently objective and discreet will it be possible to detect the character, the goodness or defect of the interrelationships between the participants of this "living organ," which do not always appear clear, manifest, and visible, but in certain cases they remain hidden, confused, unintelligible or disguised in clothing different from what the facts show. Through this deep and detailed observation, it will be revealed if conflicts of interest and mutual distrust predominate in the relationships. Even if systems and processes are adequately designed, their implementation may lead to defective and discrete results.

13. It must be kept in mind that what is stated in each cell of the matrix described is simplified and summarized. The content and specific development of each cell or several of them can be substantiated in separate technical reports prepared by each area or business system. The general manager will be able to obtain information on reports on specific areas because it will be impossible for him to monopolize detailed knowledge in various specialties (marketing, finance, operations, IT, logistics, etc.).

Therefore, when, for example, the partial result cell of the diagnosis row is described, it is expected that it must be endorsed by a specific Comprehensive Diagnostic report of the company. In the same way, the compilation of partial reports (corresponding to the rows and columns) will endorse the **total result cell** (corresponding to the last row and column of the matrix). The resulting matrix for each company, in addition to varying in greater or lesser number of cells, will be expandable depending on the size, line of business and nature of the specific company and will function as a kind of command and monitoring board and control that receives and is permanently fed with information of the performance of business systems and areas and at the same time redirects the corresponding corrective measures on-site.

The instruments described will make it easier for senior management to execute the adjustments they consider pertinent both during management and in the feedback of the entire process. The matrix will allow us to appreciate if there are problems, for example, on the Formulation side or on the Implementation side, and specifically which problems within each of them, or the imbalance of elements compared to others will also remain more transparent.

It is also clear that this matrix does not indicate, nor does it mean, a specific or generic recipe for satisfactory management. It is simply the representation of a tool (among those that exist) for process mapping, which allows managers to visualize the routes, understand the difficulties and unforeseen events of management and control the interrelationships between people, processes, and systems. In fact, it can be complemented and deepened with other well-known management platforms such as Visio, Project, Pipefy, Bitrix24, Lucid Charter and others that develop workflow diagrams and software prototypes applicable to customer relations, operational efficiency, financial forecast, human resources, specific projects, internal communication and document management, etc.

There will be so many matrices that will vary according to the combinations that their managers conceive and decide to apply. Even in companies of the same size and line of business, the resulting matrices - due to considerations of different development of their respective systems, difficulties of transition and evolution, economic and political situations, externalities, personnel qualifications, etc. – will have their own configuration that will be adjusted as a "tailor-made suit" according to their particularities and needs. Therefore, the need for personalized matrices for each user must be considered.

Due to the above, we consider that it is inappropriate to discuss whether Effectiveness is of greater or lesser importance than Efficiency and vice versa. First, we do not recommend prioritizing or weighing the greater value of one over the other. Our thesis is that, in solving management problems, both are necessary, and that the analysis of each company will determine the measures and weights of one or the other. Therefore, the pattern of analysis and evaluation suggested by the exposed matrix is intended to be seen as the set of previous analyses and examinations that will initially support an accurate diagnosis and identification of problems with their respective causes and, subsequently, a scheme to address, confront and solve the management problem.

The presented scheme clarifies the false dilemma regarding the convenience of starting the management transformation process first with the development of Effectiveness and then with Efficiency or vice versa. Reality imposes its demands, and the circumstances of the economic environment, the market and the specific needs of the company will determine the best path, which will surely combine Effectiveness with Efficiency. The manager himself is free to apply his own methods and techniques to solve specific problems detected in a certain cell, process, or procedure.

4.5 ADDED VALUE: Key determinant of successful management.

Added Value provides us with the economic instrument with one of the most important concepts that has a lot to do with satisfactory business management. We say that something incorporates added value when the product or service in question contains, involves, or has been added some element that provides greater value. Said greater value may refer to one or more intrinsic qualities of the product or service offered (some innovation, cost reduction, success in addressing a certain portion of unsatisfied or neglected demand, and others), or it may also refer to complementary aspects of a marketing nature (expenses of distribution and shipping, training, maintenance, warranties, customer service, etc.).

There are two approaches to visualizing the concept of added value: from the marketing perspective, the concept focuses on the idea of favorably differentiating the product or service provided with respect to those traditionally offered in the market. That is, we must distinguish an improvement in the intrinsic qualities of the product or also improvements in the complementary conditions of its transaction described above (maintenance, service, guarantees, credits, etc.). It is often said, for example, that such a company has added value its logistics system that facilitates efficient dispatch (e.g., Amazon), that such a car brand has as added value the cushioning system of its cars that provide ample comfort (e.g., Renault), that such a brand of smart cell phones incorporates the best photographic quality that exceeds the user's expectations (e.g. iPhone), etc.

This could, depending on the technical complexities of the product or complementary services, even raise certain incremental costs and prices that, in any case, would be marginal or manageable with respect to the satisfaction generated by having incorporated said improvements. From this perspective, **added value reinforces Effectiveness** because it allows what we previously called "hitting the target," that is, offering "that which impacts the consumer" or, in marketing terms, that which meets an unmet expectation or is poorly covered.

Many times, the attempt described has nothing original or new. The key is to offer the same product or service that the market was already usually offering, but with a mixture of nuances that combine innovation, improvement in its content, differentiated mode of offering, the correct choice of place, time and other aspects that make it possible they gain customer favoritism. The companies that have managed to hit the target were not by chance, by improvisation, etc., but because they listened, searched, found, and took advantage of that nuance of indicated combinations. In other words, it is not about waiting for the opportunity (a result that meets those favorable conditions and circumstances) to "arise by chance," but rather, said opportunity was the result of the search process and its use (patient observation, investigation, follow-up of market, trial, and error).

This exploration and discovery of opportunities has allowed these companies to offer their clientele what favorably impacts their expectations. Although it cannot be denied that there are restricted cases where the encounter with the opportunity was fortuitous, we consider this as the exception that any rule usually has. It is unlikely to think that companies like Apple, Amazon, Netflix, Starbucks, Sony, Circo de Soleil and other successful ones are in the group of exceptions instead of being in the current of companies in permanent search for opportunities towards obtaining greater added values.

The most important thing that marketing success does not mean a mere eccentricity or the passing of the snobbery of the market is that the effort corresponds with solid and stable economic results. Economists clarify this process through the analytical instruments of our discipline. Chart N° 15 presents an initial situation of market demand (D) and supply (S); the interception of both market forces at point E* determines the equilibrium price (p*) and quantities (q *) where the quantities supplied will be equated with the quantities demanded.

The price-quantity product is represented by the area 0p*E*q*, which means both the spending of consumers or demanders and the income received by producers or suppliers. If, for whatever reason, a price variation occurs, this situation will cause movements along the supply and demand curves. If prices decrease below the equilibrium level, it is altered, causing excess demand and if prices increase above the equilibrium level, excess supply is generated.

Chart Nº 15: Added Value generated by Demand

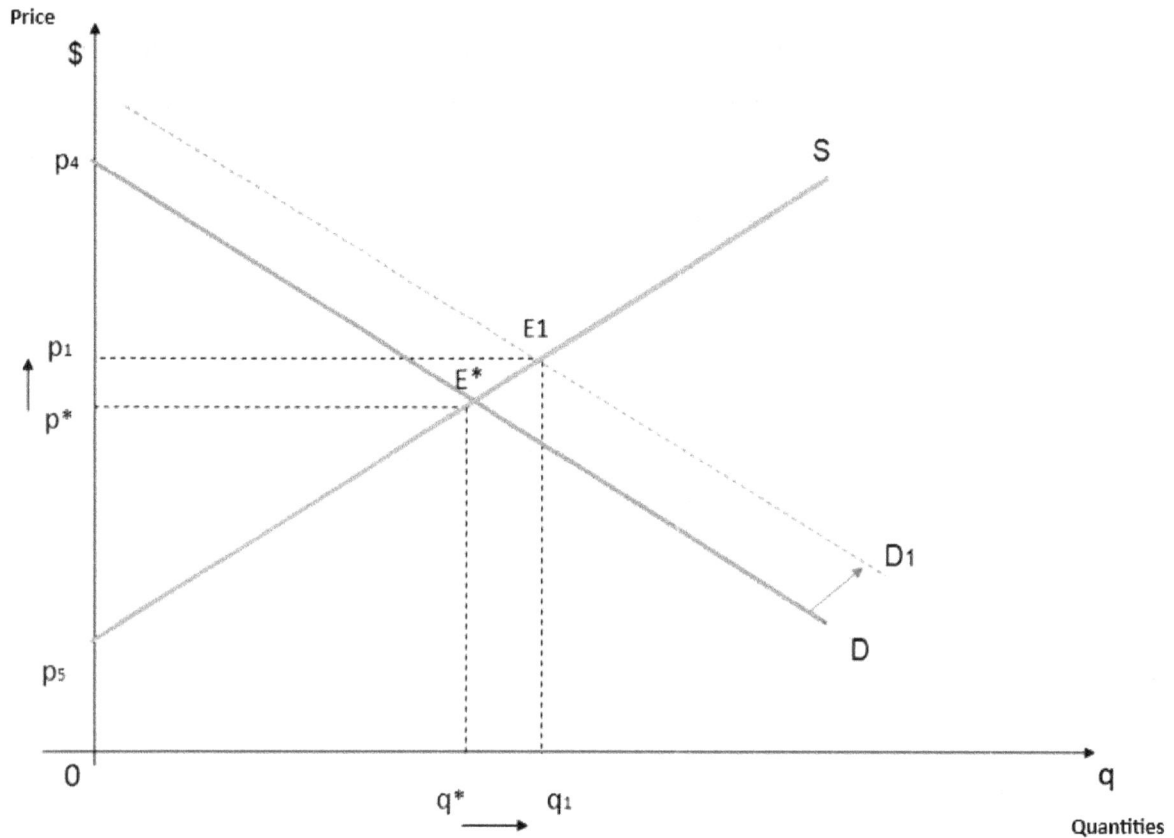

Source: Own elaboration based on graph No. 17

In this equilibrium situation, two other important effects are also constituted:

a) The consumer surplus, represented by the triangular area $p*E*p_4$. Focusing only on the demand curve, this area is called consumer surplus because, for quantities less than $q*$, consumers would be willing to pay higher prices that correspond to those determined by their demand, but in practice, they end up paying the price of market $p*$. In this way, the difference in the price you finally pay compared to the price you would be willing to pay represents a surplus. The total amount of said surplus is represented in the triangle corresponding to said quantities less than $q*$. Another way of explaining the same thing refers to the fact that the consumer's total satisfaction for acquiring $q*$ is represented in the area $0p_4 E*q*$, and what he finally pays for it is $0p*E*q*$ so that the difference between both It is your profit or surplus that is represented in the same triangular area mentioned above.

379

b) <u>The producer surplus</u>, represented by the triangular area $p*E*p_5$. It is called because focusing only on the supply curve, for quantities less than $q*$, producers would be willing to receive lower prices that correspond to those determined by their supply, but in practice, they end up receiving a higher market price corresponding to the level of $p*$. In this way, the difference in the price that they finally receive compared to the one they would be willing to receive represents a surplus whose total area corresponding to said quantities is less than $q*$, which is represented in the triangle.

Another way of explaining the same thing refers to the fact that the producer's total income for offering $q*$ is represented in the area $0p* E*q*$, and what it ultimately costs him to produce is given by the area $0p_5E*q*$ so that the difference between the two is their profit or surplus, which is represented in the same triangular area mentioned above. It should be noted that <u>the total surplus of the market</u> will be made up of the sum of the triangular areas of both surpluses, the consumer and the producer, respectively.

One of the ways to create and capture added value is when an impact is achieved in the market that is manifested through a transfer or parallel shift of the market demand curve to the right from D to D^1 (see graph No. 15). Unlike price variations that cause movements along the demand curve, the movements now indicated are generated by more intense and complicated reasons such as for example, change in consumer tastes, attention to unsatisfied demand, discovery of a market niche, reductions in transaction costs for demanders, new discoveries that allow new markets to be captured, etc.

The parallel shift implies assuming the assumption that the curves, having the same slope, maintain the same price elasticity of demand (that the percentage variations in the quantities demanded due to the percentage variations in their prices are the same before and after said shifts). Breaking the assumption of constant elasticities implies a different configuration of the changes to be described.

What is derived from this shift in the demand curve? Firstly, demanders are now willing to pay higher prices for the same amounts previously traded. It also tells us that, maintaining the same prices derived from the previous demand, the demanders would be willing to purchase quantities at levels higher than those previously existing. The displacement will have generated excess demand that will pressure higher prices. The reaction of producers will not be long in coming, and they will address these incremental excesses at higher prices that demanders are willing to pay until the new equilibrium price of E^1 is established, which also includes higher prices (p_1) and larger quantities (q_1).

In the new equilibrium situation, significant changes will have occurred: greater consumer spending due to increases in prices and quantities that correspond to greater income that producers now also receive (area $0p_1E^1q_1$). There is also an increase in the value of surpluses of consumers and producers and of the market. In this way, companies, by addressing the increase in the new and greater flow of quantities demanded for their products or services, will obtain, without substantial alterations in their operational and cost patterns, greater income and surplus. Finally, it should be noted that these added values generated by shifts in demand are in no way spontaneous or unforeseen but rather are generated, noticed, and taken advantage of by attentive direction and business management.

Another approach to visualizing the concept of added value corresponds to the perspective referring to substantive changes and improvements on the supply side and in the productive apparatus. Whether because of research processes, technological innovations, increases in productivity, reductions in producer transaction costs, adjustments to certain alterations in the environmental and economic environment, etc. - all of which translates into an impact favorable reduction in average costs, which can also be reinforced in processes of economies of scale.

These changes (see Chart No. 16) are represented in what economists call parallel transfer or shifts of the market supply curve to the right from S to S^1. In an analogous manner as described in the case of the demand curve, in this case, it is also understood that the parallel displacement of the supply curve supposes the same slope and, therefore, a constant price elasticity of the supply curve before and after said displacement (that the percentage variations in the quantities supplied due to the percentage variations in their prices are the same before and after said displacements).

The company is able, even if its demand remains unchanged, to take advantage of the rationalization of its cost structure and increase productivity to provide its offer in better conditions: for example, offer the same quantities corresponding to the previous equilibrium but at lower prices or also greater quantities offered at prices like the pre-existing ones. This being the case, excess supply will have been generated, which will put pressure on lower prices. The reaction of consumers will not be long in coming, and they will absorb said excess at lower prices until reaching the new equilibrium of E^2 agreed upon with lower prices p_2, but with greater quantities q_2.

Chart Nº 16: Added Value generated by Supply.

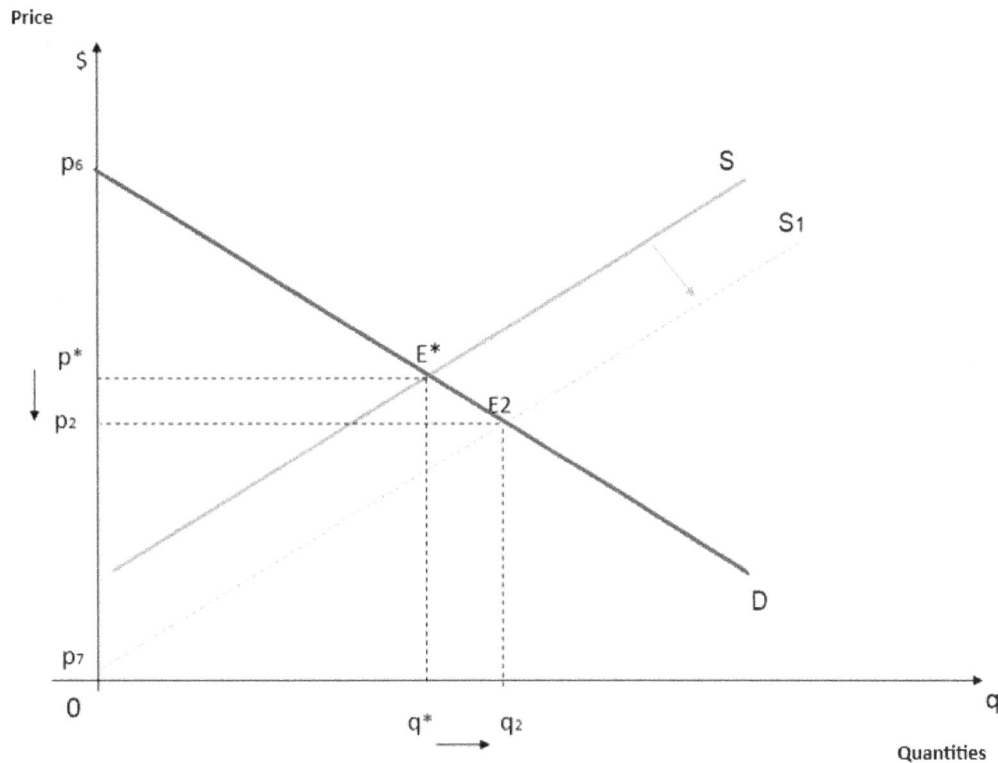

Source: Own elaboration based on graph No. 17

In the new equilibrium situation, important changes will also have occurred: While in the previous case, it was clear that higher prices and quantities generated higher expenses and income, in this case, there will be a combined effect of lower prices with higher quantities, and then the strategy will consist in sacrificing with lower prices the obtaining of greater income through greater quantities or volumes placed on the market. Therefore, the amounts that producers and consumers receive and pay (area $0p_2E^2q_2$) will be greater than the amounts traded before such changes. Here, too, there is a clear increase in the value of consumer and producer surpluses and the market.

As can be seen from this perspective, the effect of greater added value is based on what is achieved in production and costs and has a lot to do with operational (productive) improvement processes and increases in the quality and productivity of what is offered.

It is necessary to mention the last way to achieve greater added values, which corresponds to a feasible situation of combining or mixing the two options described above, which will have the advantage of reinforcing each other either by demand or by costs. In this case, both shifts to the right can be seen both in the demand curve (D^1) and in the supply curve (S^1), which generate situations of excess demand and supply with respective variations in prices and quantities that culminate in a new equilibrium situation in E^3 (see Chart No. 17).

The new equilibrium situation makes benefits clear: the product of the new and higher levels of prices p_3 and quantities q_3 generate a greater amount of income received by producers and greater spending by consumers (see area $0p_3 E^3 q_3$). It should be noted that said greater consumer spending is compatible with the acquisition of a product or service that contains a significant dose of greater added value.

Likewise, in this case of mixed displacement of demand and supply, the largest amounts of consumer and producer surplus and of the market are notable, which exceed the surpluses obtained in the initial situation (before any displacement) and are greater in comparison to cases of partial shifts in demand or supply.

Chart Nº 17: Value Added by Demand and Supply

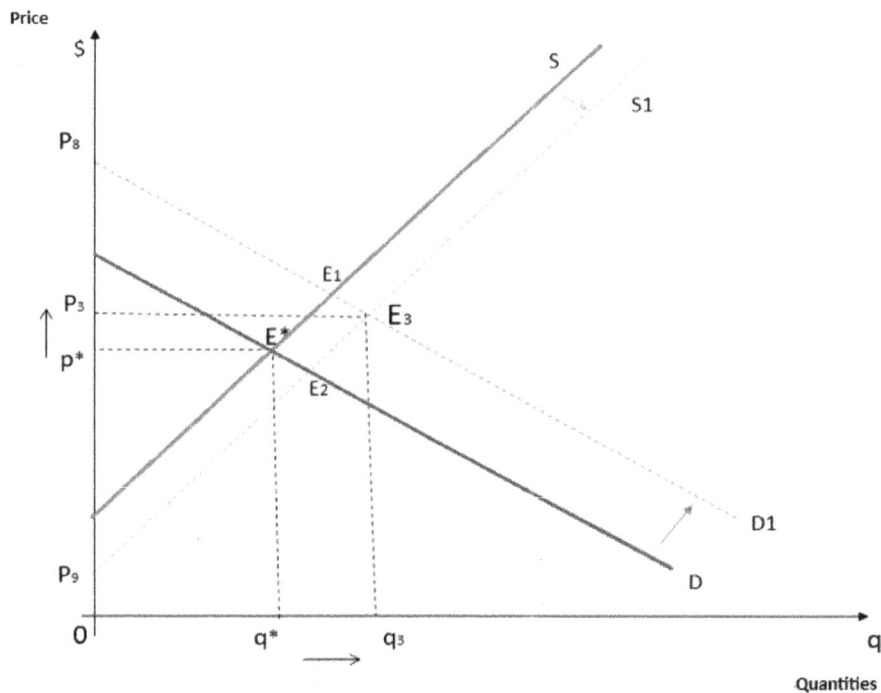

Source: Brickley, Smith, Zimmerman: "Managerial Economic and Organizational Architecture," p. 191.

In this way, business management that achieves value-added achievements promotes a simultaneity of combined effects on demand and supply with their respective impacts of effectiveness and efficiency. These, in turn, have a reciprocal impact on consolidating subsequent achievements of added values. We are talking about transfers of offers and demands growth in surpluses (of consumers and producers), all which results in favorable management performances. On the contrary, defective and erroneous management leads to ineffectiveness and inefficiencies that translate into reductions in the added values achieved and, therefore, unfavorable performances.

From the perspective of our essay, Added Value has an ambivalent connotation both from effectiveness when value is created on the demand side and from efficiency when value is created on the supply side. Except for the restrictions seen in previous chapters (blocked interrelation), an interdependence functional and reciprocal effects between both (efficiency and effectiveness) are cleared, given that improvements in one of them will impact and benefit improvements in the other and vice versa.

The search for and obtaining greater added value must be a permanent objective of business management that is aimed at successful results. Here, the basic concept is not only knowing how to react to change, nor how to anticipate the expected change but rather having the audacity **to seek or promote change**. Companies that do so through the innovation of products, services and creative processes and the research support that supports it manage to lay the key tool for their effectiveness and efficiency, and consequently for the business leadership that will differentiate them. The companies that manage to achieve greater added value are those that obtain comparative advantages because they develop that ability that allows them to surpass their competitors.

On the other hand, companies that do not adopt or get involved in these principles of obtaining greater added value and seeking change and innovation are destined to remain behind those that lead their sector and are, therefore, ultimately left behind. As noted before, changes in the environment and competition surprise these companies, and they only act reactively, fighting to survive, and over time, continuous and greater difficulties can make them disappear from the market.

In this regard, it is worth commenting that, for example, the substantial part of Peruvian exports, beyond the appreciable effort involved in the combination of resources and the challenge of their development, due to their primary-extractive nature, show a moderate pattern in the levels of added value achieved. Additionally, a simple analysis of the majority of our so-called "non-traditional exports" such as agricultural products (vegetables, fruits, cotton, etc.), the fishing sector (fish fillets, shellfish, fish meal), basic manufacturing (yarns, fabrics, and clothing), etc.; They also present a modest pattern on the value-added scale.

The substantial transformation of our productive apparatus and its lower vulnerability to the difficulties and fluctuations of the foreign market will be obtained from this goal of achieving increases in added value in products that make up our supply capacity. Due to approaches such as those just formulated and given that what is proposed sounds nice on paper, we economists earn the reputation of idealists. However, in practice, we have decades of frustration. Despite this, we insist that this approach constitutes an enormous challenge and will guarantee greater sustainability in solid and stable growth and greater competitiveness to maintain the dynamism and perspective of an emerging country.

Given the important **interrelation between added value, effectiveness, and efficiency**, added value can be considered as a reference performance indicator. This performance must be constituted as the synthesis of an integral (holistic) system of methods, procedures and techniques included in the management of an organization that, in our essay, we have called management with effectiveness and efficiency. To do this, we suggest one last imaginative exercise to visualize what has been stated using a three-dimensional graph that is explained below.

Let us remember that in the first chapter, we had built graph N° 2 where on the "x" axis we represent the Efficiency and on the "y" axis the Effectiveness and both variables were restricted to a two-dimensional plane. On this occasion, we present a new graph that, in addition to the variables, we will add a third variable, the "z" axis, that represents business performance.

Also, to avoid confusion, the difference between the current three-dimensional graph and the three-dimensional graph described in section 3.2.1 is that in the graph of said section, the "x" axis represented in the Business Systems, the "y" axis represented the Inputs, and the "z" axis represented the Results in terms of Efficiency due to the combination of inputs and systems. In the present case, the development of the relationship and effects between effectiveness ("y" axis) and efficiency ("x" axis) will be determining factors in business performance ("z" axis).

In this way, a hypothetical point "p" of the new three-dimensional space will reflect the conjunction of a determining level of efficiency, effectiveness, and its corresponding level of performance of any business management. It can also be formed based on that imaginary line of the "xy" plane constructed in graph No. 2, an imaginary diagonal (see dotted line) that starts from the vertex of origin of the three axes and "rises" in magnitudes equidistant from each axis. This diagonal imaginary represents successive and continuous equidistant combinations of effectiveness, efficiency and performance, starting from lower levels to elevated levels of the three variables (see Chart No. 18).

Chart Nº 18: Effectiveness, Efficiency and Performance

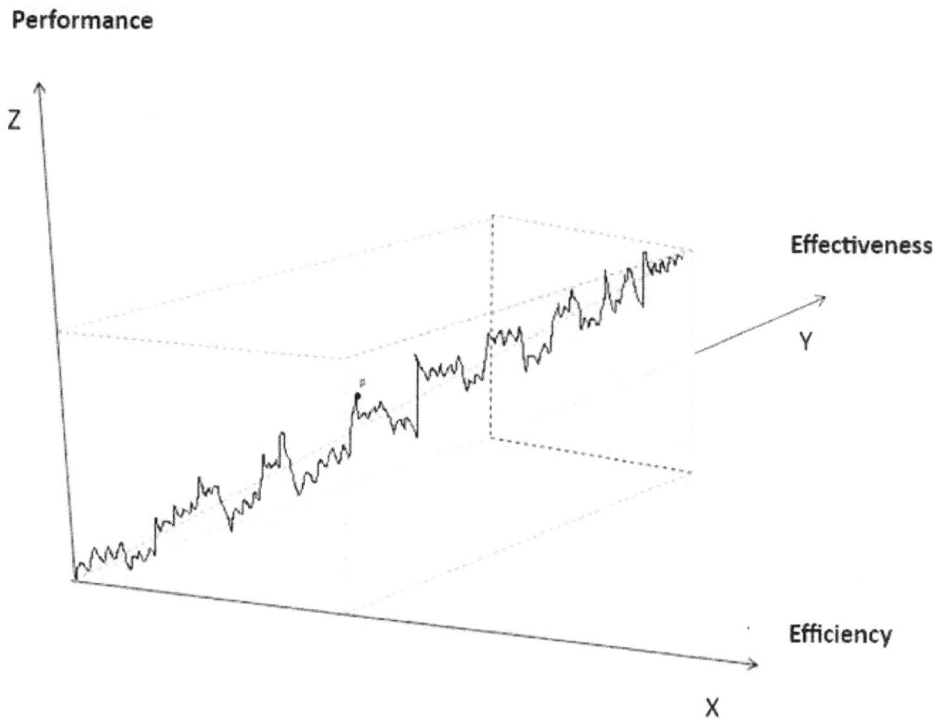

Source: Own elaboration

When relating the matrix described in the previous section and comparing it with the current graph, we must take into account the recommendation of S. Levitt and S. Dubner [28], where they remind us, within the framework of their hypothesis, that the facts present some hidden side that we must explore and that "two things that are correlated does not mean that one is a cause of the other." A correlation, in the strict sense, simply means a relationship that exists between two variables – let us call it X and Y – but it does not tell us anything about the direction of that relationship. It is possible that X causes Y; and it is also possible that Y causes X, and it may be that X and Y are both variables causing Z or vice versa. So, the interpretation of the regression and

---

[28] See: "Freakonomics" Op. cit. page 8

correlation coefficients of a statistical model depends in advance on what the researcher considers to be the dependent or independent variable.

Returning to our three-dimensional graph of effectiveness, efficiency, and performance, it should be noted that the graphed diagonal is imaginary and is presented only for analytical purposes because it represents a specific route or trajectory that projects hypothetical combinations of magnitudes of efficiency, effectiveness, and their corresponding magnitude of performance. In the facts, the hypothetical point "p" mentioned above could be close or distant to said diagonal, and its trajectory (made up of the continuity of such points) could be below said diagonal (defective pro-management) or close to and above it of it (pro-successful management).

As specified before, in practice, the "magnitudes" of efficiency and effectiveness hardly coincide, and in turn, these will not be of the same order of magnitude as the performance. In this, we must consider the out-of-phase sequence of the succession of activities and the presence of contributing and contradictory forces and elements in each component of effectiveness and efficiency.

In the three-dimensional graph shown, the time variable is implicit for all components, and therefore, we recommend considering that the relative speed in the short term in one component will not always have immediate and equivalent correspondence for the other components and vice versa. The short- and long-term perspectives and time horizons are also different for each component. With this, we want to highlight that the "performance variable" does not necessarily have immediate effects derived from the remaining variables, but rather, it will necessarily be activated "after and with a different intensity" than the rest. For this reason, the slope of the imaginary diagonal will be affected by the time restriction that the implementation processes entail, and the transition problems mentioned above. Therefore, it has been preferred to graph it with a moderate slope of 30° degrees, more in line with reality.

There is another general restriction that affects the three variables. Each of these variables will not be able to grow in a progressive, sustained, and indefinite manner. There will be a "maximum possibilities limit" for each of them based on the restrictions of each business reality. Just as in the theory of prices that makes up the economic discipline, there is an income budget line that delimits the possibilities of utility or satisfaction of the consumer. Thus, limits of maximum management possibilities will also be presented that will be of different magnitude for each variable of the model, so they are formed into a kind of fences or walls (of effectiveness, efficiency and performance) that beyond them cannot be achieved overcome them. Such stops jointly contain or encapsulate business management in a space like that of the geometric figure known as a parallelepiped, but within which they fluctuate with a wide degree of freedom. Its shape is the same as a simple shoe box, as shown in Chart N° 18.

The resulting or definitive profile of the performance variable is represented in the line that results from the succession of points within which (of the geometric figure of the parallelepiped) it will present ups and downs that could place it above or below the imaginary diagonal. Its profile will be like the teeth of a saw, or it will also be like the graph of a stock market index or the profile of the top of a mountain range (in the reinforcement of the fact that we are prisoners of our preconceptions, it depends on whether the person observing the graph be a carpenter, a stock market analyst or an environmental lover).

Let us remember that this entire diagrammatic exercise is, as we said before, an imaginative architecture that attempts, on the basis of interrelation between elements of any system, to represent or transmute concepts and ordinal and qualitative criteria into cardinal and quantitative approximations that are indicative to intuit, clarify and clear up doubts regarding the content, functionality, profile and directionality presented by the nebulous business and organizational reality. This exercise should not be classified as merely fanciful because there are indicators, ratios and other quantitative and qualitative signals in the described platforms of effectiveness, efficiency and performances, which provide sufficient support for its foundation.

Professor P. Samuelson [29] is responsible for clarifying such entanglements more categorically when he points out: "the way we perceive the observed facts depends on the theoretical lenses we put on...**we are prisoners of our preconceptions, prejudices, feelings and sordid interests**." (highlighting is ours). Also, worth highlighting is what is known as the fallacy of composition, according to which one can err by generalization when one infers that what is true and valid for one party is also necessarily true, valid (and only for that reason), for the whole. As P. Samuelson also details in the same source: "...in the field of economics, what is true for individuals is not

---

[29] see "Economía", op. Cit. page 6

always true for society. On the other hand, what seems true for everyone may be false for some individuals."

Without fear of committing the same fallacy, we can transfer this appreciation to the field of social organizations and, particularly in the field of business activity and within it. We must avoid falling into the frequent error of generalizations and pay more attention to the differences and contrasts in those elements or factors that are also part of their totality. That is, what seems true and good for one area or sector of the company is not necessarily true and beneficial for the entire company and vice versa.

Likewise, in broader scenarios, what is valid and beneficial for companies in an economic sector or industry is not necessarily valid for all sectors of the country, and what is beneficial for many companies in the country is not necessarily so for companies in particular sectors or industries. There are plenty of examples: a currency devaluation hurts importers and domestic consumers due to higher prices but initially benefits exporters because they will initially receive higher income when they are converted into local currency. A rise in interest rates benefits creditors and harms debtors due to the higher financial costs they will face.

In this same sense, tax exemptions and concessions favor certain companies and taxpayers and discriminate against others, generating a criticism of the situation of privileges. The raising of import tariffs on certain goods is also the subject of criticism for the protection of certain sectors (manufacturing) and adulteration of profit margins for others (commercials or distributors). The decrease in social spending on health and education could correct a pressing fiscal deficit in government management, but it could mean widening the gap of neglect, poverty, and well-being in dispossessed social sectors.

Different perspectives on the same event

In reinforcement of what has been stated, we propose making a brief parenthesis to graphically present what we can call the appearance of contradictions contained in different perspectives on the same fact. Below, with the help of the attached graph, two perspectives are presented that interpret the same reality in a different way. See Chart N° 19.

(See: https://blogs.sas.com/content/sascom/2016/03/23/neural-networks-demystified)

The reality referred to is an object that corresponds to a cylinder slightly suspended above the horizontal plane. Those located from the right perspective, either due to their position (frontal with respect to the observed object) or because of luminosity, will not be able to distinguish that it is a cylinder, but due to the projection of the object on the left plane, they will appreciate the silhouette of a square-shaped object.

On the other hand, those who are positioned from the left perspective will not be able to distinguish, because of their position or the light, that what they observe corresponds to a cylinder, but rather, due to the projection of the object on the right plane, they will appreciate the silhouette of a circular object. In conclusion, observers from both perspectives will have their own interpretation and "their own certainty" of what they observe, which will be different from each other (square vs. circle) and different from the truth or reality itself (cylinder).

Chart Nº 19: Different perspectives of the same reality

When these issues are analyzed from different and even contradictory perspectives on non-physical but social phenomena and events, the perspectives have greater diversity and complexity (such as the debate between pro-business and free market positions vs positions in defense of greater regulation, supervision or state participation in the economic scenario, not to mention the conflictive issue of respect and tolerance of freedoms and human rights and the conditions and restrictions to them; or also in different conceptions in matters of social coexistence such as divorce, abortion, equality gender, social and sexual discrimination, racial segregation, environmental protection, etc.). In these debates we come to appreciate that each party refers to "being right" from their own perspective and even try to generalize and even impose their vision of reality on the opposing party.

Firstly, and as if to calm tense spirits, we propose to use concepts derived from the approach of Relativity that Albert Einstein [30] left us, who exemplified to laymen the results of his work by diagramming a train station and two people, one of them located in the embankment in front of the railway line and another inside a high-speed train that was passing through said station. By assuming that two lightning bolts explode towards the left (point A) and right (point B) sides, the person who remained still on the embankment and whose location was at the equidistant or middle point where such lightning struck, said person will affirm (considering the speed of light) that the light from each lightning strike reached it at the same moment, that is, there was simultaneity in said events.

For its part, the same event observed by a person moving from inside the high-speed train along said railway track can be found before or after the person who is located on the embankment. If they are to the left of said person and close to point A, the person inside the train will affirm that they will have seen the light signal of the lightning that falls at point A (to which they are closest) before seeing the lightning that falls at point B. If he is to the right of the person on the embankment and close to point B, he will affirm the opposite, but in both cases, the person inside the train will maintain that such lightning bolts are not simultaneous.

---

[30] See: Walter Isaacson: "Einstein. Su vida y su Universo", Debate. 1ra Ed. Set 2008, pages. 151-155

Who is right? Here, Einstein's scientific rigor and precision come into play: "There is no absolute way to affirm that one of the observers is right...nor that two events are absolutely or simultaneous. Since there is no absolute simultaneity, there is no absolute time either. Every moving frame of reference has its own relative time. If time is relative, so are space and distance. For both people, the speed of light is the same, but the person on the embankment will observe that the "distance" that the light must travel "is longer than the observation of the person inside the train. From the perspective of the person on the embankment, time passes more slowly inside the moving train."

Returning to the topic of social controversies and with the help of the conceptual framework described in the previous paragraph, we can also outline that there is not always an absolute reason or certainty. Each party has its truth founded. It cannot be determined definitively who is right. The only thing that can be said, in the first instance, is that each part is in contradiction with the other part.

As a second step, It must be understood that in the field of personal relationships, it must be admitted that when it comes to social realities, living, dynamic forces, human nature is a symbiosis that brings together **elements of reason and corporeality**, such forces have the capacity to emit and receive "foundations." or arguments." If during the interrelationships between the protagonist's contradictory forces predominate (of imposition, denial, destruction, ignorance, disregard, etc.), then **corporality,** with its respective positions of individuality, instinctive and sometimes even selfish biases and myopic, will be the one that finally imposes and maintains its position and validity (e.g., the law of the strongest, the prioritization of the senses).

If, on the other hand, during relationships between participants, additive forces, collaboration, understanding, and openness to approaches other than their own predominate, then **reason** will make way because it will allow progress in the discovery of the truth. Returning to the initial graph, we will say that, <u>through a different perspective, and without abandoning the original vision of each part but incorporating them into an integral perspective (that includes both),</u> it will be possible to distinguish and discern the true object or reality, in this case, it is a cylinder and not a square figure nor a circle.

What does this digression of differentiated perspectives have to do with our business management topic? It has to do with the fact that in a business management process extreme bias of dogmatic, biased positions, improvised or spontaneous trials lacking sufficient verification and proof must be avoided. Managements that refine their direction from a comprehensive perspective will develop business systems oriented towards those innovative opportunities that involve the entire organization and not just some specific area. Such companies obtain those improvements in their product or service offered that translate into achievements of greater added value that will differentiate them from competitors and allow them greater income and surpluses.

An example of this is Sony Corporation, whose policy of encouraging and promoting innovative creativity is a characteristic of its management style. At the product level, examples of innovative companies are plenty and sufficient; there are cell phones, laptops, digital cameras, hybrid and electric cars, innovations in fast food establishments, audio and sound equipment, innovative business recreational, hotels and restaurants, etc. It is also worth considering what we describe later for the Apple company (see chapter 5, Steve Jacobs' conceptualization of "non-Apple perspectives").

It is clear, according to the examples cited, that it is the large corporations and the innovative technology products developed by them which, due to their own organizational and technical capacity, are at the forefront of these search processes for greater added value. In this rearrangement, the influential processes of technological innovation and research will be setting the tone for the new international division of labor and specifically for a new rationality that defines what to produce, how, where and for whom to produce.

Will this technological implosion be that we are experiencing in countries "icons of both social systems" (USA and China), the one that finally ends up imposing a new resource allocation mechanism that surpasses and even makes obsolete the unrestricted principles of the free market and/or central planning of said systems? After a century of those management styles that we showed in the first chapter, could the supply be the one that, through its accelerated technological processes, is recycled again to become predominant and protagonist of the new management styles?

Small and medium-sized companies turn out to be, due to their own limitations, simple takers or acquirers of available technologies, which remain stuck in circles of obsolescence whose last cycle of existence culminates in developing countries. These technological restrictions in such countries and their companies are the possibilities of development options or creation of modern technologies and only leaves open the options for technology adaptation. In this path, the performance of the technical and professional personnel who put into practice their ingenuity and inventive capacity to make workable solutions with creative variants for their specific reality and within the framework of existing technology plays a fundamental role.

From the above, it can be deduced that modern organizations will be careful to preferably select technologies and human resources that contribute to the function of adding added value. From this perspective, the business apparatus of modern and large organizations will continue to focus on technological processes of relevant contribution to value and will be subcontracted to third companies in those simpler, differentiated or complementary processes (accessories, parts and pieces and other components of different technical or strategic complexity, complementary services, etc.).

Likewise, those parts of the staff whose individual performance or in conjunction with technology generates that greater desired value will remain as permanent workers with greater job stability and will be subcontracted, through the outsourcing mentioned above (services), to the staff for routine functions, of lower qualification and technical complexity or those of temporary requirement. However, this should not lead us to the extreme of generalizing that the contracting of such peripheral services described does not add value; on the contrary, in certain cases, they could add significant value due to the greater efficiency with which they carry out their specialized work compared to that which was done by the organization itself. A notable example of this is the acquisition of microprocessors by large companies that produce personal computers, laptops, etc.

Innovation processes, as one of the supports to achieve greater added value (both from own generation and from related third parties), must be part of the business strategy, and the importance of the topic makes it worthy of ad hoc treatment to the responsibility of the top management. The development of innovative processes will be a task directed by the highest authority of the organization and will, therefore, have greater weight in its execution phase. In this effort, it must be kept in mind and ensure that the innovation processes <u>are accompanied by improvements in the resulting quality</u>. It has been observed that many times technological innovations are undertaken with the sole purpose of reducing costs and to the detriment of the quality obtained.

In countries like Peru, we still belong to the block of countries that provide raw materials, natural resources, food, fruits, etc., towards markets in developed countries and other emerging countries. We have a modest industrial development, and we share, with some countries, the production of basic or conventional technology goods and final or short-durable consumer products (clothing, footwear, processed foods, preserves, fabrics, fabrics, beverages, etc.).

Peru requires strengthening, readjusting, and complementing the domestic and export productive apparatus so that in addition to sustained growth, it gradually reorients itself towards the search for a pattern with greater added value that allows it to gain competitiveness in the domestic and foreign markets. Whether we like it or not, we will continue to be a country with enormous potential for the exploitation and export of minerals for many years. For this reason, one of the things that must be done is to take advantage of this potential advantage and channel it for the benefit of the rest of the country as a lever for internal development in complementation and support of other productive sectors.

So, when we propose strengthening the productive apparatus, the idea is not only greater growth but also maximizing its efficiency and productivity schemes. And when we propose readjusting the productive apparatus, we aspire for greater production to incorporate greater weighting of added value and a greater degree of sectoral integration or complementation. The past development models of outward growth (primary exporter), inward growth (industrialization via import substitution) or the combination of both or inserting themselves with limited possibilities into the globalization process all resulted in insufficient to generate development more autonomous.

In all these models, we reiterate the absence of greater integration of the internal productive structure was evident, where each sector or activity functions as a form of watertight behavior disconnected from the others and supplied by a strong supply of imported inputs and equipment. This explains its reduced interconnectivity, its limited industrial linkage, and an asymmetric pattern in our productive and foreign trade structure.

5. FINAL THOUGHTS

Throughout this study, we have used and even abused phrases, proverbs, adages, aphorisms, etc., with the intention of specifying or complementing certain ideas and approaches presented. They collect reflections from prominent writers, scientists, artists, and other personalities from different disciplines at separate times, as well as unpublished and anonymous expressions of popular wisdom. By remembering his teachings, we have drawn on his wisdom in those parts where the work required it and recorded our approval by citing his authorship.

Due to the intentional frequency that we have made of its use, it is worth noting that phraseological language is not exempt from limitations and must be considered with due reservations. As a favorable aspect, we note that every phrase contains and alludes to a part of the truth of the reality it describes. Therefore, it is valid as a specific reference. However, as an unfavorable aspect, given their limited length, the sentences contain content restrictions, especially when they refer to more complex situations. Therefore, when you try to go beyond the profile that a phrase describes and try to encompass greater content, there is a risk that you may fall into a distortion of reality.

Let us make a brief parenthesis to refer to the Fable of the Lamp of Diogenes. It is said that, in ancient Greece, Diogenes (413 BC) wandered around Athens with the help of a lamp in search of honest and just men. This fable is very illustrative of our current reality, where we need many Diogenes to undertake an arduous search that allows us to find a greater number of honest and just men. Even so, there is the possibility (as Diogenes considered it) of finding them closer than thought with the help of a dim light that manages to capture their special internal brilliance, often overshadowed by luminary personalities who intend to show honesty without possessing it.

In other times and scenarios, the renowned philosopher José Ortega y Gasset [31] enlightens us on this topic by noting that **the permanent virtue of a thought is that of being true**. To the extent that any phrase the author adds deviates from said postulate and embraces thoughts that are misaligned with what is true, it can force reality by adding extended concepts that do not contain it or that distort it. Such phraseology, according to Ortega, can, in certain cases, vitiate thought by preventing it from fulfilling the virtue described above (pointing towards what is true) and turning

---

[31] See "EL Espectador..." op. cit. pages 146-147

it into falsification. In this regard, we can complement that when the panorama of arguments appears artificially confused or mixed with half-truths, the phraseological deformation could shadow the falsification, taking the form of a sneaky partial adulteration of reality.

In summary, we can affirm by assimilating the lessons of Diogenes and Ortega that leaders who possess the aforementioned requirements of honesty and justice (demanded by Diogenes) and who put forward arguments that embrace concepts based on truth (posed by Ortega) do exist, although they may be rare, but they are working hard and silently at their job, they have never set themselves the label of being exemplary or important men, nor do they go out of their way to show off what they are or what they do. Unlike these, brilliant artificially luminary personalities appear on stage, false aspiring leaders who display their boasting, their lies and conduct themselves, with the tricks of their forbidden weapons, to generate and aggravate social crises in their media and hinder the advancement of potential and genuine leaders.

Just as Diogenes did in his time, the key tool to identify and separate those who appear to be leaders from those who truly do so is to use in these times a "modern lamp of discernment" that makes it easier for us to illuminate and advance in the search for honest men. That lamp is none other than our ability to identify those thoughts and actions that are unequivocally and provenly true and adjusted to the truth, that is, identifying those thoughts and men that do not lie, falsify, adulterate or distort reality.

Overlooking or omitting the use of this modern "lamp of discernment" ends up debasing the false leader and clouding the massive current of his obedient followers, leading both towards habitual and even consensual forms where deception prevails. Cognitive blindness, obtundation, stubbornness and this whole morass of confusion and obfuscation, indifference and permissiveness are clear examples of forms of **social self-deception**. But among the surreptitious forms of said self-deception (own or through the induction of third parties), we have, on the one hand, cases in which we tend to accept, trust, believe and take as true what is not true (that is, we take what is false as if it were true) and on the other hand, there are cases in which, on the contrary, we tend to discard, reject, repudiate and even refuse to accept taking as true what is actually true (that is, we reject what is true as if it were false).

The problem worsens when the debate does not remain in the scope of arguments and ideas, but rather certain people, self-convinced of their positions, arrive in an inappropriate manner and form to confront each other and attack each other (verbally or physically) and to the extent of eliminating each other against those who disagree, question, and oppose them. In such cases, especially in political scenarios, when the truth is fractured, confused, or diverted from the false, emotion prevails over reason.

The mixture of institutionalized violence (entrenched in state powers, de facto powers, and the colluding press) with prominent levels of ignorance or popular indifference are perfect ingredients that prevent greater awareness of the problems experienced. The respective citizens and voters of the American environment and the Peruvian environment could have arranged the use of that "lamp of discernment" of Diogenes to discard dishonest people and also have developed the thoroughness of Ortega y Gasset to detect the accumulation of lies and falsehoods of labeled leaders (such as Donald Trump and Keiko Fujimori) that perhaps would have led them to ostracism and not to remain as brilliant and leading figures in their respective political scenarios.

The other criticism of phraseological language is that it unconsciously encourages, both those who receive it and those who circulate it, the transmission of a certain anesthetic dose of compliance (due to the unquestionable respect and recognition of the authorship of the phrase in question). It is also argued that derived from the above, phraseology induces a certain dose of complacency, which subliminally appeases, numbs consciences, and covers with cold clothes probable initiatives that emerge as respectable criticisms and differences with respect to what predominates.

What has been described explains in part why, on the one hand, social coexistence in any society or group has been able to be endured for prolonged periods of time. For example, the typical medieval phrase "died king, long live the king" has to do with the tacit acceptance of the continuity of the monarchical system. On the other hand, it also explains the advent of political, religious, and sectarian creeds, which have questioned, through counter-cultural proposals and positions, the validity of dominant values and principles.

The problem arises when well-intentioned personalities, by devoting themselves with frenetic passion to actions to achieve certain ideals (which is laudable), have fallen prey to political or religious indoctrination from any bias, either by their own conviction or by alignment induced by third parties, so that the enchantment and enthusiasm that they impose on their commitments make the achievement of "the cause or the mission" dominate their actions, restructure the priority of their activities and impose personal reluctance and renunciations on themselves.

Along this enchanted route, where the anesthetic dose is quite strong, the border of common sense is sometimes crossed, and the brainwashing to which such people were subjected (with doctrinal extremes, political, religious or both) surreptitiously transports them into a kind of fascinating slide of "self-imposed and sacrificial apostolate" that excludes from its vision and action everything that is not fighting for the cause or the mission. Even one's own life is relegated to the point that it can become martyrology (suicidal induction of extreme indoctrination in some terrorist options), and the lives of others can also be degraded by having no qualms about sacrificing them because it is usually argued that it is a simple "collateral damage" where the end justifies the means.

Once again, Ortega calms anguish and shocks by pointing out [32]:

> "The standard of perfection is simply valid as a goal for the race. The important thing is to run toward it and whoever does not reach it is neither dead nor dishonored... Our existence should not be a paradigm, but rather a biased course between models that at the same time brings us closer to them and gently avoids them".

Indeed, the quote raises an interesting perspective on the search for perfection, but without falling into anguish or feeling of failure if the desired goals are not achieved. The idea is reinforced that our existence is our own path, in which we can approach different models and recommended patterns, but we also have the freedom to maintain a prudent distance and forge our own destiny.

Indeed, the quote raises an interesting perspective on the search for perfection, but without falling into anguish or feeling of failure if the desired goals are not achieved. The idea is reinforced that our existence is our own path, in which we can approach different models and recommended patterns, but we also have the freedom to maintain a prudent distance and forge our own destiny.

It is necessary to warn about the blind compliance that any phrase what surreptitiously aims to impose. Therefore, a balance is recommended between, on the one hand, giving course and liberality to those individual initiatives because, thanks to them, creations, innovations, and

---

[32] see: "EL Espectador..." op. cit. page. 100

advances in human knowledge have been generated and, on the other hand, developing a considered equanimity and moderation in the adoption, execution and monitoring of the route taken to avoid falling into extreme fanaticism. We close the comment, reiterating the recommendation with another well-known phrase: "Illuminate the saint with a candle, but not so close that he burns it, nor so far away that he does not illuminate it."

5.2. WORLDVIEW AND CONDITIONING

It also remains striking that human nature is invested with that kind of conceptual framework assimilated, learned, and enriched by our culture and by our own experience with which we appreciate and value things. This framework is fueled by redeemable criteria of coexistence, but it is also not free of prejudices and suspicious misgivings. All of this, with its favorable and unfavorable parts, makes up that vision of the world or cosmovision that varies according to cultures (Weltanschauung for the Germans), times and according to it, we tend, as a filter or shield, to approve what is habitual or familiar to us and disapprove that which is not.

This manifests in our personality a certain predisposition towards what we could call **"habituality subconscious,"** which is part of that "inner self," so that we tend to consider and trust that our "infallible filter of perception" leads us directly, without errors nor ramblings, towards the true and authentic. What is critical about the tendency described is that when unfavorable factors predominate in our framework, the shield becomes a strong barrier that prevents assimilating the truth from other perspectives. We forget that, although we can reach the truth, we do not have exclusive rights over it, and it is difficult for us to understand that an error or distortion of perspective and diagnosis may have unconsciously invaded us.

In attention to the care that we must take against this barrier of habituality subconscious and against the phraseological limitations previously exposed, throughout this essay, our reluctance to pigeonhole the reader into detailed forms or ways of acting and interpreting matters has been made included in business management. What has been done is simply to show a map in which alternative routes and access routes are indicated so that the manager can make his own decisions according to his considered criteria and his circumstances.

The map and its routes are descriptions that involve generic margins of errors and risks and provide valuable information, but they will not be sufficient. The journeys to be undertaken on each path are more specific, and the margin of error or risk includes imponderables that are difficult to predict, and it is up to each entrepreneur to challenge them. How do I deal with it? Through irreplaceable **contact with reality, facing the facts and developing one's own experience**.

For this reason, we have been categorical when we affirm that there is no "best strategy," a best "form of leadership," a best "organizational culture," a best "organizational structure," a "best operational or commercial system," a "better executive management system," a "better control and evaluation system," etc., which can be the subject of complete imitation of other experiences, in other realities and other times. Both the routes and maps and the experience of third parties are referential elements, but we recommend that the business manager does not waste too much time searching for magic formulas and focuses on the development of his own route. **The most crucial step after the references described in these reflections is to find, travel and continue one's own path, face it, and not avoid it.**

We have found quite similarity in the simplicity of the work of a gardener or horticulturist and the tasks that are the responsibility of the business manager. In effect, the simplicity of procedures helps and guides us to tackle more complex tasks and then once learned, such complex tasks become simple. Gardeners must approach their work with sufficient technical skill - preparation of the land, defining their purposes in terms of the type of crops or plantations to be produced, selection of seeds, sowing and adequate irrigation, and fertilizer to provide their products with quality, strength and optimal growth, etc. - combined with their experience and innovative skills, they learn to produce a variety of plants not only for food but also for ornamental, landscaping, aromatic and therapeutic plants for health. Gardeners must also apply their skills to counteract the difficulties and environmental and climatic variants and the probable effects of diseases and pests.

Only "after getting their hands dirty and participating in the field of events" of their own experience will the gardener or horticulturist be able to monitor and develop their crops and finally deservedly enjoy the harvest of their effort. The figure of a gardener or horticulturist who remains reflective or contemplative in his garden is unthinkable. Nor can they approach their work stuck to a strictly pre-established manual. Although the manuals and experiences of third parties are useful, they only constitute references. The important thing for him will be to develop and learn from his own experience, enhancing the resources of his own garden.

As a way of paralleling the above with our experience in business and financial management, we will say that: As a development of our own practical experience and just like the gardener or horticulturist who needed to get his hands dirty and actively participate in the development of his crops, the business manager or financial administrator who claims to be a professional will undertake his management only after listening and evaluating the conditions of the reality that he is going to face and his available resources. There is no room for improvisations, "jumps into the void or shots into the air."

Just as the gardener defined his production, seeds and irrigation and fertilizer systems, the manager will be, after his initial evaluation, in a better position to refine the selectivity of his production or service to offer. He will specify his objectives and goals, the quality of resources, inputs and the business models or systems to be used. Like the proactivity of the gardener, the manager does not fit the figure of being a passive observer, acquiring the pose of a simple supervisor or the figure of a manager numb at his desk.

Regarding adaptability and in an analogous way to the gardener or horticulturist when he begins and develops the planting and care of his crops, the manager, appealing to his knowledge and experience, always begins and develops his tasks in a flexible, open and honest manner. With a clear idea of his potential and risks, he will appeal to his innovative skills to face challenges and changes in the environment and the imponderables that reality presents to him, adjusting his strategy and making appropriate and timely decisions to do so. Just like the effort that the gardener makes to provide his products with quality and optimal growth, the business or financial manager does the same so that his management has that same profile and acquires the desired feasibility and strengthening.

Finally, in terms of self-learning, any entrepreneur cannot approach his or her work in a rigid manner and stick to any pre-established script. Although manuals and third-party experiences can be useful as references, a business or financial manager must be willing and committed to learning from his own experience. He cannot depend solely on what others have done or what the books dictate. Personal experience and continuous learning are essential for growth, innovation, and professional success.

In short, for both the gardener and the business or financial manager, **it will be the drive, skill and creativity applied to simple tasks that will allow them to tackle complex tasks satisfactorily**.

As Anthony de Mello points out in "The Song of the Bird," 26th Edition, Editorial Sal Terrae, 1997, page 44: "Life is like a bottle of good wine. Some are content reading the label. Others prefer to test their content". There are people who, above economic considerations regarding any event, circumstance, change, or any project, prefer a cautious state of remaining informed and remaining as observers and at a distance. There are others who choose to experience tasting and move towards a state of undertaking the new and unknown. Each person decides what is right, why to do it, how and in what way to do it, in what place and at what opportunity to undertake or avoid doing things.

Business models have a reference value in terms of background and precautions to consider, but even the most sophisticated techniques and methodological processes could not be blindly traced without the due adaptation process. For this reason, we collect the well-known phrase: "walker, there is no path, the path is made by walking," from the poet Antonio Machado (in his poem "Proverbs and Songs"), where he conveys the idea that life is a constant process of creation and discovery, and everyone must create their own path as they advance in their endeavors. For this reason, we have proposed that it be the manager himself who resolves his challenge and dares to experience his own failures or, better yet, his own successes.

Experience, the teacher of life, suggests that we must "learn by doing" and following the rule of "trial and error." Said idea is reflected in a passage from the famous work "The Alchemist" [33] where it is related: "...there is only one way to learn - the alchemist responded to the boy who was making a pilgrimage in search of treasure - and that is through action. Everything you needed to know; the trip taught you."

5.3. REGARDING REMEDIES AND RECIPES

We regret to disappoint the expectations of those who hoped that this work could provide them with a detailed list of what they should do and the magic formula or recipe that will lead them to achieve business success. This is not possible, and I distrust the guru who proposes it to you. Each

---

[33]See Paulo Coelho, op. cit. page 134.

manager, based on their own reality, with their own style, with assistance and through bumps and stumbles, will have to solve their own problems and find their own solution, which will have its own particularity and originality and will not be a mere copy or imitation of other people's situations (no matter how successful they may have been). In this, we must keep in mind what the Argentine-Spanish writer and novelist Mario Satz points out: "Perfection is a polished collection of errors."

Learning from history teaches us that business management is a complexity composed of a diversity of elements (resources, participants, environments, cycles, technology, processes, etc.), of multiple and varied convergences that tend to move it towards unstable scenarios and even chaotic. Therefore, it is inconvenient to lock and imprison business management in the straitjacket that any dogma represents. But the "gurus" are incorrigible, and in their desire to become famous, to sell themselves and their labeled proposal, they trap business management in dogmas and try to sell their "new paradigms," thus becoming dogmatists of the anti-dogmatic.

In terms of organizational management, reservations must be made when approaches with the category of absolute and permanent truths are presented. What was sacrosanct yesterday, along with the sacred cows that advocated it, are diluted and fade away to give way to the new currents of the present. But nothing guarantees its durability, which will also be affected by the discoveries, innovations, and circumstances of tomorrow.

The importance of changes in approaches to the perception of reality and the incorporation of new methods and tools different from the usual ones are happening more frequently than what happened before and are determining that predominant paradigms perish and break. For this reason, someone proposed that the social sciences have progressed from funeral to funeral. From this funereal perspective, we can understand that, in the economic and business field, the new paradigms are "gravediggers" of the old ones.

As we noted before: "the eyes see what the spirit wants, and things are not what they appear to be at first sight." On a previous visit to the city of Buenos Aires, I stopped in the center of the city in front of a magazine stand, and I was able to appreciate the genius of Quino, creator of the famous comic strip "Mafalda" who graphically presented the idea presented in a masterful way and simple. Mafalda, in a single-frame monologue, shows a feeling of great frustration and laments, saying: This is unbearable. People only understand what they want to understand!

It is worth quoting here a reflection by Steve Jobs (Co-founder of Apple) highlighting essential values such as independence of judgment and courage (such as fortitude) to undertake new things, which deserve to be highlighted for their relationship with what is described in this essay:

> "Your time is limited, so don't waste it living someone else's life. Don't get caught up in dogma, which is living with the results of other people's thoughts. Don't let the noise of others' opinions drown out your inner voice. And most importantly: have the courage to follow your heart and intuition. Somehow, they already know what you really want to be. Everything else is secondary".

Mr. Jobs, who died a few years ago (October 2011), not only contributed to the effectiveness and efficiency of his organization (which for several years has been among the five largest companies in the world) but in his capacity as Strategist, visionary and leader sowed a great seed to provide his company with a training and lifelong learning scheme. He institutionalized Apple University, but more than a conventional internal management training center, its main idea, compatible with the aforementioned phrase, has been, according to Richard Tedlow – professor of the Business History course at Harvard for 31 years and current professor of the so-called Apple University - ensuring that the company's staff develop corporate thinking different from that in force in the organization, called "non-Apple perspectives" that helps them think critically and stay open to new ideas. (See Fortune Magazine, 04/01/2015 edition, page 64).

Mr. Jobs, who died a few years ago (October 2011), not only contributed to the effectiveness and efficiency of his organization (which for several years has been among the five largest companies in the world) but in his capacity as Strategist, visionary and leader sowed a great seed to provide his company with a training and lifelong learning scheme. He institutionalized Apple University, but more than a conventional internal management training center, its main idea, compatible with the aforementioned phrase, has been, according to Richard Tedlow – professor of the Business History course at Harvard for 31 years and current professor of the so-called Apple University - ensuring that the company's staff develop corporate thinking different from that in force in the organization, called "non-Apple perspectives" that helps them think critically and stay open to new ideas. (See Fortune Magazine, 04/01/2015 edition, page 64).

In terms of leaders and leadership, a generalized recipe on what and what things are recommended is also fruitless. It usually happens that what would be useful for those who are risk averse would end up being irrelevant for those who live with it. The only thing we can recommend is that you have to know "when, where and how to run" and have the disposition to do so (take advantage of the tide in your favor) and also know "when, where and how to stop" (or take shelter from the tide against), so that, when steering the business boat, there is clarity regarding the circumstances of the winds and tides for or against and a predisposition to act and develop according to them. Someone commented, "We don't control the winds, but we do control the sails."

An organization or company cannot be conceived only as a structure limited to generating wealth or generating well-being by satisfying a need covered with a certain product or service. From a less economic and business perspective, an organization cannot separate itself from being made up of human structures that possess a culture and a set of values that they receive and project from it to society and vice versa. We could call this situation a de facto cultural condition that plays a key role in facilitating or conditioning achievements of effectiveness and efficiency.

Whether due to risks of incompetence, inexperience, or corruption, the business or organizational management and leadership function should not and cannot be subject to improvisations, to "trying trial balloons" without any foundation, nor hopeful in improbable random events, nor subject to free will of apprentices or inept people often distant from patterns of reasonableness. The strategic nature of the Management leaves no chance of leaving it prey to management incompetence. The demand for quality in private and public management becomes an indispensable condition and its non-compliance aggravates costs and waste of resources.

The managerial position should not be conceived as if it were a learning or training center, much less to do favors or offer employment opportunities. The managerial function cannot be occupied by someone who has a desire to learn but must be occupied by someone who meets the merits of ability and experience and who, accompanied by a team of top-level collaborators, executes and reinforces criteria of efficiency and effectiveness to the entire business or organizational field. We would have half the success guaranteed if the best professionals are selected, without sparing any expense, in the team responsible for leading the organization.

The character and form of relationship between the management body and employees is also crucial. Just as in a university faculty, the result (effectiveness) of good educational quality, beyond imposing infrastructures and equipment, fundamentally depends on the functioning and interrelation of this duality between teacher (committed to teaching) and student (committed to learning). Thus, we can also affirm that in terms of business management, beyond impressive physical facilities and equipment (inert capital in the absence of human energy), its result will also depend on the functioning and interrelation between the management body (committed to adequate attention to its external and internal clients) and the company's staff, workers, technicians, employees and professionals (committed to their job function and their personal fulfillment in it).

It is worth using the fiction of one of the classic works of cinema to highlight aspects of management discussed in this essay that exemplify the mixture and interrelation between formulation (with its perspective of effectiveness) and implementation (with its perspective of efficiency). Let us remember the classic movie Ben Hur and the superb performance of Charlton Heston in one of the most important scenes of said film when driving the chariots in the horse race. Ben Hur showed as a good leader not only clarity and conviction in his purpose, not only fighting spirit and courage to overcome difficulties in the competition, not only knowledge of the goodness and defects of his horses as well as the characteristics and dangers of the route, not only knowledge of the tricks of dishonest competitors (Messala), not only experience in competing in adverse environments, he knew how to manage the strength of his resources (his horses), he commanded them and with his skill and experience and achieved his goal.

Ben Hur, in addition to being a good leader and executor of his strategist, fundamentally showed virtues and values such as management capacity, confidence, self-control, resolute attitude, determination and charisma to reconcile two historic antagonists towns (Jew and Arab) towards the achievement of a specific and shared objective: the final victory in the race. It is enough to remember the encouraging exchange of greetings and the commendable words of hope spoken by the Arab sheikh who sponsored his participation in the competition: "Judah, I give you the Star of David so that it illuminates the path of your people and my people and together they blind the eyes of Rome..." Certainly, and beyond the fact that such people keep certain animosities and antagonisms alive, history is full of chapters where deposing particular positions and committing to the achievement of a comprehensive and common objective has given beneficial results for all.

5.4. INTERNAL AND EXTERNAL IMBALANCES AND DISAGREEMENTS

The delicate processes of both learning and resistance to change suggest that we must pay special attention to stimulating the predisposition and commitment of personnel to conduct their respective tasks. As Confucius noted see "The Song of the Bird" [34]: "Not teaching a man who is willing to learn is wasting a man. Teaching those who are not willing to learn is wasting words". Therefore, in each business or organizational reality, it must be evaluated whether the proposed change efforts are going to mean a waste of words or, on the contrary, the absence or postponement of changes will mean wasting personnel willing to take on the challenges of learning from them.

Initially, it was proposed that effectiveness and efficiency are something like two sides of the same coin (business management). We held this as a recognition of the importance of both factors, but this should not lead to interpreting "literally" that any management will require 50% effectiveness and 50% efficiency, respectively. The dose of one or the other will be a specific result of the diagnosis of each business reality, and approaches that are markedly biased in favor of or against efficiency, or effectiveness should not be generalized a priori. Once again, we reiterate that there are no magic formulas applicable to any organization. The harsh reality imposes certain conditions that force a certain flexibility in the planning framework and the way in which contradictions or controversies between what is formulated and what is implemented are resolved. This will be an issue that management will have to elucidate.

In relation to the presence of Control and Evaluation systems, it never ceases to draw attention: Why, in the absence of control, does a perverse predisposition increase in people to deviate from the correct path and even reach, in notorious cases, the extreme of committing a crime? Furthermore, why, even in the context of strict control systems, with the establishment of regulations and other rules to standardize procedures and behaviors, do cases occur regularly where some people deviate from the norm and follow deviant criteria? Why does excess regulation sometimes produce the opposite effect to the spirit that the norm pursues?

The answer to these intriguing questions seems to be found in human nature, and for example, Confucius (approximately 500 years BC), as one of those who know the essence of human nature, maintained: "The human being has the perverse tendency to transform what he it is forbidden to

---

[34] Anthony de Mello: "El canto del Pájaro", op. cit. page 53

him in temptation." In the scheme of Western religious doctrine, the biblical episode of Adam and Eve and the forbidden apple tree sends us the same message.

The sociopolitical envelope that characterizes any reality is not a product of chance or coincidence, although exceptional situations can be recognized. Our and foreign history is a faithful witness to terms and concepts such as aristocracy, oligarchies, plutocracies, kleptocracies, autocracies, gerontocracies, technocracies, domes, castes, dominant groups, etc., with which the realities and their protagonists are typified they make up. Strictly speaking, "the freedom involved in any business management" is relative because when interrelated with its envelope, the cycles, trends and particularities of that interrelation condition the evolution of said management.

I wonder, as a premonition, if what happened around the construction of Trump's controversial wall on his border with Mexico and the circumstances surrounding it, in addition to being an imposing monument to racism and xenophobia, is also (like what happened after the fall of the Berlin Wall), a prelude to the displacement of some current hegemonic power to make room for a new one. This is not another illusory conjecture; unlike what happened with respect to the Berlin Wall, where no one predicted its fall or the subsequent dismemberment of the Soviet Union, some analysts in geopoliticians (non-Americans) report that we have currently begun to experience a peculiar process of "translatio imperi" to refer to a struggle between the prevailing hegemony (USA) and the new rising hegemony (China) [35].

In another scenario, Peruvian society and politics have already experienced almost three decades of pernicious and perverse influence from what we could call the Fujimori dynasty. In other words, much of what happened in our sociopolitical experience revolved (and continues to revolve!) around what Fujimori, his children and their entourage did, did not do, and the illegal and unscrupulous way supporters have been starring in the Peruvian political scene. No one other than the Peruvians themselves will be responsible for accepting the continuity of the farce and lie in their politics or for proposing a prophylactic therapy to shake off and get rid of it.

The concentrated elites of political power in Peru captured, retreated, and want to recapture a platform of dominance in different instances and levels using toxic leaders, toxic political parties,

---

[35] "El porqué del populismo..." Op. cit. page 45.

toxic parliamentarians, toxic judges and prosecutors, ministers and other toxic advisors, and of course, helped by certain toxic media committed not so much to providing objective and true information but to biasing public opinion. This platform has tipped the balance so that successive right-wing and left-wing government administrations become entangled and fail (whether due to imposition, negligence, ineptitude or incompetence of management, due to crisis and lack of leadership, due to the predominance of anti-values, due to corruption and prebends or whatever).

Although the right proclaims left and right that the current problems, including corruption, are due solely and exclusively to the management of the pseudo-left former president Pedro Castillo (who, by the way, and like the liberal former president Pedro Pablo Kuczynski, only occupied the presidential seat for barely eighteen months), the truth is that focusing from a broader historical perspective and after so many cycles of repetitive frustration of the same thing, we have tried to explain the reason for this and we have asked ourselves, like so many analysts on so many occasions: "At what point did Peru get screwed?" (classic phrase taken from the character Zavalita from the novel Conversations in the Cathedral by Mario Vargas Llosa) and the answer takes us to the same roulette, that is, verification of cycles and effects repeated over so long that it transcends the republican bicentennial and transports us even until colonial times.

By continuing to investigate the reason for this, we have asked ourselves this time with the help of the Machiavellian filter and its perverse curiosity: could it be that the repeated failed efforts of authorities with conditional decision-making capacity were, from another perspective, successful results of "princes in charge" who did they execute well their script of using power in favor of the elites they served? Could it be that these circles of hidden powers repeatedly disdained and postponed necessary changes for the benefit of postponed majorities to maintain a "status quo" that suited only them?

In confirmation of such concerns, in the interview conducted by David Hidalgo (Aug. 2017) with the prominent researcher Dr. Francisco Durand following one of his recent publications, he asks him to clarify his concept of de facto powers in Peru. To which he responds that said idea obeys the concept that:

"…the government is not the power but is simply an entity that allows someone to occupy the State for a time. And that <u>behind the government there are people who have many resources, many influences, and therefore are, de facto, a shadow power</u>...I maintain that the main factual power of the moment are the corporate elites, both national and foreign, who have also been very associated... The great de facto power of the moment is national and foreign capital and, behind them, embassies and international financial organizations. That is, external forces."

https://ojo-publico.com/sala-del-poder/francisco-durand-ahora-estamos-la-republica-empresarial (the underlining is ours).

As confirmed by prominent researchers cited earlier in this work (See section 2.2.4 Leadership Crisis), maintaining this chaotic situation has been the responsibility of said political and economic elites interested mainly in obtaining in their favor the usufruct of the power. These elites used to remain hidden behind the scenes so that they were others or rather their partisan and mercenary puppets (with or without uniform), who, in an obedient performance, made the pantomime of denunciations and criticisms regarding that critical reality that they promised to change through the old resource for populist messages selling of illusion of change. Consecutively, the electorate was enthralled and many times manipulated by sentimentality and unfulfilled promises.

So, a good part of said electorate, in a confused capacity to discern what is true from what is false, without a cautious review, analysis or questioning of what and how the fake promises are exploited, ended up favoring the candidate or the outsider who had the most impact on them. As has been happening in Peru for a long time, the electorate ended up leaning toward the candidate who, in his modest opinion, represented "the lesser evil." Once the favor of the vote was obtained, the words and intentions of the elected candidate were carried away with the wind because his policies and actions colluded with said de facto powers, resulting in the facts, yet another frustration for the great majority.

There are also well-known cases where a portion of the electorate is reluctant to let itself fall into the resignation of the "lesser evil" and expresses its protest by renouncing to express its right to vote (notorious absenteeism), voting blank (because no electoral option satisfies it). or he convinces and does not wish to be complicit or be represented by any of the options in dispute) or finally he vitiates his vote because he considers that the call is irritating and outrageous.

411

Although it is a growing sector of dissenting currents with more qualitative than quantitative weight, its presence deserves serious reflection. Do they constitute a self-confessed current and consequently express a position that does not care about the immediacy of electoral results and prefers to defend a longer-term vision of different content that they do not find in any of the worn-out political representations of the medium? Are they relegated as helpless spectators, as habitual pessimists, as indifferent pusillanimous people who, due to their minority weight, are finally discarded by party interests?

It is a sector of dissidents on which a "blank slate" is made (it is a real fact whose manifest intention is not considered; it is ignored and not considered). We consider that not making use of the right to vote is finally an option of the voter that is even distorted and even manipulated in artificial tricks or dirty games of some electoral systems where the null, flawed, or blank vote is automatically awarded to the party option that turns out to get first place.

How to resolve the mess when this minority of non-conformists becomes more relevant and must be considered inclusively, or do they not even deserve that? How to resolve the mess of obtaining some form of representation for this sector of dissatisfied people who are not convinced by the successive and precarious electoral offers, nor are they convinced by the manipulation of their will in favor of an option that they do not share and that thanks to this they obtain a cheating majority? How should democracies manage this will having dissatisfied sectors so that, even though they lack representation, their relative weight is not manipulated in favor of third parties and can be respected, even if in a neutral manner and counteract the artifices of arranged congressional majorities?

5.5. DEMOCRATIC EXPERIENCES

An important part of the external envelope discussed in this essay has to do with the political sphere and with the democratic experience. We are left with the impression that the contexts of this external envelope are so variable and even contradictory to the point of having distorted democratic functioning. Democracy is presented as an armor of apparent formality in wide-ranging regimes: liberal, conservative, centrist, social democrat, right-wing, leftist, federative government regimes, presidential, parliamentary, pseudo-dictatorial, authoritarian administrations and even in the most abject and despicable regimes of our history.

Contemporary democratic experiences have gracefully become "umbrellas with a wide coverage of Tyrians and Trojans," a kind of "catch-all" where everyone fits, and in addition, each one boasts of possessing the most authentic and perfect democratic version that others. The deformation described responds in part to the fact that it is unknown that democracy represents "in strictu sensu", a scheme of legal formality whose purpose is to become a means of instrumental order to facilitate, improve and expand the potential of human existence and its social environment.

That is, democracy should not be conceived as an end but as a means at the service of citizens. Those who consider it an end have coined the term "let us fight to achieve and maintain an authentic democracy," and in that sense, they consider it as a purpose. For whom they defend this approach, they are satisfied with the fact that democracy is attached to the top of the legal structure, that is, in the constitution of a country. So, although some of its articles are a dead letter and contain gross omissions, the credentials and symbols of being reflected in the constitution seem sufficient to them even if we only remain in the realm of formalities and without determining the essence and substance of the true status of a democracy.

Caution suggests avoiding extremisms such as those currently experienced in Peru, where the legal aberration is fueled by a law modifying or reforming constitutional articles without respecting the requirements that the constitution itself establishes. There is also the risk of falling into the peculiar figure of Hyper democracy (a caricature of democracy taken to the extreme with excessive doses of deviations or distortions) when, for example, decisions are allowed to be influenced and hindered by a majority of the votes achieved with tricks and compromises "under the table" that determine manipulations in the decision-making processes. In certain cases, it becomes slow, difficult, and cumbersome and in other cases, conveniently expeditious, which makes the implementation of public policies and the solution of urgent problems difficult.

As explained before, just as in defective democracies, there is a risk of tyranny of the minority; hyper-democracy can give rise to the tyranny of questionable majorities, in which the rights and opinions of minorities can be ignored or suppressed in favor of preferences of whimsical or arranged majorities. This can undermine fundamental principles of democracy, such as the protection of individual rights and the promotion of diversity and inclusion.

In relation to comments on democracy, it is worth recalling the observations made by Mr. César Pérez Vivas, published in his article "Political Fragmentation" Op. cit. published in the newspaper La Nación on July 20, 2021. The author notes:

> "A democratic society by nature is plural...Political, ideological, and social pluralism is at the root of every society, and democracy is the system of life and government that allows this diversity to be handled in a civilized manner. When a society is not able to order and channel this diversity, it opens the way to authoritarianism and/or social decomposition, with effects as perverse as war, medium-intensity violence and ungovernability. This phenomenon occurs in societies that have experienced or are experiencing a process of deinstitutionalization."

The underlining of the quote is ours and we have done it because Mr. César Pérez Vivas was describing the Peruvian reality two years in advance. It is evident that the fragmentation of the social fabric that we mentioned before is usually accompanied and reflected in a political fragmentation where chaos and atomization prevail, and both fragmentations (social and political), in turn, expand into a generalized institutional crisis (or deinstitutionalization as the called Mr. César Perez Vivas). Crisis to which we also referred previously when we touched on both the topic of Leadership and External Conditioning. In addition, and reinforcement of the same, it is convenient to quote again Dr. Francisco Durand, who is in the internet source (interview by David Hidalgo. Aug. 2017, op. cit.) adds:

> "...the approach that we are in a democracy and that through that mechanism we decide which program to vote for and, if we dislike it, we change in the next election, is a rather naive view...Economic power has preferential access to the State. He can fill it using the revolving door (going from company executives to government functions and vice versa).
>
> So, by hidden or overt acts, we reach the same conclusion. They believe that power can be managed like this, trusting in the ignorance of the people and believing that, with the promise of modernity and technical management, Peru will improve.
>
> The underlying issue is that we have continuity of the economic model, and we continue with a policy of deregulation, and we forget to protect the consumer, we do not consider the rights of workers, and we tolerate the State making decisions that favor a privileged minority. In

reality, what we see is a very interesting phenomenon: the more concentrated and organized economic power is, the more dispersed and atomized the party system is" (the underlining is ours).

The passage of time confirms what Dr. Francisco Durand maintains, since currently (September 2024) we have in Peru the absurd number of more than forty political party options that will begin the election competition for the next year.

The democratic contradictions that many societies experience can be clarified with the masterful metaphor that José Ortega y Gasset [36] once again illustrates to us: **"The river opens its channel, and then the channel enslaves the river."** The river is formed and constituted, according to the author, by that large fluid of cultural contingent that a society creates and innovates through means, instruments, and mechanisms (State, science, morality, religion, politics, art, etc.).

This important cultural contingent corresponding to the river runs in its middle, forming the channel (legal, institutional, social, economic, and political superstructure) that contains it and once said channel is formed, it makes the course of the river viable. One of the components of that instrumental order that makes up the river is constituted by that institution that we call democracy.

According to what the author points out, it usually happens that when democracy seeks to project itself beyond the sphere of its own action and aspires to encompass different spaces of life, when democracy seeks to establish itself as a determining instrument of the content and orientation of other elements that make up the entirety of that river and also aims to be the main protagonist of the course and flow within the channel; then its denaturalization begins, and its functioning is diverted, becoming forced or disguised representations of science, art, religion, morality, etc.

We add that the responsibility for this democratic deviation falls on certain classes and political parties, which "ex professo" and deliberately have ignored that this democratic instrumental order is only one among the various instruments and mechanisms required by any society for its evolution to be liberated of obstacles, problems, and complications.

---

[36] See: El Espectador op cit. page 50

The contradictory thing is that these disastrous classes and political parties have been either due to internal meanness and their collusion with other political bodies, or due to obtundation or severe presbyopia in the discernment of the substantial from the trivial, or due to pernicious amnesia, or due to incompetence and improvisation, either because of not knowing how to respect their own boundaries with those of other disciplines and powers (constituting the river described), or because of continuous blunders aimed at camouflaging serious corruptions, or because of their complicity with impositions of power elites, etc., the only thing that they have achieved are effects that are contrary to social and economic development and hinder it.

These classes and political parties have attempted to champion the defense of an idolized democracy to try to turn it into an end and not an optimal means that facilitates social evolution, that is, they have complicated the course of the river to the point of causing risky deviations and overflows. Precisely, when the accumulation of nonsense is intense and unbridled, the polarized extremes of the political spectrum become visible (ultra-conservatism, ultra-leftism, authoritarianism), all of them tinged with loaded populism. Ortega y Gasset [37] is quite severe when maintaining:

> "Democracy, strictly and exclusively conceived as a norm of political law, seems to be an optimal thing. But when it is deformed into religion or art, into thoughts and gestures, into heart and customs... when pure legal formality is elevated to the category of an integral principle of existence, the way is opened to engender the greatest extravagances and aberrations, **false, feigned, morbid and degraded democracy is institutionalized that will lead us toward the tyranny of plebeians**" (the underlining is ours).

It is admirable how this generational viewer that philosophers and historians have enables them not only for a suitable interpretation of the historical past but also for an accurate projection of the future, since what Ortega y Gasset typified many decades ago as tyranny of plebeians is what is currently political analysts highlight "populism" as widespread, coming from different political outlets.

By juxtaposing the message of the Ortega y Gasset metaphor about the "river and its channel" and associating it with Heraclitus' perception of the principle that "everything changes, and nothing

---

[37] see: El Espectador op. cit. page 67

remains unchanged," we can agree that the river (in Ortega's conception) will continue in permanent affluence (as Heraclitus conceives it). Therefore, this unstoppable torrent of culture, science, art, politics, and their respective mutations cannot be maintained in captivity, coercion or permanent manipulation. The author jealously argues that there will be no channel, nor any feigned democratic instrument within said channel, capable of limiting and impeding the advances and other manifestations of this continuous influx of intelligence and human concerns.

So, when the channel is inappropriate or obsolete, when the channels of participation, mobilization and renewal of socioeconomic structures become stuck in stagnant routines with regressive effects, when the rupture of that elastic or implicit contract or social pact is encouraged, the inertia and dynamics of the river's content (with all its means, instruments and mechanisms) will overflow the original channel, flood new spaces and form a new channel that will direct its march toward new spaces and directions. What is described is not a mere utopia; the history of humanity has shown us how the rise and fall of various empires and nations constitute, from this perspective, uncontrollable advances of rivers that overflowed uncomfortable channels.

For the moment, we continue to experience the prevalence of an artificial and dangerous clouding in the protagonists of different political powers that make it increasingly difficult for maturity, equanimity, and good sense to prevail. The route of understanding, constructive dialogue and shared responsibilities are being lost in many cases because many of the spokespersons of the most representative political classes are more interested and attentive in considering how the media effects of their voices and poses impact the surveys and opinion polls, caring less whether the content of their statements or attacks are authentic or false and whether they address the need for change.

The main purpose of representatives and activists of the main current political currents is to continue contaminating the sociopolitical scene by adding more fuel to the fire so that vituperations, offenses, attacks and tricks between Republicans and Democrats, leftists and rightists, liberals and conservatives, centrists and socialists, etc., are common currency not only in hot pre-electoral periods but also after them, in regular confrontations between the opposition and the government in power.

In the interest of struggles for democracy (frequently and mistakenly conceived as an end), traditional party options and new conservative tendencies on the right and extreme left are establishing, revamping and anesthetic populist schemes. In this context of tug and pull, the pendulum of history seems to shift towards pro-rightist scenarios. We will have to be attentive to the details of how said populism consolidates the elite-people binomial and the complicated fabric and social coexistence. From another perspective, there will be those who maintain that this confusing "scenario of confrontations and understandings" of extreme positions are manifest symptoms (within the conceptual framework of Ortega y Gasset) of an upcoming and uncontainable overflow of the river and its renewed tributaries over its anachronistic channel.

5.6. GENUINE AND DISGUISED INDEPENDENCE OF CRITERIA

In section 4.3, "The threats of populist currents in public and private management," severe observations and criticisms of left-wing and right-wing populism were argued. At the end of this section, I had the impression that, by having criticized the expectations of one side or another of traditional and predominant doctrinal currents, I had to gratuitously earn the antipathy and annoyance of a majority membership that only considers pertinent and valid the choice of aligning itself toward one side or the other. From this obtuse perspective, any option that has shades of independence and misalignment with well-known conventions (right and left) is disqualified.

Those who adopt an independent position are often misplaced or classified as part of the so-called center or neutral categories. From the narrow linear perspective of a continuum or interval, it is considered that what does not agree with the extremes necessarily corresponds to the center. Accordingly, a centrist position corresponds to a fixed and central position that can collect partial contents from both extremes, and that typifies a characteristic ambiguity. Likewise, it is alluded to that the neutral position implies an impartiality that is sometimes used as a shield to avoid commitment and determination toward something greater and clear definition. In certain cases, it even tends to discredit neutrality due to its lack of determination or its dose of indifference regarding its circumstances.

Such centrist or neutral positions are the object of furious criticism from both sides of the ideological spectrum because they consider that they only represent positions of invalid lukewarmness, of nuance disguised as false and shadowy positions. For those on the extreme right, the center option (in the Peruvian environment) brings together despicable "caviars" (disguised communists), and for those on the extreme left, the center option brings together hidden and shadowed neoliberals or representatives of the "brute and corrupt right" (right-wing with nuances of ineptitude and violence). That is the typical aggressive characteristic of our political protagonists who, in addition, blame each other for responsibility for the crisis we are experiencing.

In contrast to the above, our point of view is that a genuine independent position as we conceive is not located in a fixed and invariant manner in the equidistant center of that hypothetical continuum between right and left, nor can it be attributed to a strict functionality, neutral or ambiguous. Its independent nature is the result of a particular analysis of reasonableness and reality. The independent position that we recognize does not remain tied to a rigid and inflexible position and is open to moving freely, without ties and with the limitations of the case, toward points of view that sometimes coincide and sometimes disagree with positions of the right or the left, (or any other position), but without remaining conditioned by rigid precepts and rather distant from whimsical extreme positions.

Independent positions are also criticized because it is stated that they lack doctrinal essence or background and for being imbued and coated with a chameleon-like and accommodating nuance. In this regard, it is worth noting that the variability that in certain cases takes an independent position responds to the fact that, being realities changing, the analysis frameworks, the instrumentation, and the tools for evaluation and solution of problems do not necessarily have to be limited to single concepts, nor to biased, exclusive processes and procedures.

An independent position classified as a center could cover a narrower space that, in addition to distancing itself from extremes, has shared areas of interrelation with the conventional right and left positions. This would give rise to specific center-right or center-left spaces. Even so, this categorization wrongly once again locks it into a fixed position. Genuine independent positions are not strictly committed to traditional party doctrines, but they can embrace or coincide with some principles and doctrines that in no way condition them.

Independence of judgment does not at all mean an irresolute or elusive neutrality because its position is imbued with a strong conviction, commitment and declared defense of what it believes in and what it proposes. This independent position does not usually identify in an unrestricted manner with predominant parties and doctrines since, when serious discrepancies arise with such trends, it has no qualms about distancing itself from them. Another significant difference is that this independent perspective does not negotiate or traffic its convictions and does not have a vocation for indoctrination (so that others follow it) and much less a sheep's instinct (to follow others). Part of the problem is identifying the authentic defenders of independent positions compared to those who deceptively attack the so-called center positions.

Curiously, one must recognize the existence of notorious representatives of extremes who, to gain followers and not reveal themselves in their extremism, camouflage themselves in center positions. For example, we must mention the elected mayor of Lima, Mr. Rafael López Aliaga, representative of the most conservative right in Peru and a sure candidate for the presidency, who, in his vein attempt to moderate his misguided extremism, has defined his National Solidarity party as Center Right and there will be no shortage of unwary people who believe him.

History is full of notable figures of genuine independent standing in politics, economics, the arts, religion and other disciplines (from Socrates, Moses, Michelangelo, Galileo, Einstein, Gandi, Mother Teresa, Krishnamurti, Steve Jacob, Orwell, etc.), where the majority of them marked a position very different from the extremes existing in their time, or from any comfortable position of center, or of neutrality or ambiguity. On the contrary, they had to battle, defend, and commit to options different from the predominant trends.

We rule out aligning ourselves in the center of this continuous imaginary, where on the far right, freedom is prioritized, arguing that it is the engine of progress and individual initiatives and that the goal of equality (which they criticize) only means the distribution of poverty. Nor do we align ourselves on the opposite side of the extreme left, where it is argued that even in the paradisiacal assumption of fulfilled freedoms, the existing inequalities continue to be striking and are confirmation of the maintenance and worsening of concentrated patterns of income and power. Without ceasing to have significant validity, many problems of this path of egalitarian experiences lie in the fact that civil rights and liberties were also relegated. Each side has true arguments and obvious flaws.

Who is right? As stated, before in Graph No. 19, "Different perspectives of the same reality," we will also say that in this case, "there is not always an absolute reason or certainty and that each part has its truth founded. It cannot be determined definitively who is right. The only thing that can be said, in the first instance, is that each part is in contradiction with the other part." In this dialectical confrontation, we witness how intellectual representatives of the right and the left argue, attack and even ridicule anyone who does not belong to their side and to leave their close intellectual and social circles happy and pleased for those who write.

We support our independent perspective based on the verification of contradictions and iniquities exposed not in the unquestionable ideals of freedom and equality but that unfortunately appear contaminated or accompanied by critical realities of both systems (totalitarian and liberal). We refuse to align both in extreme positions and in a fixed center position. In attention to the social dynamics itself, we prefer to move towards a framework of greater independence, distant from rigid ties and open to renewed currents of thought. An approach to this can be addressed in this doctrinal French legacy represented ideographically by that equilateral triangle of freedom, equality, and fraternity where any of them does not prevail or exclude the other principles and within which it is maintained not a fixed or rigid position but a mobile development and in greater harmony of balances between the three principles mentioned.

Without ceasing to recognize the validity of each principle of freedom or equality analyzed individually and theoretically, we do not discard them, but rather we try to complement them, stripping of their doctrines that only confront them, and rescue them in their principled version. In our humble understanding, their confrontation constitutes a false dichotomy that prevents or makes it difficult to mobilize (get closer or distance) between them when deviations or distortions occur in their application that detracts from them. When these principles are validated with reality, we notice that in the contemporary debate, fraternity, a principle that bases social coexistence and the adoption of solidarity criteria that facilitate consensual and peaceful coexistence, has been completely eluded. Fraternity constitutes a kind of corrective of deviations from libertarian individualism and a corrective of partial egalitarianisms concentrated in elites of socialist collectivities.

Fraternity should not be understood as a mere charitable, secondary, subordinate, or subsidiary principle to what remains from the application of the other principles but as a consubstantial, unavoidable requirement and a vital counterweight to that triangular theorem mentioned above. Its exclusion invalidates a choice that only considers libertarian or egalitarian principles. In recognition that an independent position can incorporate respectable variants and can be supported by a wide range of other existing doctrines and ideologies. We have maintained our independent position in response to common criticism that they often lack doctrinal substance or principles.

Indeed, the principles inherited from the French Revolution and its main exponents, Jean-Jacques Rousseau, Baron de Montesquieu, Voltaire, Denis Diderot, and others, have served as important references and guidelines for our independent position.

When the independence of judgment is part of an unrecognizable, denied, or lost genre, you are at the risk of your work being cataloged, classified, and pigeonholed in the disdain and contempt of specialized critics and the representative media of conventional factions. You are finally segregated and disdained without any favorable recommendation or reference. Nobody confirms it to you, but your work will become part of the group of workers tacitly discarded for having committed the sin of misalignment.

From a personal perspective, when opting for an independent option, you may be invaded by a strange sensation of seeing yourself also isolated, "in the middle of obvious loneliness, walking in the open, lost in a cold and rainy night in the middle of a public road, barefoot and against traffic." In the unrest of these tribulations, it will not seem strange to you to see drowned the hope of finding a publisher interested in accompanying you on your unpublished adventure and much worse when you lack the reputation of a "famous author," and you belong to that legion of unknowns, novices and aspiring upstarts to writer.

Disagreement with respect to traditional positions and conventions exposes us beyond the discrepancy itself and its argument to walking alone in a direction different from that marked by avant-garde trends and different from the usual route where large crowds enthusiastically head. Therefore, paraphrasing the philosopher Hegel, we reaffirm his message: "You must have the courage to make mistakes." When from both sides of the spectrum, respectable personalities and friends harass and accuse you of maintaining a lonely independence, and you refuse to shelter yourself in that warm and majority membership that they claim to represent.

When you do not accept the false dilemma that is presented to you: you are with me or against me! or when it is not understood that the discrepancy does not necessarily mean antagonism, then there is no other option than to assume "the cost of paying for the novitiate" for daring to write approaches that some people find misophonia (discrepant or unpleasant sounds) annoying and to assume it with the same modesty and integrity as this entertaining and intrepid journey began.

Personally, I am grateful in advance for the criticism and comments that this book may raise, but it is my responsibility to warn, almost at the end of this work, that it has not been written with the intention of pleasing (or exasperating) anyone's expectations specific sector (political, academic, professional, labor, etc.). In several of these sectors, there are recognizable characters with blinders who only read, appreciate, and approve of what comforts them from their perspective and discard or detest what does not agree with it.

This work is aimed at that broad multidisciplinary sector of current and potential entrepreneurs, at that group of young students with curiosity in the topic presented, also at academics who show an open willingness to appreciate and value new perspectives and businesspeople eager to learn and improve the development of their activity in its specific environment. We do not want to gain followers or sell a brand; we are only motivated by the purpose of providing a different approach and perspective. Our position independent of conventional dogmas or political parties is also fed by the appreciation made by José Ortega y Gasset [38], which we share "in extenso":

> "Reality is offered in individual perspectives. What is in the background for one is in the foreground for another. The landscape orders its sizes and distances according to our retina, and our heart distributes the accents. The visual and intellectual perspectives are complicated by the appraisal perspective.
>
> Instead of disputing, let us integrate our visions in generous spiritual collaboration, and as the independent banks come together in the thick vein of the river, let us compose the torrent of reality... I am going to describe the slope that reality sends towards me... As stated, it formally excludes the desire to impose my opinions on anyone. Quite the opposite: I aspire to infect others so that each one of them is faithful to their perspectives."

Another example of the independence of judgment can be seen in the renowned writer George Orwell, in addition to his furious sarcasm towards the Soviet regime described in his fable "Rebellion on the Farm," which was mentioned previously in the preface of his aforementioned work (op. cit. pages 7-19), a scathing criticism of that feigned freedom of the press and of the sneaky censorship that he had to face in his english environment, considered as a jealous guardian of the freedom of opinion and thought of his time. The author states that intellectual freedom, as a deeply rooted tradition of Western culture, can barely exist because intellectuals (in the circumstances of their time) have departed from that tradition and maintain:

---

[38] see: "El Espectador", op. cit. pages 21 y 22

"If the intellectual freedom that has been one of the distinctive features of western civilization means anything, it is that everyone has the right to say and publish what they consider to be true if it does not indisputably harm the rest of the community. This principle (the author highlights) is captured in the famous words of Voltaire: "I detest what you say, but I will defend to the death your right to say it."

According to the author: ...many of our intellectuals... have accepted the principle that a book should be published or suppressed, praised, or condemned, not according to its merits but according to political expediency...Such a contradiction can only be explained in one way, that is, by a cowardly desire to align oneself with the bulk of the intelligentsia. (The underline is ours)

Here, it is worth specifying that the author's objective is not only to criticize defects and excesses that he considered existing in the Soviet regime of his time but also to bring to light that deviation, rearrangement of those spheres of government and the media that in underhanded collusion prevailed in the liberal and western system of his time. According to the author, he had to experience the validity in intellectual circles of a kind of orthodoxy unregulated by government intervention, which functioned as a general tacit agreement and established what "was not appropriate or should not be said." Although it was not forbidden to say this, that or the other, anyone who challenged orthodoxy would be silenced. The author specifies:

"The sinister thing about literary censorship in England is that, for the most part, it is voluntary. Unpopular ideas can be silenced, and inconvenient facts kept in the dark without the need for official prohibition... the same veiled censorship also works in books and magazines, just as it does in plays, radio, and movies... Now what the dominant orthodoxy demands is an uncritical admiration of Soviet Russia.

It is possible that by the time this book (Rebellion on the Farm) is published, my views on the Soviet regime will become more widespread. But so, what? Changing one orthodoxy for another does not necessarily represent progress. The enemy is the gramophone mentality..." (the underlined is ours)

Faced with the described Orwellian reflection on the freedom of the press and the thought that he had to experience, we cannot fail to refer to what these freedoms have represented in the Peruvian context. Firstly, it should be noted that, as in the case of Orwell and his English media, a concentrated press also prevails in Peru. The problem of said concentration, beyond considerations related to property, has to do with its notorious capacity to exert pressure and direct public opinion toward interests of factual powers (mainly groups of economic power) and, above all, to the interests of political parties whose leader's function at the request of those in the remaining powers (executive, legislative and judicial).

This concentration not only includes written media (newspapers, magazines, books and publications) but also radio and television media and includes other media not economically linked but with open ideological affinity and coinciding purposes (Willax, Diario Expreso, La Razón, etc.). The agreed avalanche of this concentrated press was notable, for example, in the fierce opposition and harassment that, together with the parliamentary majority, they made of former president Pedro Castillo and was not limited until they managed to defenestrate him. Of course, Castillo, due to his ineptitude and deviations, also made sufficient merit for this.

However, the complacency that this same concentrated press displays toward the current president, Dina Boluarte, who, despite forming an administration lacking any direction, commits the same and even worse clumsiness than her predecessor, does not cease to draw attention. Despite flagrant violations of human rights and despite her shameless interest in screwing herself into power, she has not had any embarrassment in accompanying the legislative branch in its conspiracy to undermine the country's institutions. Despite all these widely criticizable facts in any circumstance and time, said concentrated press was exhibiting for the entire year 2023 a tolerance and a voluntary self-imposed censorship in the purest style typified by Orwell of "that which is not appropriate or should not be said" and therefore remained silent and complicit.

Freedom of the press is not unrestricted as the defenders of said press argue to defend, but rather, it is a conditional, tolerant and subordinate freedom of the press. Drawing a parallel with what Orwell denounced, we can say without fear of being wrong that the dominant and imposed orthodoxy in our country has been to maintain an uncritical position to that overwhelming duo of parliamentarism colluded with an executive power that, for the subordinate interests of both, they continue to make a fool of themselves by governing us. Daring to publish a writing or express an opinion contrary to or challenging said orthodoxy caused voluntary censorship and silencing of the concentrated press (written, radio or television) or even exposed you to experiencing grievances and even complaints of all kinds.

To be objective, we must specify some achievements that we consider salvageable in the case of the Diario El Comercio of Lima, Peru, considered the dean of the local Peruvian press. Even though said newspaper can be considered part of the group of concentrated press and the current that typifies it, it has not stopped publishing opinions of independent professionals and analysts, some of whom we have cited throughout this work and appear in the recorded bibliographic sources. In honor of the truth, these researchers have made known their points of view on the national problem in broad freedom of opinion and thought.

Many of these comments are even discrepant and distant from the newspaper's editorial line, and other commentators are, of course, related to said line. We consider that the fact of enabling, giving access and dissemination to diversity of opinions is not an exceptional rule but rather a professional practice that is part of a redeemable tradition that still maintains said newspaper. Therefore, we make the respective reservations to avoid annoying generalizations. In the end, the reading public will exercise its stern verdict of whether to maintain its preference.

We must also indicate the accentuation of two critical aspects of our conjuncture: the confirmed economic recession, its worrying consequences on poverty (with a decline to levels of previous decades and with a tendency to worsen) and the alarming citizen insecurity with a clear tendency to deteriorate even more. Faced with this reality highly felt and criticized by the population, it would be shameful for the press to hide or evade them, which is why some media outlets are marking a suggestive distance and have begun to criticize the inefficient legislative and executive powers.

In accompaniment to this bad smell scenario, there are still more events that are taking place in judicial settings, especially the recent scandals in the Public Ministry (Prosecutor's Office) that will test to what extent the tacit support of said press will be permissible or if, on the contrary, sanity will impose limits on shamelessness.

5.7. PROBABLE AND DIFFICULT MANAGEMENT SCENARIOS

Amid this mess and an increasingly complicated economic, social, and political panorama, we want to outline some Machiavellian conjectures, each one with its respective handles of becoming real possibilities:

In this attempt at futurology, we must start from a first panorama that is preceded by complicated antecedents. Firstly, the pernicious advances in institutional deterioration carried out by political parties that make up the current majority parliamentary have continued to be carried out for their benefit alone (for example, Election of members of the Constitutional Court (TC), the election of the Ombudsman, Election and dismissal of Supreme Prosecutors and Special Prosecutors, legal provisions for electoral accommodation for said majority). These parties include Fuerza Popular led by Keiko Fujimori, the Alliance for Progress party led by César Acuña, Renovación Popular party led by Rafael López Aliaga and the Perú Libre party led by Vladimir Cerrón and others of lesser representation.

However, confirming that the criminal route is not easy and that there are always loose ends in the tricks and armed entanglements, the recent dissemination of chats, audios and contacts between direct advisors of the prosecution and some congressmen have led to an abrupt scandal that left exposed a plot of covert benefits where exchanges of favors were negotiated and seriously compromised congressmen from said parliamentary majority and the current prosecutor herself, Dra Patricia Benavides.

It should be noted that the oral trial phase of important leaders of the current political parties described is also close to the beginning, and the Prosecutor's Office, as a sign of its goodwill towards its required political allies, has been committing in their favor certain changes and appointments of new prosecutors in charge of those cases. Due to the above, and even though the parliamentary majority has not obtained everything it needed to finalize its future electoral strategy, time is of the essence and is crucial for it to strengthen its alliances and strategy.

In that perspective, the prosecution will weave its well-known practice of establishing agreements "under the table" and has important things to offer. She will promise to suspend the progress of the fiscal files that contain complaints against that parliamentary majority and will also do everything possible to appoint unconditional prosecutors in the upcoming trials of the political leaders of the parties of said majority. That is, she will offer to advance in institutionalizing impunity. For its part, Congress will do everything possible to quickly activate the defenestration of all members of the National Board of Justice (JNJ) to block, delay and nullify any decision aimed at the replacement and probable dismissal of the prosecutor. This struggle between parliament (due to the intermediary need of the prosecutor) and the JNJ has just begun, and we will have a spectacle guaranteed for a long time (with parades of defensive tricks, counteroffensives, and confrontational political operators).

Given the conviction of the current prosecutor regarding that the chat and audio scandal was created by the executive and especially directed by Ex premier Alberto Otárola, her immediate and emotional response a few hours after the aforementioned scandal was incredibly fast to initiate a constitutional lawsuit against the president, her premier and other people, for human rights responsibilities in the deaths of fifty citizens in the events of December (2022) and January (2023). All this unusual change of attitude has been in contradiction with the astonishing slowness and length of said process for almost 10 months. Although the weapon of constitutional demands does not seem, for now, to have an effect, the struggle between the prosecutor and the executive has also just begun.

The executive's response could not have been more precise. Mrs. President spoke openly by declaring that the Attorney General should resign. Convinced that there are no coincidences in politics, she again set up the racket to free former president Alberto Fujimori. The smokescreen worked, and in open disregard of the provisions of the International Court of Human Rights of the OAS, the Constitutional Court (TC), together with the government, have functioned as simple puppets directed by Keiko Fujimori and her party. Giving the green light to the freedom of Mr. Fujimori does not attract the attention of the members of the TC who, since previous resolutions and in return for favors received for their appointments, have been leaving signs that they act in favor of Keiko and his party.

But in the case of the executive, it is possible that the zeal of Dina Boluarte and her Ex premier in the face of recent parliamentary questioning of several of her ministers and in the face of pressure from Keiko to release her father has led the president to give in to such pressures to ingratiate himself with Keiko and thereby also ensure their fragile alliance and obtain some support to counteract the outbursts of the prosecutor Benavides. Ms. Boluarte has come to the conviction of avoiding having Ms. Keiko declared an enemy because of the risk that it means that she will unleash a parliamentary vacancy plot against her.

Unfortunately, the myopia and ineptitude of Mrs. Boluarte lead her to make decisions only in response to her immediate interests. Cloaking oneself in the skirts of Mrs. Keiko Fujimori is a tremendous miscalculation, it is enough to review the family and political disloyalties that Keiko displays in her personal record. Ms. Boluarte's terrible decision to ignore and disregard the recommendation of the Inter-American Court of Human Rights has placed the country in the status of an international pariah and without measuring the legal and economic consequences of said decision.

In this scenario, where what happens goes according to what is planned by that parliamentary majority, everything will be ready and served for the assault on power in the next elections in 2026 or the sooner, the better. As time goes by, the only card down Mrs. Boluarte's sleeve of being able to threaten her resignation so that "they all leave" will become less relevant. For the practical purposes of the congressional majority soon, it will not matter whether Ms. Boluarte is removed from power due to vacancy or resignation.

However, settling collusion is not as easy as it seems. The dream of a happy dawn is haunted by terrible nightmares. What happens if things do not evolve according to plan and if the cards played go awry or "the shot backfires" for the protagonists? For example, the current national prosecutor, Ms. Patricia Benavides, has been suspended from her duties (Dec 07, 2023) by the JNJ for a period of six months until the investigations of complaints against her are completed for leading a possible criminal network or organization within the prosecutor's office and her probable dismissal hangs over her.

This will take away her control of her power platform and will prevent her from appointing prosecutors for cases that are about to go to trial. Of course, she will not stay with her arms crossed, and her legal attack, with parliamentary support, against the JNJ will continue in open confrontation. The tricks and legal tricks between lawyers, congresspeople, political scientists, journalists, and other observers for and against one party or another will be "the talk" (gossip of the moment) in short-term national political events.

Considering the background described, in this first hypothetical panorama characterized by crossfires, two scenarios could be triggered:

a) A first scenario could end up tipping the balance in favor of said congressional majority in collusion with the current suspended Attorney General. The pressure to defenestrate the JNJ from political leaders and their parties will be strong due to their high dependence on favors received from the Attorney General, Mrs. Patricia Benavides. She, in turn, needs to collude with the said parliamentary majority to consolidate her personal power to take over and control a large part of the judicial institutions.

Many members of this mafia parliamentary majority are risking their political future; the bitter fight has already begun, and all arguments are valid. The gross cynicism of representatives of the said parliamentary majority (and of renowned jurists, journalists, and other interested parties) does not fail to draw attention. They refer to the discovered scandal as if it were isolated personal differences between authorities or allude to attempts to "caviars" for recovering leadership positions or referring to non-existent doctrinal contradictions. This deviation underestimates the severity of the crisis and avoids its own responsibilities.

By distorting the substance of the debate and what a declared crisis between powers of the state means, the congresspeople do nothing more than expose their deformed conviction of not feeling like leading actors in the problem and their trick of excluding themselves from it, of diverting attention, becoming manifest towards other protagonists and holding them responsible for the crisis that occurred. If this tendentious trick and artificial conspiracy prevails, and despite the clear indications against the Prosecutor of the Nation, we remain attentive to the outcome of the investigative process that must continue its course without obstacles or delay.

Parliament's intention to shield the prosecutor from any misconduct is opposed to the disturbing question of who supervises, investigates, controls, and sanctions the auditors when they defect. If they are artificially shielded, not only impunity will have been institutionalized in the country, but a denatured "judicialization of politics," or as others also call it, the "politicization of justice." In any case, and despite the headwinds that the prosecution faces, the congressmen will continue vitiating the independence of powers and moving toward the subsequent step that we can call the criminalization of politics that will place us one step away from the authoritarian anarchy of a spurious and corrupt parliament.

President Dina Boluarte is not yet aware that she has only been used by the parliamentary majority to obtain what they required of her (to keep in power and make legal arrangements in favor of said congressional majority). As previously mentioned in the case of this congressional majority, Ms. Dina Boluarte, her premier, her ministers and other instances of the executive branch are also not aware of, nor do they feel part of, nor responsible for the problem of the political situation, much less make an adequate reading of the problems that they will face beyond the short term.

For this reason, she has not foreseen that as the deadline for the next elections approaches and as social discontent worsens, political parties will begin to consider the inconveniences of continuing a coexistence that harms them by dragging them down. It will not be outside their calculations to distance and get rid of her. Then, with the greatest self-confidence, this same parliamentary majority that made her president will find the perfect candidate to transfer and foist upon her a tremendous responsibility regarding the instability and social discontent generated by them.

They will thus have the excuse to expect her from power through another structured presidential vacancy (in which they would have plenty of reasons and experience to do so). This dagger in the back of parliament toward the president is not surprising nor is it new for those who lead parties accustomed to developing all their ingenuity in conspiratorial intrigues. Amid a chaotic economic and political situation, this mafia-like parliament is going to try to sell the people the deception of having satisfied their requirements that "they all leave" with Dina Boluarte at the head and that they will continue their march once they are over necessary political reforms that of course suit them and no one else.

Then the framework of what we could now call "fraud architecture," structured by the true and henchmen "fraudsters," will be refined with this feat of institutional takeover where the majority of the following organizations are captured or under control: Judicial Branch (Constitutional Court, National Prosecutor's Office, National Board of Justice, Supreme Court and Attorney General's Office), Electoral Power (National Election Jury, National Office of Electoral Processes).

In our concept, for the winners (parliamentary and executive branches), it will be a "Pyrrhic victory" (a costly victory for the winning side that will generate very unfavorable effects that are difficult to manage). Businesspeople, investors, consumers, and citizens, in general, will begin by asking themselves whether it is worth continuing to develop their activities in a scenario that has become, due to the crisis of instability and insecurity, a "no man's land or ungovernable land." All of this is aggravated by the imminent El Niño Phenomenon, for which the country has not adequately prepared, and which threatens to cause serious disturbances towards the second quarter of 2024 and worsening of the Dengue epidemic.

Additionally, what will happen when citizens, businesses and investors realize that their demands in the judicial spheres are rigged in favor of colluded interests and mafias installed in said power and that, by not finding internal justice and legality, their appeals to international courts will not be respected?

This is when the international community, certain embassies and other international entities and organizations will take "dissuasive measures" against the country and those who are responsible for the blatant emergence of institutions, democracy and other arbitrariness and attacks against human rights. We are ashamed to admit it but faced with the silence and passivity of internal actors and agents, this criminal parliament considers that it has a free way to conduct its misdeeds and is only partially stopped by the manifestation of external agents. So, given that such external agents are annoying, they are already considering a project to disaffiliate Peru from the Inter-American Court of Human Rights in the short term.

Nor do we stop worrying about what this criminal political class does not even care about. We refer to the fact of continuing to irresponsibly incubate a social implosion with unpredictable economic and political effects. The only things that will continue to rise will be recession, unemployment, inflation, the decrease and disincentive of investments, food shortages, crime and the general appreciation of an uncertain outlook that is not conducive to business management.

Unfortunately, they continue with their deformed appreciation that politics goes on separate strings with the economy; it is not perceived that said policy has a direct impact on it, discouraging it due to wrong decisions made and that economic crises require rethinking in politics that are often ignored by those responsible for its conduct. Furthermore, when foolishness and improvisation prevail among those who make decisions, anything can happen. They are convinced that nothing and no one prevents the weight of the majority votes they have.

b) In the second scenario, it is assumed that the outbursts of the prosecutor and the parliamentary majority that support her in her defense do not have the desired effects and the balance tips in favor of the JNJ. This hypothesis first proposes unmasking, with evidence, the accumulation of irregularities, crimes, and collusion between the involved parties. This situation will mean an extension of major scandals to those experienced today. To avoid alleging a lack of trial guarantees, errors in judicial processing and other legal tricks, one must act with the greatest care, with due correction, adjust to the regulations and with the greatest diligence in the case. It is not surprising that the mafias once again hire select law firms from Lima or those with political influence, which, as in the previous and failed allegations of fraud against former President Castillo, will not be assisted by reason in their vain attempts to defend what indefensible. But what they will achieve is delay the processes.

Of course, once the respective rulings are issued by the judicial authorities, the Prosecutor and the extensive list of henchmen and criminals who accompanied her and depended on her mismanagement will have to assume responsibility for her actions. The accused will always have the right to appeal, and it would not be unusual for those who now demand non-respect and departure from international courts to end up appealing and seeking justice in such courts. Otherwise, they will have to swallow the whole story when it is argued that the Constitutional Court (TC) and the government have established jurisprudence in not abiding by the provisions of the international court, such as what happened in the recent pardon of former President Fujimori.

Unmasking established mafias is difficult and expensive. As will be appreciated, we are facing a cumbersome scenario due to the legal twists and turns that it entails a long-lasting scenario due to the knowledge of the slowness of judicial processes in our environment (the case of Ms. Keiko Fujimori has been ongoing almost a decade preparatory stage and recently gone to oral trial). Although it is a scenario that will try to strengthen the rule of law and political institutions and lay the foundations for a healthy democracy and socioeconomic recovery, its gestation process will be long, arduous and the risk of being affected by these platforms of harmful influences of political and economic agents who will be on the lookout to cause deviations and recover privileges. The challenge to be achieved is, therefore, from a double perspective, both constructive tasks and defensive tasks.

Perhaps we will see the heads of notorious culprits roll, although "the chain always breaks at the weakest link," we will witness crossfire between the accused and the accusers, there will be no shortage of pressure of all kinds against authorities and witnesses, intimidation, who knows, even attacks homicides, and the possibility of elusive suicides (as has already happened before) that cannot bear the ignominy of the crime and its guilt is not ruled out. Nor are scandalously lenient sentences ruled out that include fewer years in prison than crimes for cell phone theft.

Meanwhile, the country is not ready to remain immobilized in its weak state of health and wait for the final decisions of judges that may arrive tomorrow, later, or never, so in parallel, the urgent and delicate prophylactic task must begin in the organizations and institutions that require it. Many changes and reordering of work teams will have to be implemented and justice administration systems will be improved in the shortest time possible. The actions of the ruling power represented by an independent judicial power will be decisive in the results. There remains hope that not all levels of the judiciary have been taken over by mafias and private interests, but the gaps in corruption will continue to hinder improvements.

It must also be clear that achieving the cleanliness of this flawed platform of powers that exists today must do not only with holding responsible those people who deviated and distorted the regulations but with the purpose of consolidating and recovering that rule of law where the independent functioning of the powers of the state is consolidated, and the necessary and unrestricted balance of powers between them is respected. This is an old wish that I have been hearing since my time as a university student (around fifty years ago) that our generations have left unfinished, and I have the hope that current generations adopt it as an important demand and mission to achieve.

It should be noted that, both in the first scenario and in this second scenario (constituents of the first hypothetical panorama outlined), if we do not act with objectivity, transparency while respecting all the formalities of the case, we will run the risk of incurring vendettas and excessive "witch hunts" blaming innocent people without sufficient evidence of the case that can vitiate the process (we have already seen it before). We have outlined a first hypothetical panorama with its respective two variants of contrasting scenarios that involve direct protagonists of the crisis. But let us not forget that there are, alive and well, other factual powers with a discreet profile but notoriously omnipresent and even, according to history, with a suggestive capacity to veto or admit electoral options to the political arena. We are referring to the Armed Forces and the Economic Power Groups (GPE), which we will discuss next.

We then outline a second hypothetical panorama that presents the following antecedents:

The de facto power represented by the Armed Forces is currently in an embarrassing situation, and no matter how much its members hide or deny, having used and abused weapons against the civilian population in legitimate protests in situations that have been widely documented, filmed, and ratified by international organizations, accuses senior officials of uncomfortable responsibility

434

for the 49 deaths and human rights violations that occurred in December (2022) and January (2023) in the southern region of the country.

Given this serious, objective and concrete fact, it is to be assumed that the same parliamentary clique described in previous scenarios and eager to make alliances will seek, with the same corrupt and ominous style, to offer this de facto power some legal twist to protect them and guarantee them maximum extension, freezing and mitigation of your legal liabilities. All this in exchange for said de facto power showing complacency in the face of their crude attempts to smooth their consolidation of power.

However, this same de facto power is fully aware that, in the case of human rights crimes that do not prescribe, such acts are like a stigma and in the end, sooner or later, in one way or another and no matter how many promises from third parties, necessarily all of them are going to have to face their responsibilities. The problem with this military power is not then to avoid such responsibilities but to know how and when to face them. It would not be strange if certain sectors within said power were willing to resolve the issue without further delays and setbacks.

The other de facto power, which is the Economic Power Groups, are interested in developing a climate with social and political stability that makes it easier for them to achieve continuous benefits, preferably focused on short-term horizons. We have described in the previous sections on Leadership and External Conditioning that, unfortunately, these groups are disconnected. They are a kind of fiefdom with a lot of political influence, but they lack the conviction to lead or manage a comprehensive project as a nation and with medium- or long-term perspectives. Each electoral process is only the opportunity to finance parties and place and change political agents in their favor. This situation is one of the symptoms of our problem that should call the business class to rethink its traditional role on the national scene.

The congressional clique's ruse of consolidating an alliance with economic groups does not seem as simple as the exchanges of prebends it maintains with the suspended prosecutor. These power groups already have solid economic stability, and their permanence exceeds the period of governments and parliaments in power. Many of the current congressmen with close criminal affiliations (except for a small and respectable minority) do not know who they are dealing with and will believe that the enactment of certain laws in their favor will be enough to have them as allies. Although they will not stop liking these prebends, such laws will be of no use if the underlying problem continues to deteriorate. That is, if the climate of ungovernability, legal instability and citizen insecurity continues not only to be present but to worsen.

To begin with, they have closed the pipeline of private investments; activities will be conducted at a minimum level of operation, that is, risking as little as possible. For most businesspeople, the climate of uncertainty and mistrust is growing; economic agents such as producers, consumers and local investors begin to consider continuing their activities outside the country, and the degree of impoverishment and poverty also increases. In this sense, these groups of economic power will be more inclined to even consent to the possibility of a military coup if it is provisional and guarantee them a climate of stability, governability, and security for the development of their normal activities.

Amid this, the political architecture built by the parliamentary clique, no matter how attempts at its stubborn institutional seizure of power, will not end up convincing such de facto powers because, at the end of the day, the unruly mud and filth they generate, also affects such economic powers. Said the mafia parliamentary clique is not only incapable of perceiving or being aware that they are part of the problem, but their actions even aggravate the problem. On page 79 of this study, when dealing with the problem of corruption described by Mr. Alfonso Quiroz in his article: "Historical costs of corruption" pages. 82 and 92, in the work: "The Infamous Pact. Study on corruption in Peru" op. cit. he explicitly mentioned that one of the main qualitative problems generated by said corruption has been key in institutional weakening, socioeconomic instability, and investment. Overall, there is a kind of inverse relationship that determines that the greater the corruption, the lower the investments and growth. Textually, it is worth recalling his statement:

> "…the institutional costs incurred during the infamous decade (1990-2000) were enormous in terms of both the inefficient and distorted functioning of key institutions and the damage caused to the civic community fabric…the institutions that suffered the greatest damage were the armed forces, police and intelligence system…Corruption has bequeathed to Peru perhaps the highest value and institutional costs than any other contributing factor to underdevelopment."

We must recognize that such de facto powers (armed forces and economic power groups) have a neat organization and reinforce their management with the support of their own staff of independent professionals and advisors from multiple disciplines (lawyers, economists, sociologists, psychologists, and others) who keep them aware of the situation, the socioeconomic advantages, and risks. Another thing is to verify the use they make of said advantage and the concomitant effects of damage described, which has led some obscure members of the armed forces and businesspeople to be part of that disastrous parliamentary clique. Despite this, it is clear to large sectors of the armed forces how difficult it is for this parliamentary majority to get rid of their permanent wear and tear of citizen disapproval regarding the members of parliament themselves, their political parties, and their respective leaders.

Additionally, it has also become clear to such authorities that this clique is not interested in and even despises public opinion. They conduct their misdeeds in an analogous way to thieves in shopping centers and establishments, believing that no one is watching them or recording them with secret cameras. They act believing as if no one notices what they are doing and remain faithful to their presumption that politics walks on separate strings from the economy. No matter how much this criminal parliament persists in its hidden plots and no matter how much they have the support of a certain complicit press, everything becomes known, everything is filtered, and the crude attempts remain a mere insult to the intelligence of serious local and international observers.

In summary, the conditions set out in the preceding paragraphs, the environment and circumstances are not conducive to establishing alliances or agreements with partners so discredited that they are unaware of loyalty and trust as basic criteria that should prevail among members of any agreement. Additionally, this congressional caucus cannot offer the factual powers described what they would demand as a minimum condition to sit down to negotiate; it cannot offer what they do not have either in the present or in the immediate future, that is, they cannot offer a basis minimum of acceptable economic, social, and political stability. This is the Achilles heel that this group of criminals has created, and it will be their end.

Considering the background described, we present the characteristics that typify this second hypothetical panorama:

The elites of our armed forces and police will continue to be bothered, like a stone in their shoe, by the possibility of future trials for human rights violations. It is not inappropriate to think that no matter how many promises they receive from the parliamentary clique in the sense of shielding them, they will not be predisposed to trust a partner as discredited as these congressmen, nor in their political parties, nor in their questioned leaders. In the end, the military elites are aware

437

that they can end up "without a rope and without a goat" (losing everything) and remain frustrated victims of a childish deception covered in lies and disloyalty.

So, in a country like Peru where the most random probabilities are possible, and recognizing that even within a formality accepted by all in the sense that the military are "non-deciding actors of politics," it cannot be ruled out that the democratic institutions will break through a forced **coup d'état** that, in order to calm shocks, will be announced as being provisional in nature and due to the need to deal with emergencies. It is not that we agree on the need for a coup; we only point it out as the possibility of a turbulent scenario. The problem is quite complex due to its peculiar characteristics.

For what reason would the coup be conducted?

Among the important and highly publicized reasons to justify the coup we would have the undesirable generalized crisis of ungovernability, and social upheaval caused by the current legislative-executive duo and that to get out of a situation of greater anarchy and being close to "hitting rock bottom", it will grant the military the perfect pretext of a State Question for their intervention.

Not all crises are the same, and we have argued before that social phenomena are unique and unrepeatable. And one of the typical signs of the current crisis is that complicated plot of conflicts, interpositions, and imbalances between powers of the state that we currently experience and that translates into a climate of ungovernability with anarchic profiles that no one wants. We would be in a situation like the inside of a balloon that continues to inflate and is about to burst. The socioeconomic and political system cannot withstand any longer and we continue to be trapped in conflicts whose solution requires an unraveling with the participation of external forces or factors to the direct protagonists of ungovernability.

On the other hand, in Peru, it usually occurs with curious assiduity, a kind of tradition that society, citizens, political representation parties and other social agents in general have assimilated a peculiar reaction to situations of acute crisis. The traditional citizen response has been to accept, without hesitation, the intervention of the armed forces.

We have seen it in cases of political instability of the previous Pedro Castillo government, where more than one sector demanded the intervention of the armed forces due to their reluctance

438

to resign from office. We have also seen this same claim in previous episodes to combat critical profiles of advances in drug trafficking, terrorism, or a combination of both (narcoterrorism), the coronavirus pandemic and its support in social confinement tasks and now its intervention in the face of problems is being demanded of citizen security. Regardless of whether this is good or bad, what we do is rescue it as a customary phenomenon appealed to by citizens in the face of chaotic crises that provide sufficient reasons for such de facto powers (military) to justify their intervention.

The most accurate reason for the coup, but less widespread, would be the desire of its main protagonists to "take the bull by the horns, with their own means and without trusting or hoping to receive favors from third parties." This can only be explained by the military's purpose of assuming its own defense, of safeguarding its own interests and counteracting with its own forces the judicial onslaught that it will have to face. Here, it will be decisive how the military elites, not only with imposition but with deterrence, would simultaneously be able to reach a consensus on a complex political agreement and in demanding prudential periods.

The possibilities of achieving this will depend on how different interests or points of view are recognized or satisfied: that of relatives of the victims, of international pro-human rights organizations, of prosecutors and citizens who are going to demand that, no matter how many agreements are reached, arrive, civil and criminal responsibilities must be established and it will also depend on how to build bridges with the political forces of the broadest spectrum of the environment. Depending on how their judicial concerns can be calmed, how their responsibilities can be partially mitigated and after the degree of consensus to be achieved (Uruguayan or Argentine style), the military will be able to decide or negotiate how and when to return democratic institutions to the country and its early return to the rule of law. If no agreement is formalized or agreed upon, history could repeat a new military leadership with unexpected profiles, and we will confirm the popular adage that states: "the cure was worse than the disease."

What conditions are going to be raised to mitigate the coup?

This forced exit and the abrupt break of democratic institutions with the intention of containing greater social unrest or anarchy (located especially in the south of the country) would only be permissible if the following aspects are scrupulously managed:

Let's admit that there is not going to stop being repression, nor will their stop being protests; therefore, to avoid further bloodshed and innocent victims still fresh in our memories, the key will be to know how to manage the protests in such a way that they are avoided repressive excesses and deviations that go beyond just protests are also avoided. This strategy requires a fine line in a cunning "tug of war" (adjust and tolerate) with internal political forces.

Although the military coup could partially address the platform of citizens' struggle that demands, as an initial measure, a prompt resignation of the president and the closure of Congress (everyone leave!), we know that said measure is necessary, but in no way sufficient way to face complicated problems. It must be clear that it is not a question of, under the pretext of cleansing the country of a large part of the execrable political class, it ends up supporting the institutionalization of renewed dictatorships that make a clean slate of opposition forces and that tend to remain in power.

The providential citizen consent to the coup would only be sustainable if, in addition to reestablishing democratic institutions, institutional deviations are simultaneously corrected, and the foundations are laid promptly and efficiently to restore a process of stability and socioeconomic improvement. Accordingly, the popular request to call general elections would be harmless if certain preconditions for authentic political reforms were not met and, at the same time, dismantle the reforms undertaken by the current congressional caucus for its particular benefit (e.g., Abolition of primary elections and regulatory limitations for new electoral options).

Furthermore, another obstacle must be overcome: any coup government or authoritarian civil government will be on alert for observation by the international community, which will be able to grant its recognition after evaluating what is done and how the actions are done things. Why is this "agreement" with the international community important? Because if it does not exist, we will be left in the condition of a "pariah" country or a "banana" country (despised, plagued, and isolated due to improper management of citizen rights, with nuances of ungovernability and without institutional support). With this, the possibilities of trade agreements or financial support from abroad are cut short.

Curiously, the onslaught of the parliamentary opposition would lead us to be part of that select club of countries such as Venezuela, Cuba, Nicaragua, and El Salvador that represented the models rejected by our representative right in their attacks (during the entire electoral campaign and the months before and after installed) against former President Castillo. That is to say, the blindness and ineptitude of this kleptocratic parliament direct us towards that scenario that they rejected before.

In this coup conjecture, the current parliamentary clique loses because its bread burned at the "door of the oven" (its strategy collapses in the final stretch). But they would not openly confront the military elites, but rather, they will swallow the bitter pill of having to wait patiently for the duration of the necessary institutional restructuring demanded by the citizens and by the economic power groups as a prior step to the general elections. It will not be strange if, on this occasion, these cliques now appeal to international organizations (currently vilified and denigrated) to denounce the cessation of the constitutional order and demand their participation to reestablish the prompt return to democracy.

Nor is a variant out of place given by the mixture of the previous panoramas where, as from past eras of history, "a modern civilism" can be replicated where the collusion between military and political elites with the sole purpose of maintaining that status quo is evident or order pre-established and agreed by them.

Finally, we develop a third hypothetical panorama where the profile acquired by the described scenarios seems relevant to us and where the actors play their last cards. Here are its main features:

If the conjectures of the panoramas described above are considered inappropriate, unmanageable, or misguided (predominance of the mafia parliament, predominance of the military elites, or the combination of both), the country will continue toward that inexorable path or deterioration with a tendency of growing crisis, of anarchy and social, political, and economic upheaval where contradictions that no one wants are exacerbated, except the extreme positions of the left and right.

That is to say, a climate of effervescence of social protests, increased citizen insecurity, ungovernability and power conflicts, ineptitude, blunders and corruption of executive and legislative branch officials, renewal of authorities by improvised officials, drastic reduction of private investment, worsening unemployment, lower levels of tax collection, degradation of the living standards of vulnerable populations, greater uncertainty for all socioeconomic agents (businessmen, consumers, investors, workers, students, housewives, etc.) will predominate.

But this hell under our noses is nothing new; it has been happening and being observed by most citizens with impassive bewilderment, with astonishing reactions and irresolution as if it were going to affect others and not all of us. In high social strata, such behavior is understandable, but in the majority low and middle strata, it seems that the greatest damage caused by this crisis of ungovernability has to do not so much with the increase in pauperization experienced but with having caused a daze, apathy or social apathy where it seems that citizens have lost social awareness of the degradation that accompanies it, where living in the midst of filth becomes almost normal and where nothing is questioned or done to get out of that stinking swamp of filth. The results of the survey data are not enough and are of little interest to those who make decisions.

Here, we blame the high unconsciousness of the executive and parliament. As a result of subsequent calls for popular protests, the massacres of December (2022) and January (2023), President Dina Boluarte had the nerve to publicly question the population, telling them: How many more deaths do you want? This form of deterrence suggests that such protests, despite being enshrined as a constitutional right, will inevitably be repressed with bullets.

Faced with the repressive outbursts that were experienced, we understand why the population maintains its reluctance to participate in public protests and because of the threats of all the paraphernalia of legal sanctions with criminal liability converted into laws against citizens, opposition journalists and other independent voices that can be accused of crossing that tenuous line where what are legitimate protests are not differentiated from the actions of vandals that promote disorder and riots. This is what we can call "institutionalized violence" from the power against citizens.

As a reflection, it is worth recalling the article by Mr. Carlos Lecaros: "Injustices, Claims and Repression" (page 86 of this document), regarding the suspicious speech of Don José Baquíjano y Carrillo (precursor of Peruvian independence) pronounced in front of who would occupy a new viceregal period Don Agustín de Jáuregui (1780-1784) to whom he subtly reminds him that in the face of authoritarian government tyrannies: "…improving man against his will has always been the deceptive pretext of tyranny; that the people are a spring, which, when forced more than its elasticity suffers, bursts, destroying the reckless hand that oppresses and holds it."

240 years have passed of warning of that discourse where the protagonists change, the political scenario changes, but the functionality of an oppressive system of power against majority

populations remains constant. Once again, these are demands that have been successively postponed or ignored and that cry out to be addressed.

In this same order of ideas, Basadre's previous phrase cited on page also deserves reflection. 260 of the present study, where he reminds us: "…The history of Peru in recent times is perhaps nothing more than the subversion of the provinces against Lima, for the first time or Lima concedes, and grants or evils occur that will no longer be those they passively endured the provinces, but those who emanate from their rebellion."

Lastly, just as important are the comments of Mr. Luis Guillermo Lumbreras (see page 260 of this study) where he points out:

> "…What is happening currently is a confrontation between the country of us (those from the center of Lima) and the country of others (the peripheral provinces), we have access to a series of services that the vast majority of others do not have or have them in a precarious way (education, medical and hospital care, retirement, food, etc.). We ignored each other. What is happening is that the others are starting to get up." The comments in parentheses are ours.

The social scientist maintains that we must unify nationality criteria, recognize our differences and that the claim of others is true. In this third panorama, we can also distinguish two scenarios that call into question a restless dichotomy that we describe below:

The first option includes a desirable process of progressive transition with order and freedom. To a certain extent, this scenario could represent the continuity and improvement of the variant of the first hypothetical panorama where the JNJ recovers the country's institutions, and the foundations are laid for a socioeconomic recovery. Overcoming the political, social, and economic crisis in which we are immersed will be very costly and re-entering a process of governability and manageable stability would take no less than five years. Challenging work will have to be done on different fronts, sectors, and areas of the country. One of the channels for this is to promote consensus, build bridges of understanding and, make the population feel authentically represented and have honest and honest leaders, businesspeople, professionals, and workers.

In this sense, one of the channels is to find that representativeness involves not only the conventional partocracies but also the other representative entities of society. The mechanism of the National Agreement has always been considered necessary to reach a consensus that allows recomposing, undoing, and remaking relevant improvements, changes and exploring new institutional arrangements. Simultaneously, there is also a consensus to undertake a prompt and orderly call for new elections general that previously contemplated more urgent political reforms.

Other personalities have also proposed updating the issue of a Constituent Assembly. Regardless of how controversial this initiative may be, the majority recognizes that due to the successive amendments that have been proposed to the current Constitution, urgent modifications to it are necessary. However, there is also a consensus that the current situation does not favor the best opportunity to carry them out. We know that the issue of the Constituent Assembly would take no less than a couple of years to be convened, installed, undertake its work and complete it.

Both the National Agreement and the Constituent Assembly make up two important mechanisms whose orientation fits with what we have previously called Formulation or Strategic Design for the nation. So, we have on the one hand, the contributions made to us by illustrious social scientists cited in this study (Jorge Basadre, Luis Guillermo Lumbreras, Francisco Durand and others) both in terms of the clarity of their diagnoses of our problems and the respective Vision, Mission, and Objectives to be achieved. On the other hand, we will also have the guidelines of political and economic criteria that will come from the work of a necessary National Agreement and hopefully from a possible Constituent Assembly. But we have seen throughout this work that the previous Formulation effort remains weak and incomplete without a necessary and parallel Implementation of the entire process. We ourselves will have to take on the challenge of resolving the issue of how to implement this process.

The urgency of the case requires us to address needs through practical, immediate solutions, which may not be completely refined and perfect, but which mitigate emergencies. For this reason, some analysts prefer to propose corrections "along the way" instead of postponed perfections that never arrive or that, due to whimsical obstacles, delay the sleep of the righteous. Faced with this, more temperate voices suggest that it is better to do things correctly, orderly, slowly, and not so quickly. Promptness without efficiency frameworks usually leads to improvisations, errors, and costly repetitions of processes. That is, the permissiveness of imperfections, imbalances and spontaneities end up conditioning the results with little or no effectiveness.

The crucial problem of this dilemma is then how to deal with emergency situations efficiently and effectively. The recent COVI experience provides certain guidelines to approach and treat the problem described. In this debate, it was established that the most important thing was not so much to exhaust oneself in what to do but how to move forward in preparing the conditions and the ground to pave and ensure the proper path of what to do. Advance alternately with Formulation and Implementation.

The second option corresponds to a highly conflictive scenario with exacerbated effervescence where the outcomes of violence are destabilizing. Before, we have described in greater detail that our social problems show serious limitations whose functionality has been corroded by endemic hypertrophy of a structural nature. The classification of this social scenario corresponds to a permanent situation of chaos, disorganization, non-compliance and deviations from institutional roles, lack of compliance and respect for regulations and authorities, predominance of all types of corruption, arbitrariness, conflict of interests, lack of social representation, etc. In general, it is a certain runaway anarchic scheme where "the crisis hit rock bottom."

As a result, processes of social and economic regression are generated, deterioration of the conditions and living standards of the population, worsening of poverty and a general climate of uncertainty and social unrest. How to treat this serious patient who is in intensive care? In our society, in addition to the crises exposed, it also shows, as part of said crisis, a notorious lack of honest leaders and, the predominance of a culture of anti-values and a lack of ethics in most institutions that make their treatment difficult.

The outcome of this third conjecture has to do with the answers that each one refines to the following questions: what will be the cost of not acting on the matter, of continuing to evade and hold others responsible for what we have ad-portas and is it coming upon us? What must happen to shake us from this impassivity because we consider that the problems affect third parties and not all of us? What can be done to raise the low dose of political awareness and make citizens wake up from shameful lethargy in this matter? Will Lima concede to the pressure from the provinces and especially that which comes with great force from the south of the country? How do you unify criteria for national self-awareness? Who will execute and lead the difficult implementation tasks? Who will fill this power vacuum? Will it be organized civility, de facto powers groups, or the traditional pseudo-renewed partocracy?

Some groups or political agents of organized civility will want to do so, but based on past experiences, doubts remain as to whether they will have the capacity and experience to take on the challenge of effective and efficient, quite complex public management. Technical and professional orphanhood is an obstacle that affects not only the leader of any organization but also the responsibility of the large management team that must accompany him. This has been long becoming a condition for outsiders and their parties, who only discover or become aware of this problem when they come to power. They make an enormous effort to reach power, and once in power, the disaster of processes muddied with corruption that we repeatedly know continues. What is required for this route to offer possibilities for change?

Some economic power groups can form a suitable technical team to conduct the difficult task of Implementation. But we have doubts whether they are sufficiently predisposed and motivated to conduct political management with Nation State criteria and profiles. The myopia of not considering a governance scheme with priority inclusion and attention to the requirements of displaced, segregated, and neglected sectors prevents them from seeing the potential of their own benefits in long-term horizons because they are only interested in focusing on continuing the usufruct of short-term profits. What is required for this other route to offer possibilities for change?

We are facing scenarios where there are few or no leaders or leadership teams with authentic vision, probity, and honesty. We are exposed to risks of penetration or the voracity of false leaders, of obsolete and new politically representative parties. There will also be no shortage of the well-known political vultures (from extreme sides on both the right and the left) and outsiders eager to deceive citizens with populist costumes y masks representing political center options. It seems as if we are doomed to always have more of the same. The questions raised require answers pending on the national agenda.

5.8. POLICY GUIDELINES AND OTHER CONDITIONS

When reviewing other types of external conditions, the experienced Coronavirus (COVID-19) pandemic and its unfortunate balance of people and companies injured or that ceased to exist suggests to those of us who remain in the fight that we will have to learn to continue doing the same things as before, but in some different way or start new things. This crisis has once again tested the ingenuity, innovation, creativity, and capacity of economic agents (businessmen, workers, investors, professionals, researchers, etc.) to have to perfect, adapt, modernize, and reinvent themselves. The survival of business and personal activities tells us **that to make a**

difference the important thing will be not so much what to do but rather finding the best ways to do it.

In this context of challenge, the countries of the developing world, with a narrow immediate vision of their governments in power, combined with little motivation on the part of the private sector to develop or adapt their own technology, have caused technological activity to have an alarming deficit of priority, attention and budget allocation. This will only reinforce our technological dependence on all areas of knowledge. That is, shortening or closing technological gaps and discovering, or promoting sectors with the potential for technological development, are arduous and long-range tasks that require strong conviction and persistence. It is a dream that we must dare to start, even if it is in small steps, because the future possibilities of achieving efficiency and effectiveness will depend on it.

One of the warnings that we must keep in mind is that the reference map of effectiveness and efficiency that we have described represents only one form (among many existing ones), referring to a particular pattern of analysis and evaluation of business performance. There are, in fact, other approaches that suggest different schemes for doing the same (M. Porter's competitiveness diamond, the multivariable framework of the seven "s" and the eight criteria to achieve excellence described by T. Peters and R. Waterman Jr. in his work "In Search of Excellence," the Balanced Scorecard by R. Kaplan and D. Norton, the business architecture scheme by James Brickley, Smith, Zimmerman in his work Managerial Economics & Organizational Architecture, the diagrams, archetypes and patterns of behavior that Peter Senge describes in his work "The Fifth Discipline," the Thinking in Systems scheme by Donella H. Meadows and many others).

Let us not forget that in addition to the approaches described, there are those other schemes that we referred to at the beginning of this work (section 1.1 General notion of business management) characterized by logical patterns of mathematical models that also show their respective advances and innovations. Quantum physics and mathematics have gained recognition in the field of financial investments due to their ability to analyze enormous amounts of data and make predictions with high accuracy. Quantum finance is a discipline that uses mathematical, physical, and statistical models to analyze financial markets and predict future trends. Quantum finance experts use such tools to develop models that can predict market behavior more accurately than traditional models.

As the author Donella Meadows [39] points out in her cited work (page 21),

> "Some things can be seen through the lens of the human eye, others through the lenses of a microscope, others through the lenses of a telescope, and some others through of systems theory lenses. Everything that is seen through each lens, in fact, exists. Each way of seeing allows knowledge of the world to become more complete. The world is more confused, more interconnected, more interdependent, and inconstant, the more ways of seeing it, the better."

To this, we add that different business problems do not have to be pigeonholed into exclusive schemes but may also correspond to different diagnosis and solution strategies.

The short term poses to us more frequently than before the problem of facing business management in the context of a panorama of permanent changes with increasing doses of uncertainty and unpredictability. Amid this, continuous internal and external changes and accelerated technological innovations cause a kind of atmospheric turbulence where the "crew of the business ship" becomes stunned, immobilized and, in certain cases, accused of a lack of reflexes or delayed reactions. Conventional tools appear outdated and are somewhat insufficient to successfully address the challenges of facing new problems. In this sense, the purpose of our approach, as well as the other proposals mentioned above, aims to provide us with conceptual frameworks that help us clarify these deficiencies, absences, and gaps and allow us to refine our aim and dose resources to correct deviations and face unforeseen events.

We share the reflection of the notable scientist Albert Einstein: "Do not try to be men of success, instead try to be men of value" (see Peggy Anderson: "Great quotes from great leaders," Celebrating Excellence, Inc., 1992, Page LD13). In accordance with Einstein's message, we should redefine the concept of successful business management expressed in this essay with courageous **business management**. Knowing his personality, we will say that his recommendation is to pursue management aimed at walking along unexplored routes by investigating, redefining, changing, and innovating new products and recent technologies. All this with firm conviction and persistence in achieving them.

We complement this recommendation with what was pointed out by a prominent entrepreneur, Robert T. Kiyosaki, in his well-known work: "Rich Dad's Cashflow Quadrant. Warner Business

---

[39] see: "Pensando em sistemas", op. cit. page 21

Book. New York, 2000, page 151; when he points out that: "success is not a good advisor, we learn more from our own failures, so we should not fear if we fail. Failures are part of the process of success. You cannot be successful without failure". We can only add that we must learn the lessons about our mistakes so as not to repeat them and get up again after a fall. As the Latin proverb says: "Errando corrigitur error" (by erring, the error is corrected).

The writer Paulo Coelho [40] adds more of the same to us in this beautiful message:

> "...the hearts of men are like that. They are afraid to realize their greatest desires because they find that they do not deserve it or that they will not achieve them. My heart is afraid of suffering - said the boy to the alchemist -... tell it (the alchemist responded) that <u>the fear of suffering is worse than the suffering itself</u> and that no heart ever suffered when it went in search of its dreams... While I was looking for my treasure (said the boy), I discovered things along the way that I had never dreamed of finding if I had not had the courage to try things impossible for shepherds. (emphasis is ours)

The coincidental direction of the recommendations never ceases to draw our attention: that of Steve Jobs regarding maintaining independence of judgment and fortitude to undertake new things, also Albert Einstein's recommendation regarding not pretending to be a man of success but of courage, the Robert Kiyosaki's recommendation to not fear our failures, as well as Paulo Coelho's message to face the fear of suffering when facing new goals. All the recommendations described have in common that they lead us to the necessary condition of **facing our fears**, which are part of the complex configuration of human nature.

Why is it important, in terms of organizational management and social coexistence, to face our fears instead of "forgetting about them and leaving them still, inactive and inert"? Because first, our fears have a permanent presence in our subconscious and are automatically activated to immobilizing people towards a numbing emotional state, where we remain clouded and incapable of reasoning fluently and lucidly, of inferring appropriate conclusions and even less about making the best and timely decisions. Secondly, because unlike admitted fears that we can face or minimize (for example, fear of cliffs, darkness, insecurity, material loss, fear of separation or loss of loved ones, fear of one's own death, etc.), <u>the fears that we consider to be still, never are.</u>

---

[40] "El Alquimista" op. cit. page 138

449

These fears were hidden and waiting for the slightest stimulus or neglect to make themselves present. These fears lie in apparent inactivity in the subconscious, but they are "alive and well," enjoying that deceptive anonymity granted by our resistance to admitting them openly, either because we deny them to ourselves, rationalize them in a supposed forgetfulness, or because we disguise them with the garb of negative feelings (anger, sadness, stress, anguish, shame, resentment, etc.). These are the fears wrapped in "toxic" feelings that do us the most harm because, as psychologists point out, they are free to come to the fore and exert their fatal influence.

I rescued among old personal notes an important anonymous phrase that warned: "You cannot live in fear all your life. Life is like that: you fall, you get up, and you fall again. But if you don't even move for fear of falling, you have already sunk". It is not difficult to imagine what will happen to the business or government management crew who, faced with difficulties in their management, are trapped in panic and fear.

Among the deceptive fears that do the most damage we have the **fear of success**. As contradictory as it may seem, this topic is worth reflecting on. Carlos Vallés, S.J., in one of his works: "Do Not Fear." San Pablo 1998, Spain, Pages 53-61, argues that most people are not aware of the fear of success; they do not admit it. Rather, they hide it and openly accept that they fear failure. The author maintains that the predisposition to not fear success but rather failure is what is seen in superficiality or, as we say in Peru, "from the teeth out."

In the depths of the subconscious, those ramblings of the human mind appear as complexes of guilt, inferiority, entanglements, and traumas from the past or from our training that obstruct and put obstacles on the route to success. Amid them, a close relative hides, which is the fear of risking what we already possess (personal wealth, wealthy position, or social prestige), and that could be lost on the risky path to success. From this perspective, some propose that more than fearing success, what we have is fear of assuming the risk of that set of unfavorable possibilities that the march towards success implies.

In the world of investments, one often hears the saying: "betting on the safe side is giving up on getting rich." This sentence hides the conditioned message that to overcome a condition of modesty or precariousness; one must always take risks. This is not necessarily true; it is known that achieving a well-established status of wealth cannot be obtained overnight, and you cannot burn through stages to achieve it. Except for occasional events (unexpected inheritance, winning the lottery, technological discovery, marketing beta or even illicit actions), the route to wealth is long and tedious, and you must learn from both successes and mistakes.

What is appropriate is to consider and not close ourselves in rigid conservative positions. Be aware of openings toward risk positions that allow gradual improvements in profits. Even this generic recommendation will encounter emotional resistance in people who do not show a willingness to tolerate risks and have a declared aversion to them.

Among the internal twists and turns of our existence, it can also be mentioned that it comforts us to figuratively maintain the illusion, the dream, and the distant hope of achieving success, but we are not willing to assume the risks and challenges that this entails and above all we are not willing to take actions and much less embark on the sacrifices to obtain it. However, the vicissitudes of life have taught us that achievements and compensations are not free, nor do they come from the sky. It is even said that the manna (fallen from heaven according to the Bible) took time and work to allocate with adequate criteria to order its availability, group it, store it, distribute it, and, due to its scarcity, dose it for reasonable consumption.

Despite this, we prefer to remain reluctant to undertake something new or different (which means time and work to do so). We settle for what is known, and we prefer that duality of remaining cocooned in the security of what we modestly have and, at the same time, prolonging the fantasy to continue wanting what we don't have, doing little or nothing to achieve it. That way, we stay wrapped in the lulling "poor man's hope."

In this regard, we must begin by convincing ourselves that nothing is free; people are reluctant to recognize that there is no free lunch, and some social sectors and people (especially within developing countries) have become accustomed to obtaining a good part of basic services subsidized and even free (food, water, electricity, health, and others) whether due to government assistance, the benevolence of a benefactor, or external help. Without ceasing to consider that in part of the dispossessed population, the receipt of said benefits is justified, it is also observed that part of said population, despite improving their status, demands to remain in that condition of continuing to benefit permanently.

Even in the USA, a good percentage of people who benefited from financial support from unemployment insurance, enjoying an amount even higher than the salary they had been receiving, were reluctant to try new jobs to continue enjoying said insurance while receiving income without working. It must be engraved in the brains of those directed and leaders that we ourselves must take charge of solving our own problems and that the purpose of increasing or maintaining a certain well-being requires a cost that we must assume and an effort to deploy.

Without ceasing to recognize that special circumstances warrant occasional and justified assistance in strata of extreme poverty, in any case, we must be aware that its permanence fuels costs that cannot be avoided because the rest of society ends up paying for it.

In addition to the internal mental twists and turns, it has often happened that, being close to achieving success and the desired goal, we are invaded by what we usually typify as "the procession goes inside" (internal fears), so we become paralyzed, or we go back, we get disturbed and although it may seem paradoxical, we end up convincing ourselves that we will not achieve it, that we are not worthy of success and we even conclude that it is not good for us. The author wonders why the composer Brahms kept his first symphony for twenty years without publishing it and why it took the mathematician George Cantor as many years to make known his theory of transfinite numbers.

I remember the brilliant performance of the Peruvian women's volleyball team at the Seoul Olympic Games (South Korea, 1988). Leaving category rivals out of competition, they came to play for the gold medal against the powerful team of the Soviet Union. After winning the first two sets, they faced the third and final set, which they won with a comfortable score of 12 against 7, that is, they were barely three points away from triumph and "on the way" to glory when suddenly they experienced a kind of dizziness from altitude, their mind was disturbed and according to later testimonies from some of them, they themselves did not believe what was happening, they begin to lose rhythm, coordination, concentration and finally lost successive sets and finally lost the match. What happened? Are the players seized by sudden panic and fear of success?

On the contrary, according to one of Einstein's biographers, Mr. Walter Isaacson, in his work "Einstein: His Life and His Universe" Debate. First Edition, Sep. 2008; points out that the young Einstein's temperament of marked curiosity, imagination, irreverence and even detachment from any form of established authority allowed or provided him with enough personal shield to break with the sacred parameters of Newtonian Physics in force during almost 200 years, and not to their predecessors (who had already made important advances and discoveries). Perhaps the latter were also attacked by an attack of resentment or aversion to success, and Einstein was in a better position to face it?

Other times, we have an aversion to success because it imposes subsequent sacrifices and obligations on us. The successes and triumphs the author maintains produce enthusiasm at the beginning and slavery at the end, and therefore, the fear of that nightmare and that spiral of triumphs that demand more triumphs can sabotage it. In other cases, we avoid success because it is more comfortable to take refuge in perfectionism, and we postpone finishing work, projects or studies because we consider them unfinished.

In the end, Carlos Vallés maintains in his work [41]:

> "That is the battle between mediocrity and excellence... between security and risk. The adventure is worth it, but there are many complexes within us that make us cower before the unprecedented excursion and boycott it before it begins... The fact is that we fear both success and failure, the difference is that the fear of failure is patent, while the fear of success remains hidden and for that reason, it can do more damage...it is interesting to bring it out of the shadows to address it head-on forehead."

To this, we will add the wise popular proverb: "Each one is the owner of his own fears and complexes," and these appear in our experience and ambush us suddenly and at unexpected moments, marking milestones, limits, borders and scars. But in terms of business management, it is appropriate to point out inconveniences both for excessively conservative and prudent managers (with their extreme variants of exaggeratedly indecisive and fearful) and for those who show a greater willingness to live with and accept risks (with their well-known extreme variants of permanently risk-takers and even "suicidal" for assuming too much of them). Excluding ourselves from the extreme situations described above implies a favorable disposition to face our fears and manage them with moderation, which means initial progress.

How can we deepen this progress so as not to remain in a simple, accommodating, and eclectic impartiality? Curiously, we have left the business "management problem" linked to the economic area to fall into the "manager problem" related to his psychological and behavioral profile. In this field, we cannot escape the contributions of another notable researcher and psychologist, Mr. Daniel Goleman, who, in his work "Emotional Intelligence in the Company" (Spanish title of the

---

[41] "No temas" op. cit. pages 59 y 60

original "Working with Emotional Intelligence"), 1999 Ediciones Argentinas, tells us (pp. 380-386) that:

> "…emotional intelligence is a term referring to the development of basic skills such as the ability to: recognize our own and other people's feelings, manage such emotions in ourselves and in our relationships, develop motivation to move towards set goals and persevere in the face of setbacks and frustrations, development of empathy (ability to perceive and appreciate perspectives different from one's own) that facilitates cultivating affinity with a diversity of people and finally development of social skills that facilitates adequate reading of situations to interact, overcoming difficulties and using these skills to persuade, negotiate, direct and resolve disputes through cooperation and teamwork."

The capabilities described in this quote return us to the topic of business management because, as the author points out and as we also point out throughout this work, the current situation of a globalized economy and permanent changes pose challenges of renewed tools and processes where the contribution of capabilities described in emotional intelligence is of utmost importance for the requirements of effectiveness and efficiency.

Indeed, the pressures of demanding competitiveness require a management body with the capacity for knowledge, emotional management, adequate and rapid reaction capacity in the face of such changes to develop effective, efficient, and timely decision-making. If, on the other hand, management is trapped in what we call toxic emotions (panic, fear, anger, depression, hatred, abuse, revenge, etc.), it will show a slow or inopportune capacity to react to changes, accompanied by blunders and inappropriate decision making.

Likewise, within what we call changing environments, it will be relevant to have managers with a high degree of motivation to support renewed objectives and values, with a good degree of initiative and creativity that facilitate conducting innovations in management. All of this, with the promotion of those empathic capacities (recognition of feelings of third parties in group contexts) that allow that dose of tranquility and calm so that through collaboration and affinity, they make negotiation, resolution of conflicts, setbacks, and ever-present emergencies in any organization.

Although it can be outlined that successful management requires an adequate balance between efficiency and effectiveness, this statement, while still being acceptable, leaves us in a limbo of generality. Any generic prescription could even be counterproductive since efficiency (or effectiveness) could be reinforced in inadvisable areas, times, and situations. However, companies with successful business management have been able to find in that balance or imbalance that which allows them to mobilize in a range of variability where, curiously, they move from one field to another with detachment from rigid approaches and managing with the flexibility of criteria, sometimes opposite to those initially chosen, but appropriate depending on the circumstances.

Such companies know how to give the appropriate and time the rudder stroke to change their route; they know where they are, what terrain they are on and what the environment is like. Sometimes, they are strictly ordered, and other times, they are flexible and tolerant of chaos and know how to protect themselves against it. Sometimes, they tend toward decentralization and other times towards centralization, sometimes they accelerate the pedal of growth and other times, they decelerate and even take the respective pause, sometimes they cling to the script of what is formulated in the strategy and other times, they take risks and have the courage to change it supported by the creativity, innovation and experience of the leading team. These companies are not daunted by the euphoria of success or the desperation of a crisis because they know how to restructure and rethink (particularly and comprehensively) their routes, objectives, and goals.

In distinct parts of this essay, criteria and concepts have been highlighted that, although they are projected towards the business or organizational field, in the dynamics of any management, they cannot be separated from the personal or individual basis of the manager. So that interrelation between company and manager and their complex circumstances will be the reflection of the connotations of effectiveness and efficiency learned and put into practice on a personal level by the manager and by those who accompany him in said task.

In the sustainability of satisfactory management, there must be affinity and correspondence between the individual level of intrinsic qualities of those responsible for management and the business level of proven results thereof. It is less plausible to accept that someone who was improvised, lacked leadership, unethical, disorganized, lacked direction and control, inept or corrupt in their individual experiences would simultaneously be the opposite of the head of a company or organization.

Just as on the topic of social responsibility, we propose a necessary commitment of the company with the community that goes beyond economic and legal responsibility. On this occasion we also propose the ethical commitment of those responsible for management with their workers that also goes beyond the contractual commitment of a simple remuneration. The management of efficiency and effectiveness proposed in this work is not limited to the narrow purpose of obtaining greater profits at minimum cost. We have proposed a strict commitment on the part of senior management to ensure that framework of reciprocal trust with the closest circle of collaborators (its professional, technical and labor staff) and then expand that same collaboration and trust of the same framework of ethics, in the face of that whole world of external connections (supplier companies, banking entities, tax supervisory or control authorities, clients, community, etc.) with whom it maintains a continuous relationship.

But let us not rush to prejudge; no one suggests that the company becomes a welfare institution for tasks that correspond to other instances, much less that it sacrifices its lucrative purpose. Of course, the social responsibility of the company with the community and the ethical responsibility of senior management with its internal and external clients will mean "adjusting a moderate portion of its surpluses," that is, assuming certain cost increases that will affect profits. However, we consider that the impact on the profit rate in the short term may be "manageable" without failing to consider the intention of contributing to the purposes of their work and community environment and obtaining a stable profit rate in the medium and long term.

Defenders of pure efficiency must weigh in their balance of benefits and costs. What and how much does it mean for the company to maintain, with the community where it operates, an environment of understanding and reciprocal collaboration? How much does the company earn (versus how much it spends) in collaborating with the implementation of a work of social or cultural impact so often longed for and postponed by the authorities (a highway, a hospital, a school, a museum, a recreation center, etc.)? How much does the company potentially earn by establishing a technical labor training center for activities related to its own field in its local area?

How much does the company earn for organizing an event for integration, awards and work stimulation and for participation in defining or adjusting medium-term objectives, goals and challenges? How much does the company earn for promoting and sponsoring scholarships and cultural and sporting events in the local environment? What will be the company's profit rate in a long-term perspective by undertaking the initiatives described? The answers of each company to these questions will clear up doubts and provide admirable surprises.

When investigating questions of leadership, we saw in the previous chapters that the channels of national representation, the partocracy and the conglomerate of political actors in our environment (Peru 2023) were and remained, due to past and present experiences, disqualified from assuming an authentic process of legitimizing leadership of necessary and important changes that history and the situation demand. Some well-intentioned citizens optimistically hopeful about the future possibilities of the nation suggest that, with political options being scarce, whatever force aspires to national representativeness and to govern the destinies of the nation <u>must consider the priority of establishing a balanced and compensatory of powers,</u> so that the deviations and excesses committed by one of them can be corrected by another.

This platform, as Americans say, "check and balance" has failed and has become denatured in our country and partly explains the crisis of misgovernment that we are experiencing. It is necessary to warn that, due to this shortcoming, the changes or substitutions of protagonists in each power are of little use if the distorted scheme of balance (or rather, imbalance) of powers existing in our environment remains intact and in force. To cite an example, through the artifice of changes in congressional regulations or legal subterfuges, constitutional reforms are pursued (and sometimes have been achieved) that the so-called Constitutional Court overlooked or even ratified.

The above occurs and results when, in fact, there is no clear independence of powers that prevents successive arbitrary interference of one power over another. There are plenty of examples: we have a predominant parliamentary scheme in our environment that established deformed and capricious norms that partly explain having had six presidents in five years. We have had embarrassing cases of parliamentary majorities that shielded (protected) prosecutors and other corrupt judicial authorities.

Lately, we have been witnessing regrettable cases where the actions of some prosecutors and judges have been determining the political agenda in a mix of colluding interests. There have also been successive laws "on the fly" (established without sufficient debate) vetoed by the executive but finally approved at parliamentary insistence. We have had cases where the Constitutional Court (when it still had respectable autonomy) had to amend parliament by declaring crude legal attempts on the latter's part unconstitutional. Currently, the conditioned conformation of this Constitutional Court has unfortunately made it a captive of parliament and of the Fuerza Popular party led by Keiko Fujimori.

Firstly, we consider that a requirement to achieve relative independence of State Powers will be to find the optimal ways to instrumentalize what we have called the scheme of counterweight, balance, and compensation of powers. We are even witnesses of cases where the apparent crossfire between the executive and legislative powers were only "smokescreens" and in no way impediments to failing to enact laws with agreed economic contents.

Additionally, given that judicial power has the delicate task of being a settler or guarantor in major conflicts not only between civility but also between powers, the independence of this power is much more strategically crucial and must remain untainted from its origin and formation and during its operation. To this end, we suggest that the titular members of the main institutions that comprise it (members of the Supreme Court, the Constitutional Court, the Supreme Prosecutor, and some other positions that have the nature and requirement of impartiality, neutrality and autonomy, such as senior officials of the electoral power, the Attorney General's Office, the Comptroller's Office, the Ombudsman's Office) are not subject to the exclusive election of any specific power but rather are designated with the assistance of various powers and civil institutions.

It must be clearly established that the elections for said positions must respond to strict criteria of technical and professional suitability and proven experience in the respective areas and, therefore, must be free of political-partisan nuances or political sympathies or antipathies. This situation has led to suspicions, doubts, subterfuges of manipulations and other collusion within the parties, between parties and between powers of the State.

On this complicated topic, Dr. Francisco Durand maintains in the same work cited:

> "The third reform, where there is more failure and fewer results, is that of the justice administration system. The result of this order of priorities is that we have a country with institutions that are functional to the market economy and economic globalization, while the rest fail. <u>There has never been in this elite (it refers to the economic powers) a plan, an idea, a concept that a total transformation of the State had to be carried out and, could not be abandoned, the poor sectors</u>, which required a good state education, good health services, good police, honest judges. We are paying that price. This shows that this power elite basically has a short-term vision.

> "<u>We are in a country</u> that is difficult to predict, <u>inherently unstable</u>. That has always been a characteristic of Peruvian political history. The Guano Republic collapsed with the war with Chile after a difficult transition. Then

came the oligarchic republic, which Leguía liquidated. We have had dictatorships and governments of different types. And now we are in the corporate republic, which was inaugurated in 1990 and continues from 2000 under conditions of formal democracy. <u>A purchased democracy, let's say, that does not really correspond to the aspirations of the masses</u> because each president who comes to power usually offers something that he later does not fulfill and hides his relations with the great economic powers. (underlining is ours).

When in political and business management, reason and good judgment oriented towards respect for individual rights and society as a nation are neglected, it results in inadequate channels that prioritize emotionality, sentimentality, externalities towards undesirable routes of authoritarianism, corruption, criminality and other deviations that tend to privilege the interests of power elites. However, to avoid the imprudence of biased absolute criteria, it is necessary to point out the necessary perseverance of a determined heart but committed to ethics (contrary to the anti-values described above) and consistent in gesture and spirit with it so that it feeds energy to that force required by a leadership where reason predominates and consequently, the tasks of necessary and desired changes are fulfilled.

5.9. FICTIONS, REALITIES, CULTURAL CONTRIBUTIONS, AND SOME RESTRICTIONS

Despite the contradiction of opposite concepts between, for example, fiction and reality, researchers usually use the first (fiction) to better understand the tangled panorama that the second (reality) presents to us. So, the apparent contradiction gives way to a certain complementarity. To do this, we have dared to use some imaginative devices, transfers of temporary settings, hypotheses and figurative assumptions, quotes from writers in fictional works, brief reviews of film productions and, in general, any device that confirms that the filter of fiction is of great help for scientific curiosity to penetrate the mysteries of reality. That is, it is valid to use fiction to improve knowledge of reality.

The best example of this is the prominent scientist, Mr. Albert Einstein[42], with an exaggeratedly curious and imaginative personality, who, without fear of being mistaken, would

---

[42] see: Walter Isaacson: "Einstein. Su vida y su universo…" op. cit, page 592

have expressed his approval of the statement in the preceding paragraph since we know his quote: "I don't have no special talent, I'm just passionately curious." Likewise, compiler Peggy Anderson [43] picks up the phrase: "The important thing is not to stop questioning. Curiosity has its own reason for existence...Never lose your spirit of curiosity." His imaginative devices in advancing his theory of relativity are known.

On the other hand, the imagination can, for example, take elements of reality and project and develop fantastical and magical fiction (subjective and unreal) with which we tend to sweeten, alleviate, and cope with the always hazardous reality. In this case, fiction is not the means but the end, the intangible final product that provides the public with entertainment that increases their well-being.

Without fear of being wrong, we maintain that Mr. Walt Disney and those who followed the same path as Mr. Stan Lee, creator of the successful Marvel comic strips (Spider-Man, Iron Man, Thor, Hulk, the Fantastic Four, etc.) They successfully brought their creative fiction to the cinematographic world of entertainment with the same purpose of providing that touch of charm for our complicated reality. In the same direction, Mrs. J. K. Rowling, creator of successful youth novels, also made into films in the Harry Potter saga; Mr. George Lucas and his Star Wars films and so many other writers, producers, artists, and other professionals have made brilliant use of their imagination to, through entertainment and culture, put their contribution fee in improving our quality of life.

According to what has been described, the apparent contradiction between fiction and reality is suspended in conceptual and theoretical generality. They relate harmoniously in a fine imagination and are complemented and reinforced. In fact, whether through means and motives of curiosity, the human mind structures its own imaginative arsenal to analyze reality, deduce its principles and help us to better understand it (task of Einstein and his Theory of Relativity) and also from of this reality, there are those who, making use of that same imaginative potential, have built and developed an amazing filter of fiction that transports us and makes us cope with reality in a more entertaining and improved way (task by W. Disney, his magical world of Disneyworld and those who followed that same route).

---

[43] "Great quotes from...", op cit. page LD12

Beyond what could be assumed as a simple variety of curiosities and imaginations, fiction acquires special connotations because when economists look at the "entertainment" industry, we are absorbed to see that, according to reports from The Economist magazine, Nov 16-22 2019, p. 13, the businesses included in this activity have spent a substantial amount of 650 billion dollars in acquisitions and programming in the last five years.

Given that the flow of investment usually sniffs out and precedes the flow of profits, and these, in turn, direct part of them to ensure a reciprocal spiral between both, we can conclude that, for quite some time now, **the magic of fiction has been turning into reality, huge profits for its creators.** Hopefully, the imaginative attempts developed in this work will lead us along the same route.

The note of good humor in what was written in the previous line is intended to relocate us to that contrast between fiction (desired) and reality (experienced). We can ask ourselves how, from our profession and experience, can we contribute so that this critical Peruvian socioeconomic reality breaks away from those structural rigidities that have tied it and moves toward "that fiction of an imaginary society with greater well-being and social justice? The renowned Peruvian economist Richard Webb gives us an important direction (See: "Subibaja del Economista, A reflection on the future of economic science" at www.grade.org.pe/novedades/subibaja-del-economista-por-richard-webb/ October 13, 2014).

In this article, the author expresses the disappointments in the evolution of the Economics career, and in his investigations, he points out:

> "...with the help of Google, I made a leap...to the top of the profession, where four prominent economists - including two Nobel Prize winners -they met to debate the future of economic science. Confessing their own failure to foresee and prevent the global financial crisis (which preceded the meeting), they believed that the orthodox model of economics has become more of a cult than a science and **that it was necessary to multiply scientific creativity and pay more attention to issues such as inequality, happiness, institutions, culture, and power".** (highlighting is ours).

Our curiosity in developing this work has coincided with the message of the cited article. We have tried to venture into that institutionality called companies and governments to unravel the complexity of their management and propose a management framework in terms of effectiveness and efficiency as conditions to achieve a satisfactorily administered management. In this framework, we have postulated, among other things, that the effectiveness derived from participatory leadership, identified and supported by a change-promoting organizational culture and values, plays a significant role, equal to and sometimes greater than the efficient execution of any implementation process in direction and allocation of resources. Such effectiveness and efficiency efforts converge not only for satisfactory management but also to strengthen tasks of bridging inequalities gaps and achieving greater general well-being of all economic agents (companies, governments, workers, professionals, consumers, investors, artists, from home, etc.).

How can we overcome the pessimism that is instilled by vain attempts to change and improve things? How can we overcome this latent crisis of leadership and disrupted values that threaten signs of permanence not only in Peru but in several Latin American countries (and in other regions of the world)? Ideas are fought with ideas. Culture and the values that support it open windows for us: colloquiums, debates, essays, approaches, and proposals contained in written works, film works, works of art and of course (and although it may not seem like it) in musical works and songs.

Everything we experience in this amazing cultural scenario appears with a certain veil of neutrality, unintelligible, but often as Donella H. Meadows maintains: "…in certain cases, the least obvious part of a system that is related to its function or purpose is the one that most influences the behavior of that system." (See: "Pensando em systems," Original title in English: Thinking in Systems, Translation Paulo Alfonso, 1st Ed, Rio de Janeiro, Sextante, 2022, page 31.

For this reason, we consider that, by digging deeper into said cultural scenario and deciphering the relative importance of respect to the other components of the systemic scenario, it is usually seen that this culture allows us to appreciate, whether intentionally, subliminally or surreptitiously, various forms and modalities regarding how are nourished, maintained, reinforced and modified (slightly or substantially) those conceptions, archetypes, roots and everything and all that we previously called "worldview" that guides us and clarifies a better knowledge of the entire system, of the elements that comprise it and their interrelationships.

It is now understood why the Peruvian anthropologist and historian Luis Guillermo Lumbreras supports and defends the cultural rights of our people and, within them, first, their right to preserve their native language. Sharing this approach, we also add in section 4.3.3 Populism in Peru, the right of communities to claim all other artistic expressions. Knowledge of these particularities will improve our knowledge of the integrity of any system. Before, we have rescued musical themes (El Plebeyo and Flor de Retama) to highlight that cultural expressiveness, but the same can be found in any other artistic manifestation: a painting, a sculpture, a handmade work, a poem, etc.

In this sense, and although it may seem innocent and insubstantial, I allow myself to continue this route and take the thread of the songs as an active element of this cultural scene and appeal on this occasion to the inspiration of an Argentine bard: Enrique Santos Discépolo, already deceased, to remember his tango "Cambalache" whose original version original composed it in 1934. Let us mentally transport its message to our reality to verify admirable coincidences. Let us see it:

> ♫♫ "The world was and will be crap, I know it. In five hundred and six and in two thousand too. That there have always been thieves, Machiavellians and scammed, happy and bitter, values and dublés. But that the twentieth century is a display of insolent evil, there is no longer anyone who denies it. We live wallowing in a meringue and in the same mud, we all groped each other.

> Today it turns out that it is the same to be right as to be a traitor, ignorant, wise or thief, generous or swindler. Everything is the same, nothing is better! A donkey is the same as a great teacher! There are no postponements, no ladder, the immoral have equaled us... If one lives in imposture and another steal for his ambition, it does not matter whether he is a priest, a mattress maker, king of clubs, cheeky or a stowaway.

> What a lack of respect, what an attack on reason! Anyone is a lord; anyone is a thief! Mixed with Stravinski goes Don Bosco and "La Mignon," Don Chicho and Napoleon, Carnera and San Martin… Just like the disrespectful stained-glass window of the "Cambalache" (exchanges) has mixed with life and wounded by a sword without rivets, you see the Bible cry against a heater.

> … Twentieth-century cambalache problematic and feverish, he who does not cry does not suck, and he who does not steal is a fool. Just try it, give it a go! We're going to find each other there in the oven! Don't think anymore; sit down, no one cares if you were born honorable. He who works night and day like an ox is the same, as he who lives off others, as he who kills, as he who heals, or who is outside the law..."

(see: https://letrastango.com/letra/cambalache **and**

https://www.infobae.com/sociedad/2022/10/31/los-personajes-de-cambalache-generales-santos-mafiosos-boxeadores-y-estafadores-como-retratos-de-una-epoca/ **)**

Comments:

Only for clarification purposes is it necessary to explain expressions because they are common slang or idiomatic customs at that time. The term "Cambalache" refers to a situation where, in a chaotic, disorderly, and mixed manner, things are brought together to be bought and sold, and products (valued or undervalued) of diverse natures and origins are negotiated (Like a Flea Market). Prices are normally determined based on haggling, needs and constraints of sellers and buyers. In economic terms, it is a very sui generis market that exists in all countries with informal economies and agents. However, rather than explaining the material content of the term cambalache, the author emphasizes the essence and quality that this term involves in that background of social life.

With admirable success, the author projects that disenchantment, that pessimism and appreciation that "the world was and will be a mess in 506 and in 2000 as well" (we do not know why he chose that initial year or if he only did it to accentuate the temporality of a situation that he describes in force for fifteen centuries). Given what we have been experiencing in this first quarter of this twenty-first century, it is not inappropriate to assume that we will continue to live together until we do not know when the same unpleasantness of his denunciation. That is the experience of a socioeconomic model with notable signs of permanent decay.

"There have always been swindlers, Machiavellians and scammers" refers to the fact that thieves, malicious people, and ill-intentioned people who have taken advantage of easily defrauded victims have always coexisted. Likewise, the lyrics point out that "values and dublés" coexist; that is, in society, people who exhibit credentials of values of well-known personal or professional recognition coexist in an intermingled manner with counterfeiters, imitators and mediocre careerists. "We live wallowing in a meringue, in the same mud, we all mess around." that is, we live in an adulterated society, all aggrieved because good and bad are mixed and confused.

In this twentieth century of insolent evil, the author notes with exceptional crudeness and severity, "it is the same to be upright or a traitor, ignorant or wise, generous or swindler." That is, the appreciable (or detestable) quality in the essence of people is not differentiated or distinguished. "Everything is the same... a donkey is the same as a great professor (with the forgiveness of the donkey who, according to experts, is more intelligent than supposed).

There are no postponements, no ladder, the immoral have equaled us." Since that time the author emphasizes that meritocracy ceased to exist. People and different social roles, politicians, authorities, priests, businesspeople, consumers, public officials, and citizens in general are devalued by actions of clear deterioration. Some "live in imposture (falsehood, deceit, cheating, lying), and others steal in their ambition." The author's severe denunciation of a hypocritical society with disrupted values in both the ruling classes and those led.

…" which violates reason, anyone is a lord, anyone is a thief." The song describes egalitarianism with many contrasting characters, with a notorious and recurring presence in the media press and popular gatherings: "Mixed with Stavisky (a renowned swindler of the time who prided himself on interacting in social circles with politicians of the time) goes Don Bosco (Saint creator of the Salesian order) and La Mignon (female lover in the showbiz of the time), Don Chicho (Sicilian gangster established in Rosario city, finally deported) and Napoleon (French monarch), Carnera (famous Italian boxer, European heavyweight champion) and San Martin (liberator generalissimo of several countries in America)." For this reason, the author maintains: "just like in the disrespectful shop window, life has been mixed." Of course, amid the social chaos that typifies Cambalache, respectable personalities are contrasted in media complicity with characters of dubious reputation.

"…wounded by a sword without rivets, you see the Bible crying against a heater." The sword without a rivet has nothing to do with the known weapon, nor, as I mistakenly assumed, did said sword cross a Bible from one side to the other. The rivetless sword is a unique device like the hook used by butchers that hangs the toilet paper used in any toilet at one end. In the initial decades of the twentieth century, it was well-known how expensive and scarce such toilet paper was, and a convenient substitute was found and widespread: "Bible paper" of acceptable softness, fineness and silkiness. This was facilitated by the generosity of evangelical institutions that at that time used to distribute Bibles free of charge among the community, which used to use them for uses other than religious ones. This hook was hung on one side against the water heater (old water heaters), and the other end of the hook passed through the Bible, from which it was easy to slide the pages. The truth is that when needs (economic and physiological) are urgent, religious arrests and commitments are undermined.

465

We do not know if it was because of this crude irreverence to the religious spirit or because of the popular sarcasm that the lyrics meant in their denunciation and indignation against the "establishment" (or both reasons), which resulted in their veto, prohibition, and censorship of this song by of certain intolerable regimes. In the end, and as always, the forbidden tends to leak out, and its popularity increased to become one of the most consecrated songs in the Argentine musical anthology.

"...he who does not cry does not suck." The author collects this message that, to this day, has deeply penetrated popular sentiment. The phrase advises that you must be attentive and determined to claim, protest, and vehemently demand to obtain benefits or perks because, as always, you live surrounded by a series of restrictions, limitations and unforeseen events; if you do not carry out your demands, no one cares about your situation and no one will recognize you at all. Workers, businesspeople, taxpayers, consumers, producers, bankers, savers, exporters, etc., all of them "cry."

All economic agents "cry" as a way of exerting social pressure, without which it is difficult to think that they will obtain any concession or benefit. Unfortunately, those with decision-making capacity (authorities, bosses, administrators, etc.) have made it a habit to participate in this institutionalized practice, paying attention, rewarding, and making concessions only to those who protest and forgetting about those who do not.

"...and he who does not steal is a fool". This is a more perverse sentence because it classifies as stupid the honest person who fully fulfills his role. In other words, a person who steals, commits a crime, and remains unpunished is considered smart and skilled.

"Just try it, let's go, we're going to find each other there in the oven! Don't think anymore; Sit down, ...no one cares if you were born honorable! He who labors night and day like an ox is the same as he who lives off others, he who kills or heals or is outside the law". In this last sentence the author describes with accomplished mastery the distorted and grotesque nature of a social reality that for a century has continued to be copied and reproduced to the present and with signs of remaining in the decades to come.

What is the most impactful thing about this song? It is a manifest testimony of human precariousness and a desperate wake-up call that reveals and denounces the bad with the intention of correcting it and achieving the good. The validity of his message is admirable. If we wanted to update the song, it would be enough to change the name of certain characters (both bad and good). For example, we can replace Stravinsky with Bernie Madoff (a great New York swindler), Don Bosco with John Paul II, Mignon with Ciccolina, Don Chicho with Al Capone, the monarch Napoleon with the English monarch recently deceased Elizabeth II, to the boxer Primo Carnera by Muhamed Ali and to San Martin by the also generalissimo Franco. The names are superfluous and follow one another, the characters change, the settings and circumstances change, but what remains constant is that "disrespectful window of the Cambalaches that have changed our lives." To the point of distorting and disrupting it.

Mr. Atricio Milla Mardones comments in accurate depth on the message that Discépolo left us and explains why we decided to include it in this part of the work:

> "Cambalache," the author notes, "is the national anthem of the murky things in life, which gives us a philosophical, existential, prophetic and political summary of the 20th century, but it is clear that it is valid for the 21st century… Paradoxically, such maybe a tango is responsible for awakening the civic and political consciousness of the masses so that <u>we do not live a life of tango lyrics but of consistent and thoughtful beings who can have a critical vision of their contemporary national reality</u>".

(https://miscuentosconhistoria.blogspot.com/2011/02/tango-cambalache.html), Sunday, February 20, 2011. (underlining is ours)

We pose an additional reflection on the tricky questions: will our pathetic numbness continue to haunt us as we continue to consent to that "attack on reason where anyone is a lord, or anyone is a thief?" Will we continue singing this emblematic tango: "happy or bitter... wallow in a meringue…both the honest one who works night and day like an ox and the gangster who is outside the law"? This will depend on our covert or overt sympathies and experiences. Everything indicates that dance, its tragicomedy, and its daring social collusion will continue in force, and each one will have their motivations to reaffirm themselves in doing it, avoid it or counteract it according to their civic conscience.

In a glimpse of an answer, we share the appreciation of Donella H. Meadows (see: "Thinking in systems," Op. cit. pages 15-19), who holds that the problem maintains its profile because remain constant the behavioral patterns of people and institutions that in turn, they respond to conventional thought patterns that support them. In this regard, it is necessary to reaffirm what was previously stated that if we want to change attitudes (behavior patterns) we must first change that culture and set of values that impact thought patterns. This involves a double process of learning and unlearning values.

We consider that it corresponds to this cultural scenario in its aspect of songs and musical art that the people make their own, which constitutes one of the means that help us improve the understanding of the behavior and functionality of these varied systemic components. Paraphrasing that perspective indicated by Ortega y Gasset (on the relationship between the river and its channel), we can admit that said cultural contingent and its artistic manifestations will have to "contribute to the greater fluidity of that river and as one of its tributaries of that torrent of human creation, will reinforce their impulse in uncontrollable overflow to reach new channels."

As a culmination, we close this chapter with another important final reflection coming from a literary gem written decades ago, but also of undeniable permanence and importance with our management topic. Its author, Mr. Antoine de Saint Exupéry, in his famous work "The Little Prince," R. J. Ediciones, Caracas, shows off his brilliant imagination by providing us in a figurative sense, beautiful messages that we must keep in mind as reminders and recommendations in our coexistence social and in the scope of any type of management.

The central character of this imaginative writing is a boy decked out in prince's clothing on whose interplanetary itinerary we rescue two encounters. The first is his visit to the fourth planet inhabited by a "businessman" who was counting nearly five hundred million. The little prince started a conversation and asked (op. cit. pages 55-57):

> "Millions of what? The businessman responded: One of those little things that shine... that make lazy people dream. But I'm very serious! I don't have time to dream. Oh, stars? answered the little prince, and what are you doing with five hundred million stars? The businessman responded nothing again. I own them. And what is the use of having stars? said the little prince, it helps me to be rich, and what good is it to you to be rich? To buy other stars...I own the stars since no one before me thought of owning them...and what do you do with them? I administer them, I count them, and I tell them again... The little prince said - if I have a scarf, I can tie it around my neck and take it with me. If I have a flower, I can pick my flower and take it with me. But you can't catch the stars...

The little prince had other ideas of what it means to possess things...I – he continued saying – own a flower, which I water every day. I own three volcanoes, which I sweep every week... The fact that I own them is useful for my volcanoes, it is useful for my flower. But you are no use to your stars...the businessman opened his mouth but didn't know what to answer".

In this ingenious passage, the little prince reminds us that some older people believe they own something, but they do not realize that, by not being able (or not wanting) to dispose of it, enjoy its use and consumption, deep down, it is as if they did not own anything. On the other hand, possessing something implies developing an effort to maintain, conserve and strengthen what one possesses, that is, it implies the need to do things that are useful for what one possesses.

The parallel that this passage has with the message of Christian spirituality in the parable of the talents in the Gospel of Saint Matthew (25:14-30) is curious. When men receive material or immaterial gifts or goods (represented by talents) they are under the obligation to multiply them through their dedication and effort and are rewarded for it. Otherwise, he who remains inactive without any purpose of fruitfulness, whether due to excess caution, recklessness, negligence, laziness or for any reason whatsoever, will lose what was entrusted to him in possession.

From our approach, as economists, we have proposed in this work to recommend to businesspeople and entrepreneurs a management effort developed in a complementary manner with effectiveness and efficiency. But, from a more comprehensive perspective and as a form of self-criticism, the recommendation is incomplete because it must collect and assimilate that philosophical and spiritual wisdom, which we sometimes tend to receive in messages wrapped in storytelling, parables, and songs.

These are messages that make up that theory of good living, which reminds us of and makes us meditate that not everything should focus on pure effort and that even to stay in that direction, the essential effort must be alternated with the reflective pause of partial achievements 1 and compensatory feedback from the enjoyment of what one possesses or what one has earned. The fulfillment of a cycle of reciprocal and alternating effects between effort and enjoyment of what one possesses or receives must be expected, avoiding undesirable extremes of pure effort or pure enjoyment.

The second message contains the essence of the work and happens during his visit to the seventh planet, our planet Earth. Here, he meets a fox in the middle of the desert whom he invites to play and a dialogue [44] is established:

"...I can't play with you, I'm not tamed," said the fox, "what does taming mean?" asked the little prince... it means creating bonds... if you tame me, we will need each other. You will be, for me, unique in the world. I will be the only one in the world for you... it will be as if my life were filled with sunshine. I will know the sound of footsteps that will be different from all the others. The other steps make me hide under the ground. Yours will call me out of the den, like music.

Do you see, there, the wheat fields? The wheat fields don't remind me of anything. But you have hair the color of gold. Then, when you have tamed me, it will be wonderful! The wheat, which is golden, will bring me your memory. Men no longer have time to know anything, they buy ready-made things from sellers. Since there are no sellers of friends, men no longer have friends...if you want a friend, tame me.

What is there to do?" asked the little prince. We must have patience. You will start by sitting a little far from me... I will look at you out of the corner of my eye, and you won't say anything. Language is a reason for misunderstandings. But every day, you can sit a little closer. The next day, the little prince returned; the fox told him: it would have been better if you came back at the same time. If you come, for example, at four in the afternoon, from three o'clock onwards, I will begin to be happy, and at four o'clock I will become agitated... I will discover the price of happiness! Rituals are necessary. what is a ritual? said the little prince… it is what makes a day different from other days, an hour different from other hours."

In the first paragraph of the recent quote, the author explains through his characters the meaning of establishing a relationship of friendship that, in the context of the colloquial language of the work, uses the term "tame," explained as "creating bonds." This process leads to a reciprocal need between those who establish it. It is fueled by sensations, experiences and pleasant memories that make a loyal friend unique and appreciable (if you tell me you come at four in the afternoon, I will be happy from three!). The fox told the little prince that, due to the pressures of everyday life, men, unfortunately, no longer have friends.

---

[44] see:" El Principito", op. cit. pages 81-84

So that it is not misinterpreted that the noted quote and its previous comment are simple and illusory literary fictions that are not relevant, we reaffirm what was stated before (see section 2.3.1) regarding that the management of a company, will be to <u>conduct it not only</u> in a framework of technical efficiency but must contemplate forms, channels or means that allow people who make it up to realize yourself professionally and personally. It was also stated that the sciences that study human behavior, such as psychology, maintain that the person develops the maximum of his capacity when he truly believes and trusts in what he does and believes and trusts in those who accompany him in his work do, that is say when there is **mutual reliability**.

We also reiterate the previous concept that the organization or company cannot be conceived only as a structure limited to generating wealth. From a less economic perspective, as we said, an organization cannot be separated from being made up of people who possess a culture and values that they receive and project from it to society and vice versa. For all these reasons, we consider that, in any organization, "the creation of bonds" of sincere and true friendship between members of a business team and between employees and managers is important to advance the necessary reliability and specify the achievement of shared objectives.

The second paragraph of the quote reveals to us what must be done to create bonds or "domestication," as referred to in the work. In this unique lesson in human relations, the curious tactic to achieve said domestication reveals to us that, in this process, there are two key procedures: first, understanding that forms or formalities are important to get to the bottom of things. Here, gradualness, step by step, stands out; hasty advances, burning stages, or creating shortcuts are not advisable. We must forget about temporal pressures.

Secondly, avoid abuse of language or displays of swear words. The haste of clarifications and direct confrontations may be inopportune at this stage. More important is that body language of attitudes and gestures that speak louder than words and avoid their misinterpretation (I will look at you out of the corner of my eye! pointed out the fox). With such procedures, this gradual approach will be obtained (every day you will sit closer! indicated the fox). Within these formalities, the recommendation of the reference to Rite, normally understood as that set of rules, practices and forms established in settings of religious, political, and social institutions, does not cease to surprise. In establishing ties, sticking to a recurring "modus operandi" (we will see each other regularly during a certain time of the day or week! noted the fox) will help prepare an environment of favorable expectations.

When we want to establish or strengthen a sincere relationship of appreciation, friendship, solidarity; when we extend attention, an invitation, a simple greeting, a present with its wrapping detail or anything else addressed to any person whom we want to entertain, whether in our environment (girlfriend, wife, parents, children, co-workers, friends, etc.) or people from less known or frequent backgrounds; let us keep in mind the ritual recommendation of the fox and also the advice of the French writer and playwright Pierre Corneille (1606-1684): "The way of giving is worth more than what is given."

It is worth making the reservation that several comments on Corneille's phrase have mostly pigeonholed it into trivial messages of "charity." For us, the forms, the gestures of what is given, go beyond any sphere of charity or simply good manners because this can hide or disguise covert forms of hypocrisy. Therefore, we must pay special attention to body language, which allows us to appreciate the sincerity, honesty, and spirit of the offeror. Body language does not lie and reveals to us the compatibility or discrepancy between what is mere appearance and what is substantial or true.

Writing these lines, I remembered part of the lyrics of a well-known Peruvian waltz by the famous composer Augusto Polo Campos that captures the longing for a customary rite in a heartfelt sentimental relationship that goes like this:

> "Every Sunday at twelve, I will go out to the window to wait for you as before after mass and in the lonely corner, I will see my soul, which awaits your steps, looking for my arms and without your smile, the sun will go away from the morning tomorrow, the bells will cry for you, every Sunday at twelve o'clock after, after mass."

For this reason, let us not ignore the rites and formalities. As the fox pointed out in his dialogue with the little prince, Pierre Corneille and our remembered Augusto Polo Campos, let us agree that rites, gestures, and forms are necessary and important; they have a singular and almost magical effect, and, for some reason, they are part of good social coexistence. The message represents a lesson in human relations.

But that is not all. The most important thing remains to be mentioned. Continuing with the incidents of the story, the little prince finally managed to tame the fox, and before saying goodbye and as a preview of the meaning of a "creation of bonds," the fox told the little prince [45]:

> "…go see the roses again. You will understand. That yours is unique in the world. You will come back... and I will give you a secret. When the little prince saw the roses, he told them: You are exceptionally beautiful, but you are empty... we cannot die for you... my rose looks like you, but it alone is more important than all of you: because I watered it. Because I killed the caterpillars. Because I heard her complain, boast, or even sometimes remain silent. He turned to the fox and said goodbye... This is my secret, said the fox: You only live well with your heart. The essential is invisible to the eyes… you become responsible forever for what you have domesticated."

The quote relates the crowning message of the author's work: **The essential is invisible to the eyes**. In the development and commitment of our tasks, we will establish human relationships of a personal, family, work, communal and social nature. We must keep in mind that, as we advance along our path, achievements of a material, tangible, and physical nature must be accompanied and constitute shared results with that set of invisible qualities and virtues: honesty, commitment to service, courage, creativity, loyalty, collaboration, respect, formality, and that whole group of values described in previous chapters.

These invisible pillars will be the basis that will reinforce this process of "domestication or creation of bonds" alluded to by the fox in his dialogue with the little prince and will be the ones that transform us into people who possess that reliability, probity and good aura sense in any task to undertake or in any task to which we are called.

Among these essential and invisible things, we must keep in mind not only what must be done but also what requires caution or what must be avoided. We are facing a kind of obtundation because of postmodernity, the computer revolution, idioms, consumerism, etc., which, according to Mr. Marco Aurelio Denegri in his renowned televised programs "The Function of the Word," used to make clear mention of several terms accompanied by "ism" suffixes that disrupt and weaken our criteria, judgments and confuse our perceptions. Here, we present some of them and add others for your complete understanding. For example, when dealing with the issue of choosing investment options or any business venture, we noticed a notorious **superficialism**, spontaneity

---

[45] see: "El Principito", op. cit. pages 84-85

and lack of depth or lack of foundations with which a crucial issue was approached by neophytes and improvisers who start a venture with a lack of analysis, evaluation, and monitoring.

Hand in hand with the above, we mention this propensity to do things in the easiest way by looking for the good, nice and cheap (profitable or profitable) but with minimal effort and without any sacrifice. This predisposition towards ease (that word in Spanish is "facilismo'), although it is advantageous in the production or obtaining of practical and utilitarian results, also leads us to the erroneous conception that tends to despise or discard everything that involves effort. With this, two fundamental facts are unknown: firstly, the experience of life goes hand in hand with that group of difficulties and problems which are inherent and unavoidable facts that we all face. So, leaning towards what is easy does not mean automatically discarding or freeing ourselves from problems because they will always be present to gauge our strength. Secondly, facing challenges, developing efforts and assuming responsibilities is also a way of testing capabilities and increasing one's confidence. To refuse to do so is to remain stagnant, paralyzed, fearful and to lose the opportunity to improve oneself.

Another aspect that requires caution is the tendency towards **immediatism** among social agents. In this case, a way of acting predominates, akin to thinking immediately, thoughtlessly, and reactively, that only considers short-term facts or circumstances to the detriment of more reflective and medium or long-term considerations. In addition to the temporal connotation of what is quick, urgent, and fast there is also a spatial connotation related to what is close, adjacent, or contiguous that allows a temporary advantage. All of this to the detriment of options that offer stability and gradualness and that, above considerations of time (short term) and space (proximity), allow advantages of greater sustainability. On the personal and social level, for example, selfish immediatism characterized by crises of relationships and family, work, neighborhood, and social ties are referred to.

On the political and economic level, immediatism does not think about promoting collective well-being in the long term but rather focuses its attention on making profits in the short term in accordance with some sectors and interests. As we saw in the proposal of prominent Peruvian researchers, the political and economic classes and elites have frequently been reticent and evasive in implementing or promoting plans, programs, and State policies of national coverage. In this way, projects with a comprehensive and national perspective for the benefit of future generations and, in the longer term, were, due to immediate tendencies, continually postponed and unknown.

In addition to what has been described above, it is worth emphasizing that the achievement of satisfactory organizational and business management suggests, in accordance with the previous paragraph, the demand for an inclusive social order as well as the convenience of avoiding **deviationism** and sliding into vicious circles where said elites remain many sometimes seduced by excessive ambitions for power and by that set of very visible anti-values of human temptations (corruption, bribery, betrayal, toxic feelings of hatred, antipathies, revenge, intrigues, illicit and criminal acts, worldly vices, obtaining profits at any cost, etc.).

The above is also linked to another perspective known as **fragmentalism,** through which decisions, actions and objectives tend to be made in isolation or partial, without a comprehensive consideration of how they affect the entire system to which they belong. This contrasts with the other recommended way of facing life with a holistic vision or a deep understanding of the interrelationships between various aspects of life, such as a professional or technical career, personal relationships, health, and emotional and social well-being. For example, a person who adopts a fragmentary perspective in his or her career will focus solely on professional advancement and dedicate most of his or her time and energy to work, neglecting other important aspects of life, such as personal, family relationships, or their health and communal or social commitments or responsibilities.

Finally, and to close reflections on the suffix's "-ism" of notorious and significant importance because they disrupt perceptions, we cannot fail to mention the contrasting terminology between **"triumphalism vs. pessimism."** Both with favorable and unfavorable nuances. While triumphalism has in its favor the highlighting of achievements, progress, and possibilities for improvement, all of which inspire currents of evolution, growth, and entrepreneurship; Pessimism has in its favor the fact that it makes us see problems, difficulties and adverse possibilities that induce advisable attitudes of caution and prevention of errors.

For its part, the great disadvantage of triumphalist positions is the overvaluation of their potential and the underestimation of risks that end up dislocating them and distorting their own reality. Obnubilation is their norm and the reason for their failure or fall (Hitler and Napoleon are clear examples of this). While the great disadvantage of pessimists is precisely an overestimation of difficulties and risks to the point of underestimating solutions and decreasing confidence in applying them. All of this translates into paralyzing, timid, and unproductive positions in situations that demand commitment to desirable changes. Their rule is summarized in: "why start something that will not change anything." Finally, like many things in life, each person must avoid extreme situations and, according to their circumstances, find their own optimal balance or bias.

After the varied reflections of ideas and contrasts described in this chapter, what we maintained in the Introduction of this work becomes clearer. We are going to err on the side of being redundant and reaffirm it: "The convulsive scenario and our own mental conditioning disrupt our perception of evidence, making us see what has a substantial character as if it were complementary in nature or also what is complementary as substantial. Errors in perspective are inevitable."

In this same sense, the caution that we suggest in the prologue of this work has to do with the behavior of the macrosystems in which we are immersed. On the one hand, in countries in the capitalist orbit, the onslaught of strong nationalist and protectionist winds, defense of concessions and tax advantages, reorientation of selective subsidies in response to changes in energy and technological patterns, or even revaluation and prioritization of concepts of security and national interest in all the cumbersome instruments of public policies. All of this has been translated into greater strengthening and government intervention in liberal economies. The accentuation of this trend, despite the displeasure of ultra-conservative positions, cannot be ignored because it exposes the fragility of the free market principle as the only and best mechanism resource allocator.

The staunch defenders of this free-market principle are worried and even blushing when they see that state intervention is essential to support it. Why do the most important economies of the West break the purity of the principle and have to admit and move towards this undesirable turn of state strengthening in their economies?

On the other hand, in countries with socialist systems, due to the need for openness and competition (consistent with liberal criteria), central planning must relax its precepts to mold and adapt to provide and meet the requirements, conditions and demands of the open market in which they participate. Also, due to the interdependent nature of the global market and because no country meets the conditions of self-sufficiency, in these socialist countries, it is also of utmost importance to supply themselves goods and services from liberal economies for their respective internal markets. This introduction of liberality into their economies and the benefits derived from it (quite verifiable in the Chinese economy) has also called into question the purity of the unwavering guidelines dictated by technocrats regarding central planning as the only and best mechanism for allocating resources.

In this case, the staunch defenders of central planning also find it worrying and even embarrassing to accept the essential interconnection with liberal free market economies to support and prevent the expiration of their dynamism and their planning mechanism. Why do the most important economies of the socialist orbit loosen the purity of the planning principle and have to admit and cannot discard the interconnection with liberal economies to give new vigor to their suffocating planning centralism?

In this regard, we maintain that in this contrast between, on the one hand, the pragmatism posed by realities and, on the other hand, the orientation and follow-up of doctrinal principles, policy makers and leaders of representative countries of both systems are inclined to prioritize an instrumental in favor of the first (pragmatism) partially sacrificing the second (principles and doctrines). In this sense, the unconditional defense of resource allocation mechanisms, read "free market" in neoliberal capitalist systems and "central planning" in totalitarian socialist systems, are supported by fragile columns that are being eroded by reluctant forces and countercurrents within their same systems.

The appreciation of Systems Theory seems to gain validity by maintaining that it is the components of the systems themselves that develop their own corrective forces or attractors to chaos (or boom) to, for example, balance chaos towards stability, introducing a certain order into the disorder or, on the contrary, the same systemic evolution of a relatively ordered scheme generates a certain disorder that requires compensatory adjustments. In verification of this dynamic, we put cold cloths and appease the concern of recalcitrant defenders of the purity of the principles described above (free market and central planning) to tell them to calm down, that they can remain faithful to their flags but with due diligence, prudence and reservations because we are in a transition process where some of the elements and some of their interrelationships show mutation, but the purposes and functionalities of each system as a whole are still maintained.

From this perspective, this mutation fits within a temperance scheme imposed on both macrosystems. While the hegemonic confrontations are elucidated (on the stages of economic, military, technological, etc.), we will have to get used to living with these spawns of State Capitalism current in socialist systems or of Statism strengthened with private predominance current in neoliberal systems. That will be, for now, the new troupe (with parades, suits, and costumes) in which it must develop the business and organizational management.

Just as the Industrial Revolution in its century of existence (1760-1870) led to important socioeconomic changes and was accompanied by philosophical doctrines and thought - such as liberalism and Marxism - that supported their respective realities and continued in force after it.

Almost two centuries of evolution have passed, where in recent decades, an impressive speed of scientific and technological advances has been accentuated as never seen before, and that will impact and transform the world not only in its material or physical aspect of what and how to do things but also in that other immaterial aspect of values, life expectations, human relationships between people and countries, and the predominance of cultures and hegemonies.

It is not out of place to consider that the current technological revolution, with artificial intelligence included, causes such magnitude of changes that by provoking future socioeconomic scenarios, and it is also accompanied by renewed philosophical doctrines different from the currents in vogue and against all odds, they end up burying obsolete doctrines due to their almost two hundred average years of presence. Understanding the philosophical and engineering challenges posed by the recent technological complexities opens another debate, which is in its beginning.

CONCLUSIONS

- The factors that we classify as "levers of effectiveness" have the characteristic of becoming necessary conditions to hit the bull (target) of "achieving those desired results and the right things." That is, having a planning strategy, having an institutional leadership scheme, and projecting a business culture with business sustainability values; they are factors that, regardless of their dose of content and mixtures, aim to achieve Effective processes.

- We conceptualize Strategy as a dual tool. Strategic Formulation is linked to Effectiveness, while Strategy Implementation is linked to Efficiency. Mistakes are often made with or without a Strategy, but having it allows us to examine where, how, and why we failed. In this, we must consider that, in terms of business management, improvisations and placing hopes on chance play against us.

- Leadership responds to a process of social influence of complex personal interrelationships to guide, structure and facilitate behaviors, activities and relationships oriented towards the achievement of shared goals whose results matter not because of the specific qualities of a person or an admirable group of people. (read leaders), but this process allows for achieving organizational effectiveness. Leadership allows us to anticipate, promote, and face changes because it enhances opportunities and avoids identified risks.

- The Organizational Culture is constituted as the predominant philosophy in the company; it is structured based on a set of values and beliefs that determine the "modus vivendi," the way of facing and solving problems and the degree of resulting commitment, individual and group, of the members of any organization. One of the most important reasons for the failure of many change projects (strategy changes, system changes, organizational structure changes, administrative and operational process changes, policy changes, etc.) is because they lack the intention to address something as important as cultural change based on values that in turn promote the attitudes of the proposed changes.

- Social responsibility, as one of the elements of an organizational culture, covers a variety of areas described (economic, legal, ethical, and philanthropic) and have communication and dependency channels configured between them. When this is not understood, then there are cases of companies that, despite successfully undertaking their economic and legal responsibility, will be seen as greedy entities that only enjoy for themselves the profits

479

and surpluses obtained without the intention of sharing a voluntary portion of these. with the community where they operate.

- From the perspective of efficiency and the management techniques that comprise it, business management is comprised of executive activities in the daily grind and involves the management and allocation of resources in the face of changing and unforeseen situations. The efficiency platform conceived as the "best way of doing things" includes the integrated and harmonious development of its components (Organization, Direction Management and Control and Evaluation), which will allow management to approach and adjust towards the proposed goals and will be carefully achieved by overcoming the obstacles and inconveniences that harsh reality demands.

- The "Organization" component is responsible for the formation of the support structure for the desired change, that is, the organizational architecture of the company. It is a macrosystem composed of business systems and subsystems (operational, commercial, administrative, financial, logistical, IT, etc.) that are structured as a kind of "tailor-made suit" for each user and will vary depending on the business, size of the organization, technological availability, business cycle, economic situation, budget restrictions, etc. The business organization chart and the description of its functionality and structure simply constitute the scaffolding on which this macro system will rest.

- The Implementation phase will continue with the development of another macro system, which is the execution of activities aimed at initiating, modifying, improving, or also strengthening the current business reality. That is, it is the Direction and execution itself. Here, it is up to you to decide the day-to-day management work related to the allocation of resources to evaluate and operate the operation of the different business systems. The harsh reality imposes certain conditions that force a certain flexibility in the planning framework. How contradictions or controversies between what was formulated and what was implemented are resolved will be an issue that management must elucidate. This phase will evaluate management capacity and expertise.

- Why are Control and Evaluation processes so necessary in an organization? Because behind any organization are the men who manage and develop them and some men, for assorted reasons and in the absence of control schemes, are prone and vulnerable to defect.

This is human nature; it appears confused and disturbed with old ties (of insatiable search for money, pleasure, power, etc.) in which few can unravel it, and another good part becomes disturbed, debased, clouded, succumbs and tangles more.

- Among the various restrictions and conditions that affect the achievement and permanence of satisfactory efficiency standards, we can highlight the so-called "cognitive blindness." This concept refers to certain aspects, problems, or criteria that, in certain circumstances, the governing or managerial body does not recognize, deny, or simply ignores. A respectable number of managers consider that only the efficiency achieved is sufficient to achieve subsequent effectiveness and business success.

- The previous assessment is part of a complicated situation of resistance to change, which in turn is another of the main difficulties manifested in the Implementation phase. Every process of restructuring, reorganization, and redefinition of procedures and positions involves changes. Many people see this as affecting their interests or personal positions, so they react by hindering the proposed projects and doing everything possible to make them fail or remain indifferent to their requirements.

- The implementation phase also presents other restrictions derived from transition problems that affect the proposed business systems (inadequate approaches to diagnoses and proposed solutions, unexpected economic situations, insufficient provision of human and financial resources, etc.). The adaptation process takes time and resources that are in direct proportion to two factors: From what level we start and to what level we aim, that is, the difficulties of transition must do in addition to their own problems with the magnitude of the desired change.

- When things are done correctly (understood within the framework of efficiency), one of the first symptoms is the recognition that the business engine is tuned, oiled, and prepared to show (and usually does) a growth performance continuous, stable, and sustained. Production volumes, sales income, clients served, positions worked, workers hired, facilities and material resources used, financial capital used and required, investments and new and complementary projects, etc. Everything is going within a notable framework of growth and impressive dynamics.

- Another recognized way to identify and measure efficiency is through productivity. It is a technical coefficient that measures the resulting relationship between the product and the inputs used in its production process. That is, there is a recognition of knowing that one is more efficient when one obtains more production while keeping the amount of inputs constant or also obtains the same production with a smaller amount of inputs. In both cases, productivity will have increased.

In the Peruvian informal sector, an explosion of microenterprises survives, where low-skilled labor is hired with meager remuneration and, therefore, among other things, exhibits the lowest levels of productivity and profitability. The above leads us to reveal the directly proportional relationship between levels of informality and poverty, where the increase or decrease of one of them impacts the other and vice versa. But in the middle of them, and as a backdrop, productivity comes into play. It is no coincidence that elevated levels of informality, such as those seen in the Peruvian reality, participate in low levels of productivity. This completes the vicious circle of greater informality, greater poverty, and lower productivity, consolidating a permanent spiral of deterioration and precariousness.

- Another of the symptoms and outstanding characteristics of efficiency is Quality, which we understand as a process of continuous improvement of the product or service offered. Why is quality in management so important? First, it makes efforts not only in relation to the result of the product or service offered but also involves the entire company and is not limited to the functionality of a particular area. Secondly, quality is important because when a company delivers to the consumer a high dose of quality in the form of a product or service offered, this means not only increases in the company's profits but also involves an increase in quality of life in the satisfaction of that specific need and better well-being of society.

- The business entity is conceived as a complex system, with high sensitivity to events typical of the business environment, to innovation processes and in general to internal and external changes that give it a tendency to become destabilized, unbalanced and, in exceptional cases, even a propensity towards chaos. Systemic thinking warns us about the preponderance of environmental variability that, by causing a succession of links of causes and effects, amplifies imbalances and threatens the effectiveness and efficiency of any business management.

The business complexity referred to not only concerns large companies but also small business units. In this scenario, activities with a reduced profile are permitted by authorities are formed, such as retail trade in food, clothing and footwear, outpatient food establishments, and personal services. In today's Peru, those three-quarters of the workforce employed in this informal sector contributes only one-fifth of total production. The low productivity that this implies conditions or influences the resulting productivity for the national total. It is crucial to resolve the question of how to break part of this vicious circle of poverty where a trap of precariousness persists in which many people and small businesses in our economy are involved.

- It continues to be a great headache for politicians, academics, researchers, social scientists, and other brilliant minds. The still unresolved sociopolitical debate of the disparity and imbalance between this complex trilogy of a) Production and growth achieved (what, how, where) and for whom to produce), b) Income Distribution Patterns because of such growth, and c) Individual Rights and Freedoms that accompany the entire process.

- The debate is emerging and taking shape in the economic and business sphere between, on the one hand, those who staunchly defend free enterprise and economic liberalism (with reduced participation and intervention of the State) and, on the other, those who advocate a notorious degree of state intervention and control in the economy (with restricted private participation in it). Behind each option described, there is a separate way of conceiving, specifying and prioritizing production and growth; a separate way of conceptualizing and distributing the income generated from such growth and a different way of considering individual freedoms and rights. Defenders and detractors of both approaches have found their place in government administrations at different times and in different countries with dissimilar results.

- In this continuum between liberalism and interventionism, organizational management experiences greater or lesser degrees of freedom and restrictions where it is conditioned by that socioeconomic and political envelope. Additionally, business management will also face a different variability that corresponds to unforeseen and fortuitous events such as war conflicts, natural disasters (droughts, floods, earthquakes), new technological discoveries, fires, plagues, epidemics, social disorders, work stoppages, terrorism, etc., which make up another peculiar random envelope and constitutes part of that universe of events that are statistically difficult to predict.

- As part of this socioeconomic and political envelope, Populism or populist currents emerge, identifiable by a particular democratic appearance, mixed and shaded in the broad partisan political spectrum (right, center and left). The variability of parties and principles are formalisms that matter little; the underlying reason is to use said populism as a strategic means conducted by the elites of any social formation to consolidate, control, and remain in power. To this end, the key to populism has always been to consolidate that "people-elite" binomial so that with the support of citizens it makes it easier for them to direct the system to benefit their interests. The protagonists of said populism are aware that if they must lie or manipulate the mass of citizens, there will be no choice but to do so because the end (obtaining their electoral potential) justifies the means.

- Another essential element that acts as a springboard for populism is precisely the reactions to international upheavals and one of them is the resurgence of an immaculate nationalism. In the American case, Trump and his policy on the external front caused the USA, considered for decades to be the standard-bearer of free trade, to give up on said purpose and alleging an imbalance of perceived benefits with respect to its main competitors to become the standard-bearer of a protectionist nationalism and which also finds a marked distance from several international and multilateral organizations.

- The Peruvian (and Latin American) political scene of the last decades was not exempt from the populist phenomenon. There we have in Peru the elected political outsiders such as Alberto Fujimori, Alejandro Toledo, Ollanta Humala, Pedro Pablo Kuczynski, Martin Vizcarra and Pedro Castillo, who, in the heat of the electoral processes and in an "express" manner, created, to fulfill appearances, their own political party (without substance, form, or doctrine), or they turned out to be figureheads of existing improvised political parties.

We Peruvian citizens have been spectators of how the presidents described found it easy to catch unwary people and come to power, but once in power, it was extremely difficult for them to stay in power and conduct satisfactory management. The lack of a sufficient "political background" (support and knowledge) emerged, either due to inexperience, ineptitude, inexperience in the public management, and due to getting mixed up in the cocktail shaker of corrupt temptations.

What does the described mess of external envelopes have to do with business management? It has to do with it because when turning the page from the electoral environment to the economic and social reality, the quality of any public administration is no longer determined by intentions, promises and words but by actions, progress, achievements, and setbacks. These are the true, timely and objective signals that are provided to economic agents (businesspeople, producers, investors, merchants, consumers, workers, professionals, technicians, etc.) who, based on said signals, will make their respective decisions in the economic environment that concerns them. So, when such signals do not exist, are not clear, or simply show a wrong direction that ignores the recommendations of responsible advisors, specialists and scientists, a climate of uncertain expectations and instability is fostered.

- The appearance and expansion of the Coronavirus (COVID-19) pandemic that the world suffered (2020-2022) is part of that random envelope of external variability but of a different nature and connotation than the one previously mentioned (populism). The surprising expansion of said pandemic and the implementation of confinement policies have generated an unfavorable impact on the economic sphere of magnitudes never experienced with subsequent effects like any economic recession caused by it.

The recent events of Russia's invasion of Ukraine (Feb 24, 2022) make the world panorama look different because it has unleashed political and economic effects of such magnitude that it has projected a particular border controversy of a regional nature into a controversy with effects of global character. The losing protagonist will be, as in other episodes of hegemonic controversies, the country where the theater of operations took place, in this case, Ukraine and its people. Which is devastated with a regrettable balance of greater loss of life, destruction of physical facilities (homes, hospitals, buildings, energy supply plants, water, and other material resources) and with their inalienable right to claim what they consider their own. Its reconstruction will be long and tedious and will depend (as it currently is) on help from the West.

During this futurology, we remain with the suspicion that in the coming decades, a harmful influence of the probable hegemonies of the China-Russia front will be accentuated. The dangerous profiles of individual rights and freedoms predominant in such hegemonies can expand (by consent or imposition) to the rest of the world. The leadership of two autocratic monarchs and their respective styles of government present, from our perspective, obvious signs of false and deviant democracies.

Business and organizational management was seriously affected by the Coronavirus pandemic, which has imposed a complicated future on us with greater debt and financial burdens. Additionally, the other random external conditions with bellicose overtones will impose, for several years to come, an unfortunate mixture of inflation, scarcity and increase in the cost of energy sources, food, and other goods with a significant impact on levels and structures of costs and productivity, making it difficult for us to produce the same and survival becomes more difficult.

- We have proposed an instrumental tool that is relevant to visualize this interrelation between effectiveness and efficiency and their degree of reciprocal affectation or disaffection through the presentation of a matrix that relates effectiveness and efficiency. This instrument is an adaptation of the methodology proposed by the researcher Peter Baltes in his work cited in this work, where he develops the MACORE model (which is the acronym (in Spanish) for the components: goal, analysis, conceptualization, organization, realization, and evaluation).

The model and its components are configured in a linear and consecutive sequence, and in our essay, due to the nature of the entity under analysis, the company with its management complexity, such components are articulated in an interdependent and integral manner.

- From the perspective of our work, Added Value has an ambivalent connotation both from effectiveness when value is created on the demand side and from efficiency when value is created on the supply side. Managerial management that specifies value-added achievements promotes a simultaneity of effectiveness and efficiency, and these, in turn, have a reciprocal impact on consolidating and creating the conditions for subsequent achievements of added values. We are talking about transfers in the forces of supply and demand, generating greater income and/or lower costs, and increases in surpluses (of consumers and producers), all which results in favorable performances in the company or organization and benefits for internal clients and external to the company. Currently, it is large corporations and the innovative technology products developed by them which, due to their own entrepreneurial capacity, are at the forefront of these processes of searching for and obtaining added value.

- This technological trend that promotes greater added values is setting the tone for the new international division of labor where what to produce, how, where and for whom to produce has a new rationality. Will this technological implosion that we are experiencing in countries "icons of both social systems" (USA and China) finally end up imposing a new resource allocation mechanism that surpasses and even makes obsolete the unrestricted principles of the free market and/or central planning of such systems? After a century of those "Management Styles" that we showed in the first chapter, the Offer emerges again with such force that, through its accelerated technological processes, it is recycled again to become the protagonist of the next management styles.

- The emphasis of the proposed approach on effectiveness and efficiency is not at all new, the parts and pieces that compose it are well known and widely disseminated in a copious literature more extensively developed than those shown in this work. We have presented one of those ways to understand and undertake, in the best viable way this complex business management scheme. This presentation is described within a logical framework (effectiveness and efficiency matrix) that provides instrumentation for the detection of latent or hidden problems and thus obtains adequate clarity and perspective to undertake and complement desired solutions.

BIBLIOGRAPHY

- Anderson, Peggy. Great quotes from great leaders. Celebrating Excellence, Inc. 1992.

- Baltes, Peter. La vida buena. Teoría crítica del vivir, Lima, Universidad del Pacífico, 1999.

- Banerjee, Abhijit V. y Duflo Esther. Poor Economics. A radical rethinking of the way to fight Global Poverty. Reprint Public Affairs, USA, 2012.

- Baños, Pedro. El dominio mundial. Elementos del poder y claves geopolíticas. Editorial Planeta S.A. Primera Edición 2018.

- Basadre, Jorge. El azar en la historia y sus límites. Penguin Random House Grupo Editorial. 1971.

- Basadre, Jorge. Perú: Problema y Posibilidad y otros ensayos. Pinguin Random House Grupo Editorial. 2022.

- Bolden, Richard; Hawkins Beberly; Gosling Jonathan y Taylor Scott. Exploring Leadership. Oxford, University Press. 2011.

- Boron, Atilio. El sueño del marqués. Mario Vargas Llosa. Una pluma al servicio del imperio. Monte Avila Editores Latinoamericana, 1ra. Edición, 2021.

- Brickley, James; Smith Clifford y Zimmerman Jerold. Managerial Economics and Organizational Architecture. Third Edition. McGrow Hill Irwin. 2004.

- Carrillo, Fran (coordinador) y varios autores: "El porqué de los populismos. Un análisis del auge populista de derecha e izquierda a ambos lados del Atlántico. Ediciones Deusto 2017, España.

- Coelho, Paulo. El Alquimista. Harper Collins Publishers, New York, 1ra Edición Ilustrada, mayo 2007.

- de Mello, Anthony. El canto del pájaro. 26° Edición, Editorial Sal Terrae, 1997.

- de Saint Exupéry, Antoine. El Principito, R. J. Ediciones, Caracas

- Durand, Francisco. Los doce apóstoles de la economía peruana. Una mirada social a los grupos de poder limeños y provincianos. Pontificia Universidad Católica del Perú. Fondo Editorial, 2017, Lima, Perú.

- Ferrell, O. C; Fraedrich John y Ferrell Linda. Business Ethics: Ethical Decisions Making and Cases. Houghton Mifflin Co, New York, Sixth Edition, 2005.

- García, Salvador y Dolan Shimon. La Dirección por Valores. McGraw-Hill/IESE.España,1997.

- Gerber, Michael E. The E-Myth Revisited. Why Small Businesses Don't Work and What to Do About it. Harper Business, New York, 1995.

- Goleman, Daniel. La inteligencia emocional en la empresa. 1999 Ediciones Argentinas.

- Goslings and Mintzberg. The five minds of a manager. 2003, Harvard Business Review 81(11).

- Hatten, Timothy S. Small Business Management. Entrepreneurship and Beyond. Houghton Mifflin Company Third Edition, 2006.

- Isaacson, Walter. Einstein: Su vida y su universo. Debate, 1ra Ed, Set 2008.

- Jiménez Nieto, Juan Ignacio. Política y Administración. Editorial Tecnos, Madrid, 1970.

- Jones Gareth y George Jennifer. Contemporary Management. McGraw-Hill Irwin, Third Edition, 2003

- Kiyosaki, Robert T. Rich Dad's Cashflow Quadrant. Warner Business Book. New York, 2000.

- Kumar, Krishan. Imperios. Cinco regímenes imperiales que moldearon el mundo. Ediciones Pasado y Presente, SL 2018, Barcelona.

- Levitt, S y Dubner S. Freakonomics. Harper Collins Publishers, New York, 2006.

- Meadows, Donella H. Pensando em sistemas. 1ra Ed, Rio de Janeiro, Sextante, 2022. Traducido al portugués por Paulo Alfonso.

- Mintzberg, Henry; Quinn James B. y Voyer John. El Proceso Estratégico. Conceptos, Contextos y Casos. Primera Edición 1997.

- Mokate, Karin Marie. Eficacia, eficiencia, equidad y sostenibilidad: ¿Qué queremos decir?". Documento de Trabajo del INDES. Banco Interamericano de Desarrollo, Julio de 2001. Serie de Documentos de Trabajo I-24. Washington, D.C.

- Ortega y Gasset, José. El Espectador., Salvat Editores S.A, España, 1970.

- Orwell, George. "Rebelión en la Granja", 19a ed., Ciudad Autónoma de Buenos Aires: DeBolsillo, 2022.

- Peters, Thomas j. y Waterman Jr, Robert H. In Search for Excellence. Harper &Row, Publishers, New York, 1982.

- Portocarrero, S Felipe., (editor). El Pacto Infame. Estudio sobre la corrupción en el Perú. Primera Edición, marzo 2005.

- Salomon, Robert y Martin Clancy. Morality and Good Life. Fourth Edition, McGraw-Hill Companies, 2004.

- Samuelson, Paul. Economía. Undécima Edición 1983.

- Senge, Peter; Charlotte Roberts; Richard Ross; Bryan Smith y Art Kleiner. La Quinta Disciplina en la práctica. Ediciones Granica S.A. Barcelona, 1995.

- Talbott, John. The 86 Biggest Lies on Wall Street. Seven Stories Press, First Edition, New York, 2009

- Thompson Jr, Arthur y Strickland III A. J. Strategy Formulation and Implementation. Tasks of the General Manager. Business Publications, INC. Plano, Texas. Third Edition.

- Vallés, Carlos S.J. No Temas. San Pablo 1998, España.

- Vargas Llosa, Mario. El pez en el agua. Editorial Seix Barral, S.A 1993.

Sources consulted from Internet

- https://es.wikipedia.org/wiki/Philippe_P%C3%A9tain
- https://es.wikipedia.org/wiki/Colegio_Electoral_de_los_Estados_Unidos
- https://santodomingocorre.com/index.php/categoria-noticias/937-la-honestidad-del-atleta-ivan-fernandez-al-dejar-ganar-a-un-atleta-despistado)
- https://elpais.com/deportes/2012/12/14/actualidad/1355506756_770952.html
- https://www.biografiasyvidas.com/biografia/p/poma.ht
- https://www.project-syndicate.org/onpoint/american-democracy-on-the-brink-by-joseph-e--stiglitz-2018-06
- https://www.comexperu.org.pe/articulo/659-de-los-conflictos-socioambientales-registrados-en-enero-de-2022-corresponden-a-actividades-relacionadas-con-la-mineria
- https://en.wikipedia.org/wiki/Edward_Snowden
- https://en.wikipedia.org/wiki/Facebook#Privacy
- https://en.wikipedia.org/wiki/Cambridge_Analytica
- https://es.wikipedia.org/wiki/Investigaci%C3%B3n_del_fiscal_especial_de_los_Estados_Unidos_de_2017#:~:text=La%20investigaci%C3%B3n%20del%20fiscal%20especial%20de%20los%20Estados,que%20surjan%20en%20el%20curso%20de%20esta%20investigaci%C3%B3n.
- https://es.wikipedia.org/wiki/Accidente_del_transbordador_espacial_Challenger
- https://concepto.de/productividad/
- CIDEI - Sectores de Trabajo, Productividad y Dinámica Ocupacional (inei.gob.pe)
- https://gestion.pe/economia/inei-informal-pais-sigue-creciendo-formal-266936-noticia/
- https://www.eluniverso.com/entretenimiento/television/netflix-pierde-20000-suscriptores-en-lo-que-va-del-2022-nota
- https://idoc.pub/documents/ley-de-la-variedad-requerida-d49oj3j38649
- https://sites.google.com/site/padillaparelesleonardosistemas/2-1-propiedades-de-los-sistemas/2-1-10-ley-de-la-variedad-requerida) (appointment with restriction due to temporary availability)
- https://es.wikipedia.org/wiki/Muro_fronterizo_Estados_Unidos-M%C3%A9xico

- https://www.europarl.europa.eu/news/en/headlines/world/20190214STO26415/eu-us-trade-talks-the-issues-at-stake
- https://www.nytimes.com/2017/05/26/world/europe/nato-trump-spending.html
- https://es.wikipedia.org/wiki/Veracidad_de_las_declaraciones_de_Donald_Trump
- https://news.gallup.com/poll/203198/presidential-approval-ratings-donald-trump.aspx
- https://coronavirus.jhu.edu/map.html
- https://www.bbc.com/mundo/noticias-52578840
- https://www.bancomundial.org/es/news/press-release/2022/06/07/stagflation-risk-rises-amid-sharp-slowdown-in-growth-energy-markets
- https://www.imf.org/en/Publications/WEO/Issues/2022/04/19/world-economic-outlook-april-2022
- http://enfermed.mx/wp-content/uploads/2020/04/Curva-Pandemia-Recesion-400x435.png
- https://www.infobae.com/america/agencias/2020/04/17/reabrir-demasiado-pronto-hara-mas-dano-que-bien-noah-smith/
- https://www.global-rates.com/es/estadisticas-economicas/inflacion/indice-de-precios-al-consumo/ipc/estados-unidos.aspx
- https://estadisticas.bcrp.gob.pe/estadisticas/series/mensuales/resultados/PN38067GM/html/2020-1/2022-7/
- https://www.bancomundial.org/es/news/press-release/2023/01/10/global-economic-prospects
- https://elpais.com/internacional/2022-03-21/que-son-y-como-funcionan-los-misiles-hipersonicos-kinzhal-que-rusia-ha-lanzado-contra-ucrania.html
- https://www.motorpasion.com/industria/nueva-liberacion-masiva-barriles-petroleo-tratara-relajar-precios-frenar-hegemonia-rusa-sector-energetico
- https://www.france24.com/es/minuto-a-minuto/20220308-acuerdo-petrolero-con-eeuu-servir%C3%ADa-a-venezuela-ante-sanciones-a-rusia-dice-experto
- https://www.nytimes.com/es/2022/03/22/espanol/opinion/rusia-oposicion.html)
- https://www.reddit.com/r/atheism/comments/1bjpoa/this_image_demonstrates_how_perspective_can/#lightbox

- www.grade.org.pe/novedades/subibaja-del-economista-por-richard-webb/
- https://letrastango.com/letra/cambalache
- https://miscuentosconhistoria.blogspot.com/2011/02/tango-cambalache.html
- https://es.wikipedia.org/wiki/Flor_de_Retama
- https://www.cancioneros.com/letras/cancion/739535/flor-de-retama-antologia
- https://www.youtube.com/watch?v=0IrEZvVklsc (appointment with restriction due to temporary availability)
- http://korazondeperro.com/elmundo/injusticias-reclamos-y-represion-la-espiral-de-la-violencia/).
- https://ojo-publico.com/sala-del-poder/francisco-durand-ahora-estamos-la-republica-empresarial

Sources consulted from Newspapers and Magazines.

- Diario El Comercio, Lima, Perú. Nov 13, 1994
- Diario El Comercio, Lima, Perú. Julio 28, 2018
- Diario El Comercio, Lima, Perú. Mayo 21, 201
- The Wall Street Journal. March 30, 2018
- Diario El Comercio, Lima, Perú. Abril 29, 2018
- Diario El País, Madrid, España. Jun 4, 1986.
- Diario El Comercio, Lima, Perú. Mayo 23, 2019.
- Diario El Comercio, Lima, Perú. Mayo 14, 2020
- Diario El Comercio, Lima, Perú. Diciembre 11, 2022
- Diario El Comercio, Lima, Perú. Diciembre 18, 2022
- Diario El Comercio, Lima, Perú. Enero 08, 2023
- Diario La Nación, Buenos Aires, Argentina. Julio 20, 2021. Artículo: "La Fragmentación Política",publicado por el Sr. César Pérez Vivas.
- The New York Times, Ago 07,2019
- The New York Times, May 2020, pág. 16, "Artificial Intelligence". Special Edition.
- Revista Caretas, Edición 2299. Sept 05, 2013

- Revista Time. Sept 23, 2013

- Revista The Economist, Aug 30-Sept 05, 2014. págs. 9 y 21-24

- Revista The Economist, Jul 14-20, pág. 23 "Representing Americas. The minority majority".

- Revista Fortune Sept 15, 2017 pág. 90.

- Revista The Economist, Julio 06, 2018, pág. 11 y 18

- Revista The Economist Nov 9, 2019. págs. 9 y 18

- Revista The Economist, May 16-22, 2020, págs. 7 y 57

- Revista Fortune, enero 4 2015, pág. 64

- Revista The Economist, nov16-22 2019, pág. 13

- Revista The Economist, Obituary pág. 78, Sep 3-9 2022.

- Revista The Economist, sep 17-23, 2022, pág. 25

- Revista The Economist, mayo 20th 2023, pags 16-19.

- Weekly magazine "Hildebrandt en sus trece", March 22, 2024, page 15. Lima, Peru, Year 14, No. 678).

www.ingramcontent.com/pod-product-compliance
Lightning Source LLC
Chambersburg PA
CBHW080414030426

42335CB00020B/2450